Perception of Space and Motion

Handbook of Perception and Cognition
2nd Edition

Series Editors
Edward C. Carterette
and **Morton P. Friedman**

Perception of Space and Motion

Edited by
William Epstein
Sheena Rogers

Department of Psychology
University of Wisconsin—Madison
Madison, Wisconsin

Academic Press

San Diego   New York   Boston
London   Sydney   Tokyo   Toronto

This book is printed on acid-free paper.

Copyright © 1995 by ACADEMIC PRESS, INC.

All Rights Reserved.
No part of this publication may be reproduced or transmitted in any form or by any
means, electronic or mechanical, including photocopy, recording, or any information
storage and retrieval system, without permission in writing from the publisher.

Academic Press, Inc.
A Division of Harcourt Brace & Company
525 B Street, Suite 1900, San Diego, California 92101-4495

United Kingdom Edition published by
Academic Press Limited
24-28 Oval Road, London NW1 7DX

Library of Congress Cataloging-in-Publication Data

Perception of space and motion / edited by William Epstein, Sheena J. Rogers.
     p.   cm. — (Handbook of perception and cognition (2nd ed.))
    Includes bibliographical references and index.
    ISBN 0-12-240530-7
    1. Motion perception (Vision) 2. Space perception. 3. Picture
perception. 4. Visual perception. I. Series.
    BF245.P47   1995
    153.7'5—dc20   95-2336
                                         CIP

PRINTED IN THE UNITED STATES OF AMERICA
95 96 97 98 99 00 BC 9 8 7 6 5 4 3 2 1

Contents

1   *The Metatheoretical Context*
William Epstein

2 The Perception of Spatial Layout from Static Optical Information
Barbara Gillam

3 Perceiving Layout and Knowing Distances: The Integration, Relative Potency, and Contextual Use of Different Information about Depth
James E. Cutting and Peter M. Vishton

4   *Perceiving Pictorial Space*
Sheena Rogers

7   *Perceiving Events*
Dennis R. Proffitt and Mary K. Kaiser

8   *Self-Motion: Visual Perception and Visual Control*
William H. Warren, Jr.

11 *Dynamic Touch*
M. T. Turvey and Claudia Carello

Contributors

Numbers in parentheses indicate the pages on which the authors' contributions begin.

Claudia Carello (401)
Department of Psychology
Center for the Ecological Study
   of Perception and Action
University of Connecticut
Storrs, Connecticut 06239

James E. Cutting (63)
Department of Psychology
Cornell University
Ithaca, New York 14853

William Epstein (1)
Department of Psychology
University of Wisconsin—Madison
Madison, Wisconsin 53706

Barbara Gillam (23)
School of Psychology
University of New South Wales
Sydney, 2052
Australia

Rick Jenison (365)
Department of Psychology
University of Wisconsin—Madison
Madison, Wisconsin 53706

Mary K. Kaiser (227)
NASA Ames Research Center
Moffett Field, California 94035

Philip J. Kellman (327)
Department of Psychology
University of California—
   Los Angeles
Los Angeles, California 90024

Joseph S. Lappin (165)
Department of Psychology
Vanderbilt University
Nashville, Tennessee 37240

Dennis R. Proffitt (227)
Department of Psychology
University of Virginia
Charlottesville, Virginia 22903

Sheena Rogers (119)
Department of Psychology
University of Wisconsin—Madison
Madison, Wisconsin 53706

James T. Todd (201)
Department of Psychology
Ohio State University
Columbus, Ohio 43210

M. T. Turvey (401)
Department of Psychology
Center for the Ecological Study
  of Perception and Action
University of Connecticut
Storrs, Connecticut 06239

Peter M. Vishton (71)
Department of Psychology
Cornell University
Ithaca, New York 14853

William H. Warren, Jr. (263)
Department of Cognitive and
  Linguistic Sciences
Brown University
Providence, Rhode Island 02912

Frederic L. Wightman (365)
Waisman Center and Department
  of Psychology
University of Wisconsin—Madison
Madison, Wisconsin 53705

Foreword

The problem of perception and cognition is in understanding how the organism transforms, organizes, stores, and uses information arising from the world in sense data or memory. With this definition of perception and cognition in mind, this handbook is designed to bring together the essential aspects of this very large, diverse, and scattered literature and to give a précis of the state of knowledge in every area of perception and cognition. The work is aimed at the psychologist and the cognitive scientist in particular, and at the natural scientist in general. Topics are covered in comprehensive surveys in which fundamental facts and concepts are presented, and important leads to journals and monographs of the specialized literature are provided. Perception and cognition are considered in the widest sense. Therefore, the work will treat a wide range of experimental and theoretical work.

The *Handbook of Perception and Cognition* should serve as a basic source and reference work for those in the arts or sciences, indeed for all who are interested in human perception, action, and cognition.

Edward C. Carterette and Morton P. Friedman

Preface

The perception of space and motion has been central to the analysis of perception in the 20th century. While the record has been one of steady progress, the past 25 years have been marked by special promise. Space and motion were traditionally considered separate domains in the study of perception, but it is now clear that the two are closely linked. The aim of this volume is to put the interested reader in contact with the contemporary empirical and theoretical statuses of investigation in the two domains.

The period since publication of the first edition of the *Handbook of Perception and Cognition* has been especially fruitful. The reasons are various: some theoretical, some pragmatic, and others technological. The coming of age of J. J. Gibson's ecological approach is significant. The developing concept of information in spatio–temporal optical structure has played a central role in much of the research reviewed in this volume. The demand for artificial vision systems has motivated a search for working solutions to age-old problems, and the availability of computer graphics has made the whole enterprise more tractable. Old questions have been resolved or productively recast. Important new questions, previously neglected, have been addressed with much success. While there are obvious continuities between the contents of the current volume and that of its predecessors, we have been happily impressed by how much there is in the current volume that is new and valuable.

In Chapter 1, William Epstein has the broad objective of setting out several general metatheoretical questions related to the perception of spatial layout. A stance toward these questions, for example, the inverse projection problem and the nature of information, often is a formative influence on the formulation of specific questions under investigation. In Chapter 2, Barbara Gillam reviews the large body of literature devoted to investigations of information for spatial layout in static stimulation due, for example, to ocular adjustments and retinal disparity. James Cutting and Peter Vishton, in Chapter 3, extend this review in new directions as they examine the evidence bearing on the range of effectiveness of the various "cues," promoting a distinction between personal space, action space, and vista space. They also consider the way in which multiply accessible cues may be integrated. The ease with which we perceive pictorial space belies the special challenge it poses to perceptual theory. Sheena Rogers, in Chapter 4, assesses the empirical status of the field and argues that while pictures bear a structural relationship to the real scenes they represent, and are perceived in much the same way, their success is due to the many constraints on potential ambiguity and distortion that are provided by traditional artistic practice.

Chapters 5 through 8 are concerned with the perceptual consequence of information in dynamic stimulation. Information is a fundamental construct in modern analyses. In Chapter 5, Joe Lappin examines the conceptual and quantitative specification of information in the context of perceiving structure from motion. The past 15 years has seen intense study of structure from motion. Jim Todd, in Chapter 6, reviews the contributions in this field. His analysis of the robustness of the visual system in the face of violations of computationally required constraints cautions us to take care in formulating accounts of human vision based on tests of computational algorithms. We now recognize that changing stimulation carries information not only about structure but also about events, actions, and meanings. In Chapter 7, Dennis Proffit and Mary Kaiser review this rich literature. Perceiving biomechanical motions, time to contact, and control of interceptive actions, and perceiving natural dynamics are among the topics. Chapter 8, by Bill Warren, concludes this set of chapters. The control of locomotion by information available in optic flow has provided a happy opportunity for the integration of the psychophysical, computational, and neurophysiological approaches to the study of perception. Warren's chapter is a masterly examination of the visual control of human locomotion, perception of self-motion, and the visual regulation of posture and gait.

What is the origin of the competencies described in Chapters 2 through 8? Do they appear early in infancy or are they the product of an extended personal history of experience? Does their appearance exhibit a regular order and pacing? These questions antedate experimental psychology. At mid-century, however, it was discovered that a number of surprisingly simple investigative procedures could move these questions from the armchair into the laboratory and the pace of empirical resolution has quickened. In Chapter 9, Philip Kellman reviews the methods and findings concerning the ontogeny of the perception of spatial layout, motion, and events.

The preceding chapters have been concerned with visual perception of spatial layout and motion. The human percipient is preeminently a visually dependent creature and the heavy emphasis on vision research reflects this fact. Nevertheless, humans can and do access spatial layout and motion by exploiting information in nonvisual stimulation. Fred Wightman and Rick Jenison examine the information for spatial layout in auditory stimulation in Chapter 10. While the importance of sound has long been recognized, strikingly new in this chapter is an examination of the potential information in dynamic acoustic structures. Owing to the very recent introduction of this style of investigation, results are still tentative, but if the investigation of dynamic optical structures is an apt precedent, this approach will have rich returns.

Chapter 11 is without precedent. In this chapter, Michael Turvey and Claudia Carello examine the information in the stimulation resulting from haptic stimulation. Although the prospects for this line of research may be found in J. J. Gibson's writings, development and execution of this work should be credited to Turvey and his associates. The chapter stands as the definitive review of this ambitious and systematic body of research.

We believe that this volume will be the canonical source for years to come. The credit for this belongs to our collaborators in the enterprise. We thank them.

William Epstein and Sheena Rogers
Madison, Wisconsin

CHAPTER 1

The Metatheoretical Context

William Epstein

I. INTRODUCTION

The chapters that follow this one do the essential work of a handbook. Their writers put the reader in contact with the contemporary status of the empirical and theoretical issues in the designated domains. The treatments are sharply focused and appropriately so. The present chapter seeks to discharge a different assignment. My aim is to review a diverse set of general concerns that cut across the particular domains and modalities. In some instances these concerns may be traced to the early modern history of the study of perception; in other instances they are of more recent origin. Attitudes toward these matters, sometimes explicit but typically implicit, often contribute toward shaping formulation of the question under investigation and the investigative style.

II. THE INVERSE PROJECTION PROBLEM

For any given three dimensional (3-D) structure, event in three space, or spatial layout, if the physical dimensions of the structure, event, or layout are known exactly, then application of the appropriate mathematics will allow the occurrent retinal spatiotemporal structure to be computed. Solv-

Perception of Space and Motion

ing the direct projection problem, that is, going from the distal state of affairs to the proximal affairs is a straightforward task.

The circumstances are drastically different when the inverse projection problem is assayed: When the occurrent retinal state of affairs is known, it is impossible to pick out a unique distal property, object, or event as the source. In contrast to the direct projection problem, going from the occurrent proximal state of affairs to the distal state of affairs constitutes an ill-posed problem. The difficulty arises from the fact that while a specific distal event or arrangement is compatible with only a single retinal state, a given retinal state is compatible with countless distal states.

The inverse projection problem does not seem to have troubled vision theorists before Descartes. Nor for that matter was perception of 3-D structure or spatial layout a central concern. Perhaps it was ascription to one or another variant of a copy/contact theory, intromissionist or extramissionist, that concealed the problem. Nor does the problem appear clearly in Kepler's writings, in this case very likely because Kepler was concerned with establishing the retinal image, a problem of direct projection.

It was during the century that followed Kepler, in the writings of Descartes, Mallebranch, Molyneux, and Berkeley that the inverse projection problem began to assume a shape that resembles the modern formulation: "For distance being a line directed end-wise to the eye, it projects only one point in the fund of the eye. Which part remains invariably the same, whether the distance be longer or shorter" (Berkeley, 1709, Sec. II). On first examination the Molyneux–Berkeley formulation might be taken to be the claim that since the retinal image is formed on a two-dimensional projection surface, the image cannot be the basis for perception of 3-D structure. This is a questionable reading. Descartes had already explicitly rejected resemblance between image and object as the basis for perception, and Molyneux and Berkeley followed Descartes in this regard. A better reading of the Molyneux–Berkeley premise is that since a given state of retinal stimulation is compatible with a countless number of distal arrangements, there is necessarily an irreducible equivocality in optical stimulation that makes going from optical input to distal arrangement impossible.

The inverse projection problem has been a prominent motivating factor in early modern and modern theories of perception. Berkeley's (1709) essay *An Essay Toward A New Theory of Vision* opened with an assertion of the inverse projection problem. The problem seemed intractable to Berkeley (1709), leading him to conclude that contrary to the evidence of everyday experience "neither distance nor things placed at a distance are themselves . . . truly perceived by sight" (Sec. XLV). Instead Berkeley proposed that only touch has direct access to properties of spatial layout and that the representations of spatial layout (distance, size, and location) seemingly made available by vision are in fact mediated by the ideas of touch.

Although as late as the mid-nineteenth century Berkeley's (1709) theory was considered beyond dispute (Mill, 1842, 1874); to present day readers, the theory must seem to border on the perverse. One way to come to terms with Berkeley's move is to construe it as a response, albeit an exaggerated one, to the dilemma posed by the inverse projection problem: If there is an irreducible equivocality that rules out specification of distal states and events by retinal input, and if despite this equivocality perception of the spatial layout is unequivocal, how else could this come about except through the intercession of another highly reliable correlate of spatial layout? At the heart of the matter is the inverse projection problem. Berkeley's theory is testimony to the power of this problem to drive theoretical work.

Nor has the need to address the inverse projection problem seemed less urgent to modern theorists. From Helmholtz to contemporary computationalists, the challenge of the inverse projection problem has been a formative influence. What follows is a historical survey of the diverse responses to this challenge.

A. The Constructivist Response

In the opening section of Volume 3 of his *Physiological Optics* Helmholtz (1867/1925) presented his fundamental rule of perception that "such objects are always imagined as being present in the field of vision as would have to be there in order to produce the same impression on the nervous mechanism, the eyes being used under ordinary normal conditions" (p. 2). Although this assertion is frequently treated as a claim about perceptual processes, it was not intended as such by Helmholtz who considered it to be only an empirical generalization whose correctness is not contingent on a commitment to process. Indeed, how could the assertion be incorrect given the fact that the visual system successfully sustains adaptive behavior? A visual system whose outputs could not be described by this rule would surely be maladaptive.

What sort of process underlies this ruly behavior? For Helmholtz (1867/1925), the answer was offered in his famous hypothesis of unconscious inference. The form of inference Helmholtz postulated would be considered today an inductively strong inference yielding a conclusion that is highly likely to be correct but not certain. The following are some examples:

1. under normal conditions, only 3-D structures generate patterns of binocular disparity

the occurrent retinal stimulation is a pattern of binocular disparities

therefore, the object in my visual field is very likely a 3-D structure. . . .

2. under normal conditions of illumination, when only a single light

source is present, a continuous planar surface illuminated by the source will not exhibit any abrupt discontinuity in lightness (brightness)

this surface exhibits an abrupt brightness discontinuity

therefore the surface is unlikely to be planar; it is constituted of two noncoplanar surfaces joined at the brightness border forming a 3-D structure

3. under normal conditions, the visual angle subtended by a stationary object viewed by a stationary observer remains constant

the visual angle subtended by this object is undergoing cyclic expansion and contraction

therefore, the object is not stationary; it is translating between a near and far point in three space

When the inductive structures are set out in this way it becomes clear that the heavy work has been assigned to the major premise. The major premise is assigned the task of dislodging the obstacle posed by the inverse projection problem. This is accomplished by stipulating a context that serves to disambiguate the minor premise. In the absence of the putative context, the optical circumstances specified by the minor premise are equivocal, owing to the inverse projection problem. In turn, this equivocality blocks any conclusion about the distal state of affairs. However, with the major premise in place, the inferential process can run smoothly from premises to conclusion.

Helmholtz (1867/1925) has served as a model for many twentieth century approaches. The writings of Brunswik (1956), Gregory (1993), Rock (1983), and the proponents of transactionalism very obviously bear the imprint of Helmholtz, and Helmholtz's influence is clearly present in scores of other analyses (e.g., Nakayama & Shimojo, 1992; Shepard, 1990, pp. 168–186).

1. Transactionalism

The transactionalist approach to perception prospered in the 1940s and 1950s. Although transactionalism is no longer in evidence as an actively advocated clearly demarcated position, it has left us an enduring legacy in the form of a set of remarkable demonstrations of illusions in three-space. Of these, the rotating trapezoid and the distorted room illusions are the most widely known. For the transactionalists, these experimental demonstrations highlighted both the fundamental problem that confronted the visual system as well as the nature of the process that generated the resolution of the problem. The fundamental problem is posed by the pervasive fact of *equivalent configurations*. Different distal configurations are said to be equivalent if they provide an observer with identical optical input. The transactionalists argued (and sought to prove by geometrical analysis) "that each of the visual cues (for spatial layout) defines an infinite family of equivalent configurations, or, to state the converse, for any cue there exists an infinite family of physically configurations, all of which provide the same visual cue. . . . It is essential, however, that the organism which receives these identical messages be able to distinguish between them" (Ittelson, 1960, pp. 50–51). Here we have the inverse projection problem. How is the problem resolved? The answer proffered by the transactionalists is that the perceiver brings to bear additional information in the form of assumptions about the world acquired through experience: "Apparently the organism, always forced to choose among the unlimited number of possibilities which can be related to a given retinal pattern, calls upon its previous experiences and 'assumes' that what has been most probable in the past is most probable in the immediate occasion" (Kilpatrick, 1961, p. 46). Both the assumptions and the process are presumed to be unconscious. The resulting perceptions are in the nature of best fitting predictions; the perceptions are not of the nature of apodictic assertions about the world.

Although the transactionalists (e.g., Kilpatrick, 1952, p. 90) recognized the commonalities between their viewpoint and Helmholtz's (1867/1925), they also insisted that their view was different in some important respects. Notwithstanding their insistence, the differences are not obvious. One possibility is that for the transactionalist the assumptive context is a dynamic state that is regularly updated by experience or reorganized to reflect the purposes of the percipient and the specific demands of the situation.

2. Brunswik's Probabilistic Functionalism

For most of its modern history, the analysis of visual space perception has been cue driven. The conventional list of cues can be found in every introductory perception textbook. The cues may be properties of optical input, for example, binocular disparity, occlusion, or adjustments of the oculomotor system, for example, convergence, or stored information about objects, for example, known size. The cues serve as clues to the distal state of affairs. The cues vary in reliability, some are better clues than others. For example, binocular disparity is more reliable than shading as a cue for 3-D shape, and occlusion is more reliable than relative size as a cue for depth order. However, even the most reliable of the cues are imperfectly correlated with the distal spatial layout; these may be good clues, but they are only clues. Also, the less reliable of the cues, taken in isolation, provide slender support for maintaining perceptual contact with the environment.

To account for the fact that perceived spatial layout typically is veridical, cue theorists introduced two additional considerations: One, that multiple cues are regularly available and that these cues are processed concurrently. Two, that the integration of the outputs of the processing of the different cues provides a representation of the environment that is more highly correlated with the distal state of affairs than any single cue.

The cue concept and the notion that the perceptual process is one that generates a perceptual representation that is the best fit for a set of individually imperfect cues are widely held beliefs among contemporary investigators. However, the fullest and most systematic expression of this approach is Brunswik's (1956; Postman & Tolman, 1958) *probabilistic functionalism*. For Brunswik, perception is in all respects probabilistic: The distal-proximal relationship, the mediating process, and the distal–perceptual relationship are inherently probabilistic. The term *ecological validity* was invented by Brunswik to refer to the probabilistic relationship between the distal and proximal states, for example, between spatial layout and distance cues. The ecological validities of the various cues are less than perfect and vary among each other. Ecological validities are objective correlations between physical variables. The weights assigned to the various cues in the process of information integration are plainly a different matter. The assigned weights or *criterial validities* in Brunswik's analysis may mimic the ecological validities or they may deviate from the ecological validities. The weightings and the form of the rule that governs the integration of information determine the perceptual representation. Given the probabilistic nature of the ecological and criterial validities, it is inevitable that the relationship between the perceptual and distal worlds, the perceptual achievement or *functional validity* will also be imperfect. Cutting and Vishton (this volume, chapter 3) present a contemporary assessment of cue validity.

3. Rock's Cognitive Constructivism

The most complete statement of Rock's (1983) cognitive approach is found in his monograph *The Logic of Perception*. No other writer has been as forthright as Rock in advocating the cognitive constructivist approach and in facing up to its difficulties. Among the primary prompts for Rock is the inverse projection problem:

> Logically, a given local stimulus is only an ambiguous indicator of the relevant property of the object producing it. For example, an image of a given size, measured by the visual angle that an object subtends at the eye, will be produced by a whole family of objects of varying sizes, each at a different distance. Thus the perceptual system could never determine from an image's visual angle alone what the size of the object that produced it is. The same is true analogously for image shape with respect to object shape (because the

slant of the object can vary), image velocity with respect to object velocity (because the distance of the moving object can vary), image intensity (or luminance) with respect to surface color (because illumination can vary), and so forth (Rock, 1983, p. 22).

For Rock (1983), ambiguity is pervasive. This ambiguity challenges the perceptual system and the theoretician who wishes to understand the system. How does the visual system resolve ambiguity and reliably generate a perceptual description that fits the distal state of affairs? The answer proffered by Rock is that the perceptual system possesses a repertoire of rules that are homologues of the laws that link the physical variables. For example, perceived size (S'), represented retinal size (θ'), and perceived distance (D') are linked by a rule, $S' = \theta' \times D'$, that is isomorphic to the law that links their distal counterparts. These perceptual rules are exploited by the perceptual system to resolve the inverse projection problem. Continuing with the size example, when the system has access to visual angle and distance cues, application of the rule resolves ambiguity about size: Only one size will fit the rule. Rock's answer is unabashedly cognitive: The rules are real, that is, they are represented in the perceptual system; the operations are real, not merely as if postulations, and an "executive agency" that applies the rules is openly postulated.

B. The Computationalist Response

The computationalists (e.g., Marr, 1982) are also moved by the challenge of the inverse projection problem. Poggio (Poggio, Torre, & Koch, 1985) put the matter succinctly: "In classical optics or in computer graphics the basic problem is to determine the images of three-dimensional objects, whereas vision is confronted with the inverse problem of recovering surfaces from images" (p. 314). The visual system is confronted by an ill-posed problem, one which does not admit a unique solution.

The computationalist response is to seek to identify plausible constraints on the environment that can underwrite a one:one mapping between environmental properties or events and occurrent optical input: "The main idea for 'solving' ill-posed problems, that is, for restoring 'well-posedness,' is to restrict the class of admissible solutions by introducing suitable a priori knowledge. A prior knowledge can be exploited, for example, under the form of either variational principles that impose constraints on the possible solutions or as statistical properties of the solution space" (Poggio et al., 1985, p. 315).

In a sense, postulation of the appropriate constraints dissolves the inverse projection problem: When the environment satisfies the posited constraints, there is only one distal configuration or event that is compatible with the occurrent optical input. When the constraints cannot be identified, the computational enterprise is stillborn, blocked by the inverse projection problem.

It may seem that the computationalists' constraints are merely reincarnations of the transactionalists' assumptions or of the premises in Rock's (1983) neo-Helmholtzian account. Indeed, some expressions of the computational approach may encourage this interpretation. Nevertheless, there is an important distinction between the status of assumption and rules on the one hand and constraints on the other. For the transactionalist and the cognitive constructivists, the assumptions and rules are lodged in the mind of the perceiver; that is, the assumptions and rules are explicitly represented in the visual information-processing system. Admittedly, the assumptions and rules are not readily available for conscious assessment; indeed, they may be totally inaccessible under all sensible conditions. Nevertheless, the assumptions and rules are represented and are causally active in the perceptual process. None of these claims ought to be made for computational constraints. The constraints are environmental regularities that have prevailed in the ecological niche of the species over the course of evolution of the perceptual system. As such, these regularities have acted to shape the design of the computational modules so that their output given optical input under ordinary conditions is such and such. Although it makes sense to ask how assumptions and rules are represented and who it is that uses them, these questions are not properly asked about constraints. The computationalist theorist needs to know the relevant constraints to proceed to the algorithmic level of explanation. This should not be mistaken to mean that the perceiver needs knowledge of the constraints to see the world as he or she does. The difference between the cognitive constructive stance and the computational stance may be summarized simply: For the cognitive constructivist, the perceptual system is rule following; for the computationalist, the system is rule instantiating.

C. J. J. Gibson's Response

Beginning with his earliest book in 1950 and reaffirmed in his later writings, Gibson (1950, 1966, 1979) has taken the view that the inverse projection problem is a pseudoproblem, owing its origin and persistence to a mistakenly narrow construal of both the objects of perception and the nature of stimulation. Gibson argued that the object of perception is a fully furnished world, not objects detached from settings (or isolated from any setting), and that the stimulation that counts for a perceptual system are dynamic structures of light and not static fragments of the dynamic spatiotemporal optical structures. According to Gibson, when this (ecological) stance is adopted toward the environment and stimulation, the inverse projection problem does not appear. Instead an unequivocal one:one mapping between environment and stimulation becomes apparent. Since there is no equivocality, there is no need for the moves taken by the constructivist to resolve the putative ambiguity.

It is common to present Gibson's view on this matter as a claim that when the appropriate levels of description are adopted, then one:one mappings will be discovered that are noncontingent and unqualified by any additional considerations. Indeed Gibson (1979) often writes as if this is the reading he would like to receive. Notwithstanding this evidence, on closer scrutiny it appears that Gibson's position is different, resembling very closely the stance of the computationalist. This is to say that Gibson's assertion that stimulation and the environment are unequivocally linked, or that stimulation carries "information," is tacitly contingent on the satisfaction of environmental constraints. Perhaps the reason that Gibson was reluctant to give this contingency the prominence it later received in the writings of the computationalists was a fear that talk of constraints so readily slips over onto talk about mental entities. Had Gibson become convinced that there was a noncognitive formulation of constraints he might have admitted them more explicitly.

III. CUES OR INFORMATION

In the preceding section a distinction between cues and information was suggested. In this section this distinction will be elaborated.

Reference to information is common in the experimental analysis of perception and cognition. Developments in communication engineering provided an early stimulus for consideration of information. In the Shannon–Weaver (1949) theory a signal carries information to the extent that it reduces the uncertainty concerning the object or event. Shannon and Weaver were careful to distinguish between the amount of information carried by a signal and the content or meaning of the signal. The construct information in their theory was assessed exclusively on the basis of uncertainty reduction, independent of what the signal tells the percipient. The Shannon–Weaver construct has become part of the standard repertoire of analytic tools.

A second source of encouragement for talk of information was adoption by cognitive psychologists of a paradigm inspired by the computer program metaphor called *information-processing theory*. Unlike Shannon and Weaver, cognitive psychologists who adopted this metatheory did not provide a defined sense of the construct information. In the work of cognitive psychology, information assumed a variety of forms: a property of the distal environment, a property of stimulation, and a product of the cognitive processes.

Despite the excitement that accompanied the introduction of the

Shannon–Weaver (1949) theory and the information-processing theory, neither of these approaches had a significant effect on the analysis of the classical problems of perception. Gibson's information construct has had a contrasting fate. Gradually refined by Gibson between 1950 and 1979, the Gibsonian construct was largely ignored and poorly understood throughout most of its early history. Only recently has the Gibsonian notion of information assumed a central position in the analysis of perception.

For Gibson (1979), information is a property of optical stimulation that is nomically related to a property of the environment, that is, a relationship that is grounded in natural law; a relationship between optical stimulation and the environment that is lawful, not merely ruly. As illustration, the relationship between optical motion configurations, such as continuous projective transformations, and solid form undergoing motion in 3-D space is lawful under the rigidity constraint. The relationship is not merely correlational; the relationship is assured by physical laws that stipulate the ways in which environmental events structure light. It is this grounding in natural law that is the warrant for the claim that information uniquely specifies the state of affairs.

Following closely Dretske's (1981, 1986) analysis, we may say that information specifies the state of affairs because it is in the way of a "natural sign."

> Naturally occurring signs mean something, and they do so without the participation of an interpreter. Water doesn't flow uphill; hence, a northerly flowing river means there is an elevation gradient in that direction. Shadows to the east mean that the sun is to the west. A sudden force on the passengers in one direction means an acceleration of the train in the opposite direction. . . . The power of these events or conditions to mean what they do does not depend on the way they are interpreted, or, indeed, whether the events or conditions are interpreted or recognized at all. The power of a 'natural sign' is underwritten by certain objective constraints, certain environmental regularities. . . . When these constraints are satisfied, the relation between the sign and the state of affairs constituting its meaning is counterfactual—supporting in that if the state of affairs had not obtained neither would the natural sign (Dretske, 1986, pp. 18–19).

Delineation of the nature of the properties of optical stimulation that are informative and the properties of the environment that the informative optical structures specify presupposes prior commitments to a conception of stimulation and the environment. When a Gibsonian perspective is adopted, the environment is described at a scale that is relevant to the support of effective action, and forms of optical stimulation will be sought in the spatiotemporal structures of stimulation that accompany encounters with the environment so delineated.

Note that thus far neither perceiver nor perceiving has been mentioned. There is good reason for these omissions. Information in the Gibsonian sense intended is not a commodity in the mental storehouse of the person, nor is it a property of experience. As Gibson (1966, 1979) has remarked, the perceiver does not have information, and he or she certainly does not perceive information. Information is a property of structured light. To assess the informative structures of light, no psychophysics is needed. Only an appropriate mathematical analysis is required.

Two differences between the Gibsonian concept and the earlier information theory and information-processing theory concepts stand out: (1) Unlike the information-processing concept, information in the Gibsonian sense is exclusively an objective property. The perceiver makes no contribution to information, although the design and designs of the perceiver will determine whether information is detected. (2) Unlike the Shannon–Weaver (1949) construct, information in the Gibsonian sense has an intentional character, it specifies states and events in the environment.

What about the relationship between information and cues? Three differences between cues and information deserve highlighting: (1) As noted, information is a property of optical stimulation whose relationship to the environment is underwritten by natural law. Cues have more diverse grounding that includes a history of experience and acculturation. For example, it is often suggested that the pictorial cues owe their efficacy to the acquisition of a set of conventions of symbol interpretation. (2) It has been the practice to treat cues as imperfect indicators of the distal configuration or event. (See preceding section.) Information, under specified constraints, is a perfect specifier. The ecological validity of information is 1.0. (3) The probabilistic nature of cues encourages the search for perceptual processes that make up for the unreliability of the input to achieve a reliable and distally correlated output. In one standard story this role has been assigned to an inference-like process. The unequivocal nature of information inspires a different agenda: (1) a search for a level and language of description of stimulation and environmental constraints that establishes information for spatial layout or events, (2) a program of psychophysical investigation to evaluate the relationship between perception and information, and (3) consideration of models of processing that are driven by information rather than by rules and inferences. Not surprisingly, this agenda has been promoted most vigorously in the analysis of information for spatial layout in dynamic stimulation. However, Rogers's (this volume, chapter 4) assessment of pictorial space shows that the prospects for this agenda are not necessarily limited to dynamic stimulation.

A. An Embarrassment of Information

Taking Berkeley's (1709) analysis of vision as a starting point, there has been a remarkable conversion of opinion regarding the availability of information in stimulation for spatial layout. The opinion that stimulation is informationally impoverished has been replaced by the assessment that stimulation is informationally rich. A listing of depth cues is now a common feature of textbook expositions of the problem of perceiving spatial layout. There is an embarrassment of information.

Why has the perceptual system evolved sensitivities to apparently redundant sources of information? One answer is that the redundancy is much lower than it seems. For one, different variables of optical stimulation carry different messages about the world, for example, some specify the ordinal arrangement of surface, others specify metric properties of spatial layout. In addition, the different cues can be shown to have different effective ranges; for example, the interposition cue is not affected at all by distance from the observer and thus is effective at all viewing distances, whereas binocular disparity loses effectiveness beyond the middle-distance range. These answers are developed in detail by Cutting and Vishton (this volume, chapter 3).

Another answer to the question posed by apparent redundancy is that interactions among concurrently available cues enhance the effectiveness of the perceptual system. Here are two examples.

1. Complementing

It is well-known that most cues are limited in their capability to support complete representations of spatial layout. For example, orthographic projection of optical motions simulating a 3-D object rotating in depth (e.g., Wallach & O'Connell's, 1953, kinetic depth effect display and its countless successors) can specify the shape of the simulated object, but the information carried by these optical motions cannot specify depth order (or direction of rotation). Absent complementary information, a definite shape will be seen, but it will undergo perceptual reversals. In contrast, other cues have highly reliable effects on perceived depth order but no known effects on 3-D shape. Occlusion (either static interposition or dynamic occlusion–disocclusion) is an example of a highly effective cue for depth order. The information in occlusion can be combined with the information in the optical motion configurations in a complementary fashion to produce an unambiguous 3-D perceived shape. Experimental demonstrations have been reported by Anderson and Braunstein (1983) and Braunstein (1982).

2. Accumulation

When multiple concordant cues for depth are available concurrently, the effects of the cues may combine additively to amplify perceived depth. An example is a study by Bruno and Cutting (1988) who used four sources of information for relative depth: relative size, height in the plane, occlusion, and motion parallax. All of the combinations of the presence or absence of each of these sources were generated. The results were straightforward: The magnitude of perceived relative distance (exocentric distance within a display configuration) increased linearly with the number of sources of information. The addition of cues led to amplification of the depth response. Similar results have been reported by Landy, Maloney, and Young (1991) for texture gradients and optical motion configurations and by Bülthoff and Mallot (1988) for binocular disparity and shading. The latter writers use the term *accumulation* to refer to this effect of information combination. An older demonstration of accumulation was reported by Künnapas (1968), who varied the number of distance cues in an experimental situation modeled after the classical Holway–Boring (1941) investigation of size perception. Künnapas reported that as the number of cues increased, perceived distance increased.

It is not uncommon for two or more of the effects to occur in a given set of circumstances. Here is an illustration:

Consider a structure from motion display that simulates a specific 3-D shape. The stimulation implementation will necessarily stipulate viewing distance; that is, the optical motion configuration will specify the simulated 3-D shape for a hypothetical observer at a specific viewing distance. Now suppose an observer is introduced at the prescribed viewing distance but that the observer's view of the display is limited to monocular observation through a stationary 2-mm aperture (an artificial pupil). What reports of perceived shape should we expect? In the absence of information to determine the distance of the display, we assume that the observer will make a default assignment. The reported shape will then be determined by the value of the default distance and the relative optical velocities. It is highly unlikely that the perceptual solution will match the simulated shape. Next, suppose that binocular viewing is allowed and that accommodative convergence is effective to specify distance accurately. The effect will be to bring the perceived 3-D shape closer in line with the stimulated shape. However, as was noted earlier, depth order is likely to fluctuate. The addition of occlusion–disocclusion information will eliminate fluctuation. The observer's reported shape may still underrepresent the dimensions of the simulation, owing to the presence of binocular disparity information that signals coplanarity of all points in the display. So in the final step, the display is stereoscopically presented with the appropriate disparities. The amplification resulting from the combination of motion and stereopsis leads to an enhanced and accurate 3-D shape report.

Despite a general recognition that the visual system has concurrent access to multiple sources of information, the investigation of information integration has been slow to develop. For the most part, the work that has been reported has been content to describe the data, very little has been done to delineate the perceptual process.

In a curious turn, the neo–Gibsonians who are committed to promotion of an information-based account of the perception of spatial layout have shied away from examination of concurrent multiple sources of information. It might have been expected that the neo–Gibsonians would welcome the opportunity to affirm that perception is a function of information in stimulation. However, quite the opposite seems to be the case. The facts seem to cause discomfiture among the ranks of the ecological realists, for example, Pittenger (1989), leading Burton and Turvey (1990) on occasion to deny the basic fact of informational multiplicity.

In fact, there is no incompatibility between the assertion of informational multiplicity and the conception of information advanced by Gibson (1979); (Also see Cutting, 1991, on this point.) The true cause of the discomfiture must be different, and it is not difficult to identify. The ecological realists suspect that talk about multiplicity inevitably will be followed by talk about selection among the diverse informational variables or consideration of rules for integration of different informational variables. From an assertion about facts, that is, that multiple sources of information are available, we will pass uncritically to the style of speculation about process that is anathema to the ecological realist.

In a general sense, the ecological realist analysis (or my reading of their concerns) is correct. Recognition of informational multiplicity will lead to speculation about process. Surely such a development is to be welcomed. However, it does not follow that the ensuing talk about process must entail postulation of a mental apparatus for selecting, deciding, and integrating. There are other options, among them are those that can be derived from the conception of the perceptual process as an executive-free process of spontaneous self-organization.

IV. PERCEPTUAL CONSTANCY

Despite the importance of the inverse projection problem as a motivating stimulus for perceptual theory, the problem is not directly concerned with perception. We turn next to consideration of the mapping relation between optical inputs and perceptual outputs. The facts of the perceptual constancies highlight the challenge posed by this relationship. Changing conditions of viewing, for example, viewing distance, vantage point, lighting, bring with them changes in the local optical input that is correlated with a distal object or event. Yet everyday experience and laboratory evidence demonstrates that perception is constant over a wide range of optical variations that result from the changes of viewing conditions.

Consider the simple case of the perceived shape of a 3-D configuration. Viewed from different vantage points, the configuration assumes very different projective shapes. Viewed from different distances, the visual angles subtended by the visible faces of the configuration vary inversely with variations in viewing distance; binocular disparity, a principal determinant of perceived exocentric distance (depth), will vary inversely with the square of the viewing distance. In consequence, the same observer who occupies different observation points successively or a set of observers each occupying a different observation point relative to the 3-D object will have access to different optical inputs. Despite these differences, there is likely to be very little difference among the descriptions of 3-D shape elicited from the observers occupying the various observation points.

How does the perceptual system take a variable optical input and generate an invariant perceptual output? From Koffka (1935, chapter 6) to Marr (1982, p. 29), the question is everywhere in the study of perception and has not received a definitive answer anywhere. Two principal approaches compete in the efforts to address the challenge posed by the perceptual constancies. One takes the problem to be real and proposes that the visual system resolves the problem by taking into account additional information and putting into play perceptual algorithms that assure constancy. The other approach proposes to dissolve the problem by identifying variables of optical stimulation, often called *invariants*. An invariant is a property of optical stimulation (1) that remains invariant with variations of the viewing condition, (2) that is linked in one:one relationship to the relevant environmental property or event, and (3) that controls perception of these properties or events. The first approach has a long history (for reviews see Epstein, 1973, 1977; Sedgwick, 1986); the second approach was made prominent by Gibson (1959, 1966, 1979), although clear precursors are to be found in Wallach's (1939, 1948) treatments of speed constancy and brightness constancy.

The taking-into-account or scaling approach rests on two suppositions. One, that the visual system has access to information that allows accurate monitoring of the current state of the variable that conditions the optical input. In the illustrative case of 3-D shape, the visual system is presumed to have access to information that allows monitoring of viewing distance and vantage point. Inasmuch as there is ample evidence that the visual system does in fact exploit multiple sources of information to evaluate distance, the first supposition is not controversial. The second supposition concerns perceptual algorithms: these are processing rules that are homologous with the physical laws that govern the relationships among the distal and proximal physical entities. Continuing with our illustration, the physical relationship in the case of disparity depth is disparity = (interocular separation × depth)/(viewing distance^2). It is supposed that a homologous relation, with perceived depth, perceived distance, and representation of interpupillary separation replacing their physical counterparts, is the basis of the perceptual algorithm for computing depth from disparity.

Attitudes regarding the ontological status of these algorithms vary. Some contend that the algorithms are actual rules represented in the visual system (Rock, 1983), they are internalized representations of the physical relations (Shepard, 1990). Others take the view that the algorithms are not represented in the visual system. They are only instantiations of the activity of special purpose computing modules. The modules have been designed by evolution to process inputs in a fixed way, they instantiate rules but should not be said to follow rules.

Irrespective of differences in ontological stance, there is a standard experimental paradigm for evaluating the algorithmic approach. The information that specifies the current state of the conditioning variable (e.g., distance) is manipulated so as to lead to variations of the perceptual representation of the state of variable (e.g., variations of perceived distance), and conforming variations of the dependent variable (e.g., perceived depth) are expected. Conforming variations are those variations that would occur if the computation of the dependent variable is correctly described by the putative algorithm.

Although the prospect of an invariant-based account of constancy was plainly set out by Gibson as early as 1959, the account has not progressed much beyond the initial programmatic statement offered by Gibson. However, a study by Rogers and Caganello (1989) of disparity curvature and the perception of 3-D surfaces is in the spirit of the Gibsonian approach and can serve nicely as a contrast to the scaling approach. First, Rogers and Caganello show that the second spatial derivative of disparity (disparity curvature) remains invariant with viewing distance. Second, they show that disparity curvature is specific to surface curvature. Third, they show that human observers are sensitive to differences in disparity curvature and that they exploit the information carried by disparity curvature in discriminating the curvature of 3-D shape. There is no need to posit a scaling operation that takes distance into account because disparity curvature is an invariant that preserves information over changing viewing distance.

V. LESSONS FROM ILLUSIONS

The fundamental aim of all theories of perception is to supply an account that is sufficient to explain veridical perception, that is, perception that supports successful action by keeping the perceiver in contact with the environment. Given this aim, it might seem paradoxical that so much attention has been devoted to the study of illusions, that is, to cases in which perceptual representation is at odds with the distal state of affairs. The resolution of this apparent paradox is straightforward: With one notable exception, it is the shared opinion that illusory and veridical perception result from a common set of processes so that an understanding of illusions contributes to an understanding of veridical perception. Moreover, it is widely believed that the character of illusions points to the nature of the common underlying processes that are otherwise hidden and difficult to recognize in ordinary, veridical seeing.

The consensual stance toward illusions has a venerable history. It may be noted in Berkeley's (1709, Sec. XXIX–XL) treatment of the Barrovian case involving an illusion of perceived distance when objects are viewed through appropriate lenses. It is plainly displayed in the writings of Helmholtz (1867/1925) and in the writings of the Gestalt theorists (e.g., Koffka, 1935). Some expressions of the consensual viewpoint among more contemporary writers are Kanizsa's (1979) treatment of subjective contours as products of the more general minimum principle in perception, Gregory's (1993) assessment of a variety of illusions as reflections of the general hypothesis-testing character of perception, Coren's (1986) account of illusions of extent as reflections of the contribution of efference readiness to perception, and Hoffman's (1983) computational approach to the interpretation of visual illusions.

The arguments joining illusion and general principles of perceptual processing have been both inductive and deductive. On occasion, observation and investigation of illusions have been the basis for inferences concerning general perceptual principles. Two illustrations are Wertheimer's (1912) investigations of apparent motion, which are credited with priming the Gestalt theory of the brain processes underlying perception, and the observations of diverse illusions of size, for example, the moon illusion, which have promoted the development of a general account of size perception. On occasion, the illusory effects have been inventions induced by prior general theoretical views. Two examples are the remarkable inventions of Ames (1952), the distorted room and the rotating trapezoid, which were devised to demonstrate the central tenets of transactionalism and the figural aftereffects that Köhler (1940) derived from his theory of the brain processes underlying vision. Most frequently, the relationship between the study of illusions and efforts to establish general principles of perceptual processing has been more dynamic. A typical case is the relationship between the study of the class of illusions known as specific aftereffects and the development of neurophysiological models of visual processes. In this case, the flow of influence has been bidirectional: neurophysiology has informed the study of illusion, and the study of illusion has informed models of human neurophysiology.

The exception to the consensual view concerning the place of illusion in the development of a theory of veridical perception is the position adopted by J. J. Gibson (1966, chapter 14; 1979, chapter 14). Gibson has argued that the study of illusions can contribute very little to development of a theory of perception in contact with the environment because the conditions that promote illusions are nonrepresentative of the conditions of ordinary perception. Whereas ordinary seeing occurs under conditions that are rich in information, illusions occur under conditions that are contrived to be informationally impoverished. This difference between the conditions of information limits severely the generalizability of the results of studies of illusion to understanding ordinary seeing. According to Gibson, only study of ordinary seeing can inform us about the fundamental nature of the perceptual process.

Despite Gibson's (1979) insistence that only veridical perception is worth studying, a survey of the experimental data that Gibson (1950, 1966, 1979) introduces to develop his theory reveals that very often the data are, in fact, technically instances of nonveridical perception. The standard investigative strategy deployed by advocates of Gibson's theory is to show that information controls perception by isolating individual variables of spatiotemporal stimulation that carry information and to afford subjects access to this information under the controlled conditions of the psychophysical experiment. Isolation of the informative variables is typically achieved by a simulation procedure. Before the availability of computer graphics technology, simulation involved creating actual physical arrangements, for example, Gibson's optical tunnel (Gibson, 1979, pp. 153–156) and his texture gradient displays (Gibson, 1950, chapter 6). With the introduction of computer graphics, physical arrangements were replaced by computer-generated graphic displays, for example, accretion and deletion displays (Kaplan, 1969), structure from motion displays (Todd, this volume), and optical flow (Warren, this volume, chapter 9). In all of these cases, inasmuch as the display is a simulation, it is not what it appears to be, and the perceptual impression may fairly be designated as illusory.

This observation suggests that Gibson does not, in fact, object to the study of illusion but only to the study of one type of illusion. Those illusory percepts that are linked in a principled way to informative variables of spatiotemporal stimulation are instructive. On the other hand, according to Gibson (1979), the study of illusions that occurs when the perceptual system is denied access to information or when information is impoverished or perturbed cannot form the basis for an understanding of ordinary, information-based perception.

VI. ALTERNATIVE INVESTIGATIVE PROTOTYPES

The history of the investigation of the perception of spatial layout has been dominated by a standard paradigm. The familiar realization of this paradigm is an experiment that requires the subject to occupy a fixed observation point and to report an aspect of the appearance of a test object that is presented in uniform surrounding. The principal aim of such experiments is to assess the relationship between aspects of perceived spatial layout, for example, shape-at-a-slant in depth, and individual cues In the interest of experimental control, the subject is confined to a fixed viewing position, and the object is abstracted from its typical environmental context.

The standard paradigm has been productive. Our sourcebooks (e.g., Sedgwick, 1986; also see Gillam chapter, this volume) are packed with the findings of experimentation in the standard mode. Notwithstanding this record, strong reservations have been expressed concerning the wisdom of founding an account of everyday seeing on the base provided by the findings of the standard paradigm. Brunswik (1956) and Gibson (1959, 1966, 1977; also see Haber, 1985) have been most insistent in questioning reliance on the standard paradigm. It is a curious fact that although Brunswik's and Gibson's attitudes about the fundamental nature of the perceptual process are totally incompatible, they both make common cause in criticizing the standard paradigm.

For Brunswik (1956), the fundamental defect in the standard paradigm is that the experimental isolation of cues disrupts the natural correlations among cues that are characteristic of the conditions of ordinary seeing. In doing so, the standard paradigm misses the central question of information integration; that is, the findings with single cues do not help us to understand the process that combines the information from the normally concurrent cues.

For Gibson (1979) the shortcomings of the standard paradigm are even more compromising. For Gibson the important questions are not concerned with perception of properties of objects but with perception of spatial layout, the structure of the environment. The information for maintaining contact with the environment is carried by the spatiotemporal transformations of optical structure that are generated by egomotion or environmental events. Owing to the restrictions on information and action that are mandated by the standard paradigm, studies in this mold teach us very little about ordinary seeing.

In view of these criticisms, one might expect that the experiments reported by investigators inspired by Brunswik and Gibson would have a different cast than the body of standard experimentation. However, with a few notable exceptions, Brunswikian and Gibsonian experiments are not distinctively marked. One exception that comes to mind is Brunswik's (1956, pp. 43–48) study that solicited size judgments of ordinary objects present in the observer's visual field as she went about her routine activities over the course of the day. (Two more recent studies [Toye, 1986; Wagner, 1985] of perceived spatial layout in multicue outdoor settings would probably have pleased Brunswik.) Also notable are E. J. Gibson's investigations of the affordances of spatial layout and surfaces assessed by the action patterns of young infants (Gibson, Riccio, Schmuckler, Stoffregen, Rosenberg, & Taormina, 1987; Gibson & Walk, 1960). No doubt there are other examples, but the addition of these examples would not alter the impression that the investigative styles adopted by adherents of contrasting theoretical orientations are basically alike.

Although the Brunswik–Gibson critique has had little consequence for the design and conduct of experiments, the critique has had very significant effects in redirecting considerable investigative energy from the study of information in static optical structures to the study of information in dynamic optical structure, from the study of single cues to the study of concurrent multiple cues, and from the study of the passive observer to the study of the active observer. Striking evidence of this redirection can be had by comparing the contents of the current volume with earlier treatments in the first edition of this handbook. The shifts in emphasis have not exclusively been due to the Brunswik–Gibson critique. Johansson's (1977) critique of the standard paradigm and his seminal investigations of event perception (Johansson, 1950, 1973; Johansson, von Hofsten, & Jansson, 1980) have been highly influential in promoting the move toward study of optical motion configurations (see Proffitt & Kaiser, this volume, chapter 8). Another strong influence is to be found in the machine vision community (e.g., Barrow & Tennenbaum, 1986). The early efforts to implement machine vision were cast in the image of the standard paradigm. The failure of these efforts eventually turned the machine vision community away from the standard paradigm to consideration of dynamic stimulation and the potential of integrating information over multiple concurrent cues. The emphasis on information in dynamic spatiotemporal structures is not limited to analysis of vision. The chapters by Wightman and Jenison (this volume, chapter 10) and Turvey and Carello (this volume, chapter 11) exhibit the same emphasis in the domains of auditory and haptic spatial layout, respectively.

VII. CONCLUSION

Admittedly, several of the matters considered in this chapter are not the sort that can be resolved empirically. Nevertheless, these purely conceptual matters as well as the others are likely to remain part of the background of ongoing work. It sought to be useful for most investigators to monitor the status of these matters from time to time.

References

Ames, A. (1952). The rotating trapezoid. In F. P. Kilpatrick (Ed.), *Human behavior from the transactional point of view.* Hanover, NH: Institute for Associated Research.

Andersen, G. J., & Braunstein, M. L. (1983). Dynamic occlusion in the perception of rotation in depth. *Perception & Psychophysics, 34,* 356–362.

Barrow, H. G., & Tennenbaum, J. M. (1986). Computational approaches to vision. In K. R. Boff, L. Kaufman, & J. P. Thomas (Eds.), *Handbook of perception and human performance*. New York: Wiley.

Berkeley, G. (1709). *An essay toward a new theory of vision*. London: J. M. Dent.

Braunstein, M. L. Andersen, G. J., & Riefer, D. M. (1982). The use of occlusion to resolve ambiguity in parallel projections. *Perception & Psychophysics, 31*, 261–267.

Bruno, N., & Cutting, J. E. (1988). Minimodularity and the perception of layout. *Journal of Experimental Psychology: General, 117*, 161–170.

Brunswik, E. (1956). *Perception and the representative design of psychological experiments*. Berkeley: University of California Press.

Bülthoff, H. H., & Mallot, H. A. (1988). Integration of depth modules, stereo and shading. *Journal of Optical Society of America*, 1749–1758.

Burton, G., & Turvey, M. T. (1990). Perceiving the lengths of rods that are held but not wielded. *Ecological Psychology, 2*, 295–324.

Coren, S. (1986). An efferent component in the visual perception of direction and extent. *Psychological Review, 93*, 391–410.

Cutting, J. (1991). Four ways to reject direct perception. *Ecological Psychology 3*, 25–34.

Dretske, F. (1981). *Knowledge and the flow of information*. Cambridge, MA: MIT Press.

Dretske, F. (1986). Misrepresentation. In R. J. Bogdan (Ed.), *Belief: Form content and function* (16–29). Oxford: Clarendon Press.

Epstein, W. (1973). The process of taking-into-account in visual perception. *Perception, 2*, 267–285.

Epstein, W. (1977). *Stability and constancy in visual perception*. New York: Wiley.

Gibson, E. J., Riccio, G., Schmuckler, M. A., Stoffregen, T. A., Rosenberg, D., & Taormina, J. (1987). Detection of the traversability of surfaces by crawling and walking infants. *Journal of Experimental Psychology: Human Perception and Performance, 13*, 533–544.

Gibson, E. J., & Walk, R. D. (1960). The "visual cliff." *Scientific American, 202*, 64–84.

Gibson, J. J. (1950). *The perception of the visual world*. Boston: Houghton Mifflin.

Gibson, J. J. (1959). Perception as a function of stimulation. In S. Koch (Ed.), *Psychology: A study of a science: Vol. 1* (pp. 456–501). New York: McGraw Hill.

Gibson, J. J. (1966). *The senses considered as perceptual systems*. Boston: Houghton Mifflin.

Gibson, J. J. (1977). On the analysis of change in the optic array. *Scandinavian Journal of Psychology, 18*, 161–163.

Gibson, J. J. (1979). *The ecological approach to visual perception*. Boston: Houghton Mifflin.

Gregory, R. L. (1993). Seeing and thinking. *Italian Journal of Psychology, 20*, 749–769.

Helmholtz, H. von (1925). *Handbook of psychological optics* (Vol. 3, J. P. C. Southall, Trans.). New York: Dover. (Original work published 1867)

Hoffman, D. D. (1983). The interpretation of visual illusions. *Scientific American, 249*, 154–162.

Holway, A. F., & Boring, E. G. (1941). Determinants of apparent visual size with distance variant. *American Journal of Psychology, 54*, 21–37.

Ittelson, W. H. (1960). *Visual space perception*. New York: Springer.

Johansson, G. (1950). *Configurations in event perception*. Uppsala: Almquist & Wiksell.

Johansson, G. (1973). Visual perception of biological motion and a model for its analysis. *Perception & Psychophysics, 14*, 201–211.

Johansson, G. (1977). Spatial constancy and motion in visual perception. In W. Epstein (Ed.), *Stability and constancy in visual perception* (pp. 375–420). New York: Wiley.

Johansson, G., von Hofsten, C., & Jansson, G. (1980). Event perception. *Annual Review of Psychology, 31*, 27–63.

Kanisza, G. (1979). *Organization in vision*. New York: Praeger.

Kaplan, G. A. (1969). Kinetic disruption of optical texture: The perception of depth at an edge. *Perception & Psychophysics, 6*, 193–198.

Kilpatrick, F. P. (Ed.). (1952). *Human behavior from a transactional point of view.* Hanover, NH: Institute for Associated Research.

Kilpatrick, F. P. (1961). *Explorations in transactional psychology.* New York: New York University Press.

Koffka, K. (1935). *Principles of Gestalt psychology.* New York: Harcourt, Brace.

Köhler, W. (1940). *Dynamics in psychology.* New York: Liveright.

Künnapas, T. (1968). Distance perception as a function of available cues. *Journal of Experimental Psychology, 77,* 523–529.

Landy, M. S., Maloney, L. T., & Young, M. J. (1991). Psychophysical estimation of the human combination rule. *Sensor fusion III: 3D Perception and Recognition, Proceedings of the SPIE, 1383,* 247–254.

Marr, D. (1982). *Vision.* San Francisco: Freeman.

Mill, J. S. (1842). Bailey on Berkeley's theory of vision. *Westminster Review,* October, 1842. In J. S. Mill (1874). *Dissertations and discussions.* Vol. 2 (pp. 162–191). New York: Holt.

Nakayama, K., & Shimojo, S. (1992). Experiencing and perceiving visual surfaces. *Science, 257,* 1357–1363.

Pittenger, J. B. (1989). Multiple sources of information: Threat or menace. *ISEP Newsletter, 4,* 5–8.

Poggio, T., Torre, V., & Koch, C. (1985). Computational vision and regularization theory. *Nature, 317,* 314–319.

Postman, L., & Tolman, E. C. (1958). Brunswik's probabilistic functionalism. In S. Koch (Ed.), *Psychology: A study of a science* (Vol. 1, pp. 502–564). New York: McGraw Hill.

Rock, I. (1983). *The logic of perception.* Cambridge, MA: Bradford Books/MIT Press.

Rogers, B., & Cagnello, R. (1989). Disparity curvature and the perception of three-dimensional surfaces. *Nature, 339,* 135–137.

Sedgwick, H. A. (1986). Space perception. In K. R. Boff, L. Kaufman, & J. P. Thomas (Eds.), *Handbook of perception and human performance* (Vol. 1). New York: Wiley.

Shannon, C. E., & Weaver, W. (1949). *The mathematical theory of communication.* Urbana: University of Illinois Press.

Shepard, R. N. (1990). *Mind sights* (pp. 168–186). New York: Freeman.

Toye, R. C. (1986). The effect of viewing position on the perceived layout of scenes. *Perception & Psychophysics, 40,* 85–92.

Wagner, M. (1985). The metric of visual space. *Perception & Psychophysics, 38,* 483–495.

Wallach, H. (1939). On constancy of visual speed. *Psychological Review, 46,* 544–552.

Wallach, H. (1948). Brightness constancy and the nature of achromatic colors. *Journal of Experimental Psychology, 38,* 310–334.

Wallach, H., & O'Connell, D. N. (1953). The kinetic depth effect. *Journal of Experimental Psychology, 45,* 205–217.

Wertheimer, M. (1912). Experimentelle studien über das sehen von bewegung. *Zeitschrift Psychologie, 61,* 121–163.

CHAPTER 2

The Perception of Spatial Layout from Static Optical Information

Barbara Gillam

I. INTRODUCTION

The present chapter will review the literature on absolute distance, relative distance, surface slant and curvature, and the perception of size and shape within the context of several broad issues that have influenced thinking and experimentation to varying degrees in recent years. These issues will be outlined here and referred to where relevant throughout the chapter.

One issue that has driven recent research is the way stimulus input is described, which carries implicit assumptions about how it is encoded and represented. Euclidian and other conventional frameworks may be restricting and misleading as a basis for visual theory. Koenderink and Van Doorn (1976) have been particularly influential in providing new and mathematically sophisticated analyses of the proximal stimulus for vision. Recently, Todd and colleagues (Todd & Bressan, 1990; Todd & Reichel, 1989) have proposed and tested alternatives to a metric representation of spatial layout. The question of how information is represented has also been explicitly raised by workers in computational vision, of whom the most influential has been Marr (1982), although the representation issue is implicit in some older controversies (Gibson, 1950, 1966).

Another issue raised by computational approaches is the relationship

Perception of Space and Motion

between the processing of different sources of information or cues underlying the perception of spatial layout. Machine vision has tended to treat these cues (stereopsis, structure from motion, shading, perspective, etc.) as separate modules or processing systems, a view that has also received support from psychophysics (Bruno & Cutting, 1988; Dosher, Sperling, & Wurst, 1986). These and other studies have focused on how different modules are combined. However, modularity has also been questioned. Bülthoff and Mallot (1990), for example, have found some strong interactions between stereopsis and shading. Furthermore, it will be argued later in this chapter that comparison of some seemingly separate processes, specifically perspective and stereopsis, may indicate common mechanisms. Conversely, seemingly equivalent perceptual responses may show inconsistencies and intransitivities (Gillam & Chambers, 1985; Loomis, Da Silva, Fujita, & Fukusima, 1992) because, to return to the first issue raised, they are not based on a common Euclidean map but on information or representations specific to the task required.

Distance perception has provoked speculation for hundreds of years since it fails to correspond in any obvious way to properties of the retinal image and reveals perception to be a complex achievement. It is usually assumed that some nonretinal source of information must be added to the image to give distance and depth. Berkeley (1709/1960) proposed that convergence of the eyes and accommodation of the lens are used as distance cues since they both vary systematically with the distance of an object from the observer. The tradition of thinking about distance perception as essentially observer centered continues to the present time. Marr (1982), for example, proposed that in the representation he called the $2\frac{1}{2}D$ sketch, each surface is assigned a range value, that is, distance from the observer. On this view (Marr, 1982) the distances from one object to another (exocentric distances), the depths within objects, and the relative depths of objects are all derived from observer-centered distances. Marr also proposed that surface orientation is specified initially in an observer-centered fashion; that is, relative to the normal to the direction of gaze. Geographical orientations (the orientations of surfaces relative to each other or to canonical surfaces) are on this view derived from such observer-centered representations. Another example of observer-centered thinking is the view that perceived distance necessarily underlies the constancies. The conviction that size constancy for example is achieved by a process of evaluating the angular size of an object in relation to its perceived distance from the observer persists in the face of contrary experimental evidence, as will be shown later.

An alternative view is presented by the work of Gibson (1950, 1966). In what is probably the most significant development in thinking about spatial layout in the last 50 years, he departs entirely from the idea of a third dimension added to the two dimensions of the retinal image. Gibson regards all distal properties (properties of environmental layout) as deriving from information in what he called the *optic array,* defined as the structured light arriving at a particular station point (the nodal point of the eye) at a particular time. The optic array is usually approximated by its projection onto a picture plane interposed between the scene and the station point. Further information is given by changes in the optic array produced by shifts in the station point: either simultaneous (binocular parallax) or successive (motion parallax). Insofar as Gibson emphasized the information available to be picked up, rather than the physiological means by which this is done, he influenced vision research to deal with greater complexity on the input side than had traditionally been the case. It must be recognized, however, that Gibson was himself influenced by Koffka (1935), particularly by the latter's use of the concept of *invariant* properties or relationships in the visual input that do not change with viewing position and may therefore underlie perceptual constancy. Information in the optic array or arrays may specify exocentric distances and geographical orientations just as directly as, or more directly than, observer-centered ones and may specify size and shape just as directly as distance and slant. Sedgwick (1983) has given explicit expression to Gibson's ideas in the concept of an environment-centered representation directly derived from properties of the optic array. An environment-centered representation makes specific those stable geographical properties that do not change with viewpoint or distance. This has obvious advantages in economy of representation. As will be shown later in the chapter, an environment-centered representation can be based on what Sedgwick called the *perspective structure of the optic array.*

To what degree perceived properties of spatial layout are direct responses to properties of the optic array and to what degree they are derived from observer-centered distance or orientation is an empirical question, and the evidence will be considered in detail when each aspect of spatial layout is discussed. Indeed this issue constitutes a central theme of the chapter.

II. THE PERCEPTION OF ABSOLUTE DISTANCE

Regardless of its determining role for other aspects of layout perception, the perception of the absolute distance of objects and landmarks is important for an observer's behavior, especially motor behavior. It differs from relative distance perception in that it can only be specified in metric units, whereas relative distance may involve metric units, ratios, or simply an ordinal appreciation of distance.

A. Oculomotor Cues

These have an historically primary role in the theory of distance perception and operate only at close distances. As objects move closer to the observer two major oculomotor responses occur. Accommodation, a contraction of the ciliary muscles, causes the lens of the eye to become more convex. This has the effect of fine tuning the focus of the image on the retina (much of which is already achieved by the cornea). Defocus blur has traditionally been regarded as the proximal stimulus for accommodation, although changes in size (looming) have recently been found to stimulate it (Kruger & Pola, 1985).

A second oculomotor response, convergence, is achieved by disjunctive eye movements that rotate the eyes in opposite directions toward or away from the nose. Two kinds of convergence are distinguished. So-called *fusional vergence* is stimulated by diplopia. It serves to bring the two images of an object onto the foveas where they can fuse. However, accommodation itself also produces a tendency for the eyes to verge (*accommodative vergence*). This can be demonstrated under conditions in which one eye is closed and a target moves toward the other eye along its line of sight, thus eliminating any need for that eye to change position to fixate the target. The closed eye will nevertheless verge if accommodation is free to respond to the change in distance. For both kinds of vergence, vergence angle (the angle between the two visual axes) is greater for near objects than for far objects, and vergence therefore is a potential distance cue. A good critical and historical discussion of the role of oculomotor cues in the perception of distance can be found in the chapter by Hochberg (1971).

Investigation of the role of accommodation and convergence in perceiving the distance of a target from the observer is fraught with difficulties. First, links between accommodation and convergence responses (Morgan, 1968) make it difficult to investigate their effects separately. Second, accommodation and convergence are not easy to measure, and many studies of their effects on size and distance do not measure them, assuming that by varying stimulus proximity, convergence and accommodation will automatically be triggered to the optimal degree. The degree of accommodation in particular, however, varies with target features and the depth cues present and should be measured rather than assumed to have occurred (Fisher & Cuiffrieda, 1988). Third, fusional vergence can deviate to a small degree from the object of fixation if convergence is stimulated by displacing the images laterally in opposite directions on the retina, for example, with base-in or base-out prisms, without changing the plane of accommodation. This deviation is known as *fixation disparity* (Ogle, 1950). It can be measured by placing a vertical line seen only by the left eye above the binocular fixation target and another vertical line, seen only by the right eye below the fixation target. To the extent that convergence deviates from the target, these "nonius" lines will appear misaligned.

A fourth problem that often goes unrecognized is present in studies in which fusional vergence is varied either by placing a patterned frontal plane surface at different distances in a reduction tunnel or by laterally shifting left and right eye images that have been rendered eye-specific by means of polarizing vectagraphs or red–green anaglyphs. In addition to eliciting vergence changes, these stimulus conditions introduce shape differences between the images that decrease with the distance of the surface (see Figure 1). These differences, a form of binocular disparity, occur because as a surface moves closer to the observer, the angles from which it is viewed by the two eyes become increasingly acute and increasingly different. A frontal plane surface with a regular shape and pattern produces images in which both vertical and horizontal extents form gradients of size that are opposite in direction to the two eyes and that vary in steepness with the proximity of the surface. Because binocular disparity (to be discussed in detail later) is normally associated with local depth differences between two points or with slant, it is often overlooked as a factor in the perception of the distance of frontal plane surfaces, although Helmholtz (1909/1962) drew attention to it, and Swenson (1932) referred to *binocular parallax* as a confounding factor in

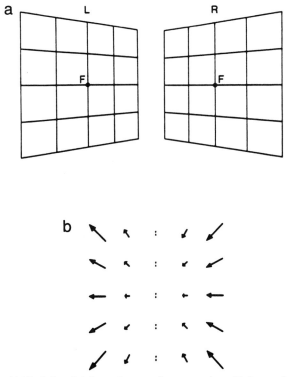

FIGURE 1   (a) The left and right eye images of a rectangular grid close to the eyes. (b) The vectors show combinations of horizontal and vertical disparity for each point on the grid (from Tyler, 1991).

convergence studies. Ames (cited in Ittelson, 1960) and Ittelson himself proposed that disparity changes are responsible for the famous "wallpaper effect" (Meyer, 1842 cited in Boring, 1942), which is usually thought of as a convergence effect. The repetitiveness of the pattern allows the eyes to verge near or far, depending on which details are locked onto. This change in vergence, however, also changes the angular relationships between the lines of sight and the congruent parts of the pattern and therefore the disparity gradients projected by the pattern. It could be these gradient changes rather than convergence per se that produce the vivid changes in apparent distance, which tend to accompany changes in vergence in the wallpaper effect.

A final complicating factor in evaluating the effects of accommodation and convergence arises from the fact that to eliminate size cues to distance, the angular size of the target is usually kept constant as accommodation and convergence are varied. Regardless of the distance effects obtained, it is always reported in such studies that an increase in accommodation and convergence is accompanied by a shrinkage in perceived size (convergence micropsia). Macropsia accompanies decreasing convergence. This is eco-logically appropriate since an object of a given angular size stimulating greater convergence would be both closer and smaller than one stimulating less convergence (Emmert's law, see Figure 2). Size scaling seems to be directly elicited by convergence. The geometrically predicted size effects are much more reliably obtained than the predicted distance effects and can themselves influence distance judgments profoundly. with subjects often

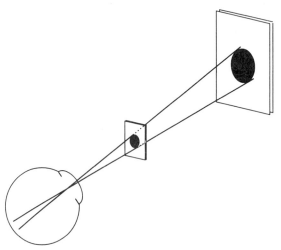

FIGURE 2   An image of constant visual angle (such as an after image) subtends an object in which physical size increases with distance from the observer (Emmert's law).

reporting that objects appear to have receded in distance when in fact the object or the vergence position has come closer. This is known as the *size–distance paradox*. It is as if the decrease in size is interpreted as an increase in distance, completely overriding any direct effect convergence might have on distance perception. The effects of size micropsia and macropsia on perceived distance vary greatly with the stimulus conditions used to elicit accommodation and convergence (Alexander, 1974). The size problem can only be eliminated, however, by using a point source, although in the case of accommodation, and probably vergence as well, a point source is not an optimal stimulus.

Bearing in mind all of these difficulties, the role of oculomotor factors in distance perception will now be considered. Only studies in which perceived distance is measured will be considered. It is known that convergence can also influence perceived stereoscopic depth (Wallach & Zuckerman, 1963) and curvature (Johnston, 1991). These scaling effects may be a secondary response to the effects of convergence on perceived distance. It is possible, however, that like the size response they are direct responses to convergence.

1. Convergence with a Point Source

When a point source is used, thereby eliminating binocular parallax and size cues, most studies find that convergence can be effective at close distances, up to about a meter (Foley, 1985; Foley & Richards, 1972; Gogel, 1977; Richards & Miller, 1969; Swenson, 1932), although there are considerable individual differences in the degree to which convergence is used.

Morrison and Whiteside (1984) found ordinally correct distance judgments up to 10 m, although there was considerable compression of range. These authors furthermore found that manipulating convergence optically was not as effective as changing the real distance of the target, and they suggested the possibility that the point source is judged to some extent on the basis of its disparity relative to the resting state of convergence in the dark. Hochberg (1971) has also pointed out that double images may play a role in producing the distance effects associated with convergence.

2. Accommodation Alone and Accommodative Vergence

In a well-conducted study, Fisher and Cuiffrieda (1988) used patterned stimuli (to be sure of optimizing the accommodation response) monocular viewing, and a kinesthetic (reaching) method for measuring perceived distance. They measured accommodation with a Badel optometer. They found that about 25% of individuals perceived distance changes related to changes in accommodation, although there was a restriction of range in apparent distance relative to accommodation distance. Like other investigators who have used a surface rather than a point source as the stimulus, they report a number of distance reversals, suggesting that size responses to the oculomotor cues were interfering with distance responses. Heineman, Tulving, and Nachmias (1959) in another well-controlled study obtained both size and distance judgments of an extended object of constant visual angle extent. They found the order of distances reversed in direction from the predicted order for seven of the eight subjects who showed distance effects at all. They attribute these distance reversals to the size micropsia induced when accommodation and accommodative vergence increased. Lens-produced accommodation and its associated vergence also seem particularly prone to distance reversals, presumably caused by the minification effect of the lens as well as size micropsia (Alexander, 1974). Although size micropsia severely interferes with attempts to investigate the effects of accommodation and convergence on perceived distance, such effects may nevertheless occur under normal viewing conditions in which they would be complemented by size cues, rather than interfered with by them.

3. Fusional Vergence and Binocular Disparities

The only studies, using extended surfaces as stimuli, which seem to be exempt from distance reversals (in that they have found, for example, that perceived distance reliably diminishes with increased convergence) tend to be those in which the surfaces at different distances are binocularly viewed (Gogel, 1961a,b, 1977; Gogel & Sturm, 1972; Komoda & Ono, 1974; Lie, 1965). This geometrically corrected effect could be due to the greater effectiveness of vergence when an extended binocular object is used, to the binocular disparity information present under these conditions, or to both of these factors. A number of such studies (e.g., Wallach & Frey, 1972) have used base-in or base-out prisms to vary vergence. These introduce distortions that are opposite in the two eyes and, therefore, may produce gradients of horizontal disparity (Linksz, 1952).

Ames (cited in Ittelson, 1960) claimed that the effect of fusional vergence on the apparent distance of surfaces is eliminated if curved surfaces are used, designed to lie on the Vieth–Müller circle (see Figure 6) so that the binocular parallax present for frontal plane surfaces is removed. He claimed that this rules out convergence as the cue responsible for the wallpaper effect. This claim was investigated by Ono, Mitson, and Seabrook (1971), who found an effect of fusional vergence on apparent distance even when such curved surfaces are used. A significantly greater effect was obtained, however, when frontal plane surfaces were used instead, thus implicating binocular parallax in stimulus arrangements of this sort. It appears from this and other experiments that disparities add significantly to the effect of convergence on the apparent distance of binocular surfaces, although they may not be effective if they conflict with convergence (Ono et al., 1971).

It is only recently that the mathematical relationship of disparity gradients to absolute distance has been studied in detail. In particular, gradients of vertical disparity have aroused considerable interest because of their special potential for providing absolute distance information (as first proposed by Helmholtz, 1867/1925). Unlike gradients of horizontal disparity, gradients of vertical disparity are little influenced by surface slant and therefore are especially informative about absolute distance and eccentricity of the surface (Gillam & Lawergren, 1983; Longuet-Higgins & Mayhew, 1982), although if the surface is taken to be in the frontal plane, gradients of horizontal disparity too can provide absolute distance information (Longuet-Higgins & Mayhew, 1982). Figure 3 (from Gillam & Lawergren, 1983) shows that the ratio of the projected size in the right eye relative to the left eye of a vertical extent increases linearly as a function of the rightward eccentricity of the extent (up to about a 40° eccentricity).[1] Significantly, as Figure 3 shows, the slope of this function decreases with observation distance of the surface and therefore provides a potential source of information about surface distance. Whether this information is used has been the subject of considerable controversy. Unfortunately most of the evidence concerning the role of vertical disparity in absolute distance perception, like some of the evidence mentioned previously concerning convergence, is not based on measurements of perceived distance as such but on the effect of vertical disparity on the scaling of various other judgments presumed to depend on perceived distance. These include stereoscopic curvature around a vertical axis (Helmholtz, 1909/1962) and stereoscopic slant around a vertical axis (Gillam, Chambers, & Lawergren, 1988a), both of which show a scaling effect of vertical disparity, and stereoscopic curvature around a horizontal axis (Cumming, Johnston, & Parker, 1991), which does not. It is possible that these scaling effects are derived from perceived distance, but it is also possible that they are direct responses to vertical disparity gradients.

---

[1] Gillam and Lawergren (1983) and Longuet-Higgins and Mayhew (1982) independently developed similar mathematical theories of vertical disparity, absolute distance, and eccentricity. Longuet-Higgins and Mayhew argued that vertical disparity specifies the eccentricity of "gaze angle," whereas Gillam and Lawergren argued that vertical disparity is a property of the optic arrays of the two eyes and specifies the eccentricity of an object independently of where the eyes are looking. Gillam and Lawergren, unlike Longuet-Higgins and Mayhew, defined vertical disparity in terms of the ratios of the vertical projections in the two eyes of a given spatial extent. This has a much simpler relationship to target eccentricity and distance than the vertical positional disparity of a point, which also depends on the distance of the point above or below the visual plane.

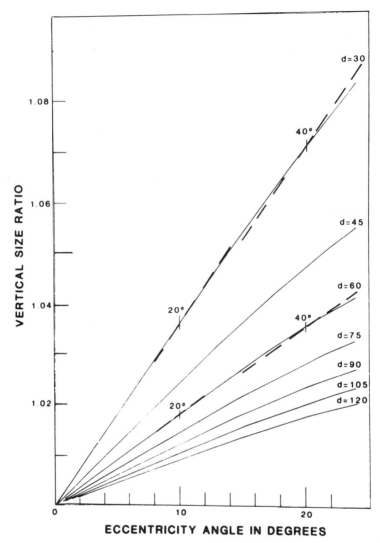

FIGURE 3   The ratio of vertical image sizes in the two eyes of vertical lines on a frontal plane centered on the visual plane at various eccentricities relative to the median plane. The parameter is the distance of the frontal plane in cm (measured along the median plane). The dashed lines each plot the vertical size ratios when the plane is slanted away from the frontal plane around an axis at the eccentricity and distance indicated by the short vertical line. The degree of slant is shown in each case. Note that slant has little effect on vertical size ratios (from Gillam & Lawergren, 1983).

Few investigators have attempted a direct test of the hypothesis that vertical disparity gradients influence distance perception. Nevertheless, the evidence from the convergence literature and the observations of Ames (cited in Ittelson, 1960) and Ono et al. (1971) strongly implicate disparity gradients in absolute distance perception, perhaps in interaction with convergence, although none of this research looks separately at vertical and horizontal disparity gradients. Rogers and Bradshaw (1993) reported however that vertical disparity gradients do influence absolute distance perception for large targets (greater than 40° of visual angle).

B. Specific Distance Tendency and Equidistance Tendency

Gogel (1965) has shown that when objects are monocularly presented in darkness without a context they are usually reported to be at a distance of approximately 2 to 4 m. He called this the *specific distance tendency,* and it constitutes a fundamental concept in other work that Gogel has carried out on size and distance perception. Owens and Liebowitz (1976) have also shown that when there is no stimulus to accommodation or convergence there is a tendency to verge and accommodate at about the distance of the specific distance tendency. They called this *the dark focus of accommodation.* The *equidistance tendency* (Gogel, 1965) describes a tendency for an observer to perceive an object of unknown distance to be at the same distance as a neighboring object. This effect decreases in strength as the angular separation of the objects increases.

C. Size as a Cue to Distance

The geometric relationship between size, distance, and visual angle is given by Equation 1, assuming that tan s approximately equals s.

$$S/D = s, \tag{1}$$

where S = physical size,
  D = distance, and
  s = visual angle (in radians).

Assuming that visual angle is always given, it is theoretically possible to derive size given distance or distance given size. The size–distance invariance hypothesis asserts that physical size, distance, and visual angle information are also perceptually related so that for a given visual angle size, the greater the distance perceived the greater the perceived size, and vice versa. This is known as the *size–distance invariance hypothesis.* The claim that perceived size is derived from perceived distance will be considered in the section on size perception. Here the concern will be on the adequacy of the claim that distance perception can be influenced by known object size given visual angle. Object size can be given either by instructing an observer as to the object's size or more commonly by relying on the observers knowledge of the sizes of familiar objects (Epstein, 1963). The literature in this area (summarized well by Hochberg, 1971, and Sedgwick, 1986) is problematic because it is possible for an observer to infer the approximate distance an object of a given familiar size or apparent size must be to subtend a visual angle of the magnitude it has, while perception in the sense of an automatic and immediate impression of distance is not affected. It is quite difficult to decide between these alternatives. The current consensus seems to be that the effect of familiar size is largely judgmental rather than perceptual (Gogel & Da Silva, 1987; Predebon, 1991). Gogel and colleagues' account of the relationship between familiar size and perceived distance (Gogel, 1977; Gogel & Da Silva, 1987; Gogel, Loomis, Newman & Sharkey, 1985) raises a number of interesting methodological and substantial questions concerning size and distance perception and will be considered in detail.

1. Gogel and Da Silva's Theory of Off-Size Perception

Gogel and Da Silva (1987) claim that although the reported distances of familiar objects viewed monocularly in the dark vary with known physical size roughly as one would expect from the size–distance invariance hypothesis, this is not the explanation. They found that the objects appeared either too small or too large (off sized). They attribute these size effects to the fact that the objects are seen at the specific distance tendency (SDT). An object whose combination of angular and familiar size would place it closer than the SDT will then appear too large when seen at the SDT, whereas one whose combination of angular and familiar size would place it further than the SDT would appear too small. According to Gogel and Da Silva, these perceived (off) sizes will be compared with the object's familiar size, and the difference will be attributed (cognitively) to distance. The too large object will be reported as close and the too small object as far, thus mimicking the effect one would expect if familiar size directly influenced perceived distance. Gogel and Da Silva support the claim that the familiar objects in their experiment were in some sense perceived at the SDT, even though not reported to be at that distance, on the basis of results obtained with an indirect method of measuring perceived distance; a method that Gogel and colleagues (Gogel, 1977; Gogel & Da Silva, 1987; Gogel & Sturm, 1972; Gogel & Tietz, 1980; Gogel, et al., 1985) have applied very widely in size–distance studies. (Indirect measures can be useful in avoiding cognitive intrusions in perceptual responses.) Gogel's method is based on position constancy during head movements. When a target is fixated and the head moved from side to side, the eyes must counterrotate to keep the target fixated. This is achieved by a combination of the vestibular–ocular reflex and pursuit eye movements (Hine & Thorn, 1987). The closer the target, the more the eyes must move to compensate for the displacement on the retina that a given head movement would cause. The magnitude of this response, if monitored, could obviously serve as a distance cue and was reported to do so by Johansson (1973, although there were some other possible cues in his experiment). Gogel asserts that the degree of ocular rotation during head movements does not in itself provide a cue to distance but that an experimenter can infer the distance at which a subject perceives a target from the degree of concomitant movement of the target he or she reports during lateral head movements made while viewing a target in the dark. Gogel claims that if the target is seen as closer than its true distance it will undergo "with" motion with the head; if it is seen as further it will undergo "against" motion. Position stability is a sign that the target is seen at its true distance. By having subjects report on these motions, Gogel claims to be able to measure perceived distance objectively, that is, uncontaminated by "cognitive" distance. There are some problems however with this account. Sedgwick and Festinger (1976) found only a poor relationship between pursuit eye movements and perceived target motion. It is also possible that eye movements do not fully compensate for head movements and that retinal slippage of the target rather than an error in perceived distance is to some degree responsible for the apparent motion. While it is clear that concomitant motion with head motion does vary with object distance (Gogel et al., 1985), it is unlikely that it has the precision necessary for use as a measure of perceived distance; especially since it does not give estimates that agree with those that are based on other measures (Gogel, 1977). An alternative account of both the size and the distance percepts in Gogel's experiment is as follows: The perceived distances were influenced by familiar size but not completely determined by it, being closer to the SDT. The apparent sizes were somewhat influenced by familiar size but also by apparent distance, which was closer to the SDT than the true distance. This led to the objects appearing somewhat off sized. Thus, both the distance and size effects can be explained in a manner that avoids the awkward distinction Gogel makes between perceived and cognitive distance.

Gogel's concept of perceived distance to refer to a distance that is different from the one reported by subjects and that nevertheless enters into the size–distance invariance equation resembles the concept of "registered" distance. This concept, the use of which in the older German literature was already criticized by Koffka (1935), is further discussed below.

2. Complexities of Distance Responses

There are really two distinctions in the distance response domain that need to be made. The first is the distinction between physical distance inferred by the subject (perhaps on the basis of apparent size or familiar size) and apparent or perceived physical distance. Depending on instructions, subjects' responses may reflect one or the other. This distinction seems quite legitimate and has been well developed by Carlson (1977) and Predebon (1991). On the other hand, there is the distinction between apparent physical distance (consciously available) and registered distance (not consciously available). This distinction is much less legitimate in that the distinction is not tied, like that between inferred and apparent distance, to stimulus conditions such as instructions nor generally to response criteria. (Gogel & Da Silva, 1987, is the exception here.) Registered distance is normally postulated to account for the subject's judgment of some property such as size, on the assumption that this can only have been derived from distance on the basis of the size–distance invariance hypothesis. Often distance is not measured but is simply inferred from size judgments (Wallach & Frey, 1972; Gogel et al., 1985). In more extreme cases in which perceived size is not predictable from the observers' distance reports (such as the size-distance paradox), it is assumed that some other distance, registered unconsciously, determines the size response (Higashiyama, 1977; Rock & Kaufman, 1962). Rock and Kaufman give a good exposition of this position.

The concept of registered distance is a post hoc one that is based on a theoretical assumption of the necessary truth of the size–distance invariance hypothesis. Instead, however, the very observations that make the postulation of registered distance necessary can be regarded as violations of the hypothesis. Indeed, for years the empirical basis of the size–distance invariance hypothesis has been challenged (Epstein, Park, & Casey, 1961; Gruber, 1954; Kilpatrick & Ittelson, 1953; Sedgwick, 1986). In support of this position, it will be argued in the section on size perception that just because size judgments vary with distance cues, it does not logically follow that these cues have their effect through the mediation of distance judgments.

3. The General Issue of Assumed Properties in Absolute Distance Perception

The proposition that familiar size might be used in perceiving absolute distance can be thought of as one example of a much more general class of distance cues that is rarely considered: namely the information available from the projected properties of configurations if they can be assumed to have certain physical or distal properties. Another example of the same genre of cues was already mentioned: Horizontal disparities would provide absolute distance information if they can be assumed to arise from a frontal plane surface. Absolute distance could in theory also be derived from the form ratio (Braunstein & Payne, 1969); that is, the relationship between the projection of the width to the depth of an object assumed to be a cube lying on the ground or a horizontal disc, for example, the top of a wastebasket. This is so because, to anticipate the next section, the diminution of projected widths is approximately proportional to distance, whereas the diminution of projected depths is approximately proportional to distance squared. The ratio of width to the disparity of the depth of an assumed regular object could also potentially serve this function. Few of these factors have ever been investigated, and some may be a rich source of useable information about absolute distance. Gogel and Tietz (1980) are some of the few investigators to realize the potential of combining sources of information to determine absolute distance. They pointed out that absolute distance can be specified by the combination of relative size and motion parallax. They did not find that subjects were able to make use of this information. Other information of this general type may, however, be used.

D. Far Distance Perception

In general, studies of distance perception in the open air have concentrated on exploring the accuracy with which it can be done. They have not tried to isolate the sources of distance information, which is of course difficult to do over large areas of space. Levin and Haber (1993) had subjects verbally estimate the distances in feet between stakes placed around a flat grassy area approximately 20 ft in diameter (up to 40 ft from the observer.) Binocular vision was used. They found that subjects were extremely accurate. Judged distance was a linear function with a slope of 1 and an intercept of 1. (In these experiments, it should be noted that the targets were all the same real size which could have provided a cue to relative egocentric distance.) There was a small tendency to overestimate distances perpendicular to the line of sight, but subjects were no more inaccurate in estimating exocentric distances than egocentric distances. Other studies (e.g., Loomis et al., 1992) have found, however, that frontal distances must be considerably greater than distances lying in depth in order to appear to be of equal extent.

Some studies have measured perceived distance by means of motor responses such as ball throwing (Eby & Loomis, 1987) or walking toward a previously viewed scene with eyes closed (Thomson, 1983; Loomis et al., 1992). Eby and Loomis eliminated size as a cue and found increasing deviations from accuracy beyond approximately 10 m. In Thomson's study, subjects were able to walk with accuracy toward targets up to 25 m away. More recent studies using walking with the eyes closed have, however, found increasing error with distance but impressive accuracy up to 12 m (Loomis et al., 1992). The motoric data in general indicates that distance perception is very accurate, whereas matching methods may indicate considerable error. For a discussion of the issues raised by this discrepency see Hochberg (1971), Loomis et al. (1992), and Cook and Griffiths (1991).

Another approach is to use fractionation measures. This allows apparent distance to be plotted as a power function of real distance, although, since fractionation measures are distance ratios, they do not allow conclusions to be drawn about the accuracy of distance perception in metric units. Cook (1978) showed that the same exponent was found for a given individual over a range of distance tasks, thus supporting the scalability of distance perception. He found that the exponent averages approximately one, but there are considerable stable individual differences.

1. Perspective and Distance: The Ground Plane

Another approach to the study of distance perception at greater distances is to analyze the pictorial information available (information available in a picture plane projection of a single optic array). This approach was pioneered by Gibson and his students (Gibson, 1950, 1966) but there is little actual data concerning the degree to which the various sources of information are used. Sedgwick (1986) provides an excellent account of the pictorial information about spatial layout, only some of which will be discussed here.

Fundamental to Gibson's (1950, 1966) account is the concept of the ground plane on which objects rest and which may therefore be used to locate them in space. The layout of surfaces, including the ground plane, is given by both the explicit and implicit structure of the optic array (Hay, 1974; Sedgwick, 1986). Equally sized and spaced texture elements on the ground plane form a gradient of size and spacing in the optic array. The further they are in the scene, the more closely spaced the elements are in the optic array. The gradient provides a scale of equivalent exocentric distances and can also specify egocentric distance by the relationship of the nearest elements to the body. There are two ways in which texture can vary that influence its effectiveness in providing information about distance. (Perceived slant and curvature, to be discussed later, are also influenced by these factors.) They are (1) whether the texture is regular or stochastic and (2) whether the elements and spacings forming the gradient are parallel to the picture plane (widths and heights) or orthogonal to the picture plane (depths). For dot patterns, gradients of regular texture are more effective than gradients of stochastic texture, and among regular textures, gradients of extents parallel to the frontal plane (widths and heights) are more effective than gradients of extents orthogonal to the frontal plane (depths, Vickers, 1971). The former is known as linear perspective, the latter as compression (or foreshortening). Figure 4 illustrates these two gradients. Linear perspective and compression differ in several ways. In a linear perspective gradient, element widths (or heights) diminish proportionally to their distance from the eye (or camera). In a compression gradient, element depths diminish approximately proportionally to the square of their distance from the eye (Gibson, 1950). This arises from the fact that in the latter case not only does projected size diminish with distance of the texture

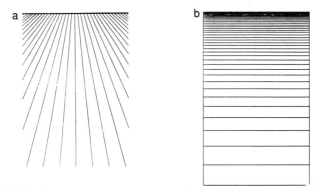

FIGURE 4   (a) A linear perspective gradient. (b) A compression gradient.

element from the eye, but also the surface forms an increasingly steep angle with the line of regard as distance increases, which causes an increased foreshortening of extents in the picture plane. In other words, a compression gradient is subject to two independent sources of diminution as distance increases.

A second difference between the two types of gradient that is of perceptual significance is that there is an emergent feature associated with linear perspective (which gives it its name). The implicit or explicit parallel lines joining the endpoints of widths or heights of a set of identical objects on a receding ground plane are not parallel in the optic array. For example, each line on the ground plane parallel to the median plane has an orientation that deviates from vertical as its lateral deviation from the median plane increases (see Figure 4). These lines converge implicitly or explicitly to a vanishing point. Line convergence gives an extremely powerful impression of distance. There is no equivalent emergent feature in the case of compression.

The vanishing point of a set of parallel lines will vary with the orientation of the lines on the ground plane, but all sets of parallel lines on a common planar surface will have vanishing points that line up in a horizon. The horizon of the ground plane (as for all horizontal planes) is horizontal and at eye level in the optic array. The horizon of the ground plane itself provides information about distance. An object on the ground plane is more distant the closer it is to the horizon in the optic array. (This is known as the cue of *height in the field.*) Sedgwick (1986) showed that the angular deviation in the optic array of the base of an object on the ground from the horizon specifies absolute distance relative to a scale factor (the observer's eye height). Also, the more distant an object, the more the gaze must be raised to look at it if it is above the horizon or lowered if it is below the horizon (Wallach & O'Leary, 1982). An object at infinity will require a level gaze.

Figure 5 shows that vanishing points and their horizon are implicitly

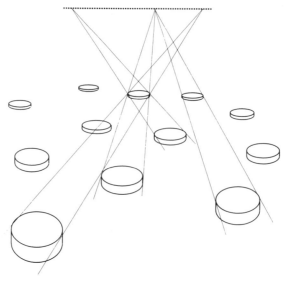

FIGURE 5   A figure in which objects are arranged stochastically. The vanishing points of lines joining any two objects form a horizon (shown by the dotted line).

specified even for stochastic arrangements of objects on a plane that have identical size and shape (Sedgwick, 1986), an observation supported experimentally by Cutting and Millard (1984). It is not surprising then that stochastic arrangements of objects of finite size give a much better impression of distance than the same stochastic arrangement of dots, which do not provide implicit vanishing points. There has been little research in which texture gradients, linear perspective, and the horizon have systematically been varied to determine their role in distance perception, although some or all of these factors are assumed to play a major role in the perception of far distances and to provide an assumed source of accurate distance information in evaluating other cues (Gogel, 1977; Johansson, 1973). It should be noted that texture gradients provide information about the distance between objects in any direction just as well as they provide range information, or the distance of an object to the observer, so long as the objects are seen to be in contact with the ground plane.

III. THE PERCEPTION OF RELATIVE DISTANCE

A. Relative Angular Size

Although familiar size is not well supported as a determinant of perceived distance, many studies confirm that in the absence of any other depth cues, the relative angular size of objects of similar shape is perceived as a difference in relative distance rather than as a difference in size at the same distance (Hochberg & Hochberg, 1952). There is some evidence that a relative angular size effect occurs even when objects are not the same shape (Epstein & Franklin, 1965). Relative distance can also be given by texture gradients on a plane. Twice as many texture elements will specify twice the distance even if the scale factor, which gives a texture element a metric unit value, is not available.

B. Stereopsis

One of the most effective sources of relative distance (depth) information is binocular disparity. The sense of relative distance based on disparity is known as *stereopsis*. Although it is not the business of this chapter to consider motion, it should be mentioned that motion parallax unlike binocular disparity is poor in giving a strong impression of the relative distance for two objects (Gibson, Gibson, Smith, & Flock, 1959) or for sparse fields of objects (Rock, 1984).

Binocular disparity is best understood as the difference between the two perspective views of a configuration or scene which are available in binocular vision (Wheatstone, 1838). The relationship between the two views varies with the depth within the configuration viewed, its distance from the observer, its eccentricity and, of course, the interocular distance or the difference in station points. Identical images on the two eyes (cover points) only occur for points in external space placed on the *geometric horopter*.[2] The significance of the horopter for stereopsis is to provide a useful geometric reference for mapping binocular images onto external space.

The geometric horopter is a horizontal circle (the Vieth–Müller circle, Figure 6) and a line passing vertically through the fixation point (Nakayama, 1977). All other points will be imaged on noncorresponding positions in the two eyes, that is, they will have *positional disparity*. If a Euclidean framework is imposed, such noncorrespondence can be described as horizontal disparity, vertical disparity, or a combination of the two.

It can be seen from Wheatstone's (1838) stereograms (Figure 7) that there are many ways in which the difference between the two binocular views may be described. There are differences in orientation, curvature, and spatial frequency. Any of these could potentially be a primitive for the stereoscopic system. The simplest difference, however, and the one that has until recently received almost all the research attention is the difference in horizontal angular separation between the left and right eye images of two points at different depths (angular disparity, see Figure 8). Whereas posi-

---

[2] Other horopters are defined visually by using criteria of common visual direction and fusion (Ogle, 1950; Tyler, 1991).

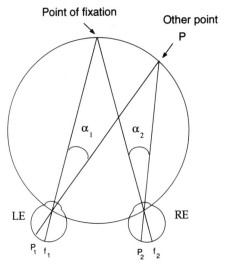

FIGURE 6   The Vieth–Müller circle. All points on the circle stimulate corresponding points (cover points on the two eyes; LE = left and RE = right eye). Any two points on the circle also have zero angular disparity.

tional disparity (the degree to which a single point in space projects to geometrically noncorresponding points in the two eyes) varies with the fixation point, angular disparity is invariant across fixation points. The equation giving the approximate relationship between the angular disparity, the depth and distance of the configuration, and the interocular distance is approximately given by Equation 2.

$$\eta = \frac{\delta a}{\gamma(\gamma + \delta)}, \qquad (2)$$

where
η = disparity,
a = interocular distance,
γ = distance, and
δ = depth.

It should be noted that angular disparity decreases approximately with the square of the distance, assuming that δ is small relative to γ. Again, as in the case of the monocular cue of compression, this is because there are two independent factors determining the shrinkage with distance. One is that the two eyes' views become more and more similar as distance increases. The second is that all projected extents and, therefore, the differences between them diminish with distance (Wallach & Zuckerman, 1963).

Stereoacuity, the smallest angular difference between the images of two lines that can be perceived as a depth difference is a hyperacuity (Westheimer & McKee, 1978); that is, the angular difference that can be resolved is

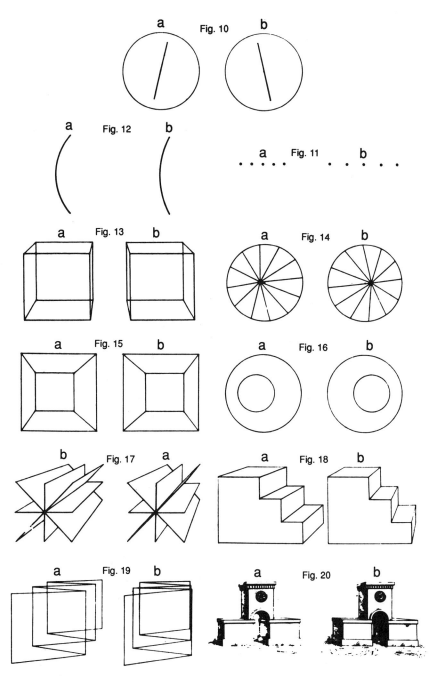

FIGURE 7   Wheatstone's (1838) stereograms showing a variety of image differences that can give rise to depth when the images are combined stereoscopically.

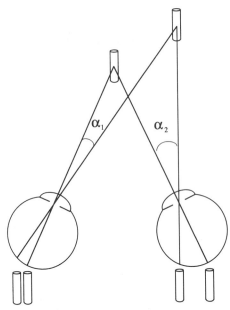

FIGURE 8 Angular disparity for two objects in depth. Disparity is conventionally specified as $\alpha_1 - \alpha_2$.

smaller than the angular subtense of a single cone and must be based on an evaluation of the distribution of activity among several receptors. Stereoacuity is typically between 3 and 30 s/arc but varies with a number of stimulus factors (see Amigo, 1964, for a summary of the older literature; Schor & Badcock, 1985; Westheimer & McKee, 1978). It is more resistant than vernier acuity to a vertical separation of the targets (Berry, 1948) and not affected by their common lateral motion (Westheimer & McKee, 1978). It also decreases with the lateral separation of the targets (Graham, Riggs, Mueller, & Solomon, 1949; Hirsch & Weymouth, 1948; McKee, Welch, Taylor, & Brown, 1990). Indeed stereoscopic acuity, binocular fusability (Burt & Julesz, 1980), and the magnitude of perceived depth (Bülthoff, Fahle, & Wegmann, 1991; Tyler, 1973) are functions not of disparity per se but of *the disparity gradient* (the ratio between the angular disparity of two elements and their angular separation). In other words, the greater the separation of two elements, the more their disparity must be increased to maintain the same effect as for two elements in close proximity. Ogle (1950) and Foley and Richards (1972) showed, however, that at greater lateral separations, stereoscopic acuity can be considerably increased by eye movements between the targets. The reasons for this are not known, but see Enright (1991).

It has been shown that the depth between a pair of objects in binocular vision is not only given by their own disparity but by the disparity of neighboring items (Mitchison & Westheimer, 1984; Westheimer, 1986) and by the proximity of the objects to surfaces whose orientation in depth is given by stereopsis (Gulick & Lawson, 1976; Mitchison & Westheimer, 1984) or monocularly (Agee & Gogel, 1967; Kumar & Glaser, 1992). Unlike the pictorial location of isolated objects by means of their perceived attachment to the ground plane, stereoscopically viewed objects do not need to be seen to be attached to stereoscopically viewed surfaces for such surfaces to mediate the depth between them.

The high acuity of stereoscopic depth perception makes it important for fine motor responses with the hands (Servos, Goodale, & Jakobson, 1992). Stereopsis is not just a near vision sense, however. It is also crudely useful at considerable distances. On the basis of stereoscopic acuity, it is possible to work out the greatest observation distance at which stereopsis can distinguish differences in depth. For a relatively poor stereoscopic acuity of 30 s/arc, objects approximately half a kilometer away are distinguishably nearer than infinity.

Although fusion of the left and right eye image is only possible up to about 14 min of arc angular disparity in the fovea (a much lower disparity than can be fused in the periphery, Ogle, 1950), a qualitative sense of depth can be obtained up to about 2° disparity, despite the presence of double images (Foley, Applebaum, & Richards, 1975). Double images should be much more phenomenologically ubiquitous than they are, given the extreme disparities that occur all of the time at far distances while viewing near objects, and vice versa. Suppression takes care of some potentially double images. When looking at a far scene, for example, there are two unfuseable images of a near object. If one of those corresponds to an image of the background in the other eye and the other background image is occluded, the sole background image will be seen, with the corresponding foreground image being suppressed. This has the effect of making the maximum amount of detail available from a scene. The process responsible is probably related to the suppression studied by Levelt (1965) in which the image with less blur and higher contrast, higher spatial frequency, or both suppresses its corresponding but nonfuseable image in the other eye. For more recent accounts of the processes of suppression and the related process of binocular rivalry see Blake (1989) and Wolfe (1986).

Since disparity for a given depth decreases with the square of the distance, it is obvious that disparity needs to be scaled for distance, that is, to be subject to a constancy process, for depth perception to be veridical (see Figure 9). Stereoscopic depth constancy was first demonstrated by Wallach and Zuckerman (1963), who used real pyramids with the square base away from the observer and obtained both size (the base) and depth (base to apex) matches for two equivalent distances (produced by setting an arrangement

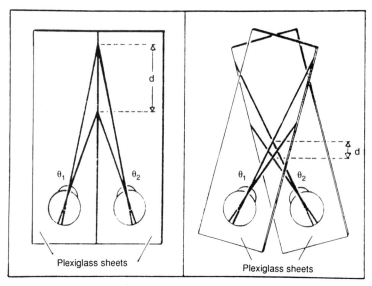

FIGURE 9   Illustration of how the same angular disparity can be produced by different depth intervals (d) for configurations at different distances from the eyes (from Ono & Comerford, 1977).

of mirrors). They found both judgments to be rather accurate, with depth for a constant disparity increasing with the square of the distance, whereas size increased proportionally with distance. They attribute the distance effects to convergence. For a good summary of the older literature on stereoscopic depth constancy, see Ono and Comerford (1977). Familiar size and linear perspective cues to distance (O'Leary & Wallach, 1980) and the frontal size of the target or neighboring targets (Gogel, 1960; Collett, Schwartz, & Sobel, 1991) also influence the degree of depth perceived for a given disparity. Sobel and Collett (1991), however, failed to find any depth scaling effect when changes in viewing distance from 12.5 to 100 cm were simulated by manipulating disparity gradients with convergence constant. Seen depth was always appropriate to the convergence distance (50 cm). It is possible that disparity gradients are effective in stimulating distance scaling only for more complex patterns of stimulation and only in co-operation with convergence.

Cormack (1984) purported to confirm depth constancy out to distances as great as 100 m. He had subjects match a probe to the apparent depth of a target. This task, however, does not reveal the apparent depth of the target and probe whose depth difference has been nulled; a problem that is common in nulling tasks (see, for example, Lie, 1965; Ritter, 1977). Foley (1985) used verbal estimates and reaching with an unseen hand and confirmed his theory that the perceived depth between two points is based on the "effective distance," which is not the same as the physical distance when convergence is the only distance cue. The question arises for depth scaling as it does for size scaling as to whether it is an indirect effect of distance perception or a direct effect of distance cues such as convergence.

Much of the work that bears on the question of stereoscopic constancy scaling has concerned the scaling of stereoscopic slant and curvature rather than depth per se and will be dealt with in the next section, which is concerned with these judgments.

IV. SURFACE PERCEPTION—SLANT AND CURVATURE

A. Pictorial Information

Although the role of texture gradients in the perception of absolute distance has been little investigated empirically, they have received a great deal of attention in relation to judgments of slant and more recently curvature.

Despite Gibson's (1950) initial claims, it has been known since the fifties that gradients of stochastic dot texture give a poor impression of slant (Braunstein, 1968; Clark, Smith, & Rabe, 1956; Gillam, 1968; Rosinski & Levine, 1976). Texture density has also been found to give a poor perception of curvature (Cutting & Millard, 1984; Todd & Akerstrom, 1987).

The early finding that outline convergence led to accurate slant judgments of isolated objects (Clark, et al., 1956) foreshadowed later findings that linear perspective is the major determinant of effective monocular pictorial slant (Braunstein, 1968; Gillam, 1968; Rosinski & Levine, 1976). Unlike texture density, it also shows considerable dominance when placed in conflict with stereopsis in a slant-matching task (Gillam, 1968; Stevens, Lee, & Brooks, 1991). Perspective curvature is also found to be dominant over stereoscopic curvature when introduced for regular checkerboard type patterns (Stevens & Brookes, 1988). Compression on its own gives a very poor slant impression even with regular patterns (Braunstein & Payne, 1969; Gillam, 1968). The form ratio (the projected depth to width ratio of a regular object), although a poor slant cue compared with linear perspective (Braunstein & Payne, 1969), appears to play a role in the perception of curvature (Cutting & Millard, 1984).

Linear perspective has several properties that may contribute to its effectiveness compared with compression in supporting perception of slant. Sedgwick (1986) points out that the slant of a surface is given by the angle of the line of regard to the horizon of the surface (the locus of the vanishing points of all the sets of parallel lines on the surface). Vanishing points are implicitly specified by the converging lines or implicit lines always present in configurations providing linear perspective even when they are not explicitly represented. There is no emergent feature in the compression of depths in the scene that can imply or specify a vanishing point so directly. Vanishing points can also be used to evaluate relative geographical slant. Surfaces that have the same geographical slant will have the same horizon since they are parallel to each other.

At the beginning of this chapter the computational view was presented that geographical slant, defined as the slant of a surface relative to a canonical slant such as the ground plane or alternatively the slant of one surface relative to another, is derived from optical slant or viewer-centered slant, which is defined as the local slant of a surface relative to the direction of gaze (Marr, 1982). The ground plane, for example, changes optical slant with distance from the observer as it forms an increasingly acute angle with the direction of gaze, whereas its geographical slant remains constant. Gibson (1950) himself believed initially that the latter was derived from the former but realized later that this is not necessary. As mentioned previously, the implicit structure of the optic array provides information from which geographical slant can be derived directly. Sedgwick and Levy (1985) conducted an experiment that further supported the hypothesis that geographical slant is directly perceived rather than derived from optical slant. They had subjects view two surfaces that were placed in different directions relative to the observer. Subjects had to match the surfaces either for optical slant, which would result in different geographical slants, or for geographical slant, which would result in different optical slants. They found that subjects were significantly more precise in matching geographical slants, which makes it unlikely that geographical slant is derived from optical slant.

B. Stereoscopic Slant

Stereoscopic slant perception, like stereoscopic surface perception generally, could be achieved by responding to the gradients of positional disparity for elements on the surface. Gillam, Flagg, and Finlay (1984) called this *the surface mode* of stereoscopic slant perception. Alternatively, stereoscopic slant could be achieved by responding to the local depth information provided by disparity discontinuities at the boundaries between surfaces at different depths and extrapolating from the boundary across the surface. Certain similarities with brightness perception are obvious. (See Brookes and Stevens,, 1989b, for a general discussion of this analogy.) Gillam et al. (1984) called this the *boundary mode*. These two modes will be considered in turn because they raise different issues.

1. The Surface Mode and Slant Anisotropy

Stereoscopic slant was first studied and analyzed in detail by K. N. Ogle in his landmark book *Researches in Binocular Vision* (1950). Much of the book is given to the study of the slant perception resulting from the imposition of disparity gradients on frontal plane surfaces. Before the days of computers this was done by the aniseikonic lenses invented by Ames (1946), which create disparity gradients by differentially magnifying the images in the two eyes in various meridians. Gradients of horizontal disparity in both the vertical and horizontal meridians were found by Ogle to elicit geometrically predicted slants around the horizontal and vertical axes, respectively (the geometric effect), although surprisingly he did not discover the strong axis anisotropy in these responses, favoring slant around the horizontal axis, perhaps because he studied mostly vertical axis slant always under optimal conditions.

The anisotropy, however, has been of considerable interest during the last 10 years since it cannot be explained at the level of local positional disparity and implicates more global factors in stereoscopic slant perception.

Under what conditions does the anisotropy occur?

In studying stereoscopic slant perception, other slant cues cannot easily be eliminated. They will either conflict with or contribute to the slant perceived on the basis of stereopsis. One way to examine the effects of stereopsis without this complication is to do as Ogle (1950) did and impose disparity gradients on surface patterns that are known to be poor monocularly, such as patterns of random dot texture.[3] Under these conditions, slant around a horizontal axis (floor plane) is quickly perceived (Gillam, Chambers, & Russo, 1988b), has a low-detection threshold (Rogers & Graham, 1983), and is approximately as geometrically predicted by the disparity gradient present (Gillam & Rogers, 1991). Under the same conditions, slant around a vertical axis is often very difficult to perceive. It has a higher threshold for detection (Rogers & Graham, 1983), is attenuated in degree (Gillam et al., 1984; Holliday & Braddick, 1991; Mitchison & McKee, 1990), can have a very long latency (Ames, 1946; Gillam et al., 1988b; Seagrim, 1967) and even be reversed in direction (Gillam, 1967; Gillam, 1993; Seagrim, 1967).

The horizontal–vertical anisotropy is a striking effect. The problem of its origins is by no means solved, but there are a number of clues as to its nature that have considerable interest because they link stereoscopic slant to other forms of slant perception and suggest that it is not as modular as it is usually considered to be.

The global difference between the images when a horizontal disparity gradient is imposed in the horizontal meridian (slant around a vertical axis) is a difference in spatial frequency or a compression of one image relative to

---

[3] Even then, however, accommodation and accommodative convergence (although not fusional vergence) are in conflict with stereoscopic slant (Buckley & Frisby, 1993).

the other (see Figure 10[a]). This is quite unlike the global difference resulting from the imposition of a gradient of horizontal disparity in the vertical meridian (slant around a horizontal axis). Globally this can be described as the horizontal shearing of one image relative to the other (see Figure 10[b]). The shear transformation introduces orientation disparity relative to the vertical but not relative to the horizontal. The particular stereoscopic effectiveness of horizontal shear, which they called *transverse disparity* as opposed to simple *width disparity,* was first pointed out by Wallach and Bacon (1976). Although there has been some speculation that it is the disparity of the angle between the vertical and horizontal orientations that is critical (in line with Koenderink and Van Doorn's, 1976, theory that slant is given by the deformation of the disparity field), research has not supported this view (Gillam & Rogers, 1991). The possibility has also been ruled out that the difference between the effectiveness of uniocular compression and horizontal shear can be eliminated by using oblique line stimuli, which equate the absolute magnitudes of orientation disparity in the two cases (Gillam & Ryan, 1992; Mitchison & McKee, 1990). It must be concluded that there is something particularly effective about horizontal shear.

The really interesting point about stereoscopic anisotropy, when the global differences between the disparate images are considered, is that it is similar to the differential effectiveness of monocular slant perception on the basis of linear perspective and compression as discussed previously. Linear perspective, which involves a shearing of the image, is highly effective, whereas texture compression is ineffective. Rogers and Graham (1983) also found a similar anisotropy in the perceptual response to gradients of motion parallax. The geometric similarity between stereopsis and motion parallax is well recognized as is the geometric equivalence between motion parallax

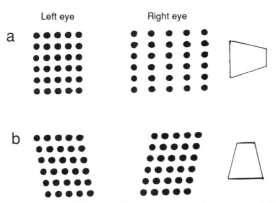

FIGURE 10   Global image differences for (a) slant around a vertical axis (horizontal gradients of disparity) and (b) slant around a horizontal axis (vertical gradients of disparity; Gillam et al., 1988b).

(the relative motions in the changing optic array when the head is moved) and structure from motion (the relative motions in the changing optic array when a configuration is moved relative to a fixed head). It is not often recognized however, that stereopsis is to monocular perspective in the static domain as motion parallax is to structure from motion in the motion domain.

The only caveat is that unlike motion parallax, stereopsis only provides horizontally separated views and therefore it cannot mimic the perspective effects of displacing elements vertically or obliquely in the visual field. The similarity is confined to the effects of lateral displacements: With this restriction, the two modes of attaining an appreciation of static spatial layout can be shown to be geometrically equivalent, just as motion parallax and structure from motion are. The argument is as follows: For a surface slanted around a horizontal axis, for example, the ground plane, the two stereoscopic views of a line or implicit line extending into depth differ by a shear transformation (see Figure 10b). In monocular perspective, likewise, such a line on the ground plane will undergo a shear transformation if shifted laterally from the center of vision (see Figure 4). This is the basis of linear perspective or the convergence of parallel lines in the picture plane. For a surface slanted around a vertical axis (e.g., a wall plane), the two stereoscopic views differ in the degree to which details are compressed (see Figure 10a). Similarly, if such a plane is viewed monocularly from positions that vary in lateral displacement from the center of vision, details will undergo a change in the compression of details along the meridian perpendicular to the axis of slant (see Figure 4).

The fact that in all three modes of perceiving spatial layout, motion, perspective, and stereopsis shear is highly effective, whereas compression is ineffective, suggests that stereoscopic anisotropy is at least partly to be explained by a general difficulty the visual system has with processing certain geometries as opposed to others.[4] There is, however, a major difference between stereopsis, motion parallax, and structure from motion, on the one hand, and monocular perspective on the other; namely, that the former are able to recover the shear even when the stimulus is a random dotted texture, whereas the latter cannot. This can, however, easily be explained. The reason that shear is not retrievable from a slanted random dot pattern in monocular perspective is that it is carried by unrelated pattern elements. It can only be picked up when there are elements in different parts of the pattern that can be assumed to have the same real-world orientation, such as rectilinear forms. That is why linear perspective is not available for stochastic dotted patterns. In stereopsis, on the other hand, it does not

---

[4] Nakayama et al. (1985) found a much lower threshold for motion per se in random dots when the motion was based on shear rather than compression.

matter what the pattern is; it is basically the same in the two eyes' views so that the shear can in principle (and in fact) be recovered even when the pattern is random. The same applies to the successive views provided by motion parallax or structure from motion.

Given that the visual system has difficulties with compression in all modes of depth processing, it seems likely that the global cue of a difference in compression or spatial frequency (which amounts to the same thing) is not available to perception, whereas the global cue of shear is available perceptually.

Gillam et al. (1988b) have emphasized the long latency in resolving stereoscopic slant around a vertical axis. They have attributed the latency to the fact that given the absence of an effective global transformation between the images, such as horizontal shear, the slant must be retrieved by local processes. Given, however, considerable evidence that the visual system fails to encode absolute positional disparities and gradients of positional disparity (Gillam et al., 1988b), resolution of the slant can only proceed by processing successive angular disparities between neighboring points across the surface. These angular disparities are, however, all identical and must be integrated to give slant. This may take time, especially when stereopsis is not supported by other cues; hence the long latencies obtained.

2. The Boundary Mode

There is one condition in which there is no difficulty in resolving slant around a vertical axis. Under this condition it is immediate, fully developed, and resistant to conflicting perspective information (Gillam et al., 1984; Gillam et al., 1988b). This dramatic improvement occurs when the stereoscopically slanted surface is seen immediately above or below a frontal plane surface. The facilitation of slant does not occur when the two surfaces are placed beside each other. Hence, the effect cannot simply be attributed to slant contrast. It occurs even when the discontinuity between the surfaces is what Julesz (1971) calls cyclopean (not visible monocularly) and therefore cannot be attributed to monocular information. Why then is slant so effectively resolved under these conditions? It appears that the significant new factor introduced into the relationship between the two images by the presence of the second surface is a *gradient of angular disparity* among pairs of points spanning the discontinuity between the two surfaces (see Figure 11a). It may also be significant that this is also a gradient of horizontal shear. Unlike gradients of positional disparity, this gradient is immediately perceptually available and results in slant of the entire surface.

Gillam et al. (1988b) have generalized from this finding to argue that the processing of disparity discontinuities at the boundaries of surfaces under-

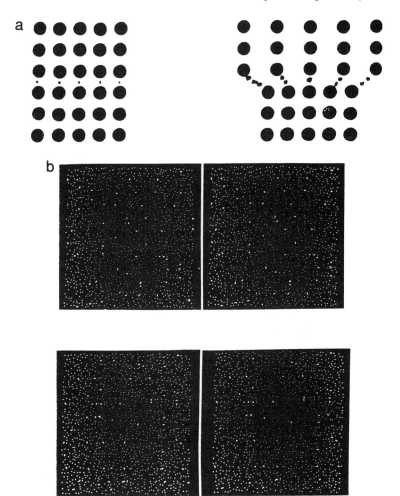

FIGURE 11   (a) A schematic diagram of the left and right images of an upper surface stereoscopically slanted back on the right above a lower surface in the frontal plane. (b) Upper pair: A random dot stereogram of a surface slanted back on the right (schematically shown in Figure 10[a]). Lower pair: A random dot stereogram representing the same stereoscopic slant as in the upper pair but viewed above a surface stereoscopically in the frontal plane (as shown in 11[a]; Gillam et al., 1988b).

lies much of stereoscopic surface perception so that, for example, the resolution of the depth of a central cyclopean square in a Julesz (1971) stereogram is likely to be based on discontinuities at the boundaries, rather than on a comparison of the positional disparities of the surface and the background as is assumed in most computational theories of stereopsis (such as that of Marr & Poggio, 1979). In the case of the Julesz square, there is a horizontal shear in the disparity field corresponding to the upper and lower boundaries of the square and the background. This is likely to be a major contributing factor in its resolution. The data of Anstis, Howard, and Rogers (1978) and Brookes and Stevens (1989a) also attest to the effectiveness of depth processing at disparity discontinuities. Attention has also been paid in recent years to the facilitating role of the monocular regions at the side boundary discontinuities of a Julesz square (Gillam & Borsting, 1988; Nakayama & Shimojo, 1990). Such monocular regions provide cues to occlusion, which is fundamental to form perception and object recognition and has rapidly become a major focus of research interest. Occlusion appears to be determined early in visual processing with stereopsis participating in its resolution (see Nakayama, Shimojo, & Silverman, 1989).

It has sometimes been asserted that the critical stimulus for the effective stereoscopic slant of surfaces is the presence of nonzero second or third derivatives of disparity (Stevens & Brookes, 1988). It may be that they are more effectively processed than first derivatives. However, data on vertical stereoscopic ridges (Buckley & Frisby, 1991; Gillam et al., 1988b) do not support the view that the presence of second or third derivatives per se has a strong facilitating effect on stereoscopic slant around a vertical axis unless the slant is very extreme.

3. Stereoscopic Slant Constancy

Stereoscopic slant constancy refers to the ability to perceive slant correctly by stereopsis despite changes in observation distance. Just as with stereoscopic depth constancy, the disparity gradient varies with observation distance. As the first derivative of disparity, it is proportional to distance. Therefore, in order for a disparity gradient to be correctly converted into depth, absolute distance or information correlated with it must be available on some basis. Stereoscopic slant constancy is extremely good when observation distance is varied up to about one meter (Gillam et al., 1988a; Ogle, 1950; Wallach, Gillam, & Cardillo, 1979), but its origin is not known. Both convergence and vertical disparity gradients are possible sources of information. Gillam et al. (1988a) found that stereoscopic slant constancy is excellent for a random dot pattern and very poor for a horizontal line of dots. This suggests that vertical disparity does play a role in scaling for distance because convergence is available for both stimuli, but only the random dot pattern has vertical disparity.

Another source of ambiguity for horizontal disparity gradients is that they can be influenced by the eccentricity as well as the distance of a surface. This only applies to temporal–nasal eccentricity, which shifts the image nearer to one eye than the other, thereby increasing the overall size of the image on the one eye and decreasing it on the other and introducing both horizontal and vertical disparities. Up–down eccentricity does not place the object closer to one eye than to the other, which means that gradients of horizontal disparity in the vertical meridian are not influenced by the eccentricity factor and are therefore not ambiguous. (The ambiguity of disparity gradients in the horizontal meridian and not the vertical meridian could contribute to the horizontal–vertical slant anisotropy [Mitchison & Westheimer, 1990]. It cannot be the whole story, however, since Gillam et al. (1988b), and Rogers and Graham (1983) have found that horizontal–vertical anisotropies are also obtained in resolving sinusoidal modulations of depth or Craik–O'Brien–Cornsweet depth profiles. Eccentricity can mimic the effect of planar slant on disparity gradients, but not these more complex variations in depth.)

If gradients of disparity in the horizontal meridian are to be used for slant perception there must be a process by which horizontal disparity attributable to eccentricity is parsed out. What evidence is there that such a process exists and on what basis could the different sources of horizontal disparity be separated? An obvious factor would be that an eccentric surface would require asymmetric convergence of the eyes to fixate it. Ebenholtz and Paap (1973) found that introducing asymmetric convergence by means of a haploscope (a Wheatstone stereoscope with the mirrors mounted on moveable arms), while keeping all visual information constant, resulted in the predicted change in the slant perceived. There also seem to be some purely visual factors that are produced by surface eccentricity and appear to scale the response to horizontal disparity gradients. Vertical disparity is one such factor since it is strongly affected by moving a surface into an eccentric position but not by slanting it. As mentioned previously, Figure 3 shows that the vertical disparity of an object (expressed as the ratio of the image sizes in the two eyes) increases approximately linearly with eccentricity at a given observation distance. A very strong indication that vertical disparity is implicated in the scaling of slant to take account of eccentricity is the so-called induced effect described by Ogle (1950). This is a slant induced by magnifying one image vertically while keeping horizontal disparities at zero. The slant perceived under these conditions represents the correct geometric interpretation of a zero horizontal disparity surface at the eccentricity indicated by the vertical enlargement of one image (Gillam & Lawergren, 1983; Longuet-Higgins & Mayhew, 1982).

Another indicator of eccentricity, which may be used to scale horizontal disparity gradients, is related to surface perspective. It arises from the fact that whereas in the center of the visual field the horopter (defined here as the tangent to the Vieth–Müller circle) and the normal to the line of sight coincide, in the eccentric visual field, they do not. Furthermore, the angular separation of these surfaces equals the angle of eccentricity. This difference and therefore surface eccentricity (Figure 12) can be derived for any binoc-

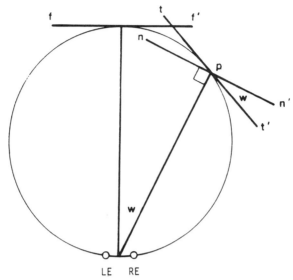

FIGURE 12   In eccentric positions, the horopter (tt, tangent to the Vieth–Müller circle) and the normal (nn) do not coincide as they do in a central position where both lie on the frontal plane (ff). The difference between them equals (w) the angle of eccentricity (from Gillam & Lawergren, 1983).

ularly viewed surface with sufficient perspective information to indicate the orientation of a surface relative to the normal (the surface, which because all parts of it are equidistant from the eye, gives zero perspective convergence and compression). The difference between the angular deviation of a surface from the normal, given by perspective, and the angular deviation of the same surface from the horopter, given by stereopsis, also equals the eccentricity of the surface. Furthermore, this difference also specifies the geographical slant of the surface relative to the frontal plane. Gillam (1993) has shown that when a disparity gradient is introduced for a surface without altering the perspective gradient, slants are often reported that are appropriate to the eccentricity consistent with this discrepancy. These slants are in the opposite direction to the slant specified by the same disparity gradient in the center of the field where the disparity and perspective gradients agree. The fact that reverse slants are reliably obtained under these conditions strongly indicates that perspective is not just dominating disparity. A perspective gradient of zero would on its own give a zero slant, and a positive disparity gradient would on its own give a positive slant. These cannot be added so as to give a negative slant. This is only possible when the implications of their combination for spatial geometry is taken into account by the visual system. Interestingly, this suggests that perspective and stereopsis are intimately interactive and are not, as is typically hypothesized, independent modules, contributing separately and independently derived slants to a high-level mechanism that combines them according to a weighted sum.

V. THE PERCEPTION OF SIZE AND SHAPE

There are four questions that dominate the study of size perception. The first is the accuracy with which observers can judge the physical size or shape of objects of unknown size and shape at different distances and the effect of stimulus factors on this accuracy. The second is the degree to which the accurate perception of objective size depends on a calculation that is based on angular size and distance (the size–distance invariance hypothesis) and to what degree on a direct response to stimulus information. (The same question can be asked about shape and slant.) A third and related question, is to what degree are people able to respond to visual angle size or retinal shape under conditions in which there are plenty of cues to objective size and shape? Finally, it can be asked whether size is a primary perceptual quality, like motion, or whether it is derived from position information.

Size perception is such an old problem that the first of these questions is well-handled in previous accounts and will not be dealt with in detail here. In real scenes size is judged rather accurately even at very large distances (Gibson, 1950), although there is a well-established tendency for size to be overestimated at far distances (overconstancy). Sedgwick (1986) gave a thorough account of the accuracy of size and shape perception under various conditions and the causes of overconstancy.

Even though perceived size is frequently not as predicted by the size–distance invariance hypothesis, it is nevertheless a function of stimulus factors that are potential cues to distance. This has led to the view that it must depend on perceived distance if not explicitly then implicitly as a response to "registered distance". This way of thinking about the problem is based on a failure to recognize that cues to distance are also in almost every case cues to size as well (and cues to slant are also cues to shape). This is generally recognized in the case of ground plane cues. There is widespread acceptance of Gibson's (1950) statement, "The size of any particular object is given by the scale of the background at the point to which it is attached" (p. 181). It has also been shown empirically that at least some of the size scaling that occurs under these conditions is not derived from the distance response to the background. In Figure 13, the backgrounds provide equivalent distance information regardless of test line orientation. If perceived or registered distance were responsible for size scaling, the upper line in each figure should always be perceptually enlarged to the same degree relative to the lower line. In fact, the size scaling is restricted to Figure 13 (a) and (c), the cases in which the background scale is present along the same dimension as the test lines. These figures were devised in the context of the

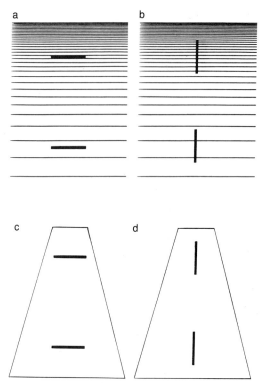

FIGURE 13   Size scaling depends on the direction of the background scale. Only test lines (b) and (c) show an enhancement of the upper line relative to the lower (Gillam, 1980).

Ponzo illusion, and indeed, illusions provide many clues concerning the direct scaling effects of contexts of various kinds. Morgan, Hole, and Glennerster, 1990, for example, have shown that size can be scaled by line orientation.

Sedgwick (1986) has drawn attention to another important pictorial size cue: the horizon ratio. The ratio in the picture plane of the height of an object on the ground plane to the height from its base to the horizon equals the ratio of the physical height of the object to eye height since the horizon is always at eye level in the picture plane. Although there has been little research on the degree to which such information is used, there is widespread acceptance of the possibility of direct size perception in this case. A direct effect of context on size perception is also well established for object surrounds or frames (Rock & Ebenholtz, 1959).

It is the effects on size perception of the oculomotor cues—accommodation and convergence—and the facilitating effects of binocular disparity on both size and shape that pose the real stumbling block for direct theories of size perception (Hochberg, 1971; Rock & Ebenholtz, 1959) because the tradition of regarding these exclusively as distance cues is so strong. Yet accommodation and convergence influence size perception much more reliably than they influence distance perception, and it seems reasonable to conclude that the effect of these oculomotor factors on size is a direct one. Size micropsia and macropsia are adaptive responses in normal circumstances in which angular size alters with distance in that these responses perceptually counteract such size changes. The size effects of accommodation and accommodative vergence are modest (approximately 25% of the scaling effect necessary to compensate completely for normal angular size changes with distance; Heineman et al., 1959). However, under conditions of fusional vergence with an extended object, the size scaling effect is much greater. It is sufficient to produce complete constancy, at least up to the distance of one meter (Leibowitz, Shiina, & Hennessy, 1972; Oyama & Ikawaki, 1972). This too could be a direct effect of stimulus information. Figure 14 shows that fusional vergence with an extended binocular object specifies size just as directly as it specifies distance.

What about shape at a slant? Again, this has been shown to be greatly

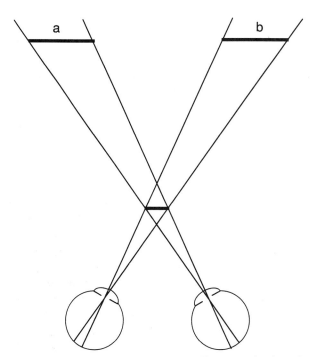

FIGURE 14   The eyes are converged on two laterally separated polarized images (a) and (b). These geometrically specify an object both close and small.

improved in the presence of binocular vision (Kaiser, 1967), a fact, it is often assumed (Hochberg, 1971), that can only be explained by means of the shape–slant invariance hypothesis since no direct information is available. Again it can be shown that this assumption is not necessary. Binocular information specifies shape just as directly as it specifies slant (Gillam, 1967).

Another line of evidence concerns the priority of angular size. It has been convincingly argued by McKee and Welch (1992) that if objective size is based on angular size, the latter should be judged with greater precision than the former. On the contrary, these authors found that angular size judgments are less precise than objective size judgments. It has generally been found that angular sizes are very difficult to match accurately under cue-enriched conditions. Sedgwick (1986) points out in a reanalysis of past data that the traditional use of the Brunswik constancy ratio made angular size matches appear much better than they in fact were. Of special note, Morgan et al. (1990) have shown that there is no loss of precision associated with the bias in size produced by the arrow heads in the Müller–Lyer illusion. This suggests that various contextual size scaling effects are direct low-level processes. Many illusions may well be functional in viewing normal three-dimensional scenes as opposed to line drawings (Gillam, 1980; Morgan et al., 1990).

Morgan et al. (1990) have argued that size is based on position. Gillam and Chambers (1985) have argued against this view on the grounds that perceived position is not affected by the Müller–Lyer illusion. Subjects were able to place markers very accurately below the physical positions of the arrow heads. Morgan et al. argued that Gillam and Chamber's subjects were judging orientation rather than position. This is possible, in which case perceived orientation is independent of position. Either way, there is an intransitivity that points to highly judgment-specific representations that do not map onto each other.

Finally it should be pointed out that although there is every reason to suppose that much more of size and shape perception is a direct response to information in the optic array or to oculomotor information than is normally considered to be the case, there is no reason on that account to rule out a direct link between apparent distance and apparent size. It is difficult to separate direct effects from indirect ones by experiment since both are a function of the so-called distance cues. One condition, however, in which the information remains the same while apparent distance changes (the converse of the situation illustrated in Figure 13) is the 3-D wire Necker cube. In viewing this stimulus reversals of depth are frequent and are accompanied by a marked change in the apparent relative sizes of the front and back faces of the cube. This points to the existence of strong percept–percept couplings (Hochberg. 1974). In this form, the size–distance invariance hypothesis would seem to be playing a role in space perception, although it is difficult to tease out how much of a role under more complex circumstances.

VI. CONCLUSION

There has been much emphasis in recent years on the role of motion in perceiving spatial layout and structure. Perhaps this has gone too far. A rich apprehension of the surrounding scene can be gained from a static view, especially with binocular vision. This chapter has specified much of the information on which such an achievement may be based, with evidence concerning the manner in which human vision is able to use such information. In many cases we show that perceptual responses that are often regarded as inferred or derived can be better explained as direct responses to features or relationships in the optic array or to other visual information such as convergence. In this spirit we also show that perceptual responses may not map on to each other in a Euclidean manner and yet that different cues can interact in surprising ways to disambiguate each other. It is also clear from this outline that there are still many serious gaps in our knowledge.

References

Agee, F. L., Jr., & Gogel, W. C. (1967). Equidistance judgments in the vicinity of a binocular illusion. *Journal of Experimental Psychology, 74*(1), 87–92.

Alexander, K. R. (1974). The foundations of the SILO response. *Optometric Weekly, 9*, 446–450.

Ames, A., Jr. (1946). Binocular vision as affected by relations between uniocular stimulus patterns in commonplace environments. *American Journal of Psychology, 59*, 333–357.

Amigo, G. (1964). The stereoscopic threshold of the human retina. *The Australian Journal of Optometry, 47*, 87–97.

Anstis, S., Howard, I. P., & Rogers, B. (1978). A Craik-O'Brien-Cornsweet illusion for visual depth. *Vision Research, 18*, 213–217.

Berkeley, G. (1709). *An essay towards a new theory of vision.* (Reprinted from *Berkeley: A new theory of vision and other writings*, 1960, London: J. M. Dent & Sons)

Berry, R. N. (1948). Quantitative relations among vernier, real depth, and stereoscopic depth acuities. *Journal of Experimental Psychology, 38*, 708–721.

Blake, R. (1989). A neural theory of binocular rivalry. *Psychological Review, 93*, 145–147.

Boring, E. (1942). *Sensation and Perception in the history of experimental Psychology.* New York: Appleton-Century Company.

Braunstein, M. L. (1968). Motion and texture as sources of slant information. *Journal of Experimental Psychology, 78*(2), 247–253.

Braunstein, M. L., & Payne, J. W. (1969). Perspective and form ratio as determinants of relative slant judgments. *Journal of Experimental Psychology, 81*(3), 584–590.

Brookes, A., & Stevens, K. A. (1989a). Binocular depth from surfaces versus volumes. *Journal of Experimental Psychology: Human Perception and Performance, 15*(3), 479–484.

Brookes, A., & Stevens, K. A. (1989b). The analogy between stereo depth and brightness. *Perception, 18*(5), 601–614.

Bruno, N., & Cutting, J. E. (1988). Minimodularity and the perception of layout. *Journal of Experimental Psychology: General, 117*(2), 161–170.

Buckley, D., & Frisby, J. P. (1993). Interaction of stereo, texture and outline cues in the shape perception of three-dimensional ridges. *Vision Research, 33*(7), 919–933.

Bülthoff, H., Fahle, M., & Wegmann, M. (1991). Perceived depth scales with disparity gradient. *Perception, 20*(2), 139–280.

Bülthoff, H. H., & Mallot, H. A. (1990). Integration of stereo, shading and texture. In A. Blake & T. Troscianko (Eds.), *AI and the eye* (pp. 119–146). New York: Wiley.

Burt, P., & Julesz, B. (1980). A disparity gradient limit for binocular fusion. *Science, 208*, 615–617.

Carlson, V. R. (1977). Instructions and perceptual constancy judgments. In W. Epstein (Ed.), *Stability and constancy in visual perception* (pp. 217–254). New York: Wiley.

Clark, W. C., Smith, A. H., & Rabe, A. (1956). The interaction of surface texture, outline gradient, and ground in the perception of slant. *Canadian Journal of Psychology, 10*, 1–8.

Collett, T. S., Schwarz, U., & Sobel, E. C. (1991). The interaction of oculomotor cues and stimulus size in stereoscopic depth constancy. *Perception, 20*, 733–754.

Cook, M. (1978). The judgment of distance on a plane surface. *Perception & Psychophysics, 23*(1), 85–90.

Cook, M., & Griffiths, K. (1991). Representation of spatial structure in reaching to a visual target. *Journal of Experimental Psychology: Human Perception and Performance, 17*(4), 1041–1056.

Cormack, R. H. (1984). Stereoscopic depth perception at far viewing distances. *Perception & Psychophysics, 35*(5), 423–428.

Cumming, B. G., Johnston, E. B., & Parker, A. J. (1991). Vertical disparities and perception of three-dimensional shape. *Nature (London), 349*,(6308), 411–413.

Cutting, J. E., & Millard, R. T. (1984). Three gradients and the perception of flat and curved surfaces. *Journal of Experimental Psychology: General, 113*(2), 198–216.

Dosher, B. A., Sperling, G., & Wurst, S. A. (1986). Tradeoffs between stereopsis and proximity luminance covariance as determinants of perceived 3D structure. *Vision Research, 26*, 973–990.

Ebenholtz, S. M., & Paap, K. R. (1973). The constancy of object orientation: Compensation for ocular rotation. *Perception & Psychophysics, 14*(3), 458–470.

Eby, D. W., & Loomis, J. M. (1987). A study of visually directed throwing in the presence of multiple distance cues. *Perception & Psychophysics, 41*(4), 308–312.

Enright, J. T. (1991). Exploring the third dimension with eye movements: Better than stereopsis. *Vision Research, 31*, 1549–1562.

Epstein, W. (1963). Attitudes of judgment and the size–distance invariance hypothesis. *Journal of Experimental Psychology, 66*, 78–83.

Epstein, W., & Franklin, S. (1965). Some conditions of the effect of relative size on perceived relative distance. *American Journal of Psychology, 78*, 466–470.

Epstein, W., Park, J., & Casey, A. (1961). The current status of the size–distance hypotheses. *Psychological Bulletin, 58*(6), 491–514.

Fisher, S. K., & Cuiffrieda, K. J. (1988). Accommodation and apparent distance perception. *Perception, 17*(5), 609–621.

Foley, J. M. (1985). Binocular distance perception: Egocentric distance tasks. *Journal of Experimental Psychology: Human Perception and Performance, 11*(2), 133–149.

Foley, J. M., Applebaum, T., & Richards, W. (1975). Stereopsis with large disparities: Discrimination and depth magnitude. *Vision Research, 15*, 417–421.

Foley, J. M., & Richards, W. (1972). Effects of voluntary eye movement and convergence on the binocular appreciation of depth. *Perception & Psychophysics, 11*, 423–427.

Gibson, E. J., Gibson, J. J., Smith, O. W., & Flock, H. R. (1959). Motion parallax as a determinant of perceived depth. *Journal of Experimental Psychology, 58,* 40–51.

Gibson, J. J. (1950). *The perception of the visual world.* Boston: Houghton Mifflin.

Gibson, J. J. (1966). *The senses considered as perceptual systems.* Boston: Houghton Mifflin.

Gillam, B. (1967). Changes in the direction of induced aniseikonic slant as a function of distance. *Vision Research, 7,* 777–783.

Gillam, B. (1968). Perception of slant when perspective and stereopsis conflict: Experiments with aniseikonic lenses. *Journal of Experimental Psychology, 78,* 299–305.

Gillam, B. (1980). Geometrical illusions. *Scientific American, 242*(1), 102–111.

Gillam, B. (1993). Stereoscopic slant reversals: A new kind of "induced" effect. *Perception, 22,* 1025–1036.

Gillam, B., & Borsting, E. (1988). The role of monocular regions in stereoscopic displays. *Perception, 17,* 603–608.

Gillam, B., & Chambers, D. (1985). Size and position are incongruous: Measurements on the Müller–Lyer figure. *Perception & Psychophysics, 37,* 549–556.

Gillam, B., Chambers, D., & Lawergren, B. (1988a). The role of vertical disparity in the scaling of stereoscopic depth perception: An empirical and theoretical study. *Perception & Psychophysics, 44*(5), 473–483.

Gillam, B., Chambers, D., & Russo, T. (1988b). Postfusional latency in stereoscopic slant perception and the primitives of stereopsis. *Journal of Experimental Psychology: Human Perception and Performance, 14*(2), 163–175.

Gillam, B., Flagg, T., & Finlay, D. (1984). Evidence for disparity change as the primary stimulus for stereoscopic processing. *Perception & Psychophysics, 36*(6), 559–564.

Gillam, B., & Lawergren, B. (1983). The induced effect, vertical disparity, and stereoscopic theory. *Perception & Psychophysics, 34*(2), 121–130.

Gillam, B., & Rogers, B. (1991). Orientation disparity, deformation, and stereoscopic slant perception. *Perception, 20,* 441–448.

Gillam, B., & Ryan, C. (1992). Perspective, orientation disparity, and anisotropy in stereoscopic slant perception. *Perception, 21,* 427–439.

Gogel, W. C. (1960). Perceived frontal size as a determiner of perceived binocular depth. *Journal of Psychology, 50,* 119–131.

Gogel, W. C. (1961a). Convergence as a cue to absolute distance. *Journal of Psychology, 52,* 287–301.

Gogel, W. C. (1961b). Convergence as a cue to the perceived distance of objects in a binocular configuration. *Journal of Psychology, 52,* 305–315.

Gogel, W. C. (1965). Equidistance tendency and its consequences. *Psychological Bulletin, 64*(3), 153–163.

Gogel, W. C. (1977). An indirect measure of perceived distance from oculomotor cues. *Perception & Psychophysics, 21*(1), 3–11.

Gogel, W. C., & Da Silva, J. A. (1987). Familiar size and the theory of off-sized perceptions. *Perception & Psychophysics, 41*(4), 318–328.

Gogel, W. C., Loomis, J. M., Newman, N. J., & Sharkey, T. J. (1985). Agreement between indirect measures of perceived distance. *Perception & Psychophysics, 37*(1), 17–27.

Gogel, W. C., & Sturm, R. D. (1972). A test of the relational hypothesis of perceived size. *American Journal of Psychology, 85,* 201–216.

Gogel, W. C., & Tietz, J. D. (1980). Relative cues and absolute distance perception. *Perception & Psychophysics, 28,* 321–328.

Graham, C. H., Riggs, L. A., Mueller, C. G., & Solomon, R. L. (1949). Precision of stereoscopic settings as influenced by distance of target from a fiducial line. *Journal of Psychology, 27,* 203–207.

Gruber, H. (1954). The relation of perceived size to perceived distance. *American Journal of Psychology,* 411–426.

Gulick, W. L., & Lawson, R. G. (1976). *Human stereopsis: A psychological analysis.* New York: Oxford University Press.

Hay, J. C. (1974). The ghost image: A tool for the analysis of the visual stimulus. In R. B. MacLeod & H. L. Pick, Jr. (Eds.), *Perception: Essays in honor of James J. Gibson* (pp. 268–275). Ithaca, NY: Cornell University Press.

Heineman, E. G., Tulving, E., & Nachmias, J. (1959). The effect of oculomotor adjustments on apparent size. *American Journal of Psychology, 72,* 32–45.

Helmholtz, H. von (1925). *Handbook of physiological optics* (J. P. C. Southall, Trans.). New York: Dover. (Original work published in 1867)

Higashiyama, A. (1977). Perceived size and distance as a perceptual conflict between two processing modes. *Perception & Psychophysics, 22,* 206–211.

Hine, T., & Thorn, F. (1987). Compensatory eye movements during active head rotation for near targets: Effects of imagination, rapid head oscillation and vergence. *Vision Research, 27*(9), 1639–1657.

Hirsch, M. J., & Weymouth, F. W. (1948). Distance discrimination. *AIMA Archives Ophthalmology, 39,* 210–223.

Hochberg, C. B., & Hochberg, J. E. (1952). Familiar size and the perception of depth. *Journal of Psychology, 34,* 107–114.

Hochberg, J. E. (1971). Perception: Space and movement. In J. W. Kling & L. A. Riggs (Eds.), *Experimental psychology* (3rd ed., pp. 475–546). New York: Holt, Rinehart & Winston.

Hochberg, J. E. (1974). Higher-order stimuli and inter-response coupling in the perception of the visual world. In R. B. MacLeod & H. L. Pick, Jr. (Eds.), *Perception* (pp. 17–39). Ithaca, NY: Cornell University Press.

Holliday, I. E., & Braddick, O. J. (1991). Pre-attentive detection of a target defined by stereoscopic slant. *Perception, 20,* 355–362.

Ittelson, W. H. (1960). *Visual space perception.* New York: Springer.

Johansson, G. (1973). Monocular movement parallax and near-space perception. *Perception, 2,* 135–146.

Johnston, E. B. (1991). Systematic distortions of shape from stereopsis. *Vision Research, 31*(7/8), 1351–1360.

Julesz, B. (1971). *Foundations of cyclopean perception.* Chicago: University of Chicago Press.

Kaiser, P. K. (1967). Perceived shape and its dependence on perceived slant. *Journal of Experimental Psychology, 75,* 345–353.

Kilpatrick, F. P., & Ittelson, W. (1953). The size–distance invariance hypothesis. *Psychological Review, 60*(4), 223–231.

Koenderink, J., & Van Doorn, A. (1976). Geometry of binocular vision and a model of stereopsis. *Biological Cybernetics, 22,* 29–35.

Koffka, K. (1935). *Principles of Gestalt psychology.* New York: Harcourt, Brace & World.

Komoda, M., & Ono, H. (1974). Oculomotor adjustments and size–distance perception. *Perception & Psychophysics, 15*(2), 353–360.

Kruger, P. B., & Pola, J. (1985). Changing target size is a stimulus for accommodation. *Journal of the Optical Society of America, 2,* 1832–1835.

Kumar, T., & Glaser, D. A. (1992). Shape analysis and stereopsis for human depth perception. *Vision Research, 32*(3), 499–512.

Leibowitz, H. W., Shiina, K., & Hennessy, R. T. (1972). Oculomotor adjustments and size constancy. *Perception & Psychophysics, 12,* 497–500.

Levelt, W. J. M. (1965). *On binocular rivalry.* Soesterberg, the Netherlands: Institute for Perception RVO–TNO.

Levin, C. A., & Haber, R. N. (1993). Visual angle as a determinant of perceived interobject distance. *Perception & Psychophysics, 54*(2), 250–259.

Lie, I. (1965). Convergence as a cue to perceived size and distance. *Scandinavian Journal of Psychology, 6,* 109–116.

Linksz, A. (1952). *Physiology of the eye: Vol. 2. Vision*. New York: Grune & Stratton.

Longuet-Higgins, H. C., & Mayhew, J. E. W. (1982). A computational model of binocular depth perception. *Nature, 297*, 376–378.

Loomis, J. M., Da Silva, J. A. Fujita, N., & Fukusima, S. S. (1992). Visual space perception and visually directed action. *Journal of Experimental Psychology: Human Perception and Performance, 18*(4), 906–921.

Marr, D. (1982). *Vision*. San Francisco: Freeman.

Marr, D., & Poggio, T. A. (1979). A computational theory of human stereo vision. *Proceedings of the Royal Society of London, 204*, 301–328.

McKee, S., & Welch, L. (1992). The precision of size constancy. *Vision Research, 32*(8), 1447–1460.

McKee, S. P., Welch, L., Taylor, D. G., & Bowne, S. F. (1990). Finding the common bond: Stereoacuity and the other hyperacuities. *Vision Research, 30*(6), 879–891.

Mitchison, G. J., & McKee, S. P. (1990). Mechanisms underlying the anisotropy of stereoscopic tilt perception. *Vision Research, 30*(11), 1781–1791.

Mitchison, G. J., & Westheimer, G. (1984). The perception of depth in simple figures. *Vision Research, 24*(9), 1063–1073.

Mitchison, G. J., & Westheimer, G. (1990). Viewing geometry and gradients of horizontal disparity. In C. Blakemore (Ed.), *Festschrift for H. B. Barlow* (pp. 302–309). Cambridge, England: Cambridge University Press.

Morgan, M. J., Hole, G. J., & Glennerster, A. (1990). Biases and sensitivities in geometrical illusions. *Vision Research, 30*(11), 1793–1810.

Morgan, M. W. (1968). Accommodation and vergence. *American Journal of Ophthalmology, 45*, 417–454.

Morrison, J. D., & Whiteside, T. C. D. (1984). Binocular cues in the perception of distance of a point source of light. *Perception, 13*, 555–566.

Nakayama, K. (1977). Geometrical and physiological aspects of depth perception. *Image Processing Proceedings SPIE, 120*, 1–8.

Nakayama, K., & Shimojo, S. (1990). Toward a neural understanding of visual surface representation. *Cold Spring Harbor Symposium on Quantitative Biology, 40*, 911–924.

Nakayama, K., Shimojo, S., & Silverman, G. (1989). Stereoscopic depth: Its relation to image segmentation, grouping, and the recognition of occluded objects. *Perception, 18*, 55–68.

Nakayama, K., Silverman, G., MacLeod, D., & Mulligan, J. (1985). Sensitivity to shearing and compressive motion in random dots. *Perception, 14*, 225–238.

Ogle, K. N. (1950). *Researches in Binocular Vision*. New York: Hafner.

O'Leary, A., & Wallach, H. (1980). Familiar size and linear perspective as distance cues in stereoscopic depth constancy. *Perception & Psychophysics, 27*(2), 131–135.

Ono, H., & Comerford, T. (1977). Stereoscopic depth constancy. In W. Epstein (Ed.), *Stability and constancy in visual perception: Mechanisms and processes* (pp. 91–128). New York: Wiley.

Ono, H., Mitson, L., & Seabrook, K. (1971). Change in convergence and retinal disparities as an explanation for the wallpaper phenomenon. *Journal of Experimental Psychology, 91*(1), 1–10.

Owens, D. A., & Leibowitz, H. W. (1976). Specific distance tendency. *Perception & Psychophysics, 20*, 2–9.

Oyama, T., & Iwaki, S. (1972). Role of convergence and binocular disparity in size constancy. *Psychologishe Forschung, 35*, 117–130.

Predebon, J. (1991). Spatial judgments of exocentric extents in an open-field situation: Familiar versus unfamiliar size. *Perception & Psychophysics, 50*(4), 361–366.

Richards, W., & Miller, J. F., Jr. (1969). Convergence as a cue to depth. *Perception & Psychophysics, 5*(5), 317–320.

Ritter, M. (1977). Effect of disparity and viewing distance on perceived depth. *Perception & Psychophysics, 22*(4), 400–407.

Rock, I. (1984). *Perception*. San Francisco: Freeman.

Rock, I., & Ebenholtz, S. (1959). The relational determination of perceived size. *Psychological Review, 66,* 387–401.

Rock, I., & Kaufman, L. (1962). The moon illusion: II. *Science, 136,* 1023–1031.

Rogers, B. J., & Bradshaw, M. F. (1993). Vertical disparities, differential perspective and binocular stereopsis. *Nature, 361,* 253–255.

Rogers, B. J., & Graham, M. E. (1983). Anisotropies in the perception of three-dimensional surfaces. *Science, 221,* 1409–1411.

Rosinski, R. R., & Levine, N. P. (1976). Texture gradient effectiveness in the perception of surface slant. *Journal of Experimental Child Psychology, 22,* 261–271.

Schor, C., & Badcock, D. (1985). A comparison of stereo and vernier acuity within spatial channels as a function of distance from fixation. *Vision Research, 25,* 1113–1119.

Seagrim, G. N. (1967). Stereoscopic vision and aniseikonic lenses: I and II. *British Journal of Psychology, 58,* 337–356.

Sedgwick, H. A. (1983). Environment-centered representation of spatial layout: Available visual information from texture and perspective. In J. Beck, B. Hope, & A. Rosenfeld (Eds.), *Human and machine vision* (pp. 425–458). San Diego, CA: Academic Press.

Sedgwick, H. A. (1986). Space perception. In K. Boff, L. Kaufman, & J. Thomas (Eds.), *Handbook of perception and human performance* (ch. 21, pp. 1–57). New York: Wiley.

Sedgwick, H. A., & Festinger, L. (1976). Eye movements, efference, and visual perception. In R. A. Monty & J. W. Senders (Eds.), *Eye movements and psychological processes* (pp. 221–230). Hillsdale, NJ: Erlbaum.

Sedgwick, H. A., & Levy, S. (1985). Environment-centered and viewer-centered perception of surface orientation. *Computer Vision, Graphics, and Image Processing, 31,* 248–260.

Servos, P., Goodale, M. A., & Jakobson, L. S. (1992). The role of binocular vision in prehension: a kinematic analysis, *Vision Research, 32,* 1513–1522.

Sobel, E. C., & Collett, T. S. (1991). Does vertical disparity scale the perception of stereoscopic depth? *Proceedings of the Royal Society: London B, 244,* 87–90.

Stevens, K. A., & Brookes, A. (1988). Integrating stereopsis with monocular interpretations of planar surfaces. *Vision Research, 28*(3), 371–386.

Stevens, K. A., Lees, M., & Brookes, A. (1991). Combining binocular and monocular curvature features. *Perception, 20,* 425–448.

Swenson, H. A. (1932). The relative influence of accommodation and convergence in the judgment of distance. *Journal of General Psychology, 7,* 360–380.

Thomson, J. A. (1983). Is continuous visual monitoring necessary in visually guided locomation? *Journal of Experimental Psychology and Performance, 9,* 427–443.

Todd, J. T., & Akerstrom, R. A. (1987). Perception of three-dimensional form from patterns of optical texture. *Journal of Experimental Psychology: Human Perception and Performance, 13*(2), 242–255.

Todd, J. T., & Bressan, P. (1990). The perception of 3-dimensional affine structure from minimal apparent motion sequences. *Perception & Psychophysics, 48*(5), 419–430.

Todd, J. T., & Reichel, F. D. (1989). Ordinal structure in the visual perception and cognition of smoothly curved surfaces. *Psychological Review, 96*(4), 643–657.

Tyler, C. W. (1973). Stereoscopic vision: Cortical limitations and a disparity scaling effect. *Science, 74,* 958–961.

Tyler, C. W. (1991). The horopter and binocular fusion. In D. Regan (Ed.), *Binocular vision* (pp. 19–37). London: Macmillan.

Vickers, D. (1971). Perceptual economy and the impression of visual depth. *Perception & Psychophysics, 10*(1), 23–27.

Wallach, H., & Bacon, J. (1976). Two forms of retinal disparity. *Perception & Psychophysics, 19,* 375–382.

Wallach, H., & Frey, K. J. (1972). Adaptation in distance perception based on oculomotor cues. *Perception & Psychophysics, 11,* 77–83.

Wallach, H., Gillam, B., & Cardillo, L. (1979). Some consequences of stereoscopic depth constancy. *Perception & Psychophysics, 26,* 235–240.

Wallach, H., & O'Leary, A. (1982). Slope of regard as a distance cue. *Perception & Psychophysics, 31,* 145–148.

Wallach, H., & Zuckerman, C. (1963). The constancy of stereoscopic depth. *American Journal of Psychology, 76,* 404–412.

Westheimer, G. (1986). Spatial interaction in the domain of disparity signals in human stereoscopic vision. *Journal of Physiology, 370,* 619–629.

Westheimer, G., & McKee, S. P. (1978). Stereoscopic acuity for moving retinal images. *Journal of the Optical Society of America, 68*(4), 450–455.

Wheatstone, C. (1838). Contributions to the physiology of vision: I. On some remarkable and hitherto unobserved phenomena of binocular vision. *Philosophical Transactions of the Royal Society: London, 128,* 371–394.

Wolfe, J. M. (1986). Stereopsis and binocular rivalry. *Psychological Review, 93,* 261–282.

CHAPTER 3

Perceiving Layout and Knowing Distances: The Integration, Relative Potency, and Contextual Use of Different Information about Depth*

James E. Cutting
Peter M. Vishton

In general, the visual world approaches the Euclidean ideal of veridical perception as the quantity and quality of perceptual information increases.

Wagner (1985, p. 493)

How do we see and understand the layout of objects in environments around us? This question has fascinated artists and philosophers for centuries. Indeed, the long-term cultural success of painting, and more recently of photography and cinema, is largely contingent on their convincing portrayal of spatial relations in three dimensions. Of course, the information about spatial layout available in pictures and in the real world has also fascinated psychologists for 125 years. Indeed, the problems of perceiving and understanding space, depth, and layout were among those that helped forge our discipline.[1] Moreover, their sustaining importance is reflected in this volume.

Perhaps the most curious fact about psychological approaches to the study of layout is that its history is little more than a plenum of lists. Lists have been generated since Hering and Helmholtz (see, for example, Boring, 1942; Carr, 1935; Gibson, 1950; Graham, 1951; Woodworth & Schlosberg,

---

* This research was supported by National Science Foundation Grant SBR-9212786 and by a John Simon Guggenheim Memorial Fellowship during 1993–1994 both to James E. Cutting.

[1] Consistent with Gibson (1966, 1979), we prefer to use the term *perception of layout* rather than the perception of depth or of space. Strictly speaking, observers do not perceive depth but objects in depth, and they do not perceive space but objects in space.

Perception of Space and Motion

1954) and are found today in every textbook covering the field. These lists typically include a selection of the following: accommodation, aerial perspective, binocular disparity, convergence, height in the visual field, motion perspective, occlusion, relative size, relative density, and often many more. As an entrée into the field, such a list is prudent and warranted. Taxonomy is, after all, the beginning of science, of measurement, and is an important tool in pedagogy. What is most remarkable about such a list is that in no other perceptual domain can one find so many generally intersubstitutable information sources, all available for the perception of the same general property—the layout of objects in the environment around us.[2] However, after 125 years more than list making is needed for our science.

Three fundamental questions about the perception of our surrounding world are, to our minds, too seldom asked. All are before the summary statement by Wagner (1985) given above. First, why does the human visual system make use of such a wide variety of sources of information—often called *cues*[3]—in understanding and in deriving the structure in depth of a complex natural scene? Second, how do we come to perceive the three-dimensional layout of our environment with reasonable, even near metric, accuracy when taken singly, none of the visual sources of information yields metric information throughout the range of distances we need? Third, given all of these sources, does anything lay beyond list making that might allow us to begin to understand why so many sources are used and are necessary?

The purpose of this chapter is to attempt to answer all three questions. In Wagner's (1985) terms, we want to be concrete about the quantity and quality of information about depth and to provide the framework for a theory of environmental context and physiological state supporting the perception of layout. We claim also that these three questions are linked in important ways, but before addressing them we must acknowledge that historically psychology has had serious qualms with the formulation of the second. Two such qualms have dominated discussion of the topic, those pertaining to illusions and to the non-Euclidean nature of perceived space.

---

[2] Not all psychologists accept the existence of multiple sources of information for a given object or event (see Burton & Turvey, 1990, vs. Cutting, 1991a, 1992a). We claim this belief separates those who espouse direct perception from directed perception (Cutting, 1986).

[3] The term *cue* comes from sixteenth century theater documentation, and the abbreviation *q*, for *quando*, is Latin for *when*. As appropriated by psychology, but continuing theatrical play, a cue entails a knowledgeable observer, one with foreknowledge about when and how to act on layout information. The term cue, then, is heavily aligned with an empiricist position in any nativist–empiricist debates about layout. We prefer the term *source of information*, despite its length, so as to remain neutral in this debate.

A. Illusions of Layout

First, it is not overly difficult to fool the eye, even of a wizened observer, about the layout of some small corner of the world. If one has sufficient skill, one can paint *trompe l'oeil* or carpenter nonrectilinearly joined surfaces, place individuals in confined viewpoints so they can peer at those surfaces or into those spaces, and then demonstrate that those observers do not correctly understand the layout of what they see. Indeed, the Pozzo ceiling (Pirenne, 1970) and the Ames room (Ames, 1955; Ittelson, 1952) are compelling and important examples of such large-scale visual illusions of layout. In particular, under certain controlled circumstances, we perceive the Ames room as it is not, conventionalizing its layout to that of a rectilinear chamber. The typical theoretical statement about its perception is a variant of a traditional argument in philosophy, *the argument from illusion* (e.g., Hirst, 1967). That argument states that if the senses can be deceived, how can we be sure they do not deceive us all of the time? The particular answer given for the Ames room illusion by transactionalists concerns the useful, but occasionally misleading, idea that knowledge and experience necessarily intervene in perception.

Whereas one would be foolish to deny the utility of knowledge and experience as it can shape perception, current perceptual theory suggests that that molding process is not omnipotent. Moreover, the physical world is hardly the plastic and ambiguous place that the transactionalist psychologists might have had us believe. For example, if the purpose of the Ames room (Ames, 1955) illusion is to deceive the eye, the perceiver must severely be fettered, typically monocular, and motionless. As demonstrated by Gehringer and Engel (1986), when the observer is allowed to use two eyes and to move even a modest amount, the illusion almost completely disappears (see also Runeson, 1988).

Thus, one should conclude that when perception of an environment's layout is important to us—and we would claim it almost always is—our perception of that layout is typically adequate, even near veridical, when exploration is allowed. Therefore, in the place of the argument from illusion, we offer a pragmatic retort, which one might call the *argument from evolution* (see also Cutting, 1993). This argument states that if the senses were deceived too frequently, we as a species would surely have, without extensive divine guidance, become extinct long ago. The pragmatics of potential failure over the long span of every evolutionary test of our senses render null the possibility of their gross defectiveness. Thus, we suggest the measurement abilities of the senses are typically as good as they need to be under everyday requirements (see Cutting, Springer, Braren, & Johnson, 1992b), and for measuring layout, we think they need to be quite good.

Gehringer and Engel's (1986) result presages a main point of this chapter. Through the combination of multiple sources of information—motion parallax, stereopsis, and so forth—in a cluttered, well-lit environment we come to perceive, with reasonable accuracy, the layout of the world around us. Of course, the key phrase here is "with reasonable accuracy." As a working assumption, we claim that temporary, and relatively small, errors in judgment of distance—say, those of up to 15%—are not likely to have consequence in normal, day-to-day livelihood; relatively large errors, on the other hand—say, those of an order of magnitude or even of simply 50%—might begin to tax our survival.

B. Euclidean and Non-Euclidean Layout

The second qualm about the accuracy of perceived layout concerns the "shape" of space. Physical and perceptual layouts have not always been modeled by mathematicians and psychologists in an Euclidean manner (see, for example, Blank, 1978; Luneburg, 1947). Even in moderately complex environments straight lines can be perceived as curved (Battro, Netto, & Rozestraten, 1976; Helmholtz, [1867/1925]; Indow, 1982; Indow & Watanabe, 1984). Indeed, anyone with relatively high-powered glasses (1.5 or more diopters)can, on taking them off and putting them back on, verify this fact by looking near and along the corners of a room. Such curvature, whether seen binocularly or monocularly, occurs in the periphery of the eye(s). Assessments of such curvature have often been placed in a Riemannian framework and used in accounting for the perception of both three-dimensional environments and illusions in two-dimensional images (Watson, 1978). Such results have led philosophers to argue whether visual space is Euclidean or non-Euclidean (e.g., Daniels, 1974; Grünbaum, 1973; Putnam, 1963; Suppes, 1973).

Perhaps the most damning empirical evidence against systematic accounts of non-Euclidean (curved) space is that, when individual perceivers' spatial judgments are modeled, they vary widely in curvature (Foley, 1964, 1966; but see also Wagner, 1985, for other problems). To accept curved perceptual space, then, is also to accept that each of us lives in a perceived world with different curvature. Embracing such a view leads one to the philosophical antinomy more typical in discussions of language—that of how private minds with quite different ideas can communicate about shared experiences.

We think the best solution to the problem of curved space is an elaboration of the pragmatic approach of Hopkins (1973): The degree of curvature of physical space is so small that, on a local level, it cannot be decided whether it and phenomenal space, which generally follows physical space, are Euclidean or only a good approximation thereof (see also Cutting,

1986). Again, notice the implication of "reasonable accuracy," or in this case reasonable Euclidean approximation. We strongly suspect that with modest exploration on the part of any observer, the curvature modeled to his or her perceptual judgments of layout will vary both with the environment modeled and with the particular individual perceiving it, but the overall mean curvature of all terrestrial spaces that we might find ourselves in is very nearly zero (see also Wagner, 1985). This would mean that perceptual spaces are sufficiently close to being Euclidean that little of practical import is gained by considering Riemannian curvatures, perhaps with the exception of understanding how a Riemannian space becomes a Euclidean space with additional sources of information.

I. ON THE ACCURACY OF PERCEIVED SPACE

> An observer's ability to perceive distance varies with number of circumstances, most prominent of which is the degree to which the experimental situation makes available information for distance.
>
> *Sedgwick (1986, p. 22–28)*

As implied by Sedgwick (1986), it is not difficult in the laboratory to make the perception of layout difficult. Escaping artificial confinements and following general tenets of Gibson (1950, 1979), many researchers have conducted studies using various experimental techniques in large outdoor spaces. Most of these suggest that our ability to perceive layout and distances is quite good in situations with many sources of information. We appear to have rough metric knowledge in making distance judgments (E. Gibson & Bergman, 1954) that improve with feedback; relative distance judgments, on the other hand, do not appear to improve with feedback (Wohlwill, 1964).

A. Distance Estimation by Stationary Observers

In psychophysical terms, the power function for distance judgments is well described by an exponent with the value near 1.0 (see Baird & Biersdorf, 1967; Cook, 1978; Da Silva, 1985; Purdy & Gibson, 1955; Teghtsoonian & Teghtsoonian, 1969; see also Flückiger, 1991); such a result means that metric relations are fairly well perceived and preserved. Indeed, in keeping with the notion of reasonable accuracy, Cooks's data show stable exponents of individuals varying between about 0.78 and 1.22, with a mean close to 0.95; with several different methods, Da Silva (1985) reported ranges of about 0.60 to 1.30, and means around 0.94.

An important fact about results from distance judging experiments is that mean egocentric depth (distance away from the observer) is systematically foreshortened when compared with frontal depth (distances extended laterally in front of the observer and orthogonal to a given line of sight).[4] Thus, even with an exponent of 0.95, objects at egocentric distances of 10, 100, and 1,000 m would be seen to be at only 9, 79, and 710 m, respectively; whereas frontal distances would tend to show no such diminution. These egocentric foreshortenings represent 10, 21, and 29% errors in judgment, respectively, and might seem to impugn a claim of reasonable accuracy in perceiving layout, particularly in the great distance. However, there are two sets of facts available suggesting we generally have a more accurate perception of layout than even these experiments suggest.

B. Distance Estimation by Moving Observers

In defense of the idea of reasonable accuracy, the first set of facts comes from research on visually directed action. Thomson (1980), Laurent and Cavallo (1985), and Rieser, Ashmead, Talor, and Youngquist (1990), for example, showed that individuals are quite accurate in walking blindly to the distance of an object previously seen—indicating little, if any, foreshortening. Moreover, Loomis, Da Silva, Fujita, and Fukushima (1992) combined tasks in the same subjects and found the typical foreshortening effect in the distance estimation task and general accuracy in a directed action task. Thus, with Loomis et al. we conclude that acting on static visual information yields accurate estimates of space, but numerical or algebraic estimates in the same space often do not yield these accurate estimates.

A second important fact concerns motion information available to a moving observer. In standard psychophysical distance estimation tasks, the exponents reported are for stationary observers. By allowing an observer to move more than minimally with eyes open, the egocentric origin of the foreshortened space (be it affine or vectorially defined; see Wagner, 1985) must also change. Such changes would make any simple foreshortening model of perceived distances unlikely and would necessarily transform the space to a more Euclidean format.

C. Perceived Interobject Distances Are Multiply Constrained

Another avenue of research supporting accurate perception of depth and layout concerns the following kind of experiment: Individuals are placed in a cluttered environment and then asked to make judgments of distances

---

[4] Indeed, many would suggest that such judgments would be foreshortened still further. Direct scaling and related methods are often criticized as being open to "cognitive correction"; most adults know that distances foreshorten as they increase and could easily compensate judgments with this knowledge (Baird, 1970; Carlson, 1977; Gogel, 1974). However, in the context of this chapter, we see no reason to separate cognition and perception.

among the various objects in that space (e.g., Kosslyn, Pick, & Fariello, 1974; Toye, 1986). The half matrix of interobject judgments is then entered into a multidimensional scaling program (e.g., Kruskal, 1964; Shepard, 1980), and the two-dimensional solution is compared with the real layout in which observers made their judgments. Toye, for example, had observers judge the distances between all 78 possible pairs of 13 posts in a courtyard set among four tall buildings. These judgments were treated nonmetrically (i.e., as ranked information) and scaled in two dimensions. The original and the best fitting derived solutions revealed detailed and accurate correspondence between the two. Since absolute distances were judged with reasonable accuracy, the overlap of the two spatial representations is correct in scale and in general configuration.

We take Toye's (1986) methods and results as an important analogy for everyday commerce in our environment. That is, judgments about the distances among objects in a cluttered environment can vary, even vary widely. However, when taken together, they constrain each other in a manner well captured by nonmetric multidimensional scaling (NMDS) procedures (see also Baird, Merrill, & Tannenbaum, 1979; Baird & Wagner, 1983). Any psychological process for understanding the layout of objects in a visual scene would do well to mimic such a multiple-constraints procedure. Incidental, anomalous over- and underestimates of distance would then be corrected through consideration of other distances between various objects under consideration.

II. INFORMATION INTEGRATION: RULES, WEIGHTS, AND THE FEASIBILITY OF COMPLETE EXPERIMENTATION

There are two general empirical phenomena associated with experiments that have viewers estimate depth and that vary the number of sources of information available about layout. Künnapas (1968) found both. That is, adding information to a stimulus display generally increases the amount of depth seen, and adding information generally increases the consistency and accuracy with which judgments are made. The latter effect is surely the more important, but most investigations have focused on the former.

A. Nearly Linear Systems, Combination Rules, Cooperativity, and Data Fusion

An early indication that more depth is often seen with more sources of information stems from research by Jameson and Hurvich (1959). Kaufman (1974) called this the *superposition principle* from linear systems theory. More recently, Bruno and Cutting (1988) investigated the perception of exocentric depth from four sources of information: occlusion, relative size, height in the visual field, and motion perspective. By manipulating the image of three vertically oriented and parallel planes, Bruno and Cutting orthogonally varied the presence and absence of these four sources of information. Using a variety of techniques (direct scaling, preference scaling, and dissimilarity scaling), they found evidence of nearly linear additive combination of the four sources of information. That is, although different viewers weighted the four different sources differently, each source was generally intersubstitutable, and each addition generally yielded the perception of more exocentric depth.

After reanalyses of the direct scaling data of Bruno and Cutting (1988), Massaro (1988) questioned the conclusion of additivity. Massaro compared the fits of an additive and multiplicative model [the fuzzy-logical model of perception (FLMP) see Massaro, 1987, 1989; Massaro & Cohen, 1993; Massaro & Friedman, 1990], and found that, among the ten individual viewers, the data of five were better fit by the additive model and those of five others by FLMP. Moreover, Dosher, Sperling, and Wurst (1986) found similar multiplicative results in the integration of information from stereopsis and size. Thus, Massaro (1988) claimed Bruno and Cutting's (1988) results were indeterminant with respect to additivity. Cutting, Bruno, Brady, and Moore (1992a) then ran additional studies similar to those of Bruno and Cutting (1988). They found that among a total of 44 viewers, the data of 23 were better fit by an additive model, and the data of 21 by FLMP. Clearly, it is still indeterminant which model fits the data better, but it is equally clear that the data are almost linear in the middle range of the scale. The near linearity of these data suggests that, in an approach to the study of information combination, the notion of "nearly decomposable systems" (Simon, 1969)—what Marr (1981) and Fodor (1983) later called *modules*—is not far wrong.

Others have investigated the integration of various sources of information about layout (e.g., Berbaum, Tharp, & Mroczek, 1983; Braunstein & Stern, 1980; Nawrot & Blake, 1991; Rogers & Collett, 1988; Stevens & Brookes, 1988; Terzopoulos, 1986; van der Meer, 1979; Wanger, Ferwerda, & Greenberg, 1992). From a theoretical perspective these, and the previously outlined research, can be discussed in terms of two concepts: *cooperativity* (e.g., Kersten, Bülthoff, Schwartz, & Kurtz, 1992) and *data fusion* (e.g., Luo & Kay, 1989, 1992). Unfortunately, across the larger literature cooperativity is a term that seems to mean little more than the possibility of finding all possible combinations of additivity and interactions as dependent on context. Nonetheless, a particularly useful cooperative approach to integration was suggested by Maloney and Landy (1989; Landy, Maloney, & Young, 1991). They proposed that each source of information may leave one or more parameters about depth unknown and that various parameters from various sources can disambiguate one another. For example, within their system, they suggest that absolute metric qualities of stereopsis can scale the unanchored metrics of relative size, and size can offer depth order to the rotations of kinetic depth information. Robust estimators are also used to reduce the weight of any source of information generally out of line with the others.

Data fusion, on the other hand, is a term from robotics. Luo and Kay (1992), for example, discussed the integration of information in terms of four levels: integrating signals, pixels, features, and symbols. The first two forms of integration generally deal with relatively low-level electronics, but the latter two can be used to distinguish the approaches of Cutting et al. (1992a) and Massaro (1987; Massaro & Cohen, 1993). The approach of Cutting et al. is, as extended in this chapter, one of integrating many features looking for geometrical correspondence among sources of information; the approach of Massaro, on the other hand, is one of integrating symbols and increasing the truth value of what is perceived. Thus, in this context, the computational goal of feature fusion is to build a map; the computational goal of symbol fusion is to measure the surety of a percept and the grounds on which that surety is based.

B. Not Rules but Weights

Consider a modeling context. Whereas an understanding of the rules of information integration in visual perception is important, it is surely less interesting than an understanding of the weights. That is, what we and everyone else really want to ask are the following questions: Which sources of information are most important? When are they important? and Why? How much does relative size contribute to impressions of layout, say, as compared with stereopsis? How important is accommodation compared with aerial perspective? And so forth. These are the questions about weights for the various sources of information. In this chapter we provide a framework within which to suggest answers, but in the past, for at least two reasons, this type of exercise has proven extremely difficult.

First, through a process called *ecological sampling*, Brunswik (1956) and Brunswik and Kamiya (1953) tried to assess the cue validity of various sources of information—essentially the probability any proximal source is lawfully connected to distal affairs—then imputing weights to these probabilities. However, as principled as this approach is, it is logistically unfeasible. It has never been able to deliver a proper ecological survey of sources of information about depth, and in principle it probably cannot (Hochberg, 1966).

Second, the study of information weights is context and adaptation-level dependent. For example, Wallach and Karsh (1963a, 1963b; Wallach, Moore, & Davidson, 1963), have shown that stereopsis is extremely malleable as a source of information about depth. One day of monocular viewing even by an otherwise stereoscopically normal individual will, immediately after eye patch removal, render temporarily useless the stereoscopic information in judgments about depth. Moreover, through the use of random-dot stereograms (which remove all other depth information), Julesz (1971) reported that stereoblindness and stereoweakness were not uncommon in the normal population. For our purposes, however, we suggest that the variability found in stereopsis is unusual for an information source about layout; most other sources seem not to show large individual differences nor adaptational differences (but see Wallach & Frey, 1972a, 1972b).

C. Can One Empirically Study the Perception of Layout Given All Its Sources of Information?

The sheer number of information sources renders implausible any blindly systematic and thorough experimentation of the perception of layout. Consider the list of sources given above—accommodation, aerial perspective, binocular disparity, convergence, height in visual field, motion perspective, occlusion, relative size, and relative density—plus others that have been suggested in the literature, such as linear perspective (e.g., Carr, 1935), light and shading (e.g., Gibson, 1948; Graham, 1951), texture gradients (Gibson, 1948, 1950), kinetic depth (e.g., Maloney & Landy, 1989), kinetic occlusion and disocclusion (Kaplan, 1969; Yonas, Craton, & Thompson, 1987), and gravity (Watson, Banks, Hofsten, & Royden, 1992). Granting that each source be singular—and the texture gradients clearly are not (see Cutting & Millard, 1984; Stevens, 1981)—and granting further that this list be complete, there are 15 different sources to be considered and integrated by the visual system. Given such a lengthy list, it is a wonder how the visual system can function. Moreover, it is a wonder as to what researchers should do.

In general, we researchers have studied selected combinations of sources almost as an effort to avoid thinking about a full-fledged frontal attack on the general problem of layout and its perception. We have explored the effectiveness of pairs, triples, or even quadruples of the various sources of information in a given context. Examples of this strategy are rife (Bülthoff & Mallot, 1988; Bruno & Cutting, 1988; Dees, 1966; Dosher et al., 1986; Landy et al., 1991; Nakayama, Shimojo, & Silverman, 1989; Ono, Rogers, Ohmi, Ono, 1988; Terzopoulos, 1986; Uomori & Nishida, 1994; Wanger et al., 1992), and such research is important. However, given these 15 sources of information, there would be 105 possible pairs of information sources to study, 455 possible triples, and 1,365 possible quadruples, not to mention higher order combinations. These are surely more than enough to keep visual scientists busy well past the millennium; because they are also sufficiently plentiful, one wonders how overall progress is ever to be made. Such combinatorics suggest that researchers must set aside global experimentation as being simply unfeasible. As an example, if one uses only two levels (presence or absence) of each source listed above, he or she would need 2^{15} (or more than 32,000) different stimuli for a complete orthogonal design; with three levels per source (necessary for thorough assessment of additivity; Anderson, 1981, 1982), there would be 3^{15} or more than 14,000,000 different stimuli. This explosion negates thorough experimentation and even most theoretically selective experimentation. The major impetus of this chapter, then, is to explore logically the separateness of these sources, and their efficacy at different distances, in an attempt to prune the apparent richness of information about layout at all distances to a more manageable arrangement within particular domains. This will also provide a set of concrete predictions.

III. NINE SOURCES OF INFORMATION ABOUT LAYOUT: MEASUREMENT, ASSUMPTIONS, AND RELATIVE EFFICACY

In this section we compare and contrast nine sources of information about depth and then eliminate six others from consideration as either being not independent of those previously analyzed or not demonstrably useful for understanding general layout. Each source of information here is discussed in three ways. First, each source provides information inherently measured along a particular scale type. Second, each is based on a different set of assumptions about how light structures objects in the world, and these will play a role in our discussion. Third, and most important, many sources vary in their effectiveness at different distances, but some do not.

We use the weakest common scale for each source of information—the ordinal scale—and plot the threshold for judging two objects at different distances by using previous data where available and logical considerations elsewhere. Reduction to a common scale is an example of scale convergence (Birnbaum, 1983), a powerful tool for any discussion of perception, of psychology, and of science in general. We next compute distance thresholds by analogy to the computation of contrast sensitivity in the spatial-frequency domain. That is, in considering the distances of two objects, D_1 and D_2, we plot the ratio of the just-determinable difference in distance between them over their mean distance, $2(D_1 - D_2)/(D_1 + D_2)$, as a function of their mean distance from the observer, $(D_1 + D_2)/2$. In this manner our metric compensates for the often-noted decrease in accuracy with distance, such as that noted by Gogel (1993) in the following:

> Distance or depth errors are apt to occur in distant portions of the visual field because cues of depth are attenuated or are below threshold and therefore are unable to support the perception of depth between distant objects at different positions. (p. 148)

We also assume that distance judgments are made on the two objects separated by less than, say, about 5° of visual angle measured horizontally. This latter assumption is necessary in order that the environment is sufficiently cluttered with objects and surfaces to let all sources of information operate as optimally as conditions might allow. Having converted ordinal distance judgments to the same axes, we can then compare the efficacy of the various sources of information. Nagata (1991) was the first to present such plots and comparisons, but we offer much in contrast to what he proposed. As a working assumption, we regard depth thresholds of 10%, or 0.1 on the ordinate of Figure 1, as the useful limit in contributing to the perception of layout.

Before presenting these thresholds, however, we must discuss two important caveats. First, we assume the observer can look around, registering differences in each source of information on the fovea and neighboring regions of the retina. Thus, thresholds will typically be discussed in terms of foveal resolution even though the perception of layout, by definition, must extend well beyond the fovea at any instant. Clearly, then, we also assume

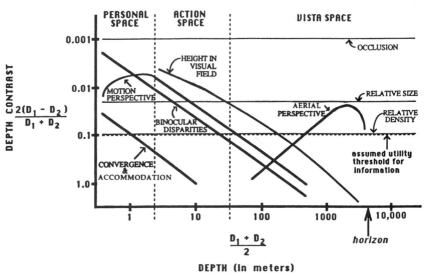

FIGURE 1   Just-discriminable depth thresholds as a function of the log of distance from the observer, from 0.5 to 5,000 meters, for nine different sources of information about layout. Such plots were originated by Nagata (1981) and are extensively modified and elaborated here; they are plotted with analogy to contrast sensitivity functions. Our assumption is that more potent sources of information are associated with smaller depth-discrimination thresholds and that these threshold functions reflect suprathreshold utility. These functions, in turn, delimit three types of space around the moving observer—personal space, action space, and vista space—each served by different sources of information and with different weights. This array of functions, however, is idealized. Figure 2 shows variations on the themes shown here.

visual stability and the integration of information across saccades (see, for example, Bridgeman, Van der Heijden, & Velichkovsky, 1994). Second, we assume that each source of information pertains to a set of objects at an appropriate retinal size. Thus, although an observer will surely not be able to discern from the distance of a kilometer the relative distance of two postage stamps, we claim that this is a problem of object resolution, not a problem reflecting source threshold. The relative distance of two buildings at the same distance is in many circumstances quite easily seen. Thus, in the context of our discussion, we always assume that the observer can easily resolve what he or she is looking at.

We begin our discussion with five more or less traditional pictorial sources of information (historically, often called *secondary cues,* for example, Boring, 1942), then move to the discussion of motion, and then finally to the ocular and physiologically based sources of information (often called *primary cues*).

A. Occlusions

Although the principle [of occlusion] is too obvious ordinarily to receive special mention as an artistic technic, it eventually got into the lists of secondary criteria for the perception of distance, as for example in Helmholz's in 1866.

Boring (1942, p. 264)

1. Measurement

Occlusion occurs when one object hides, or partially hides, another from view. It is ordinal information; it offers information about depth order but not about the amount of depth. At an occluding edge, one knows nothing other than that there is discontinuity in egocentric depth and that along each surface on either side of the edge the depths are likely to change more or less smoothly and continuously. Thus, a given pair of objects—occluding and occluded—might be at 5 and 10 cm from the observer, at 50 and 100 m, or equally at 5 cm and 1,000 m. Initially, ordinal information may not seem impressive, as suggested in the quote by Boring (1942, p. 264). Indeed, some researchers have not considered occlusion as information about depth at all (e.g., Maloney & Landy, 1989). However, two facts must be considered. First, an NMDS procedure that is based only on ordinal information can yield near-metric information in a scaling solution (Shepard, 1980). Second, for occlusion to yield ordinal information, one need make only four assumptions: the linearity of light rays, the general opacity of objects, the Gestalt quality of good continuation of boundary contours, and luminance contrast.

2. Assumptions

The first assumption—the rectilinearity of rays—is a general principle of light. Its failures are neither common nor generally consequential; they occur only with changes in densities of transmitting media, whether graded (such as those yielding mirages, fata morgana, and the like; see, for example, Forel, 1892; Minnaert, 1993) or abrupt (such as those at lens surfaces or at reflective surfaces). This assumption is further based on considering the eye (or any dioptric light registration device) as a pinhole camera, an assumption known as the *Gaussian approximation* (Pirenne, 1970). However, the rectilinearity of rays has been an axiom of optics and visual perception since Euclid (see Burton, 1945); it is an assumption that must be made for all visual sources of information about layout; and thus it need not be considered again.

The second assumption—the general opacity of objects—holds in most circumstances. Light does not usually pass through most of the things that make up our world. This assumption is pertinent, strong, and useful. Moreover, it can be violated to quite some degree in cases of translucency and transparency (see the discussion of aerial perspective below). That is, even when light does pass through objects, it is often changed in luminance, chromaticity, or both such that depth order can be maintained (Gerbino, Stultiens, & Troost, 1990; Metelli, 1974).

The third assumption, sometimes called Helmholtz's rule (Hochberg, 1971, p. 498), is that the contour of an object in front does not typically change its direction where it intersects the object seen as being behind it. The extreme unlikelihood of alignment of the eye, the location of sudden change in a contour of an occluding object, and the point of occlusion is, in modern parlance, a nonaccidental property (Witkin & Tenenbaum, 1983).[5]

Finally, for occlusion information to be useful, the luminance contrast at the occluding edge must be above threshold, and probably considerably above. Contrast is importance because the world does not unusually present itself in line-drawing form, the structure implied by any straightforward application of Helmholtz's (1867/1925) rule.

3. Effective Range

The range over which occlusion works is extremely impressive. Quite simply, occlusion can be trusted at all distances in which visual perception holds. As shown in Figure 1, the effectiveness of occlusion does not attenu-

---

[5] Despite Helmholtz's (1867/1925) formulation, and the more technical version of it offered by Ratoosh (1949), Chapanis and McCleary (1955) found more to occlusion than good continuation. Figural properties entered as well, an idea well captured by Leeuwenberg (1971) and Kellman and Shipley (1991).

ate with distance, and indeed the threshold for ordinal depth judgments generally exceeds all other sources of information. We suggest that with conventional natural objects and artifacts, occlusion can, throughout the visible range, provide constant depth thresholds about 0.1%. This is the width of a sheet of paper seen at 1.0 m or the width of a car against a building seen at 2 km. The separate functions for paper, for plywood, for people, for cars, and for houses are shown in the first panel of Figure 2. In a deep sense, the efficacy of occlusion is limited only by the physical properties of objects in the world. If we could make large opaque objects vanishingly thin, occlusion thresholds would increase with that ability. The caveat, of course, is that an occluding edge does not guarantee a difference of 0.1%; the difference in depth might equally be 1000%.

B. Relative Size and Relative Density

> There is no object so large . . . that at a great distance from the eye it does not appear smaller than a smaller object near. Among objects of equal size, that which is most remote from the eye will look the smallest.
>
> *Leonardo (Taylor, 1960, p. 32)*

1. Measurement and Assumptions

Relative size is the measure of the projected retinal size of objects or textures that are physically similar in size but at different distances. Relative density concerns the projected retinal density of a cluster of objects or textures, whose placement is stochastically regular, as they recede into the distance. Unlike occlusion, relative size and relative density can, in principle, both yield more than ordinality, they can yield scaled information. Making the similar physical size assumption for similarly shaped objects, the ratio of their retinal sizes or the square root of their ratio of their densities will determine the inverse ratio of their distances from the observer. However, there are three assumptions.

First, for relative size there must be more than one object, and they cannot be too large and too near. For example, if the center of one planar surface of an object is orthogonal to the line of sight and subtends a visual angle of 45°, an identical object half its distance would subtend 79°, not 90°.[6] When objects are smaller than about 20°, which will include virtually everything seen, this submultiplicativity is minimal. For example, a rectilinear

---

[6] Where is the angular subtense, d is the distance to the object, and h is the height of the object. Where that object has a planar face at right angles to the observer, and where the observer is looking at the middle of the measured surface extent are represented by the following formula: $\partial = 2 \times \arctan [h/(d \times 2)]$.

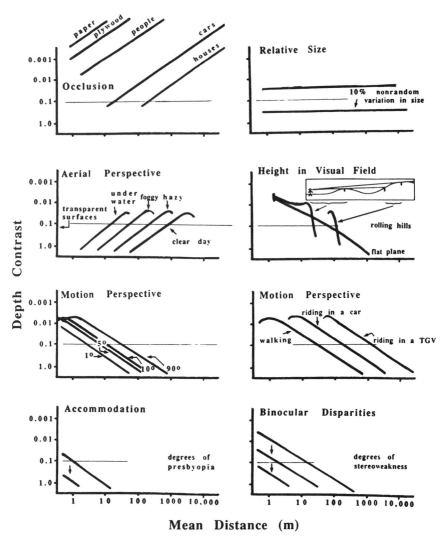

Mean Distance (m)

FIGURE 2 Eight variations in the depth-threshold functions for various sources of information under conditions that are either nonideal or violate some assumptions made in Figure 1. The first panel shows occlusion depth-threshold functions for five different substances: paper, plywood, people, cars, and townhouses. The function in Figure 1 is flat because of the parallel cascade of these rising functions. The second panel shows the decrease in effectiveness of relative size, when there is a 10% variation in size. When there is 10% random variability in size across the whole layout, it is not clear there would be any diminuation of this function. The third shows the functions for aerial perspective under different atmospheric conditions, plus the function underwater and a suggestion about transparency. The fourth panel shows the change in threshold function of height in the visual field, when the surface of support is nonplanar. The fifth panel shows four functions for motion perspective; that for 90° to the observer's linear path (as shown in Figure 1) and those for 10°, 5°, and 1° from the path. The sixth panel shows the 90° function for a pedestrian, a passenger in an automobile, and a passenger in a fast train (the TGV in France). The seventh panel shows the decrease of the

object that subtends 10° will, at half the distance, subtend 19.85°, a near-perfect doubling or retinal size.

Second, without assuming knowledge of the particular objects themselves (which transforms this source of information into "familiar size" or "assumed size"; see, for example, Epstein, 1963, 1965), differences in retinal size of 3:4:5 and differences in retinal density of 9:16:25 occur equally for three objects (or sets of objects or textures) at 1, 1.33, and 1.67 cm and at 50, 66.5, and 83.3 m. Thus, differences are metrically scaled but without absolute anchor. If the objects are known to the observer, then relative size becomes familiar size, and absolute information is available. Aside from knowledge, the only other difference between the two is that with familiar size there need be only one object present; with relative size, more than one must be visible, and with relative density there must be many. In general, we do not assume knowledge of objects here.

Third, the assumption of similarity in physical size must not be taken too strictly. For example, mature trees of the same kind, age, and shape will be roughly, but not exactly, the same size (e.g., Bingham, 1993). A 10% range in variability in size in strategically placed objects could cause a similar variability (error) in the assessment in distance. This can reduce the power of the scaling factor, but even in its reduction the information scale has stronger assumptions than that of mere ordinality; it might be called *fuzzily scaled* information.[7]

2. Ordinal Conversion and Effective Ranges

Although relative size can offer scaled information, for our purposes we must reduce it to ordinal judgments. Teichner, Kobrick, and Wehrkamp (1955) measured the just-noticeable distance thresholds for large objects mounted on jeeps stationed in a desert and similar terrains.[8] These data are replotted and shown in Figure 1, with the same value as given by Nagata

---

efficacy of accommodation with age. The eighth shows the possibilities of different degrees of stereoweakness. We claim that these types of variations in these functions occur across contexts and individuals and modify the orderings of importance (the weights) in the integration of information about layout.

[7] The assumption of similarity, and not identity, is also important when considering texture. A texture surface, by conventional definition, is one peppered with similar texture elements; these typically lie flat on the object surface and will be at various orientations to the observer, yielding nonidentical retinal projections.

[8] The experiments of Teichner et al. (1955) appear to have covaried relative size and height in the visual field. Our analysis suggests height is the more powerful sources of information than relative size in the near field. Nonetheless, it makes sense that relative size should not attenuate with distance and that its threshold value should be near 3%.

(1991). Notice that, like occlusion, relative size can generally be trusted throughout the visible range of distances, from say 0.5 m to 5,000 m (the horizon for an average adult standing on an earthen surface approximating a flat plane or at the edge of a large calm lake) and beyond. However, relative size provides a depth threshold of about 3%, a bit more than an order of magnitude worse than occlusion. Moreover, if natural objects are allowed to vary in size by 10%, the effectiveness of size is further diminished, as shown in the top panel of Figure 2.

On logical grounds alone, Nagata (1991) suggested that one's sensitivity to density ought to be the square root of two times greater than relative size. However, the data of Cutting and Millard (1984) have shown that density is psychologically less than half as effective as the size gradient in revealing exocentric depth (see also Stevens, 1981). Thus, we have plotted it as weaker than relative size in Figure 1, at just about our 10% threshold, equal to our margin for considering a source of information effective for determining layout. This means that a viewer ought to be able to just discriminate the difference between two patches of random elements; one containing 95 and the other containing 105 dots. For further discussions of density, see Allik and Tuulmets (1991), Barlow (1978), and Durgin (1995). Since we have already assumed stochastic regularity in textures, any effects of variability in element spacing would seem likely to be related to the parameters modeling the stochastic regularity. However, since we know of no data relevant to this concern, no panel in Figure 2 is devoted to factors of variation that would generate a function different than that shown in Figure 1.

C. Height in Visual Field

> In the case of flat surfaces lying below the level of the eye, the more remote parts appear higher.
>
> *Euclid (Burton, 1945, p. 359)*

1. Measurement and Assumptions

This fourth source of information is in the projected relations of the bases of objects in a three-dimensional environment to the viewer. Such information, moving from the bottom of the visual field (or image) to the top, yields good ordinal information about distance from the point of observation (see, for example, Dunn, Gray, & Thompson, 1965). Height in the visual field also has the potential of yielding absolute distances. The assumptions that must be made for such information, however, may in many situations be unacceptably strong. They are four and in decreasing acceptability, if not plausibility, they are (1) opacity of the ground plane, (2) gravity and that each object has its base on the surface of support (it is not suspended, or floating), (3) that the observer's eye is at a known distance (say, about 1.6 m for any individual about 5 ft 9 in. in height) above the surface of support, and (4) that the surface of support is generally planar and orthogonal to gravity. If all assumptions are valid, then 10° of visual angle below the horizon, the width of a fist held vertically at arm's length, is 9 m away, assuming an eye height of 1.6 m for an observer standing on level ground, and 2° below the horizon, the width of the thumb at arm's length, is about 50 m away.[9] However, the plethora of assumptions needed to validate height in the visual field may occasionally impugn its effectiveness, as suggested in our later section on source conflict. We feel that Assumptions (1) and (2) are the only ones generally valid.

2. Effective Range

Unlike occlusion, size, and density, the effectiveness of height in the visual field attenuates with distance. Since the bases of seen objects must be touching the ground plane for it to be useful, since we are considering an upright and moving observer, and since the observer's eye is already at a height of 1.6 m, no base closer to the eye than 1.6 will generally be available.

We assume that height-in-visual-field differences of 5 min of arc between two nearly adjacent objects are just detectable. This is an order of magnitude above standard resolution acuity (which is about 0.5 min), but it allows for quite a few degrees of separation in the visual field for the two objects under consideration. Moreover, a different value would simply shift the function up or down a bit. Under these assumptions and considerations, as shown in Figure 1, the utility of height in the visual field is truncated short of about 2 m, at 2 m it is nearly as effective as occlusion (provided one is looking at one's feet), and beyond 2 m its effectiveness diminishes curvilinearly. At about 1,000 m its threshold value has fallen to a value of 10%, our benchmark for assumed utility. However, when Assumption 4 is violated, ordinal information can even improve beyond what is shown in Figure 1 for objects in which bases are still visible. This is due to the rotation of

---

[9] However, even without a metric assumption, size can still be scaled in terms of eye height. There is, for example, information in the horizon–ratio about size (e.g., Sedgwick, 1973). It is useful to assume that the projected height of the horizon is at the same height as the eye, which Edgerton (1975) called the *horizon-line isocephaly*. In the flattest terrestrial situations, it is at an angle of about 89.98° with respect to the gravitational vertical (Cutting, 1986). Thus, anything intersecting the projection of the horizon line at the point of observation (the eye) is at the same height as the eye; anything or anyone whose height is half the distance from its base to the horizon line is half the height of the point of observation; and anything that has the horizon line bisect its vertical extent is twice the height of the point of observation. In this manner, scaled information is available in the optical array relative to the point of observation. Again, if eye height is known, then absolute size and absolute distance information are available, although they will not necessarily be used.

the particular region of the ground plane toward the eye of the observer; sample functions are shown in the third panel of Figure 2.

D. Aerial Perspective

> There is another kind of perspective which I call aerial perspective because by the atmosphere we are able to distinguish the variations of distance. . . . [I]n an atmosphere of equal density the remotest objects . . . appear blue and almost of the same hue as the atmosphere itself.
>
> *Leonardo (Taylor, 1960, pp. 37–38)*

Aerial perspective is determined by the relative amount of moisture, pollutants, or both in the atmosphere through which one looks at a scene. When air contains a high degree of either, objects in the distance become bluer, decreased in contrast, or both with respect to objects in the foreground. Such effects have been known in art since before Leonardo and are called effects of *participating media* in computer graphics.

1. Measurement and Assumptions

In principle, aerial perspective ought to allow interval information about depth. By assuming, as Leonardo did, that the participating medium is uniform, then the increasing blueness or lightness of objects in the distance will be linear with their increasing distance from the observers. In practice, however, it would seem that aerial perspective allows only ordinal comparisons; we know of no data on the topic, although contemporary computer graphics technology would easily allow preliminary study. Nonetheless, real-world experimental control of participating media would be extremely difficult to obtain.

2. Effective Range

As shown in Figure 1, and unlike all other sources of information, the effectiveness of aerial perspective increases with the logarithm of distance. This is due to the fact that, assuming the medium is uniform across linear distance, logarithmic increases in distance will encompass logarithmically increasing amounts of the medium. The limitation, however, is that with great distances objects become indistinct, and the source of information becomes rapidly ineffective. The function shown in Figure 1 is Nagata's (1991), but as shown in fourth panel of Figure 2, the effective range can vary greatly, depending on whether there is fog, haze, or clear air.

The concept of aerial perspective is also easily modified to consider underwater environments, condensing the range still further, and is also justifiably applied to the perception of transparency (Gerbino et al., 1990; Metelli, 1974). That is, the study of the depth order of two or more colored but transparent sheets is no different than aerial perspective, except that the sheets become the medium and that rather than being a graded continuous function, the transparency generates a discrete-valued step function. Transparency is the only source of information about layout that does not assume the opacity of objects.

With these five sources, our assessment of the pictorial sources of information is complete. Other sources of information might be added to this list, but we defer discussion of them until our full list is complete. We now move to the discussion of motion, then to accommodation, convergence, and binocular disparities.

E. Motion Perspective

> In walking along, the objects that are at rest by the wayside stay behind us; that is, they appear to glide past us in our field of view in the opposite direction to that in which we are advancing. More distant objects do the same, only more slowly, while very remote bodies like the stars maintain their permanent positions in the field of view.
>
> *Helmholtz (1867/1925, p. 295)*

Motion is omnipresent for a mobile observer, it is even claimed to be the foundation of human vision (Lee, 1980). To be sure, when stabilized images are projected onto the retina, removing all motion, the world disappears; without motion, it is very difficult to get infants to respond to any aspects of layout (Yonas & Granrud, 1985). Nonetheless, we think the role of motion in our perception of layout may have been overplayed; indeed, in landscape paintings there is no motion and yet these have pleased people in many cultures for many centuries. Moreover, empirically, Schwartz and Sperling (1983) have shown that relative size can dominate motion information in judgments of depth, and Vishton, Nijhawan, and Cutting (1994) have shown that size and other sources of information can dramatically influence observers' judgments of their heading in sequences simulating observer motion through cluttered environments. In this light, then, we would expect motion information to be relatively important for the perception of layout, but not all encompassing.

The relative movement of the projections of several stationary objects caused by observer movement is called *motion parallax;* the motions of a whole field of such objects is called *motion perspective* (Gibson, 1950, 1966). Ferris (1972) and Johansson (1973) demonstrated that, through motion perspective, individuals are quite good at judging distances up to about 5 m (but see Gogel, 1993; Gogel & Tietz, 1973). Introspection suggests our accuracy would be high at considerably greater distances as well.

1. Measurement and Assumptions

Motion perspective assumes little other than that one is moving through a rigid environment. Some depictions of that environment also assume planarity of the surface of support (Gibson, 1966, 1979; Gibson, Olum, & Rosenblatt, 1955; see also Bardy, Baumberger, Flückiger, & Laurent, 1992; Flückiger & Baumberger, 1988), but this second assumption is typically made only for purposes of pedagogical or methodological clarity. In principle, the complete array of motions specifies to a scaling factor the layout of the environment and the instantaneous position of the moving observer (e.g., Gibson, 1966, 1979; Koenderink, 1986; Lee, 1980; Prazdny, 1983). That is, with no other information available, one can mathematically discern from the flow both the relative position of objects and one's own relative velocity (in eye heights per second).

What is relative in this context concerns clutter and reveals two interrelated sources of motion information—edge rate and global flow rate (see, for example, Larish & Flach, 1990). Assume that one is moving at a constant height and velocity over a flat ground plane with textures at regular separation and that one is in a vehicle with a windscreen and maintaining constant orientation with respect to the plane. Edge rate is the number of countable objects, or edges, per unit time that pass any point on the windscreen as one moves forward and is related to relative density as discussed above. Given a uniformly textured ground plane, edge rate will be constant everywhere there is texture.[10] Global flow rate is the pattern of relative motions everywhere around the moving observer; rapid beneath one's feet, decreasing with distance, nearly zero at the horizon all around, and generally following a sine function as one moves from 0° (directly ahead) to 180° (directly behind) and then back to 360°. This hemispherical pattern is multiplied as a function of velocity, or as the reciprocal of altitude.

More concretely, edge rate is dependent on velocity and texture density but not on altitude; flow rate is dependent on velocity and altitude but not on texture density. Larish and Flach (1990) demonstrated that impressions of velocity depend much more on edge rate than flow rate, accounting for the efficacy in Denton's (1980) study of car drivers slowing down at tollbooths and roundabouts on motor ways through the use of decreasingly spaced markers. It may be that impressions of layout and depth are similarly governed more by edge rates than flow rates, but the relation between the functions for density and motion perspective in Figure 1 suggests it may not. In any event, since regular or even stochastically regular textures are often not available to a moving observer, we concentrate on flow rates at 2 m/s, about the speed of a pedestrian.

---

[10] It is said that Israeli pilots flying over the Negev desert often have problems maintaining altitude. The Negev has stochastically regular texture (dunes), but the frequencies and amplitudes gradually change north to south. In maintaining edge rates, the pilots must increase altitude as the texture density decreases (Shimon Ullman, 15 February 1991, personal communication).

2. Ordinal Conversion and Effective Range

Again, and with others who have assessed the efficacy of motion perspective such as Nagata (1991), we assume that the moving observer is a pedestrian and free to move his or her eyes about (although all considerations are monocular). Thus, the thresholds plotted in Figure 1 are foveal for a roving eye (one undergoing pursuit fixation during locomotion and saccadic movement, see Cutting et al., 1992b), where motion detection is best, and our situation then equally assumes an individual has sampled many locations in the visual field over a period of time.

Unlike the monotonic function shown by Nagata (1991), we have indicated that motion perspective acuity declines below about 2 m because of the difficulty in tracking and even seeing differences in rapid movement. Graham, Baker, Hecht, and Lloyd (1948), Zegers (1948), and Nagata measured the difference thresholds for motion detection. If the experimental values are used as input measures for the pedestrian motion perspective at relatively short distances (<10 m), and if the absolute motion threshold (1 min of arc/s) is used for distances beyond (see also Graham, 1951),[11] the function shown in Figure 1 is generated. However, that function also assumes that one is looking at 90° to the direction of movement, a somewhat unusual situation for a pedestrian. Thus, a family of threshold functions is shown in the fifth panel of Figure 2 for an observer looking at 1°, 2°, and 10° from his or her direction of movement. Since observers do not usually change direction to assess layout, the function in Figure 1 probably overestimates the importance and power of motion perspective for a pedestrian; but, of course, when riding in a car or fast train (TGV in France), the function would amplify and slide to the right, as shown in the sixth panel of Figure 2.

F. Convergence and Accommodation

We alter the disposition of our eyes, by lessening or widening the distance between the *pupils*. This disposition or turn of the eyes is attended with a sensation, which seems to me to be that which in this case, brings the *idea* of greater or lesser distance into the mind.

Berkeley (1709, sections 16–20)

Convergence is measured by the angle between the optical axes of the two eyes. When this angle is large, the two eyes are canted inward as if to

---

[11] Data are available for relative depth-through-motion threshold up to the equivalent of 10 m for a pedestrian (Zegers, 1948). Beyond 10 m there are no data, but the motion generated by the pedestrian is so slow that any object could easily be fixated during pursuit motions. Once fixated, the absolute motion thresholds can be used.

focus on a spot very near the nose; when this angle approaches 0°, the two eyes are parallel, aligned as if to focus on the horizon or beyond. Accommodation is the change in the shape of the lens of the eye, allowing it to focus on objects near or far while still keeping the retinal image sharp. The effective degree to which accommodation can change in a given eye is defined by the distance between the near point (the point measured along the optical axis—from the fovea, through the middle of the pupil, outward—to the nearest orthogonal plane at which something can be placed and remain in focus because of the thickening of the lens) to the far point (that point along the same axis farthest away at which an object can remain in focus because of the thinning of the lens). These points vary considerably across individuals and, with age, within individuals. At any instant, the effectiveness of accommodation may not be very great since blur occurs equally for objects nearer and farther than the mean focal depth, providing measures that fail ordinality. However, across fixations at different depths accommodation has the potential of offering such information.

Convergence and accommodation are reflexively yoked (Fincham & Walton, 1957; Kersten & Legge, 1983; Morgan, 1968) thus, we have considered them together.[12] Both can be measured in diopters, or the reciprocal of distance in meters; therefore, the changes in distance from 0.33 to 0.5 m, from 0.5 to 1.0 m, and from 1 m to infinite distance are each 1 diopter.

1. Measurement and Assumptions

The assumptions of these two sources of information are few: For convergence to be effective one must have an object to fixate and knowledge of (or familiarity with) the distance between one's eyes—for an adult usually about 6.4 cm. In addition, for both convergence and accommodation to be effective, the target must have reasonable luminance contrast and a relatively complex spatial frequency distribution (Fisher & Ciuffreda, 1988). Thus, in principle, these sources could be extremely effective in measuring distance, yielding metric information within the near distance.

2. Ordinal Conversion and Effective Range

As suggested by the metric of diopters, neither convergence nor accommodation is effective at great distance. Indeed, evidence suggests that the effectiveness of convergence alone as a source of information for depth is confined to a range up to only about 2 m or so (see Gogel, 1961; Hofsten, 1976; Lie, 1965; Richards & Miller, 1969), and accommodation a bit less so (Fisher & Ciuffreda, 1988), although both can interact with other sources

---

[12] Of course, convergence is also yoked to stereopsis, and when the vergence system runs awry, rendering it difficult or impossible to foveate the same part of an object with both eyes, strabismus results.

(Wallach & Norris, 1963). Even when combined their useful range still seems to be less than 3 m (Liebowitz, Shina, & Hennessy, 1972). The function shown in Figure 1 stems from the experiments and logical considerations of Nagata (1991) and shows the utility of both sources declining linearly with distance. The functions shown in the seventh panel of Figure 2 remind us that since the ability to accommodate generally declines with age, its efficacy as a source of information about layout must also change.

G. Binocular Disparity, Stereopsis, and Diplopia

[T]he mind perceives an object of three dimensions by means of two dissimilar pictures projected by it on the two retinae.

Wheatstone (1838, p. 373)

Binocular disparities are the differences in relative position of the projections of the same object on the retinas of the two eyes. When looking at an object at a given distance, there are other locations in the environment that, if objects are located there, fall on a zero-disparity surface called the *horopter,* generally circular in depth according to Thales theorem (see Arditi, 1986) and linear along declining planes when measured vertically (Nakayama, 1977). When these disparities are sufficiently small, they yield stereopsis or the impression of solid space. When greater, they yield diplopia—or double vision—also a good source of information about relative depth (Ogle, 1952; Duwaer & van den Brink, 1981). No other source of information about layout has been more studied than binocular disparity and we cannot do justice here to its vast literature. For a lucid discussion see Kaufman (1974) and for comprehensive overviews, see Arditi (1986) and Gulick and Lawson (1976).

1. Measurement and Assumptions

The measurement scale implied by retinal disparities and stereopsis has often been taken to be the strongest among all sources of information about layout. Indeed, many have claimed that disparities offer an absolute metric for distance (Dees, 1966; Maloney & Landy, 1989). The assumptions underlying stereopsis are few and seldom violated—one must have, first, some knowledge of or familiarity with the distance between the eyes,[13] the state

[13] It is clear our visual system makes some roughly accurate assumption about interocular distance. In this vein, it is interesting that early stereoscopic pictures—showing cityscapes and other scenes of large expanse—enhanced the distance between the eyes. In turn, these diminished the effective size of the objects seen. Thus, many early American stereoscopic pictures were visual oxymorons, presenting sequoias (which are large, but then diminished to near normal size in appearance by intercamera distance) in conjunction with people. Rather than impressing the (late twentieth century) observer with the size of sequoias, they impress one with the diminutive nature of the people next to them.

of vergence (which beyond 2 m is always less than 1°), and then one must find the locations of appropriately corresponding points with generally lateral retinal displacements in the two eyes. These corresponding points need not be identified with parts of objects, indeed random dots will do (Julesz, 1971), and the relative luminance and relative size of those dots is not vitally important. The paucity of assumptions associated with the utility binocular disparities may reinforce their effectiveness in perception.

2. Ordinal Conversion and Effective Range

Ordinal thresholds for depth can be computed from existing discussions and data (Arditi, 1986; Berry, 1948; Bülthoff, Fahle, & Wegmann, 1991; Ebenholtz & Walchli, 1965; Foley, 1991; Nagata, 1991; Ogle, 1952, 1958) and are shown in Figure 1. Critically, these assume that vergence can vary across fixations at different distances and that both stereopsis and diplopia are useful for depth judgments. Clearly, disparities are most effective in the near field (regardless of fixation depth), and their relative effectiveness attenuates linearly with distance. Notice also the similarity in threshold acuity for binocular disparity and motion perspective when both are at their best for pedestrians, a result that fits snugly with the comparative results of Dees (1966), who assessed the accuracy of perceived depth by using these two sources of information independently and in combination. Since stereoweakness and stereoblindness are not uncommon, the functions in the eighth panel of Figure 2 are designed to capture this fact.

H. Sources Not Considered

In our list of nine sources of information about layout, we have left out several commonly accepted candidates. Their omission has been purposeful, but needs explanation; so let's consider each in turn.

1. Texture Gradients

Gibson (1950) was first to note the importance of texture gradients for the perception of layout, and we agree that they are powerful sources of information (e.g., Cutting & Millard, 1984). However, there are at least three gradients of texture in surfaces receding in depth: the gradients of size, density, and compression. The size gradient (the change in the largest extent of a texture element, measured parallel to the axis of tilt) is effectively no different than relative size working continuously on many elements across a surface.[14] It has thus already been considered and plotted in Figure 1. Like-

---

[14] Size gradient here was called the *perspective gradient* by Cutting and Millard (1984) and the *scaling gradient* by Stevens (1981).

wise, the effectiveness of relative density has also been given in Figure 1. The compression gradient is isomorphic with the slant gradient considered by Nagata (1991), and his analysis, on the basis of the results of Freeman (1966), suggested that it is quite powerful (indeed about three times as effective as relative size) and unchanging with distance. However, we find Nagata's analysis unconvincing; the data of Cutting and Millard suggest that compression is extremely ineffective in its psychological effect of revealing depth—much less so than even density—and it is thus not included in our list. Instead, compression (or slant) is good information about object shape, particularly its curvature near the object's self-occluding contour (Marr, 1981).

2. Linear Perspective

It will surely strike some as surprising that we have not placed linear perspective in our list. Our reason is not because its effects are not powerful, they are (e.g., Kubovy, 1986). We omit discussion here because linear perspective is a systematic combination (even an asystematic combination, see Elkins, 1992) of several other sources of information and a choice of display elements. For example, it combines all three texture gradients—size, density, and compression—with occlusion and then is separated from natural perspective (see Leonardo, in Taylor, 1960) by the copious use of parallel lines. Receding parallel lines are an extremely effective way of reducing noise in the measurement of object sizes, densities, and compressions; but all of the relevant elements of linear perspective have already been considered.

3. Brightness, Light, and Shading

Some conflation of these terms has appeared on many lists of sources of information about layout (e.g., Boring, 1942; Nagata, 1991), but we find their inclusion anomalous (as did Gibson, 1950). To be sure, it has been demonstrated that gradually increasing the luminance of an object causes it to appear to move forward. However, this appears to be something of a "theatrical" effect, one which assumes either that the foreground is better lit than the background or that the light source of a scene is necessarily near and at roughly the same distance from the object as one's eye. Since the position of the sun negates both of these assumptions, we think something else is at work. In fact, we believe that luminance in such cases may be acting as a surrogate for relative size, and indeed it has been used experimentally in just this manner (Dosher et al., 1986). More ecologically, the play of light on a form yields shadows, which have also been construed as a source of information about depth (e.g., Bülthoff & Mallot, 1988; Yonas & Granrud, 1985). However, with Cavanagh and Leclerc (1990), we think it is better to consider shadows as information about object shape, not depth per se. Moreover, shadows can be considered an application of the phenomenon of transparency, which in turn was considered a variant of aerial perspective.

4. Kinetic Depth

Quite a number of researchers have discussed kinetic depth (Wallach & O'Connell, 1953)—structural information revealed through motion (e.g., Ullman, 1979, 1983)—as an important source of information about depth (e.g., Maloney & Landy, 1989). However, we suggest that this information, like shading, concerns object shape and contributes little to the study of layout. Moreover, in rotating wireframe forms it often fails the criterion of ordinality—figures reverse in depth, even when perspective information is added (Braunstein, 1962, 1976)—and a rotating, generally solid object in silhouette often does not even allow perception of rigidity (Wallach & O'Connell, 1953).

5. Kinetic Occlusion and Disocclusion

Kaplan (1969) and Yonas et al. (1987), among others (e.g., Andersen & Braunstein, 1983), have discussed the property of kinetic occlusion—sometimes called *accretion* and *deletion of texture*—as a source of information about depth. However, we regard kinetic occlusion as covered in our list in two ways. First, kinetic occlusion is simply occlusion as revealed through motion; it differs only in that it need not assume any luminance contrast at the occluding edge. Under conditions of low visibility, such as approaching a descending set of textured steps at night, kinetic occlusion may be the only source of information available to the pedestrian. Nonetheless, aside from small differences in the assumptions on which it is based, kinetic occlusion does not have separate qualities or properties from occlusion. Second, kinetic occlusion can also be considered a two-valued function of motion perspective, yielding ordinal information, but again already considered in our list.

6. Gravity

It is interesting that researchers continue to discover more sources of information about layout and depth, and we expect this trend to continue at a slow pace. Recently, for example, Watson et al. (1992) postulated that gravity can serve as a source of information. That is, since the acceleration patterns of dropped or thrown objects on the retina will vary with distance, these patterns are available as information. Clever as this idea is, gravity is not likely to be very useful in determining layout because one seldom sees objects thrown or in free fall when viewing one's surroundings. In addition, gravity as such appears to be a source of information about an isolated object not about layout.

I. Overview

The functions in Figure 1 are ordinal depth-threshold measures for various sources of information about layout as a function of mean distance from the observer. If we assume that the relations among these threshold functions can generalize to suprathreshold situations, then we may have a powerful tool. However, these functions are somewhat idealized and may not apply to all situations. The functions shown in Figure 2 show the variability that can be obtained according to different environments and states of the observer. Nonetheless, we assume that in every environment for every observer, one can, in principle, plot a similar array of functions and that that array can be used to understand how we perceive layout as we do.

IV. A SITUATION-SENSITIVE DOMINANCE HIERARCHY OF INFORMATION SOURCES

> Objects and events in a natural environment can be multiply specified by many different sources of information, each of which is detected by a specialized processing module with its own individual limitations. In any given situation, we would expect to obtain erroneous outputs from some of these modules because of inappropriate viewing conditions, but it would be most unlikely for two or more of them to fail in exactly the same way.
>
> *Todd (1985, p. 708)*

Why are there so many sources of information about layout? Part of the answer must be that environments are typically rich, but they can also be extremely varied, with certain kinds of information present in some situations but not in others. Another part of the answer must be that perceiving layout is extremely important to us, as it must have been to our forebears and is to other organisms so that systems with multiple mechanisms for the gathering of information about layout have an advantage over those with single mechanisms. Now, the analysis of the relationships in Figure 1 suggests many things that allow us to go beyond such vague notions and beyond Todd's instructive beginning.

Why might a source of information fail? Figure 1 suggests that with varying distance some sources fail to deliver an adequate quality of information. The panels of Figure 2 suggest that with varying environments (and with varying states of the organism) this adequacy will also vary. The differential adequacies as a function of distance may account for some traditional findings in the field.

A. Conflicting Information

In Figure 1 we find rationale for certain well-known results in experimental situations of what is often called *cue-conflict*—when two or more sources of information are presented yielding discrepant ordinal information about depth. If we assume that our threshold analyses were properly carried out and that they can be used to generalize to superthreshold considerations, then certain predictions can be made.

Let us consider four examples. First, occlusion would appear to dominate all other sources of information for layout (see Bruno & Cutting, 1988, Figure 7; Krech & Krutchfield, 1958) and in all contexts. In fact, in situations of conflict, these functions suggest only binocular disparity (Nakayama et al., 1989), and perhaps height in the visual field would seem to come close to the power of occlusion. Second, we also find evidence as to why accommodation and convergence are generally so weak and in situations of conflict will generally dominate no other information. Their role in such situations seems simply to modify perceived layout through the use of other sources (Wallach & Frey, 1972a, 1972b). Third, our threshold functions also suggest that height in the visual field would dominate relative size information out to about 500 m, but that size would dominate beyond. We know of no data on this matter.

Fourth, consider a potential problem for our hierarchy. The data shown in Figure 1 would seem to predict that height in the visual array would always dominate binocular disparity, at least beyond about 2 m. However, this seems implausible, and within 1 m, Gilchrist (1977, 1980) has provided empirical proof. One possible rationale for this reversal in our system is through consideration, not simply of the functions shown, but also of the validity of the assumptions underlying each source. The assumptions of height in the visual field entail objects resting on a flat ground plane as seen from one's usual eye height, and they all seem almost cognitive. In contrast, the assumptions for binocular disparity are physiologically given. It seems likely, then, that certain classes of disparities on certain objects could easily invalidate an assumption made for height in the visual field; thus, disparity differences at the base of an object compared with those of the ground immediately in front of the object would render invalid the assumption of the object resting on the support surface, and binocular disparity would then dominate height in the visual field. Such an analysis offers some empirical force to the otherwise weak notion of "cooperativity" among sources of information about layout.

B. Three Categories of Source–Distance Relations

In addition, the relations among the various functions in Figure 1 suggest that there are three categories of information sources for layout: those that do not vary with the logarithm of distance, those that dissipate with distance, and one that increases with the logarithm distance.

1. Sources Invariant with Distance

Three sources of information are unaffected by logarithm of distance from the observer—occlusion, relative size, and relative density—and all are pictorial sources of information. Such effective consistency across distances suggests that in experimental situations information conflict occlusion will always dominate size, which in turn will always dominate density. Moreover, in natural situations, these three sources can be used as anchors across different depth ranges to coordinate perception of layout from arm's length to the horizon along a logarithmic scale. Indeed, elaboration of Birnbaum's (1983) terms indicates that the similarity of function shape of these sources within the same measurement scale should well reinforce one another.

2. Sources Dissipating with Distance

Members of the second category generally decrease in effectiveness with distance and would do so whether measured logarithmically or linearly. These are height in the visual field and motion perspective (both assuming objects are not too close) and the physiologically coordinated cluster of ocular sources: binocular disparity, convergence, and accommodation. Throughout the relevant range of distances, these five sources maintain their relative ranking and, given the same general function shape and scale, we would expect them to act in consort, therefore, reinforcing each other's measurements.

3. A Source Increasing with Distance

Finally, the only source of information that generally increases its effectiveness with the logarithm of distance is aerial perspective. In typical situations, however, this source is likely to become effective only with great distance. It may even help compensate for (cooperate with) the declining effectiveness of the information sources in the previous group by enhancing occlusion information.

Given three classes of ordinal depth-threshold functions—those constant with the logarithm of distance, those decreasing, and one increasing—we speculate that one can go beyond Birnbaum (1983) and, given the shared ordinal scale, postulate the utility of function shape contrast. That is, in addition to the possibility of members of each category reinforcing one another, the existence in optimal situations of different function shapes can serve to diversify and solidify judgments of distance. We claim these functions serve to separate at least three different types of distance.

C. Segmenting the Space around Us

As an attempt to satisfy the primary goal of this chapter, the relations in Figure 1 suggest a framework for a theory of contextual use of the various sources of information about layout. From the pattern of threshold results and calculations in Figure 1, we suggest that the layout around a moving perceiver can be divided into three circular, egocentric regions that grade into one another. For the purposes of this discussion, we eliminate relative density from further consideration since it appears to be on the margin of utility throughout the visible range.

1. Personal Space

The zone immediately surrounding the observer's head, generally within arm's reach and slightly beyond, is quite personal. Typically, others are allowed to enter it only in situations of some intimacy or in situations of public necessity, such as when one rides in a crowded subway car (e.g., Hall, 1966; Sommer, 1969). The perception of people and of objects in this space is served by a number of sources of information, but this number is smaller and experimentally more tractable than the complete array we have been discussing. Somewhat arbitrarily we delimit this space to be within 2 m, and typically this is the space worked within by a stationary individual. Thus, motion perspective is not typically generated by the observer through his or her own motion, but instead, motion parallax (and perhaps kinetic depth information) is generated by observer manipulation.

Within this region, and according to our framework as we have laid it out, six sources of information are generally effective. Five are as they appear in Figure 1: occlusion, retinal disparity, relative size, convergence, and accommodation. We suggest that, when each is available, these five roughly dominate each other in that order. Motion information is also used, but it is not typically the information from motion perspective since this is a space typically perused by a stationary observer, not a pedestrian. Indeed, the useful motion within this domain will most typically be the motion generated by observer head motion or observer manipulation of objects. We also suggest that in most circumstances this collection of these six sources of information is selected from the background of the other three (or more) sources (which have generally null value), integrated, and combined—each constraining the other—to produce the ability of human observers to accurately manipulate objects around them. Notice that four of these sources decline in effectiveness with distance in near space, with the declining effectiveness of accommodation and convergence (and the intrusion of height in plane) helping to delimit it from more distance spaces; two other functions (those for occlusion and size) are constant.

2. Action Space

In the circular region just beyond personal space is a space of an individual's public action. Relatively speaking, we move quickly within this space, we can talk (even teach) within it without too much difficulty, and if need be, we could toss something to a compatriot within it or throw a projectile at an object or animal. This space is also served by a different collection and ranking of sources of information. There are five sources of information: occlusion, height in the visual field, binocular disparity, motion perspective (here for a pedestrian), and relative size. These are selected from the background of the other four sources, which have essentially no substantive value. The first and the last of these sources are constant with the logarithm of distance, and the other three decline. Because the utility of disparity and motion perspective decline to our effective threshold value of 10% at about 30 m, we suggest this effectively delimits space at 30 m.

3. Vista Space

Beyond about 30 m very little changes for the binocular pedestrian, except over a period of several seconds. For example, the motion of an object is considerably less salient than its displacement, and the benefits to perceiving layout from two eyes are also greatly diminished. The only effective sources of information are four sources that have traditionally been called the *pictorial cues:* occlusion, height in the visual field, relative size, and aerial perspective. We suggest that these are selected from the background of other five, uninformative sources. Since the effectiveness of binocular disparity and motion perspective has diminished substantially in this space, we regard their inputs as relatively modest; what lies beyond about 30 m for a pedestrian, we claim, is the layout of a vista, generally unperturbed by the motions of the observer. However, let us be clear, this is not to say we do not see objects in depth beyond 30 m, clearly we do. What we are claiming is that only the monocular and static sources of information are typically available in any quality to the pedestrian. Vista space is also the region in which very large paintings are most effective in either revealing layout or deceiving the eye so that extended layout is seen, such as in the Pozzo ceiling in the Church of St. Ignazio in Rome (Pirenne, 1970).

4. Source Potency Ranked within Spaces

With egocentric space segmented in this manner, we can now rank order the relative importance of the various sources of information within the three spaces (again, given the assumption that we can generalize from threshold

TABLE 1   Rankings of Information Sources by the Areas under Their Curves in Figure 1 within the Three Kinds of Space

Source of information	Personal space	Action space All sources	Action space Pictorial sources	Vista space
1. Occlusion and interposition	1	1	1	1
2. Relative size	4	3.5	3	2
3. Relative density	7	6	4	4.5
4. Height in visual field and height in the picture plane	—[a]	2	2	3
5. Aerial perspective and atmospheric perspective	8	7	5	4.5
6. Motion perspective and motion parallax	3	3.5	—	6
7. Convergence	5.5	8.5	—	8.5
8. Accommodation	5.5	8.5	—	8.5
9. Binocular, disparity, stereopsis, and diplopia	2	5	—	7

[a] Dashes indicate data not applicable to source.

to suprathreshold considerations). Such a set of rankings is shown in Table 1. This is done by integrating the area under each depth-threshold function within each spatial region, then comparing relative areas. Notice several things. First, we ranked convergence and accommodation as tied throughout. Second, within personal space we ranked convergence and accommodation as superior to relative density since although all three might appear to be tied, we have chosen to emphasize the fact that the logarithmic scale of distance is truncated at the near end of the scale. Third, we ranked height in the visual field above relative density in vista space to emphasize the near field (it is not everywhere that one can see farther than, say, 200 m into the distance), but we did not include it at all in personal space (unless one is crawling, as an infant might, on the floor). Finally, we ranked aerial perspective as tied with density in vista space since under many atmospheric conditions the function is slid leftward and subsumes more area in the nearer part of vista space than does density.

We assume these rankings by area beneath each curve reflect the general importance of the sources of information within each segment of space. With these rankings in place, we wish to apply our scheme in three ways: looking at the relational development of their use representative art, looking at the ontogeny of the use of the various sources of information, and looking at scientific research.

V. THREE APPLICATIONS FOR THE SYSTEM OF PERSONAL, ACTION, AND VISTA SPACES

A. Layout, Pictorial Art, and a Hierarchy of Information Sources

Let us consider the general development of pictorial art as it has represented space. Before beginning, however, several caveats are in order. First, this is not the place to give a full treatment of the psychological study of space in pictorial art, only an extremely brief sketch can be given. Second, we consider pictorial art only through the Renaissance and certainly not through the development of photography. This constraint eliminates consideration of the last half of the nineteenth and all of the twentieth century, by removing motion perspective from consideration and the three ocular and binocular sources (accommodation, convergence, and disparity), this leave us with only the five pictorial sources of information: occlusion, relative size, relative density, height in the visual field, and aerial perspective. Third, although some interesting things have been said by psychologists about the development of art—sometimes briefly (e.g., Gregory, 1966) and sometimes in detail (e.g., Blatt, 1984; Hagen, 1986; Kubovy, 1986)—there has also been considerable mischief (e.g., Gablik, 1976), which we do not wish to replicate. In our context, perhaps the worst sin would be to suggest an invariant order in the application of pictorial sources of information across cultures and time.

1. Method

We sampled widely from images in many traditions of pictorial art, we focused on single pictures, and within those images we noted the sources of information about layout from our list that are used. In this manner, we are definitely not attempting an analysis of the history of art. Instead, we are deliberately ahistorical, focusing sequentially on single artists (or schools) at a particular time, who composed a particular piece of art for a particular purpose. If within this image a single source of information is used alone to depict depth, then it is at the top of the hierarchy; if a second source is used only in the context of the first and without any others, then it is ranked second; and so forth.

2. Results and Discussion

If only one source of information about three-dimensional layout is used by an artist, that source is almost certainly occlusion. For example, occlusion is the only such information seen in paleolithic art from about 12,000 years ago; it is used in the Hall of the Bulls cave paintings in Lascaux, those in Niaux, and those in Altamira (see the images in Biederman, 1948, and Hobbs, 1991). Occlusion is also typically the only depth information used in Egyptian art of 2500 B.C. (see, for example, the images in Hagen, 1986, and Hobbs, 1991). We take this finding as evidence that occlusion is at the head of the hierarchy for information about layout.

If a second source of information is used to portray three-dimensional layout, that information is typically height in the visual field. The conjunction of occlusion and height, with no other sources, can be seen in high classical Greek art (fourth century B.C.); in Roman wall paintings (first century B.C.); in traditional Chinese landscapes (tenth–thirteenth centuries); in Japanese art (twelfth–fifteenth centuries); in the works of Cimabue (thirteenth century), Duccio di Buoninsegna and Simone Martini (fourteenth century), and Giovanni di Paolo (fifteenth century) in Western art; and in Persian drawings (fifteenth century; see, for example, the images in Blatt, 1984; Cole, 1992; Hagen, 1986; Hobbs, 1991; Wright, 1983). This widespread array of sources suggests that height in the visual field is second in the hierarchy.[15]

If a third source of information is used, that information is typically relative size. Before the systematization of linear perspective, many of the images of Giotto, Gaddi, and Lorenzetti (fourteenth century), for example, use relative size information coupled with occlusion and height. Some traditional Chinese art and Japanese art also add size variation to occlusion and height (see, for example, the images in Cole, 1992; and Hagen, 1986). The layout in these images suggests that relative size is the third source in the hierarchy.

After these three sources, however, the ordering in our hierarchy is less clear. In the Western tradition, it would appear that relative density is next. Coupled with occlusion, height, and size, the use of density first appeared with the use of local perspective, particularly in the tilings of floors such as those of Lorenzetti, and was complete with the global perspective of Alberti, Donatello, Massachio, and Uccello (fifteenth century; see, for example, the images in Cole, 1992). Only later did Leonardo (fifteenth–sixteenth centuries) systematically use the blueness of aerial perspective. This ordering makes sense within our system. Linear perspective took occlusion as granted and made a coherent system out of height and size, creating a tool to represent density information in a system of parallel lines. This feat makes the registration of information about layout in action space quite clear and allows for the separation of action space from extreme vista space through the use of aerial perspective.

On the other hand, in Roman art, in Chinese landscapes, and in many

---

[15] It is sometimes difficult to be sure that height in the visual field is being used in pre-Romanesque art or art outside of the Western tradition. In Greek vases and in Egyptian wall paintings, smaller people and objects are often found in the interstices between major figures, but it is not clear whether this is done for reasons of balance and other esthetic concerns or whether depth and distance layout are being portrayed.

Romanesque works, artists often used a dimming and fuzziness of contour of shapes in the distance that can be said to mimic aerial perspective. These artists did this without any clear use of relative density and sometimes without clear variation in size.[16] Nonetheless, because the systematic use of aerial perspective (with Leonardo) followed the systematicity of linear perspective (with Alberti), we rank density fourth in our hierarchy and aerial perspective fifth. The complete orderings are given in Table 2.

With this ordering in place, let us discuss our segmentation of space in the context of pictorial art. The space in pictures is traditionally neither too far nor too near in action space. Few pictures (even portraits) are composed to portray objects too near in personal space, and only with the full development of Renaissance art is vista space clearly represented. If we consider the region of action space shown in Figure 1, from about 2 to 30 m, and consider the rankings of their importance given in Table 1, we can then compare those with the rankings within our hierarchy given in Table 2. Interestingly, that rank-order correlation is perfect ($r_s = 1.00$, $p < .01$). Moreover, in vista space, the correlation is high as well ($r_s = .87$). These results are also shown in Table 3.

Thus, there is a sense in which the depth-threshold data of the various sources of information shown in Figure 1 and the rankings generated from them given in Table 2 predict well the hierarchical use of the sources in pictorial art. Why would this be so? We follow the suggestion of Blatt (1984) who stated, "The history of art is the history of the artist's overcoming limitations and widening the range of representational possibilities" (p. 26). We suggest that the discovery and the use of the various sources of information about depth are reflected in a concomitance of their obviousness and their ease of implementation. Occlusion is relatively obvious and easy to implement, height and relative size are perhaps a bit less obvious (requiring more of the "artist's perspective" of registering information as it is projected to the eye) and certainly a bit more difficult to implement in a systematic manner, and relative density and aerial perspective are not very obvious and technically quite difficult to implement.[17]

B. Layout and the Ordering of Successful Source Use in Ontogeny

A second arena in which to apply our system of spatial segmentation and rankings of information sources concerns the perceptual development of

[16] Related, but separate, from aerial perspective in Japanese art is the cloud convention (Hagen, 1986), in which clouds are inserted in the image so that a story line can be told. The clouds separate one story line from another.

[17] Yonas and Granrud (1985), like many others, composed a list of information sources that is different than ours. We have not included reference to their discussion of shading, familiar size, and the accretion and deletion of texture.

TABLE 2   Sources of Information about Depth, Hierarchical Development in Pictures, Age of Their Onset for Use by Children, and Citations from PsycINFO[a]

Source of information	Development in art	Onset age in infants (mo)	Number of scientific articles
1. Occlusion, interposition	1. Used alone	3.0	33
2. Relative size	3. Used with occlusion and typically with height in the visual field	5.5	29
3. Relative density	4. Used only with full development of linear perspective and typically before systematic aerial perspective in Western tradition	7+	4
4. Height in plane and height in visual field	2. Used with occlusion	7+	19
5. Aerial perspective and atmospheric perspective	5. Perfected after linear perspective, but also used before	7+	0
6. Motion parallax and motion perspective	—[b]	5.0	38
7. Convergence	—	4.5	24
8. Accommodation	—	4.5	15
9. Binocular disparity, stereopsis, and diplopia	—	3.5	229

[a] Citations from PsychINFO are from the years from 1984 to 1993.

[b] Dashes indicate data not applicable to source.

infants and children. Considerable research has been devoted to the discovery of the onset of the use of various types of information about depth and layout, and Yonas and Granrud (1985), in particular, discussed this evidence directly.[18] Thus, our method is a straightforward literature search. The onset values for the use of the various sources of information about layout are given in Table 2. The age values for relative size and motion perspective stem from work reported by Yonas and Granrud for convergence from Hofsten (1977), for stereopsis from Fox, Aslin, Shea, and Dumais (1980), and for occlusion from Baillargeon (1987) for situations of kinetic occlusion.[19] We assume the value for accommodation is the same as that for

[18] Stereopsis and motion, of course, are technically quite difficult and could only develop artistically with the development of photography and cinema. Blur (the photographic analog to misaccommodation) is also generally not found in art until after photography.

[19] We also have evidence of Peter M. Vishton working in the laboratory of Elizabeth Spelke that dynamic occlusion information is used by infants of 3 months and younger in many situations.

convergence (e.g., Kellman & Spelke, 1983), since they are reflexively linked, although Banks (1980) and Haynes, White, and Held (1965) have shown full accommodative responses in infants by 3.5 months. Finally, the values for relative density, height in the visual field, and aerial perspective are unknown, but they clearly arise after the others.

1. Results and Discussion

We consider three rank-order correlations, those between ranks of the onset of source use by infants and the rank of their importance as determined by the area under their ordinal depth-threshold functions within each region of space around the observer. Despite the relatively coarse information about the use of some sources, the rank-order correlation between onset and potency within personal space is impressive ($r_s = .80$, $p < .01$), but those between for action and vista space are not ($r_s = .09$ and $-.14$, respectively). These results are shown in Table 3.

This pattern of correlations makes sense. For the young infant, personal space is the only space that matters; outside of a meter or so little interaction of import occurs. Only later, with toddlerhood and beyond, will action space become important. Indeed, our own experience is that many young children have little, if any, appreciation of vista space. A memorable example of this can be found at Grand Canyon National Park. There, in various book shops in concession areas, one can peruse numerous, beautifully produced photographic books of the vistas around the Colorado river basin. However, these books are for adults. The children's sections carry books of photographs of indigenous animals and plants—all composed within 10 or so meters of the camera. Apparently, young children cannot easily appreciate the absence of motion perspective and binocular disparity information.

TABLE 3   Rank-Order Correlations of the Prominence of the Sources of Information within Each Space with Ordered Use of Sources across the History of Art, with Ordered Development in Infants, and with Ordered Popularity in Scientific Research

Domain	Regions of egocentric space		
	Personal	Action	Vista
Hierarchy in art	—[a]	1.00	0.87
Onset of use by infants	0.80*	0.09	−0.14
Scientific articles	0.92*	0.49	0.02

[a] Dash indicates too few sources to assess by correlation.

* $p < .01$.

C. Layout and Its Corpus of Scientific Research

A third arena in which to apply our system of depth segmentation and rankings is scientific research. However crudely this "system" may be, one can reflect on the overall study of the perception of layout by simply counting the number of articles published on each or several of these sources. The number of reports concerned with each source of information might then be taken as a rough estimate of scientific interest in it and indirectly as an estimate of its importance in understanding how human beings appreciate depth and layout.

1. Method

The relevant searches can be done through the use of PsycINFO, a database published and updated annually by the American Psychological Association (APA) that includes 1,300 scholarly journals, plus dissertations and other reports, collected since 1984. Thus, at the time this analysis was done, ten years of research (1984–1993) could be combed for each source of information (as listed in Table 2).

Searches are not necessarily straightforward. First, one must discern the appropriate set of keywords. Since some of these sources go by multiple names (e.g., motion parallax and motion perspective), all names must be searched. Second, one must be sure that each source of information is studied in the context of the perception of layout, which the APA defines as *depth perception*. For example, a key word search for *binocular* turned up over 700 studies, but a conjunctive search of *binocular* and *depth* yielded only 149 studies. Similarly, a search for *stereoscopic* turned up over 300 studies, but a search of *stereoscopic* and *depth* yielded only 137 studies. A search for *diplopia* and *depth* found only one study. Since a conjunctive search for *stereoscopic* and *binocular* and *depth* turned up 58 studies, the total number of relevant entries is 149 + 137 + 1 − 58 = 229. Conjunctive searches of each source with *depth* are also needed to disambiguate a keyword. For example, a search for *occlusion* by itself brought up over 200 entries, but most of these are about teeth; a search for *accommodation* found nearly 650 studies, but not surprisingly, most of these are Piagetian in character; and a search for *convergence* yielded almost 1,000 studies, but these are about everything from economics to mathematics to psychoanalysis. Finally, once the searches were complete, each entry was perused to make sure it was a relevant study.

2. Results and Discussion

Again we consider three rank-order correlations, those between ranks of the scientific articles produced on each source of information and the rank of importance within each region of space around the observer. Of interest, we found a pattern similar to that with infants. Whereas the rank-order correlation between scientific articles and personal space is impressive ($r_2 = .92$, $p < .01$), those for farther spaces declines rapidly ($r_s = .49$ for action space and $r_s = .02$ for vista space). These results are shown in Table 3. If the across-source publishing record of our discipline can be taken as an indication of what we researchers regard as important about the perception of layout, then we are indeed a very near-sighted lot.

VI. CONCLUSION

In the beginning of this chapter we asked three questions: Why are there so many sources of information about layout? How is it that we perceive layout with near-metric accuracy when none of these sources yield metric information about it? Can we not do better, theoretically, in understanding our perception of layout than simply make a list?

Our answer to the first question begins with Todd's (1985) answer previously given. Perceiving layout is extremely important to human beings, so important that it must be redundantly specified so that the redundancy can guard against the failure of any given source or the failure of any of the assumptions on which a given source is based. However, information redundancy is only part of the answer. Different sources of information about layout metrically reinforce and contrast with each other, providing a powerful network of constraints.

Our answer to the second proceeds from this idea. Through the analysis of depth-threshold functions for nine different sources of information about layout, one can begin to understand how those sources of information sharing the same-shaped functions across distances can help ramify judgments of layout by serving to correct measurement errors in each. Equally important, those resources differing in function shape across distance serve to enhance resolution generally at the near edge of some distance domains: those immediately around us, those within which we can act, and those that we simply observe. Together, same-shaped and different-shaped functions constrain each other, providing a better global metric of egocentric distance than any single source provides on its own.

Third, on the basis of our analyses and the pattern of functions shown in Figure 1, we suggest that list making has mislead us about space and layout. Psychologists and other vision scientists have generally considered layout, space, and distance as a uniform commodity in which observers carry out their day-to-day activities. Moreover, as noted by our analyses of scientific studies of the sources of information about layout, our discipline has not done justice to our perception of the far field, of landscapes, and the like. We claim there are at least three kinds of space around each of us, each perceived by means of different combinations of different sources of information, each combination dependent on the context in which the information is presented. Researchers, we hope, can now focus on particular combinations of sources within each type of space in an effort to understand how they constrain one another and help provide the near-metric quality of perceived space.

References

Allik, J., & Tuulmets, T. (1991). Occupancy model of perceived numerosity. *Perception & Psychophysics, 49,* 303–314.

Ames, A. (1955). *An interpretive manual for the demonstrations in the Psychology Research Center, Princeton University.* Princeton, NJ: Princeton University Press.

Andersen, G. J., & Braunstein, M. L. (1983). Dynamic occlusion in the perception of rotation in depth. *Perception & Psychophysics, 34,* 356–362.

Anderson, N. H. (1981). *Foundations of information integration theory.* San Diego, CA: Academic Press.

Anderson, N. H. (1982). *Methods of information integration theory.* San Diego, CA: Academic Press.

Arditi, A. (1986). Binocular vision. In K. R. Boff, L. Kaufman, & J. P. Thomas (Eds.), *Handbook of perception and human performance* (Vol. 1, pp. 1–41). New York: Wiley.

Baillargeon, R. (1987). Object permanence in 3.5 and 4.5-month-old infants. *Developmental Psychology, 23,* 655–664.

Baird, J. C. (1970). *Psychophysical analysis of visual space.* Oxford, England: Pergamon Press.

Baird, J. C., & Biersdorf, W. R. (1967). Quantitative functions for size and distance. *Perception & Psychophysics, 2,* 161–166.

Baird, J. C., Merrill, A. A., & Tannenbaum, J. (1979). Studies of the cognitive representation of spatial relations: II. A familiar environment. *Journal of Experimental Psychology: General, 108,* 92–98.

Baird, J. C., & Wagner, M. (1983). Modeling the creation of cognitive maps. In H. L. Pick, Jr. & L. P. Acredolo (Eds.), *Spatial orientation: Theory, research, and application* (pp. 321–366). New York: Plenum.

Banks, M. S. (1980). The development of visual accommodation during early infancy. *Child Development, 51,* 646–666.

Bardy, B. G., Baumberger, B., Flückiger, M., & Laurent, M. (1992). On the role of global and local visual information in goal-directed walking. *Acta Psychologica, 81,* 199–210.

Barlow, H. B. (1978). The efficiency of detecting changes of density in random dot patterns. *Vision Research, 18,* 637–650.

Battro, A. M., Netto, S. P., & Rozestraten, R. J. A. (1976). Riemannian geometries of variable curvature in visual space. Visual alleys, horopters, and triangles in big open fields. *Perception, 5,* 9–23.

Berbaum, K., Tharp, D., & Mroczek, K. (1983). Depth perception of surfaces in pictures: Looking for conventions of depiction in Pandora's box. *Perception, 12,* 5–20.

Berkeley, G. (1709). An essay towards a new theory of vision. (Reprinted from *The works of George Berkeley,* 1837, pp. 86–116, London: Thomas Tegg & Son)

Berry, R. N. (1948). Quantitative relations among vernier, real, and stereoscopic depth acuities. *Journal of Experimental Psychology, 38,* 708–721.

Biederman, C. (1948). *Art as the evolution of visual knowledge.* Red Wing, Minnesota: Charles Biederman.

Bingham, G. (1993). Form as information about scale: Perceiving the size of trees. *Journal of Experimental Psychology: Human Perception and Performance, 19,* 1139–1161.

Birnbaum, M. H. (1983). Scale convergence as a principle for the study of perception. In H. Geissler (Ed.), *Modern issues in perception* (pp. 319–335). Amsterdam: North-Holland.

Blank, A. A. (1978). Metric geometry in human binocular vision: Theory and fact. In E. L. J. Leeuwenberg & H. F. J. M. Buffart (Eds.), *Formal theories of visual perception* (pp. 82–102). New York: Wiley.

Blatt, S. J. (1984). *Continuity and change in art*. Hillsdale, NJ: Erlbaum.

Boring, E. G. (1942). *Sensation and perception in the history of experimental psychology*. New York: Appleton-Century-Crofts.

Braunstein, M. L. (1962). Depth perception in rotating dot patterns: Effects of numerosity and perspective. *Journal of Experimental Psychology, 64*, 415–420.

Braunstein, M. L. (1976). *Depth perception through motion*. New York: Academic Press.

Braunstein, M. L., & Stern, K. R. (1980). Static and dynamics factors in the perception of rotary motion. *Perception & Psychophysics, 27*, 313–320.

Bridgeman, B., Van der Heijden, A. H. C., & Velichkovsky, B. M. (1994). A theory of visual stability across saccadic eye movements. *Behavioral and Brain Sciences, 17*, 247–292.

Bruno, N., & Cutting, J. E. (1988). Minimodularity and the perception of layout. *Journal of Experimental Psychology: General, 117*, 161–170.

Brunswik, E. (1956). *Perception and the representative design of psychological experiments*. Berkeley: University of California Press.

Brunswik, E., & Kamiya, J. (1953). Ecological cue-validity of "proximal" and other Gestalt factors. *American Journal of Psychology, 66*, 20–32.

Bülthoff, H. H., Fahle, M., & Wegmann, M. (1991). Perceived depth scales with disparity gradient. *Perception, 20*, 145–153.

Bülthoff, H. H., & Mallot, H. A. (1988). Interpreting depth modules: Stereo and shading. *Journal of the Optical Society of America, A, 5*, 1749–1758.

Burton, G., & Turvey, M. T. (1990). Perceiving lengths of rods that are held but wielded. *Ecological Psychology, 2*, 295–324.

Burton, H. E. (1945). The optics of Euclid. *Journal of the Optical Society of America, 35*, 357–372.

Carlson, V. R. (1977). Instructions and perceptual constancy. In W. Epstein (Ed.), *Stability and constancy in visual perception: Mechanisms and processes* (pp. 217–254). New York: Wiley.

Carr, H. (1935). *An introduction to space perception*. New York: Longmans.

Cavanagh, P., & Leclerc, Y. G. (1990). Shape from shadows. *Journal of Experimental Psychology: Human Perception and Performance, 15*, 3–27.

Chapanis, A., & McCleary, R. A. (1955). Interposition as a cue for the perception of relative distance. *American Journal of Psychology, 48*, 113–132.

Cole, A. (1992). *Perspective*. London: Dorling Kindersley.

Cook, M. (1978). Judgment of distance on a plane surface. *Perception & Psychophysics, 23*, 85–90.

Cutting, J. E. (1986). *Perception with an eye for motion*. Cambridge, MA: MIT Press/Bradford Books.

Cutting, J. E. (1991a). Four ways to reject directed perception. *Ecological Psychology, 3*, 25–34.

Cutting, J. E. (1991b). Why our stimuli look as they do. In G. Lockhead & J. R. Pomerantz (Eds.), *Perception of structure: Essays in honor of Wendell R. Garner* (pp. 41–52). Washington, DC: American Psychological Association.

Cutting, J. E. (1993). Perceptual artifacts and phenomena: Gibson's role in the 20th century. In S. Massin (Ed.), *Foundations of perceptual theory* (pp. 231–260). Amsterdam: North-Holland.

Cutting, J. E., Bruno, N., Brady, N. P., & Moore, C. (1992a). Selectivity, scope, and simplicity of models: A lesson from fitting judgments of perceived depth. *Journal of Experimental Psychology: General, 121*, 364–381.

Cutting, J. E., & Millard, R. M. (1984). Three gradients and the perception of flat and curved surfaces. *Journal of Experimental Psychology: General, 113*, 198–216.

Cutting, J. E., Springer, K., Braren, P., & Johnson, S. (1992b). Wayfinding on foot from information in retinal, not optical, flow. *Journal of Experimental Psychology: General, 121,* 41–72.

Daniels, N. (1974). *Thomas Reid's inquiry.* New York: Burt Franklin.

Da Silva, J. A. (1985). Scales of perceived egocentric distance in a large open field: Comparison of three psychophysical methods. *American Journal of Psychology, 98,* 119–144.

Dees, J. W. (1966). Accuracy of absolute visual distance and size estimation in space as a function of stereopsis and motion parallax. *Journal of Experimental Psychology, 72,* 466–476.

Denton, G. G. (1980). The influence of visual pattern on perceived speed. *Perception, 9,* 393–402.

Dosher, B. A., Sperling, G., & Wurst, S. A. (1986). Tradeoffs between stereopsis and proximity luminance covariation as determinants of perceived 3D structure. *Vision Research, 26,* 973–990.

Dunn, B. E., Gray, G. C., & Thompson, D. (1965). Relative height on the picture–plane and depth perception. *Perceptual and Motor Skills, 21,* 227–236.

Durgin, F. H. (1995). Texture density adaptation and the perceived numerosity and distribution of texture. *Journal of Experimental Psychology: Human Perception and Performance, 21,* 149–169.

Duwaer, A. L., & van den Brink, G. (1981). What is the diplopia threshold? *Perception & Psychophysics, 29,* 295–309.

Ebenholtz, S. M., & Walchli, R. M. (1965). Stereoscopic thresholds as a function of head and object orientation. *Vision Research, 5,* 455–461.

Edgerton, S. Y. (1975). *The Renaissance discovery of linear perspective.* New York: Basic Books.

Elkins, J. (1992). Renaissance perspectives. *Journal of the History of Ideas, 53,* 209–230.

Epstein, W. (1963). The influence of assumed size on apparent distance. *American Journal of Psychology, 76,* 257–265.

Epstein, W. (1965). Nonrelational judgments of size and distance. *American Journal of Psychology, 78,* 120–123.

Ferris, S. H. (1972). Motion parallax and absolute distance. *Journal of Experimental Psychology, 95,* 258–263.

Fincham, E. F., & Walton, J. (1957). The reciprocal actions of accommodation and convergence. *Journal of Physiology (London), 137,* 488–508.

Fisher, S. K., & Ciuffreda, K. J. (1988). Accommodation and apparent distance. *Perception, 17,* 609–612.

Flückiger, M. (1991). La perception d'objets lointains [The perception of distant objects]. In M. Flückiger & K. Klaue (Eds.), *La perception de l'environnement* (pp. 221–238). Lausanne, Switzerland: Delachaux et Niestlé.

Flückiger, M., & Baumberger, B. (1988). The perception of an optical flow projection on the ground surface. *Perception, 17,* 633–645.

Fodor, J. A. (1983). *Modularity of mind.* Cambridge, MA: MIT Press/Bradford Books.

Foley, J. M. (1964). Desarguesian property in visual space. *Journal of the Optical Society of America, 54,* 684–692.

Foley, J. M. (1966). Locus of perceived equidistance as a function of viewing distance. *Journal of the Optical Society of America, 56,* 822–827.

Foley, J. M. (1991). Stereoscopic distance perception. In S. R. Ellis, M. K. Kaiser, & A. C. Grunwald (Ed.), *Pictorial communication in virtual and real environments* (pp. 559–566). London: Taylor & Francis.

Forel, F. A. (1892). *Le Lèman* (Vol. 2). Geneva, Switzerland: Slatkine.

Fox, R., Aslin, R. N., Shea, S. L., & Dumais, S. T. (1980). Stereopsis in human infants. *Science, 207,* 323–324.

Freeman, R. B. (1966). Absolute threshold for visual slant: The effect of size and retinal perspective. *Journal of Experimental Psychology, 71*, 170–176.

Gablik, S. (1976). *Progress in art*. London: Thames and Hudson.

Gehringer, W. L., & Engel, E. (1986). The effect of ecological viewing conditions on the Ames distortion room illusion. *Journal of Experimental Psychology: Human Perception and Performance, 12*, 181–185.

Gerbino, W., Stultiens, C. J., & Troost, J. M. (1990). Transparent layer constancy. *Journal of Experimental Psychology: Human Perception and Performance, 16*, 3–20.

Gibson, E. J., & Bergman, R. (1954). The effect of training on absolute estimation of distance over the ground. *Journal of Experimental Psychology, 48*, 473–482.

Gibson, J. J. (1948). Studying perceptual phenomena. In T. G. Andrews (Ed.), *Methods of psychology* (pp. 158–188). New York: Wiley.

Gibson, J. J. (1950). *Perception of the visual world*. Boston: Houghton Mifflin.

Gibson, J. J. (1966). *The senses considered as perceptual systems*. Boston: Houghton Mifflin.

Gibson, J. J. (1979). *The ecological approach to visual perception*. Boston: Houghton Mifflin.

Gibson, J. J., Olum, P., & Rosenblatt, F. (1955). Parallax and perspective during aircraft landings. *American Journal of Psychology, 68*, 40–51.

Gilchrist, A. L. (1977). Perceived lightness depends on perceived spatial layout. *Science, 195*, 185–187.

Gilchrist, A. L. (1980). When does perceived lightness on perceived spatial arrangement. *Perception & Psychophysics, 28*, 527–538.

Gogel, W. C. (1961). Convergence as a cue to absolute distance. *Journal of Psychology, 52*, 287–301.

Gogel, W. C. (1974). Cognitive factors in spatial responses. *Psychologia, 17*, 213–225.

Gogel, W. C. (1993). The analysis of perceived space. In S. Masin (Ed.), *Foundations of perceptual theory* (p. 113–182). Amsterdam: North-Holland.

Gogel, W. C., & Tietz, J. D. (1973). Absolute motion parallax and the specific distance tendency. *Perception & Psychophysics, 13*, 284–292.

Graham, C. H. (1951). Visual perception. In S. S. Stevens (Ed.), *Handbook of experimental psychology* (pp. 868–920). New York: Wiley.

Graham, C. H., Baker, K. E., Hecht, M., & Lloyd, V. V. (1948). Factors influencing thresholds for monocular movement parallax. *Journal of Experimental Psychology, 38*, 205–223.

Gregory, R. L. (1966). *Eye and brain*. New York: McGraw-Hill.

Grünbaum, A. (1973). *Philosophical problems of space and time* (2nd ed.). Boston: Reidel.

Gulick, W. L., & Lawson, R. B. (1976). *Human stereopsis*. New York: Oxford University Press.

Hagen, M. A. (1986). *Varieties of realism: Geometries of representational art*. Cambridge, England: Cambridge University Press.

Hall, E. T. (1966). *The hidden dimension*. New York: Doubleday.

Haynes, H., White, B. L., & Held, R. (1965). Visual accommodation in human infants. *Science, 148*, 528–530.

Helmholtz, H. von (1925). *Treatise on physiological optics* (Vol. 3, J. P. C. Southall, Ed. and Trans.) New York: Dover. (Original work published 1867)

Hirst, R. J. (1967). Illusions. In P. Edwards (Ed.) *The encyclopedia of philosophy* (Vol. 4, pp. 130–133). New York: Macmillan and The Free Press.

Hobbs, J. A. (1991). *Art in context* (4th ed.). Fort Worth, TX: Harcourt Brace Jovanich.

Hochberg, J. (1966). Representative sampling and the purposes of perceptual research: Pictures of the world, and the world of pictures. In K. R. Hammond (Ed.), *The psychology of Egon Brunswik* (pp. 361–381). New York: Holt, Rinehart & Winston.

Hochberg, J. (1971). Perception. In J. W. Kling & L. A. Riggs (Eds.), *Handbook of experimental psychology* (3rd ed., pp. 396–550). New York: Holt, Rinehart & Winston.

Hofsten, C. von (1976). The role of convergence in space perception. *Vision Research, 16,* 193–198.

Hofsten, C. von (1977). Binocular convergence as a determinant of reaching behavior in infancy. *Perception, 6,* 139–144.

Hopkins, J. (1973). Visual geometry. *Philosophical Review, 82,* 3–34.

Jameson, D., & Hurvich, L. M. (1959). Note on the factors influencing the relation between stereoscopic acuity and observation distance. *Journal of the Optical Society of America, 49,* 639.

Indow, T. (1982). An approach to geometry of visual space with no a priori mapping functions: Multidimensional mapping according to Riemannian metrics. *Journal of Mathematical Psychology, 26,* 205–236.

Indow, T., & Watanabe, T. (1984). Parallel- and distance-alleys with moving points in the horizontal plane. *Perception & Psychophysics, 26,* 144–154.

Ittelson, W. H. (1952). *The Ames demonstrations in perception.* Princeton, NJ: Princeton University Press.

Johansson, G. (1973). Monocular movement parallax and near-space perception. *Perception 2,* 136–145.

Julesz, B. (1971). *Foundations of cyclopean perception.* Chicago: University of Chicago Press.

Kaplan, G. A. (1969). Kinetic disruption of optical texture: The perception of depth at an edge. *Perception & Psychophysics, 6,* 193–198.

Kaufman, L. (1974). *Sight and mind.* New York: Oxford University Press.

Kellman, P. J., & Shipley, T. F. (1991). A theory of visual interpolation of object perception. *Cognitive Psychology, 23,* 141–221.

Kellman, P. J., & Spelke, E. S. (1983). Perception of partly occluded objects in infancy. *Cognitive Psychology, 15,* 483–524.

Kersten, D., Bülthoff, H. H., Schwartz, B. L., & Kurtz, K. J. (1992). Interaction between transparency and structure from motion. *Neural Computation, 4,* 573–589.

Kersten, D., & Legge, G. (1983). Convergence accommodation. *Journal of the Optical Society of America, 73,* 322–388.

Krech, D., & Crutchfield, R. S. (1958). *Elements of psychology.* New York: Knopf.

Koenderink, J. J. (1986). Optic flow. *Vision Research, 26,* 161–180.

Kosslyn, S. M., Pick, H. L., & Fariello, G. R. (1974). Cognitive maps in children and men. *Child Development, 45,* 707–716.

Kruskal, J. B. (1964). Multidimensional scaling by optimizing goodness of fit to a nonmetric hypothesis. *Psychometrika, 29,* 707–719.

Kubovy, M. (1986). *The psychology of perspective and Renaissance art.* Cambridge, England: Cambridge University Press.

Künnapas, T. (1968). Distance perception as a function of available visual cues. *Journal of Experimental Psychology, 77,* 523–529.

Landy, M. S., Maloney, L. T., & Young, M. J. (1991). Psychophysical estimation of the human depth combination rule. In P. S. Shenker (Ed.), *Sensor fusion III: 3-D perception and recognition: Proceedings of the SPIE, 1383,* 247–254.

Larish, J. F., & Flach, J. M. (1990). Sources of optical information useful for perception of speed of rectilinear–linear self-motion. *Journal of Experimental Psychology: Human Perception and Performance, 16,* 295–302.

Laurent, M., & Cavallo, V. (1985). Roles des modalités de prise d'informations visuelles dans un pointage locomoteur [The role of visual inputs in a locomotion task], *L'Année Psychologique, 85,* 41–48.

Lee, D. N. (1980). The optic flow field. *Philosophical Transactions of the Royal Society, London, B, 290,* 169–179.

Leeuwenberg, E. (1971). A perceptual coding language for visual and auditory patterns. *American Journal of Psychology, 84,* 307–347.

Leibowitz, H. W., Shina, K., & Hennessy, H. R. (1972). Oculomotor adjustments and size constancy. *Perception & Psychophysics, 12,* 497–500.

Lie, I. (1965). Convergence as a cue to perceived size and distance. *Scandinavian Journal of Psychology, 6,* 109–116.

Loomis, J. M., Da Silva, J. A., Fujita, N., & Fukushima, S. S. (1992). Visual space perception and visually directed action. *Journal of Experimental Psychology: Human Perception and Performance, 18,* 906–921.

Luneburg, R. K. (1947). *Mathematical analysis of binocular vision.* Princeton, NJ: Princeton University Press

Luo, R. C., & Kay, M. G. (1989). Multisensor integration and fusion in intelligent systems. *IEEE Transactions on Systems, Man, and Cybernetics, 19,* 901–931.

Luo, R. C., & Kay, M. G. (1992). Data fusion and sensor integration: State-of-the-art 1990s. In M. A. Abidi & R. C. Gonzalez (Eds.), *Data fusion in robotics and machine intelligence* (pp. 7–135). San Diego: Academic Press.

Maloney, L. T., & Landy, M. S. (1989). A statistical framework for robust fusion of depth information. *Visual Communication & Image Processing, IV: Proceedings of the SPIE, 1199,* 1154–1163.

Marr, D. (1981). *Vision.* San Francisco: Freeman.

Massaro, D. W. (1987). *Speech perception by ear and eye: A paradigm for psychological research.* Hillsdale, NJ: Erlbaum.

Massaro, D. W. (1988). Ambiguity in perception and experimentation. *Journal of Experimental Psychology: General, 117,* 417–421.

Massaro, D. W. (1989). Multiple book review of *Speech perception by ear and eye: A paradigm for psychological inquiry. Behavioral and Brain Sciences, 12,* 741–794.

Massaro, D. W., & Cohen, M. M. (1993). The paradigm and the fuzzy logical model of perception are alive and well. *Journal of Experimental Psychology: General, 122,* 115–124.

Massaro, D. W., & Friedman, D. (1990). Models of integration given multiple sources of information. *Psychological Review, 97,* 225–252.

Metelli, F. (1974). The perception of transparency. *Scientific American, 230*(4), 90–98.

Minnaert, M. (1993). *Light and color in the outdoors.* New York: Springer-Verlag. (Originally published in Dutch in 1973)

Morgan, M. W. (1968). Accommodation and convergence. *American Journal of Optometry and Archives of American Academy of Optometry, 45,* 417–454.

Nagata, S. (1991). How to reinforce perception of depth in single two-dimensional pictures. In S. R. Ellis, M. K. Kaiser, & A. C. Grunwald (Ed.), *Pictorial communication in virtual and real environments* (pp. 527–545). London: Taylor & Francis.

Nakayama, K. (1977). Geometric and physiological aspects of depth perception. *SPIE: Three-Dimensional Image Processing 120,* 2–9.

Nakayama, K., Shimojo, S., & Silverman, G. H. (1989). Stereoscopic depth: Its relation to image segmentation, grouping, and the recognition of occluded objects. *Perception, 18,* 55–68.

Nawrot, M., & Blake, R. (1991). The interplay between stereopsis and structure from motion. *Perception & Psychophysics, 49,* 230–244.

Ogle, K. O. (1952). On the limits of stereoscopic vision. *Journal of Experimental Psychology, 48,* 50–60.

Ogle, K. O. (1958). Note on stereoscopic acuity and observation distance. *Journal of the Optical Society of America, 48,* 794–798.

Ono, H., Rogers, B. J., Ohmi, M., & Ono, M. E. (1988). Dynamic occlusion and motion parallax in depth perception. *Perception, 17,* 255–266.

Pirenne, M. H. (1970). *Optics, painting, & photography.* Cambridge, England: Cambridge University Press.

Prazdny, K. (1983). Information in optic flows. *Computer Vision, Graphics, and Image Processing, 22,* 235–259.

Purdy, J., & Gibson, E. J. (1955). Distance judgments by the method of fractionation. *Journal of Experimental Psychology, 50,* 374–380.

Putnam, H. (1963). An examination of Grünbaum's philosophy of geometry. In S. Baumrin (Ed.), *Philosophy of science* (pp. 205–215). New York: Interscience.

Ratoosh, P. (1949). On interposition as cue for the perception of distance. *Proceedings of the National Academy of Sciences, Washington, 35,* 257–259.

Richards, W., & Miller, J. F. (1969). Convergence as a cue to depth. *Perception & Psychophysics, 5,* 317–320.

Rieser, J. J., Ashmead, D. H., Talor, C. R., & Youngquist, G. A. (1990). Visual perception and the guidance of locomotion without vision to previously seen targets. *Perception, 19,* 675–689.

Rogers, B. J., & Collett, T. S. (1989). The appearance of surfaces specified by motion parallax and binocular disparity. *Quarterly Journal of Experimental Psychology, 41,* 697–717.

Runeson, S. (1988). The distorted-room illusion, equivalent configurations, and the specificity of static optic arrays. *Journal of Experimental Psychology: Human Perception and Performance, 14,* 295–304.

Schwartz, B. J., & Sperling, G. (1983). Luminance controls the perceived 3-D structure of dynamic 2-D displays. *Bulletin of the Psychonomic Society, 21,* 456–458.

Sedgwick, H. (1973). The visible horizon: A potential source of visual information for the perception of size and distance. *Dissertation Abstracts International, 34,* 1301–1302B. (University Microfilms No. 73-22530)

Sedgwick, H. (1986). Space perception. In K. R. Boff, L. Kaufman, & J. P. Thomas (Eds.), *Handbook of perception and human performance* (Vol. 1, pp. 1–57). New York: Wiley.

Shepard, R. N. (1980). Multidimensional scaling, tree-fitting, and clustering. *Science, 210,* 390–398.

Simon, H. A. (1969). *The sciences of the artificial.* Cambridge, MA: MIT Press.

Sommer, R. (1969). *Personal space.* Englewood Cliffs, NJ: Prentice Hall.

Stevens, K. A. (1981). The information content of texture gradients. *Biological Cybernetics, 42,* 95–105.

Stevens, K. A., & Brookes, A. (1988). Integrating stereopsis with monocular interpretations of planar surfaces. *Vision Research, 28,* 371–386.

Suppes, P. (1977). Is visual space Euclidean? *Synthese, 35,* 397–421.

Taylor, P. (Ed., & Trans.) (1960). *The notebooks of Leonardo da Vinci.* New York: The New American Library.

Teghtsoonian, M., & Teghtsoonian, R. (1969). Scaling apparent distance in a natural outdoor setting. *Psychonomic Science, 21,* 215–216.

Teichner, W. H., Kobrick, J. L., & Wehrkamp, R. F. (1955). The effects of terrain and observation distance on relative depth perception. *American Journal of Psychology, 68,* 193–208.

Terzopoulos, D. (1986). Integrating visual information from multiple sources. In A. Pentland (Ed.), *From pixels to predicates* (pp. 111–142). Norwood, NJ: Ablex.

Thomson, J. (1980). How do we use visual information to control locomotion? *Trends in Neuroscience, 3,* 247–250.

Todd, J. T. (1985). Perception of structure from motion: Is projective correspondence of moving elements a necessary condition? *Journal of Experimental Psychology: Human Perception and Performance, 11,* 689–710.

Toye, R. C. (1986). The effect of viewing position on the perceived layout of scenes. *Perception & Psychophysics, 40,* 85–92.

Ullman, S. (1979). *The interpretation of motion.* Cambridge, MA: MIT Press.

Ullman, S. (1983). Recent computational studies in the interpretation of structure from motion. In J. Beck, B. Hope, & A. Rosenfeld, (Eds.), *Human and machine vision* (pp. 459–480). New York: Academic Press.

Uomori, K., & Nishida, S. (1994). The dynamics of the visual system in combining conflicting KDE and binocular stereopsis cues. *Perception & Psychophysics, 55,* 526–536.

van der Meer, H. C. (1979). Interrelation of the effects of binocular disparity and perspective cues on judgments of depth and height. *Perception & Psychophysics, 26,* 481–488.

Vishton, P. M., Nijhawan, & Cutting, J. E. (1994). Moving observers utilize static depth cues in determining their direction of motion. *Investigative Opthamology & Visual Science, 35,* 2000.

Wagner, M. (1985). The metric of visual space. *Perception & Psychophysics, 38,* 483–495.

Wallach, H., & Frey, K. J. (1972a). Adaptation in distance perception based on oculomotor cues. *Perception & Psychophysics, 11,* 77–83.

Wallach, H., & Frey, K. J. (1972b). The nature of adaptation in distance perception based on oculomotor cues. *Perception & Psychophysics, 11,* 110–116.

Wallach, H., & Karsh, E. B. (1963a). Why the modification of stereoscopic depth-perception is so rapid. *American Journal of Psychology, 76,* 413–420.

Wallach, H., & Karsh, E. B. (1963b). The modification of stereoscopic depth-perception and the kinetic-depth effect. *American Journal of Psychology, 76,* 429–435.

Wallach, H., Moore, M. E., & Davidson, L. (1963). Modification of stereoscopic depth-perception. *American Journal of Psychology, 76,* 191–204.

Wallach, H., & Norris, C. M. (1963). Accommodation as a distance cue. *American Journal of Psychology, 76,* 659–664.

Wallach, H., & O'Connell, D. N. (1953). The kinetic depth effect. *Journal of Experimental Psychology, 45,* 205–217.

Wanger, L. R., Ferwerda, J. A., & Greenberg, D. P. (May, 1992). Perceiving the spatial relationships in computer-generated images. *IEEE Computer Graphics, 21,* 44–59.

Watson, A. B. (1978). A Riemannian geometric explanation of the visual illusions and figural aftereffects. In E. L. J. Leeuwenberg & H. F J. M. Buffart (Eds.), *Formal theories of visual perception* (pp. 139–169). New York: Wiley.

Watson, J. S., Banks, M. S., von Hofsten, C., & Royden, C. S. (1992). Gravity as a monocular cue for perception of absolute distance and/or absolute size. *Perception, 12,* 259–266.

Wheatstone, C. (1838). Contributions to the physiology of vision: I. On some remarkable and hitherto unobserved, phenomena of binocular vision. *Philosophical Transactions of the Royal Society, London, 128,* 371–394.

Witkin, A. P., & Tennebaum, J. M. (1983). On the role of structure in vision. In J. Beck, B. Hope, & A. Rosenfeld (Eds.), *Human and machine vision* (pp. 481–543). New York: Academic Press.

Wohlwill, J. F (1964). Changes in distance judgments as a function of corrected and uncorrected practice. *Perceptual and Motor Skills, 19,* 403–413.

Woodworth, R. S., & Schlosberg, H. (1954). *Experimental psychology* (2nd ed.). New York: Wiley.

Wright, L. (1983). *Perspective in perspective.* London: Routledge & Kegan Paul.

Yonas, A., Craton, L. G., & Thompson, W. B. (1987). Relative motion: Kinetic information for the order of depth at an edge. *Perception & Psychophysics, 41,* 53–59.

Yonas, A., & Granrud, C. E. (1985). The development of sensitivity to kinetic, binocular, and pictorial depth information in human infants. In D. J. Ingle, M. Jeannerod, & D. N. Lee (Eds.), *Brain mechanisms and spatial vision* (pp. 113–145). Dordrecht, the Netherlands: Martinus Nijhoff.

Zegers, R. T. (1948). Monocular movement parallax thresholds as functions of field size, field position, and speed of stimulus movement. *Journal of Psychology, 26,* 477–498.

CHAPTER 4

Perceiving Pictorial Space

Sheena Rogers

I. INTRODUCTION

Representational pictures are simple to see. Their ubiquity in Western life reminds us of this and at the same time belies the fact that they pose a special challenge to theories of perception. A common belief is that pictures are simply slices of reality, peeled from an imaginary window and fixed to paper or canvas. (It is at least, a common aesthetic belief that they should look as though they are [Parsons, 1987].) Surely, then, any theory that explains how we perceive the world has also explained how we perceive pictures. Some careful thought, however, reveals a paradox. Pictures are flat yet represent the world that is not. We move our heads, and the objects depicted do not change their aspect. There is no pattern of relative motion between near and far objects, no binocular disparity. The range of color and intensity is limited, the surface is textured, sometimes shiny. Worse still, when we move our heads, we transform the optical geometry of the picture, systematically deforming the depicted layout.

Pictures seem to do more to demonstrate their objective flatness than to represent a three-dimensional (3-D) world, yet we have no trouble perceiving the sizes, shapes, and distances of depicted objects. For some, this paradox presents an ineffable mystery (Gregory, 1966, 1970). For many, it is no mystery at all: Pictures are perceived like everything else (Gibson, 1971). Their dual reality as both objects and representations of objects simply entails a secondary or subsidiary awareness of the picture's objective properties (Polanyi, 1970). An economical theorist would want a single perceptual theory to account for both the facts of perceiving the real world and the facts of perceiving depicted worlds. Surprisingly, two otherwise starkly contrasting approaches to perception agree on this. Both traditional, constructivist theories and the more recent ecological approach have simply subsumed pictures under their general theories of perception. It is the thesis of this chapter that neither view is adequate (although the ecological approach comes closest) since neither theory takes into account the historical development of the role of the artist in constructing meaningful pictures that are simple to see.

This chapter will review the empirical literature on the quality of perceived pictorial space under a variety of viewing conditions both ideal and ordinary. In particular, the effects of viewing pictures away from their center of projection will be reviewed and evaluated to address theoretical issues in perceiving pictorial space. The empirical evidence supports the idea that pictures bear a close structural relation to the real scenes they represent, but it will be argued that the concept of constraint is an essential one. Pictures have great potential to be ambiguous and to present systematically distorted spaces. The fact that they are rarely perceived as ambiguous or distorted is due to traditional artistic practice that provides constraints on the construction and observation of pictures and that almost guarantee their success.

A. Theoretical Approaches to Picture Perception

There is a long history of scholarship on the construction of pictorial space (Alberti, 1435–1436/1966), but interest in the perception of pictorial space is much more recent. Perhaps this is because early scholars such as Alberti felt that their enterprise was based on vision itself, but certainly because, for centuries, the perception of the world has been thought to be based on pictures: the retinal images formed in our eyes. The ubiquitous and compelling analogy between the eye and the camera has ensured a central role for the retinal image (conceived as an image or picture) in classical accounts of visual perception. What we see is not the world but its image. The analogy has become explicit in current computational approaches to vision. Still or video cameras provide images for intelligent machines to "see." Pictures are simply assumed to be the appropriate input for such devices and their equivalence to the real scenes they represent is rarely questioned. Gibson (1967/1982c) has observed that "psychologists and artists have misled one another; we have borrowed the so-called cues to depth from the painters, and they in turn have accepted the theory of perception we deduced from their techniques" (p. 20).

Once the perceiver is considered as the viewer of images, no special theory of picture perception is needed. Standard accounts of perception can simply be adapted to the case of painting and photography (e.g., Gombrich, 1960/1977; Helmholtz, 1968; Hochberg, 1980). A central feature of traditional constructivist theories has been the essential poverty and ambiguity of images, both retinal and artificial. At most, they contain cues or clues to the layout of the scene depicted. These cues require interpretation or some process of intellectual supplementation to recover the lost third dimension (Gregory, 1974; Helmholtz, 1881/1968). Thus, perception is constructed by the perceiver. Gombrich (1960/1977) has elaborated most on this theme with respect to pictures. The beholder's share contributes not only an interpretation of the conventions of perspective (or cues) but of the culturally determined conventions we call *pictorial style*. Goodman (1968) has gone farther, arguing that all of these conventions are arbitrary and pictures are meaningful only to the extent that viewers share the code that was used to create them.

The possibility that existing accounts of pictures were inadequate arose with Gibson's challenge to traditional theories of perception (Gibson, 1950b, 1966, 1979). He insisted that the camera metaphor for the eye is a "seductive fallacy" (Gibson, 1979, p. 64) and that "the common belief that vision necessarily depends on a retinal image is incorrect" (Gibson, 1960/1982b, p. 261). Ambiguity and uncertainty are not qualities of our perceptual experience because perception depends on the richly informative spatiotemporal optical structures present in the transforming optic array of an active, exploring perceiver. These structures are uniquely specific to their source and are therefore unambiguous and informative: When a certain optical structure is present so too is a certain environmental state. The task for perception, then, is not one of construction of perception, but one of detection of information (Gibson, 1966). The value of this approach to perception is evident in many of the chapters in the present volume (see Warren, for example).

In direct contrast to pictures, the optic array not only surrounds the perceiver but is continuously transformed by the perceiver's activity within the environment. Informative structure specific to the unchanging properties of the environment (the sizes of objects, for example) remains invariant under transformations of the optic array and is thus revealed by them. Indeed, Gibson (1966/1982d) argued that a frozen array must be ambiguous since "invariants can be detected only where there is opportunity to distinguish them from the variations" (p. 178), that is, under transformation of the optic array (see also Gibson, 1979, p. 10, 42, and 147).

Furthermore, the ecological approach emphasizes the role of perception in the control of action. Pictured worlds obviously have no potential for action in any straightforward sense. Nevertheless we can perceive object qualities such as size, shape, and distance, and perhaps we can even make action-based judgments about these objects. (Is this climbable? Graspable? Huggable? Jumpable?) Also, the ability to perceive pictorial space has no obvious evolutionary advantage. It barely makes sense to talk of picture perception as adaptive. The implication is that the perceptual skills that evolved to help us survive in the real world also work when we are confronted by a picture of the real world. From here it is a short step to say that a single theory can and should explain both. Yet the emphasis on the information available to an active perceiver in a transforming optic array, and the argument that the snapshot view of the world is the exceptional case, appears to preclude an information-based account of pictures. Pictures present a frozen array that cannot be explored by the perceiver. Thus, it would seem that pictures can contain no information.

The paradox is that Gibson and his followers have not developed a special theory to account for the perception of pictures but have been surprisingly eager to subsume them under a general theory of visual perception (see Gibson, 1971, 1979; Hagen, 1980). Gibson proposed the following definition of pictures: "A picture is a surface so treated that a delimited optic array to a point of observation is made available that contains the same kind of information that is found in the optic arrays from an ordinary environment" (Gibson, 1971, p. 31). Gibson, at least, was aware of the inherent paradox in his position (e.g., Gibson, 1973, p. 45). His answer was to suggest that although "these features are present in an unchanging array, they are best revealed in a changing array" (Gibson, 1973, p. 45). He later suggested that pictorial invariant structures are simply weaker than those emerging under transformation (Gibson, 1979, p. 271).

The paradox was never adequately resolved by Gibson (see Gibson, 1979, p. 73, 84, 168, and compare p. 271) and has not been addressed by researchers on picture perception. The resolution of the paradox, however, lies in a fuller understanding of the notion of information and of the limiting conditions that engender a unique relationship between an optical structure and a state of the environment. It is clear that some structures hold no prospect of providing information in a single, frozen array. Lee's (1980) time-to-contact variable and Koenderink's (1986) differential invariants are examples. However, Warren (1984; Warren & Whang, 1987) has found that the necessary information for perceiving the climbability of stairs and the passability of apertures is present in frozen arrays. The clearest examples of pictorial invariants are provided by the horizon relations. Sedgwick (1973) identified the horizon as the basis of a series of optic array relations between the horizon and the projection in the optic array of all objects on the ground plane. These relations fully specify the size, distance, slant, and direction of objects and surfaces. He subsequently has considered how these relations might be defined in terms of the projective geometry of linear perspective (Sedgwick, 1980). One of them, the horizon–ratio relation, has been subject to experimental test and is considered later.

The task for researchers in perception is two-fold. First, we must identify optical structures capable of specifying the properties or affordances of the environment and determine whether this information is available in static or moving, monocular or binocular viewing conditions. Some structures may be present only in transforming arrays, some may be present in both static binocular and transforming arrays, and finally, some structures may qualify as pictorial invariants: optical structures available in frozen arrays and hence in pictures. The second task is the empirical one, we must discover whether the identified invariants provide affective information for perception and under what conditions. It is likely that pictorial invariants are more heavily constrained than their "real" counterparts. A complete account of the effectiveness of any pictorial invariant will require a full account of the constraints under which the information it provides can go through. Pictures are inherently ambiguous. The argument that picture perception is based on informative structure need not deny this fact. Artists and experimental psychologists can exploit pictorial ambiguity, or they can constrain it. It will be argued later that many of the necessary constraints are built in to traditional artistic practice.

II. SCALING PICTORIAL SPACE

A. Veridicality and the Representation of Reality

One of the goals of this chapter is to examine the extent to which pictures succeed in representing reality: their veridicality. Pictures are rarely so successful that they can trick the viewer, as did the legendary Pygmalion, into believing that the creation is the real thing (see Gombrich, 1960/1977). They could, however, capture the information for the layout of the objects and surfaces in the scene such that an observer's judgments about the depicted scene match those made when the real thing is presented. By supposing that the information in the picture is indeed of the same kind as that available from the corresponding real array, there is still a limitation on the success of pictures in accurately representing reality. The problem is that of scaling the pictorial space. To be clear, the question of veridicality properly concerns the match between perception of spatial layout in pictures and the perception of spatial layout in real-scene controls and not the match between picture perception and the objective measurements of the original scene layout. This is because depth and distance in real scenes are themselves usually underestimated (for reviews, see Cutting & Vishton, this volume, chapter 3; Sedgwick, 1986; Gillam, this volume, chapter 2). Toye (1986) and Wagner (1985) have both reported that there is a compression of depth extents relative to frontal extents and that compression increases as distance increases.

Scaling real or pictorial space depends on the availability of some metric. This could be provided by the presence in the scene of a yardstick or another object of known size. Recently, researchers have focused on intrinsic units of measurement such as the observer's eye height, although, of course, if eye height is known in some other metric, it could be used to scale absolute dimensions in that metric (Sedgwick, 1973, 1980). Knowledge of one's own eye height in a real, ambient optic array is probably no less reasonable than knowledge of one's interocular separation to scale binocular disparities, and a number of researchers have shown that eye height may indeed be used to scale size and distance (Mark, 1987; Mark, Balliett, Craver, Douglas, & Fox, 1990; Warren, 1984; Warren & Whang, 1987).

Sedgwick (1980) has described several optic-array structures that can provide information for the absolute dimensions of a pictorial layout when the height of the station point is known. Gradients of texture size, for example, can provide information for the angle at which a visual ray from the station point intersects the ground surface. Gibson and Cornsweet (1952) have called this angle *optical slant*. Optical slant covaries with distance, and so any structure providing information for optical slant also specifies distance from the observer relative to the height of the station point, that is, in eye-height units (cf. Purdy, 1960). Sedgwick (1973) has also shown that knowledge of the height of the point of observation would allow accurate estimates to be made of the height and width of all objects standing on the ground plane, which are also vertical and parallel to the picture plane (see the horizon relations below).

In the case of a picture, knowledge of the eye height used in its construction (the height of the station point) poses a problem. The observer could use her own eye height as a scaling factor, but unless her eye height is coincident with the height of the picture's actual station point, errors in scaling pictorial space would occur. It would not be sufficient to simply position one's eyes at the level of the picture's horizon. The original station point may have been at any height: on a hillside, at a skyscraper window, or reclining on the floor. Often, though, a picture's station point is at an average person's eye height above the ground, and an observer positioning herself at the station point could use her own eye height to scale pictorial space with little ill-effect. However, Bingham's (1993b) study of tree size indicated that people do not use their own eye height in making size judgments in pictures, at least not when other information in the picture (here, tree form) indicates that it is inappropriate. It is possible, of course, that the position of the horizon relative to the depicted objects (and perhaps the picture frame) informs us not about the absolute size of the objects but about the height of the original point of observation. Photographs taken from a high viewpoint usually look as though they were. In this case, depicted objects do not look unusually small as they would if the observer assumed a 1.6-m eye height. However, Hagen and Giorgi (1993) report that observers asked to judge the position of a camera used to take a photograph tend to judge its height to be around 5 ft.

Further research is needed to discover whether absolute sizes and distances vary with an observer's own eye height while viewing a picture, whether they vary with the position of the horizon relative to the frame, with indications from the content of the picture for the height of the station point, or with other potential scaling factors.

B. Relative Size and the Horizon–Ratio Relation

The sizes and distances of objects relative to each other are specified by the horizon relations, even when the height of the station point is not known (Sedgwick, 1980). The horizon may therefore be the basis of important sources of information in both pictorial and environmental optic arrays. The horizon is a feature of the optic array and of perspective pictures. It is the infinitely distant limit of a ground plane and its position in the array is always at eye level. (The earth's horizon is not at infinity and is therefore lower than the true horizon, though it is usually very close.) The height of an object from its base on the ground to the point where it intersects the horizon is always the same as the height of the point of observation above the ground. In a picture, however, the height of the point of observation (used in taking or constructing the picture) may not be known. If more than one object is present in the scene, however, their relative sizes are fully specified by the horizon–ratio relation. Figure 1 illustrates such an example. Object A is intersected at its midpoint by the horizon and is therefore twice the height of the point of observation. A second object, B, is intersected at one third of its height and is thus three times the height of the point of observation. Object B is therefore one and one half times as tall as A. Objects of the same height, B and C in the example figure, are intersected in the same proportion by the horizon, regardless of the distance between the objects and the observer.[1] More generally, the ratio of the distance between the bottom of the object and its top (S) to the distance between the bottom of an object and the horizon (H) invariantly specifies the size of the object relative to the height of the station point and the sizes of objects relative to

---

[1] Note that the observation that relative size may be specified independently of distance marks an important deviation from the existing assumption of a close link between the two. There are some data to support their perceptual independence (see Smith, 1958b).

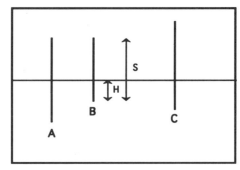

FIGURE 1   The relative sizes of objects A, B, and C are fully specified by the horizon–ratio relation, S:H.

each other (see Figure 1). This more general account allows for the fact that the size of objects lower than the station point, and therefore entirely below the horizon, is also determined by the horizon–ratio relation. The horizon ratio, then, concerns two distances measured on the picture plane (or measured in terms of visual angle in the optic array): S and H. Notice that the ratio S:H (the horizon ratio) is identical for Objects B and C, indicating their equality.

Sedgwick's (1980) analysis of the horizon relations shows that the horizon is a basis of a potentially powerful source of information for spatial relations in pictures. Although Sedgwick has shown that the information is available, the essential task of providing evidence that it is actually used by picture viewers has barely begun (Bingham, 1993a; Rogers, 1995; Rogers & Costall, 1983), yet the question of the information's effectiveness in the perception of depicted spatial relations is a crucial one.

A series of studies by Rogers suggests that the horizon–ratio relation can indeed provide an effective basis for relative size judgments in pictures (Rogers, 1994; Rogers & Costall, 1983). Using a simple drawing response, subjects estimated the appropriate height on the picture plane of a comparison object, given a same real-size standard (a single, vertical line). The horizon–ratio relation, unlike traditional cues such as height in the picture and diminishing size with distance, specifies relative height precisely, and, therefore, accurate responses should be expected if the observers' judgments are based on this structure. Many participants in these experiments produced highly accurate responses, indicating that they were indeed making use of the available horizon-based information. There was some evidence that the horizon ratio was most effective when the depicted objects were tall enough to be intersected by the horizon and when additional information was present in the pictures to indicate that the given line was in fact the horizon. In addition, Sedgwick (1980) has suggested that observers may be able to recover an implicit horizon from the geometric features of a picture or perhaps by imposing their own eye level on the picture. Rogers's results lend some support to this idea, but more research is needed.

Bingham (1993a, 1993b) indirectly investigated the effectiveness of the horizon–ratio relation while examining the effects of the form of trees on their perceived absolute size and the perceived sizes of a set of cylinders on the ground surface. When the cylinders were presented alone, on a ground plane with a texture gradient and horizon, the horizon–ratio relation proved less effective than in Rogers's (1995) experiments. However, Bingham's (1993a, 1993b) cylinders were not only mostly below the horizon, they were also all of the same image size and may not have fully been integrated into pictorial space. They may have appeared, instead, to be affixed to the surface of the picture, and the horizon ratio would not then apply.

Further research is needed to discover the variables that affect the utilization of the horizon–ratio relation in pictures. For example, the content of a picture could indicate the nature of a given horizontal line, it could indicate the height of the original point of observation, and it could imply the position of the horizon when it is not explicitly represented. As yet, no research exists on the effectiveness of the other horizon relations described by Sedgwick (1973, 1980) that specify relative distance, slant, and direction.

III. VARIABLES THAT AFFECT PERCEPTION OF PICTORIAL SPACE

How close is the match between an observer's judgments of the layout of a depicted scene and those made when the real thing is presented? Most researchers have found that perceived pictorial depth is underestimated relative to perceived real depth (Hochberg, 1962; Schlosberg, 1941; Wilcox & Teghtsoonian, 1971; Yonas & Hagen, 1973), even when the geometric array from the picture is isomorphic with that from the real scene (Adams, 1972; Hagen, Jones, & Reed, 1978). Hagen et al., for example, found that depicted distances of 10 to 50 in. between objects standing on a checkered ground were underestimated by an average of 50% (monocular viewing).

The additional compression of pictorial depth is often attributed to the conflict between flatness information that specifies a picture's objective surface and pictorial information for the depicted 3-D layout. Binocular and motion parallax, the texture of the picture surface, and the presence of a frame could all reveal a picture's flatness. Some writers have also pointed to the truncation of the visual field as a cause of the compression of pictorial depth (Hagen et al., 1978; Lumsden, 1980).

A. Truncation of the Visual Field

Viewing a picture is like viewing a real scene through an aperture. The picture frame or aperture boundary interrupts or obscures some of the foreground extending from objects in the scene (depicted or real) to the eyes of the observer. This missing portion of the optic array could otherwise have provided information for the distance from the observer to those objects and surfaces. The loss of this information could therefore have consequences for perceived depth in the scene. Underestimation of distance to the picture (or scene) would mean that the rate of change of visual angles over a depth extent in the scene would appear relatively slow for that distance, consistent with a shorter extent. Depth compression is therefore predicted. (If Gogel's 1965, equidistance tendency applies here, there should be consistent effects on perceived depth between observers). Hagen et al. (1978) reported results supporting this hypothesis. Truncation of the visual field by viewing a real scene through a peephole or through a rectangular occluding frame, and by viewing a picture of the scene, all led to a compression of perceived depth relative to the depth perceived in the untruncated real scenes (all four conditions used an unmoving, single eye).

Increasingly long focal length lenses reduce the angle subtended by the area of view in a decreasing, negatively accelerated function of the focal length of the lens. It is possible that some of the depth compression perceived in photographs taken with telephoto lenses (as described below) is due to this truncation of the visual field. Lumsden (1983), however, was unable to find an effect of the degree of truncation on perceived depth in a study intended to separate the effects of magnification from the effects of truncation produced by the use of telephoto lenses.

B. The Monocular Advantage

It has long been observed that the appearance of three dimensions in a picture is more striking under certain viewing conditions, such as viewing the picture with one eye only and by using a peephole or a lens in a reduction screen or viewbox (Ames, 1925; Eaton, 1919; Emerson, 1863; Enright, 1991; Koenderink, van Doorn, and Kappers, 1994b; Leeman, Elffers, & Schuyt, 1976; Nagata, 1991; Schlosberg, 1941). A number of old viewing devices make use of one method or another to produce their sometimes powerful effects. The usual explanation is that the restricted view enhances the effectiveness of pictorial-depth information by reducing the conflicting flatness information that specifies a picture's objective surface (and which seems to contribute to the compression of pictorial space described above). The monocular view avoids disparity information for the flatness of the picture surface that one would expect to conflict with the monocular information for depth. In Helmholtz's (1881/1968) words, "in binocular vision the picture distinctly forces itself on our perception as a plane surface" (p. 141). Typically, the observer's eye is fixed in place by using a chin rest or a bite board, which also removes additional information for the picture's flat surface normally available from motion parallax. Surprisingly, the difference in perceived depth between binocular and monocular views of a picture has only recently been quantified.

In a study of pictorial relief (i.e., the 3-D shape of a depicted object), Koenderink et al. (1994b) had their observers adjust a gauge figure so that it appears to be painted on the surface of a photographed 3-D sculpture. Repeated adjustments made at many points over the surface provide local attitude measurements allowing the perceived surface to be reconstructed. Comparisons among the surfaces produced under different viewing conditions and by different observers could then be made. Observers viewed the image *en face,* at a fixed distance, using a head and chin rest but with no further restrictions. The station point for the photograph used was unknown and is unlikely to have coincided with the actual viewing point. (One consequence of this is that the veridicality of perception cannot be assessed by the present results.) By closing one eye this as much as doubled the depth perceived with both eyes open, corroborating the long held, but previously unmeasured, belief in the vivid effects of monocular picture viewing. Koenderink et al. also tested the perceptual effect of removing stereo information during binocular viewing by using a device called a *synopter* by its inventor, Moritz von Rohr (patented by Carl Zeiss in 1907). The synopter produces optical coincidence of the eyes so that they receive identical optical inputs. The result for at least some observers is a further increase in perceived depth, up to a factor of three, over natural binocular viewing. This result probably gives a better indication of the powerful flattening effect of stereo information on perceived pictorial depth during ordinary two-eyed picture viewing. Koenderink et al. (1994b)[2] concluded that "human vision involuntarily strikes some kind of 'compromise' between the *flatness* of the picture surface and the *relief* due to monocular cues."

C. Peephole Picture Viewing

Peephole viewing is monocular and head motion is prevented, and this should enhance perceived depth as described above. A peephole or a lens also restricts the observer's view to the picture itself, hiding the frame and surrounding surfaces. Loss of the visible frame and discontinuous surrounding surfaces reduce information for the picture as a flat object (perhaps even for the presence of a surface at all), potentially enhancing the illusion of depth in the picture. This is the oft-cited reason for the success of the various picture-viewing devices. Peephole viewing should therefore result

[2] See Cutting and Vishton (this volume, Chapter 3) for more on the topic of information integration.

in optimal perceived depth and the greatest illusion of a real 3-D scene. However, the earlier discussion of the truncation of the visual field applies here also: The loss of the foreground should result in an underestimation of distance to the depicted objects and thus a flattening of pictorial depth. A hint that truncation does diminish perceived depth despite peephole viewing is provided by the truly stunning effects produced by Dutch perspective boxes such as the famous one in Britain's National Gallery by Von Hoogstraden (see Leeman et al., 1976). Here, the painted foreground is not truncated but extends all the way to the eye of the observer at the peephole.

Two predictions follow. First, peephole viewing should produce a compelling impression that the observer is looking at a real 3-D scene. Second, it should also lead to greater perceived pictorial depth than monocular viewing, but some compression will remain relative to the depth perceived in an untruncated, real-scene control. A number of studies provide support for our predictions concerning peephole viewing.

Schlosberg (1941) showed that a monocular, peephole view of a photograph does indeed provide a very strong illusion of a real 3-D scene. The appearance of three dimensionality is as compelling as that found in the familiar handheld stereoscope. That the strong impression of real depth is accompanied by accurate perception of layout is demonstrated by Smith and Smith (1961). Their subjects were asked to toss a ball at a target on the floor of a room, they could see through a 152-mm lens in a peephole (over a range of 3 to 8 m depicted distances). Performance was remarkably accurate despite the fact that they unknowingly saw a black and white photograph of the room, it was not the room itself. Ball tosses in the real room under identical viewing conditions were slightly more accurate and less varied.

Adams (1972), however, was unable to find a significant difference between peephole viewing and unrestricted (but without head motion) binocular viewing. Subjects adjusted the shape of a vertical rectangular reference "tile" to match the apparent shape of rectangular tiles on the depicted floor (the projected depth of the floor was 24 in., and the station point was 24 in. from the picture). At the station point, the tiles were projectively square, though they always appeared shorter than squares to the subjects. Adams's analysis combined results from two sizes of peephole: 6 mm and 0.75 mm. There appears to be much less depth compression with the larger peephole (about 10%) than with either the binocular viewing or the tiny pinhole when viewing was at the station point (about 50%), but the difference between the two peepholes was not significant. (Adams also varied viewing distance. These results are discussed in the appropriate section below.)

D. Implications of Compressed Depth for Pictorial Relief

It is clear from the foregoing section that perceived pictorial space tends to be somewhat flatter or more compressed than its objective, environmental counterpart. Most studies have considered the sizes and distances of objects laid out on the ground before an observer, but the compression of pictorial depth also has implications for pictorial relief; that is, the spatial layout of the surfaces of a single object. We saw, as previously discussed, that the depth dimension of the perceptual object varied systematically with the presence or absence of binocular information for the flatness of the picture surface. Four questions arise. First, do observers perceive a stable, consistent 3-D surface (deformed or not) from the information provided by a pictorial representation? Second, do different observers agree on the shape of this 3-D surface? Third, to what extent does the perceived surface conform to the objective true shape of the depicted object? Fourth, to what extent does the perceived pictorial surface correspond to the surface perceived when the observer inspects the real 3-D object? (These last two questions are different if one does not assume veridicality in the perception of real scenes.) Koenderink and his colleagues (Koenderink & van Doorn, 1992; Koenderink et al., 1994b) have recently turned their attention to some of these questions.

The rich data provided by Koenderink et al. (1994b), and an earlier experiment using the same paradigm probing local surface attitude (Koenderink & van Doorn, 1992), demonstrated remarkable internal consistency in the shape of the perceptual surfaces. Individual subjects' response settings appear to track closely a stable and consistent perceived surface. Furthermore, different observers produce identically shaped and finely resolved 3-D surfaces, indicating that they all exploit the same optical information provided by the photographs. In the early experiment the depicted sculpture was a smooth, rounded object (Brancusi's *The Bird,*) and 3-D shape information was probably based principally on photographic chiaroscuro (the distribution of light and dark areas) and contour. The later photographs, of a river-worn Greek stone torso and a clay sculpture by Medardo Rosso of a veiled head, were richer in texture gradients, perspective, and other potential sources of information for the 3-D shape of the depicted objects. Of special interest, although the shapes of the different observers' response surfaces were in strong agreement, the amount of depth, that is the degree of extension in the z dimension, varied by as much as a factor of two between subjects in both studies. This is reflected in the pattern of scatter in the data both within and between subjects: estimates of surface tilt (i.e., the direction in which a pictorial surface points away from frontoparallel) are much less variable than estimates of surface slant (how much it points away). Slant is affected by perceived depth, whereas tilt is not. Scatter in the slant settings accounted for 94%–97% of the total variance in the 1992 experiment. In the later experiment (Koenderink et al., 1994b), the amount of spread in the slant settings (but not the tilt data) was dependent on magnitude of the gradient, in accord with a Weber fraction of about 20%.

Koenderink et al. (1994b; Koenderink & van Doorn, 1992) did not address our third question, the veridicality of pictorial perception, in the two studies previously described. Given the variability between subjects in the scaling of the depth dimension, it can be inferred that this aspect of pictorial layout at least is not veridical. Certainly, a common finding in studies of slant perception utilizing pictorial displays is that slants appear more frontal (the depth dimension more compressed) than expected from the geometry of the optic array (Clark, Smith, & Rabe, 1955; Flock, 1965; Freeman, 1965, 1966a, 1966b; Gibson, 1950a; Gruber & Clark, 1956; Perrone & Wenderoth, 1991; Purdy, 1960; Smith, 1956; Thouless, 1931; Wenderoth, 1970). Further research is needed to assess the correspondence between perceived and veridical shape. Koenderink and van Doorn's (1993, 1994a) description of shape in terms of local surface orientation, the location of depth extrema, the presence of features such as ridges, islands and so forth, which are independent of the variations in depth scaling, will undoubtedly prove helpful.

Few studies have included the appropriate real-scene controls that would enable us to assess our fourth question and determine the correspondence between perceived pictorial 3-D layout and perceived environmental 3-D layout. If veridicality is assumed in the latter case, then one would conclude that pictures are somehow deficient in information for spatial layout. We need to know whether people exhibit similar variability in the depth dimension and lack of sensitivity to surface slant in the perception of real 3-D objects and scenes. Indeed, a recent study by Koenderink et al. (in press) indicates that the earlier results tell us more about the visual system than about pictures. The "deficiency" is ours. Lack of sensitivity to the degree of surface slant is not unique to pictorial displays. Their study probed local surface attitude by using a real 3-D object (a rough sphere) instead of a picture as the stimulus (a direct comparison to pictorial stimuli was not made in the experiment, but the two studies (Koenderink et al., in press, 1994b) are generally comparable). As before, observers adjusted a local gauge figure projected onto the object until it appeared to be a circle painted on the surface. Settings were obtained at numerous points over the object's surface, allowing the perceived surface to be reconstructed and its conformity to the actual surface to be assessed.

Koenderink et al. (in press) obtained results very similar to those in the pictorial relief study (Koenderink et al., 1994b). Perceptual surfaces were internally consistent and well articulated, though somewhat paraboloid and not spherical. The perceptual surfaces produced by different observers were very similar in shape, although, once more, there were marked differences between subjects in scaling the depth of the object. As in the case of pictorial relief, the amount of spread in the slant settings (but not the tilt data) was dependent on magnitude of the gradient, in accord with a Weber fraction of 20%–30%. The direction of surface tilt was again quite precisely estimated with repeated settings. The perceived depth of the sphere was dependent on viewing conditions, with relief more pronounced with binocular viewing (and overestimated by 30%–40% for two subjects), less pronounced with monocular viewing (roughly veridical), and flatter still with synoptic viewing (underestimated by up to 40% for one subject). Notice that this ordering for perceived depth from a real 3-D object is the reverse of that obtained for pictorial relief in the companion experiment (Koenderink et al., 1994b). This is as expected, binocular information in the present case is for depth rather than for flatness.

Thus, nonveridicality appears to be the case not just for pictorial perception but for the perception of real scenes also. One important implication for research in picture perception is that adequate interpretation of results will often depend on knowing about performance in real-scene comparison conditions. Similar performance in the two cases implies that similar processes underlie the perception of pictures and the perception of real scenes.

IV. THE PROBLEM OF THE STATION POINT

A. Is the Station Point a Privileged Viewing Position?

In constructing a perspective picture, the artist begins by identifying a precise viewpoint for the scene to be depicted, which will be the center of projection for the picture. If the resulting picture is then viewed from this unique station point (by a single, stationary eye), there will be a geometric isomorphism between the optic array projected from the picture and that projected from the original scene. The perspective picture is considered to be a slice through the visual pyramid, preserving the whole array of visual angles subtended at the eye by the original objects. (Of course, there will be differences in color, luminance, etc. between the picture and the real scene. See Pirenne, 1970, and Helmholtz, 1968.)

This fact has led to the idea that the station point is also a privileged viewing position for the picture. Pictures work their magic because of this geometrical identity, but then the magic should only work (or work best) under very restricted viewing conditions. Leonardo pointed out that for a pictured, near object "to have the effect of nature" the spectator must have "his eye at the very distance and height and direction where the eye or the point of sight was placed in doing this perspective" (Leonardo da Vinci cited in Richter, 1970). Helmholtz (1981/1968)wrote, "By a correct perspective drawing we can present to the eye of an observer who views it from a *correctly chosen point of view* [italics added], the same forms of the visual image as the inspection of the objects themselves would present to the same eye, when viewed from the corresponding point of view" (p. 141). Ordinary picture-viewing almost never includes a peep hole or other device for positioning the eye at the station point. The possibility that the observer might locate the station point was discussed earlier. Pictures are usually viewed from too far or too near, from too low or too high, and from one side or another. Thus, the optic array projected from the picture to the eye of the observer is rarely isomorphic with that projected from the real scene. Systematic distortions are introduced, with each change in viewpoint, which are always consistent with some other 3-D layout of surfaces: the virtual space of the picture.

The impact of these geometrical distortions on perception has been a subject of speculation since the system of linear perspective was invented, and more recently, of analysis and experimentation. Of particular concern is the fact that picture viewers rarely complain that depicted scenes appear distorted. More commonly, people marvel over the compelling impression of reality a picture can provide. They are enchanted by the illusion of a world seen through the window of the picture frame. Cutting (1986a, 1986b, 1987) has named this paradox for La Gournerie,[3] and Kubovy (1986) refers to the *robustness of perspective*.

However, it is useful to distinguish between the perceiver's awareness of a distorted layout (i.e., the transformation of shapes and layout is noticed and looks odd) from the perceiver's perception of a distorted layout (i.e., the transformed optic array determines perceived spatial layout), which may or may not be accompanied by awareness of the distortions. With this distinction in mind, four possible explanations exist for the apparent absence of perceived distortions, and they are not necessarily exclusive alternatives.

1. Relying on intuition mostly, many commentators have concluded that picture viewers are somehow correcting the distortions produced by ordinary picture viewing: the *compensation hypothesis*.
2. Distortions are minimal and so are not noticed or do not matter.
3. Some pictorial information for layout is unaffected by ordinary viewing away from the station point, remaining invariant.
4. Distortions of the virtual space of the picture are perceived and affect judgments about the depicted layout.

1. The Compensation Hypothesis

In an early paper Gibson (1947/1982a) suggested "that there exists an automatic compensation in visual perception" on the basis of the "simultaneous perception of the [picture surface] as oblique" (p. 233). This idea continues to have currency. A very similar idea was proposed by Pirenne (1970) and taken up by Hagen (1974), Haber (1980), Kubovy (1986), and Rosinski and Farber (1980; Farber & Rosinski, 1978; see also Greene, 1983). Pirenne

---

[3] La Gournerie (1859) reconstructed the transformations of virtual space of pictures produced by viewing away from the pictorial station point.

(1970) wrote that "an unconscious intuitive process of psychological compensation takes place, which restores the correct view when the picture is looked at from the wrong position" (p. 99). The mechanism is dependent on an awareness of "some of the surface characteristics of the picture at the same time as [we] perceive the scene represented by the picture. This gives stability to [our] percept of the depicted scene when [we] view it from the wrong position" (Pirenne, 1970, p. xxii). Distortions will be apparent when "the spectator is unable to see the painted surface *qua* surface" (Pirenne, 1970, p. 84). Kubovy's (1986) scheme is somewhat similar, he stated the following: "Observers are not aware of distortions in virtual space because a part of the visual system (whose workings are unconscious) registers both the nature of the virtual space and the orientation of the surface of the picture, and corrects the former in the light of the latter" (p. 55).

Writers have differed in how they see the operation of the mechanism, but all describe a seemingly rational process. Farber and Rosinski (1978; Rosinski & Farber, 1980) argue that an observer could not know whether any particular viewpoint is correct or incorrect from the geometry of the picture. (Although see Sedgwick, 1980, for an account of how an observer might recover the station point for a picture. See also Adams, 1972, Greene, 1983, and Farber and Rosinski, 1978. As yet, there is no evidence that people are able to do this.) Picture viewers must, therefore, make "certain assumptions about the . . . nature of picture viewing and base . . . compensation on such assumptions" (Farber & Rosinski, 1978, p. 281). One assumption concerns the location of the correct viewing point for pictures: typically along a line perpendicular to the picture plane. Another concerns the correct viewing distance and is perhaps based on picture size. Viewers may also make assumptions about the content of pictures: "Distortions or irregularities in the virtual space will have little effect on perception if the observer assumes that regularity in fact exists in the environment" (Farber & Rosinski, 1978, p. 281). Pirenne (1970) also claims that our preconceived ideas about the depicted contents of a picture are relevant.

Hagen (1976) added that the compensatory mechanism would be acquired through experience with pictures, implying that normal pictorial space does appear distorted to children and pictorially naive adults. This idea has not yet adequately been tested (but see Hagen, 1976; Rogers, 1986).

The compensation hypothesis fits easily within traditional constructivist or cognitivist accounts of perception and plainly borrows from Helmholtz's (1867/1925) notion of unconscious inference. Recent attempts to overturn the idea that seeing is like thinking (Epstein, 1993; Gibson, 1966, 1979; Kaniza, 1979, 1985) also present a challenge to this putative compensatory mechanism. The alternative explanations look to the facts of projective geometry and the limitations of the visual system to avoid resorting to a cognitive correction process.

2. Distortions Are Minimal

While developing his ecological approach to perception with its reliance on the information available in spatiotemporal optical structure, Gibson struggled with the special problems posed by pictures for his account (Gibson, 1971, 1979, 1980). He eventually concluded that although viewing from the station point is "the only way to prevent distortions of the virtual layout," it must be that "the distortions themselves are not all that serious" (Gibson, 1979, p. 284). More recently, Cutting has proposed (1) that the optical distortions are usually minimal and (2) that they are too small to matter to the visual system (Busey, Brady, & Cutting, 1990; Cutting, 1987).

3. Pictorial Invariants

The notion of *pictorial invariants* appears to be an oxymoron, yet an information-based account of pictures requires their existence. The invariants may be sufficient to preserve the experience of an undistorted space, important enough to underpin veridical perception of at least some aspects of the layout, or both. Given the long-held belief in the essentially distorted nature of pictorial space when Leonardo's conditions for capturing "the effect of nature" are not met, there is a surprising abundance of pictorial structures that actually remain invariant under a variety of ordinary picture-viewing conditions: structures that can specify much of the 3-D layout of a pictured scene. Remember that no psychological claims are being made here. Whether the following invariant structures are important for perception is an empirical question and is addressed in the next section.

A promising class of mathematically invariant structures available in pictures is based on the horizon (Rogers, 1986, 1995; Rogers & Costall, 1983; Sedgwick, 1980; see above). The horizon in pictures is the basis of a number of geometrical structures that are able to specify relative size, distance, and slant (Sedgwick, 1980, 1986). The horizon–ratio relation, for example, is invariant under changes in viewing position when the eye remains in the horizontal plane extending out of the picture from the horizon; that is, under perpendicular displacements and horizontal, lateral displacements. Vertical displacements of viewing position result in changes in the visual angles subtended by vertical extends on the picture plane, changing the ratio, and thus changing the object's specified size, slant, and distance. No research has yet tested the perceptual effects of these change on perception.

Gibson (1950b) noted a means by which relative size may be specified, which is plainly invariant with viewing-position changes. "Texture numerosity" indicates the relative size of objects by the number of ground-surface texture elements occluded by the objects at the point at which they are attached (Gibson, 1950b, p. 181). (Note, though, that an object of constant height occludes more texture the further it is from the center of projection, Gillam, 1981. This, too, is unaffected by changes in viewing position.) Again, no research explicitly addresses the usefulness of this source of information for perception.

Lumsden's (1980), Farber and Rosinski's (1978), and Sedgwick's (1991) analyses of magnification and minification, produced by too near or too far a viewing position, show that all angular relationships are uniformly transformed, thus all relationships are invariant. The relative sizes, shapes, slants, and distances of pictured objects are preserved when the observer is too close to or too far from the picture. Rosinski and Farber's analyses indicate that, even in the case of the shear transformations produced by lateral displacements, the relative sizes of frontal surfaces and extents are unaffected (Rosinski, 1976; Rosinski & Farber, 1980). (See below for accounts of these transformations and reviews of the relevant literature.)

A number of studies have found that relative size is rather accurately estimated in pictures under a variety of changes in viewing position, and despite simultaneous transformations in perceived relative distance. The size–distance invariance hypothesis implies a close link between the two, yet the empirical evidence seems to indicate their independence (Bengston, Stergios, Ward, & Jester, 1980; Hagen, 1976; Rosinski, 1976; Smith, 1958b). It is possible that some or all of the above sources of invariant information for relative size may have been present in the experimental displays and that this information is effective for human observers. Further research is needed directly manipulating the availability of information that is invariant under viewpoint changes and measuring the effects on perception.

Koenderink and van Doorn (1993, 1994a) have described invariants of pictorial relief (i.e., the depth structure of single objects) that preserve information for the shape of the object in terms of the partial depth order of locations on the object's surface under transformations of the object's depth dimension. A useful analogy, introduced by Koenderink, is to consider the depth dimension as a bellows that can be stretched and compressed under certain viewing conditions (e.g., perpendicular displacements of the viewing position and monocular versus binocular picture viewing). Some features of surface relief are preserved, or remain invariant, under this monotonic transformation of the depth scale: The relief of a pictured face, for example, will retain its local depth extrema (Morse singular points), its saddles, ridges, courses, and islands (identified by Hildebrand, 1893, and fully described by Koenderink and van Doorn, 1993, 1994a). Some preliminary evidence has been obtained that indicates that these invariants are important for perception (Koenderink & van Doorn, 1994a, personal communication, May, 1994).

4. Geometry Determines Perception

Finally, it has rarely been considered that the perceived spatial layout in a picture may actually be determined by the transformed optical geometry. The picture may look odd under certain conditions (say, in the extreme case of anamorphic art) but it need not, and the distortions may not be noticed. For example, Gombrich (1960/1977) has suggested that if distortion is mostly not apparent it is because "if trees appear taller and narrower, and even persons somewhat slimmer, well there are such trees and such persons" (p. 144). Of course, real people and real trees do not wax as we approach a frontal view of them and wane as we walk past them. It is an empirical question, so far not addressed, whether these distortions of pictorial space are apparent to a moving observer.

A serious discussion of the problem of the station point and the explanations presented depends on (1) a full analysis of the nature of the optical transformations that occur during ordinary picture viewing and (2) experimental evidence of the perceptual effects that result. In recent years, both have become available in the literature and will be reviewed here.

B. Viewpoint-Dependent Transformations of Pictorial Space

Ordinary picture viewing involves a variety of displacements of viewing position all of which result in some transformations of the array of visual angles subtended by parts of picture. Every transformed array corresponds to a new spatial layout of the pictured scene, different in systematic ways from the original, environmental layout. The transformed layout specified at any particular viewpoint is known as the virtual space of the picture. Detailed accounts of the viewpoint-dependent transformations of virtual space are provided by Adams (1972), Cutting (1986a and 1986b), La Gournerie (1859), Kubovy (1986), Lumsden (1980), Farber and Rosinski (1978), and Rosinski and Farber (1980). Sedgwick (1991) gives a particularly complete analysis. The transformations are summarized here, and the experimental literature on the perceptual effects of these transformations are reviewed.

1. Perpendicular Displacement: Magnification and Minification

a. Geometry

Positioning the eye too near a picture but on a line perpendicular to the picture plane and passing through the center of projection is optically equivalent to a uniform magnification of all the visual angles in the optic array. Similarly, too far a viewing point minifies all visual angles (Lumsden,

1980). Magnification and minification have consequences for depth and slant in virtual space with the transformations produced by minification being in the opposite direction to those described below for magnification.

The depth dimension of the virtual space of a picture is compressed by magnification and stretched by minification. Lumsden (1980) demonstrates that the projected visual angle subtended by a frontal dimension of a depicted object is proportional to $1/D$ (where D is the distance of the eye from the picture plane): Visual angle is a decreasing, negatively accelerated function of viewing distance. If a picture viewer is closer to the picture plane than the station point, all the visual angles will uniformly be magnified, maintaining the relationships among them (Lumsden, 1980). So, a three-power magnification of a depicted cube (with the front face parallel to the picture plane and centered about the line of sight) that, at the station point has a front face 10° visual angle and a back face 8.5°, will have a front face 30° and a back face 25.5°. In both cases, the rear face subtends an angle 85% the size of the front face. If an observer were to view a (real) wire-frame cube at increasing distances and to compare the front and back faces, close up, then the difference in visual angles subtended by the front and back faces is large, but as the viewing distance approaches infinity, the difference becomes vanishingly small. Similarly, equal intervals marked out at increasing distances along the ground plane subtend smaller and smaller visual angles (another decreasing, negatively accelerated function). As Lumsden (1980) observed, "such large projections of the nearer objects [here, face] with minimal decrease in projection of the farther ones, and minimal vertical displacement in the locus of contact with the ground, would normally specify a much closer arrangement of [faces] separated by much lesser distance" (p. 98). That is, the rate of change of textural density and the degree of perspective convergence over a given visual angle are altered and specify a different spatial layout to the unmagnified array. In fact, the virtual front-to-back depth corresponds to the real depth divided by the power of magnification. So a three-power magnification results in a projection consistent with a compression to one third of the real depth. Similarly, a three-power minification with the eye at three times the proper viewing distance results in a tripling of the depth dimension relative to the depth specified at the station point.

The slants of receding surfaces become more frontal in virtual space under magnification and less frontal under minification (Farber & Rosinski, 1978; Lumsden, 1980; Sedgwick, 1991). A "cube" will respectively be squashed or stretched out of shape and its sides will no longer meet the front and back faces at right angles. Surfaces and lines that are either frontal or perpendicular to the picture plane are unaffected by magnification and minification. The maximum distortion occurs for intermediate orientations

(Lumsden, 1980; Sedgwick, 1991). So far, no research has looked explicitly at perceived slant during perpendicular displacements of viewing position. All studies have examined perceived depth and distance.

b. Perception

If perception were determined by optical geometry, then one would predict severe consequences for microscopists and astronomers in determining the spatial layout of their respective objects of interest. Indeed, Lumsden's (1980) description of some hair-raising consequences of the massive magnifications typical of microscopy (and astronomy) has led one commentator to wonder aloud whether Galileo's critics were on to something (Costall, 1981). That there are perceptual implications for the lower, everyday, range of magnification also is apparent from the well-known telephoto effect. The long focal-length cameras of newspaper and television photojournalists lead to the strong impression of batsmen far too close to catchers and pitchers for safety. The empirical evidence is at least qualitatively consistent with this common observation. There is considerable evidence that perceived depth varies systematically with perpendicular displacement of viewing position and in the direction predicted. The degree to which the perceptual layout "fits" the virtual layout varies among the reported experiments and there seem to be a number of additional variables that affect perceived pictorial space, which need further investigation.

Magnification and minification have been produced by experimenters both by varying the viewing distance to a picture of constant size and by the use of lenses. (Lumsden, 1983, compared the two methods.) In the latter case, viewing distance is held constant, and either the image size is varied or the area of view is varied within a constant image size. A very wide range of image sizes, depicted depth intervals, and viewing distances have been used. Some studies have used peephole or aperture viewing, and some have used unrestricted viewing. Some studies have found that magnification and minification produce almost exactly the perceived distances predicted by the geometric analysis, and some do not—though there is usually some change in perceived depth in the predicted direction. Most authors have concluded that these changes in perception support the hypothesis that geometry determines perception. Some, however, have taken the discrepancies between perceived depth and predicted depth to imply the operation of a compensatory mechanism (e.g., Farber & Rosinski, 1978). A closer examination of the literature suggests that this explanation is premature. Alternative hypotheses are offered.

Not all studies have reported sufficient quantifiable information for the match between the geometrically predicted depth and perceived depth to be accurately assessed. Nicholls and Kennedy (1993a), for example, asked subjects to compare two line drawings of a wire-frame cube and rate the comparison as a better or worse depiction of a cube than the standard. If the ratings change with changes in viewing distance from the picture, then the virtual space is affecting perception. Using powers of minification and magnification ranging from 0.05 to 3.7 (over three experiments) for two drawings differing in the degree of perspective convergence (strong and moderate), Nicholls and Kennedy found significant effects of viewing distance, thus the perceived shape of the cube was affected by both magnification and minification. Both perspective drawings received their highest rating at their correct viewing points. A parallel projection was included in the study (the station point is technically at infinity) and viewed from the same set of viewing distances. It was rated most cube like at all of the longer viewing distances and disliked only at the closest viewing point. Magnification led to decreasing preference ratings for all three drawings as the viewing point approached the picture plane, as the geometry would predict.

Smith and Gruber (1958) found that the transformed virtual space quite precisely determined perceived depth. They showed subjects both a 360 ft (110 m) corridor and a large photograph of it through peepholes. The photograph was positioned at distances from 1 m to 2.8 m so that it varied in visual angle (33° to 12°) and in the degree of magnification and minification. The station point was at 2.1 m, so there was a range from a 2.1 power magnification to a minification power of 0.75. In other words, transformed pictorial distances between the nearest and farthest viewing position differed by a factor of 2.8. The task was to estimate distances in the photographed corridor as proportions of the same distances in the real corridor. Farber and Rosinski's (1978) reanalysis of the data reveal an almost perfect match between perceived and predicted distances (nearest and farthest condition differing by a factor of 2.86), and Smith and Gruber themselves report a match within 6% of the predictions.

Less close matches were found in two experiments by Smith (1958a). Smith provided two different viewing distances (2 ft [62 cm] and 9.5 ft [2.9 m]) for photomurals similar to Smith and Gruber's (1958; depicted distances up to 110 m) and asked subjects to estimate distances in paces. The station point was not given, but transformed pictorial distances between the near and far viewing position differed by a factor of 4.5. The manipulation did affect perception, but the obtained difference was only a factor of 2.5. It is possible that minification resulted in less expansion of depth than predicted, magnification resulted in less compression, or both, but not enough information is provided to be certain.

Several studies have found that the effects of magnification are more precisely predicted from the geometry than the effects of minification. Smith's (1958b) second study used photographs of outdoor scenes of white stakes in a plowed field (depicted distances up to 410 m). Two pictorial viewing distances (15 in. [38 cm] and 50 in. [1.27 m]) provided a magnification power of 1.33 and a minification power of 0.4, thus transformed pictorial distances between the near and far viewing position differed by a factor of 3.3. The obtained distance judgments differed by a factor of 2.7, with underestimation of distances particularly great in the minified array (but still expanded relative to the objective distances).

One of the few studies to manipulate magnification and minification by varying the focal length of the lens used to photograph a scene and holding viewing distance and image size constant found similar results. Kraft and Green (1989, see also Kraft, Patterson & Mitchell, 1986) photographed naturally occurring target objects at distances from 20 m to 320 m with lenses of focal length 17 mm, 28 mm, 48 mm, 80 mm, and 135 mm. Slides were viewed by groups of subjects sitting between 2 m and 4 m in front of a projection screen, with unrestricted ordinary viewing conditions. Observers were asked to estimate distance in meters to the target. Given the ordinary viewing conditions there are many sources of error variance, but the effect of the different lenses on perceived distances was nonetheless pronounced.

By reanalyzing Kraft and Green's (1989) data, it is apparent that the magnification conditions produce almost exactly the predicted degree of compression, whereas minification produces perceived distances shorter than predicted. By taking the 48-mm lens as "normal" with no magnification, we can first assess distance estimation in this control condition and then look for relative expansion and compression of perceived distance in the other conditions. With the 48-mm lens, (no magnification) distance estimation is close to veridical at 20 m and 40 m but is increasingly underestimated as distance to the target object increases (underestimated by almost 40% at the farthest distance of 320 m). This underconstancy at greater distances is commonly observed in the perception of real scenes also. The 135 mm magnifies the array and should compress the perceived distance by a factor 0.36 relative to the 48-mm lens. Averaging across the five target distances, perceived depth was in fact compressed by a factor of 0.37.[4] Magnification with the 80-mm lens predicts a compression factor of 0.6, and the obtained average was also 0.6. Minification with a 28-mm lens predicts an expansion factor of 1.71. The obtained average factor of 1.39 reflects a constant underestimation at all distances. Similarly, a 17-mm lens should produce distance increases of a factor of 2.82 over the 48-mm lens condition, but the obtained average was only a factor of 2.06.

Adams (1972) also found underestimation of depth intervals in his study, especially under minification. Using a picture of a shallow square-tiled floor, 24 in. (61 cm) deep, and relatively close viewing distances (at 12 in.

---

[4] Numbers are approximate as they are based on data reported in graph form in Kraft and Green (1989, Figure 1).

[31 cm] at the station point at 24 in. [62 cm] and at 48 in. [1.22 m]), Adams generated a two-power magnification and a 0.5-power minification. The task required observers to estimate the depth of tiles drawn in perspective on a ground plane by adjusting the height of a comparison tile on a frontal wall in the same scene. By reanalyzing Adams data and by averaging across binocular and monocular viewing conditions, perceived depth was compressed by 16% relative to the objective space when the display was minified (instead of the predicted doubling of depth). Compression was still greater at the station point (38%) where none was predicted and greater still in the magnified condition (62% compared with a predicted 50% compression). The near and far viewpoints predict a difference in depth of a factor of 4, but a difference of only a factor of 2.7 was obtained. However, the average tile depth in the magnified condition was exactly half that in the untransformed condition, as the geometry would predict, thus in this case the relative depths were accurately perceived, despite the underestimation of absolute depth.

Perceived pictorial depth seems to be reliably shallower than predicted. Lumsden (1983) compared a four-power magnification to an unmagnified display with the manipulation produced either by changing viewing distance from the picture or by using a 200-mm telephoto lens to take the picture. Slides depicted two 6 ft (1.83 m) white posts spaced 12 ft (3.66 m) apart: the closest one at 84 ft (25.60 m) from the camera, and the farthest at 96 ft (29.26 m). Both methods of magnification led to significant reductions in the estimated distance between the poles compared with that perceived in the unmagnified pictures, though Lumsden reports that compression was less than expected by the geometry (actual data not reported). Depth was substantially underestimated (by about half), even in the latter condition. Lumsden points to the very small difference in the visual angles subtended by the two poles (0.4°) and in their vertical separation in the field (0.22°) as a possible explanation for the underconstancy obtained. I return to this point below.

Bengston et al. (1980) also reported that the degree to which pictorial space is compressed and expanded by the viewpoint, manipulation is limited, although perceived depth varied in the direction predicted by magnification and minification. Bengston et al.'s observers were required to estimate the depth interval between two Russian dolls, photographed against an untextured background, in units of doll heights (the actual depth interval of 9.5 in. [24.13 cm] = 2.6 doll heights). Photographs were viewed from distances ranging from 5 in. (12.7 cm) to 100 in. (2.54 m). Their data show a slower than predicted rate of compression under magnification factors of approximately 2, 4, 8, 10, and 20. Instead of the predicted difference of a factor of 20 in perceived depth between the station point and the viewing point nearest to the picture plane, these conditions differed by only a factor of 1.48, averaging across the image set used. Viewing points too far from the picture plane generated minifications of approximately 0.5, 0.25, 0.12, 0.1, and 0.05. Geometrically, these would expand the depicted interval from 9.5 in. (24 cm) up to 190 in. (4.38 m) in the farthest viewing position (a factor of 20). However, this latter condition expanded the interval perceived at the station point by an average of only a factor of 1.63. The depth interval was increasingly underestimated as the specified distance expanded.

It seems that there is a perceptual limit to the degree of expansion produced by minification and to the degree of compression produced by magnification. Explanations given for the flattening of perceived depth relative to the geometrically specified depth are somewhat post hoc. For example, one factor contributing to the minimal effects of magnification in Bengston et al.'s study may be the very shallow space specified by the geometry: from less than half an inch to the objective value of 9.5 in. A magnification "floor" here may well be due to this small objective depth interval. Some depth was always perceived and at very small values they may be indiscriminable, resulting in a fixed small interval being reported. Alternatively, Bengston et al. suggest that their subjects had some trouble using the prescribed metric at small values below 1 doll length.

Some more general explanations are relevant to several studies, however. One factor that probably contributed to the flattening of pictorial depth in Kraft and Green's (1989) study, in Lumsden's (1983) study, and in Bengston et al.'s (1980) study is the use of relatively unrestricted viewing conditions that allow information for the flatness of the picture itself to conflict with pictorial information for a 3-D scene. (See the section on the monocular advantage above). Lumsden's observers were seated at the appropriate distance, but otherwise viewing was unrestricted and binocular. A chin rest was used to position the observer's head at the appropriate distance from the picture in Bengston et al.'s study. Viewing was monocular, but no peephole was used. Thus, respectively, observers could see the projection screen or the frame and tripod used to display the pictures and there was no possibility of observers mistaking the photographs for real scenes.

In Bengston et al.'s (1980) study, a second factor may have contributed to the flattening of pictorial depth: The untextured background of the photographs ensured very minimal information for distance in the pictures. Gogel's (1965) equidistance tendency may apply here: Objects of unknown distance are perceived to be the same distance as their neighbors, hence the underestimation of the depth interval between them. In other words, no (or little) information for distance may be the same thing for the perceptual system as information for no (or little) distance.

There is a third factor contributing to the flattening of pictorial space in general and to the restriction in the degree to which perceived depth can be manipulated by magnification and minification in particular. The equidistance tendency especially applies when the angular separation between the objects is small. Small angular separations in the elevation of depicted objects are apparent in most of Bengston et al.'s (1980) stimuli, in those of Lumsden (1983), and possibly in other earlier experiments. Studies that report a compression in perceived depth, even when pictures are viewed from the station point (most of those reviewed here), may well be reflecting poor sensitivity to depth information over very small visual angles. If the array is then magnified some further compression may occur, but it would not be surprising to find that compression is limited for these perceptually shallow intervals and does not occur at the rate expected. The argument can be extended to the case of minification. Bengston et al. suggest that the equidistance tendency predicts greater underconstancy for depth intervals that are at greater distances from the observer and that this effect should occur in pictures just as it does in the perception of real scenes. "The proportion of Dg [geometrically specified depth] should decrease," they argue, "both as Dg increases and/or as the distance to the interval increases" (Bengston et al., 1980, p. 753).

Bengston et al. (1980) and Nicholls and Kennedy (1993a) provide some relevant data. Both studies included a manipulation of the distance of the correct station point (the camera position or center of projection) from the depicted objects. This manipulation varies the "strength" of perspective: the degree of foreshortening in the picture, the rate of convergence of parallel lines, and the rate of size diminution with distance. Near station points produce very strong perspective, and very far camera positions result in weak perspective. A scene of two 6 ft (1.83 m) poles, the near one 84 ft (25.6 m) from the camera and the far one 96 ft (29.26 m) away (camera height at 3 ft [.91 m]), will have a vertical angular separation on the picture plane of 0.22°. The difference in visual angle subtended by the two poles is 0.4° (Lumsden's, 1983, stimuli). Moving the camera closer to the objects, 12 ft from the near pole and 24 ft from the far one, will increase the angular separation to 6.9° and the difference in visual angle between the two poles to 13.8°. These two pictures look very different. Of course, if the observer views each picture from its correct station point, the geometry is still isomorphic with that of the original array and one might predict that this station point manipulation would have no effect on the perceived distance between the two poles. However, Bengston et al. and Nicholls and Kennedy found that distance of the center of projection does make a difference to perception. Nicholls and Kennedy's subjects rated a moderately convergent drawing of a cube as better than either a strongly convergent drawing or a parallel projection, even when each is viewed from its correct station point. Bengston et al. found a significant effect of camera position on the perceived depth interval between two dolls. Perceived depth declined systematically with the decreasing angular separation and angular difference produced by increasing camera distance. The compression of depth that resulted from the camera position manipulation was more dramatic than that produced by the viewing-position manipulation over the same range of distances: a factor of 472 compared with a factor of 1.54 in the most affected case, the strong convergence condition. Of most relevance to the issue of the perceptual effects of displacing the observer from the station point is the interaction between camera position (the degree of perspective convergence) and viewing distance found in the Bengston et al. study. Perpendicular displacement of view point did not affect perceived depth when the depth interval was grossly underestimated because of a far camera position and very weak perspective. Perceived depth appears to be more affected by viewpoint-dependent transformations as the degree of perspective convergence increases. There are two implications: First, weak perspective or parallel projections may be more robust and less susceptible to the distortions of ordinary picture viewing; second, the benefit of robustness is gained at the expense of perceived depth.

More research is needed to determine the validity of these statements. First of all we need fully to determine the effect of camera position (the degree of perspective convergence) on pictorial spatial layout. What are the respective contributions of angular separation and the usually concomitant gradient of angular size? Is the effect dependent on very small angles of some absolute value or are they determined as a proportion of object size? If the latter is true, then the uniform magnification of visual angles should not change the effect of camera position on perceived depth. If the former is true, it should. We need to know the effect of the depth of the depicted scene on perception. Are shallow scenes more robust than scenes of greater depth? No study has yet manipulated this variable systematically or tested its interactions with camera station point and observer viewing position.

A reading of the art history and art theory literature reveals that these questions have long been of interest to artists, and we have much to learn from their endeavors. Memo board *trompe l'oeil* pictures, for example, depict extremely shallow 3-D spaces and conjure their illusion of reality to any viewing point. The magic of *trompe l'oeil* depicting much deeper spaces is invariably tied to observation from the station point (see Leeman et al., 1976). In between these two extremes, the aesthetics literature from Leonardo to the present has advised against too-close station points (producing strong convergence) in the construction of pictures, and the concern has been with the perception of distortion during ordinary picture viewing. An experimental program of the kind suggested could quantify and perhaps explain the artists' rules of thumb on this matter.

Further research is also needed to determine the shape of the functions comparing perceived distance with predicted distance under varying degrees of minification and magnification. The functions may well be linear with a slope near one when the degree of minification or magnification is relatively small (as in Smith & Gruber, 1958), but the functions may well level off when larger values are used (as in Adams, 1972; Bengston et al., 1980, Smith, 1958b). Further research is also needed to examine the contribution of other variables such as those that indicate the objective nature of the picture: image size and angular subtense (smaller pictures may seem more object-like than pictures that take up more of the optic array), surface information, and the presence of a visible frame. Does conflicting flatness information serve to flatten the functions? To what extent? Does varying the amount of flatness of information vary the degree to which the function is flattened? These questions have implications for the compensation hypothesis. It has been suggested that the compensation mechanism is dependent on information of this kind for its operation. If compensation is "all or none," then a very different pattern of results should emerge than if the effect of added flatness information is some kind of perceptual compromise between flatness and depth (see Cutting & Vishton, this volume, chapter 3, for more on models of information integration).

2. Displacements Parallel to the Picture Plane

a. Geometry

Horizontal displacements that shift the eye from the station point to the left or right, parallel to the picture plane, result in the shearing of all angular relationships (Rosinski & Farber, 1980). As the eye moves laterally to the left, for example, points, lines, and planes in the virtual space of the picture shift to the right. The further these are from the picture plane, the greater their displacement, resulting in this case, in a clockwise rotation in the direction of all lines and planes that are not frontoparallel. The tiles on the floor in a Vermeer interior, and indeed the room itself, would no longer be rectangular. Distances between points in the scene are altered with consequences for relative size, shape, slant, and orientation. The relative size, shape, and orientation of frontal lines and surfaces, however, are unaffected.

In an analysis on the basis of vanishing points, Sedgwick (1991) shows that distortions of the orientation (slants) of lines and planes produced by shifting the viewpoint laterally and parallel to the picture plane can be enormous. Virtual orientation is affected by the degree of objective orientation and by the angle through which the viewpoint is shifted. Distortion tends to increase as both of these angles increase, but the objective orientation angle at which distortion is maximal also depends on viewing angle: As viewing angle increases distortion will be maximal for increasingly large objective orientations. Distortion (the difference between the objective and virtual orientation) can approach 180° as the observer's viewing point approaches a 90° displacement to the side (the observer would be looking along the picture plane).

Vertical displacements (too high or too low a viewpoint) produce identical transformations, but the shear will be vertical not lateral. As the eye moves upward, for example, points, lines, and planes rotate downward. Hang your picture too low on the wall and the ground plane will slope downward in virtual space at the same angle as your line of sight to the picture's horizon (Sedgwick, 1991).

Ordinary picture viewing typically involves both normal and parallel displacements that produce a picture plane slanted about either the vertical or the horizontal axis. The geometric transformations here are the additive combination of the separate compression and shear effects described above (Farber & Rosinski, 1978; Rosinski & Farber, 1980).

b. Perception

Just as the telephoto effect is a familiar, visible distortion produced by perpendicular displacements of viewing position, so there is remarkable, visible distortion of pictorial space produced by lateral displacements, that is, the oft-noted rotation of depicted objects that occurs as we walk past a picture. A portrait's eyes seem to follow us around the room, and there is no escaping Lord Kitchener's pointing finger in the famous World War I recruiting poster (later borrowed by Uncle Sam). Nevertheless, early work on the perception of slanted pictures was mostly concerned with demonstrating the existence of a compensation mechanism by showing that distortions of shape (Perkins, 1973; Wallach & Marshall, 1986), size (Hagen, 1976), and slant (Rosinski, Mulholland, Degelman, & Farber, 1980), are either absent or minimal, at least when observers are aware of the picture surface orientation. More recently, however, others have demonstrated strong effects of vertical displacement on the perceived slant of a ground plane (Johansson & Borjesson, 1989) and the rotational distortions described for some objects (Ellis, Smith & McGreevy, 1987; Goldstein, 1979) and for slanted surfaces (Halloran, 1989, 1993), mostly in line with the geometric predictions (Cutting, 1988; Goldstein, 1988). Often, however, perceived distortion is less than predicted and there is some evidence that relative spatial position of depicted objects is preserved even in pictures showing marked deformations when viewed from the side (Goldstein, 1979, 1987; Halloran, 1989). In some cases, the visual system appears to tolerate small distortions (Busey, Brady, & Cutting, 1990; Cutting, 1987). In others, information for picture surface orientation given by the frame does seem to be relevant in limiting distortion. These results do not necessarily imply the action of a special pictorial compensation process, however. Alternatives are discussed after this literature is reviewed.

Two sets of studies by Goldstein indicate that the orientation of depicted objects is systematically distorted when pictures are viewed from the side. With a series of depictions of horizontal rods, varying in orientation from parallel to perpendicular to the picture plane, Goldstein (1979) found that the rods appeared to rotate by different amounts as the viewing angle changed, with those pointing directly out of the picture (like Kitchener's finger or the Mona Lisa's eyes) rotating most, and rods parallel to the picture plane rotating least. Goldstein calls the effect *differential rotation*. He also obtained it with a more complex scene (Theodore Rousseau's *Village of Becquigny*), later (Goldstein, 1987) with pairs of vertical dowels set at different orientations, and in portraits, manipulating gaze direction and head orientation. Similar differential rotation effects were obtained by Ellis et al. (1987) and by Halloran (1989) for Winslow Homer's *The Fog Warning*. Goldstein (1979) and Halloran (1993) also found that even virtually depthless depicted objects will appear to rotate a little with viewing angle (e.g., flat disks, arrows, and even depicted and real picture frames), although to a lesser degree than objects extending in depth.

Different amounts of rotation (orientation distortion) for different objective orientations are predicted from Sedgwick's (1991) analysis of orientation distortions described above. Indeed, Cutting (1988) applied affine geometry on the basis of La Gournerie's (1850) analyses to Goldstein's (1987) experimental stimuli and found a reasonably close fit between the geometrical predictions and the data.

Conflicting evidence was obtained by Rosinski et al. (1980) in a study that has been influential among those promoting a compensation mechanism in picture perception (see Kubovy, 1986). Unlike Goldstein (1979, 1987) Rosinski et al. studied perceived slant of a planar surface that composed the whole picture. Photographs were taken of a rectangular board painted with black and white vertical stripes set at a range of objective slants from 30° to 150° (where 90° is a frontal surface, and angles below and above 90° indicate a right and left-wall surface, respectively). Pursuit of evidence in support of the compensation hypothesis has usually involved the manipulation of information specifying the presence and orientation of the picture surface, which is supposed to trigger the mechanism. Rosinski et al., for example, used cross-polarized filters to minimize surface reflections from their photographic stimuli and a darkened viewing box in Experiment 1 and compared results with a second experiment in which no such devices were used, viewing was binocular, and the picture surface and frame were clearly visible. In Experiment 1, viewing was from the correct station point or from 45° to the right. In Experiment 2, it was from 45° to the left or right, with no station point comparison. In the viewing-box experiment, the slanted surface rotated—perceived slant was closer to virtual slant (i.e., geometrically specified slant) than to the objective slant, though always somewhat flattened. In the visible surface condition, however, perceived slant seemed closer to the objective, depicted slant, though again flattened, and there was no difference between the two viewing positions. Rosinski et al. concluded that a compensatory mechanism, dependent on awareness of the picture surface and orientation, operates to provide a percept like that obtainable at the station point.

In an extension of Rosinski et al. (1980), Halloran's data (1989) indicate that the conclusion is unwarranted. Halloran suspected that distortions of virtual space would be more apparent when depicted slants are large and viewing position is extreme, and, indeed, Sedgwick's (1991) analysis predicts that this is when distortion is maximal. Halloran increased the range of depicted surface slants by adding 15° (extreme left wall) and 165° (extreme right wall) slants and increased the number and range of viewing positions (30° through 150° [90° is perpendicular]). Pronounced effects of viewing point on judged slant were obtained, with more rotation for the more extreme slants at more extreme viewing points, as the geometry predicts. The slanted surfaces were all perceived as flatter (closer to the picture plane) than specified, and the effects are therefore weaker than predicted and weaker than those obtained by Goldstein (1979). In accord with Rosinski et al.'s findings, there was no effect of viewing position when depicted slants were 60°, 130°, or frontal (90°), except for the most extreme viewing angles where the slanted surfaces rotated.

Similarly, Perkins (1973) found considerable tolerance for shape distortion in viewing line-drawn parallelepipeds from the side. Subjects classified each drawing as rectangular or not and tended to judge the drawing as if they were seeing it from the front (picture plane-relative shape), whether the viewing angle was 26° (70% of observers) or 41° (77% of observers) from perpendicular, and not according to the virtual space (observer-relative shape). More extreme viewing positions were not tested, and the degree of distortion predicted for the drawings is not clear.

It might be tempting to conclude that Perkins's (1973) observers were able to compensate for oblique viewing, "correcting" the drawings to a frontal view. It would be perverse to conclude, however, that compensation occurred in Rosinski et al.'s (1980) and Halloran's (1989) study only for those slants in which distortion is minimal and not at all for those in which it is maximal (see Sedgwick, 1991, Figure 10).

Three factors may contribute to the limit on perceived distortion here. First, slant underestimation or regression to the frontal plane (Thouless, 1931) is typical of depicted planar surface slants like these and may result in some loss of distortion (Braunstein & Payne, 1969; Clark et al. 1955; Epstein, 1981; Epstein, Bontrager, & Park, 1962; Flock, 1965; Freeman, 1965, 1966a, 1966b; Gibson, 1950; Gruber & Clark, 1956; Perrone, 1980; Perrone & Wenderoth, 1991; Purdy, 1960; Smith, 1956; Wenderoth, 1970). Halloran

(1993) found that slanted picture frames also regress to a frontal plane. He found that frame regression subtracts from object rotation within the picture space, suggesting that this regression component is a constant and does not vary with depicted object slant and depth. Small shifts of viewing position would, therefore, be unlikely to result in distortion. Although this process constitutes a correction of some kind, it is not unique to pictures. Second, observers may be insensitive to distortions at the lower end of the range (Cutting, 1987). Thresholds of sensitivity to orientation and shape distortion have not yet been established, but there is some suggestive evidence that they are quite high. Pictures of faces rotated (around a vertical axis) as much as 22° away from the frontal plane do not appear more distorted than unslanted faces (Busey et al., 1990). Faces, of course, may have different thresholds than more regular objects such as planar surfaces or rods. To paraphrase Gombrich (1960/1977), if faces appear somewhat slimmer, well there are such faces, and some distortion may be acceptable (observers were not so accepting of faces slanted around a horizontal axis). Meister (1966) noted that moviegoers will not notice distortions if they are seated within 22° of the perpendicular, and Cutting provides further support for this idea. Rotating rectangular objects appeared equally rigid when the movie is viewed frontally or slanted at 22.5°, but noticeable distortions occurred at a 45° viewing angle. Cutting and Busey et al. therefore suggest that no compensation is needed for moderately slanted pictures for which distortions may simply be subthreshold, and no compensation is evident for more extremely slanted pictures. Further research is needed to explore distortion thresholds and avoid a potentially tautological argument. A third alternative (not necessarily exclusive) provides a role for picture frame information for the orientation of the picture surface, without requiring a psychological compensation process of the kind described.

3. The Effect of the Picture Frame and Surface Information

Compensation theorists all point to the important role of information for the presence of the picture surface "to restore the correct view when the picture is looked at from the wrong position" (Pirenne, 1970, p. 99). The orientation of the slanted pictures in Perkins (1973) study was clear to subjects, who, he suggested could have used this information in compensating for viewing position. However, in this and in other studies in which the picture plane slant is specified, it is often unclear whether subjects are instructed to make judgments of the depicted object as it looks from their view point (e.g., observer-relative slant) or to make judgments relative to the slant of the picture plane (e.g., picture plane-relative slant). Striking effects of instructions on perceptual judgments have been noted before (Carlson, 1977). In Rosinski et al.'s (1980) study observers were asked to adjust a palm board to match surface slant "depicted in the photograph" (p. 522). In Experiment 1 with the viewing box, this is equivalent to asking how a surface slant looks "from here" that is, observer-relative slant. In Experiment 2, in which the frame and surface are visible, observers could interpret this to mean they should judge the surface slant relative to the slant of the picture. This would almost certainly lead to a difference in the results of the two experiments and does not necessarily implicate a compensation process of the kind proposed. There is evidence that relative slant judgments like these are readily made and are based on geometric information in the array. Halloran (1989), for example, simulated oblique viewing of a picture of a slanted lattice. Observers judged the slant of the depicted lattice relative to a black field, which was also depicted as slanted. Results closely matched the judgments made of lattice slant in pictures actually viewed obliquely when observers were explicitly asked to judge slant relative to the picture plane. In general, in the absence of explicit instructions but in the presence of picture plane-slant information, the obviously slanted picture surface leads to picture plane-relative judgments. Halloran (1993) considers that "the frame, or picture surface, simply becomes the coordinate reference for orienting parts of the depiction, whenever the task suggests that this surface, rather than a frontal plane or the line of sight be the orthogonal referent" (p. 506). The absence of information for the orientation of the picture surface may lead to an observer-relative judgment because there is no alternative (e.g., Rosinski et al., 1980). Observer-relative judgments are also obtained if the instructions explicitly ask for them, even in the clear presence of surface information (Goldstein, 1979, 1987).

Possible supporting evidence that object-to-frame comparisons are made is found in Wallach and Marshall (1986). When the picture frame slant was congruent with physical picture slant, a depicted cube was judged the same shape as from a frontal view. When the two were incongruent, the picture was slanted and the frame frontal, the cube was judged distorted. Wallach and Marshall concluded that observers' visual systems compensated for the evident shape distortion in the former condition. However, the cubes were depicted with a face close to parallel to the picture plane, and the authors note that ordinary shape constancy processes could account for their finding.

Halloran (1989) and Wallach and Marshall (1986) both indicate that the slant specified by the picture frame is more important than the physical slant of the picture itself. Furthermore, manipulating picture surface information by comparing back-projected photographic transparencies with prints (Hagen, 1976; Rogers, 1986) does not have the effect predicted by the compensation theorists. The less obvious surface of the former should impair the ability to compensate for viewing position-dependent distortions since "the compensation process is operative only in the presence of a visible picture surface" (Hagen, 1976, p. 57). However, Hagen and Rogers both found that judgments of relative size in the pictures were more accurate in the case of the transparencies, not less.[5]

Halloran (1993) argued that the comparison of frame and depicted object might be a kind of "rectifying principle" but it does not seem to be quite the kind of perceptual mechanism of compensation that Pirenne (1970), Rosinski and Farber (1980), and Kubovy (1986) had in mind. It is based entirely on optical geometry and requires no assumptions about ordinary picture viewing and no reconstruction of the scene from the correct viewing point. Simply put, the whole optic array from the scene containing a picture is relevant to picture perception, not just the array projected from within the picture itself.

4. Spatial Layout

Both the geometry and the empirical evidence indicate that some parts of a depicted scene distort more than others when an observer views the picture from the side and that the degree of distortion changes as the observer moves around. Nevertheless, there is some evidence that despite these marked transformations in perceived pictorial space, judgments about the relative positions of objects in the scene are surprisingly unaffected (Goldstein, 1979, 1987, 1991). In Goldstein's (1987) experiments, the picture surface and frame were always visible and the observers were required to judge both orientation and spatial position of pairs of vertical dowels pictured in a triangular grouping. Orientation distorted while spatial position did not do so even within the same picture. Perhaps the positional displacements are subthreshold, even when orientation distortions are not (Cutting, 1987), or perhaps the corrective effect of the frame lends stability (Halloran, 1993). However, it seems more likely that the above analysis of the orientation experiments applies here. Orientation and spatial layout were judged in the same picture but in separate experiments. Orientation judgments were explicitly observer relative, which, as we have seen, leads to reported distortions. It is very likely, however, that observers judged layout relative to the picture plane. Actual instructions are not given, but Goldstein (1987) reports that observers "judged the spatial layout of the dowels by arranging three disks on a piece of paper to duplicate the positions of the bases of the dowels in the picture" (p. 257).

Careful experiments are needed that clearly manipulate instructions

---

[5] Hagen (1976) offers her study as support for the compensation hypothesis. However, she chose to assess perceived size as an indicator of perceived depth. The relative size of frontal objects is not affected by the affine shear of lateral viewing angles, so no compensation is required. Hagen's experiment is criticized on logical grounds by Rogers (1986), who also reports a failure to replicate Hagen's principal findings.

about the required frame of reference for judgments about orientation, shape, and spatial position of depicted objects. There is evidence that such instructions matter and that observers are able to make both observer-relative and picture plane-relative judgments. In the absence of picture plane information, judgments of spatial position may also be observer relative and hence show the expected distortions. So far, no experiments have examined the perception of relative object positions during oblique viewing under view box conditions that remove information for the orientation of the picture surface.

Of course, it is still possible that a compensation process is active here that corrects spatial layout even if orientation remains uncorrected. Cutting (1988), for example, argued that spatial layout is derived from optical information about orientation (distortions and all) from the picture and from optical information about picture surface slant. Taking the latter into account, he argues, allows a process of Euclidean rectification (compensation) to take place for spatial layout and orientation would be unaffected.

A further possibility remains that would allow spatial layout to appear relatively undistorted despite distortions of orientation when a picture is viewed obliquely. Aspects of spatial layout may, of course, be determined by a number of sources of pictorial information, and some of these are invariant with viewing angle (see above). Careful manipulation of these pictorial invariants would allow an estimate of their importance in ordinary picture viewing. It would be a mistake to conclude that a compensation process acts for layout but not for orientation on the basis of current evidence.

5. Traditional Artistic Practice and Constraints on Distortion

There is another factor relevant to the perception of distortion in the projective space of pictures, one that has received little serious consideration from psychologists: the significant contribution made by the artist in constraining the potential for distortion inherent in perspective pictures. There has been a long tradition in painting (and more recently in photography) of developing practices designed to minimize perceived distortion. The very success of these practices ensures their transparency to the picture viewer and their neglect in theories of picture perception.

Writers from Leonardo to the present have made recommendations to artists concerning the construction of pictures. Dubery and Willats (1983), for example, repeat the traditional prescription that the visual angle subtended by the width of the picture at the station point should not exceed 25°. If it does, distortions of shape and position will appear at the edges of the picture when it is viewed away from the station point. The skilled artist can hide these distortions, however. Dubery and Willats (1983) show two examples. The perspective of Vermeer's *Music Lesson* is constructed so accurately that it is possible to calculate the artist's precise location in relation to the scene, revealing that the angle of view for the picture is 45°. To hide the square floor tiles that would have visibly distorted at the bottom of the picture, Vermeer draped a rug over them on the right-hand side and cut them with the picture frame on the left (Dubery & Willats, 1983, p. 77). They show similar masterful framing in the work of another seventeenth century Dutchman, Pieter Saenredam (1595–1665). In a reconstruction of *The Grote Kerk at Haarlem,* Dubery and Willats removed the picture frame and revealed severely distorted columns at the edges of the picture. An alternative recommendation is that the artist should avoid placing very regularly shaped objects near the edges of the picture as these distort the most obviously.

Leonardo advised avoiding the problem altogether by positioning the station point at a distance equal to about 10 times (elsewhere at least 3 or as much as 20 times) the length of the longest dimension of the object to be drawn. The greater distance allows the observer the most freedom of viewing position (Richter, 1970; see also Jones & Hagen, 1978). These rules affect the degree or strength of perspective convergence in the picture. There is some evidence that people prefer pictures with the minimal convergence produced by a 10-times rule (Hagen & Elliott, 1976; Hagen & Jones, 1978; see also Nicholls & Kennedy, 1993a) and that they reject pictures with strong convergence (Hagen & Glick, 1977). The pictorial stimuli in these studies, however, were extremely spare, and in the case of Hagen and Glick, inaccurate perspective renderings were used (see Rogers, 1986).

If there are such observer preferences for the degree of perspective, it is not clear whether they precede or follow artistic practice. In a sense, the degree of perspective convergence that is acceptable and even the selection of appropriate viewing positions are "agreed" on by picture makers and picture viewers. Pictures are essentially social products after all (Costall, 1984). The historical development of artistic and social practices in constructing and viewing pictures has ensured their success. The more skillfully the artist exploits this knowledge of picturing, the less "work" is needed on the part of the observer. For this reason, it is usually not necessary for picture viewers to make any assumptions about picture-making practices to successfully perceive pictorial space (see Rosinski & Farber, 1980). However, when the artist constructs a picture in such a way that distortion will be inevitable in ordinary picture viewing she or he can insist that the painting be viewed only from the correct station point by providing a floor mark or a peephole. Anamorphic art and certain forms of *trompe l'oeil* make use of these devices to good effect (Leeman et al., 1976).

Further research is needed, with carefully constructed pictures, to determine the effects of the degree of perspective convergence on perceived distortions when viewing position is systematically displaced. The constraints on construction and observation of perspective pictures should emerge, and artistic rules of thumb could usefully be quantified.

6. Evaluating the Station Point Problem

From the rather mixed bag of experiments reviewed above several conclusions emerge. The principal finding is that distortions of the virtual space of pictures are perceived and they do affect judgments about the depicted layout. However, the consequences of this finding for ordinary picture viewing need not be as drastic as one might suppose. Usually, the distortions and ambiguities inherent in pictorial space are limited first by the artist or picture maker and secondly by the conditions of ordinary picture viewing.

Most important, the amount of potential distortion can be limited during construction of the picture. A number of picture variables are directly relevant to the acceptability of a picture: the degree of perspective convergence used in constructing the picture in terms of both the distance of the station point from the picture plane and the distance of depicted objects within the picture, the width of the visual angle subtended by the picture, the orientation of objects within the picture, and so forth.

Furthermore, some sources of information for spatial layout are invariant with shifts in viewing position. It remains to be demonstrated that they are important in ordinary picture viewing, but if they are they would be expected to provide some stability to pictorial space and perhaps reduce the experience of distortion. We would also expect coherent use of the structures by artists when a stable pictorial space is intended and less coherent use of them when the artist's intent is to suggest otherwise (see, for example, Giorgio de Chirico's use of a dissociated horizon to invoke a surreal space).

Distortion may be further restricted by avoiding extreme displacements of viewing position. Distortions will be minimal in most ordinary picture-viewing situations if the construction rules have been followed and only moderate displacements of viewing position occur. This is usually the case when viewing pictures at a gallery, watching television, and watching movies at the cinema. The more the artist constrains distortion, the less restrictions need to be placed on the observer (e.g., in memo board type *trompe l'oeil*) and, similarly, the less the artist wishes to follow the rules of construction to limit distortion, the more she or he must restrict the position from which the observer may view the work (anamorphic art is an example and the Italian painted ceiling *trompe l'oeil* such as Pozzo's famous ceiling in the church of Saint Ignatius in Rome).

Finally, in the light of the foregoing, there seems to be no need to postulate a process of psychological compensation to explain the perceptual stability of pictorial space. There is no evidence that picture viewers engage in a thought-like process in which they juggle deformed and ambiguous optical input with knowledge about the picture surface and their assumptions about picture viewing in order to correct pictorial space.

V. THE SPECIAL STATUS OF PICTURES

Our enchantment with pictures may lead us to overlook a very important fact that pictures have a special status as perceptual objects because they are artifacts. Their undeniable success in representing reality is largely due to traditional artistic practices that impose constraints on pictures' intrinsic ambiguity and potential for distortion. Does this special status imply that a special theory is needed to explain their perception? The constraints are certainly limited to pictures and are irrelevant to the perception of the real scenes they represent. The information provided by the optical horizon, for example, is constrained only by the physical laws that place it always at eye-level and ecological laws that underwrite the adaptation of a visual system capable of detecting the information. The existence of additional constraints in the picture domain marks a firm distinction between it and the perception of real scenes. This point is important. One motivation for the present study was the question of the existence of pictorial invariants and their relationship to the invariant optical structure available in the perception of real scenes. Gibson (1971) has written that pictures make available the "same kind of information" as real scenes and that the perception of pictorial spatial relations is due to the same kind of process, the direct detection of the informational structure (see also Gibson, 1979).

The need for constraints, however, does not undermine the theory that pictures can provide information. The concept of constraint is an essential one in any theory of perception (see, for example, Marr, 1982; Ullman, 1979) and has recently received much attention (Barwise & Perry, 1983; Dretske, 1981; Runeson, 1988). For a structure to be truly informative, the conditions under which that structure unambiguously specifies some aspect of reality must be satisfied. Those conditions may well be different when the structure is not revealed through the continuous transformations of the optic array (in the perception of real scenes) but is frozen on a picture surface. Available information may be effective only when important features are adequately identified, when the degree of perspective convergence used is within tolerable limits, and when appropriate viewing conditions are met, for example. Future research should address the nature of these constraints and of their operation more fully.

VI. CONCLUSION

Pictures are notorious for their ambiguity—witness the standard catalog of visual illusions. That notoriety may be ill-deserved, however. Professionally made pictures are rarely as confusing as the products of our laboratories. However, pictures are not randomly frozen slices from a visual pyramid of light rays converging at an arbitrary station point. They are designed. Pictures seem to be as easy to see as anything else, but this fact reflects the special character of pictures as made objects, as human artifacts.

Artistic practice has a long and important history that should not be ignored. Artists have learned how to ensure that constraints are met so that information available in their pictures can be effective. The job for the perceiver then is indeed simple and need be no different from the perception of real scenes. An information-based theory of picture perception is possible but not without important qualification. Pictures are not natural objects but made ones. They can conspire with us to be meaningful in a way that the natural environment cannot, and in this sense pictures are something more than Gibson's (1971) definition will allow.

In conclusion, pictures can contain information. This information is the same kind as that found in the optic array from real scenes but it requires the satisfaction of additional constraints to be fully effective. Any successful treatment of pictures must consider their special status as objects that are made to be meaningful.

References

Adams, K. R. (1972). Perspective and the viewpoint. *Leonardo, 5,* 209–217.

Alberti, L. B. (1966). *On painting* (J. Spencer, Trans.). New Haven: Yale University Press. (Original work published 1435–36)

Ames, Jr., A. (1925). The illusion of depth from single pictures. *Journal of the Optical Society of America, 10,* 137–148.

Barwise, J., & Perry, J. (1983). *Situations and attitudes.* Cambridge, MA: MIT Press.

Bengston, J. K., Stergois, J. C., Ward, J. L., & Jester, R. E. (1980). Optic array determinants of apparent distance and size in pictures. *Journal of Experimental Psychology: Human Perception and Performance, 6,* 751–759.

Bingham, G. P. (1993a). Perceiving the size of trees: Biological form and the horizon ratio. *Perception & Psychophysics, 54,* 485–495.

Bingham, G. P. (1993b). Perceiving the size of trees: Form as information about scale. *Journal of Experimental Psychology: Human Perception and Performance, 19,* 1139–1161.

Braunstein, M. L., & Payne, J. W. (1969). Perspective and form ratio as determinants of relative slant judgments. *Journal of Experimental Psychology, 81,* 584–589.

Busey, T. A., Brady, N. P., & Cutting, J. E. (1990). Compensation is unnecessary for the perception of faces in slanted pictures. *Perception & Psychophysics, 48,* 1–11.

Carlson, V. R. (1977). Instructions and perceptual constancy judgments. In W. Epstein (Ed.), *Stability and constancy in visual perception: Mechanisms and processes* (pp. 217–254). New York: Wiley.

Clark, W. C., Smith, A. H., & Rabe, A. (1955). Retinal gradients of outline as a stimulus for slant. *Canadian Journal of Psychology, 9,* 247–253.

Costall, A. P. (1981). [Review of *The perception of pictures: Vol. 1. Alberti's window: The projective model of pictorial information.*] *Perception, 10,* 117–121.

Costall, A. P. (1984). How meaning covers the traces. In N. H. Freeman and M. V. Cox

(Eds.), *Visual order: The nature and development of pictorial representation* (pp. 17–30). Cambridge: Cambridge University Press.

Cutting, J. E. (1986a). *Perception with an eye for motion*. Cambridge, MA: Bradford Books/MIT Press.

Cutting, J. E. (1986b). The shape and psychophysics of cinematic space. *Behavior Research Methods, Instruments, & Computers, 18*, 551–558.

Cutting, J. E. (1987). Rigidity in cinema seen from the front row, side aisle. *Journal of Experimental Psychology: Human Perception and Performance, 13*, 323–334.

Cutting, J. E. (1988). Affine distortions of pictorial space: Some predictions for Goldstein (1987) that La Gournerie (1859) might have made. *Journal of Experimental Psychology: Human Perception and Performance, 14*, 305–311.

Dretske, F. I. (1981). *Knowledge and the flow of information*. Cambridge, MA: MIT Press.

Dubery, F., & Willats, J. (1983). *Perspective and other drawing systems*. London: Herbert Press.

Eaton, E. M. (1919). The visual perception of solid form. *British Journal of Ophthalmology, 3*, 349–363 and 399–408.

Ellis, S. R., Smith, S., & McGreevy, M. W. (1987). Distortions of perceived visual directions out of pictures. *Perception & Psychophysics, 42*, 535–544.

Emerson, E. (1863). On the perception of relief. *The British Journal of Photography, 10*, 10–11.

Epstein, W. (1981). The relationship between texture gradient and perceived slant-in-depth: Direct or mediated? *Perception, 10*, 695–702.

Epstein, W. (1993). On seeing that thinking is separate and on thinking that seeing is the same. *Giornale Italiano di Psicologia, XX*, 731–747.

Epstein, W., Bontrager, H., & Park, J. (1962). The induction of nonveridical slant and the perception of shape. *Journal of Experimental Psychology, 63*, 472–479.

Farber, J., & Rosinski, R. R. (1978). Geometric transformations of pictured space. *Perception, 7*, 269–282.

Flock, H. R. (1965). Optical texture and linear perspective as stimuli for slant perception. *Psychological Review, 72*, 505–514.

Freeman, R. B., Jr. (1965). Ecological optics and visual slant. *Psychological Review, 72*, 501–504.

Freeman, R. B., Jr. (1966a). Absolute threshold for visual slant: The effect of stimulus size and retinal perspective. *Journal of Experimental Psychology, 71*, 170–176.

Freeman, R. B., Jr. (1966b). Function of cues in the perceptual learning of visual slant. *Psychological Monographs: General and Applied, 80*(2) (Whole No. 610).

Gibson, J. J. (1950a). The perception of surfaces. *American Journal of Psychology, 63*, 367–384.

Gibson, J. J. (1950b). *The perception of the visual world*. Boston: Houghton Mifflin.

Gibson, J. J. (1966). *The senses considered as perceptual systems*. Boston: Houghton Mifflin.

Gibson, J. J. (1971). The information available in pictures. *Leonardo, 4*, 27–35.

Gibson, J. J. (1973). On the concept of "formless invariants" in visual perception. *Leonardo, 6*, 43–45.

Gibson, J. J. (1979). *The ecological approach to visual perception*. Boston: Houghton Mifflin.

Gibson, J. J. (1980). Foreword. In M. A. Hagen (Ed.), *The perception of pictures: Vol. 1. Alberti's window: The projective model of pictorial information* (pp. 3–31). New York: Academic Press.

Gibson, J. J. (1982a). Pictures as substitutes for visual realities. In E. Reed & R. Jones (Eds.), *Reasons for realism: Selected essays of James J. Gibson* (pp. 231–240). Hillsdale, NJ: Erlbaum. (Original work published in 1947)

Gibson, J. J. (1982b). Pictures, perspective and perception. In E. Reed and R. Jones (Eds.), *Reasons for realism: Selected essays of James J. Gibson* (pp. 258–268). Hillsdale, NJ: Erlbaum. (Original work published in 1960)

Gibson, J. J. (1982c). Autobiography. In E. Reed & R. Jones (Eds.), *Reasons for realism: Selected essays of James J. Gibson* (pp. 7–22). Hillsdale, NJ: Erlbaum. (Original work published in 1967)

Gibson, J. J. (1982d). The problem of temporal order in stimulation and perception. In E. Reed & R. Jones (Eds.), *Reasons for realism: Selected essays of James J. Gibson* (pp. 171–179). Hillsdale, NJ: Erlbaum. (Original work published in 1966)

Gibson, J. J., & Cornsweet, J. (1952). The perceived slant of visual surfaces—optical and geographical. *Journal of Experimental Psychology, 44*, 11–15.

Gillam, B. (1981). False perspectives. *Perception, 10*, 313–318.

Gogel, W. C. (1965). Equidistance tendency and its consequences. *Psychological Bulletin, 64*, 153–163.

Goldstein, E. B. (1979). Rotation of objects in pictures viewed at an angle: Evidence for different properties of two types of pictorial space. *Journal of Experimental Psychology: Human Perception and Performance, 5*, 78–87.

Goldstein, E. B. (1987). Spatial layout, orientation relative to the observer, and perceived projection in pictures viewed at an angle. *Journal of Experimental Psychology: Human Perception and Performance, 13*, 256–266.

Goldstein, E. B. (1988). Geometry or not geometry? Perceived orientation and spatial layout in pictures viewed at an angle. *Journal of Experimental Psychology: Human Perception and Performance, 14*, 312–314.

Goldstein, E. B. (1991). Perceived orientation, spatial layout and the geometry of pictures. In S. R. Ellis (Ed.), *Pictorial communication in virtual and real environments* (pp. 480–485). New York: Taylor & Francis.

Gombrich, E. H. (1977). *Art and illusion: A study in the psychology of pictorial representation*. Fifth edition. London: Phaidon Press. (Original work published in 1960)

Goodman, N. (1968). *The languages of art*. Indianapolis: Bobbs-Merrill.

Greene, R. (1983). Determining the preferred viewpoint in linear perspective. *Leonardo, 16*, 97–102.

Gregory, R. L. (1966). *Eye and brain*. London: Weidenfeld and Nicholson.

Gregory, R. L. 1970). *The intelligent eye*. London: Weidenfeld and Nicholson.

Gregory, R. L. (1974). *Concepts and mechanisms of perception*. London: Duckworth.

Gruber, H., & Clark, W. C. (1956). Perception of slanted surfaces. *Perceptual and Motor Skills, 6*, 97–106.

Hagen, M. A. (1974). Picture perception: Toward a theoretical model. *Psychological Bulletin, 81*, 471–497.

Hagen, M. A. (1976). Influence of picture surface and station point on the ability to compensate for oblique view in pictorial perception. *Developmental Psychology, 12*, 57–63.

Hagen, M. A. (Ed.). (1980). *The perception of pictures: Vol. 1. Alberti's window: The projective model of pictorial information*. New York: Academic Press.

Hagen, M. A., & Elliott, H. B. (1976). An investigation of the relationship between viewing condition and preference for true and modified linear perspective with adults. *Journal of Experimental Psychology: Human Perception and Performance, 2*, 479–490.

Hagen, M. A., & Girogi, R. (1993). Where's the camera? *Ecological Psychology, 5*, 65–84.

Hagen, M. A., & Glick, R. (1977). Pictorial perspective: The perception of size, linear and texture perspective in children and adults. *Perception, 6*, 675–684.

Hagen, M. A., & Jones, R. K. (1978). Differential patterns of preference for modified linear perspective in children and adults. *Journal of Experimental Child Psychology, 26*, 205–215.

Hagen, M. A., Jones, R. K., & Reed, E. S. (1978). On a neglected variable in theories of pictorial perception: Truncation of the visual field. *Perception & Psychophysics, 23*, 326–330.

Halloran, T. O. (1989). Picture perception is array-specific: Viewing angle versus apparent orientation. *Perception & Psychophysics, 45*, 467–482.

Halloran, T. O. (1993). The frame turns also: Factors in differential rotation in pictures. *Perception & Psychophysics, 54*, 496–508.

Helmholtz, H. von (1925). Treatise on physiological optics: Volume 3, 3rd ed. (J. P. C. Southall, Trans.). New York: Optical Society of America. (Original work published 1867; translation reprinted New York: Dover, 1962.)

Helmholtz, H. von (1968). On the relation of optics to painting. In R. M. Warren & R. P. Warren (Eds.), *Helmholtz on perception* (pp. 137–168). New York: Wiley. (Original work published 1881)

Hildebrand, A. (1893). *Das problem der form in der bildenden kunst* (The problem of shape in the visual arts). Strassburg.

Hochberg, J. E. (1962). The psychophysics of pictorial perception. *Audio-Visual Communication Review, 10,* 22.

Hochberg, J. E. (1980). Pictorial functions and perceptual structures. In M. A. Hagen (Ed.), *The perception of pictures: Vol. 1. Alberti's window: The projective model of pictorial information* (pp. 47–93). New York: Academic Press.

Johansson, G., & Borjesson, E. (1989). Toward a new theory of vision studies in wide-angle space perception. *Ecological Psychology, 1,* 301–331.

Jones, R. K., & Hagen, M. A. (1978). The perceptual constraints on choosing a pictorial station point. *Leonardo, 11,* 191–196.

Kaniza, G. (1979). *Organization in vision.* New York: Praeger.

Kaniza, G. (1985). Seeing and thinking. *Acta Psychologica, 59,* 23–33.

Koenderink, J. J. (1986). Optic flow. *Vision Research, 26,* 161–179.

Koenderink, J. J., & van Doorn, A. J. (1993). Local features of smooth shapes: Ridges and courses. In B. C. Vemuri (Ed.), *Geometric methods in computer vision II. Proceedings SPIE 2031* (pp. 2–13).

Koenderink, J. J., & van Doorn, A. J. (1994a). Two-plus-one-dimensional differential geometry. *Pattern Recognition Letters, 15,* 439–443.

Koenderink, J. J., & van Doorn, A. J., (1992). Surface perception in pictures. *Perception & Psychophysics, 52,* 487–496.

Koenderink, J. J., van Doorn, A. J., & Kappers, A. M. L. (in press). Depth relief. *Perception.*

Koenderink, J. J., van Doorn, A. J., & Kappers, A. M. L. (1994b). On so-called "paradoxical monocular sterescopy." *Perception, 23,* 583–594.

Kraft, R. N., & Green, J. S. (1989). Distance perception as a function of photographic area of view. *Perception & Psychophysics, 45,* 459–466.

Kraft, R. N., Patterson, J. F., & Mitchell, N. B. (1986). Distance perception in photographic displays of natural settings. *Perceptual & Motor Skills, 62,* 179–186.

Kubovy, M. (1986). *The psychology of perspective and Renaissance art.* Cambridge, England: Cambridge University Press.

La Gournerie, J. de (1859). *Traite de perspective lineare contenant les traces pour les tableaux, plans et courbes, les bas-reliefs et les decorations theatrales, avec une theorie des effets de perspective* (Treatise on linear perspective containing drawings for paintings, plans and graphs, bas-reliefs, and theatrical set design, with a theory of the effects of perspective). Paris: Dalmont et Dunod.

Lee, D. N. (1980). The optic flow field: The foundation of vision. *Philosophical Transactions of the Royal Society of London, B, 290,* 169–179.

Leeman, F., Elffers, J., & Schuyt, M. (1976). *Hidden images.* New York: Harry N. Abrams.

Lumsden, E. A. (1980). Problems of magnification and minification: An explanation of the distortions of distance, slant, shape, and velocity. In M. A. Hagen (Ed.), *The perception of pictures: Vol. 1. Alberti's window: The projective model of pictorial information* (pp. 91–135). New York: Academic Press.

Lumsden, E. A. (1983). Perception of radial distance as a function of magnification and truncation of depicted spatial layout. *Perception & Psychophysics, 33,* 177–182.

Mark, L. S. (1987). Eyeheight-scaled information about affordances: A study of sitting and stair climbing. *Journal of Experimental Psychology: Human Perception and Performance, 13,* 683–703.

Mark, L. S., Balliett, J. A., Craver, K. D., Douglas, S. D., & Fox, T. (1990). What an actor must do in order to perceive the affordance for sitting. *Ecological Psychology, 2,* 325–366.

Marr, D. (1982). *Vision: A computational investigation into the human representation and processing of visual information.* San Francisco: Freeman.

Meister, R. (1966). The iso-deformation of images and the criterion for delimitation of the usable areas in cine-auditoriums. *Journal for the Society of Motion Picture & Television Engineers, 75,* 179–182.

Nagata, S. (1991). How to reinforce perception of depth in single two-dimensional pictures. In S. R. Ellis (Ed.), *Pictorial communication in virtual and real environments* (pp. 527–545). New York: Taylor & Francis.

Nicholls, A. L., & Kennedy, J. M. (1993a). Angular subtense effects on perception of polar and parallel projections of cubes. *Perception & Psychophysics, 54,* 763–772.

Nicholls, A. L., & Kennedy, J. M. (1993b). Foreshortening and the perception of parallel projections. *Perception & Psychophysics, 54,* 665–674.

Parsons, M. J. (1987). *How we understand art.* Cambridge: Cambridge University Press.

Perkins, D. N. (1973). Compensating for distortion in viewing pictures obliquely. *Perception & Psychophysics, 14,* 13–18.

Perrone, J. A. (1980). Slant underestimation: A model based on the size of the viewing aperture. *Perception, 9,* 285–302.

Perrone, J. A., & Wenderoth, P. (1991). Visual slant underestimation. In S. R. Ellis (Ed.), *Pictorial communication in virtual and real environments* (pp 496–503). New York: Taylor & Francis.

Pirenne, M. H. (1970). *Optics, painting and photography.* Cambridge, England: Cambridge University Press.

Polanyi, M. (1970). What is a painting? [Foreword to *Optics, painting and photography*]. Cambridge, England: Cambridge University Press.

Purdy, W. C. (1960). *The hypothesis of psychophysical correspondence in space perception.* (General Electric Tech. Info. No. R60ELC56)

Richter, J. P. (1970). *The notebooks of Leonardo da Vinci: Vol. 1.* New York: Dover.

Rogers, S. (1986). *Representation and reality: Gibson's concept of information and the problem of pictures.* Unpublished doctoral dissertation, Royal College of Art, London.

Rogers, S. (1995). *The horizon–ratio relation as information for relative size.* Manuscript submitted for publication.

Rogers, S., & Costall, A. (1983). On the horizon: Picture perception and Gibson's concept of information. *Leonardo, 16,* 180–182.

Rosinski, R. R. (1976). Picture perception and monocular vision: A reply to Hagen. *Psychological Bulletin, 83,* 1172–1175.

Rosinski, R. R., & Farber, J. (1980). Compensation for viewing point in the perception of pictured space. In M. A. Hagen (Ed.), *The perception of pictures: Vol. 1. Alberti's window: The projective model of pictorial information* (pp. 137–176). New York: Academic Press.

Rosinski, R. R., Mulholland, T., Degelman, D., & Farber, J. (1980). Picture perception: An analysis of visual compensation. *Perception & Psychophysics, 28,* 521–526.

Runeson, S. (1988). The distorted room illusion, equivalent configurations, and the specificity of static optic arrays. *Journal of Experimental Psychology: Human Perception and Performance, 14,* 295–304.

Schlosberg, H. (1941). Stereoscopic depth from single pictures. *American Journal of Psychology, 54,* 601–605.

Sedgwick, H. A. (1973). The visible horizon: A potential source of visual information for the perception of size and distance. *Dissertation Abstracts International, 34,* 1301B–1302B. (University Microfilms No. 73-22530)

Sedgwick, H. A. (1980). The geometry of spatial layout in pictorial representation. In M. A. Hagen (Ed.), *The perception of pictures: Vol. 1. Alberti's window: The projective model of pictorial information* (pp. 33–90). New York: Academic Press.

Sedgwick, H. A. (1986). Space perception. In K. R. Boff, L. Kaufman, & J. P. Thomas (Eds), *Handbook of perception and human performance: Vol. 1. Sensory processes and perception* (pp. 21.1–21.57). New York: Wiley.

Sedgwick, H. A. (1991). The effects of viewpoint on the virtual space of pictures. In S. R. Ellis (Ed.), *Pictorial communication in virtual and real environments* (pp. 460–479). New York: Taylor & Francis.

Smith, A. H. (1956). Gradients of outline convergence and distortion as stimuli for slant. *Canadian Journal of Psychology, 10,* 211–218.

Smith, O. W. (1958a). Comparison of apparent depth in a photograph viewed from two distances. *Perceptual and Motor Skills, 8,* 79–81.

Smith, O. W. (1958b). Judgments of size and distance in photographs. *American Journal of Psychology, 71,* 529–538.

Smith, O. W., & Gruber, H. (1958). Perception of depth in photographs. *Perceptual and Motor Skills, 8,* 307–313.

Smith, P. C., & Smith, O. W. (1961). Ball throwing responses to photographically portrayed targets. *Journal of Experimental Psychology, 62,* 223–233.

Thouless, R. H. (1931). Phenomenal regression to the real object. *British Journal of Psychology, 21,* 339–359.

Toye, R. C. (1986). The effect of viewing position on the perceived layout of scenes. *Perception & Psychophysics, 40,* 85–92.

Ullman, S. (1979). *The interpretation of visual motion.* Cambridge, MA: MIT Press.

Wagner, M. (1985). The metric of visual space. *Perception & Psychophysics, 38,* 483–495.

Wallach, H., & Marshall, F. J. (1986). Shape constancy in pictorial representation. *Perception & Psychophysics, 39,* 233–235.

Warren, W. H., Jr. (1984). Perceiving affordances: Visual guidance of stair climbing. *Journal of Experimental Psychology: Human Perception and Performance, 10,* 683–703.

Warren, W. H., Jr., & Whang, S. (1987). Visual guidance of walking through apertures: Body-scaled information for affordances. *Journal of Experimental Psychology: Human Perception and Performance, 13,* 371–383.

Wenderoth, P. M. (1970). A visual spatial after-effect of surface slant. *American Journal of Psychology, 83,* 576–590.

Wilcox, B. L., & Teghtsoonian, M. (1971). The control of relative size by pictorial depth cues in children and adults. *Journal of Experimental Child Psychology, 11,* 413–429.

Yonas, A., & Hagen, M. A. (1973). The effects of static and motion parallax depth information on perception of size in children and adults. *Journal of Experimental Child Psychology, 15,* 254–265.

CHAPTER 5

Visible Information about Structure from Motion

Joseph S. Lappin

I. INTRODUCTION: CHANGING IMAGES AND VISIBLE INFORMATION

As I look through the window of my office, past a computer screen, cluttered desk, potted plant, dust-specked glass, and window frame to the outside scene, I see a dense and changing collection of objects scattered through a broad space: Spread over a rolling lawn freckled with light brown leaves, several sidewalks cross, curve, and disappear among the trees. People are coming and going, some strolling slowly, some hurrying, some on bicycles, some in groups moving and gesturing together, carrying books, backpacks, and briefcases, wearing fabrics of varying styles, shapes, sizes, and colors. Their shadows dance and glide beside them. Dark trunks rise from the grass and the pine needle tree beds, stretching a thick web of crooked limbs and fine branches toward a clear blue sky. Branches shift and sway in the breeze. Leaves are mostly gone now, though clusters of light-brown leaves cling to a couple of oaks, and several large magnolias densely covered in dark-green leaves are visible through the contrasting thicket of branches. Buildings flank the scene, walled in brick and stone, embellished in varying styles by windows, spires, ornamental roof lines, and other architectural decorations. A tower rises above the trees ahead, its clock

Perception of Space and Motion

partly hidden by the branches, and the building below hidden by magnolias in the foreground. Shiny hints of a car are barely visible through the branches and magnolia leaves as it moves in front of the hidden building. A smoke cloud rises, deforms, and drifts away above a chimney protruding above the trees and roofs. Several birds in the distance flap into the clear sky, turn together and swirl in the wind as if to land, and then fly out of sight beyond the edge of the window. Beautiful, but not unusual.

The complexity of these changing images exceeds what words can describe. The countless objects visible in this or any other scene appear in an unlimited range of sizes and shapes. Their images continually move and deform, if not because the objects move, then because the observer moves. The relative motions of the images vary with the objects' distances from the observers' gaze. Moving images obscure one another in changing tangles of occlusion. Many objects are stationary, persisting in the same form and location relative to their surroundings, but their images shift, deform, and occlude one another with changes in the observer's position. Highlights, shading, and shadows change with the relative positions of both observer and illumination. The clarity of the images depends on the observer's focus of gaze, and perception is guided by attention.

Despite the infinite variability of the optical images and perceptions, vision provides compelling, intricate, and trustworthy information about the shapes, sizes, and locations of environmental objects.

How is such quality and quantity of information obtained from such insubstantial and variable optical images? Despite what may seem their overwhelming complexity, the image changes themselves constitute a principal form of visual information. The purpose of this chapter is to examine how changing images constitute information for vision.

The concept of *information* is critical to understanding the relationship between objects, images, and perceptions. Environments and objects are visible by virtue of the information their images contain. Differences among theories of perception usually stem from differing assumptions about the form of image information.

The term *information* has become ubiquitous in psychology, but all too often the term has little or no meaning or is even misleading. Before considering how information may be contained in changing images, it is useful to clarify the concept of information.

II. THE NATURE OF INFORMATION

A. Information Differs from Energy

A physical input to the senses is usually called a *stimulus,* and perception is sometimes considered a response to a stimulus—a cause–effect transfer of energy analogous to movements caused by colliding billiard balls. This conception is inadequate for understanding perception, however. A more contemporary conception of causal relations is necessary, involving a transfer of information rather than energy.

The distinction between information and energy was implicit in Fechner's (cf. Fechner, 1860/1966) insight about the form of psychophysical relations. The intensity of a perceptual experience is incommensurate with the intensity of a physical stimulus, and no meaningful quantitative relation can exist between such variables; but a quantitative relation does exist between *changes* in sensation and *changes* in physical intensity—that is, a correspondence between differences or derivatives in two separate physical domains. Furthermore, this correspondence can be specified by a mathematical function that maps relationships in one domain into relationships in the other. This was a profound insight that is fundamental for the study of perception. The psychophysics of perception requires a psychophysics of information.

The concept of information and an associated new conception of causal mechanisms emerged most clearly in the late 1940s. Shannon (1948) provided an explicit definition of information along with an elegant mathematical framework. Other important related developments at about the same time included (1) the publication of Wiener's (1948) book on *Cybernetics,* (2) reports in 1945–1946 by von Neuman and collaborators on the design of a universal computer that could store programs in a memory, and (3) the release in 1950 of UNIVAC, the first commercially available computer. The impressive powers of these new machines derived from their organization rather than their energy. As Wiener (1954) pointed out, the modern world depends more on the transport of information than on mere physical transportation.

The information in a message or pattern resides in its organization or *form* rather than its physical substance. Unlike energy, information is not conserved. Information is not limited to a particular location in either space or time; the same organization may be copied in many physically separate locations and substances.

B. The Statistical Theory of Information

Shannon's (1948) mathematical theory of communication used the following simple model:

$$\text{SOURCE} \rightarrow \text{transmitter} \rightarrow \text{channel} \rightarrow \text{receiver} \rightarrow \text{DESTINATION}$$
$$\uparrow$$
$$\text{noise}$$

The *source* and the *destination* choose messages from sets of alternatives; the *transmitter* and the *receiver* are interfaces that transform input messages into signals formatted for the channel and transform these signals into output messages; and *noise* is uncontrolled random perturbations of the transmitted signals. *Information* effects a *correlation* between input and output events.

The quantity of information is measured in this theory by the *entropy* or uncertainty of the set of alternative messages—defined on the probability distribution over the set of possible messages. The quantity of information, H, produced by choices from a set of discrete alternatives with probabilities p_i, $i = 1, n$, and $\sum_i p_i = 1$ is given by the well-known formula

$$H = -K \sum_i [p_i \log (p_i)], \tag{1}$$

where K is a positive scalar specifying the unit of measure. The convention is to measure H in "bits"—corresponding to the minimum number of binary digits required to represent the message, where $K = 1/\log(2)$—but this unit is essentially arbitrary.

The principal property of this measure is that it is a function of the *probabilities* of the set of messages. The amount of information in an event does not involve physical characteristics of the event itself but depends on the set of alternatives that *might have* occurred. The logarithmic transform of the probabilities yields the useful property that the total information from independent messages equals the sum of the information in these components.[1]

The amount of information transmitted from source to destination depends not only on the complexity of the message but also on the fidelity of the correlation between input and output. The quantity of information transmitted, say T, may be measured by the entropy of the input message minus the conditional entropy of the input given the output

$$T = H(x) - H(x \mid y) = H(y) - H(y \mid x), \tag{2}$$

where $H(x)$ is the entropy of the input message and $H(x \mid y)$ is its conditional entropy given the output, and $H(y)$ and $H(y \mid x)$ are corresponding measures of the output message. Shannon's "fundamental theorem for a discrete channel with noise" (Shannon & Weaver, 1949, pp. 70–74) states that the rate of information transmission by a given channel has a fixed upper limit,

---

[1] An occasional misunderstanding is that information is carried by discrete events or symbols. Equation 1 is readily generalized to continuous variables. If x is a continuous variable, Equation 1 may be written $H = -\int p(x) \log p(x) \, dx$. In the continuous case, however, the measurement depends on the coordinate system; if the coordinates change, the entropy changes. If the coordinates change from x to y, then the entropy becomes $H(y) = \int p(x) (\partial x/\partial y) \log p(x) (\partial x/\partial y) \, dy$. Despite this change in the entropy measure, the derived measures of rate of information transmission and channel capacity are invariant with the coordinate system because these depend on the difference in the input and output entropies, both of which are changed by the same amount (cf. Shannon & Weaver, 1949, pp. 54–58).

regardless of the rate of input information and regardless of its encoding by the transmitter.

The mathematical theory of information had a large impact on experimental psychology during the 1950s and 1960s. Experiments seemed to show that both the accuracy and speed of identifications are limited by a generalized channel capacity (cf. Garner, 1962; Hyman, 1953; Miller, 1956). These applications of information theory departed significantly from behavioristic conceptions involving stimuli and responses: The control of behavior by information rather than by stimulation implies causation by a set of *possible* events, by what might have occurred rather than by what actually did occur (Garner, 1974).

Limitations on the usefulness of information theory became apparent by the 1970s, and its applications in psychological research virtually disappeared by 1980. The general idea that perception and cognition entailed *information processing* became the prevailing conceptual paradigm in the 1970s and 1980s, though these newer ideas were often unrelated to the form of the information as such.

A chief limitation of the definition of information given by Equation 1 is that the relational structure of the sets of input and output messages is very restricted. Relations among members of these sets are merely categorical, involving just two relations: equivalence or nonequivalence of two events. This simple relational structure is implicit in Equation 1, but it is not essential to a general conception of information as form or organization.

Information in the general sense is also embodied in forms in space and time. To understand how information about environmental objects is given by images on the retina, we must investigate potential correspondences between the structure and motion of objects and the structure and motion of their images. To understand how perception derives from such information, we must investigate its visibility.

C. A Generalized Concept of Information

In Fechner's (1860/1966) psychophysical theory, physical events are related to perceptual events by an abstract correspondence between derivatives. In Shannon's (1948) theory, the transmission of information entails a statistical correlation between two sets of events. The essence in both cases is *a correspondence between two relational structures.*

A *relational structure* consists of (1) a set of *elements,* (2) *relations* among these elements, and, in some cases, (3) a set of *operations* (e.g., concatenation and motion) applied to the elements. Information theory may be generalized by extension to other forms of relational structures. In the present application we explore its extension to the spatiotemporal structure of images of moving objects.

At least five basic issues are involved in describing and analyzing the communication of information. The same issues are involved in analyzing both computation and perception because the essence of both of these is also a mapping from input into output.

1. Representation

What are the specific relational structures that correspond to one another? What is the nature of this correspondence, for example? Isomorphism? Isometry? The representation issue is the most fundamental problem in describing information. This has been the focus of modern research on the theory of measurement (e.g., Krantz, Luce, Suppes, & Tversky, 1971), and it is the principal concern of the present chapter.

2. Complexity

How many parameters or degrees of freedom are required to represent or encode a given pattern or message? In Shannon's (1948) theory, the complexity of a message is quantified by the entropy measure, H. Comparable general measures do not now exist for information defined by most other relational structures, and this has hindered the development of generalized theories of information. Two aspects of complexity are usefully distinguished: (1) *uncertainty*—defined on the set of alternative events and (2) *organizational complexity*—defined on the spatiotemporal form of a given event or pattern. The relevant relationships involved in these two aspects of complexity may be quite different, although in classical information theory the same categorical relations are involved in both cases. These two aspects of complexity usually involve different issues in the study of vision: Uncertainty involves the observer's knowledge about the environment in which events and images occur; the set of alternative optical patterns often is not easily or meaningfully specified. The organizational complexity of a given image, however, involves its spatiotemporal structure. The nature and visibility of these spatiotemporal parameters are the main concerns of the present chapter.[2]

3. Fidelity

What is the fidelity, resolution, or degree of correlation between two relational structures? In Shannon's (1948) theory, fidelity is measured by the

---

[2] Despite the apparent distinction between these two aspects of complexity, they may have joint and indistinguishable effects on the speed and accuracy of recognition. These apparently different aspects of complexity also become less distinct in situations involving temporally connected events in the same environmental context, in which individual events and images may be continuous in time and space, and in which the spatial form of an image at one time may be physically and cognitively related to the form of previous images in both recent and distant past.

quantity of information transmitted, Equation 2. Statistical measures of correlation serve a similar purpose. The modulation transfer function (MTF) is a very useful measure of fidelity for many linear systems and for optical systems in particular. The MTF also has many useful applications in the study of vision (cf. De Valois & De Valois, 1988). The MTF applies, however, only to pairwise relations in spatial or temporal patterns. Another measure of fidelity that is useful in many psychophysical applications is the Weber fraction, which is a dimensionless (scale-free) measure of the precision of discrimination and identification judgments.

4. Uniqueness

What are the transformations by which elements in one relational structure may be changed and still preserve a representation of the other structure? In the theory of measurement, the uniqueness problem is to specify the group of permissible transformations of the real numbers that preserve a representation of the empirical relations. (An interval scale is one in which the numerical representation is unique up to a linear transformation.) In the psychophysics of object perception, we may investigate whether discriminations of a given spatial structure remain invariant under a given group of image transformations such as translations or rotations. Invariance under translations and rotations of retinal position, for example, would imply that the perceived structures entail relative distances among pairs of points. Investigations of uniqueness constitute an important psychophysical method.

5. Mechanism

What is the physical mechanism by which correspondence between two relational structures is established? What is the medium in which the message or pattern is transmitted? What types and amounts of energy are involved? What is the speed of the communication, computation, or perception? Questions about mechanisms in visual perception are often questions about the anatomy and physiology of the visual nervous system. The analysis of mechanisms, however, depends on knowledge about representation— about the form of the information.

D. Two Correspondence Issues

Information generally cannot be specified by extensive measures of physical dimensions, in contrast to physical properties involving mass and energy. One reason is that information requires communication: a correspondence between two separate relational structures. To describe information for vision, description of objects or images or behaviors alone is insufficient; correspondence or correlation is necessary.

Two such correspondence issues are pertinent to visual psychophysics:

(1) *image information* concerns the correspondence between properties of objects and their images, and (2) *visibility* involves the visual sensitivity to particular image properties as information about properties of objects. Visibility is assessed by behavioral performance in discrimination and recognition tasks. These two issues are examined in sections III and IV of this chapter.

III. IMAGE INFORMATION AND THE SPATIAL STRUCTURE OF IMAGES

A. Spatial Primitives

An initial theoretical issue is the representation problem: What are the spatial primitives, the elementary relational structures from which images are composed? This issue is so basic that usually it is not even recognized.

One general family of potential primitives is based on spatial derivatives of local image regions. Potential alternative spatial primitives may be distinguished by their *order:* the zero-, first-, and second-order derivatives in one or two spatial dimensions. (We focus here on the spatial dimensions and assume that these spatial primitives may also involve first-order derivatives in time.) Theoretical rationale for describing this family of alternatives has been developed by Koenderink and van Doorn (1992a). An important aspect of this approach is that the spatial derivatives are computed on local image regions blurred by Gaussian point-spread functions. This operation is equivalent to the use of local operators that are the derivatives of Gaussians, achieving the differentiation by local linear integration (cf. Koenderink, 1990, pp. 32–40). The spread of the Gaussian blur defines the scale of resolution, and indeed this is the only feasible method for varying the spatial scale independently of the form of the local operators.

A simple scheme for distinguishing the structures of these local differential operators is by the number and arrangement of zero-crossings between regions with opposite-signed weights. This scheme is related to the statistical geometry developed by Julesz and his collaborators (Caelli & Julesz, 1978; Caelli, Julesz, & Gilbert, 1978; Julesz, 1981; Julesz, 1984; Julesz, Gilbert, & Victor, 1978) to describe texture on the basis of spatial distributions of *n-gon* primitives (e.g., dipoles). Individual points in the n-gon can be regarded as located in the oppositely weighted regions of the differential operator. The number of points in the n-gon is therefore one greater than the order of the local differential operator.

Five alternative descriptions of the primitive components of spatial images correspond to properties detected by local operators of differing complexity.

1. *Zero order:* A zero-order operator has just one region, either positive or negative, essentially a blurred point.

2. *First order:* A first-order operator has two regions, positive and negative, sensitive to relations between two points, one on either side of the zero
crossing. These provide information about length and orientation.

3. *Second order, one-dimensional (1-D):* Relative distances among three
collinear points. Deformations carry information about surface curvature in
one direction.

4. *Second order, two-dimensional (2-D):* Triangular shapes of three points.
Deformations of this structure carry information about the tilt and slant of a
local surface patch (Koenderink & van Doorn, 1976a). An important special
case of such deformation is a transverse shear, which alters the allignment of
three quasi-collinear points.

5. *Fourth order, 2-D:* Five points in a cross-like pattern, composed of two
orthogonal sets of three collinear points. Deformations carry information
about local surface shape associated with curvature in perpendicular directions.

Schematic illustrations of each of these linear operators are shown in
Figure 1. Other higher order image properties to which vision may be
sensitive can also be described, but currently available evidence concerns
mainly these five alternatives.

These five image properties constitute potential alternative descriptions
of image information. Distinctions among the zero-, first-, and higher-
order properties are of particular interest, corresponding to images of
points, edges, or surfaces.

B. Concepts of Space

A related basic issue in describing images involves the conception of space.
The traditional approach has been to describe the structure of objects and
their positions and motions by reference to an extrinsic spatial framework,
which is conceived as fixed and given beforehand, independently of the
objects and motions it contains. The 2-D spatial structure of retinal images
is usually assumed to be anatomically defined.

An alternative conception is that visual spaces are derived rather than
fundamental, derived from objects and motions rather than from extrinsic
reference frames. Seeing the shape of an object entails seeing a space defined
by its surface. Different surfaces involve different spaces, and different projective maps from surface space onto image space.

Spatial relations among separate environmental objects, between objects
and the observer, and among the successive positions of moving objects all
involve 3-D relationships for which the image information is quite different
from that involved in the 2-D relationships within a single connected sur-

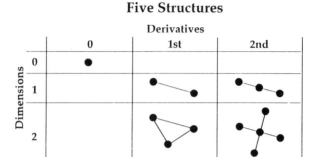

FIGURE 1 Illustrations of five primitive spatial structures and five local operators sensitive to these spatial primitives. The local operators are the derivatives of 2-D Gaussians in cartesian coordinates. The order of the operator corresponds to the number of zero crossings and equals the product of the number of dimensions and the order of the derivative. Koenderink and van Doorn (1992a) describe and discuss the larger family of such local operators.

face. The chapters in this volume by Vishton and Cutting and by Warren address the perception of such extrinsic global 3-D spaces. Because the image information differs for these extrinsic global 3-D and intrinsic local 2-D spaces, the perceived shape of a surface may be partially independent of its perceived embedding into a globally consistent 3-D space. Indeed, the visual effectiveness of photography and cinema seems to illustrate the flexible local nature of visual space (Cutting, 1987; Lappin & Love, 1992; Lappin & Ahlström, 1994).

Visual space may be structured and scaled to various degrees of specificity by the objects and motions it contains. Wason (1993) provides the following categorization of scale types relevant to visual information about structure in depth.

1. *Sequencing:* unsigned order. Connectedness and betweenness are specified, but relative proximity to the observer and relative distances between points are unspecified. Motion parallax among disconnected objects, for example, often yields only visible sequencing (Kottas, 1978).

2. *Ordination:* an ordered sequence (e.g., near to far).

3. *Cardination:* Cardinal scaling establishes relative distances (ratios of distances) between points within a given direction, but not in different directions. Cardinal scaling is preserved by affine transformations of space (by arbitrary linear transformations of the coordinate axes).

4. *Metrification:* relative scaling of distances invariant under directions in space. Mathematically, the critical axiom for a metric space is the triangle inequality. Metric scaling of 3-D space may occur by recursive images of congruent elements in neighboring positions within a volume of space. Figure 2 provides a simple illustration. Such metric scaling can also be produced by certain forms of motion (Lappin & Ahlström, 1994; Lappin & Love, 1992; Lappin & Wason, 1993; Wason, 1993). The principle can be expressed as follows: If the same object occupies two different spaces, then these spaces are congruent. Specific conditions under which visual space might metrically be scaled by motion, stereopsis, or both remain current research issues (Durgin, Proffitt, Olson, & Reinke, in press; Johnston, Cumming, & Landy, 1994; Norman & Todd, 1993; Tittle, Todd, Perotti, & Norman, in press; Todd & Norman, 1991).

5. *Absolute scaling:* through reference to a known standard, such as a familiar object. The spatial metric may be scaled by concatenating these known reference standards.

C. Spatial Resolution and Descriptions of Form

The intuitive concepts of object and shape involve solid and coherent structures, with measurable lengths of their surfaces and perimeters. Such conceptions make sense, however, only at some macroscopic scale; at a microscopic physical scale, structures are generally porous and fractal, with ambiguous measures of length. Clouds are an example, continually changing at a microscopic scale, with a coherent persisting form existing only macroscopically. Similar ambiguities apply to images as well. Descriptions of image shape depend on their scale of resolution. Equivalence classes and similarities among shapes are likewise scale dependent.

Koenderink (1990, pp. 32–40) offers the following approach for resolving these fundamental ambiguities:

FIGURE 2   A schematic illustration of a metric scaling of space by recursion of congruent structural elements.

1. Define the σ-*neighborhood* of a point as a region of radius σ centered on the point. The σ-neighborhood of an arbitrary region of points then consists of the union of the σ-neighborhoods of all the points in that region. The σ-*distance* between two shapes can be defined as the smallest value of σ such that each shape is contained with the σ-neighborhood of the other, after the two are superimposed.

2. The equivalence class of a given shape at a given σ-scale can be defined as the set of shapes that lie within some criterion σ-distance of each other. The σ-scale of resolution can then be taylored to yield appropriate equivalence classes.

3. Spatial derivatives are useful for describing images, especially images of surfaces. Both mathematical and physical measurement problems are associated with the scale dependency of spatial derivatives, however, where derivatives at finer resolutions are increasingly spuriously sensitive to noise.

These problems are avoided by convolving the image with a *blurred differentiator*—a spatial derivative of a Gaussian—that accomplishes the differentiation by integrating over a region scaled by the width, σ, of the Gaussian (see also Koenderink & van Doorn, 1992a). Such operators resemble some of those found in the visual system (Adelson & Bergen, 1991).

4. Since scale is fundamental to shape, this dependency may explicitly be recognized by descriptions at multiple scales.

D. Images of Points: Zero-Order Primitives

The traditional presumption has been that the spatial primitives are essentially points: environmental points in a 3-D space, and corresponding image points on the 2-D retina (Helmholtz, 1867/1925). Objects and their images are regarded as corresponding sets of neighboring points. The spatial coordinate or reference systems that specify the positions and arrangements of these points are extrinsic, independent of the points or objects themselves.

Ullman's (1979) *structure-from-motion theorem* is based on this conception of the spatial primitives and on the related conception of space as scaled by the extrinsic coordinates of the image plane. A similar representation is implicit in Simpson's (1993) recent review of literature on computing and perceiving depth from optic flow and is explicit in Todd's (this volume) formulation of the equations for describing the images of moving objects. These equations are useful for designing displays, but they may be misleading as descriptions of the visible information.

Because of the ambiguities inherent in the one-to-many mapping from points in 2-D image space into points in 3-D object space, the computational problem of vision is often considered ill-posed (e.g., Marroquin, Mitter, & Poggio, 1987; Poggio, Torre, & Koch, 1985). Computational solutions demand heuristics, logical inference, and use of physical and probabilistic constraints on potential 3-D reconstructions.

One such problem associated with this representation is the *correspondence problem* (e.g., Marr, 1982). How can a local motion analyzer establish which point in an image of a moving object corresponds to a given object point in another image? This problem seems especially acute in random-dot patterns used in many psychophysical experiments, in which each successive frame may contain thousands of identical image points displaced differing distances when an object is rotated in depth. The correspondence problem is also widely recognized in theories of stereopsis. This problem depends, however, on the spatial primitives. Ambiguity of correspondence diminishes with increasing complexity and distinctiveness of the spatial primitives.

E. Images of Edges: First-Order Primitives

Another description of spatial primitives has been based on first-order spatial primitives—edges, lines, and contours—especially boundary contours in images corresponding to the edges of objects (e.g., Marr, 1982). The important experiments by Wallach and O'Connell (1953) on the *kinetic depth effect* used line-based images of solid wire-frame shapes rotating in depth. Wallach and O'Connell theorized that image information about the 3-D shape was carried by changes in the projected lengths and angles of these lines.

Outlined images of the edges of objects have often been regarded as key to the shape of an object. An edge-based description is often treated as an early objective of image analysis. Like point-based descriptions, those that are based on edges also involve projections from 3-D to 2-D, entailing a similar loss of spatial structure.

One well-known problem in representing moving objects by edge-based images is the *aperture problem* (Hildreth, 1984a, 1984b; Marr & Ullman, 1981): The direction of motion of an edge is ambiguous when described by local motion analyzers with spatially restricted receptive fields. If the edge is straight and contains no textural marks at specific points, then a given shift within the aperture could have been produced by an almost 180° range of potential alternative directions of motion, with concomitantly varying velocities (minimum perpendicular to the edge). An additional problem is that boundary contours in the images of smooth surfaces do not generally correspond to the same locations on the object surface after the object rotates in depth relative to the observer.

F. Images of Surfaces: Second- and Fourth-Order Primitives

The single most important fact about vision is probably the following: *Retinal images are images of surfaces.*[3] This conception of images is relevant to Properties 3, 4, and 5, involving second- and fourth-order derivatives.

1. Background

Gibson (e.g., 1950, 1966) emphasized that images reflect the structure of surfaces, but until recently this idea had little impact on vision research and theory. The prevailing assumption has been that surfaces are derived global

---

[3] This proposition may be regarded as one working hypothesis. The potential importance of this idea has only recently been recognized, and psychophysical study has just begun. Readers would be wise to maintain a critical attitude about this hypothesis, although the correspondence between surfaces and their images now seems to the author so compelling and fundamental that alternative hypotheses are only barely imaginable.

structures that must be inferred from images on the basis of points or edges. Visual mechanisms up through early cortex have usually been thought to measure first-order properties such as contrast, spatial frequency, and edges. Surface structure was regarded as a visual product to be explained (e.g., Marr, 1982).

Contemporary understanding of the relationship between surfaces and their images owes mainly to the work of Koenderink and van Doorn. Their first work on this topic was stimulated by Gibson's (1950, 1966) descriptions of images of environmental layout and optic flow patterns (Koenderink, 1986, Koenderink & van Doorn, 1975, 1976a, 1976b, 1977). In contrast to previous approaches, Koenderink and van Doorn considered the second-order structure (first-order spatial derivatives in 2-D) of images and showed that *deformations*[4]—changes in shape of the images of local surface patches—carry information about the local tilt and slant of the surface, separable from the divergence, curl, and translations of the images. Their analysis departed from conventional conceptions of moving images as zero- and first-order patterns involving 1-D shifts in position measured by reference to extrinsic retinal coordinates.

The broader and more important contribution of Koenderink and van Doorn has been to explicate the differential geometry of surfaces and images, revealing the rich information in images of surfaces (e.g., Koenderink, 1984, 1987, 1990; Koenderink & van Doorn, 1976c, 1979, 1980, 1982, 1986, 1992a, 1992b, 1993a, 1993b). The following ideas about image information derive from Koenderink and van Doorn's research.

From both a mathematical and visual perspective, environmental surfaces and their images may be regarded as smooth 2-D manifolds.[5] Mathe-

---

[4] The algebraically defined deformation component, also known as *pure shear*, involves expansion in one direction and equivalent contraction in an orthogonal direction such that the area of a local image patch remains constant. Two algebraically independent measures of this deformation can be defined, involving pure shear in relation to two different coordinate systems, offset by a 45° rotation.

The image deformation produced by the rotation of a surface in depth ordinarily involves divergence as well as pure shear because the image area of a surface patch changes when it rotates in depth. The information about local surface orientation is provided by the change in image shape. We speak of the image deformation as if it were only this change in shape, ignoring the technicality that it involves both pure shear and divergence.

[5] A *manifold* is a topological space that can locally be described as a Euclidean vector space. This means that within any sufficiently small local region spatial positions and displacements can be described by a 2-D Euclidean coordinate system at that location, and any one such local coordinate description can be transformed into another by a linear coordinate transformation (i.e., with matrix operators). The geometry of surfaces and images does not require a local Euclidean description, however. Generalized coordinates that uniquely specify locations and displacements will suffice. The coordinate axes need not be orthogonal and do not require measures of metric distance along a given coordinate axis.

matically, smoothness means differentiability (in which mixed partial derivatives of all orders can be defined). Surfaces may be treated as smooth, even if they contain discontinuities such as gaps or sharp edges or points because these discontinuities exist only at infinitely small, isolated regions surrounded by regions that remain smooth up to the discontinuity. Such surfaces are said to be smooth "almost everywhere."

Many, perhaps all, natural surfaces violate even this generalized concept of smoothness: Clouds and leafy trees, for example, are continuous only at a course-scale approximation. Random-dot patterns used in laboratory experiments are also clearly spatially discrete rather than continuous. Many natural surfaces are fractal (Mandelbrot, 1983) and exhibit a different form of discontinuity, not differentiable anywhere at any order. The *perceived* structure of even these clearly discontinuous patterns, however, may be smooth. Gilden, Schmuckler, and Clayton (1993) recently studied discriminations of random fractal contours and found that their self-similarity across spatial scales was not perceived. The visible irregularities of these patterns were found to be perceived as incoherent noise added to underlying smooth contours. A smooth-structure visual description presumably applies to surfaces as well as contours.

The demonstrated effectiveness of random-dot patterns for displaying smooth surfaces rotating in depth indicates that the discrete dots are seen as positioned on a smooth surface (e.g., Norman, 1990; Norman & Lappin, 1992; Saidpour, Braunstein, & Hoffman, 1992). When this surface structure is violated, when the dot patterns form 3-D volumes rather than 2-D surfaces, then both coherent organization and depth are much less detectable in both moving (Lappin, 1994; Norman & Lappin, 1992) and stereoscopic patterns (Norman, Lappin, & Zucker, 1991; Stevenson, Cormack, & Schor, 1989). Vision is evidently especially sensitive to smooth surfaces.

2. Second-Order Primitives and Linear Maps between the Surface, Image, and 3-D Space

Treating retinal images as images of surfaces simplifies the problem of vision, mainly because both can be treated as 2-D manifolds. Any position on a surface may uniquely be specified by two coordinates, and any displacement over the surface may be specified by changes in two coordinates (in a generalized coordinate system that is only locally Euclidean). The surface and its image are *locally diffeomorphic,* meaning that there is a differentiable map from the surface onto its image and a differentiable inverse from the image onto the surface (see Gray, 1993). The local restriction means that the diffeomorphism holds only for open subsets, the visible regions of the surface.

If an extrinsic and globally uniform Euclidean coordinate system is used to describe spatial positions on a curved surface, then these extrinsic coordinates must be 3-D. Such a 3-D space is needed to position and scale the surface relative to other environmental objects and relative to the observer. A 3-D embedding of the surface is also implicit in its metric structure and shape. Questions about how such 3-D structural information might be contained in images of objects are particularly important in research on perception. The schematic correspondences among the spaces and coordinate systems for a surface, its image, and 3-D framework are illustrated in Figure 3.

Suppose that a local (infinitesimal) tangent vector at a point on the object surface is given by 2×1 column vector, $(\mathbf{dO}) = (do_1, do_2)^T$, and suppose that its image is given in retinal coordinates by a similar vector, $(\mathbf{dR}) = (dr_1, dr_2)^T$. Then the relation between these two coordinate descriptions is given by

$$(\mathbf{dR}) = V(\mathbf{dO}), \tag{3}$$

where $\mathbf{V}$ is a 2×2 matrix of first-order partial derivatives, $\mathbf{V} = (\partial r_a / \partial o_i)$, $a = 1$ and 2 and $i = 1$ and 2, in which the upper term varies over the rows, and the lower term varies over the columns. The coordinate transformation $\mathbf{V}$ is given directly by the optical projection of the surface onto its retinal image, and it summarizes the relationship between the surface and its image in the

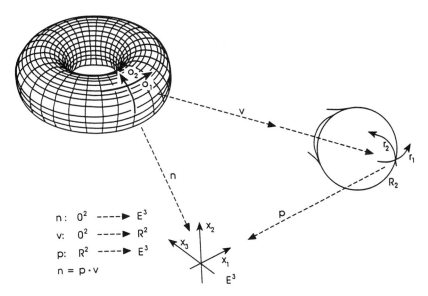

FIGURE 3 A schematic illustration of the relation between the coordinate systems on the surface, the image, and Euclidean 3-D space.

local neighborhood of any given point. Since the two coordinate systems, O^2 and R^2, serve merely to order spatial positions, without any assumed metric structure, we need not think of either of these vectors or the coordinate transformation **V** as involving numerical quantities or estimated parameters. The values of **V** vary smoothly over the visible regions of the surface. The inverse of this coordinate transformation, V^{-1}, is optically defined in the same manner.

The embedding of this same vector into Euclidean three-space, E^3, with real-valued metric structure, is given by the similar equations

$$(\mathbf{dX}) = N\ (\mathbf{dO}) \tag{4}$$

and

$$= P\ (\mathbf{dR}), \tag{5}$$

where $(\mathbf{dX}) = (dx_1, dx_2, dx_3)^T$ is a 3×1 column vector, and **N** and **P** are 3×2 matrices of partial derivatives, $\mathbf{N} = (\partial x_m / \partial o_i)$ and $\mathbf{P} = (\partial x_m / \partial r_a)$, $m = 1$, 2, and 3. Equation 5 gives the Euclidean description of the image. An alternative expression in terms of the constant coordinates of the surface, $(\mathbf{dO})$, rather than the changing coordinates of its image, $(\mathbf{dR})$, is obtained by substituting Equation 3 into Equation 5:

$$(\mathbf{dX}) = PV\ (\mathbf{dO}). \tag{6}$$

Both the Euclidean embedding of the surface, **N,** and the corresponding embedding of its image, **P,** describe the orientation of the surface in a 3-D Euclidean framework and also determine the metric size and shape of the surface. These local Euclidean descriptions are given by six independent parameters, the entries in each of these matrices. These six parameters cannot be obtained from the local image structure of either stationary or moving objects.[6]

Local diffeomorphism of the surface and its image means that both have the same differential topology, with the same ordered arrangement of intrinsic topographical features: planar, parabolic, elliptic, hyperbolic regions, and local discontinuities. Elliptic regions (with the same sign of curvature in two orthogonal directions) are hills and valleys. Parabolic lines (flat in one direction, curved in the orthogonal direction) separate hills and valleys, at inflections in curvature. Hyperbolic regions (with opposite signs of curvature in orthogonal directions) are saddlepoints at passes between peaks. The local shape of every smooth surface is one of these four types. These are intrinsic properties of the surface, invariant under affine transformations of the coordinate space. These four qualitative shape categories are illustrated in Figure 4.

[6] Ullman, 1979, showed that such structural characteristics might in principle be obtained from three or more successive images of a moving object, but such information is evidently not visible (see Todd, this volume).

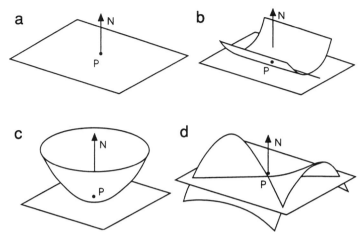

FIGURE 4   Four possible categories of the local shape of smooth surfaces: (a) planar; (b) parabolic, (c) elliptic, (d) hyperbolic.

Images of surface structure involve implicit reference to a third extrinsic dimension, perpendicular to the image plane, polarizing the surface in a near–far direction. Spatial derivatives of image properties reflect changes in orientation of the surface relative to the image plane. Consider orthographic images of surfaces marked by dense and uniformly distributed texture elements and consider the inverse texture density, the spacing among retinal coordinates relative to the spacing among texture elements. The local values of these inverse texture densities serve as an indices of the partial derivatives $(\partial r_a / \partial o_i) = V$ which map the surface onto its image, $(\mathbf{dR}) = V (\mathbf{dO})$. The maxima of these image measures correspond to points at which the surface tangent is parallel to the image plane. If the values of these maxima are scaled to one and smaller values are scaled in proportion, then these inverse densities measure local surface slant (absolute value of the cosine of the angle) relative to the image plane.

Note that the differential structure defined by these first spatial derivatives of the image (first order 1-D and second order 2-D) changes as the object moves in depth. The differential image structure at this order is not an invariant characteristic of the surface. Local information about surface structure is given, however, by the second spatial derivatives of image texture (second order 1-D and fourth order 2-D), invariant with changes in surface orientation.

Approximately the same conception applies to images defined by motion and stereopsis, in which relative velocity and binocular disparity of textured images correspond to a similar form of inverse density. The velocity and disparity fields provide additional information about the sign of the derivatives, corresponding to opposite directions of motion or disparity. Moving images also differ from textured images because the tilt and slant of the surface are generally changing over time. As Koenderink and van Doorn (1975, 1976a, 1976b) pointed out, information about surface slant is associated with deformations of the 2-D motion or disparity fields. These deformations are defined by changes in the 2-D first spatial derivatives (second-order properties).

Images defined by luminous intensity differ in two respects: (1) the implicit third dimension depends on the direction of illumination and the image normal, and (2) photometric units of intensity are incommensurate with geometric units of height. One invariant of these shaded images is that the image intensity tends to be maximized at parabolic lines, independent of the directions of illumination and view (Koenderink & van Doorn, 1980, 1993a). An important problem associated with the image intensities of moving objects is that extrema and gradients of the image intensities are not attached to fixed positions on the surface and move with respect to both the surface and image when the object rotates in depth. The intensity pattern in the momentary image provides information about the tilt and slant of the surface relative to the image plane and the illumination. However, the structure of the image intensities is not attached to fixed surface positions on the moving object (see Todd, this volume, chapter 6).

3. Surface Shape and Fourth-Order Properties

Surface shape may be described in many ways (see especially Koenderink, 1990). Three different levels of description differ in specificity of their reliance on the structure of an extrinsic 3-D framework: *extrinsic, intrinsic,* and *affine*. The distinctions among these three levels of description are relevant to the present examination of image information.

Descriptions of surface shape in differential geometry are usually extrinsic—based on the surface's orientation within the isotropic metric framework of E^3. Shape is described in terms of curvature, and curvature is measured by derivatives of the direction of the surface normal relative to surface position. The direction of the surface normal is specified by reference to the axes of E^3 hence the present label *extrinsic shape*. Specifying the orientation of a local surface patch involves six parameters, as discussed in the preceding section, and formulas for computing the surface curvature involve these parameters (see Gray, 1993; Koenderink, 1990; Lipschutz, 1969). These extrinsic parameters are not given by the local image properties.

Descriptions of extrinsic shape at a given point on the surface involve measures of curvature in two independent directions. The curvature in a particular direction is equal to the reciprocal of the radius of the best fitting circular arc touching the surface at the given point: $k = 1/r$, where r is the radius of the osculating circle, and k is the measure of curvature. The two principal curvatures, k_1 and k_2, are the curvatures in the directions with minimum and maximum curvature, respectively, and these directions are perpendicular. For a planar patch, $k_1 = k_2 = 0$; at a parabolic patch, either $k_1 = 0$ or $k_2 = 0$, but not both; at an elliptic patch, k_1 and k_2 both have the same sign, either positive or negative; and at a hyperbolic patch, k_1 and k_2 have opposite signs. These measures of extrinsic surface shape are not available either in stationary images or in momentary velocities of moving images.

The *intrinsic shape*, however, does not depend on orientation in $\mathbf{E}^3$ and may be specified by as few as three parameters, in contrast to the six parameters (matrix $\mathbf{N}$) needed to specify the local orientation of the surface. The intrinsic shape can be measured by spatial relations on the surface itself without a 3-D framework. The intrinsic shape is given in terms of extrinsic curvature by the Gaussian curvature, $K = k_1 k_2$. Although it may be defined extrinsically, K is fully determined by the intrinsic metric[7] structure of the surface (Gauss's *thereoma egregium*), invariant with orientation in $\mathbf{E}^3$ and also under bending.

The metric structure of a local surface patch is determined by three parameters which specify the Euclidean distances of local displacements over the surface coordinates. Let ds^2 be the squared length of a local displacement. For a vector in Euclidean space, this metric quantity is given by the Pythagorean theorem:

$$ds^2 = \sum_m (dx_m)^2 = (dx)^{\mathrm{T}}(dx). \tag{7}$$

This metric quantity can also be written in terms of the intrinsic coordinates of the surface, by substituting from Equation 4 into Equation 7

$$ds^2 = (d\mathbf{O})^{\mathrm{T}} (\mathbf{N}^{\mathrm{T}} \mathbf{N})(d\mathbf{O}) = (d\mathbf{O})^{\mathrm{T}} \mathbf{G}(d\mathbf{O})$$
$$= g_{11} (do_1)^2 + 2 g_{12} do_1 do_2 + g_{22} (do_2)^2, \tag{8}$$

where $\mathbf{G} = (g_{ij}) = [\sum_m (\partial x_m / \partial o_i) (\partial x_m / \partial o_j)]$. Equation 8 is known as the "first fundamental form," and the 2×2 symmetric matrix of coefficients, $\mathbf{G} = \mathbf{N}^{\mathrm{T}} \mathbf{N}$, is the metric tensor for the local surface patch.

The metric tensor for the image may be obtained by substituting the equality $\mathbf{N} = \mathbf{P}\mathbf{V}$ into the formula for $\mathbf{G} = \mathbf{N}^{\mathrm{T}} \mathbf{N}$

$$\mathbf{G} = \mathbf{V}^{\mathrm{T}} \mathbf{P}^{\mathrm{T}} \mathbf{P} \mathbf{V} = \mathbf{V}^{\mathrm{T}} \mathbf{P}^* \mathbf{V}, \tag{9}$$

---

[7] "Metric" is used in the standard mathematical sense to refer to a measure that is positive, symmetric, and satisfies the triangle inequality for all triples of points. This provides a ratio scale of distance on the surface, determining contour lengths, angles, and areas on the surface. Bending changes curvature in a given direction, but it does not change the metric structure nor the Gaussian curvature, K.

where $\mathbf{P}^T\,\mathbf{P} = \mathbf{P}^* = (p_{ab}) = [\sum_m (\partial x_m/\partial r_a)(\partial x_m/\partial r_b)]$. As may be seen, $\mathbf{P}^*$ is a symmetric 2×2 matrix of sums of products of partial derivatives, similar in form to $\mathbf{G}$, providing metric tensor coefficients for the retinal image of a local surface patch.

The values of these intrinsic metric parameters are determined by the momentary image flow field only in special cases in which an object rotates in depth in such a way that the trajectory of its surface is also a surface, producing a flow field in the image that remains constant over time, for example, a planar object rotating (around a point away from its center) within a slanted plane (Hoffman & Flinchbaugh, 1982; Lappin & Ahlström, 1994; Lappin & Love, 1992) or a surface of revolution (e.g., sphere and cylinder) rotating around its axis of symmetry. The metric structure of space can be derived in these cases from the congruence of the moving objects. In the more general case of objects rotating in depth, the structure of the image flow field changes over time with the changing orientation of the surface, and the intrinsic metric structure of the surface cannot be determined from the first-order temporal derivatives of the flow field. (Lappin, 1990, concluded incorrectly that metric structure could be obtained in this more general case, but such local metrification is possible only in the special case in which the motion is confined to a surface.)

In general, neither the extrinsic nor intrinsic metric shape of an object can be obtained from the local second-order image properties defined by first spatial derivatives in 2-D.

Deformations of fourth-order structure, however, carry local information about the qualitative or *affine shape*—characteristics of shape that remain invariant under affine transformations of the 3-D coordinates. Planar, parabolic, elliptic, and hyperbolic surface patches remain structurally distinct even under arbitrary stretching of the depth axis, for example. Schematic illustrations of the form of these fourth-order image deformations are shown in Figure 5 (see Koenderink & van Doorn, 1992a, for slightly different descriptions). Because these fourth-order image deformations are defined by difference relations among three points in any direction, they remain invariant even when an object moves in depth and alters the second-order image properties of pure shear, curl, and divergence.

These fourth-order image deformations are stable correlates of affine surface shape. They seem, therefore, potential forms of visible information about surface shape.

4. Boundary Contours

The surface of a solid object from an observer's perspective at a given instant consists of two sets of regions: the visible and the nonvisible. The visible regions are bounded in the image by *contours*, which are images of

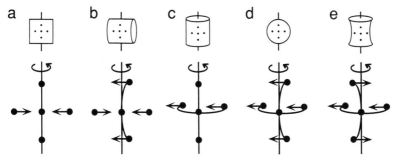

FIGURE 5 Schematic illustrations of fourth-order deformations produced by rotations in depth of five alternative surface shapes: (a) plane, (b) horizontal cylinder, (c) vertical cylinder, (d) ellipsoid, (e) saddle point. Surface curvature in the direction of rotation yields differential compression of the image of collinear surface points. Curvature perpendicular to the direction of rotation produces transverse shear in the image of quasi-collinear points aligned with the axis of rotation. (Adapted from Lappin et al., 1995, p. 146, with permission from MIT Press.)

points on the surface at which *visual rays* (vectors from the nodal point of the eye to points on the surface) are tangent to the surface. The inner product of the visual ray and the surface normal is zero at surface points projecting to the contour, and it is positive within the visible regions of the surface.[8] The boundary contours therefore provide important information about the shape of the object. The following brief discussion of this topic is taken from Koenderink (1987, 1990) and Koenderink and van Doorn (1976c, 1982), who provide more complete analyses and discussions.

The contours of smoothly curved surfaces exist in only five alternative local shapes, as illustrated in Figure 6: (1) a *convex arc,* which belongs to an elliptic surface patch; (2) a *concave arc,* which belongs to a hyperbolic patch; (3) an *inflection,* which belongs to a parabolic patch; (4) a *T-junction,* which occurs where one surface occludes another belonging to a separate part or to a separate object; and (5) an *ending contour,* which occurs in a hyperbolic patch where the direction of the rim of surface points corresponding to the contour coincides with the direction of the visual ray. Contour endings

---

[8] Note that the surface may contain other nonvisible points at which this inner product is positive and nonvisible points at which it is zero, which are hidden from view by nearer points of the surface. These nonvisible points at which the inner product of the visual ray and surface normal is greater than or equal to zero may be said to be "potentially visible" in that they belong to the same generic view of the object and may become actually visible by a small change in viewpoint that only changes the area of the same visible regions without changing the number of visible regions or the number of contours. These potentially visible points may be distinguished from other "invisible" points at which the inner product of the visual ray and surface normal is negative, meaning that the surface normal is pointed away from the image. If the object is convex everywhere, then the contour includes all the points at which the visual rays are tangent to the surface, and all potentially visible points are actually visible.

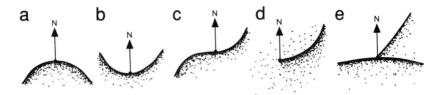

FIGURE 6   Five possible shapes of image contours of smooth objects. The shapes of corresponding surfaces are (a) elliptic, (b) hyperbolic, (c) parabolic, (d) hyperbolic, and (e) occlusion of one surface by another. (Adapted from Koenderink, 1987, p. 263, with permission from Ablex Publishing Corporation.)

occur only within hyperbolic patches, and contour ends are therefore always concave. Contours in drawings of artificial objects also often include long straight lines, which belong to a parabolic (cylindrical) surface or to a dihedral edge at the junction of two planar faces. With the exception of the T-junction, the sign of curvature of the contour equals the sign of Gaussian curvature of the surface patch. These correspondences between the shapes of contours and surfaces imply that contours constitute information about affine surface shape.

When the observer or the object moves, the rim of surface points projecting to image contours changes. These changes are informative about the surface shape. Sometimes these changes occur only within the same generic view, affecting only the extent, tilt, slant, and image area of the visible regions without altering the qualitative shape of the object's contours in the image. More generally, however, the contours may also undergo qualitative changes corresponding to the emergence of a new generic view. An entirely new visible region may appear, in which the surface normals previously pointed away from but now point toward the image; or an entire visible region may disappear, altering the number and curvatures of the contours. The potential sequences of these different generic views constitute a qualitative model of the whole object, describing the set of possible images that it affords. The alternative forms in which these contours appear, disappear, and change are described and discussed by Koenderink and van Doorn (1976c) and Koenderink (1987, 1990).

IV. FROM IMAGES TO PERCEPTIONS OF MOVING OBJECTS

The preceding review of image information raises two basic psychophysical issues. First, what spatial primitives carry visible information? Second, what information about object structure is visually acquired from the image information?

The answers to these questions are much less clear than one would expect from the extensive literature on perceiving structure from motion. The first question has seldom been recognized as an issue to be investigated. The spatial primitives have usually been taken for granted. Numerous experiments relevant to the second issue have been reported, but both the conception of issues and the experimental methods have shifted in recent years. Quantitative evaluations of the precision and reliability of discriminations of object structure have occurred mainly within the past few years, and several basic questions are currently under investigation and debate. The chapter by Todd in this volume reviews literature relative to this second question. This chapter focuses on the first question about visual primitives.

A. What Are the Visual Primitives?

Few experiments have directly addressed this issue, but several lines of indirect evidence indicate that visible information about spatial structure from motion is obtained mainly from deformations of second- or fourth-order primitives. This evidence comes from three groups of studies: (1) those in which perceived depth relations were found to be unreliable, (2) those in which perceived 3-D structure was found to be compelling and reliable, and (3) those specifically aimed at testing hypotheses about the visual primitives.

1. Differential Velocity Is Insufficient

Before the modern era of computer-controlled experiments on structure from motion, before the 1960s, researchers usually assumed that the visual primitives were points and that the essential stimulus for perceiving depth from motion was the differential velocity of neighboring points. Motion parallax, as in the images seen through the window of a moving train, was a paradigmatic illustration. Differential velocity of perceptually disconnected objects is insufficient, however.

One illustrative failure to obtain depth from motion parallax is described by Rock (1984, pp. 66–67). Spots mounted on three separate planes at different egocentric distances in depth were viewed by monocular observers who moved their heads from side to side to obtain motion parallax. Most observers reported seeing only variations in motion in a single plane. Similar results were obtained by Kottas (1978) when three vertically separated dots translated horizontally with different velocities and when these appeared subjectively as spatially disconnected. When observers reported that the dots appeared subjectively connected in depth, as vertices of a rotating triangle, then judgments were reliable about which of the three dots was between the other two, but discriminations of near versus far were uncorrelated with velocity. Similar results have been found when motion parallax is produced by images of textured surfaces superimposed in the frontal-parallel plane (Gibson, Gibson, Smith, & Flock, 1959). Judgments of the distance and even the order in depth have been quite variable, inconsistent with older ideas about depth from differential velocity.

2. Image Deformations of Connected Objects Are Necessary

When a moving pattern is seen as a connected surface, with image deformations of connected surface structure produced by either lateral motion parallax or object rotation in depth, then compelling subjective impressions and consistent judgments of 3-D structure have been found in many experiments (Braunstein, 1976; Todd, this volume). Although weak impressions of motion in depth can sometimes be obtained from changing velocities of a single point, these are neither compelling nor reliable and have not inspired experimental investigation. The image deformations of extended or perceptually connected features are evidently necessary.

3. First-Order Deformations

Relative motions that change the orientation and length of two-point structures are evidently sufficient though often not visually compelling, as shown in experimental analyses of two-dot patterns by Börjesson and von Hofsten (1972). They found that differential relative motions, changing the image distance between the two dots, were necessary but not sufficient for perceiving rigid structure and motion in 3-D. Concurrent contractions and expansions collinear with the imaginary line segment between the two dots were sometimes judged as motions in the image plane and other times as rigid translations in depth, rotations in depth, or combinations of translations and rotations in depth. Consistent judgments of rigid rotations in depth were produced only by concurrent relative motions that changed both the length and angle between the two dots.

The sufficiency of deformations of these first-order local primitives is also suggested by Johansson's (1973) demonstrations of perceived biological motion (see also Bertenthal, Proffitt, & Cutting, 1984; Blake, 1993). These complex motion patterns, however, also involve additional heirarchically synchronized common and relative motions of multiple structural components, and the coordination of these multiple components seems to carry visually salient global information. The visual effectiveness of these simple first-order deformations is also compatible with Wallach and O'Connell's (1953) demonstrations of kinetic depth from shadow-cast projections of rotating shapes of twisted wire.

Such first-order deformations may be visually sufficient, but this does not imply that deformations of second- and fourth-order spatial primitives do not also carry visible information. Vision may well be more sensitive to these higher order deformations.

4. Differential Compressions of 1-D Second-Order Structure

Changes in the relative 1-D spacing among three or more image features may carry information about the intrinsic surface structure in two different ways, one of which is evidently visually effective and the other may not be.

a. Isometry under Motion over a Surface

When the spatial separations among three collinear features represent local surface distances that remain isometric under motion over a surface in 3-D, then vision is sensitive to the deforming image separations as information about the surface distances among these three points. Lappin and Fuqua (1983) displayed three collinear dots rotating in the image as if on a plane slanted in depth around the horizontal axis. The Weber fraction for discriminating whether the center dot bisected the 3-D distance between the outer two dots was only about 2.5%, independently of the slant in depth. The patterns were displayed with strong polar perspective so that bisection in the slanted plane did not correspond to bisection in the image plane. The visual information was evidently based on the second- rather than first-order relations among these points because when the center dot did bisect the image separation in these perspective displays, the center dot appeared to change its position along the imaginary line as it rotated in depth, and observers were inaccurate in discriminating bisection of the image separation.

The perceived spatial relations in this experiment must have involved the visual derivation of a space defined by congruence under rotation over a plane in depth (see Lappin, 1990; Lappin & Ahlström, 1994; Lappin & Love, 1992; Lappin & Wason, 1993). The changing 3-D directions of the rotating object seem to induce an isometric scale common to these multiple directions. The same form of information for scaling space from congruence under motion also seems to be effective as a basis for perceiving the metric structure of 2-D shapes rotating in a slanted plane (Lappin & Ahlström, 1994; Lappin & Love, 1992). Observers are not very reliable, however, in judging the extrinsic slant of the implicit surface relative to the image plane.

b. Curved Surfaces Rotating in Depth

A much more common situation that produces differential compressions of 1-D image separations occurs when a curved surface rotates in depth so that the direction of image motion coincides with the direction of surface curvature (see Figures 5C, 5D, and 5E). Available evidence suggests that this form of information does not constitute a visual primitive, however. Lappin, Ahlström, Craft, & Tschantz (1995) tested whether detection of these second-order deformations was derived from first-order expansions. Simple five-dot patterns like those in Figure 5 underwent rapid random jittering motions which included random rotations in depth around a vertical axis. Observers discriminated cylindrical versus planar surfaces (Figures 5A vs. 5C) on the basis of the presence or the absence of differential compression. Detectability of these deformations was found to be masked by extraneous noisy first-order expansions, indicating that detection of the second-order deformations was derived from perceived differences in first-order expansions. A limitation of this study, however, was that these simple patterns and small random motions were not perceived as motions of surfaces in depth.

Evidence from studies with densely dotted surfaces that yield compelling impressions of rigid rotation in depth also indicates that vision is relatively insensitive to this form of deformation: Surface curvature is much less detectable in the direction of image motion than in the perpendicular direction (Cornilleau-Pérès & Droulez, 1989; Norman & Lappin, 1992; Rogers & Graham, 1983). Cornilleau-Pérès and Droulez and Norman and Lappin found that anisotropies in detecting and discriminating curved surfaces were quantitatively attributable to the magnitude of transverse shear (described in the next section), with little or no effect of differential compression.

5. Shearing Deformations of 2-D Second-Order Structure

Images of local patches on textured surfaces undergo shearing deformations when the surface rotates in depth. The best known case involves pure-shear deformations of the image shape defined by spatial relations among at least three neighboring points. An important special case of this class of deformations involves transverse shear in the positions of three quasi-collinear points aligned in a direction perpendicular to the image motion.

a. Pure-Shear Deformations of Image Shape

Koenderink and van Doorn (1975, 1976a; Koenderink, 1986) showed that deformations of second-order structure in 2-D patches corresponded to changes in the 3-D orientation of the local surface patch. Although this form of image information is now well-known, little psychophysical evidence assesses its effectiveness as a potential visual primitive.

Börjesson and von Hofsten (1973) studied the perceived structure and motion of a systematic range of three-dot motion patterns and found that nearly all of these patterns evoked reports of triangular shaped objects moving rigidly in 3-D space. Essentially all of the six possible rigid translations and rotations in 3-D space could be produced by vector combinations of in-phase motions converging (diverging) toward a point or a line, indicating that vision performs a type of 3-D vector analysis on the coherent motions of these structures. The visibility of this form of information suggests that it might be a visual primitive.

Contrasting evidence that vision is less sensitive to these pure-shear de-formations than to other forms of relative motion has been obtained in two more recent studies. Börjesson and Ahlström (1993) found that parallel relative motions, which produce pure shear and perceived rotation in depth around an axis in the image plane, were less effective in producing percep-tual grouping than other forms of motion in three-dot patterns involving translation, rotation, or divergence in the image plane. Lappin, Norman, and Mowafy (1991) also found that the detectability of coherent structure defined by pure-shear deformations was masked by coherent translations, rotations, or divergence that were added as independent vector components in randomly jittering motions of various multidot patterns. This evidence suggests that perception of these pure-shear deformations might be derived from other more primitive motions.

b. Transverse Shear of Quasi-Collinear Points

A visually important special case of these shearing deformations occurs to the image of three quasi-collinear texture points aligned on a curved surface when the surface rotates in depth perpendicularly to the alignment of the three points, thereby altering the image alignment of the points (see Figures 5B, 5D, and 5E). This may be the most effective carrier of visual informa-tion about shape from motion.

Cornilleau-Pérès and Droulez (1989) and Norman and Lappin (1992) found that magnitudes of this deformation could account quantitatively for detections and discriminations of surface curvature. Lappin et al. (1995) tested whether these second-order deformations were directly detectable or derived from perceived differences in first-order image rotations (curl) or zero-order translations. Small magnitudes of these second-order deforma-tions were found to be readily detectable, approximately independent of added extraneous noise in the zero- and first-order structure produced by random translations and rotations. This form of second-order deformation provides information about surface curvature and might be sufficient to account for most perceptions of the affine shape of textured surfaces rotat-ing in depth.

An independent suggestion that this form of information may serve as a visual primitive is provided by the finding in Julesz's research program that quasi-collinearity is a visual primitive for perceiving static textures (e.g., Caelli & Julesz, 1978; Caelli et al., 1978; Julesz, 1981).

6. Deformations of Fourth-Order Structure

The deformations of fourth-order structure as illustrated in Figure 5 consti-tute image information about the shapes of images of surfaces rotating in depth. Because shape information is provided by these image deformations, vision seems likely to be sensitive to this information. Evidence to support this hypothesis is not now available, however. These fourth-order deformations are composed of two second-order deformations: differential compressions in the direction of image motion (see Figure 5C), and transverse shear of points aligned perpendicular to the image motion (see Figure 5B). As noted above, the results of Lappin et al. (in press) and the substantially lower visibility of surface curvature in the direction of image rotation both indicate that the differential compressions are not directly visible as visual primitives. This same evidence suggests that fourth-order deformations do not constitute visual primitives, although currently available evidence does not rule out this possibility.

7. Boundary Contours

Several recent experiments (see Todd, this volume) demonstrate that the image deformations of contours of rotating objects are usually sufficient to produce perceived solid objects rotating in depth. The shapes defined this way often appear nonrigid, however and are often inaccurately discriminated. The few experimental studies of this problem have not yet provided a comprehensive study of visual sensitivity to the variety of contour shapes and contour deformations and changes that Koenderink and van Doorn (1976c) and Koenderink (1987, 1990) have described. Precisely how this form of local information about object shape is combined with other information about surface shape in the interior regions of the image is not well studied nor well understood. The textureless silhouettes used in experiments on perceiving shape from the contours of rotating objects might provide conflicting information about shape and curvature at the interior regions of the image. Generally speaking, too little psychophysical evidence is available to evaluate the visual information obtained from local contour deformations or to judge which specific image properties might serve as primitive forms of such visible information.

8. Summary Comments about Primitive Forms of Visible Information

This review of psychophysical evidence about the visibility of local image information does not permit a definitive identification of the local visual primitives. Much of the evidence is only suggestive, primarily because this issue has seldom explicitly been addressed. Three general statements seem justified, however. (1) The primitive forms of visible information are probably of more than one type, perhaps detected by more than one form of local operator. (2) Available evidence provides clearest support for 2-D second-order operators sensitive to quasi-collinearity. (3) Additional investigation of this fundamental issue is needed.

B. Perceiving Intrinsic and Local versus Extrinsic and Global Space

Recent research on perceiving structure from motion suggests a change in the conception of visual space. Space has traditionally been conceived as an extrinsic and global framework in terms of which the structure and motion of objects may be described. This conception is inadequate for understanding either the nature of local image information or its visibility. It has also led to confusions about the perception of space, motion, and shape.

A basic notion needed for describing image information and mechanisms that detect it involves the differential structure of spatial patterns. Differential geometry permits local descriptions of the intrinsic structure of surfaces and images. Image motion provides information primarily by deforming the space-differential structure of the image, and these image deformations probably provide visible information mainly about affine surface shape. Perception of both the surface slant and the scale of the depth axis is often incorrect and unreliable.

The conception of space indicated by this differential geometric description of surfaces, images, and motions is one in which space is induced by the shapes and motions it contains. Vision is evidently adept in deriving such spaces to describe shapes and motions within a restricted local region—as illustrated by everyday perceptions of structure in photographs, cinema, and other such pictorial illustrations (e.g., Figure 2). The visual space that describes one object may be somewhat independent of the space of another, and both may be structured more fully than the empty space between them. Little is now known, however, about the visual relations among neighboring local spaces and among local and global spaces.

These comments are necessarily a bit speculative. Current experimental evidence is insufficient. Recent evidence indicates that visual space can be scaled in certain cases by congruence of moving objects. The generality of the conditions under which this phenomenon may be effective and the limitations on its effectiveness are not now known, however.

V. CONCLUSION

The impressive quality and quantity of information obtained by vision from moving images might be explained in part by the hypothesis that the local structure and deformations of the image constitute visible information about surface shape.

Acknowledgments

Preparation of this chapter was supported in part by National Institutes of Health Vision Core Grant P30EY08126. I am grateful to Warren Craft for comments on drafts, discussion of theoretical issues, and help in preparing illustrations.

196   Joseph S. Lappin

References

Adelson, E. H., & Bergen, J. R. (1991). The plenoptic function and the elements of early vision. In M. S. Landy & J. A. Movshon (Eds.), *Computational models of visual processing* (pp. 3–20). Cambridge, MA: MIT Press.

Bertenthal, B. I., Proffitt, D. R., & Cutting, J. E. (1984). Infant sensitivity to figural coherence in biomechanical motions. *Journal of Experimental Child Psychology, 37*, 213–230.

Blake, R. (1993). Cats perceive biological motion. *Psychological Science, 4*, 54–57.

Börjesson, E., & Ahlström, U. (1993). Motion structure in five-dot patterns as a determinant of perceptual grouping. *Perception & Psychophysics, 53*, 2–12.

Börjesson, E., & von Hofsten, C. (1972). Spatial determinants of depth perception in two-dot motion patterns. *Perception & Psychophysics, 11*, 263–268.

Börjesson, E., & von Hofsten, C. (1973). Visual perception of motion in depth: Application of a vector model to three-dot motion experiments. *Perception & Psychophysics, 13*, 169–179.

Braunstein, M. L. (1976). *Depth perception through motion.* New York: Academic Press.

Caelli, T., & Julesz, B. (1978). On perceptual analyzers underlying visual texture discrimination: Part I. *Biological Cybernetics, 28*, 167–175.

Caelli, T., Julesz, B., & Gilbert, E. (1978). On perceptual analyzers underlying visual texture discrimination: Part II. *Biological Cybernetics, 29*, 201–214.

Cornilleau-Pérès, V., & Droulez, J. (1989). Visual perception of surface curvature: Psychophysics of curvature detection induced by motion parallax. *Perception & Psychophysics, 46*, 351–364.

Cutting, J. E. (1987). Rigidity in cinema seen from front row, side aisle. *Journal of Experimental Psychology: Human Perception and Performance, 13*, 323–334.

De Valois, R. L., & De Valois, K. K. (1988). *Spatial Vision.* New York: Oxford University Press.

Durgin, F. H., Proffitt, D. R., Olson, T. J., & Reinke, K. S. (in press). Comparing depth from binocular disparity to depth from motion. *Journal of Experimental Psychology: Human Perception and Performance.*

Fechner, G. (1966). *Elements of psychophysics.* (H. E. Adler, Trans., D. H. Howes & E. G. Boring, Eds.) New York: Holt, Rinehart and Winston. (Original work published in 1860.)

Garner, W. R. (1962). *Uncertainty and structure as psychological concepts.* New York: Wiley.

Garner, W. R. (1974). *The processing of information and structure.* Hillsdale, NJ: Erlbaum.

Gibson, E. J., Gibson, J. J., Smith, O. W., & Flock, H. (1959). Motion parallax as a determinant of perceived depth. *Journal of Experimental Psychology, 58*, 40–51.

Gibson, J. J. (1950). *The perception of the visual world.* Boston: Houghton Mifflin.

Gibson, J. J. (1966). *The senses considered as perceptual systems.* Boston: Houghton Mifflin.

Gilden, D. L., Schmuckler, M. A., & Clayton, K. N. (1993). The perception of natural contour. *Psychological Review, 100*, 460–478.

Gray, A. (1993). *Modern differential geometry of curves and surfaces.* Boca Raton, FL: CRC Press.

Helmholtz, H. von (1925). *Handbook of physiological optics* (Vol. 3, J. P. C. Southall, Trans.). (Original work published in 1867) New York: Dover.

Hildreth, E. C. (1984a). Computations underlying the measurement of visual motion. *Artificial Intelligence, 23*, 309–354.

Hildreth, E. C. (1984b). *The measurement of visual motion.* Cambridge, MA: MIT Press.

Hoffman, D. D., & Flinchbaugh, B. E. (1982). The interpretation of biological motion. *Biological Cybernetics, 42*, 195–204.

Hyman, R. (1953). Stimulus information as a determinant of reaction time. *Journal of Experimental Psychology, 45*, 188–196.

Johansson, G. (1973). Visual perception of biological motion and a model for its analysis. *Perception & Psychophysics, 14*, 201–211.

Johnston, E. B., Cumming, B. G., & Landy, M. S. (1994). Integration of stereopsis and motion shape cues. *Vision Research, 34,* 2259–2275.

Julesz, B. (1981). Textons, the elements of texture perception, and their interactions. *Nature, 290,* 91–97.

Julesz, B. (1984). Toward an axiomatic theory of preattentive vision. In G. M. Edelman, W. E. Gall, & W. M. Cowan (Eds.), *Dynamic aspects of neocortical function* (pp. 585–612). New York: Wiley.

Julesz, B., Gilbert, E. N., & Victor, J. D. (1978). Visual discrimination of textures with identical third-order statistics. *Biological Cybernetics, 31,* 137–140.

Koenderink, J. J. (1984). The structure of images. *Biological Cybernetics, 50,* 363–370.

Koenderink, J. J. (1986). Optic flow. *Vision Research, 26,* 161–179.

Koenderink, J. J. (1987). An internal representation for solid shape based on the topological properties of the apparent contour. In W. Richards & S. Ullman (Eds.), *Image understanding 1985–86* (pp. 257–285). Norwood, NJ: Ablex.

Koenderink, J. J. (1990). *Solid shape.* Cambridge, MA: MIT Press.

Koenderink, J. J., & van Doorn, A. J. (1975). Invariant properties of the motion parallax field due to the movement of rigid bodies relative to the observer. *Optica Acta, 22,* 773–791.

Koenderink, J. J., & van Doorn, A. J. (1976a). Local structure of movement parallax of the plane. *Journal of the Optical Society of America, 66,* 717–723.

Koenderink, J. J., & van Doorn, A. J. (1976b). Geometry of binocular vision and a model for stereopsis. *Biological Cybernetics, 21,* 29–35.

Koenderink, J. J., & van Doorn, A. J. (1976c). The singularities of the visual mapping. *Biological Cybernetics, 24,* 51–59.

Koenderink, J. J., & van Doorn, A. J. (1977). How an ambulant observer can construct a model of the environment from the geometrical structure of the visual inflow. In G. Hauske & E. Butenandt (Eds.), *Kybernetik.* Munich: Oldenberg.

Koenderink, J. J., & van Doorn, A. J. (1979). The internal representation of solid shape with respect to vision. *Biological Cybernetics, 32,* 211–216.

Koenderink, J. J., & van Doorn, A. J. (1980). Photometric invariants related to solid shape. *Optica Acta, 27,* 981–996.

Koenderink, J. J., & van Doorn, A. J. (1982). The shape of smooth objects and the way contours end. *Perception, 11,* 129–137.

Koenderink, J. J., & van Doorn, A. J. (1986). Dynamic shape. *Biological Cybernetics, 53,* 383–396.

Koenderink, J. J., & van Doorn, A. J. (1992a). Generic neighborhood operators. *IEEE Transactions on Pattern Analysis and Machine Intelligence, 14,* 597–605.

Koenderink, J. J., & van Doorn, A. J. (1992b). Second-order optic flow. *Journal of the Optical Society of America, A, 9,* 530–538.

Koenderink, J. J., & van Doorn, A. J. (1993a). Illuminance critical points on generic smooth surfaces. *Journal of the Optical Society of America, A, 10,* 844–854.

Koenderink, J. J., & van Doorn, A. J. (1993b). Local features of smooth shapes: Ridges and courses. In B. C. Vemuri (Eds.), *Geometric methods in computer vision II* (pp. 13). Belingham, Washington: SPIE.

Kottas, B. L. (1978). *Visual three-dimensional information from motion.* Unpublished doctoral dissertation, Vanderbilt University.

Krantz, D. H., Luce, R. D., Suppes, P., & Tversky, A. (1971). *Foundations of measurement, Volume 1.* New York: Academic Press.

Lappin, J. S. (1990). Perceiving the metric structure of environmental objects from motion, self-motion, and stereopsis. In R. Warren & A. H. Wertheim (Eds.), *Perception and control of self-motion* (pp. 541–547). Hillsdale, NJ: Erlbaum.

Lappin, J. S. (1994). Seeing structure in space-time. In G. Jansson, S. S. Bergström, & W. Epstein (Eds.), *Perceiving events and objects* (pp. 357–382). Hillsdale, NJ: Erlbaum.

Lappin, J. S., & Ahlström, U. B. (1994). On the scaling of visual space from motion: In response to Pizlo and Salach-Golyska. *Perception & Psychophysics, 55*, 235–242.

Lappin, J. S., Ahlström, U. B., Craft, W. D., & Tschantz, S. T. (1995). Spatial primitives for seeing 3D shape from motion. In T. Papathomas, C. Chubb, A. Gorea, & E. Kowler (Eds.), *Early vision and beyond.* (pp. 145–153). Cambridge, MA: MIT Press.

Lappin, J. S., & Fuqua, M. A. (1983). Accurate visual measurement of three-dimensional moving patterns. *Science, 221,* 480–482.

Lappin, J. S., & Love, S. R. (1992). Planar motion permits perception of metric structure in stereopsis. *Perception & Psychophysics, 51,* 86–102.

Lappin, J. S., Norman, J. F., & Mowafy, L. (1991). The detectability of geometric structure in rapidly changing optical patterns. *Perception, 20,* 513–528.

Lappin, J. S., & Wason, T. D. (1993). The perception of structure from congruence. In S. R. Ellis, M. K. Kaiser, & A. C. Grunwald (Eds.), *Pictorial communication in virtual and real environments* (pp. 425–448). London: Taylor & Francis.

Lipschutz, M. M. (1969). *Differential geometry.* New York: McGraw Hill.

Mandelbrot, B. B. (1983). *The fractal geometry of nature.* San Francisco: Freeman.

Marr, D. (1982). *Vision.* San Francisco: Freeman.

Marr, D., & Ullman, S. (1981). Directional selectivity and its use in early visual processing. *Proceedings of the Royal Society of London, B, 211,* 150–180.

Marroquin, J. M. S., & Poggio, T. (1987). Probabilistic solution of ill-posed problems in computational vision. *Journal of the American Statistical Association, 82,* 76–89.

Miller, G. A. (1956). The magical number seven, plus or minus two. *Psychological Review, 63,* 81–97.

Norman, F., & Todd, J. T. (1993). The perceptual analysis of structure from motion for rotating objects undergoing affine stretching transformations. *Perception & Psychophysics, 53,* 279–291.

Norman, J. F. (1990). *The perception of curved surfaces defined by optical motion.* Unpublished doctoral dissertation, Vanderbilt University.

Norman, J. F., & Lappin, J. S. (1992). The detection of surface curvatures defined by optical motion. *Perception & Psychophysics, 51,* 386–396.

Norman, J. F., Lappin, J. S., & Zucker, S. W. (1991). The discriminability of smooth stereoscopic surfaces. *Perception, 20,* 789–807.

Poggio, T., Torre, V., & Koch, C. (1985). Computational vision and regularization theory. *Nature, 317,* 314–319.

Rock, I. (1984). *Perception.* New York: Scientific American Books/Freeman.

Rogers, B. J., & Graham, M. E. (1983). Anisotropies in the perception of three-dimensional surfaces. *Science, 221,* 1409–1411.

Saidpour, A., Braunstein, M. L., & Hoffman, D. D. (1992). Interpolation in structure from motion. *Perception & Psychophysics, 51,* 105–117.

Shannon, C. E., & Weaver, W. (1949). The mathematical theory of communication. In *The mathematical theory of communication,* pp. 3–91. Urbana, IL: University of Illinois Press. (Original work published in 1948.)

Simpson, W. A. (1993). Optic flow and depth perception. *Spatial Vision, 7,* 35–75.

Stevenson, S. B., Cormack, L. K., & Schor, C. M. (1989). Hyperacuity, superresolution and gap resolution in human stereopsis. *Vision Research, 29,* 1597–1605.

Tittle, J. S., Todd, J. T., Perotti, V. J., & Norman, J. F. (in press). The systematic distortion of perceived 3-D structure from motion and binocular stereopsis. *Journal of Experimental Psychology: Human Perception and Performance.*

Todd, J. T., & Norman, J. F. (1991). The perception of smoothly curved surfaces from minimal apparent motion sequences. *Perception & Psychophysics, 50,* 509–523.

Ullman, S. (1979). *The interpretation of visual motion.* Cambridge, MA: MIT Press.

Wallach, H., & O'Connell, D. (1953). The kinetic depth effect. *Journal of Experimental Psychology, 45,* 205–217.

Wason, T. D. (1993). *Construction and evaluation of a three-dimensional display from a two-dimensional projection surface based on theoretical considerations of metrification and affine space,* Unpublished doctoral dissertation, North Carolina State University.

Wiener, N. (1948). *Cybernetics, or control and communication in the animal and the machine.* Cambridge, MA: MIT Press.

Wiener, N. (1954). *The human use of human beings: Cybernetics and society (2nd ed.).* Garden City, NY: Doubleday.

CHAPTER 6

The Visual Perception of Three-Dimensional Structure from Motion

James T. Todd

One of the most perplexing phenomena in the study of human vision is the ability of observers to perceive the three-dimensional (3-D) layout of the environment from patterns of light that project onto the retina. Indeed, were it not for the facts of our day-to-day experiences, it would be tempting to conclude that the perception of 3-D form is a mathematical impossibility because the properties of optical stimulation appear to have so little in common with the properties of real objects encountered in nature. Whereas real objects exist in 3-D space and are composed of tangible substances such as earth, metal, or flesh; an optical image of an object is confined to a two-dimensional (2-D) projection surface and consists of nothing more than flickering patterns of light. Nevertheless, for many animals including humans these seemingly uninterpretable patterns of light are the primary source of sensory information about the layout of objects and surfaces in the surrounding environment.

There are many different aspects of optical stimulation that are known to provide perceptually salient information about an object's 3-D form. Some of these properties—the so-called pictorial depth cues—are available within individual static images. These include texture gradients, linear perspective, and patterns of shading. Others are defined by the systematic transformations among multiple images, including the disparity between each eye's view in binocular vision and the optical deformations that occur when objects are observed in motion.

This chapter is designed to review our current knowledge about how observers are able to perceive an object's 3-D structure from image motion. The chapter is organized into several parts: It provides (1) a formal analysis of the specific patterns of optical transformations that are produced by different types of rigid body motions, (2) a historical overview of various factors that can influence observers' perceptions of structure from motion, (3) a summary of existing computational models of how image motion could theoretically be analyzed, (4) a review of current psychophysical evidence about the psychological validity of these models, and (5) a discussion of several issues that remain for future research.

I. OPTICAL PROJECTION

To appreciate existing research and theory on the visual perception of structure from motion, it is first necessary to consider how the physical motions of objects in 3-D space influence the patterns of optical stimulation at a point of observation. The top portion of Figure 1 shows the geometry that arises when an observer views a set of points in 3-D space through a planar projection surface (i.e., a window). The position of a point $\mathbf{P}(x, y, z)$ at any given instant of time (t) can be defined within a Cartesian coordinate system, whose origin is located at the point of observation, and whose z-axis is parallel to the line of sight. If the image plane is located a unit distance from the origin along the z-axis, then the projected position $\mathbf{P}'(x', y')$ of the point is defined by the following equations:

$$x' = x / z \tag{1}$$

and

$$y' = y / z \cdot \tag{2}$$

If the point has an instantaneous velocity $\mathbf{V}(dx/dt, dy/dt, dz/dt)$, then its projected velocity $\mathbf{V}'$ $(dx'/dt, dy'/dt)$ in the image plane is given by

$$dx'/dt = \frac{dx/dt}{z} - \frac{x(dz/dt)}{z^2} \tag{3}$$

and

$$dy'/dt = \frac{dy/dt}{z} - \frac{y(dz/dt)}{z^2}. \tag{4}$$

The geometry shown in the upper portion of Figure 1 is often referred to as *polar or central projection* because the rays connecting each visible point in 3-D space with its corresponding point in the image plane all converge at

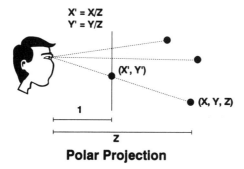

Polar Projection

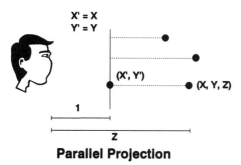

Parallel Projection

FIGURE 1   Two types of optical projection used in the analysis of structure from motion.

the point of observation. This geometry is appropriate to model almost any situation in natural vision. The lower portion of Figure 1 shows another alternative geometry called *parallel or orthographic projection* that is a reasonable approximation to natural vision whenever an observed object's extension in depth is relatively small in comparison to its distance from the observer. When using parallel projection, the image plane positions $\mathbf{P}'$ and velocities $\mathbf{V}'$ are defined by the following equations:

$$x' = x \tag{5}$$

$$y' = y \tag{6}$$

$$dx'/dt = dx / dt \tag{7}$$

$$dy'/dt = dy / dt. \tag{8}$$

Note in Figure 1 that if the depicted configuration of points under polar projection were moved farther and farther from the point of observation, the angular difference between their visual directions would become closer and closer to zero, and the resulting optical pattern would become a closer and closer approximation to a true parallel projection. One way of quantifying the appropriateness of this approximation is to measure the perspective ratio of an object's extension in depth relative to its distance from the observer (cf. Braunstein, 1962). As a general rule of thumb, any observed object with a perspective ratio smaller than 0.1 can for all practical purposes be considered as a parallel projection.

Figure 2 shows the patterns of optical motion produced by different types of rigid body motions under both parallel and polar projection. Let us first consider the case of rigid translation. Note in Figure 2 that the projected motion of an object translating under parallel projection provides no information about the object's 3-D form. In the special case of translation in depth there is no optical motion at all, and in all other cases the optical motion is identical for every point, regardless of its position in depth (see Equations 7 and 8). For objects translating under polar projection, however, there is potentially useful information available from the relative image motion of different points. As is evident from Equations 3 and 4, the optical velocities under polar projection are scaled by their positions in depth such that far away points produce slower projected velocities than do points that are closer to the observer. For components of translation perpendicular to

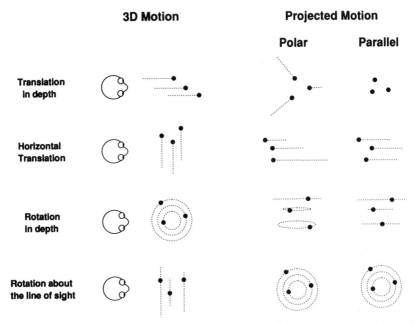

FIGURE 2   The optical projections produced by several different types of rigid body motions.

the line of sight, this produces a pattern of parallel velocities in the image plane whose magnitudes vary as a function of depth. For components of translation that are parallel to the line of sight, this produces an overall image expansion for translations toward the observer and an overall image compression for translations away from the observer. Such variations of image velocity as a function of depth are often referred to as *motion parallax*.

The analysis of rigid body rotations is somewhat more complicated than the analysis of translation. For objects rotating about fixed axes, each point **P'** in the image plane will move in an elliptical trajectory whose minor axis coincides with the optical projection of the axis of rotation (see Todd, 1982). The eccentricities of these elliptical trajectories are determined by the slant of the rotation axis with respect to the image plane. For parallel projections, the trajectories of every point will all have the same eccentricity; whereas for polar projections, the eccentricities will vary monotonically along the axis of rotation. For both types of projection, the image plane velocity **V'** is determined by the distance of a point in depth from the axis of rotation. The velocity reaches a maximum in one direction when a point is at its closest position to the observer in depth, and it reaches a maximum in the opposite direction when it is farthest away in depth. A degenerate case of rotary motion can occur when the axis of rotation is coincident with the line of sight. All of the image points in that case move along circular trajectories, and their relative instantaneous velocities are mathematically unrelated to an object's 3-D structure.

II. METHODOLOGICAL ISSUES

A. Display Generation

The importance of motion for the visual perception of 3-D form was discussed anecdotally in the writings of Mach (1886/1962) and Helmholtz (1867/1925), but a more systematic scientific investigation of this phenomenon did not occur until much later. To pursue such an investigation, it was first necessary to develop appropriate technologies for isolating the effects of optical flow from other potential sources of information such as shading, texture, or binocular disparity. The earliest experiments on the visual perception of structure from motion used a shadow projection technique to satisfy this requirement (e.g., Flock, 1964; Gibson & Gibson, 1957; Metzger, 1934; Fieandt & Gibson, 1959; Wallach & O'Connell, 1953; White & Mueser, 1960). Objects were placed on a moving track or turntable between a light source and a translucent display screen. Naive observers on the other side of the screen were then asked to report their subjective impressions while viewing the optical deformations of the objects' projected shadows. The most systematic investigation of this type was performed by

Wallach and O'Connell, who used shadows cast by a wide variety of objects on a rotating turntable. For many of these displays, observers spontaneously reported the perception of solid objects rotating in depth. Wallach and O'Connell named this phenomenon the *kinetic depth effect,* which is sometimes abbreviated in the literature as KDE.

In the early 1960s a new technology was invented that allowed researchers to create images of 3-D objects on a computer-controlled cathode ray tube. This technology was exploited almost immediately to study the perception of structure from motion in a pioneering series of experiments by Green (1961), Braunstein (1962, 1966, 1968), and Johansson (1964). When computer graphics first became available, the creation of 3-D motion displays was a rather arduous process. Because laboratory computers in the 1960s were not fast enough to simulate and display complicated 3-D motions in real time, each frame of the motion sequence was photographed individually so that the sequence could be played back in an experimental setting by using a standard motion picture projector. As computer technology has advanced, however, this limitation has long since vanished, and most modern research in this area is now performed by using real-time displays.

B. Response Tasks

There are several different response tasks that have been used over the years to assess observers' perceptions of 3-D structure from motion. In many of the earliest experiments on this topic, observers were simply asked to report their subjective experiences while viewing various types of moving displays (e.g., Gibson & Gibson, 1957; Metzger, 1934; Fieandt & Gibson, 1959; Wallach & O'Connell, 1953; White & Mueser, 1960). This is a good "quick and dirty" method to reveal qualitative aspects of an observer's perceptions, but it cannot provide precise quantitative information about an object's perceived shape or the nature of its perceived motion. Other common response tasks that are designed to overcome this difficulty include magnitude estimations of specific 3-D properties such as depth or slant or rating the perceived rigidity or coherence of an object's motion (e.g., Braunstein, 1962, 1966, 1968; Gibson & Gibson, 1957; Green, 1961). More recent investigations have also used discrimination procedures to measure how accurately observers can distinguish rigid from nonrigid motion (e.g., Todd, 1982; Braunstein, Hoffman, & Pollick, 1990) or to detect small differences in various aspects of 3-D structure (e.g., Braunstein, Hoffman, Shapiro, Andersen, & Bennett, 1987; Norman & Lappin, 1992; Todd & Bressan, 1990; Todd & Norman, 1991).

One important issue that needs to be considered in selecting a response task is the extent to which it encourages observers to rely on artifactual sources of information (Braunstein & Todd, 1990; Sperling, Landy, Dosher, & Perkins, 1989). This is especially true for experiments that use discrimination procedures with response feedback. Suppose, for example, that observers are shown two objects oscillating back and forth about a vertical axis and are asked to discriminate which one has the largest extension in depth. If both objects rotate at the same angular velocity, then their relative extensions in depth will covary linearly with the relative range of their projected image velocities. Thus, with the benefit of immediate response feedback, an observer could potentially learn to perform this task accurately, without knowing anything about the relative 3-D structures of the depicted objects. One way of revealing if observers' judgments are based on artifactual sources of information is to ask them to describe their strategies for performing the experimental task. A better technique, however, is to identify these potential artifacts in advance and to systematically control for them. In the experiment described above, for example, the covariation between depth and image velocity can be eliminated by having the objects rotate at different angular velocities.

III. GENERAL FACTORS THAT CAN AFFECT PERCEIVED THREE-DIMENSIONAL STRUCTURE FROM MOTION

A. Different Types of Motion

In the four decades that have elapsed since Wallach and O'Connell (1953) first reported their experiments on the kinetic depth effect, numerous other researchers have investigated how observers' perceptions of moving displays are influenced by a wide variety of stimulus variables. One important class of variables that has been studied extensively involves the specific nature of an object's depicted motion. It has been shown, for example, that observers' perceptions can be influenced significantly by the orientation of an object's axis of rotation (Green, 1961; Loomis & Eby, 1988, 1989; Todd, 1982). Ratings of depth and rigidity are highest for axes that are parallel to the image plane and are reduced significantly for axes that are precessing or slanted in depth. Indeed, when the axis of rotation is at its most extreme possible slant such that it is coincident with the line of sight, a projected pattern of rotary motion generally produces no impression of 3-D structure whatsoever. The one exception to this general rule occurs for image plane rotations of closed concentric contours, which can produce a compelling illusion of a moving 3-D object (Musatti, 1924; Proffitt, Rock, Hecht, & Shubert, 1992; Wallach, Weisz, & Adams, 1956; Zanforlin, 1988). This phenomenon is often referred to as the *stereokinetic effect*.

There are several other aspects of an object's motion that can also influence observers' perceptions of its 3-D structure. For example, the amount of perceived depth for a rotating object tends to increase with angular velocity (Todd & Norman, 1991) or the angular extent of rotation (Loomis & Eby, 1988, 1989; Liter, Braunstein, & Hoffman, 1994). Similarly, the perceived rigidity or coherence of an object can vary significantly with the length of an apparent motion sequence and the timing between each frame (Todd, Akerstrom, Reichel, & Hayes, 1988; Todd & Bressan, 1990; Todd & Norman, 1991). For minimal apparent motion sequences consisting of only two frames presented in alternation, perceived rigidity is greatest when there are relatively long time intervals of about 200 ms between each frame transition. As the length of an apparent motion sequence is increased, however, the optimal time interval can be reduced to as low as 50 ms or less.

B. Perspective

Another important stimulus factor that can influence the perception of structure from motion is the amount of perspective used to create the experimental displays (Braunstein, 1966; Dosher, Landy, & Sperling, 1989; Todd, 1984). Objects viewed with high levels of perspective appear to have a greater extension in depth than those viewed under parallel projection. If the perspective is larger than what is appropriate for the actual viewing distance, then objects may sometimes appear to distort nonrigidly as they rotate. For motion parallax displays of objects undergoing translation, perspective is necessary to get any perceived depth at all. Perspective can also have an effect on the perceived direction of rotation (Andersen & Braunstein, 1983; Braunstein, 1977a; Braunstein, Andersen, & Riefer, 1982). For objects viewed under parallel projection the direction of rotation is completely ambiguous, unless other information is available such as the accretion or deletion of texture at occlusion boundaries. Under strong polar perspective, however, the true direction of rotation can perceptually be specified by the image plane velocity differences between near and far surface regions.

C. Structural Configuration

Still another important class of variables that can influence the perception of structure from motion includes specific aspects of a depicted object's structural configuration (Braunstein, 1962; Dosher et al., 1989; Green, 1961; Petersik, 1980; Todd et al., 1988). For example, it has been reported that patterns of connected lines produce greater perceived coherence than patterns of random dots and that opaque surfaces appear more coherent than volumes or transparent surfaces. Increasing the number of moving elements can increase perceived coherence up to a point, but coherence can break down for very large numbers of elements on transparent surfaces or in random volumes, probably because of difficulties in matching elements over time.

An object's perceived 3-D structure can also be affected by how it is oriented in space. Research has demonstrated that the perception of surface curvature exhibits a large anisotropy with respect to how an object is oriented relative to the direction of rotation. Observers are most sensitive to curved surfaces when they are curved in a direction parallel to the axis of rotation, (Cornilleau-Pérès, & Droulez, 1989; Norman & Lappin, 1992). Similarly, other experiments have shown that object discriminations and magnitude estimates of perceived shape can dramatically be influenced by how an object is oriented with respect to the observer's line of sight. Consider, for example, the perceived structure of a horizontally oriented cylindrical surface rotating back and forth in depth about a vertical axis as depicted schematically in Figure 3. Tittle, Todd, Perotti, and Norman (in press) have recently reported that if the surface oscillates over a 10° angular extent such that its central axis is centered within the frontoparallel plane, then its eccentricity (i.e., its depth) will perceptually be overestimated by approximately 20%. If, however, the same surface is viewed from a different orientation such that its central axis is oriented at a 30° angle from the frontoparallel plane, then its eccentricity will be underestimated by approximately 20%. Similar effects of stimulus orientation have also been reported by Reichel and Todd (1990), Todd and Norman (1991), and Braunstein, Liter, and Tittle (1993).

D. Conflicting Sources of Information

One final class of variables that is known to have a significant effect on observer's perceptions of structure from motion is the presence of conflict-

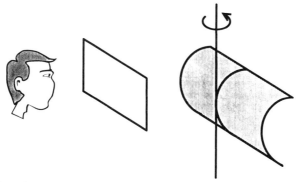

FIGURE 3 The experimental arrangement used by Tittle et al. (in press) to study the effects of object orientation on the visual perception of structure from motion.

ing cues from other potential sources of information. These effects can be observed informally by viewing the projected image of a rotating object while alternately opening and closing one eye. When such a display is observed monocularly, it appears to have a greater extension in depth than when it is observed binocularly because, in the latter case, there is conflicting information from binocular disparity to indicate that the pattern is confined to the image plane.

Most of the existing research on how other sources of information can conflict with motion has primarily been concerned with information about static slant such as texture gradients, linear perspective, or patterns of occlusion (Ames, 1951; Braunstein, 1968, 1971; Braunstein & Payne, 1968; Braunstein & Stern, 1980; Mingolla & Todd, 1981). A particularly compelling phenomenon arising from conflicts between motion and static slant information can be obtained by direct viewing of a rotating trapezoid, as was first reported by Ames (1951). When a static trapezoid is observed monocularly in the frontoparallel plane, it is typically perceived as a rectangle slanted in depth. When the object begins to rotate, however, the pattern of image motion provides conflicting information about its true orientation. This conflict can result in some startling perceptual illusions. Under appropriate conditions, a trapezoid in continuous rotation will appear instead to oscillate. It may also appear to undergo severe nonrigid deformations or even to pass through other solid objects.

IV. THEORETICAL ANALYSES

Most research on the visual perception of structure from motion that was performed before 1980 was basically exploratory in nature. The closest thing resembling a theory that was available to guide the empirical investigations of these early researchers was a hypothesis by Wallach and O'Connell (1953) stating that the perceptually relevant information for the kinetic depth effect consisted of simultaneous changes in the projected lengths and angles of moving line elements. Unfortunately, however, this hypothesis proved to be of little value for explaining how moving patterns are perceptually analyzed or even to predict their perceptual appearance. For example, it was demonstrated early on that compelling kinetic depth effects can be obtained from length changes alone (Braunstein, 1977b; Borjesson & Hofsten, 1972, 1973; Johansson & Jansson, 1968; Metzger, 1934; White & Musser, 1960), thus providing strong evidence that simultaneous changes in length and angle do not constitute a necessary condition for perceiving structure from motion. Nor do they constitute a sufficient condition, as can be demonstrated by the fact that a pattern of line segments whose lengths and angles are changed at random in different directions will appear as nothing more than random deformations in the image plane.

A. The Computational Analysis of Multiple-View Motion Sequences

The first computational analysis of how it might be possible to determine an object's 3-D structure from its pattern of projected motion was developed by Ullman (1977, 1979, 1983). Ullman's analysis was designed to be used with configurations of discrete points rotating in depth under parallel projection, in which corresponding images of each point could be identified over successive intervals of time. Given these conditions, he was able to prove that a unique rigid interpretation could be obtained (up to a reflection in depth) provided that a display contains at least three distinct views of four noncoplanar points. Subsequent analyses have confirmed that these minimum numbers of points and views are both necessary and sufficient for arbitrary configurations of moving elements, but these minimal conditions can vary somewhat in certain special case situations (see, for example, Bennett & Hoffman, 1986; Hoffman & Bennett, 1985, 1986). For example, if the motion is constrained to be at a constant angular velocity about a fixed axis of rotation that is parallel to the image plane, then a unique rigid interpretation can be obtained from three views of only two identifiable points (Hoffman & Bennett, 1986).

Ullman (1984) later developed an incremental rigidity scheme for computing structure from motion that was designed to cope with objects whose motions are not perfectly rigid. This analysis attempts to maintain an internal model of an observed object and to modify that model at each instant of time by the minimal amount of change required to account for the observed transformation. One problem with this approach is that it does not always converge on a stable interpretation when applied to rigid configurations, and even when it does converge, it may only do so after an object has rotated in depth for several complete oscillations (Grzywacz & Hildreth, 1987).

Still another class of models has been developed by Webb and Aggarwal (1981) and Todd (1982) to compute an object's 3-D structure from the relative trajectories of each element's projected motion rather than from their positions at discrete moments in time (see also Johansson, 1974). These models have identified specific conditions for distinguishing rigid from nonrigid motion, and they are applicable to both parallel and polar projections. They share one of the limitations of incremental rigidity schemes, however, by requiring that an object's motion be observed over a sufficiently long interval of time to specify the structure of each element's projected trajectory.

B. The Computational Analysis of Two-View Motion Sequences

In contrast to the analyses of multiple-frame apparent motion sequences described above, other theorists have focused their attentions on the potential information that is available within the instantaneous field of image velocities defined by two-frame motion sequences. The qualitative structure of these instantaneous velocity fields was first described by Gibson (1950, 1967, 1979), who was primarily concerned with how different patterns of optical flow provide information about an observer's movements relative to a fixed rigid environment. A more formal mathematical description was later developed by Gibson, Olum, and Rosenblatt (1958) and Gorden (1965).

There are several possible strategies that have been proposed for computing an object's 3-D structure from its instantaneous field of image velocities under polar projection. For example, if the velocity of the observer is known, then that knowledge can be used to compute the position of any visible point in a rigid environment (see, for example, Lee, 1974; Nakayama & Loomis, 1974). Without knowledge of the observer's velocity, a unique 3-D interpretation can still be obtained from the optical displacements of a small number of identifiable points (see, for example, Longuet-Higgins, 1981; Nagel, 1981), provided that they are viewed with a sufficient amount of perspective.

Another possible strategy first proposed by Koenderink and van Doorn (1975, 1977, 1986) and Koenderink (1986) involves a decomposition of smooth velocity fields into three independent components called *divergence, curl, and shear* (see Figure 4), which are sometimes referred to as *differential invariants*. The utility of this decomposition is that each component is affected by distinctly different aspects of environmental events. Although all three can be influenced by a moving object's 3-D structure, divergence is also affected by the time to contact with the point of observation for objects translating in depth (see Todd, 1981), whereas curl is influenced by rotations around the line of sight (see Figure 2). The shear component of smooth flow fields is unique in that it provides information about certain aspects of local surface structure such as relative slant or the sign of Gaussian curvature without being contaminated by other stimulus factors. Similar analyses have also been developed by Longuet-Higgins & Prazdny (1984) and Waxman and Ullman (1985) that use differential invariants of optical flow to determine an object's complete Euclidean metric structure.

For object's viewed under parallel projection, an instantaneous field of image velocities is somewhat less informative, but it does contain sufficient information to distinguish rigid from nonrigid motion and to constrain an object's 3-D structure to a one-parameter family of possible rigid interpretations (Bennett, Hoffman, Nicola, & Prakash, 1989; Huang & Lee, 1989; Koenderink & van Doorn, 1991; Todd & Bressan, 1990; Ullman, 1977, 1983). A unique 3-D interpretation can be obtained, however, for the special case of object motions that are confined to a fixed plane (Hoffman & Flinchbaugh, 1982; Lappin, 1990). It is also possible to obtain a unique

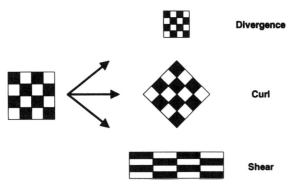

FIGURE 4   Three types of optical deformation called *divergence, curl,* and *shear* that can occur from the motions of smoothly curved surfaces. Whereas divergence and curl are influenced by the nature of an objects motion, shear provides pure information about its 3-D structure.

solution for more general configurations by imposing additional constraints (e.g., Aloimonos & Brown, 1989).

V. EMPIRICAL TESTS OF THE COMPUTATIONAL MODELS

As computational models for determining 3-D structure from motion have begun to proliferate in the literature, there has been a complementary effort to determine how closely the capabilities and limitations of these models correspond with those of actual human observers. Much of this research has centered on two basic issues: What are the specific aspects of object structure that an analysis of motion should be designed to compute, and what assumptions (i.e., constraints) are required to be satisfied for an analysis to function effectively? Whereas most existing computational models are designed to generate precise metrical descriptions of 3-D form within a narrowly constrained context, there is a growing amount of evidence to suggest that human perception is primarily concerned with more qualitative aspects of object structure and that it can function effectively over a surprisingly broad range of viewing conditions.

A. Perceived Three-Dimensional Structure from Nonrigid Configurations

One important limitation of existing computational analyses of 3-D structure from motion is that they all involve some form of rigidity hypothesis. Most models require that an object's motion must be globally rigid, though there are others that can tolerate Euclidean bendings that preserve distances measured along a surface (e.g., Koenderink & van Doorn, 1986) or piecewise rigid motions composed of locally rigid parts whose relative spatial arrangements can deform arbitrarily (e.g., Hoffman & Flinchbaugh, 1982; Todd, 1982). As a general rule, these models do not degrade gracefully. That is to say, if there is no possible rigid interpretation, then they will be unable to determine anything at all about a depicted object's 3-D structure.

There is considerable evidence to indicate, however, that the perceptual processes of actual human observers do not behave in this manner. There have been numerous studies reported in the literature that have used various types of nonrigid displays, including both locally rigid bending transformations (Jansson, 1977; Jansson & Johansson, 1973; Jansson & Runeson, 1977) and stretching transformations that are locally nonrigid (e.g., Braunstein & Andersen, 1984; Braunstein et al., 1990; Cutting, 1987; Todd, 1982, 1984). What is surprising about these displays from the perspective of current theory is that they can produce compelling kinetic depth effects of objects moving in 3-D space—albeit nonrigidly. Indeed, in those studies that have examined perceived 3-D structure rather than rigidity (i.e., Braunstein & Andersen, 1984; Todd, 1984), the results have indicated that a nonrigid stretching transformation in one direction can have little or no effect on perceived surface curvature in an orthogonal direction.

B. Effects of Number of Views

Perhaps the most well-known result from theoretical analyses of structure from motion is that a unique Euclidean interpretation of an arbitrary configuration of points under parallel projection requires a minimum of three distinct views. This finding defines the minimum amount of information required for an ideal observer who can measure the projected position of each point and perform all subsequent computations on those measures with perfect accuracy. It would not be surprising, however, if additional information were required for real observers, whose perceptual processes may be less than perfect.

In an effort to compare the performance of a theoretically ideal observer with that of actual human perception, numerous investigators have examined how the number of distinct frames in an apparent motion sequence influences observers' judgments of rigidity (Braunstein et al., 1990; Doner, Lappin, & Perfetto, 1984; Lappin, Doner, & Kottas, 1980; Petersik, 1987; Todd, Akerstrom et al., 1988) and 3-D form (Braunstein et al., 1987; Hildreth, Grzywacz, Adelson, & Inada, 1990; Liter et al., 1994; Todd & Bressan, 1990; Todd & Norman, 1991). Although it would be reasonable to expect on the basis of current computational models that the perception of structure from motion should require a minimum of three distinct views, the empirical results have shown clearly that two-frame motion sequences provide sufficient information to obtain compelling kinetic depth effects.

Moreover, if a two-frame sequence is presented in continuous alternation to eliminate any confounds with stimulus duration, increasing the sequence length with additional views has little or no effect on objective response tasks (Liter et al., 1994; Todd & Bressan, 1990; Todd & Norman, 1991). Similar results can also be obtained by limiting the lifetimes of individual points for objects viewed in continuous rotation if the overall level of noise is equated in all displays (Dosher, Landy, & Sperling, 1990; Husain, Treue, & Andersen, 1989; Todd, 1985; Treue, Husain, & Andersen, 1991).

To make sense of these seemingly impossible results, it is important to recognize that the theoretical limits on the number of distinct views needed to compute 3-D structure from motion are only applicable to the analysis of Euclidean distance relations between arbitrary pairs of points. Although two-frame motion sequences under orthographic projection are theoretically insufficient to specify an object's Euclidean metric structure, they do provide potentially useful information about any object property that is invariant under affine-stretching transformations (Koenderink & van Doorn, 1991; Todd & Bressan, 1990; Todd & Norman, 1991). What may not be obvious at first blush, moreover, is that the vast majority of tasks that have been used to investigate observers' perceptions of 3-D form could in principle be performed accurately solely on the basis of a two-frame analysis of affine structure.

Consider, for example, one of the first objective response tasks for measuring perceived structure from motion, which was developed by Lappin and Fuqua (1983). Observers in this experiment were presented with a linear configuration of three dots rotating in a slanted plane under strong polar projection and were asked to judge which endpoint the middle dot was closest to in 3-D space. The results showed that observers could perform this task with a high degree of accuracy. Although it might be tempting to conclude from this result that the perception of 3-D structure from motion is close to veridical, a more careful evaluation of the task reveals that this is not necessarily the case. Suppose, for example, that perceived intervals in depth are expanded relative to those in the frontoparallel plane, as has been demonstrated more recently by Todd and Norman (1991), Braunstein et al. (1993), and Tittle et al. (in press). If perceived depth is linearly expanded (or contracted) in depth such that the perceived shape of an object is an affine distortion of its true physical structure, then there would be no effect at all on the perceived ratios of parallel distance intervals in any given direction, and distance bisection judgments would be unimpaired. Thus, the task used by Lappin and Fuqua can only tell us about observers' perceptions of affine structure, and there is no reason to assume that the results should generalize to Euclidean tasks that require a comparison length intervals in different orientations.

There are many other tasks that have commonly been used to investigate perceived structure from motion that do not require a precise determination of Euclidean distance relations. These include most types of object discrimination and the detection of nonrigid deformations (Bennett et al., 1989; Huang & Lee, 1989; Koenderink & van Doorn, 1991; Todd & Bressan, 1990; Ullman, 1977, 1983). It is interesting to note in surveying the psychophysics literature on this topic that observers typically perform with high levels of accuracy on tasks that are theoretically possible with only two distinct views, but performance can deteriorate dramatically for tasks that require a three-view analysis of Euclidean distance relations. For example, when observers are asked to discriminate the relative 3-D lengths of moving line segments in different orientations, their discrimination thresholds are typically around 25%, which is an order of magnitude higher than those obtained for length discriminations of parallel lines in the frontoparallel plane (Norman, Todd, Perotti, & Tittle, in press; Todd & Bressan, 1990). Such findings provide strong evidence that the human visual system may be incapable of performing the higher order time derivatives needed to analyze Euclidean structure and that it must rely instead on whatever information is available within the first-order field of image velocities (see Todd, 1981).

C. Planar Motion and Perspective

There are some potential exceptions to the preceding conclusions that are useful to consider. Let us assume, as suggested above, that the perceptual analysis of structure from motion can only make use of first-order velocity information that is available within two-frame motion sequences. Such information would be mathematically insufficient to compute the Euclidean metric structure of arbitrary configurations, but it would make it possible— at least in principle—to obtain a unique rigid interpretation of an object's 3-D form in certain special-case situations. One such special case occurs for object motions that are confined to a fixed plane (Hoffman & Flinchbaugh, 1982; Lappin, 1990). Lappin and Love (1993) and Lappin and Ahlstrom (1994) have recently argued that human observers can indeed discriminate Euclidean distance relations in this situation. They found that observers can accurately judge the relative 3-D lengths of nonparallel line segments that are rotating together within a slanted plane under orthographic projection. The interpretation of this result has been challenged, however, by Pizlo and Salach-Golyska (1994) as arising from artifactual sources of information. Because the relative 3-D lengths of the depicted line segments in the Lappin and Love paradigm were allowed to covary with their relative 2-D projected lengths, to which observers are highly sensitive, it is possible that successful performance on this task need not have been based on a perceptual analysis of 3-D structure.

A second special case to consider includes objects viewed under strong polar perspective. Although perspective is known to increase the perceived depth of moving displays, the evidence does not suggest that it produces an accurate perception of Euclidean metric structure. There have been numerous experiments reported in the literature on observers' perceptions of moving surfaces translating perpendicular to the line of sight under polar projection (Braunstein & Andersen, 1981; Braunstein & Tittle, 1988; Braunstein et al., 1993; Caudek & Proffitt, 1993; Farber & McKonkie, 1979; Gibson, Gibson, Smith, & Flock, 1959; Flock, 1964; Ono, Rivest, & Ono, 1986; Ono & Steinbach, 1990; Rogers & Collett, 1989; Rogers & Rogers, 1992). The most typical pattern of results is that perceived depth is systematically underestimated relative to its true simulated value. There have also been a few studies on the accuracy of perceived 3-D structure for objects rotating in depth under strong polar perspective. The results have shown that observers are quite good at estimating relative distance intervals in a given direction (Lappin & Fuqua, 1983) but that performance deteriorates dramatically for distance intervals that are oriented in different directions (Tittle et al., in press; Norman et al., in press). When motion is the only source of information available, perceived depth intervals of rotating objects tend to be systematically overestimated relative to length intervals in the frontoparallel plane, as is also the case for objects viewed under orthographic projection (see Braunstein et al., 1993; Tittle et al., in press; Todd & Bressan, 1990; Todd & Norman, 1991).

VI. PROBLEMS FOR FUTURE RESEARCH

A. The Scaling Problem

Although there is a growing amount of evidence that computational models of two-frame motion sequences under parallel projection have many properties in common with observers' perceptions of structure from motion, there are other aspects of the psychophysical data that these models cannot explain. It is important to keep in mind that a two-frame display of an arbitrary configuration under parallel projection does not have a unique rigid interpretation. It will either have no possible rigid interpretation at all or an infinite one-parameter family of possible interpretations. This would explain why observers typically exhibit large errors in judgments of Euclidean metric structure from motion and why they are unable to discriminate different structures within the one-parameter family, even when a motion sequence contains more than two distinct frames (e.g., Liter et al., 1994; Todd & Bressan, 1990; Todd & Norman, 1991). The aspect of the data that is hard to explain, however, is the existence of systematic biases in observers' magnitude estimations of perceived depth. If the available information is infinitely ambiguous, then why should an object appear to have any specific depth at all? To the extent that it does, there would have to be some other constraint or heuristic at work to restrict the set of possible perceptual interpretations.

There have been a number of hypotheses proposed in the literature about what this constraint might be. For example, Loomis and Eby (1988, 1989) have proposed that perceived depth from motion is scaled by the amount of shear that is present within the overall pattern of optical flow (cf. Koenderink & van Doorn, 1975, 1977, 1986). Others have suggested that perceived depth is scaled by the amount of compression within the overall flow pattern (Braunstein et al., 1993), the magnitude of relative motion following the removal of image curl (Liter et al., 1993), or a compactness constraint, in which it assumed that an object's depth will be approximately equal to its width (Caudek & Proffitt, 1993). Unfortunately, however, none of these suggestions is particularly general. Each one was devised to account for the results of a relatively small set of experiments, but none of them is consistent with the entire corpus of data that has been reported in this area.

B. The Perceptual Representation of Three-Dimensional Form

The fact that observers can misperceive an object's extension in depth relative to its width while correctly identifying that it is undergoing rigid rotation leads to an interesting conundrum. Suppose, for example, that an observer overestimates intervals in depth by a factor of 25%, as has been reported by Todd and Norman (1991) and Tittle et al. (in press). If such an observer were to view a rotating ellipsoid whose extension in depth is 25% smaller than its width at a particular moment in time, it should appear at that moment as a sphere. At a later point in its rotation cycle, however, its width would be 25% smaller than its depth and it should appear as a flattened ellipsoid. Why would not this change in shape be perceived as a nonrigid deformation? This puzzle was first noted by Helmholtz (1867/ 1925) in considering the systematic distortions of stereoscopic space, but it is also applicable to the visual perception of structure from motion.

One possible resolution of this conundrum, first suggested by Gibson (1979), is that Euclidean metric distances in 3-D space are not a primary component of an observer's perceptual experience. Although he had proposed in his earlier writings that surfaces are perceptually defined by the absolute depth and slant of each local patch, he eventually concluded that this hypothesis was a mistake. Gibson noted that many of the most salient aspects of structure from motion involve ordinal relationships. For example, the presence of an occlusion as optically specified by the accretion or deletion of texture provides important information that one surface is in front of another, but it cannot indicate how far the two surfaces are separated in depth. Similarly, the presence of optical expansion or "looming" can perceptually specify the time to contact with an approaching object, but it does not provide information about the object's physical distance in depth or how fast it is moving (see Todd, 1981).

This hypothesis has been developed more fully in a recent series of papers by Todd and Reichel (1989), Todd and Bressan (1990), Todd and Norman (1991), Norman and Todd (1992, 1993), and Tittle et al. (in press). These authors have presented evidence that an observer's knowledge of 3-D form may involve a hierarchy of different perceptual representations. Their findings indicate that observers are quite accurate and reliable at judging an object's topological, ordinal, or affine properties and that perception of rigid motion occurs when these properties remain invariant over time. Although observers can exhibit a conceptual understanding of Euclidean metric structure, this knowledge may be more cognitive than perceptual. The available psychophysical evidence suggests that if observers are required to make judgments about lengths or angles of visible objects in 3-D space, they will resort to using ad hoc heuristics, which typically produce low levels of accuracy and reliability and can vary unpredictably among different individuals or for different stimulus configurations.

C. Analyses of Different Types of Optical Deformations

All of the research described thus far has exclusively been concerned with the optical displacements of identifiable features such as reflectance contours or the edges of polyhedra, for which multiple views of any given image point must all correspond to the same physical point in 3-D space—what is sometimes referred to as the *condition of projective correspondence* (Todd, 1985). In natural vision, however, the overall pattern of optical stimulation can contain a variety of other structures such as occlusion contours, cast shadows, and smooth variations of surface shading, for which this condition need not be satisfied. This can have important theoretical implications for the analysis of 3-D structure from motion. When objects move or are viewed stereoscopically, these different aspects of optical structure do not always change in the same way, and analyses that are designed to be used with one type of optical deformation will not in general be appropriate for others.

Consider, for example, the occlusion contour that forms the silhouette of a human head. If the head rotates in depth about a vertical axis, the optical contour that bounds its projection will be deformed systematically, but the locus of surface points to which it corresponds will also be continuously changing, that is, for a frontal view the occlusion contour will pass through the ears, and for a profile view it will pass through the nose. Analyses that assume projective correspondence will be of little use with this type of optical deformation, even as a local approximation. Indeed, it is often the case that the optical motion of the bounding contour will be in one direction while the projected motion of any identifiable point on that contour is in the opposite direction. (see Todd, 1985).

There are other types of image structure involving shadows and shading for which motions of the observer and motions of the observed object produce different patterns of optical deformation. For matte surface materials that scatter light in all directions, the shading in an image is determined by how each local surface patch is oriented with respect to its sources of illumination. This is sometimes referred to as a *diffuse or Lambertian shading*. For shiny surfaces, in contrast, that reflect light like a mirror, the image shading is affected by the position of the observer and the direction of illumination. This is referred to as *specular shading*. When an observer moves in an otherwise rigid environment, visible objects will all maintain a constant relationship with their sources of illumination. Because shadow borders and gradients of Lambertian shading in this context remain bound to fixed positions in 3-D space, their resulting patterns of optical deformation will satisfy the condition of projective correspondence and can therefore be analyzed by using conventional techniques for determining structure from motion. When an object moves relative to its light source, however, shadow borders and gradients of shading will move over its surface. Because this violates the condition of projective correspondence, existing computational models would be unable to generate a correct rigid interpretation.

Figure 5 provides a summary of all of the different categories of optical deformation described above. The rows of this figure represent different types of optical structure, whereas the columns are used to distinguish observer motion from object motion. Note that some of the borders between cells in this figure have been removed. These open areas define classes of deformation that are formally equivalent. For example, the deformations of reflectance contours, sharp corners, cast shadows, and Lambertian shading caused by observer motion and the deformations of reflectance contours and sharp corners caused by object motion are all formally equivalent in that they satisfy the condition of projective correspondence. This is the category on which most of the existing research in this area has been focused.

Although the remaining cells in Figure 5 have attracted much less attention, they have not been ignored altogether. There have been several demonstrations reported in the literature that human observers can obtain compelling KDEs from the optical deformations of smooth occlusion contours (Cortese & Andersen, 1991; Norman & Todd, 1994; Pollick, Giblin, Rycroft, & Wilson, 1992; Todd, 1985), and there have also been a few mathematical analyses of how this might be theoretically possible (Cipolla & Blake, 1990; Giblin & Weiss, 1987; Koenderink & van Doorn, 1977). There is some evidence to suggest that the optical deformations of shadows and shading may provide useful information as well (Norman & Todd, 1994; Todd, 1985), but the generality of this evidence remains to be deter-

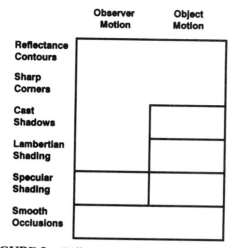

FIGURE 5   Different categories of optical deformation.

mined. One important factor that has limited research on these topics is the difficulty of creating controlled laboratory displays of moving shaded images. This difficulty is quickly diminishing, however, with the continuing advance of computer graphics technology so that this is likely to be a more active area of research within the next several years.

References

Aloimonos, J., & Brown, C. M. (1989). On the kinetic depth effect. *Biological Cybernetics, 60*, 445–455.

Ames, A. (1951). Visual perception and the rotating trapizoidal window. *Psychological Monographs, 65*, (7, Whole No. 324).

Andersen, G. J., & Braunstein, M. L. (1983). Dynamic occlusion in the perception of rotation in depth. *Perception & Psychophysics, 34*, 356–362.

Bennett, B., & Hoffman, D. (1986). The computation of structure from fixed axis motion: Nonrigid structures. *Biological Cybernetics, 51*, 293–300.

Bennett, B., Hoffman, D., Nicola, J., & Prakash, C. (1989). Structure from two orthographic views of rigid motion. *Journal of the Optical Society of America, 6*, 1052–1069.

Borjesson, E., & Hofsten C. von (1972). Spatial determinants of depth perception in two dot patterns. *Perception & Psychophysics, 11*, 263–268.

Borjesson, E., & Hofsten C. von (1973). Visual perception of motion in depth: Application of a vector model to three dot motion patterns. *Perception & Psychophysics, 13*, 203–208.

Braunstein, M. L. (1962). Depth perception in rotating dot patterns: Effects of numerosity and perspective. *Journal of Experimental Psychology, 64*, 415–420.

Braunstein, M. L. (1966), Sensitivity of the observer to transformations of the visual field. *Journal of Experimental Psychology, 72*, 683–689.

Braunstein, M. L. (1968). Motion and texture as sources of slant information. *Journal of Experimental Psychology, 78*, 247–253.

Braunstein, M. L. (1971). Perception of rotation in figures with rectangular and trapezoidal features. *Journal of Experimental Psychology, 91,* 25–29.

Braunstein, M. L. (1977a). Perceived direction of rotation of simulated three-dimensional patterns. *Perception & Psychophysics, 21,* 553–557.

Braunstein, M. L. (1977b). Minimal conditions for perception of rotary motion. *Scandinavian Journal of Psychology, 18,* 216–223.

Braunstein, M. L., & Andersen, G. J. (1984). Shape and depth perception from parallel projections of three-dimensional motion. *Journal of Experimental Psychology: Human Perception and Performance, 10,* 749–760.

Braunstein, M. L., Andersen, G. J., & Riefer, D. M. (1982). The use of occlusion to resolve ambiguity in parallel projections. *Perception & Psychophysics, 31,* 261–267.

Braunstein, M. L., Hoffman, D. D., & Pollick, F. E. (1990). Discriminating rigid from nonrigid motion. *Perception & Psychophysics, 47,* 205–214.

Braunstein, M. L., Hoffman, D. D., Shapiro, L. R., Andersen, G. J., & Bennett, B. M. (1987). Minimum points and views for the recovery of three-dimensional structure. *Journal of Experimental Psychology: Human Perception and Performance, 13,* 335–343.

Braunstein, M. L., Liter, J. C., & Hoffman, D. D. (1993), Inferring structure from two-view and multi-view displays. *Perception, 22,* 1441–1467.

Braunstein, M. L., Liter, J. C., & Tittle, J. S. (1993). Recovering three-dimensional shape from perspective translations and orthographic rotations. *Journal of Experimental Psychology: Human Perception and Performance, 19,* 598–614.

Braunstein, M. L., & Payne, J. W. (1968). Perspective and the rotating trapezoid. *Journal of the Optical Society of America, 58,* 399–403.

Braunstein, M. L., & Stern, K. R. (1980). Static and dynamic factors in the perception of rotary motion. *Perception & Psychophysics, 4,* 313–320.

Braunstein, M. L., & Tittle, J. S. (1988). The observer relative velocity field as the basis for effective motion parallax. *Journal of Experimental Psychology: Human Perception and Performance, 14,* 582–590.

Braunstein, M. L., & Todd, J. T. (1990). On the distinction between artifacts and information. *Journal of Experimental Psychology: Human Perception and Performance, 16,* 211–216.

Caudek, C., & Proffitt, D. R. (1993). Depth perception in motion parallax and stereokinesis. *Journal of Experimental Psychology: Human Perception and Performance, 19,* 32–47.

Cipolla, R., & Blake, A. (1990). The dynamic analysis of apparent contours. *Proceedings of the Third International Conference of Computer Vision,* 616–623.

Cortese, J. M., & Andersen, G. J. (1991). Recovery of 3-D shape from deforming contours. *Perception & Psychophysics, 49,* 315–327.

Cornilleau-Pérès, V., & Droulez, J. (1989). Visual perception of curvature: Psychophysics of curvature detection induced by motion parallax. *Perception & Psychophysics, 46,* 351–364.

Cutting, J. E. (1987). Rigidity in cinema seen from the front row, side aisle. *Journal of Experimental Psychology: Human Perception and Performance, 13,* 323–334.

Doner, J., Lappin, J. S., & Perfetto, G. (1984). Detection of three-dimensional structure in moving optical patterns. *Journal of Experimental Psychology: Human Perception and Performance, 10,* 1–11.

Dosher, B. A., Landy, M. S., & Sperling, G. (1989). Ratings of kinetic depth in multidot displays. *Journal of Experimental Psychology: Human Perception and Performance, 15,* 816–825.

Dosher, B. A., Landy, M. S., & Sperling, G. (1990). Kinetic depth effect and optic flow: I. 3D shape from Fourier motion. *Vision Research, 29,* 1789–1814.

Farber, J. M., & McKonkie, A. B. (1979). Optical motions as information for unsigned depth. *Journal of Experimental Psychology: Human Perception and Performance, 15,* 494–500.

Fieandt, K. von, & Gibson, J. J. (1959). The sensitivity of the eye to two kinds of continuous transformation of a shadow pattern. *Journal of Experimental Psychology, 57,* 344–347.

Flock, H. (1964). Some sufficient conditions for accurate monocular perceptions of surface slants. *Journal of Experimental Psychology, 67,* 560–572.

Giblin, P., & Weiss, R. (1987). Reconstruction of surfaces from profiles. *Proceedings of the IEEE First International Conference on Computer Vision,* 136–144.

Gibson, E. J., Gibson, J. J., Smith, O. W., & Flock, H. (1959). Motion parallax as a determinant of perceived depth. *Journal of Experimental Psychology, 58,* 40–51.

Gibson, J. J. (1950). *The perception of the visual world.* Boston: Houghton Mifflin.

Gibson, J. J. (1967). *The senses considered as perceptual systems.* Boston: Houghton Mifflin.

Gibson, J. J. (1979). *The ecological approach to visual perception.* Boston: Houghton Mifflin.

Gibson, J. J., & Gibson, E. J. (1957). Continuous perspective transformations and the perception of rigid motion. *Journal of Experimental Psychology, 54,* 129–138.

Gibson, J. J., Olum, P., & Rosenblatt, F. (1958). Parallax and perspective during aircraft landings. *American Journal of Psychology, 68,* 372–385.

Gorden, D. A. (1965). Static and dynamic visual fields in human space perception. *Journal of the Optical Society of America, 55,* 1296–1303.

Green, B. F., Jr., (1961). Figure coherence in the kinetic depth effect. *Journal of Experimental Psychology, 62,* 272–282.

Grzywacz, N., & Hildreth, E. (1987). Incremental rigidity scheme for recovering structure from motion: Position-based versus velocity-based formulations. *Journal of the Optical Society of America, A4,* 503–518.

Helmholtz, H. von (1925). *Handbook of physiological optics* (J. P. C. Southall, Trans). New York: Dover. (Original work published 1867).

Hildreth, E. C., Grzywacz, N. M., Adelson, E. H., & Inada, V. K. (1990). The perceptual buildup of three-dimensional structure from motion. *Perception & Psychophysics, 48,* 19–36.

Hoffman, D., & Bennett, B. (1985). Inferring the relative three-dimensional positions of two moving points. *Journal of the Optical Society of America A, 2,* 242–249.

Hoffman, D., & Bennett, B. (1986). The computation of structure from fixed axis motion: Rigid structures. *Biological Cybernetics, 54,* 1–13.

Hoffman, D. D., & Flinchbaugh, B. E. (1982). The interpretation of biological motion. *Biological Cybernetics, 42,* 195–204.

Huang, T., & Lee, C. (1989). Motion and structure from orthographic projections. *IEEE Transactions on Pattern Analysis and Machine Intelligence, 11,* 536–540.

Husain, M., Treue, S., & Andersen, R. A. (1989). Surface interpolation in three-dimensional structure-from-motion perception. *Neural Computation, 1,* 324–333.

Jansson, G. (1977). Perceived bending and stretching motions from a line of points. *Scandinavian Journal of Psychology, 18,* 209–215.

Jansson, G., & Johansson, G. (1973). Visual perception of bending motion. *Perception, 2,* 321–326.

Jansson, G., & Runeson, S. (1977). Perceived bending motion from a quadrangle changing form. *Perception, 6,* 595–600.

Johansson, G. (1964). Perception of motion and changing form. *Scandinavian Journal of Psychology, 5,* 181–208.

Johansson, G. (1974). Visual perception of rotary motions as transformations of conic sections. *Psychologia, 17,* 226–237.

Johansson, G., & Jansson, G. (1968). Perceived rotary motion from changes in a straight line. *Perception & Psychophysics, 6,* 193–198.

Koenderink, J. J. (1986). Optic flow. *Vision Research, 26,* 161–179.

Koenderink, J. J., & van Doorn, A. J. (1975). Invariant properties of the motion parallax field due to the motion of rigid bodies relative to the observer. *Optica Acta, 22,* 773–791.

Koenderink, J. J., & van Doorn, A. J. (1977). How an ambulant observer can construct a model of the environment from the geometrical structure of the visual flow. In G. Hauske & F. Butenandt (Eds.), *Kybernetik* (pp. 224–247). Munich: Oldenberg.

Koenderink, J. J., & van Doorn, A. J. (1986). Depth and shape from differential perspective in the presence of bending deformations. *Journal of the Optical Society of America A, 3,* 242–249.

Koenderink, J. J., & van Doorn, A. J. (1991). Affine structure from motion. *Journal of the Optical Society of America A, 8,* 377–385.

Lappin, J. S. (1990). Perceiving metric structure of environmental objects from motion, self-motion and stereopsis. In R. Warren and A. H. Wertheim (Eds.), *The perception and control of self-motion* (pp. 541–576). Hillsdale, NJ: Erlbaum.

Lappin, J. S., & Ahlstrom, U. B. (1994). On the scaling of visual space from motion: In response to Pizlo and Salach-Golyska. *Perception & Psychophysics, 55,* 235–242.

Lappin, J. S., Doner, J. F., & Kottas, B. L. (1980). Minimal conditions for the visual detection of structure and motion in three dimensions. *Science, 209,* 717–719.

Lappin, J. S., & Fuqua, M. A. (1983). Accurate visual measurement of three-dimensional moving patterns. *Science, 221,* 480–482.

Lappin, J. S., & Love, S. R. (1993). Metric structure of stereoscopic form from congruence under motion. *Perception & Psychophysics, 51,* 86–102.

Lee, D. N. (1974). Visual information during locomotion. In R. B. MacLeod & H. Pick (Eds.), *Perception: Essays in honor of James Gibson* (pp. 250–268). Ithaca, NY: Cornell University Press.

Liter, J. C., Braunstein, M. L., & Hoffman, D. D. (1994). Inferring structure from motion in two-view and multi-view displays. *Perception, 22,* 1441–1465.

Longuet-Higgins, H. C. (1981). A computer algorithm for reconstructing a scene from two projections. *Nature, 293,* 133–135.

Longuet-Higgins, H. C., & Prazdny, K. (1984). The interpretation of a moving retinal image. *Proceedings of the Royal Society of London B, 208,* 385–397.

Loomis, J. M., & Eby, D. W. (1988). Perceiving structure from motion: Failure of shape constancy. In *Proceedings From the Second International Conference on Computer Vision* (pp. 383–391). Washington, DC: IEEE Computer Society Press.

Loomis, J. M., & Eby, D. W. (1989). Relative motion parallax and the perception of structure from motion. In *Proceedings From the Workshop on Visual Motion* (pp. 204–211). Washington, DC: IEEE Computer Society Press.

Mach, E. (1962). *The analysis of sensations* New York: Dover. (Original work published in 1886).

Metzger, W. (1934). Tiefinericheinungen in optichen bewengungsfelden [Depth Perception in visually moving fields]. *Psychologische Forschung, 20,* 195–260.

Mingolla, E., & Todd, J. T. (1981). The rotating square illusion. *Perception & Psychophysics, 29,* 487–492.

Musatti, C. L. (1924). Sui fenomeni stereocinetici [On stereokinetic phenomena] *Archivio Italiano de Psicologia, 3,* 105–120.

Nagel, H. -H. (1981). On the derivation of 3D rigid point configurations from image sequences. *Proceedings of the IEEE Conference on Pattern Recognition and Image Processing* (pp. 103–108). New York: IEEE Computer Society Press.

Nakayama, K., & Loomis, J. M. (1974). Optical velocity patterns, velocity sensitive neurons, and space perception: A hypothesis. *Perception, 3,* 53–80.

Norman, J. F., & Lappin, J. S. (1992). The detection of surfaces defined by optical motion. *Perception & Psychophysics, 51,* 386–396.

Norman, J. F., & Todd, J. T. (1992). The visual perception of 3-dimensional form. In G. A. Carpenter & S. Grossberg (Eds.), *Neural networks for vision and image processing* (pp. 93–110). Cambridge, MA: MIT Press.

Norman, J. F., & Todd, J. T. (1993). The perceptual analysis of structure from motion for rotating objects undergoing affine stretching transformations. *Perception & Psychophysics, 3,* 279–291.

Norman, J. F., & Todd, J. T. (1994). The perception of rigid motion in depth from the optical deformations of shadows and occlusion boundaries. *Journal of Experimental Psychology: Human Perception and Performance, 20,* 343–356.

Norman, J. F., Todd, J. T., Perotti, V. J., & Tittle, J. S. (in press). The visual perception of 3-D length. *Journal of Experimental Psychology: Human Perception and Performance.*

Ono, M., Rivest, J., & Ono, H. (1986). Depth perception as a function of motion parallax and absolute distance information. *Journal of Experimental Psychology: Human Perception and Performance, 12,* 331–337.

Ono, H., & Steinbach, M. J. (1990). Monocular stereopsis with and without head movement. *Perception & Psychophysics, 48,* 179–187.

Petersik, J. T. (1979). Three-dimensional constancy: Coherence of a simulated rotating sphere in noise. *Perception & Psychophysics, 25,* 328–335.

Petersik, J. T. (1980). The effects of spatial and temporal factors on the perception of stroboscopic rotation simulations. *Perception, 9,* 271–283.

Pizlo, Z., & Salach-Golyska, M. (1994). Is vision metric: Comment on Lappin and Love (1992). *Perception & Psychophysics, 55,* 230–234.

Pollick, F. E., Giblin, P. J., Rycroft, J., & Wilson, L. L. (1992). Human recovery of shape from profiles. *Behaviormetrika, 19,* 65–79.

Proffitt, D. R., Rock, I., Hecht, H., & Shubert, J. (1992). The stereokinetic effect and its relation to the kinetic depth effect. *Journal of Experimental Psychology: Human Perception and Performance, 18,* 3–21.

Reichel, F. D., & Todd, J. T. (1990). Perceived depth inversion of smoothly curved surfaces due to image orientation. *Journal of Experimental Psychology: Human Perception and Performance, 16,* 953–664.

Rogers, B. J., & Collett, T. S. (1989). The appearance of surfaces specified by motion parallax and binocular disparity. *Quarterly Journal of Experimental Psychology, 41A,* 697–717.

Rogers, B., & Graham, M. (1979). Motion parallax as an independent cue for depth perception. *Perception, 8,* 125–134.

Rogers, B., & Graham, M. (1982). Similarities between motion parallax and stereopsis in human depth perception. *Vision Research, 22,* 216–270.

Rogers, S., & Rogers, B. J. (1992). Visual and nonvisual information disambiguates surfaces specified by motion parallax. *Perception & Psychophysics, 52,* 446–452.

Sperling, G., Landy, M. S., Dosher, B. A., & Perkins, M. E. (1989). Kinetic depth effect and identification of shape. *Journal of Experimental Psychology: Human Perception and Performance, 15,* 826–840.

Tittle, J. S., Todd, J. T., Perotti, V. J., & Norman, J. F. (in press). The systematic distortion of perceived 3D structure from motion and binocular stereopsis. *Journal of Experimental Psychology: Human Perception and Performance.*

Todd, J. T. (1981). Visual information about moving objects. *Journal of Experimental Psychology: Human Perception and Performance, 7,* 795–810.

Todd, J. T. (1982). Visual information about rigid and nonrigid motion: A geometric analysis. *Journal of Experimental Psychology: Human Perception and Performance, 8,* 238–251.

Todd, J. T. (1984). The perception of three-dimensional structure from rigid and nonrigid motion. *Perception & Psychophysics, 36,* 97–103.

Todd, J. T. (1985). The perception of structure from motion: Is projective correspondence of moving elements a necessary condition? *Journal of Experimental Psychology: Human Perception and Performance, 11,* 689–710.

Todd, J. T., Akerstrom, R. A., Reichel, F. D., & Hayes, W. (1988). Apparent rotation in 3-dimensional space: Effects of temporal, spatial and structural factors. *Perception & Psychophysics, 43,* 179–188.

Todd, J. T., & Bressan, P. (1990). The perception of 3-dimensional affine structure from minimal apparent motion sequences. *Perception & Psychophysics, 48,* 419–430.

Todd, J. T., & Norman, J. F. (1991). The visual perception of smoothly curved surfaces from minimal apparent motion sequences. *Perception & Psychophysics, 50,* 509–523.

Todd, J. T., & Reichel, F. D. (1989). Ordinal structure in the visual perception and cognition of smoothly curved surfaces. *Psychological Review, 96,* 643–657.

Treue, S., Husain, M., & Andersen, R. A. (1991). Human perception of structure from motion. *Vision Research, 31,* 59–76.

Ullman, S. (1977). *The interpretation of visual motion.* Unpublished doctoral dissertation, Massachusetts Institute of Technology.

Ullman, S. (1979). *The interpretation of visual motion.* Cambridge, MA: MIT Press.

Ullman, S. (1983). Recent computational studies in the interpretation of structure from motion. In J. Beck & A. Rosenfeld (Eds.), *Human and machine vision* (pp. 459–480). New York: Academic Press.

Ullman, S. (1984). Maximizing rigidity: The incremental recovery of 3-D structure from rigid and nonrigid motion. *Perception, 13,* 255–274.

Wallach, H., & O'Connell, D. N. (1953). The kinetic depth effect. *Journal of Experimental Psychology, 45,* 205–217.

Wallach, H., Weisz, A., & Adams, P. A. (1956). Circles and derived figures in rotation. *American Journal of Psychology, 69,* 48–59.

Waxman, A., & Ullman, S. (1985). Surface structure and three-dimensional motion parameters from image flow kinematics. *International Journal of Robotics Research, 4,* 79–94.

Webb, J. A., & Aggarwal, J. K. (1981). Visually interpreting the motions of objects in space. *Computer, 8,* 40–46.

White, B., & Mueser, G. (1960). Accuracy of reconstructing the arrangement of elements generating kinetic depth displays. *Journal of Experimental Psychology, 60,* 1–11.

Zanforlin, M. (1988). The height of the stereokinetic cone: A quantitative determination of a 3-D effect from 2-D moving patterns without a "rigidity assumption." *Psychological Research, 50,* 162–172.

CHAPTER 7

Perceiving Events

Dennis R. Proffitt
Mary K. Kaiser

An event is an occurrence entailing change over time. Visually perceivable events involve moving objects, observers, or both. Since events encompass just about everything that occurs in our everyday lives, one might reasonably wonder how event perception came to be a distinct topic within the field of visual space perception. Historically, the distinction arose between those perceptions that could be based on static optical information and those that could not. Thus, perceptions of space from primary and secondary depth cues are typically taken to be distinct topics. Moreover, the perceptions of depth obtained from observing object rotations and motion parallax have received so much individual attention that they are distinct topics in their own right.

Events are omnipresent in the phenomenology of everyday experience. Indeed, awareness seems to be composed entirely of events. Even when we observe a completely stationary surrounding, we arrived on the scene by locomotion and observe it with moving eyes, heads, and bodies. Moreover, most natural environments possess some moving objects, with animate creatures being of special interest.

We restrict our discussion to studies of events involving moving objects. Gibson (1979) provided a useful means for distinguishing such events from the optical transformations produced when an observer moves in a station-

Perception of Space and Motion

ary environment. Global optical flow occurs during self-motion and consists of a transforming array of optical information projected to a moving point of observation. On the other hand, whenever an object moves relative to an observer, there is a local change in the optical array. This local disturbance in optical structure is the informational basis for environmental events. Although rotating objects are events, perceiving depth from object rotations—the kinetic depth effect (Wallach & O'Connell, 1953)—is a distinct topic covered in other chapters within this volume.

Events cause changes in optical structure. Inherent within these changes are regularities—abstract relationships—that pertain to environmental properties. Consider the example of perceiving surface segregation from motion. Whenever one object passes in front of another along the line of sight, dynamic occlusion occurs in which portions of the far object's surface are deleted and accreted at the leading and trailing edges of the near object. Gibson and his colleagues have shown that people can detect the presence of distinct surfaces on the basis of dynamic occlusion alone (Gibson, Kaplan, Reynolds, & Wheeler, 1969). Movies were created of randomly textured surfaces that overlapped relative to the line of sight (Gibson, 1968). When the surfaces were stationary, a single uniform texture was seen. When one or both surfaces moved, however, they were immediately observed to segregate into two surfaces separated in depth. Yonus, Craton, and Thompson (1987) have shown that surface segregation can be observed in displays containing only the relative motions of sparsely distributed point lights that disappear and reappear consistent with their simulated location on a pair of partially overlapping moving surfaces.

The perception of surface segregation in these situations exemplifies how environmental properties can be extracted from changes in optical structure. It also exemplifies Gibson's (1970; 1977) perspective on event perception. For Gibson, events are always accompanied by an accretion and deletion of optically specified surface textures. Others have viewed events without holding to this restriction, and we develop their approach next and then note Gibson's critique of their approach.

I. PRINCIPLES OF PERCEPTUAL GROUPING: ABSOLUTE, RELATIVE, AND COMMON MOTIONS

The field of event perception finds its origin in the law of common fate, one of the Gestalt principles of perceptual grouping proposed by Wertheimer (1923/1937). The law states that elements that move together tend to become perceptually grouped. Wertheimer described a situation in which an array of points is horizontally aligned. The points oscillate up and down, with every other point moving together in counterphase relative to adjacent points. In this situation, one perceives two groups of points, each sharing a common motion.

One of the first experiments in event perception was conducted by Rubin (1927). He constructed an apparatus that caused a wheel to revolve inside a ring that was twice the diameter of the wheel. Lights could be placed on the wheel that was observed in an otherwise dark room. When one light was present, observers reported seeing it move linearly back and forth. The absolute motion of the light relative to the projection plane is, in fact, a linear sinusoidal oscillation having an extent equalling the diameter of the ring. The addition of more lights caused observers to see similar linear motions having different orientations until, with six lights, the appearance of a wheel became evident. This latter percept consisted of seeing the lights revolve around the wheel's apparent center as the whole wheel revolved within the ring. Rubin argued that this demonstration provided strong support for the claim that one does not perceive the motion of a uniform whole by perceiving individually the movement of its various parts.

Duncker (1929/1937) conducted a similar experiment, one that has since become quite familiar to readers of the event perception literature. He placed a light on the rim on an unseen rolling wheel and observers reported seeing the light move through a series of arching curves called *cycloids*. When a second light was placed at the wheel's center, observers reported one or the other of two percepts. Either the outer light was seen to revolve around the light at the wheel's hub, with this latter light moving linearly, or both lights appeared to revolve around the ends of a "tumbling stick."

These two studies set the basic paradigm for research in event perception: the creation of moving point-light displays. Obviously, if the wheels and the surfaces over which they traversed had been apparent, then the motions of the single light would have been organized relative to its visible contexts. In fact, Rubin (1927) reported that Galileo, who is generally credited with discovering the cycloid, first noticed the curve when attending a peasant festival at which wagons were rolled down hills with a single torch attached to each wheel. The use of point lights allows one to observe the perceptual influence of motion in isolation from other informational sources. Unfortunately, the contraptions required to move point lights in more complex patterns placed severe restrictions on event perception research until computer simulations became possible.

Johansson established event perception as a distinct field of study. His innovations were both methodological and theoretical. On the methodological side, he introduced two techniques that revolutionized the field. First, Johansson (1950) used a computer to display moving point lights on an oscilloscope and, thereby, freed event perception research from the constraints of constructing elaborate mechanical devices. Second, Johansson

(1973) placed lights on people and filmed them moving about in the dark. When shown to naive observers, these films evoked compelling percepts of people engaged in activities appropriate for what was intended by the filmed actors. This latter innovation spawned an enormous amount of interest in what he called the *perception of biological motions*. Both types of displays can be seen on a pair of commercially available films (Mass, Johansson, Janson, & Runeson, 1971).

Among Johansson's (1950, 1973) theoretical contributions was his articulation of perceptual vector analysis. This analysis can be illustrated with reference to one of his best known displays that is depicted in Figure 1. The display consists of seven point lights. The central light moves diagonally, whereas the banks of three lights move horizontally with an equivalent motion to the horizontal motion component of the central light. When the central point is viewed without the six surrounding lights, its diagonal motion is observed. When the surrounding lights are present, the central light appears to move vertically and the whole group of seven lights moves back and forth.

Perceptual vector analysis distinguishes three types of motion. *Absolute motions* are the trajectories of each element relative to some environmental coordinate system, typically the projection plane for the display. *Relative motions* are the trajectories of elements relative to other elements with which they are grouped. In Johansson's (1950) display, the central light has a vertical motion relative to the surrounding lights. *Common motions* are the trajectories that all of the lights share, and for this display, these compose the horizontal motion component. The assignment of perceptually orga-

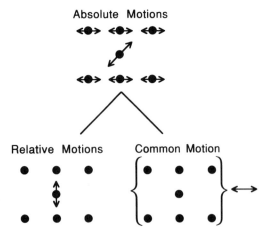

FIGURE 1   One of Johansson's (1950) best known displays. Seven points of light move as depicted at the top. These point lights are perceptually organized into the relative and common motion components shown at the bottom.

nized motions to relative and common motion categories varies somewhat within the literature and for a slightly different account from what is presented here, see Borjesson and Ahlstrom (1993). An implication of perceptual vector analysis is that the sum of perceived relative and common motions is equal to the perceptually registered absolute motions. To date, this motion preserving relationship has not been put to a systematic empirical test; however, at least for certain wheel-generated motion displays, it has been shown not to hold (Vicario & Bressan, 1990).

Wallach (1965, 1976) made essentially the same distinction; however, he referred to relative and common motions as *object-relative motions* and *observer-relative motions,* respectively. Object-relative motions are centered within the object and for rigid objects are constrained to be rotations, whereas nonrigid motions can also involve translations. Observer-relative motions are centered on the observer and can consist of rotations and translations. As Cutting (1983) pointed out, Wallach's approach is quite similar to that developed later by Marr (1982), who made a similar distinction between object- and observer-centered coordinate systems in his approach to visual processing.

Cutting and Proffitt (1981; Proffitt & Cutting, 1980) presented a somewhat more elaborate version of perceptual vector analysis with an emphasis on the role of perceptual centers in organizing event percepts. Their approach can be illustrated with reference to wheel-generated motions. Depicted in the top panel of Figure 2 are the absolute motions of two points separated by 90° on the rim of a wheel. If the wheel is rolled across a surface and only the two points are visible, then the perception is as shown in the middle panel (Borjesson & Hofsten, 1975; Proffitt, Cutting, & Stier, 1979). The bottom panel represents the organization of this display's absolute motions into the perceived object-centered relative and observer-centered common motion components. Proffitt and Cutting (1979) noted that to perceptually specify object-centered motions, a perceptual center must be derived. In the case of wheel-generated motions, this perceptual center corresponded to the center of the configuration of point lights. For the event depicted in Figure 2, this is the midpoint between the points. For greater numbers of lights, the centroid of the configuration approximates the location of the perceived center (Proffitt & Cutting, 1980). In addition, Cutting and Proffitt (1981; Proffitt & Cutting, 1980) argued that object- and observer-relative motions have vastly different perceptual significances. Object-relative motions are used to specify what the object is—its three-dimensional configuration. For rigid objects, relative motions are constrained to be rotations and, of course, people are known to be quite facile at extracting three-dimensional perceptions when observing object rotations (Wallach & O'Connell, 1953). Observer-relative motion corresponds to the motion of the event's perceptual center and specifies where the object is

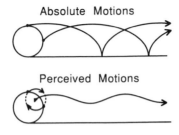

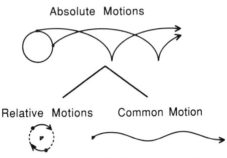

FIGURE 2 Depicted at the top are the absolute motions of two points on the rim of a rolling wheel. Below, the perceptual organization of these motions is shown.

going. Cutting and Proffitt further speculated that it is only this observer-relative motion component that is given perceptual significance in evoking intuitions about dynamics. We return to this proposal in the section on perceiving dynamics.

Perceptual vector analysis is a descriptive framework. It suggests that the perceptual system organizes the absolute motions of elements within a scene into two motion components. However, the approach does not make explicit claims about the processes by which the organization is achieved. In principle, relative motions could be organized around any stationary or moving point within the array, and the perceived common motion would then become the motion of that point. The Gestalt notion of pragnanz, or the minimum principle, has explicitly been evoked by two different approaches in an attempt to account for the specific relative and common motion components that are perceived.

Restle (1979) adapted Leeuwenberg's (1971, 1978) perceptual coding theory to handle moving configurations. Leeuwenberg developed a system for coding the complexity of visual patterns. Being highly sensitive to regularities and redundancies, this system can be used to assign a numerical value corresponding to the number of descriptors needed to describe any static pattern. The larger this coding value, the more complex the pattern.

Restle adapted this system so that it could deal with moving point-light configurations. In essence, he developed a system by which rotations and translations could each be described with a small number of distinct parameters. When applied to an array of moving points, different organizations could be compared in terms of the number of distinct motion parameters needed to describe them. If an array of moving points is not organized, then the number of parameters needed to describe it will be the sum of all of the parameters needed to describe each of its element's absolute motions. However, when organized so that one or more elements share some set of parameters, then this coding value decreases. Restle proposed that people will perceive the organization achieving the minimal coding value, that is, the organization in which elements share the greatest number of motion parameters. He applied this model to a large number of Johansson's (1950) original displays and found that it provided an extremely good prediction for the relative and common motions that people reported seeing in these displays. Cutting (1981) later adapted Restle's coding model to deal with the biomechanical motions present when point lights simulated the motions of locomoting people.

A drawback of coding theory is that it is not an account of process. That is, it can be used to evaluate the complexity of organizations once they have been defined by some other means. However, coding theory does not, itself, derive any organization.

Cutting and Proffitt (1982) proposed a minimum principle for the perception of relative and common motions with more implications for process. They proposed that the visual system seeks to minimize both relative and common motions. For rigid object motions, relative motions are always rotations, and these are minimal when their origin is at the centroid of the configuration. For a rotating configuration, the sum of all instantaneous motion vectors is zero if, and only if, rotations are specified relative to the configuration's centroid. It was further proposed that common motions are minimized when they are linear. In their examination of wheel-generated motions, they found that relative motion minimization accounted well for perceived events such as that shown in Figure 2. In all cases but one, relative motions were seen to occur around the center of the point-light configurations. The exception was the situation that Duncker (1929/1937) had described in which a light was present at the center of the wheel and another was placed on its circumference. In this situation, the perception is bistable. Sometimes the outer point is seen revolving around the one at the hub, and at other moments the pair of lights is seen to revolve around their midpoint. The first organization minimizes common motions, whereas the latter minimizes relative motions. Only when a point light coincides to the wheel's hub is this bistability observed; in all other cases, organizations manifesting a minimization of relative motions are observed (Cutting & Proffitt, 1982).

Although both of these minimum principle approaches predict the perceptual grouping of absolute motions into relative and common motion components, they do not specify what configuration will be seen. The perceptual grouping of absolute motions does not, in itself, solve the problem of extracting three-dimensional configurations from the derived motion components. On the other hand, projected rotations are an informational basis for the perception of three-dimensional form, and extracting relative motions from more complex absolute motions may be a step in the form perception processes.

It should be noted that most models of the extraction of three-dimensional form from motion are focused on rigid object motions (e.g., Ullman, 1985). Many of the displays in the event perception literature are seen as nonrigid objects (Cutting 1982; Janson & Johansson, 1973; Johansson, 1964). Moreover, other displays, such as that depicted in Figure 1, appear as organized motions more than as particular objects. The connection between the perceptual grouping of motions and the extraction of form from these motions has not yet been made.

II. PERCEIVING BIOMECHANICAL MOTIONS

During the 1960s, a dance company from Prague, Czechoslovakia, discovered a means for presenting themselves as ensembles of moving points of light. Called the *Black Light Theatre,* the dancers would cover themselves entirely in black and attach patches of material to their head and joints that would glow under blacklight illumination. When posed in stationary positions, their human form was not discernible, but when dancing, their form and actions were immediately identified.

Johansson (1973; Mass et al., 1971) developed a similar technique and used it to study the perception of biomechanical events. As can been seen in the Mass et al. films, movies were made of actors wearing luminous patches on their heads and major joints who were filmed under dark conditions such that only the patch lights were visible. The arrangement of patch lights for a walking person is shown in Figure 3.

The moving point-light displays created by Johansson (1973) are extremely engaging and entertaining to watch. One is immediately struck by the contrast between the minimality of the display's content and the richness of their perceptual meaning. Static images from these displays rarely evoke perceptions of the human form, whereas moving displays are identified very rapidly. In fact, Johansson showed that, on viewing an animated sequence of as little as 200 ms, people can identify the display as depicting a person and also identify the person's action. The filmed actors engaged in a variety of activities such as walking, climbing stairs, doing push-ups, and so forth, and these activities were easily detected.

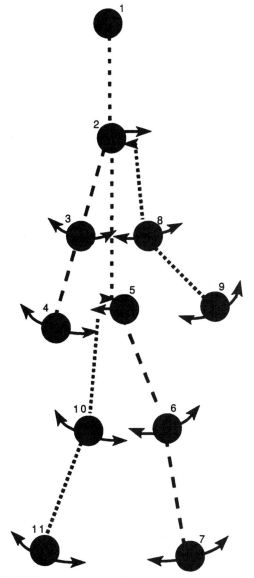

FIGURE 3   An example of point-light walker is shown.

Not only can actions be identified, but these actions can also provide useful information about physical properties. Runeson and Frykholm (1981) created videotapes of patch-light actors lifting a box with patch lights attached to its corners. In each recorded sequence, the actors lifted the box and its weight was varied across episodes. Runeson and Frykholm found that observers of the videotape sequences were able to provide estimates of the weights that were being lifted.

Cutting and his colleagues used Johansson's (1973) technique to create videotape sequences of walking people. Each sequence presented a single walker; the set of walkers was composed of a group of friends. When these sequences were shown to the group, it was found that the individuals involved could reliably identify themselves and one another (Cutting & Kozlowski, 1977). When shown to other observers who were unfamiliar with the initial actors, it was found that they could reliably identify the gender of the walkers (Kozlowski & Cutting, 1977; Barclay, Cutting, & Kozlowski, 1978). The finding that gender could be identified was surprising since, after all, most of the anatomical features associated with gender are not present in a point-light walker display.

Cutting and colleagues (Cutting, Proffitt, & Kozlowski, 1978) analyzed their displays and came to the conclusion that gender information was manifested in the relative motions of the hip and shoulder lights. The ratio of shoulder-to-hip widths differs across gender: Men have wider shoulders than hips, whereas these dimensions for women are about the same. The result of this is that, even for a point-light walker seen only in side view as it traverses the screen, the relative motions of the shoulder and hip lights reflect the differences in the shoulder and hip dimensions. Cutting et al. proposed that the relative motions of the shoulders and hips specify the twisting torso and its relative dimensions. As is shown in Figure 4, the dimensions of the torso affect its twisting motion such that the center of torque is somewhat higher in women than in men. Called the *center of moment* by Cutting et al., the location of this center of relative motions is informative about gender. Cutting (1978b) developed a means for simulating point-light walkers on computers and used this method to test the center of moment proposal. He created displays that were identical except

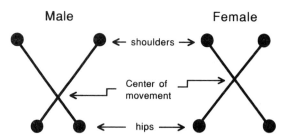

FIGURE 4   An exaggerated depiction of the relative shoulder and hip widths of men and women. In natural gait, the shoulders and hips twist in opposite directions, and a center of movement is defined that is higher in women than in men. (After Cutting, Proffitt, & Kozlowski, 1978.)

for the location of the center of moment and found that observers' gender judgments were affected by this manipulation in the manner predicted: The higher the simulated center of moment, the more likely the display was judged to be a woman.

As with other point-light displays discussed in the previous section, point-light walkers are perceived in a manner that implies an analysis of their absolute motions into relative- and common-motion components (Johansson, 1973). The specification of relative motions requires an object-centered frame of reference having a specific origin. Cutting and Proffitt (1981) proposed that the center of moment within the torso serves as the primary center and that a hierarchical analysis follows. By this account, the shoulder and hip motions are defined relative to the torso's center of moment. The shoulder and hip positions then serve as centers for the specification of the next joint's relative motion, that is, the elbow and the knee. These positions, in turn, serve as centers for the wrist and ankle. In this manner, the perception of a hierarchy of nested pendular motions is extracted by a process that determines the body's primary center and then proceeds to analyze the limbs in a joint-by-joint fashion. Each joint's motion is specified relative to the joint preceding it in the skeletal hierarchy. The point-light walker's observer-relative motion corresponds to the displacement of the torso's center of moment.

Point-light walker displays have extensively been used in studies of infant's sensitivities to motion-carried information. It has been shown that by 3 months of age, infants can extract some global structure from these displays (Bertenthal, Proffitt, & Cutting, 1984; Fox & McDaniels, 1982). Definite changes occur between the ages of 3 and 9 months in infants' responses to various manipulations of these displays, and it is only at the later ages that evidence suggests that infants may be identifying the human form (Bertenthal, Proffitt, Spetner, & Thomas, 1985). Assessment of the meaningful significance of these displays for prelinguistic infants is a problematic but not an intractable endeavor (Proffitt & Bertenthal, 1990).

Recently, Blake (1993) has shown that cats can discriminate point-light displays of walking cats from foils consisting of identical local motion vectors lacking the appropriate global organization. Blake also showed that cats lose their ability to discriminate between point-light cats and foils when the images are turned upside down. This orientation specificity has also been found when people view point-light walker displays. Adults rarely identify the human form when viewing inverted displays (Sumi, 1984). Infants begin to show orientation sensitivities at about 5 months of age (Bertenthal et al. 1985).

Some attempts have been made to describe the processes by which structure is recovered from point-light displays. Although they are descriptive, the vector analysis models of Johansson (1973, 1976) and of Cutting and

Proffitt (1981) are not really processing models of this sort since they do not derive three-dimensional structures, nor do they establish a connectivity pattern among the projected point lights. Cutting adapted Restle's (1979) coding theory to deal with point-light walker displays. As was discussed earlier, coding theory evaluates the information load of perceptual organizations only after these organizations have been derived by some other means.

A class of models, called *fixed-axis approaches,* has been developed to extract the connectivity pattern inherent in point-light walker displays (Hoffman & Flinchbaugh, 1982; Webb & Aggarwal, 1982). Unlike other structure-from-motion approaches that seek to recover the three-dimensional form of rigid solids (e.g., Ullman, 1979), fixed-axis models seek to recover the connection pattern for objects, such as the human body, that have rigid components connected by joints. Points within a rigid component can only move relative to each other along circular trajectories. These relative motions will project as circles or ellipses so long as the axis about which the rotation is occurring does not, itself, revolve. As is depicted in Figure 5, fixed-axis models can recover connectivity patterns between pairs of points by assessing whether their relative motions are circular or elliptical. These models will fail to recover rigid connections between pairs of points whenever their axes of rotation are not fixed in their direction.

Proffitt and Bertenthal (1988) examined whether the perception of connectivity in point-light displays was influenced by whether the axis of rotation was fixed in its direction. It was found that whenever the axis of rotation was itself revolving, people reported that the points in the display were unconnected or were moved together in an elastic manner. This finding is predicted by the fixed-axis models. Other findings, however, are not well assimilated by these models. The following are the most notable exceptions (1) The Mass et al. (1971) film shows two twirling point-light dances that are easily identified even though their motions violate the fixed-axis assumption. (2) Occlusion affects the perception of point-light walkers. Proffitt, Bertenthal, and Roberts (1984) created computer-generated point-light walkers with and without occlusion. Occlusion occurs in naturally produced displays whenever a luminance patch on a far limb passes behind the body. After a 1.5 min viewing period, displays without occlusion were identified only 33% of the time as compared with 85% for those having occlusion. (3) Proximity has been found to influence the perceived organization of relative motions in moving point-light displays. Gogel (1974) showed that relative motion organizations occur between near as opposed to far point lights. (4) Finally, there is evidence that people can extract connectivity from displays presenting elastic motions (Janson & Johansson, 1973).

Recently, a new approach has been taken toward understanding the processes by which biomechanical motions are perceived. Bertenthal and Pinto (1993) point out that biomechanical motions manifest regularities inherent

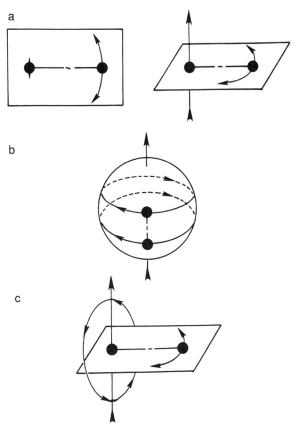

FIGURE 5   Fixed-axis models can recover connectivity in Panels *a* and *b* but not in *c*. (After Proffitt & Bertenthal, 1988.)

to the processes entailed in producing coordinated movements. For example, the motions of all of the limbs have the same frequency and are in either phase or counterphase. Bertenthal and Pinto suggest that people may perceive biomechanical motions by detecting the dynamical constraints inherent in their production. This proposal implies that biomechanical motions are special in the sense that their perception is based on a detection of regularities specific to mechanical systems, such as animals, that possess a high degree of coordination among their component structures. Some support for this approach is found in Cutting, Moore, and Morrison's (1988) study, in which it was found that point-light walker displays are masked best by scrambled walker elements that share the same gait parameters as the walker target.

As was alluded to at the beginning of this chapter, Gibson (1970) and

Johansson (1970) were of two minds as to what could be concluded about everyday human perception from studies of minimal stimuli such as point-light walker displays. Gibson (1977) argued:

> Johansson's analysis will work for what might be called a *flat* event seen from the front, or a *transparent* event, with the essential parts of the machine or the man always projected in the array. It will work for the motions and collisions in a frontal plane of objects like billiard balls. But it will not work for an ordinary event where one part goes out of sight behind another part and then comes back into sight again. (p. 163)

For Gibson, ordinary events always entailed local disturbances in optical structure in which, as some surfaces pass in front of others, deletion and accretion of optically specified texture always occurs. Since in Johansson's displays this optical information is absent, Gibson felt that they lacked the information that normally engages the perceptual system.

In this section, we have surveyed phenomena and approaches to studying biomechanical motions without questioning the ecological validity of generalizations drawn from studies utilizing Johansson's patch-light technique. We are persuaded by the evocative nature of these displays that they engage enduring and robust processes of the perceptual system. At this date, ecological approaches to perception are not developed to the point that they can provide agreed on principles that could decide the matter (Proffitt, 1993).

III. PERCEIVING APPROACHING OBJECTS

Many of our behaviors depend on temporally coordinating our actions with the approach of objects in the environment. This approach may be due to our own motion (e.g., we drive an automobile down the street and want to turn at a given point) or the motion of objects (e.g., a tennis ball comes toward us and we want to hit it back to our opponent's court). How do we time our actions?

One possible strategy would involve perceiving the relevant event kinematics and spatial layout (e.g., distance, velocity, and acceleration) and performing the necessary calculations on these physical variables to determine the time of approach. However, it has been demonstrated that if certain simplifying assumptions hold, an elegant mapping between the event kinematics and optical variables emerges. These optical variables, termed *visual tau*, are scaled to a temporal metric. Thus, an observer need not know the distance to an object or the speed of approach; the optical information is sufficient to specify the time until the object collides or passes. We examine how these optical variables can, in principle, be used to determine time to contact or passage and to control braking. We then consider their utility in a particular arena of skilled activity: baseball.

A. Time to Contact–Time to Passage

Perhaps the first derivation of visual tau was put forth by astrophysicist F. Hoyle, (1957) in his science fiction novel, *The Black Cloud*. In the book, Hoyle allows his Dr. Weichart to discover that the time until an approaching astrobody (the black cloud) reaches earth can be calculated without knowing its actual physical size or distance or performing a Dopler shift analysis. Using discrete images taken 2 months apart, the scientist can determine the object's current visual angle of extent and the rate of change of the angle. By assuming that the object is a fixed physical size (i.e., the cloud itself is not expanding or contracting) and that it is approaching earth at a constant relative velocity, the time to contact (TTC) can be estimated as

$$TTC \approx \theta \; / \; \delta\theta/\delta t, \tag{1}$$

where θ is the current angular extent (in radians), and $\delta\theta/\delta t$ is its rate of change. The derivation is straightforward. Let O be the linear diameter of the approaching object, D is the distance to the object, and V is the velocity of approach. θ can be approximated by O/D (by using the law of small angles). Taking the temporal derivative of $\theta = O/D$ yields

$$\delta\theta/\delta t = (-O/D^2) \cdot \delta D/\delta t. \tag{2}$$

Since $\delta D/\delta t$ equals $-V$ and $D/V = TTC$, Equation 2 simplifies to

$$\delta\theta/\delta t = (O/D) \; / \; TTC \text{ or } \delta\theta/\delta t = \theta \; / \; TTC, \tag{3}$$

and rearranging it yields Equation 1. The geometry of this event is shown if Figure 6a.

Lee introduced the concept of visual tau information for control of action (Lee, 1974, 1976, 1980). One important extension was to demonstrate that tau information is available for noncollision situations. In such cases, the time to passage (TTP) is specified by a mathematical analogue

$$TTP \approx \phi \; / \; \delta\phi/\delta t, \tag{4}$$

where ϕ is the angle between a moving observer's heading vector and the target object, and $\delta\phi/\delta t$ is the rate of change of that angle, as shown in Figure 6b. Since Lee has proposed a number of potential tau-type optical variables (and some nonvisual tau variables as well), it is useful to use the taxonomy proposed by Tresilian (1991). Visual tau that can be defined local to the image of an approaching object is termed *local tau,* or τ_L. (Tresilian makes the further distinction of local tau operating on the distance between two points of the object, termed $\tau_L{}^1$, and local tau calculated on the entire image area, termed $\tau_L{}^2$). Local tau is distinguished from *global tau* (τ_G), which involved processing the global velocity field produced by the observer's motion. Global tau is only available to a moving observer and

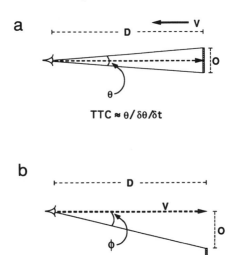

FIGURE 6   The geometry for time to contact (TTC) as shown in (a) and time to passage (TTP) events as shown in (b). (a) In the TTC event, an object, O, directly approaches the observer with a constant velocity, V. At any given distance, D, the TTC is estimated by the ratio of the object's current angular extent, θ, divided by the angle's rate of change, $\delta\theta/\delta t$. (b) In the TTP event, an object is offset a distance O from the observer's heading vector. If the observer moves at a constant velocity, V, the TTP is estimated by the angle of the object relative to the heading vector, ϕ, divided by the angle's rate of change, $\delta\phi/\delta t$.

requires that the observer be able to extract his or her heading from the optic flow. Both local and global tau require constant relative observer–object velocity to be mathematically valid. (The above derivations use a spherical coordinate system and thus require the law of small angle assumption. Lee often used a planar coordinate system. Whereas this coordinate system does not require the tangent approximation, it does require that the retina be approximated by a planar projection surface.)

Most empirical research has focused on humans' and other animals' sensitivity to τ_L. Early work demonstrated that the symmetrical dilatation of visual images results in avoidant behavior for human adults and animals (Schiff, 1965) and for human infants (Bower, Broughton, & Moore, 1970). Yonis and his colleagues (Yonis et al., 1977) examined the development of sensitivity to information for impending collision and demonstrated that image expansion becomes clearly associated with avoidant behavior by 9 months of age. Subsequent studies have demonstrated that, within certain temporal ranges, people make reasonably accurate relative and absolute TTC judgments (McLeod & Ross, 1983; Schiff & Detwiler, 1979; Schiff & Oldak, 1990; Simpson, 1988; Todd, 1981).

All visual tau-based strategies require an assumption of constant approach velocity. If the object–observer velocity is not constant, temporal error will be introduced. This error will depend on the magnitude of the acceleration (i.e., greater acceleration creates larger errors) and the time from contact or passage (i.e., the less time until contact or passage, the smaller change in velocity results from acceleration). There is some controversy regarding whether tau strategies are used in situations involving acceleration. Some evidence has been presented to suggest that humans (Lee, Young, Reddish, Lough, & Clayton, 1983) and birds (Lee & Reddish, 1981) make TTC judgments that are consistent with an assumption of constant velocity, even when acceleration is present. However, it is not clear that these studies were sufficiently sensitive to discriminate between timing based on constant velocity and timing based on nonconstant velocity (Tresilian, 1994).

More recently, investigators have examined observers' sensitivity to τ_G information, both in the presence (Schiff & Oldak, 1990) and absence (Kaiser & Mowafy, 1993) of τ_L cues. These later studies suggest that TTP judgments are not as precise as TTC judgments (e.g., Todd found reliable relative TTC judgments with less than 100-ms difference in arrival time, but Kaiser and Mowafy's observers required a 500-ms difference). Nonetheless, observers did demonstrate reasonable competence with τ_G information. Processing of τ_G information requires that observers be able to extract their heading, the position of the target object relative to the heading, and the rate of change of that position. Thus, whereas τ_G is a mathematical analogue to τ_L, its performance requirements are quite different, especially since the visual system may possess processing mechanisms specific to local expansions. Such neural mechanisms have been found in both birds (Wang & Frost, 1992) and monkeys (Tanaka & Saito, 1989) and might account for the performance advantage in TTC judgments.

B. Controlled Braking

In addition to timing intercept behavior, Lee (1976) also suggested that visual tau information can be used to control braking behavior. Specifically, Lee demonstrated that if the temporal derivative of tau, $\dot{\tau}$, is held at a constant value of -0.5, a constant deceleration resulting in a velocity of zero at the point of impact will occur. Clearly, a $\dot{\tau}$ of -1.0 corresponds to a zero deceleration and impact at the initial velocity. A $\dot{\tau}$ of 0.0 will produce an exponentially decaying velocity and deceleration to a zero velocity, with an infinite time to impact. (In practice, maintaining a $\dot{\tau} = 0.0$ would be appropriate for all but the last few feet of a helicopter pilot's approach to hover. The optimal approach protocol requires the pilot to reduce speed proportional to distance to go.)

Interpreting $\dot{\tau}$ braking strategies for intermediate values is somewhat problematic. Kim, Turvey, and Carello (1993) argued that a $\dot{\tau}$ of -0.5 represents a "critical value" for behavior and control: values from 0 to -0.5 (inclusive) will result in safe braking; more extreme values (i.e., between -0.5 and -1.0) will result in hard contact. Further, they argued, observers spontaneously classify stimuli into safe and unsafe events on the basis of this criteria. Kaiser and Phatak (1993) disputed Kim et al.'s thesis. They argued that all constant $\dot{\tau}$ profiles less than 0 and greater than -1.0 result in zero velocity at the point of impact, but the more negative profiles require extreme deceleration late in the trajectory, which may be physically unrealizable (top panel of Figure 7). However, if the braking is not obtained, $\dot{\tau}$ will not be constant. They suggested that the actual limit will be a function of the braking system's dynamics. Further, they contended, there is little empirical evidence to suggest that people actually use constant $\dot{\tau}$ braking strategies; to do so, for most $\dot{\tau}$ values, requires a complex deceleration curve (bottom panel of Figure 7) not observed in vehicle-control studies. Even Spurr's (1969) study on automobile braking from which Lee derived his $\dot{\tau} = 0.5$ strategy showed that drivers demonstrate little consistency in their braking patterns.

Clearly, a vehicle's dynamics (or an animal's biodynamics) will play a large role in determining what braking strategies are viable. In a very simple control system (e.g., where control input maps linearly with deceleration), the following strategy that is based on $\dot{\tau}$ nulling would be viable: Input a constant decleration and observe $\dot{\tau}$. If $\dot{\tau}$ increases (i.e., becomes less negative), then the deceleration is too great and should be reduced until $\dot{\tau}$ remains constant. If $\dot{\tau}$ decreases (i.e., becomes more negative), then the deceleration is insufficient and should be increased until $\dot{\tau}$ is constant. This strategy exploits the fact that the only constant $\dot{\tau}$ with a constant nonzero deceleration is -0.5 and results in a zero velocity at impact. On the basis of empirical studies to date, however, there is insufficient evidence to conclude that humans are able to utilize $\dot{\tau}$ as a control variable, even in such simple dynamic environments.

Let us consider critically timed performance in a specific domain, one that has challenged both physicists and psychologists (and more than a few statisticians) to provide adequate models of events: professional baseball. The physics of baseball are not entirely understood, despite the efforts of such distinguished scientists as R. T. Adair, who held the honorary appointment of Physicist to the National League in the late 1970s (and whose book, *The Physics of Baseball,* 1990, provides a wonderful overview of the science of pitching and hitting). Nonetheless, the simplified physical models are adequate to understand the performance challenges facing the batter and fielder.

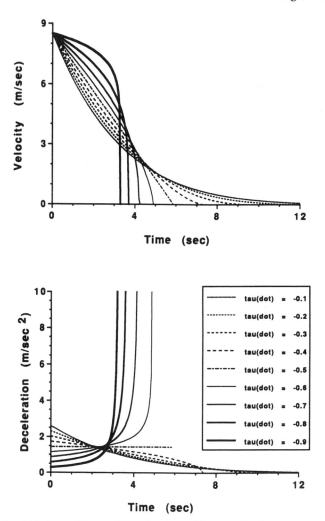

FIGURE 7 Velocity × Time and Deceleration × Time profiles for 0.1 intervals of −1<
τ(dot) < 0 by using an initial velocity of 8.5 m/s and an initial distance of 25 m. (Note that all
values yield a velocity of zero at the point of contact.)

C. Baseball

As Crash Davis succinctly explained in the film *Bull Durham,* the game of
baseball is extremely simple: you hit the ball, you catch the ball, you throw
the ball. Leaving aside the task of throwing the ball, how can visual tau (or
other optical cues) direct the player's hitting and catching behaviors?

1. You Hit the Ball

Over the history of the sport, professional baseball players have amassed a cumulative batting average of approximately 0.26. This means that, on average, the batter achieves a base hit on about a quarter of his trips to the plate. Even this success rate is remarkable when one considers the precision of action required to even hit the ball inbounds: swing a bat no more than 2 3/4 in. in diameter at a ball just under 3 in. in diameter that is approaching at a speed usually between 70 and 100 miles per hour (mph). To complicate matters, magnus and drag-crises forces may act on the ball (because of the ball's spin and irregular surface), dynamically modifying its trajectory. Since the distance from the pitcher's mound to home plate is 60.5 ft, the total travel time is less than 6/10ths of a s: a high-speed fast ball (90 mph) will cross the plate only 0.4 of a s after leaving the pitcher's hand. Given that a functional power swing requires about 0.2 s to execute (the latter half of which is largely a ballistic action), all timing-relative information must be extracted while the ball is more than 20 ft from the batter. The temporal error tolerance is small: swinging .01 s late or early will result in the ball being hit foul. At a distance of 20 ft, the ball subtends 0.7° visual angle; the expansion rate is 3.5°/s (for a 70 mph pitch). Given these daunting parameters, it is no wonder that Ted Williams pronounced hitting a baseball the hardest single act in all of sports (Williams & Underwood, 1986).

It is unlikely that τ_L, in the absence of additional visual cues, would provide sufficient information for the batter to time his swing. The best reported discrimination threshold for τ_L is about 10% and that was for stimuli in which TTC was between 1 and 4 s (Regan & Hamstra, 1992). Even if the proportional threshold generalizes to the short TTC batting requires, the associated error would be unacceptably high (e.g., around 20 ms).[1] It is possible, of course, that professional baseball players are that much more skilled in the perceptual pickup of τ_L information. However, McLeod's (1987) studies with cricket players suggest that skill level is not related to the speed of processing visual information but rather to "the organization of the motor system that uses the output of the perceptual system" (p. 49). Some researchers (e.g., Fitch & Turvey, 1978) have argued that the consistency of batters' swing execution time is evidence for a tau-margin timing strategy. That is, since the batter consistently takes 200 ms to swing, he must be using a cue like τ_L to determine when the ball is 200 ms from the plate. However, this is not a strong argument; swing-time consistency may be the result of motor programming economy or the fact that

---

[1] Bahill and Karnavas (1993) argued that a batter *should* be able to determine the ball's arrival time from τ alone. However, they base this conclusion on the assumption that since θ and $\delta\theta/\delta t$ are suprathreshold (citing Regan & Beverley's, 1978, article on expansion detection), τ can be computed with adequate accuracy.

players attempting to achieve maximum bat velocity will produce swings of consistent duration.

McBeath (1990) argued that the batter brings cognitive schemata with him to the plate. Such mental models are especially necessary if the batter does not track the ball for its entire approach but rather makes an anticipatory saccade to where to ball is predicted to cross the plate. Such an eye movement strategy is often used by batters since the ball speed makes continuous tracking virtually impossible for the last segment of the trajectory (Bahill & LaRitz, 1984). Having expectations concerning the speed of the pitch, McBeath argued, can explain batters' hitting errors with off-speed pitches and can account for the illusion of the rising fastball. McBeath (1990) maintained the following:

> If the batter maintains correct line of sight on the ball during the beginning and middle portions of its trajectory, a speed under-estimation will cause the ball to appear both slightly farther away and slightly lower than its actual location. . . . When the ball crosses the plate and the batter perceives its actual location, the experienced trajectory will be adjusted. Because the ball arrives a few milliseconds early and as much as a third of a meter above the anticipated arrival point, it will appear to hop up. (p. 548)

Whereas McBeath's account is consistent with many errors and trajectory misjudgments that batters make, it does not explain how batters hit as well as they do. A swing execution strategy that is based on nominal pitching speed would not provide the temporal precision required (and observed) in successful batters.

In all likelihood, skilled batters bring a repertoire of perceptual and cognitive skills to the task. They are able to "read" the pitcher's wind up and throwing motion for cues concerning the likely spin on the ball (and possess heuristics about the effect such spin will have on the ball's trajectory). In addition to τ_L, batters can apply their familiar size knowledge to judge the ball's depth. There are static and dynamic stereoscopic and convergence cues to the ball's distance and motion (although these may be subthreshold given the distances and temporal durations involved; see Regan, Kaufman, & Lincoln, 1986). Finally, there is a wealth of "baseball smarts" the batter brings to bear that may refine his "nominal pitch speed" expectation, including the current ball and strike count, base runner position and number of outs, and level of fatigue in the opposing pitcher. This knowledge, in addition to his finely honed perceptual skills, allows the batter to "get lucky."

2. You Catch the Ball

For discussion, we consider the problem of fielding a fly ball. Successfully catching the baseball can be divided into two subcomponents: getting to the general area of the field where the ball will land and executing a properly timed grasp of the ball. Chapman (1968) proposed a set of intriguingly simply visual cues a fielder can use to perform the first task.

Allowing several simplifications (e.g., neglecting air resistance), Chapman (1968) showed that a fly ball traces a parabolic trajectory. From the eye point of its landing site, the ball produces an image-plane trajectory with a constant range of change in elevation. Thus, to a fielder positioned correctly, the tangent of the ball's elevation angle increases linearly until the ball is caught (see Figure 8). Of interest, Chapman demonstrated that this constant tanψ rate strategy generalizes to a player who is initially in front of or behind the landing point if he moves with a constant velocity to the appropriate position. Thus, if a fielder moves at a constant speed (which is zero if he is already at the right spot) so as to maintain a constant rate of increase in tanψ, he will be in position to catch the ball when it lands. Chapman also suggested a second visual strategy that allows the fielder to position himself laterally: move so as to keep the ball at a constant relative angle. This will position the fielder correctly because two moving bodies that maintain constant relative headings are on a collision course.[2] Thus, Chapman (1968) proposed an ideal fielder operating on the following two visual cues: "If the player runs so as to maintain the bearing of the ball constant . . . and the rate of change of tanψ, constant, he is in the right place to catch the ball at the right time" (p. 870).

It is somewhat equivocal, on the basis of empirical evidence, whether outfielders actually utilize the strategies Chapman proposed. Several studies (Babler & Dannemiller, 1993; Michaels & Oudejans, 1992; Todd, 1981) have examined whether observers could accurately judge the landing point of an object (e.g., in front or behind them) on the basis of its image-plane trajectory. In Todd's study, observers performed poorly when judging the motion of a single point; judgments whether the object would land at the observation point or 30 ft in front were correct less than 65% of the time (if object expansion information was also present in the stimuli, observers were correct over 80% of the time). Babler and Dannemiller reported far better performance, which they attribute to the longer duration of their stimuli. By showing a longer portion of the trajectory (1–1.25 s compared with 0.75 s in Todd's study), larger velocity ratios (i.e., change in velocity divided by average velocity) were instantiated. Given people's relative insensitivity to acceleration (Babler & Dannemiller reported thresholds of -0.22 and 0.16), it is not surprising that Todd's "short ball" stimuli (with a

---

[2] Kaiser and Mowafy (1993) discuss cases in which this "constant-bearing" cue creates problems. Specifically, an unknown object that maintains a constant bearing can be either a distant stationary object or a moving object on a collision course; the τ_G information is equivalent. These two situations can be very difficult to distinguish in an impoverished visual environment (e.g., during night flight).

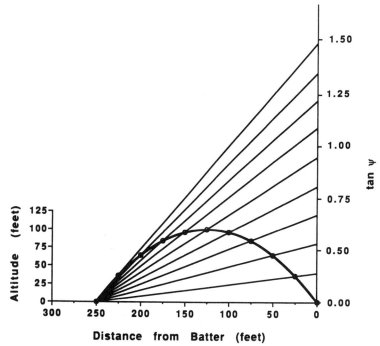

FIGURE 8 Trajectory of a fly ball and the corresponding image-plane trajectory for an observer positioned at the ball's landing site. Ball positions are shown at 0.25 s intervals.

median velocity ratio of −0.17) proved daunting for observers. Michaels and Oudejans (1992) reported passive judgment performance similar to Babler and Dannemiller and presented evidence that fielder movement is consistent with an acceleration-nulling strategy. Still, it is yet to be convincingly demonstrated that fielders use image acceleration–motion nulling strategies to visually control their positioning.

Of course, for the fielder to get to the landing point is only necessary, not sufficient. There is still the matter of catching the ball. Fielders' gloves assist in this task: their size creates a larger target area, and their "trapping action" relieves the fielder of some of the critical timing that a bare-hand grasp would require. Nonetheless, the fielder will require fairly precise visual information to guide his spatiotemporal coordination of catching, that is, getting the glove to the right place at the right time. With regard to getting to the right place, Peper, Bootsma, Mestre, and Bakker (1994) recently proposed an active control strategy that allows the fielder to modulate his hand motion on the basis of a combination of optical and kinaesthetic information. The optical information is scaled in ball-size units, requiring the fielder to augment the optical information with a familiar-size metric.

As to timing, Savelsbergh, Whiting, and Bootsma (1991) examined the use of τ_L information in controlling the grasp movements involved in catching a ball. They introduced nonveridical optical expansion by using a ball whose size could be altered during the trajectory and demonstrated that the time of the maximal closing velocity of the hand was later if the ball were deflated as it approached. Their findings suggest that grasping behavior is modified to reflect changes in τ_L, at least when the ball is caught fairly close to the eye point. When fielding a baseball, however, the ball is often caught some distance from the fielder's eye. This eyepoint and glove displacement introduces error in τ_L. Fielders must then either utilize cues that are not affected by this displacement or make an adjustment to correct for the error. Both Tresilian (1991) and Bootsma and Oudejans (1993) proposed optical variables that are more robust to eyepoint and intersect displacements. However, these optical variables tend to be far more complex than the elegant tau variables. And, like the tau variables themselves, their actual utilization as control variables is yet to be convincingly demonstrated.

IV. PERCEIVING NATURAL DYNAMICS

Perceived events are rich in meaning. Moving point–light displays of human actors not only evoke perceptions of people but also of their gender, actions, and intentions (Kozlowski & Cutting, 1977; Johansson, 1973; MacArthur & Baron, 1983, respectively). In fact, movies of simple two–dimensional geometrical shapes that move about as if in chase can evoke perceptions of highly elaborate social scenarios (Heider & Simmel, 1944). Michotte (1963) demonstrated that impressions of causality are spontaneously evoked when displays that can be construed as collisions are observed. Runeson and Frykholm (1983) showed that observers of point–light displays could report on the weight of boxes that actors had lifted. These latter two findings show that people form dynamic impressions when observing motions. In physics, descriptions of motions without regard for their causes are called *kinematics*. When a description of an object's motions includes such considerations as its mass and the forces acting on it, then the description falls within the domain of *dynamics*. Issues of causality appeal to dynamic descriptions. It is, of course, a fact that the proximal stimulation for visual event perception can completely be described in terms of kinematics. That people perceive such attributes as gender, actions, intentions, social dispositions, and dynamic relations when observing events implies that these perceptions cannot be reduced to the kinematic level of description that is sufficient for describing their stimulus bases (Gilden, 1991). Relative to the other perceived attributes, perceiving dynamics has received the most attention in the event perception literature. The most agreed on generalization that can be made from this literature is that ongoing events often evoke much more accurate dynamical intuitions than those elicited when people are assessed with static materials.

There has developed an extensive literature on people's commonsense beliefs about natural dynamics as assessed with drawings and paper-and-pencil tests. Called *Intuitive Physics* by McCloskey (1983), many studies indicate that people will make quite erroneous predictions about natural object motions, even in apparently simple situations. Consider an example from McCloskey, Caramazza, and Green (1980). Suppose that you observe a C-shaped tube that is lying flat on a table top. In the study a drawing is provided. Now suppose that a ball is placed in one end of the tube and is given a push so that it rolls through the tube and out of the other end. What will be the path taken by the ball after it exits the tube? Subjects would be asked to draw the trajectory on the drawing provided. The correct answer is that the ball should roll along a straight path tangent to the curvature of the tube at the point of exit. Many people get this problem wrong and draw, instead, a curved path that continues the curvature of the tube and gradually straightens out. Other studies using similar paper-and-pencil assessment procedures have shown that many people make erroneous dynamical predictions in a variety of other simple situations. The following are two examples: (1) When a tether on a pendulum breaks at the apex—highest position—of its swing, then the bob is not predicted to fall straight down but rather to continue to move beyond its maximum horizontal extent and to fall along a parabolic curve (Caramazza et al., 1981). When an object is dropped by a moving carrier—such as a bomb dropped from a plane—then the object is predicted to fall straight down rather than to maintain its forward momentum (McCloskey, Washburn, & Felch, 1983).

Essentially all of the situations studied in the "Intuitive Physics" literature have also been investigated by using animated events and having people make naturalness judgments. These studies have shown that people's intuitions about what looks natural conforms well with what is dynamically correct (Kaiser, Proffitt, Whelan, & Hecht, 1992). In these studies, events were created in which objects moved in a physically correct manner and also in a variety of anomalous ways including those that were predicted by people who got the paper-and-pencil problems wrong. Thus, for example, animations were created for the C-shaped tube problem in which the ball exited the tube and rolled along an appropriate straight path and also ones in which it followed a variety of curved paths. In this study, it was found that almost everyone, including people who had originally drawn curved paths, chose as most natural the canonical event (Kaiser, Proffitt, & Anderson, 1985).

There are, of course, limitations in the effectiveness of animation to evoke accurate dynamical intuitions. The least interesting of these limits are those in which the relevant dynamical quantities are imperceptible. In fact, most of the domain of physics involves objects that are either too small or too fast or slow to be seen. Of relevance to theories relating perception to dynamical reasonings are those macroscopic events in which the dynamical intuitions that are evoked are in conflict with the motions that are seen. An excellent example of such an event is the behavior of a spinning top or gyroscope. The behavior of a spinning top seems magical because its motions appear to be dynamically impossible.

Proffitt, Kaiser, and Whelan (1990) studied a situation involving the conservation of angular momentum. A computer simulation was made of a satellite spinning in space. The satellite had solar panels that could be extended or contracted in a manner that influenced its moment of inertia. The natural outcome of extending the panels would be a decrease in the satellite's angular velocity. This situation is essentially the same as a spinning ice skater who extends her or his arms and, thereby, decelerates her or his spin. In the study, events were created in which the satellite's behavior took a variety of outcomes following an extension or contraction of its solar panels. Observers were asked to make naturalness judgments, and it was found that the event was judged to be unnatural only when the satellite stopped spinning altogether or reversed in its spin direction. All other outcomes were judged to appear equally good. For a satellite extending its panels, these included various magnitudes of both decelerations and accelerations.

Howard (1978) conducted a study to determine whether animation would improve performance on the Piagetian water-level problem. In this problem, subjects are asked to predict the orientation of a liquid's surface contained within a tilted container. Typically, a drawing is provided and subjects draw a line indicating the liquid's surface. Dozens of studies have demonstrated that approximately 40% of the adult population do not draw horizontal lines but rather incline the depicted surface by more than 5° off the horizontal (McAfee & Proffitt, 1991). Howard created animated displays in which an initially upright container was tilted and the liquid's surface level sometimes remained horizontal and sometimes was misoriented in concordance with people's predictions on the paper-and-pencil test. It was found that the animations did not improve performance. McAfee and Proffitt conducted a pilot study that replicated this finding.

Clearly, viewing events sometimes evokes accurate naturalness judgments and sometimes does not. Kaiser et al., (1992) provided an account that related performance to an account of dynamical event complexity. This account is presented in more detail at the end of this section. In essence, the account suggests that performance will be good when observers can base their naturalness judgment on just one-object dimension such as the motion of the object's center of mass. Performance will be poor when more than one-object dimension is, in fact, relevant or is believed to be relevant. These situations require observers to notice such multidimensional quantities as an object's shape, orientation, and rotation.

Dynamical events have not only been studied relative to their influence in evoking naturalness judgments but also in terms of the dynamical quantities that are sometimes perceived. In this latter regard, Runeson (1977) initiated a line of research on people's ability to perceive dynamical quantities from kinematical variables. He demonstrated that there are situations in which dynamical variables are specified by relationships among kinematical variables. The most clearly articulated of these situations was that of two balls colliding. Runeson showed that the relevant conservation of linear momentum equations could be written such that the relative masses of the balls could be determined by a representation involving the pre- and postcollision velocities of the balls.

A number of studies have shown that people do, indeed, perceive dynamical quantities when viewing events. As previously mentioned, Runeson and Frykholm (1983) showed that people can make judgments about the weight of a box being lifted by a point-light actor. Bingham (1987) extended these findings to perceiving weight in a one-arm curl situation. Todd and Warren (1982) and Kaiser and Proffitt (1984) showed that people are able to make judgments about which object is heavier after watching them collide.

Given that people do perceive dynamical quantities in a variety of situations, the questions of interest become: What are people doing? Are they accurate? Are the relevant perceptual processes consistent with the physics of the situation? The studies that address these questions point to the conclusion that people form their dynamical judgments on the basis of simple heuristics that yield fairly accurate performance in some situations but not in others.

Gilden and Proffitt (1989) examined the perception of relative mass when viewing collisions. They created computer simulations of collisions in which one ball rolled across a surface and struck another stationary ball. As Runeson (1977) had shown, the kinematics in this event specify the mass ratio between the two balls. Gilden and Proffitt found that people did not base their judgments of relative mass on an appropriate physical representation of the event but rather on two implicit heuristics. One heuristic stated that after a collision, the ball with the greatest speed—that which left the screen first—was the lightest. The second heuristic stated that if the striking ball ricocheted back after the collision, then it was lighter. Two findings are especially revealing relative to these heuristics. First, the size of the judged mass ratio was found to depend on the magnitude of the variable relevant to the effective heuristic not on the actual simulated mass ratios. If the first heuristic were the effective one, then the magnitude of the mass ratio judgment depended on the difference in the balls' postcollision speeds; if the second heuristic were effective, then the angle of ricochet determined relative mass. Second, people were found to make judgments that appealed to one or the other of the heuristics, they never combined them. This means that people based their judgment solely on the ratio of speed or on angle of ricochet, and they never used both of these dimensions within the same event.

Gilden (1991) and Pittenger (1991) surveyed the literature and both concluded that the evidence favors the position that heuristical processes are at work in all of the dynamical situations investigated. Lifted-weight events are difficult to evaluate since the manner in which weight is specified by kinematic variables has never been formally articulated; however, Gilden showed that the data from the Runeson and Frykholm (1983) and the Bingham (1987) studies are consistent with the perceptual use of simple heuristics that relate to single-stimulus dimensions. Gilden reanalyzed a study on the perception of elasticity conducted by Warren, Kim, and Husney (1987). Warren et al. created displays simulating bouncing balls that had varying degrees of elasticity. Gilden showed that the data were better fit by a heuristic relating the difference in bounce heights between successive bounces than by a canonical analysis of the event in which the square root of the ratio of bounce heights was used. Pittenger (1990, 1991) came to a similar conclusion in evaluating his 1990 study showing that people are sensitive to the relationship between the length of a pendulum's arm and the duration of its period. He concluded that his subjects' relatively good performance was based on a heuristic related to arm length and not to a physical representation in which the square root of arm length is appropriate.

Heuristics are overly simplistic decision rules that yield relatively accurate conclusions in some situations and erroneous ones in others. Proffitt and Gilden (1989) proposed an account of dynamical event complexity that prescribes when dynamical heuristics ought to succeed and when they should fail. This account has two parts. First, it shows that mechanical systems can be divided into two classes differing in their physical complexity. Second, it argues that this division has relevance for the sort of heuristics that people use in assessing dynamics.

Physical representations for object motions have a categorical limit with respect to their complexity. There is a class of motions, *particle motions,* in which the only object descriptor of relevance to the object's dynamical behavior is the location of the object's center of mass. That is, the equations of motion that describe the object's behavior treat the object as if it were a particle since its form and orientation are dynamically irrelevant. All other motions are called *extended-body* motions since form and orientation are dynamically relevant. As an example, consider a wheel. If the wheel is dropped in a vacuum, then its velocity is simply a function of the distance that its center of mass has fallen. Ignoring air resistance, free fall is a particle motion. On the other hand, suppose that the wheel is placed on an inclined plane and released. In this context, the shape of the wheel—its moment of inertia—is dynamically relevant. This is an extended-body motion context.

The defining characteristic of particle motions is that their dynamical descriptions require only one object descriptor. Proffitt and Gilden (1989) proposed that people's heuristics about natural dynamics are limited to single object descriptors. People might possess a number of different heuristics related to a particular situation; however, each of these heuristics makes reference to only one object descriptor. Thus, people ought to be able to form relatively good heuristics about particle motions since these situations only require a single heuristic. On the other hand, people ought to make poorer judgments in extended-body contexts since these require representations over multiple object descriptors. Commonsense heuristics only refer to one object descriptor; people do not combine heuristics when appropriate.

Proffitt and Gilden (1989) surveyed the literature and found considerable support for this account. Recall Gilden and Proffitt's study on mass ratio judgments formed when viewing collisions. There it was found that people possessed the following two heuristics: (1) After the collision, the faster moving object is lighter, and (2) after the collision, the object that ricocheted is lighter. These heuristics yielded relative accurate judgments of which object is lighter when either relative speed or ricochet was highly salient since they are associated with the correct decision. On the other hand, when both relative speed and ricochet angle were highly salient, people never combined the heuristics and decisions of which was the lighter object were little better than chance. Proffitt et al. (1990) assessed a variety of simple extended-body situations involving rotational systems such as wheels and found that people's dynamical intuitions were highly inaccurate, even when the people tested were physics teachers and athletes—bicycle racers—who were familiar with the motions. As discussed earlier, Kaiser et al., (1992) showed that animation facilitates dynamical intuitions in particle motion contexts but not in extended-body ones.

The particle/extended-body motion distinction is only a first attempt at defining the contextual limits on human dynamical reasoning. The essence of the proposal is simply that people attend to only one thing at a time when making dynamical judgments. Judgments are relatively accurate in particle motion contexts since decisions can be based on a single object descriptor. In many situations, such as wheel-generated motions, this descriptor coincides with the observer-relative common motion, component that is seen in the event. In some simple extended-body situations such as viewing collisions, dynamical judgments are relatively accurate in some cases but not in others. In other extended-body contexts such as viewing a wheel on a ramp, dynamical judgments are more often wrong than right. Finally, in more complex extended-body contexts such as observing a spinning top, dynamical intuitions are so clearly violated that the event appears magical.

V. CONCLUSION

We take it to be self-evident that all experience is composed of events. Even a controlled tachistoscope experiment entails an occurrence that changes over time: the stimulus pattern is presented and removed. The field of event perception has focused on a few selected topics, the principal ones being those discussed in this chapter. What is common to all of these events is that the relevant perceptual information is manifested only in the change. A point-light walker display, for example, is perceived as a person only when it moves. Without motion, none of the events surveyed in this chapter would be perceived to have the meanings that are experienced when ongoing displays are observed.

The meanings experienced when viewing events include answers to the following *wh*-questions: (1) Who? Friends and gender are identified in point-light walker displays. (2) What? Three-dimensional structure is seen in object rotations (the kinetic depth effect), in moving jointed objects (point-light walkers), and in observer-relative translations (motion parallax). (3) Where? Motions are organized so that a common motion is extracted that perceptually specifies where an object is going. (4) When? Regularities, such as visual tau, are present in object motions that can inform an observer about when an object will contact or pass their point of observation. (5) Why? People form dynamical intuitions that relate to the causal necessity of events.

To these questions, perception provides answers that vary in veracity in accordance with their practical consequences. Pittenger (1991) pointed out that "people tend to have more accurate knowledge of systems with which they actually interact rather than simply observe" (p. 247). We believe this to be an important and true generalization. Perceiving the where and when of approaching objects has practical consequences demanding accurate performance. The perceptual answer to other questions can suffice with far less precision. Perceptual abilities reflect not only inherent biases and limitations but also the task demands of everyday purposive behavior.

References

Adair, R. T. (1990). *The physics of baseball*. New York: Harper & Row.

Babler, T. G., & Dannemiller, J. L. (1993). Role of image acceleration in judging landing location of free-falling projectiles. *Journal of Experimental Psychology: Human Perception and Performance, 19*, 15–31.

Bahill, A. T., & Karnavas, W. J. (1993). The perceptual illusion of baseball's rising fastball and breaking curveball. *Journal of Experimental Psychology: Human Perception and Performance, 19*, 3–14.

Bahill, A. T., & LaRitz, T. (1984). Why can't batters keep their eyes on the ball? *American Scientist, 72,* 249–253.

Barclay, C. D., Cutting, J. E., & Kozlowski, L. T. (1978). Temporal and spatial factors in gait perception that influence gender recognition. *Perception & Psychophysics, 23,* 145–152.

Bertenthal, B. I., & Pinto, J. (1993). Complementary processes in the perception and production of human movements. In E. Thelan & L. Smith (Eds.), *A dynamic systems approach to development: Applications* (pp. 209–239). Cambridge, MA: MIT Press.

Bertenthal, B. I., Proffitt, D. R., & Cutting, J. E. (1984). Infant sensitivity to figural coherence in biomechanical motions. *Journal of Experimental Child Psychology, 37,* 171–178.

Bertenthal, B. I., Proffitt, D. R., Spetner, N. B., & Thomas, M. A. (1985). The development of infants' sensitivity to biomechanical displays. *Child Development, 56,* 531–543.

Bingham, G. P. (1987). Kinematic form and scaling: Further investigations on the visual perception of lifted weight. *Journal of Experimental Psychology: Human Perception and Performance, 13,* 155–177.

Blake, R. (1993). Cats perceive biological motion. *Psychological Science, 4,* 54–57.

Bootsma, R. J., & Oudejans, R. R. D. (1993). Visual information about time-to-collision between two objects. *Journal of Experimental Psychology: Human Perception and Performance, 19,* 1041–1052.

Borjesson, E., & Ahlstrom, U. (1993). Motion structure in five-dot patterns as a determinant of perceptual grouping. *Perception & Psychophysics, 53,* 2–12.

Borjesson, E., & Hofsten, C. von (1975). A vector model for perceived object rotation and translation in space. *Psychological Research, 38,* 209–230.

Bower, T. G. R., Broughton, J. M., & Moore, M. K. (1970). The coordination of visual and tactile input in infants. *Perception & Psychophysics, 8,* 51–53.

Caramazza, A., McCloskey, M., & Green, B. (1981). Naive beliefs in "sophisticated" subjects: Misconceptions about trajectories of objects. *Cognition, 9,* 117–123.

Chapman, S. (1968). Catching a baseball. *American Journal of Physics, 36,* 868–870.

Cutting, J. E. (1978a). Generation of synthetic male and female walkers through manipulation of a biomechanical invariant. *Perception, 7,* 393–405.

Cutting, J. E. (1978b). A program to generate synthetic walkers as dynamic point-light displays. *Behavior Research, Methods, & Instruments, 7,* 71–87.

Cutting, J. E. (1981). Coding theory adapted to gait perception. *Journal of Experimental Psychology: Human Perception and Performance, 7,* 71–87.

Cutting, J. E. (1982). Blowing in the wind: Perceiving structure in trees and bushes. *Cognition: 12,* 25–44.

Cutting, J. E. (1983). Perceiving and recovering structure from events. *ACM Interdisciplinary workshop on motion: Representation and perception* (pp. 141–147). Toronto, Canada: ACM.

Cutting, J. E., & Kozlowski, L. T. (1977). Recognizing friends by their walk: Gait perception without familiarity cues. *Bulletin of the Psychonomic Society, 9,* 353–356.

Cutting, J. E., Moore, C., & Morrison, R. (1988). Masking the motions of human gait. *Perception & Psychophysics, 44,* 339–347.

Cutting, J. E., & Proffitt, D. R. (1981). Gait perception as an example of how we may perceive events. In R. D. Walk & H. L. Pick (Eds.), *Intersensory perception and sensory integration* (pp. 249–273). NY: Plenum.

Cutting, J. E., & Proffitt, D. R. (1982). The minimum principle and the perception of absolute, common, and relative motions. *Cognitive Psychology, 14,* 211–246.

Cutting, J. E., Proffitt, D. R., & Kozlowski, L. T. (1978). A biomechanical invariant for gait perception. *Journal of Experimental Psychology: Human Perception and Performance, 4,* 357–372.

Duncker, K. (1937). Induced motion. In W. D. Ellis (Ed.), *A source-book in Gestalt psychology.* London: Routledge & Kegan Paul. (Originally published in German, 1929).

Fitch, H. L., & Turvey, M. T. (1978). On the control of activity: Some remarks from an ecological point of view. In D. Landers & R. Christinia (Eds.), *Psychology of motor behavior and sport* (pp. 3–35). Champaign, IL: Human Kinetics.

Fox, R., & McDaniels, C. (1982). The perception of biological motion by human infants. *Science, 218,* 486–487.

Gibson, J. J. (1968). *The change form visible to invisible: A study of optical transition* [Film]. Psychological Cinema Register, State College, PA.

Gibson, J. J. (1970). On theories for visual perception. A reply to Johansson. *Scandinavian Journal of Psychology, 11,* 75–79.

Gibson, J. J. (1977). On the analysis of change in the optic array. *Scandinavian Journal of Psychology, 18,* 161–163.

Gibson, J. J. (1979). *The ecological approach to visual perception.* Boston: Houghton Mifflin.

Gibson, J. J., Kaplan, G. A., Reynolds, H. N., & Wheeler, K. (1969). The change form visible to invisible: A study of optical transition. *Perception & Psychophysics, 5,* 113–116.

Gilden, D. L. (1991). On the origins of dynamical awareness. *Psychological Review, 98,* 554–568.

Gilden, D. L., & Proffitt, D. R. (1989). Understanding collision dynamics. *Journal of Experimental Psychology: Human Perception and Performance, 15,* 372–383.

Gogel, W. C. (1974). The adjacency principle in visual perception. *Quarterly Journal of Experimental Psychology, 26,* 425 –437.

Heider, F., & Simmel, M. (1944). An experimental study or apparent behavior. *American Journal of Psychology, 57,* 243–259.

Hoffman, D. D., & Flinchbaugh, B. E. (1982). The interpretation of biological motion. *Biological Cybernetics, 42,* 195–204.

Howard, I. (1978). Recognition and knowledge of the water-level problem. *Perception, 7,* 151–160.

Hoyle, F. (1957). *The black cloud.* London: Heineman.

Janson, G., & Johansson, G. (1973). Visual perception of bending motion. *Perception, 2,* 321–326.

Johansson, G. (1950). *Configuration in event perception.* Uppsala, Sweden: Almqvist & Wiksell.

Johansson, G. (1964). Perception of motion and changing form. *Scandinavian Journal of Psychology, 5,* 181–208.

Johansson, G. (1970). On theories for visual space perception. A letter to Gibson. *Scandinavian Journal of Psychology, 11,* 67–74.

Johansson, G. (1973). Visual perception of biological motion and a model for its analysis. *Perception & Psychophysics, 14,* 210–211.

Johansson, G. (1976). Spatio-temporal differentiation and integration in visual motion perception. *Psychological Research, 38,* 379–393.

Kaiser, M. K., & Mowafy, L. (1993). Optical specification of time-to-passage: Observers' sensitivity to global tau. *Journal of Experimental Psychology: Human Perception and Performance, 19,* 1028–1040.

Kaiser, M. K., & Phatak, A. V. (1993). Things that go bump in the light: On the optical specification of contact severity. *Journal of Experimental Psychology: Human Perception and Performance, 19,* 194–202.

Kaiser, M. K., & Proffitt, D. R. (1984). The development of sensitivity to causally relevant dynamic information. *Child Development, 55,* 1614–1624.

Kaiser, M. K., Proffitt, D. R., & Anderson, K. (1985). Judgments of natural and anomalous trajectories in the presence and absence of motion. *Journal of Experimental Psychology: Learning, Memory, and Cognition, 11,* 795–803.

Kaiser, M. K., Proffitt, D. R., Whelan, S. M., & Hecht, H. (1992). Influence of animation on dynamical judgments. *Journal of Experimental Psychology: Human Perception and Performance, 18,* 669–690.

Kim, N.-G., Turvey, M. T., & Carello, C. (1993). Optical information about the severity of upcoming contacts. *Journal of Experimental Psychology: Human Perception and Performance, 19*, 179–193.

Kozlowski, L. T., & Cutting, J. E. (1977). Recognizing the sex of a walker from a dynamic point-light display. *Perception & Psychophysics, 21*, 575–580.

Lee, D. N. (1974). Visual information during locomotion. In R. B. McLeod & H. Pick (Eds.), *Perception: Essays in honor of J. J. Gibson* (pp. 250–267). Ithaca, NY: Cornell University Press.

Lee, D. N. (1976). A theory of visual control of braking based on information about time-to-collision. *Perception, 5*, 437–459.

Lee, D. N. (1980). Visuo-motor coordination in space-time. In G. E. Stelmach & J. Requin (Eds.), *Tutorials in motor behavior* (pp. 281–293). Amsterdam: North-Holland.

Lee, D. N., & Reddish, P. E. (1981). Plummeting gannets: A paradigm of ecological optics. *Nature, 293*, 293–294.

Lee, D. N., Young, D. S., Reddish, P. E., Lough, S., & Clayton, T. M. H. (1983). Visual timing in hitting an accelerating ball. *Quarterly Journal of Experimental Psychology, 35A*, 333–346.

Leeuwenberg, E. L. J. (1971). A perceptual coding language for visual and auditory patterns. *American Journal of Psychology, 84*, 307–349.

Leeuwenberg, E. L. J. (1978). Quantification of certain visual pattern similarities: Salience, transparency, similarity. In E. L. J. Leeuwenberg & H. F. J. M. Buffart (Eds.), *Formal theories of visual perception*. New York: Wiley.

MacArthur, L. Z., & Baron, R. M. (1983). Toward an ecological theory of social perception. *Psychological Review, 90*, 215–238.

Marr, D. (1982). *Vision*. San Francisco: Freeman.

Mass, J. B., Johansson, G., Janson, G., & Runeson, S. (1971). *Motion perception I and II* [Film]. Boston: Houghton Mifflin.

McAfee, E. A., & Proffitt, D. R. (1991). Understanding the surface orientation of liquids. *Cognitive Psychology, 23*, 483–514.

McBeath, M. K. (1990). The rising fastball: Baseball's impossible pitch. *Perception, 19*, 545–552.

McLeod, P. (1987). Visual reaction time and high-speed ball games. *Perception, 16*, 49–59.

McLeod, R. W., & Ross, H. E. (1983). Optic-flow and cognitive factors in time-to-collision estimates. *Perception, 12*, 417–423.

McCloskey, M. (1983). Intuitive physics. *Scientific American, 248*(4), 122–130.

McCloskey, M., Caramazza, A., & Green, B. (1980). Curvilinear motion in the absence of external forces: Naive beliefs about the motion of objects. *Science, 210*, 1139–1141.

McCloskey, M., Washburn, A., & Felch, L. (1983). Intuitive physics: The straight down belief and its origin. *Journal of Experimental Psychology: Learning, Memory, and Cognition, 9*, 636–649.

Michaels, C. F., & Oudejans, R. R. D. (1992). The optics and actions of catching fly balls: Zeroing out optical acceleration. *Ecological Psychology, 4*, 199–222.

Michotte, A. (1963). *The perception of causality*. (T. R. Miles and E. Miles, Trans.). London: Methuen.

Peper, C. E., Bootsma, R. J., Mestre, D. R., & Bakker, F. C. (1994). Catching balls: How to get the hand to the right place at the right time. *Journal of Experimental Psychology: Human Perception and Performance, 20*, 591–612.

Pittenger, J. B. (1990). Detection of violations of the law of pendulum motion: Observers' sensitivity to the relation between period and length. *Ecological Psychology, 2*, 55–81.

Pittenger, J. B. (1991). Cognitive physics and event perception: Two approaches to the assessment of people's knowledge of physics. In R. R. Hoffman & D. S. Palermo (Eds.),

Cognition and the symbolic processes: Applied and ecological perspectives (pp. 233–254). Hillsdale, NJ: Erlbaum.

Proffitt, D. R. (1993). A hierarchical approach to perception. In S. C. Masin (Ed.), *Foundations of perceptual theory* (pp. 75–111). Amsterdam: Elsevier.

Proffitt, D. R., & Bertenthal, B. I. (1988). Recovering connectivity from moving point-light displays. In W. N. Martin & J. K. Aggarwal (Eds.), *Motion understanding: Robot and human vision* (pp. 297–328). Boston: Kluwer.

Proffitt, D. R., & Bertenthal, B. I. (1990). Converging operations revisited: Assessing what infants perceive using discrimination measures. *Perception & Psychophysics, 47,* 1–11.

Proffitt, D. R., Bertenthal, B. I., & Roberts, R. J., Jr. (1984). The role of occlusion in reducing multistability in moving point-light displays. *Perception & Psychophysics, 36,* 215–232.

Proffitt, D. R., & Cutting, J. E. (1979). Perceiving the centroid of configurations on a rolling wheel. *Perception & Psychophysics, 25,* 389–398.

Proffitt, D. R., & Cutting, J. E. (1980). An invariant for wheel-generated motions and the logic of its determination. *Perception, 9,* 435–449.

Proffitt, D. R., Cutting, J. E., & Stier, D. M. (1979). Perception of wheel-generated motions. *Journal of Experimental Psychology: Human Perception and Performance, 5,* 289–302.

Proffitt, D. R., & Gilden, D. L. (1989). Understanding natural dynamics. *Journal of Experimental Psychology: Human Perception and Performance, 15,* 384–393.

Proffitt, D. R., Kaiser, M. K., & Whelan, S. M. (1990). Understanding wheel dynamics. *Cognitive Psychology, 22,* 342–373.

Regan, D., & Beverley, K. I. (1978). Looming detectors in the human visual pathway. *Vision Research, 19,* 415–421.

Regan, D., & Hamstra, S. (1992). Dissociation of discrimination thresholds for time to contact and for rate of angular expansion. *Investigative Ophthalmology & Visual Science, 33,* 1138.

Regan, D. M., Kaufman, L., & Lincoln, J. (1986). Motion in depth and visual acceleration. In K. R. Boff, L. Kaufman, & J. P. Thomas (Eds.), *Handbook of perception and human Performance* (pp. 19-1–19-46). New York: Wiley.

Restle, F. (1979). Coding theory of the perception of motion configurations. *Psychological Review, 86,* 1–24.

Rubin, E. (1927). Visuell whrgenommene wirkliche Bewegungen [Visually perceived actual motion]. *Zeitschrift fur Psychologie, 103,* 384–392.

Runeson, S. (1977). On visual perception of dynamic events. *Acta Universitatis Upsaliensis: Studia Psychologia Upsaliensia* (Series 9).

Runeson, S., & Frykholm, G. (1981). Visual perception of lifted weight. *Journal of Experimental Psychology: Human Perception and Performance, 7,* 733–740.

Runeson, S., & Frykholm, G. (1983). Kinematic specification of dynamics as an informational basis for person and action perception: Expectation, gender recognition, and deceptive intention. *Journal of Experimental Psychology: General, 112,* 585–615.

Savelsbergh, G. J. P., Whiting, H. T. A., & Bootsma, R. J. (1991). Grasping tau. *Journal of Experimental Psychology: Human Perception and Performance, 17,* 315–322.

Schiff, W. (1965). Perception of impending collision: A study of visually directed avoidant behavior. *Psychological Monograph: General and Applied, 79* (11, Whole No. 604).

Schiff, W., & Detwiler, M. L. (1979). Information used in judging impending collision. *Perception, 8,* 647–658.

Schiff, W., & Oldak, R. (1990). Accuracy of judging time-to-arrival: Effects of modality, trajectory, and gender. *Journal of Experimental Psychology: Human Perception and Performance, 16,* 303–316.

Simpson, W. A. (1988). Depth discrimination from optic flow. *Perception, 17,* 497–512.

Spurr, R. T. (1969). Subjective aspects of braking. *Automobile Engineer, 59,* 58–61.

Sumi, S. (1984). Upside down presentation of the Johansson moving light spot pattern. *Perception, 13*, 283–286.

Tanaka, K., & Saito, H. (1989). Analysis of motion of the visual field by direction, expansion/contraction, and rotation cells in the dorsal part of the medial superior temporal area of the Macaque monkey. *Journal of Neurophysiology, 62*, 626–641.

Todd, J. T. (1981). Visual information about moving objects. *Journal of Experimental Psychology: Human Perception and Performance, 7*, 795–810.

Todd, J. T., & Warren, W. H., Jr. (1982). Visual perception of relative mass in dynamic events. *Perception, 11*, 325–335.

Tresilian, J. R. (1991). Empirical and theoretical issues in the perception of time to contact. *Journal of Experimental Psychology: Human Perception and Performance, 17*, 865–876.

Tresilian, J. R. (1994). Approximate information sources and perceptual variables in interceptive timing. *Journal of Experimental Psychology: Human Perception and Performance, 20*, 154–173.

Ullman, S. (1979). *The interpretation of visual motion.* Cambridge, MA: MIT Press.

Ullman, S. (1985). Maximizing rigidity: The incremental recovery of 3-D structure from rigid and nonrigid motion. *Perception, 13*, 255–274.

Vicario, G. B., & Bressan, P. (1990). Wheels: A new illusion in the perception of rolling objects. *Perception, 19*, 57–61.

Wallach, H. (1965). Visual perception of motion. In G. Keyes (Ed.), *The nature and the art of motion* (pp. 52–59). New York: George Braziller.

Wallach, H. (1976). *On perception.* New York: Quadrangle.

Wallach, H., & O'Connell, D. N. (1953). The kinetic depth effect. *Journal of Experimental Psychology, 45*, 205–217.

Wang, Y., & Frost, B. J. (1992). Time to collision is signalled by neurons in the nucleus rotundus of pigeons. *Nature, 356*, 236–238.

Warren, W. H., Jr., Kim, E. E., & Husney, R. (1987). The way the ball bounces: Visual and auditory perception of elasticity and control of the bounce pass. *Perception, 16*, 309–336.

Webb, J. A., & Aggarwal, J. K. (1982). Structure from motion of rigid and jointed objects. *Artificial Intelligence, 19*, 107–130.

Wertheimer, M. (1937). Laws of organization in perceptual forms. In W. D. Ellis (Ed.), *A source-book in Gestalt psychology.* London: Routledge & Kegan Paul. (Originally published in German, 1923).

Williams, T. S., & Underwood, J. (1982). *The science of hitting.* New York: Simon & Schuster.

Yonas, A., Bechtold, A. G., Frankel, D., Gordon, F. R., McRoberts, G., Norcia, A., & Sternfels, S. (1977). Development of sensitivity to information for impending collisions. *Perception & Psychophysics, 21*, 97–104.

Yonas, A., Craton, L. G., & Thompson, W. B. (1987). Relative motion: Kinetic information for the order of depth at an edge. *Perception & Psychophysics, 41*, 53–59.

CHAPTER 8

Self-Motion: Visual Perception and Visual Control

William H. Warren, Jr.

We perceive in order to move, but we must also move in order to perceive.

Gibson (1979, p. 223)

I. INTRODUCTION

Locomotion is one of the most fundamental of animal behaviors, playing an integral role in many other basic biological activities. To be adaptive, it must be guided by information about the environment, and hence the visual control of locomotion is a similarly fundamental perceptual ability. Locomotion, and self-motion in general, thus provides a model system for understanding basic principles of perception and the control of action. In the last fifteen years the topic has proven a natural point of contact between research in perception, computational vision, and neurophysiology. This chapter focuses on the visual control of human locomotion, including our current understanding of the information available in optic flow, the perception of self-motion, and the regulation of posture and gait.

A. Perception and Action

Broadly speaking, the biological function of perception is the control of action, for adaptive behavior is the evolutionary bottom line. Traditionally, the problems of perception and action have been treated as logically independent. It has been assumed that the goal of perception is to recover

Perception of Space and Motion

objective quantities such as size, distance, shape, color, and motion, yielding a general-purpose description of the scene that can provide the basis for any subsequent behavior. Considering vision in the context of action has potentially important implications for this view of perception.

First, the set of action-relevant quantities recovered by the visual system may look different. There is long-standing evidence that perceptual judgments of distance, size, and shape are markedly inaccurate and non-Euclidean (Todd, Tittle, & Norman, in press). Given the assumed accuracy of everyday movements, this seems to present a paradox. However, metric information may be unnecessary for may tasks ranging from obstacle avoidance to object recognition, and metric tasks such as reaching could be governed by specific visuomotor mappings to which such perceptual "distortions" are transparent. On this view, the goal of perception is not to recover a general-purpose scene description but to extract *task-specific information* for the activity at hand.

Second, the linear causality of sensory input to motor output is replaced by the circular causality expressed in the quote above. Animals are coupled to the environment in two ways: informationally, so they are apprised of the current state of affairs (perception), and mechanically, so they can alter that state of affairs (action). When the animal moves, this changes the state of affairs and generates new information that can reciprocally be used to guide subsequent movements, in a perception-action loop. Perception is consequently an act that unfolds over time, rather than a momentary "percept" (Shaw, Turvey, & Mace, 1981). Judgments at any instant may be qualitative or even nonveridical, and yet over the course of the act adaptive behavior emerges from the animal–environment interaction. This notion of what might be called *pragmatic control* descends from Gibson's (1966, 1979) emphasis on the active, exploring observer.

B. Information for Locomotor Control

Four perceptual systems could potentially contribute to the control of posture and locomotion: (1) the *visual* system; (2) the *vestibular* system, including the semicircular canals sensitive to angular acceleration and the otolith organs sensitive to linear acceleration (Howard, 1986a); (3) the *somatosensory* system, including joint, muscle, and cutaneous receptors (Clark & Horch, 1986; Sherrick & Cholewiak, 1986; Turvey and Carello, this volume, chap. 1); and (4) the *auditory* system (Dodge, 1923; Wightman and Jenison, this volume, chap. 10). The mechanical senses provide information about disturbances after the fact, whereas vision and audition can guide behavior in an anticipatory or prospective manner. Although this chapter focuses primarily on vision, several points about the other modalities should be noted.

There is an ongoing debate about the relationship between these types of information for orientation and self-motion. Under normal conditions, they often redundantly specify a postural state or disturbance (Gibson, 1966), but there are situations in which they apparently conflict. Some have argued that one modality simply dominates in such situations (Lishman & Lee, 1973; Talbot & Brookhart, 1980), but there is considerable evidence for a more subtle relation. Classical sensory integration theories argue that perception results from integrating multiple ambiguous cues, often via an internal model of body orientation (Oman, 1982). Others have argued that information is defined across the modalities such that any combination of stimulation will specify a possible state of affairs, without ambiguity or interpretation (Stoffregen & Riccio, 1988, 1991). On this view, for example, standing on a rigid surface while the visual surround is moved does not present a conflict between vision and somatosensory information for upright posture, but specifies sway on a nonrigid surface. A fourth possibility is that perceptual systems are specialized to obtain information about different but overlapping aspects of the environment, which may be redundant or in conflict but is normally specific.

For example, there appears to be a division of labor between modalities, such that the vestibular system is primarily sensitive to high-frequency stimulation and brief acceleration, whereas the visual and somatosensory systems are primarily sensitive to low-frequency stimulation and (for vision) constant velocity motion (Howard, 1986b). The latter are more relevant to normal postural and locomotor control. Spontaneous postural sway is concentrated below 0.5 Hz in standing and 1.0 Hz in walking (Kay & Warren, 1995; Lestienne, Soechting, & Berthoz, 1977; Yoneda & Tokumasu, 1986), the same range in which sway responses and vection can be induced visually (Berthoz, Lacour, Soechting, & Vidal, 1979; Berthoz, Pavard, & Young, 1975; Dichgans & Brandt, 1978; Kay & Warren, 1995; van Asten, Gielen, & van der Gon, 1988a). Cutaneous information has also been shown to contribute to the stabilization of standing posture at frequencies below 1 Hz (Diener, Dichgans, Bruzek, & Selinka, 1982; Diener, Dichgans, Guschlbauer, & Mau, 1984), possibly via the distribution of pressure over the soles of the feet. On the other hand, vestibular responses to linear acceleration are only elicited at frequencies of stimulation above 1 Hz (Diener et al., 1982, 1984; Melville-Jones & Young, 1978), and the vestibular system is an order of magnitude less sensitive to the direction of linear acceleration than are the visual and somatosensory systems (Telford, Howard, & Ohmi, 1992). It thus appears that stance and locomotion are regulated primarily by visual and somatosensory information, whereas vestibular information contributes to recovery from high-frequency perturbations (Allum & Pfaltz, 1985; Nashner, Black, & Wall, 1982) and gaze stabilization during locomotion (Grossman & Leigh, 1990).

II. OPTIC FLOW

When an observer moves in a stationary environment, the light reflected to the moving eye undergoes a lawful transformation called *optic flow*. In addition to the static information about the three-dimensional (3-D) layout of the environment available to a stationary observer (Gillam, this volume, chap. 2; Rogers, this volume, chap. 4), optic flow contains information about both 3-D layout (Lappin, this volume, chap. 5; Todd, this volume, chap. 6) and the observer's self-motion. Helmholtz (1867/1925, p. 295) first pointed out the significance of *motion parallax* as a source of information for distance on the basis of the optical velocities of elements at different distances. Gibson (1947, 1950) subsequently generalized this notion to gradients of velocity 360° about the observer, produced by surfaces in depth (see Figure 1). He represented the flow pattern as an instantaneous two-dimensional (2-D) velocity field $\mathbf{V}(x, y)$, in which each vector corresponds to the optical motion of an environmental element and possesses a magnitude or speed and a direction.[1] The gradient of speed contains information about distance along a surface, which Gibson called *motion perspective,* whereas the pattern of vector directions provides information about self-motion, which he called *visual kinesthesis.* In particular, Gibson discovered that the *focus of expansion* corresponds to the current direction of self-motion or *heading* in the case of pure observer translation and suggested that this could be used to control steering. He noted, however, that an added rotation of the observer, such as a pursuit eye or head movement, annihilates the focus of expansion and significantly complicates the retinal flow pattern. A persistent question has been how the visual system determines heading from this complex pattern.

A general curvilinear motion of the observer can be described instantaneously as the sum of a translation and a rotation (Whittaker, 1944). Considering the resulting flow pattern on a spherical projection surface that moves with the eye (see Figure 2), observer translation generates radial flow along the meridians called the *translational component,* and observer rotation generates solenoidal flow[2] along the parallels called the *rotational component.* Although the term is often used loosely, I reserve *optic flow* proper for

---

[1] A field is a region of n-dimensional space characterized by a quantity such as velocity that has a unique value at every point and is a continuous function of position. The instantaneous structure of the velocity field is captured by *streamlines,* continuous field lines to which the vectors are tangent at every point. They are distinct from *path lines,* the actual trajectories of elements over time, and *streak lines,* which connect the current locations of elements that have previously passed through location (x, y). The three sets of lines coincide in the special case of *steady flow,* a stationary field in which the velocity at any point (x, y) does not change over time (Eskinazi, 1962).

[2] That is, without sources or sinks.

FIGURE 1   Optic flow field generated by observer translation parallel to a ground plane. The flow pattern is represented as an instantaneous velocity field, in which dots correspond to environmental elements, and line segments represent the associated optical velocity vectors. Vertical probe indicates the heading point.

change in structure of the optic array that is due to displacement of the point of observation, before being sampled by an eye (Gibson, 1966). Thus, optic flow is unaffected by eye rotations[3] but is influenced by movement of the point of observation on a straight or curved path. *Retinal flow* refers to the change in structure of light on the receptor surface, in retinal coordinates, which is affected by both translation and rotation of the eye. Optic flow thus defines the informational constraints within which all adaptive behavior evolved. How such information is detected by a moving eye is a contingent question, for retinal flow depends on the structure of the eye and oculomotor behavior, and different visual systems provide different solutions (Junger & Dahmen, 1991). Both issues must be addressed for a complete understanding of the use of optic flow information.

A. Formal Analysis of the Flow Field

Formal analysis of the flow field involves two reciprocal problems: (1) a description of the flow field itself—that is, how flow is generated by observer movement relative to the environment, and (2) a description of infor-

[3] This assumes that the center of rotation is at the nodal point of the eye, which is not strictly true (Bingham, 1993). However, optic flow induced by displacement of the nodal point during an eye rotation is probably negligible for a mobile observer.

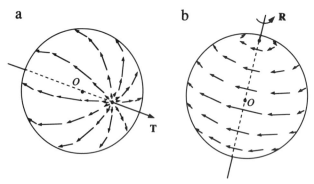

FIGURE 2   Flow pattern represented on a spherical projection surface. (a) *Translational component*: observer translation yields radial flow along meridians. (b) *Rotational component*: observer rotation yields solenoidal flow along parallels.

mation in the flow field—the inverse problem of how flow specifies properties of the environment and self-motion. In what follows I sketch existing approaches to both. I assume that local velocities can be determined from the changing intensity field that characterizes the optic array (Hildreth & Koch, 1987), although this step could be bypassed in special cases (Horn & Weldon, 1988; Negahdaripour & Horn, 1989). Given that there is likely to be considerable noise in such motion extraction, any biologically plausible heading model must be highly robust.

1. Observer Translation

Consider first a local description of optic flow for the case of pure translation, in spherical coordinates (after Gibson, Olum, & Rosenblatt, 1955; Nakayama & Loomis, 1974; see Figure 3). The observer moves with translational velocity **T** relative to a fixed environmental point P, which is a distance D from the observer and a visual angle β from the heading direction.[4] The point's optical angular speed is

$$\dot{\beta} = \frac{T \sin \beta}{D}, \tag{1}$$

and its direction of optical motion is along a meridian. Significantly, the direction of this vector is determined solely by the observer's heading, whereas its magnitude is influenced by both its position relative to the heading and the distance to the element. Several things follow immediately about the information in optic flow.

[4] Vector quantities shall be in bold (e.g., velocity **V** with magnitude V and direction $\hat{V}$), physical variables in uppercase, and optical variables in lowercase.

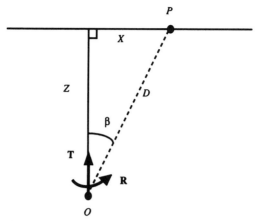

FIGURE 3   Spherical coordinate system for describing observer motion. Observer O moves with translation $\mathbf{T}$ or rotation $\mathbf{R}$ with respect to point P, which is at distance D from the observer and visual angle β from the axis of translation or rotation.

a. Heading

First, as noted earlier, heading is specified by the eccentricity and elevation of the focus of expansion (Figure 1). Because vector direction is independent of distance, this radial flow pattern specifies heading in any environment. Even when the focus itself is not in view, heading is specified by triangulating two or more vectors to find their common point of intersection (Gibson, 1950). However, assuming some noise in local motion, triangulation error necessarily increases as the flow field is sampled farther from the focus and the vectors become more parallel (Koenderink & van Doorn, 1987), which was confirmed empirically by Crowell and Banks (1993). Thus, the region of the flow field that is most informative is that near the focus of expansion.

b. Scaled Distance and Time-to-Contact

Second, the distance D to a point at position β in the field is specified only up to a scale factor of observer speed T:

$$\frac{D}{T} = \frac{\sin \beta}{\dot{\beta}}. \tag{2}$$

Thus, absolute distance can be determined only if speed is known, and vice versa. However, the ratio D/T has the dimension of time. Lee (1974, 1976, 1980) showed that the time-to-contact T_c with the plane containing P that is perpendicular to the direction of travel is specified by the optic variable *tau*, under the assumptions of constant velocity and a rigid environment:

$$T_c = \frac{\beta}{\dot{\beta}} = \tau_g. \qquad (3)$$

This version has been dubbed *global tau* because it requires that β be known and hence depends on the perception of heading (Tresilian, 1991). The derivation incorporates a small angle approximation ($\beta = \tan^{-1} X/Z \cong X/Z$) that introduces slight overestimations of T_c when β becomes large, for example, at short times-to-contact. *Local tau* specifies time-to-contact for a moving object approaching a stationary observer (or vice versa), given any two points on the object such as the contour defining a visual angle θ, and is equal to the inverse of the relative rate of expansion (Lee, 1976; Todd, 1981):

$$T_c = \frac{\theta}{\dot{\theta}} = \tau_l. \qquad (4)$$

However, this requires two additional assumptions: the path of approach must be directly toward the observer, and the object must either be spherical or not rotating.[5] Violations can lead to large errors, such as significant overestimations of T_c with an off-axis approach (Kaiser & Mowafy, 1993; Tresilian, 1991). A more general formulation specifies the time-to-contact with an off-axis interception point, as would be needed for catching, by incorporating information about the visual angle ψ between the object and the interception point (Bootsma & Oudejans, 1993; Tresilian, 1990, 1994):

$$T_c = \frac{\tau_l}{1 + \tau_l \dot{\psi} \cot \psi}. \qquad (5)$$

c. Relative Distance

Finally, the relative distance of two elements at different positions in the field is specified by

$$\frac{D_1}{D_2} = \frac{\dot{\beta}_2 \sin \beta_1}{\dot{\beta}_1 \sin \beta_2} = \frac{\tau_1}{\tau_2}, \qquad (6)$$

which also requires that heading be perceived. Equivalently, this can be considered in the time domain as the relative time-to-contact of the two elements. Thus, specific information for heading, time-to-contact, and rela-

---

[5] In the case of a rotating object, one can use the average visual angle over a cycle of rotation.

tive depth is available in the optic flow field, providing universal constraints on the evolution of visual control.

2. Observer Rotation

Consider the retinal flow produced by a pure rotation of the observer, equivalent to a rigid rotation of the world about the eye. If the observer has an angular velocity **R,** the optical angular speed of a point P at a visual angle β from the axis of rotation is

$$\dot{\alpha} = R\sin\beta, \tag{7}$$

and its direction of motion is along a parallel. In this case, both the direction and the magnitude of the flow vector are independent of distance D, and thus observer rotation yields no information about environmental structure. The magnitude is simply a sinusoidal function of position, with rotary flow about the poles and approximately lamellar flow near the equator, yielding a displacement of the retinal image (Figure 4). Thus, the retinal flow pattern specifies the axis and speed of rotation, information about self-motion that is not available in optic flow per se.

3. Translation and Rotation

Retinal flow becomes more complex in the case of combined translation and rotation. A general curvilinear motion has six degrees of freedom: transla-

FIGURE 4   Retinal flow field generated by observer rotation with respect to a ground plane about a diagonal axis.

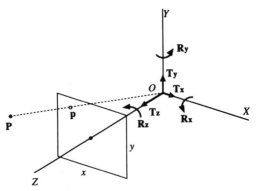

FIGURE 5   Cartesian coordinate system for describing observer motion, with a planar projection surface that moves with the observer. Observer O at the origin moves with translation (T_x, T_y, T_z) and rotation (R_x, R_y, R_z) relative to point $P = (X, Y, Z)$.

tion along $(T = T_x, T_y, T_z)$ and rotation about $(R = R_x, R_y, R_z)$ three axes; that is, the direction $\hat{T}$ (azimuth and elevation) and speed T of translation and the orientation $\hat{R}$ (azimuth and elevation) of the rotation axis and speed R of rotation. The resulting flow is more easily described in a Cartesian coordinate system with a planar projection surface that is a unit distance from the eye and moves with it, as in Figure 5.[6] Following Longuet-Higgins and Prazdny (1980), the relative physical motion of a point $P(X, Y, Z)$ is given by

$$V = -T - R \times P, \tag{8}$$

which can be expanded to

$$\begin{aligned}
\dot{X} &= -T_x - R_y Z + R_z Y \\
\dot{Y} &= -T_y - R_z X + R_x Z \\
\dot{Z} &= -T_z - R_x Y + R_y X.
\end{aligned} \tag{9}$$

The polar projection of P onto the plane at position (x, y) is

$$\begin{aligned}
x &= X/Z \\
y &= Y/Z.
\end{aligned} \tag{10}$$

The optical velocity of P is then given by differentiating Equation 10 with respect to time and substituting Equation 9:

$$\begin{aligned}
v_x &= [(-T_x + xT_z)/Z] + [xyR_x - R_y - x^2R_y + yR_z] \\
v_y &= [(-T_y + yT_z)/Z] + [(R_x + y^2R_x) - xyR_y - xR_z].
\end{aligned} \tag{11}$$

[6] The choice of coordinate system and projection surface is arbitrary; they are simply related by a coordinate transformation.

The left-hand term in Equation 11 is the translational component, which depends on distance Z, and the right-hand term is the rotational component, which is independent of Z.

The resulting retinal flow pattern, illustrated in Figure 6, is the vector sum of the field due to translation (Figure 1) and the field due to rotation (Figure 4), as would occur with a pursuit eye movement to fixate a point on the ground while walking. Note that the focus of expansion at the heading point has been replaced by a new singularity at the fixation point. Thus, if observers simply relied on the singularity in the field to determine heading, they would see themselves as heading toward the fixation point. Formally, one would like to invert Equation 11 and solve for Z and all six motion parameters, but as noted above, only the ratio of depth to speed can be known. This leaves six unknown parameters: three for rotation, two for the direction of translation, and the scaled depth Z/T. Further, to determine heading, relative depth, and time-to-contact from this retinal flow, it is necessary to decompose the translational and rotational components of flow. I return to this problem in section II C.

4. Curved Paths

Observer movement on a curved path is common in locomotion, most obviously during driving. For movement on a circular path with radius r

FIGURE 6   Retinal flow field generated by a combined translation and rotation of the observer. Observer is translating toward the probe line while simultaneously rotating because of pursuit fixation of the O on the ground plane. This velocity field is the vector sum of those in Figures 1 and 4, into which it can be decomposed.

and curvature $\kappa = 1/r$, the resulting flow lines form a family of hyperbolae in the projection plane (Figure 7)—not, as it might seem, a radial pattern centered on the instantaneous translational heading, the tangent to the curved path. Although circular motion can be analyzed instantaneously as the sum of a translation and a rotation, it would be advantageous for the observer to perceive the future curved path per se. One solution is to recover the instantaneous translational heading $\hat{T}$ from the velocity field (Cutting, 1986; Prazdny, 1981) and then integrate over time,

$$\kappa = \frac{(d\hat{T}/dt)}{T}, \tag{12}$$

although this assumes the speed T is known. Equivalently, Rieger (1983) showed that the component of optical acceleration that is perpendicular to the translational component of the velocity vector is proportional to path curvature and speed. Alternatively, the future path could be directly perceived from the curvature of the flow field itself (Lee & Lishman, 1977; Warren, Mestre, Blackwell, & Morris, 1991). For a circular path on a ground plane, Warren et al. (1991) showed that the center of rotation (and

FIGURE 7   Optic flow field generated by observer motion on a circular path parallel to the ground plane. An identical retinal flow field is produced by combined translation toward the probe line and rotation about a vertical axis, induced by pursuit fixation of the circle at eye level.

hence the radius of the path) is specified by the normals to two or more vectors in the ground plane.

5. Ambiguities of the Velocity Field

An important limitation of the velocity field representation is that it is an instantaneous description that does not capture the evolution of flow over time. Two known ambiguities result. First, there are two possible inter-pretations of the flow field produced by translation relative to a plane: the veridical one, and one in which the axis of translation and the surface normal are switched while the observer undergoes a rotation (Longuet-Higgins, 1984; Tsai & Huang, 1984b; Waxman & Ullman, 1985). This ambiguity is resolved by two or more successive velocity fields, by a non-planar environment, or if both hemispheres are visible (cf. Nelson & Aloimonos, 1988).

Second, as noted earlier, movement on a curved path in any environment is instantaneously equivalent to a translation plus a rotation. It follows that the velocity fields produced in these two cases are identical, and hence ambiguous. For example, the same field is produced by movement on a circular path in the horizontal plane and by movement on a straight path with an eye rotation about a vertical axis (Figure 7). This ambiguity is also resolved by successive velocity fields. Rieger (1983; Tsai & Huang, 1984a) showed that the two cases are distinguished by higher order accelerative flow components defined over two successive velocity fields (i.e., three frames). Further, movement on a circular path generates a stationary field such as Figure 7, whereas translation plus rotation yields a field that deforms over time (Warren et al., 1991). Thus, these ambiguities are resolved if the flow field is allowed to evolve over three or more frames and the visual system can detect such changing field structures.

B. Differential Invariants

A higher order description of the velocity field is based on its spatial deriva-tives (Koenderink & van Doorn, 1975, 1976; Longuet-Higgins & Prazdny, 1980; Regan, 1986; Waxman & Ullman, 1985). Any locally smooth flow field can be decomposed uniquely as the sum of a translation, an expansion, a rotation, and a shear at each point (see Figure 8), where *div* is the rate of expansion and *curl* is the rate of rotation. Shear is produced by a contraction in one direction and an expansion in the orthogonal direction, preserving area, and can be described by the rate of deformation or *def* and the orienta-tion of the contraction axis. These are the *differential invariants* of the flow field, which do not depend on a particular coordinate system.

Following Koenderink (1986; Koenderink & van Doorn, 1975), consider an observer moving with translational velocity $\mathbf{T}$ and rotational velocity $\mathbf{R}$

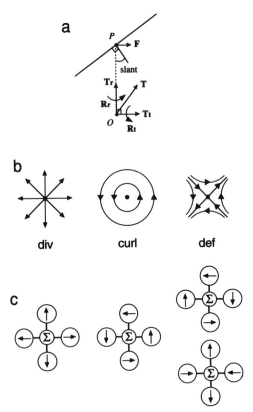

FIGURE 8   Differential invariants of the flow field. (a) Coordinate system for describing observer motion. Observer O moves relative to point P with components of translation along the radial axis to P ($\mathbf{T_r}$) and transverse to that axis ($\mathbf{T_t}$) and a component of rotation about that axis ($\mathbf{R_r}$) and transverse to that axis ($\mathbf{R_t}$). The surface patch at P has a slant $\mathbf{F}$ with respect to the line of sight, in the direction of surface tilt. (b) Elementary flow components of div, curl, and def. (c) Higher order motion units that could detect div, curl, and the two components of def. (Adapted from Koenderink & van Doorn, 1978)

relative to a local surface patch containing point P at distance D (Figure 8a). The translation can be resolved into a radial component along the line of sight to P ($\mathbf{T_r}$) and a transverse component perpendicular to the line of sight ($\mathbf{T_t}$); similarly, the rotation is resolved into a radial component about the line of sight ($\mathbf{R_r}$) and a transverse component about the orthogonal axes ($\mathbf{R_t}$). The orientation of the patch is represented by a tangent vector $\mathbf{F}$ perpendicular to the line of sight, whose magnitude is the tangent of slant (the angle between the surface normal and the line of sight) and whose direction is the tilt about the line of sight (the direction of the patch's steepest gradient, where γ is the angle between **F** and **T**$_t$). The differential components can then be defined as

$$\text{div} = -F\frac{T_t}{D}\cos\gamma + 2\frac{T_r}{D}$$

$$\text{curl} = -F\frac{T_t}{D}\sin\gamma - 2R_r \qquad (13)$$

$$\text{def} = F\frac{T_t}{D}.$$

It follows that both div and def are unaffected by **R** and are thus invariant under observer rotation, such as eye movements. Only curl is influenced by rotation about the line of sight (R_r); in addition, it is influenced by translation orthogonal to, but not toward, the point. Def is likewise produced by translation orthogonal to the point (T_t), not toward it (T_r). Finally, all three components are influenced by surface slant (F).

These differential invariants provide information about both surface orientation and heading, as shown by inverting Equation 13. First, def contains information about the slant of the patch to the line of sight, given that T_t/D can be determined at a vertex joining three or more patches (see Koenderink, 1986). Further, the affine curvature of the patch can be determined from the second-order spatial derivatives of the flow (Droulez & Cornilleau-Pérès, 1990; Koenderink & van Doorn, 1975, 1992; Waxman & Ullman, 1985). Second, once surface slant is known, heading can be determined from the maximum of divergence (div_{max}), which is invariant under eye rotation (Koenderink & van Doorn, 1981; see section II.C.2). Third, div also contains information about time-to-contact, for T_r/D is its inverse. When heading straight toward P, the first term in the equation drops out ($T_t = 0$) and div specifies the time-to-contact with P. Otherwise, T_r/D specifies P's nearness in time, even though there will be no contact, and can be determined once **F** and T_t/D are known.

These variables could in principle be extracted by various cortical mechanisms, although they would have to provide high-resolution measures to be useful in determining shape. Most obvious are higher order motion units that are based on combinations of local velocity signals, illustrated in Figure 8c (Koenderink & van Doorn, 1978). Large-field units selective for expansion, rotation, and translation have been reported in primate medial superior temporal area (MST; Saito, Yukie, Tanaka, Hikosaka, Fukada, & Iwai, 1986), but they do not have sufficient spatial resolution for a local differential analysis of the flow field and do not appear to decompose a complex flow pattern into elementary components (Orban et al., 1992; see section

III.A.5). Less obvious would be higher order units that are based on other properties such as spatial frequency or orientation (Koenderink, 1986). For example, div could be determined from changes in local texture density, curl from changes in local orientation, and def from changes in the relative orientation of neighboring contours.

C. Decomposing Translation and Rotation

As noted earlier, a combined observer translation and rotation eliminates the focus of expansion in the retinal flow field and creates a new singularity at the fixation point. How, then, do observers distinguish the direction they are heading from the direction they are looking? Gibson (1950) recognized this problem, but it was not until the 1980s that computational solutions were derived. Some approaches first estimate the rotational component and subtract it from the retinal flow field to recover the translation (Longuet-Higgins & Prazdny, 1980; Perrone, 1992; Prazdny, 1980; van den Berg, 1992). Others determine the translation directly from the retinal flow, eliminating the rotational component (Cutting, Springer, Braren, & Johnson, 1992; Heeger & Jepson, 1990; Koenderink & van Doorn, 1981; Longuet-Higgins & Prazdny, 1980; Rieger & Lawton, 1985). Both approaches *decompose* the complex flow pattern in the sense of separating its translational and rotational components.[7] Most of these models were developed for computer vision applications and were not intended as models of biological vision. I describe several classes of solutions here and turn to the perceptual evidence in the next section.

1. Discrete Models

Early efforts computed the five motion parameters and scaled depth from the optical positions of some minimum number of points (Longuet-Higgins, 1981; Mitiche, 1984; Nagel, 1981; Prazdny, 1980; Roach & Aggarwal, 1980; Tsai & Huang, 1981, 1982, 1984a, 1984b; Weng, Huang, & Ahuja, 1989). Essentially, they solved for the parameters simultaneously

---

[7] Cutting et al. (1992) identify the former as "optical flow theories" that involve a decomposition and the latter as "retinal flow theories" that do not. To the contrary, both approaches are actually based on the retinal flow pattern and both separate its translational and rotational components. The first achieves this by explicitly estimating the rotational component and subtracting it from the retinal flow, the second by determining the translational component (heading) directly from the retinal flow. Cutting et al.'s claim that heading is perceived "from information in retinal, not optical, flow" is acknowledged by both approaches and is trivially true since retinal flow is the proximal stimulation. In a deeper sense, heading information is necessarily in both: Optical and retinal flow are related by a simple coordinate transformation (addition of a constant), leaving properties such as parallax, divergence, and deformation invariant.

using four to seven corresponding points in two images, assuming coplanar points or a rigidity constraint. This had the virtue of demonstrating that the problem was well posed or overdetermined. Most such models are general in that they do not depend on 3-D structure, but they rely on precise measurements of a few points and proved highly vulnerable to noise (Verri & Poggio, 1987).

2. Differential Models

Other models determine the motion parameters and local structure from first- and second-order spatial derivatives of the flow field, such as the differential invariants (Koenderink & van Doorn, 1975; Longuet-Higgins & Prazdny, 1980; Subbarao & Waxman, 1986; Waxman & Ullman, 1985). These models are general in that they do not depend on spatial layout, although several assume planar patches. Koenderink and van Doorn (1981) proposed a simpler version in which the direction of translation is derived from the maximum of divergence, which is invariant under rotation. As evident in Equation 13, div also depends on surface slant F, and thus $\text{div}_{\max}$ does not uniquely correspond to the heading. Rather, the direction of $\text{div}_{\max}$ bisects the angle between the direction of heading and the normal to the surface. Consequently, the number and locations of local divergence maxima depend on environmental structure, such that there is a $\text{div}_{\max}$ defined for each planar surface. Perception of heading thus depends on first recovering 3-D structure. Such information requires a sufficiently continuous field and a sufficiently high resolution to define a slant and divergence maximum for each surface, implying a smoothness constraint. Differential models thus fail with discontinuous or sparse flow fields and were sensitive to noise in their original formulation. However, recent versions that determine differential components from line integrals around a closed contour are more noise tolerant (Poggio, Verri, & Torre, 1991).

3. Dynamical Models

Verri, Girosi, and Torre (1989) analyzed the flow field as the phase portrait of a dynamical system. Movement parameters can be determined from the time evolution of the local structure of the flow pattern in the neighborhood of singular points, which are structurally stable and thus resistant to noise. However, the model also assumes a smoothness constraint and requires dense flow about singular points, and thus faces difficulties with discontinuous or sparse flow fields.

4. Motion Parallax Models

Several theories are based on motion parallax, the relative motion between elements at different depths. As seen in Equation 11, the translational component of flow depends on distance Z, but the rotational component does not. Thus, two elements at a depth edge (i.e., at different depths in the same visual direction) have the same velocity due to rotation, and any relative motion between them is due solely to translation. Longuet-Higgins and Prazdny (1980) first demonstrated that these *difference vectors* radiate outward from the heading point, preserving the focus of expansion. Thus, edge parallax is invariant under rotation, isolating the translational component of flow. Rieger and Lawton's (1985) *differential motion* model generalized this approach to nonoverlapping elements in the same visual neighborhood. Although this introduces some error into individual difference vectors, they retain a global radial pattern that approximates the heading point and tolerates some noise, assuming sufficient depth variation within a neighborhood. Heading error increases to about 5° with 5% noise in vector speed and direction. Heeger and Jepson (1992; Jepson & Heeger, 1992; Prazdny, 1983) subsequently devised an exact solution without the neighborhood restriction, precomputing a coefficient matrix for differential motion between two points in different visual directions. The model is more robust than Rieger and Lawton's algorithm, but there is still a heading error of 5° with 10% noise in local vectors.

The motion parallax approach provides a particularly elegant solution to the decomposition problem. It makes no smoothness assumptions, but it does require depth variation in the environment and fails in the special case of a frontal plane. Although it is more robust than the discrete models, it still depends on reasonably accurate detection of relative motion. This might be achieved by center-surround opponent-motion units found in the monkey and pigeon (Allman, Miezin, & McGuinness, 1985; Frost & Nakayama, 1983), but they do not appear to posses the necessary characteristics for determining local relative motion with sufficient resolution.

A weaker hypothesis is Cutting's (1986) *differential motion parallax*. When fixating a point in the middle distance, elements that are farther away move across the line of fixation toward the heading point, while elements that are nearer move in the opposite direction. Under certain conditions, elements that are less than halfway to the fixation point will have the highest velocity such that the largest vector indicates heading relative to the fixation point. This could guide a sequence of fixations to the heading point, although it is known that multiple fixations are unnecessary for absolute heading judgments. Cutting et al. (1992) subsequently argued that the magnitude of the largest vector correlates with the absolute heading, although they did not show this formally. However, this relation depends on the distances of the fixation point and the highest velocity element. They also proposed that two additional variables are used at large gaze-heading angles: inward motion (IM) toward the fixation point and outward deceleration (OD) away from the fixation point, although the distances of the corresponding elements must be known. Thus, the hypothesis relies on several different variables, assumes known depth in some cases, and only specifies heading relative to the fixation point. To my mind, it is more likely that the visual system has adapted to specific information in the flow pattern as a whole, rather than to such contingent local features.

5. Error Minimization and Template Models

Rather than computing heading analytically, another class of models searches the space of possible motion parameters to best account for the global flow pattern. Bruss and Horn (1983) formulated this as an error-minimization problem, using an iterative method to reduce the least squares error between the observed and expected flow patterns. Because this approach uses information throughout the flow field rather than just a few points, it is quite robust (see also Adiv, 1985; Ballard & Kimball, 1983; Heeger & Jepson, 1992; Jain, 1982; Lawton, 1983; Maybank, 1986; Prazdny, 1981). Although on the face of it these techniques appear unrelated to biological vision, such a parameter search could be implemented as a set of neural templates for the flow fields produced by different $T + R$ combinations. The templates would be tested in parallel against the observed field, with the peak of activity in the population corresponding to the minimum-error solution. A complicating factor is that because the translational component of flow depends on depth, affecting both the magnitudes and directions of vectors in the $T + R$ flow field, there are an indefinite number of possible flow patterns.

Hatsopoulos and Warren (1991) developed such a neural model for the simple case of translation that is based on the properties of motion-selective cells in the middle temporal area (MT) and MST. After training, the output layer formed a heading map with units selective for large-field radial flow patterns at each retinal location. Perrone and Stone (1994) extended this approach to the general $T + R$ case, with a separate heading map for each possible rotation. To address the depth problem, each template was selective for a family of flow patterns produced by elements in different depth planes. Even with a coarse distributed coding of the parameter space, the model was quite accurate. Because it incorporated constraints from gaze stabilization, the model predicts certain patterns of errors with rotations that are not induced by pursuit fixation. Lappe and Rauschecker (1993) proposed a similar neural model that directly encoded Heeger and Jepson's (1992) coefficient matrix into the pattern of synaptic weights.

While this constitutes something of a brute force approach, such template models are highly noise tolerant, and the use of neural filters, spatial maps, and distributed coding is consistent with current views of neural architecture.

6. Subtracting Rotation

An alternative to determining the translation directly is to first estimate $\mathbf{R}$ and subtract it from the flow field to obtain $\hat{T}$ (Longuet-Higgins & Prazdny, 1980; Prazdny, 1980). Whereas the translational component of flow decreases with element distance (Figure 1 and Equation 1), the rotational component does not (Figure 4 and Equation 7), and thus the retinal flow from distant elements is dominated by rotation. Consequently, the visual system could use independent depth information to identify distant elements and estimate $\mathbf{R}$ from them (van den Berg, 1992). In contrast, Perrone's (1992) original template model estimated $\mathbf{R}$ quite accurately by using large-field translational motion units to sum over all flow vectors, regardless of depth. This is consistent with cells in the rabbit selective for large-field translational motion aligned with the semicircular canals (Simpson, Graf, & Leonard, 1981; see also Frost, Wylie, & Wang, 1990). One prediction of the rotation subtraction models is that rotation estimates, and consequently heading judgments, should improve with rotation rate (Perrone, 1992).

7. Oculomotor Signal

A traditional view is that information about eye rotation is provided by an oculomotor signal, such as an efference copy or proprioceptive feedback from the extraocular muscles (Matin, 1982; Holst, 1954), which is then subtracted from the flow field to recover heading (Royden, Crowell, & Banks, 1992, 1994). To its advantage, an oculomotor signal does not depend on environmental structure and would resolve visually ambiguous cases such as motion relative to a plane or on a circular path. However, the gain of the oculomotor signal is only 0.8 or less and would thus yield systematic heading errors (Hansen, 1979; Mack & Herman, 1978; Wertheim, 1987). However, the gain increases to 1.0 with a large, structured visual background, indicating that optic flow actually contributes to the perceived rotation (Gibson, 1968). Given these observations, is unlikely that the decomposition is based solely on an extraretinal signal. My concern has been to demonstrate that optic flow is both theoretically and empirically sufficient to specify heading, but it is certainly possible that redundant oculomotor information may play a role when visual information is inadequate.

8. Summary

From this survey, we can identify several key variables by which to compare the performance of computational models and human observers: (1) flow field noise, (2) number of elements, (3) element lifetime, (4) depth variation and flow field continuity, (5) rate of rotation relative to translation, (6) pursuit fixation of a point in the scene, (7) size of field of view, (8) sample of flow field, (9) display duration, and (10) independent depth information. Koenderink and van Doorn (1987) used a least squares method to assess the influence of several of these variables on the information in the flow field itself, assuming 10% noise, thus specifying limits on any model. As might be expected, the root-mean-square error in estimated translation and rotation increased with noise and decreased with the square root of the number of elements. Further, accuracy depended critically on a large field of view and declined as the ratio of rotation to translation speed increased. These factors are important to bear in mind when interpreting the experimental evidence.

III. VISUAL PERCEPTION OF SELF-MOTION

The perception of self-motion is manifested in three distinct phenomena: (a) *heading,* the perceived direction of self-motion, (b) *vection,* the subjective sensation of self-motion, and (c) *postural adjustments* such as body sway induced by optic flow. To the extent that vection and postural sway are directionally specific, they must involve the extraction of heading information. On the other hand, these phenomena are to some extent independent, for they are dissociable and have different time courses. For instance, postural sway can be elicited without vection, particularly at low optical velocities (Delorme & Martin, 1986; Lee & Lishman, 1975; Stoffregen, 1986), and the latency of vection is often over 1 s, whereas accurate heading judgments can be made within 300 ms (Berthoz et al., 1975; Crowell, Royden, Banks, Swenson, & Sekuler, 1990; Dichgans & Brandt, 1978). In this section I discuss perceptual judgments of self-motion, including heading, time-to-contact, and vection and in the following section turn to the regulation of posture and gait.

A. Perception of Heading

A preliminary question is whether humans can indeed perceive heading from optic flow with any accuracy. Cutting (1986; Cutting et al., 1992) has estimated that a heading accuracy of 1°–3° is required for obstacle avoidance at speeds relevant to walking, running, skiing, and driving. Consider first the simplest case of pure translation.

1. Translation

Observer translation yields a radial flow pattern, relevant to Gibson's original hypothesis that heading is specified by the focus of expansion. Early experiments found surprisingly poor performance, with mean unsigned errors of 5°–10° (Johnston, White, & Cumming, 1973; Llewellyn, 1971), although R. Warren (1976) reported that performance was better when the focus of expansion was on screen (3° error) than off screen (8° error). These initial results cast doubt on Gibson's hypothesis. More recently, a series of experiments in my laboratory found heading accuracies on the order of 1°, well within Cutting's criterion. In this paradigm, observers viewed moving random-dot displays and judged whether they appeared to be heading to the right or left of a probe that came on at the end of the display; mean unsigned error was represented by a "heading threshold," the visual angle between the heading and the probe at which performance was 75% correct. Under the best conditions, the mean threshold was as low as 0.5°. Key effects are summarized here.

Consistent with Gibson's hypothesis, performance is comparable in different environments, with a ground plane, a frontal plane, and a 3-D cloud of dots (Warren, Morris, & Kalish, 1988; Warren, Blackwell, Kurtz, Hatsopoulos, & Kalish, 1991). The flow field thus need not be continuous, violating assumptions of surface smoothness. Optic flow is detectable even at slow walking speeds, with thresholds better than 2° at 1 m/s and improving only slightly at higher speeds (Crowell et al., 1990; Warren et al., 1988; Warren, Blackwell, & Morris, 1989). Extraction of this information is a rapid process, such that performance asymptotes with a display duration of only 280 ms (Crowell et al., 1990; Warren & Blackwell, 1988). Further, thresholds are unaffected by reducing the lifetime of each individual dot to only two frames in a 3-s display, indicating that "instantaneous" velocity field information is sufficient for translational heading, as most models assume (Warren et al., 1991).

More important, several findings indicate that the effective heading information is the global radial structure of the flow pattern rather than a local feature such as a fixed element at the focus of expansion. First, as the number of dots is increased, performance improves linearly with $\sqrt{N}$ dots ($r = .97$), although thresholds are still better than 2° with only three dots (Warren et al., 1988, 1989; Warren & Blackwell, 1988). This is indicative of spatial summation such that the visual system is exploiting the redundancy in the radial flow pattern. Second, observers tolerate large amounts of flow field noise (Warren et al., 1991). Random perturbations of the directions of individual vectors yield a gradual decline in performance (e.g., a threshold of 2.6° with a 90° perturbation envelope), indicating that the visual system pools over local motion signals. In contrast, perturbations of vector magnitude ("speed noise") had little effect on performance, suggesting that the radial pattern of vector directions provides the most salient heading information. However, systematic biases in vector magnitude can influence perceived heading, such as increasing all magnitudes on one side of the focus of expansion, consistent with a circular path (Dyre & Andersen, in press). Third, it appears that the visual system even pools over local motions that are due to independently moving objects rather than segmenting them before determining heading (Warren & Saunders, in press; see section III.A.4). All three of these effects are observed in expansion cells in MST and in template models with large-field expansion units (Hatsopoulos & Warren, 1991; Perrone, 1992).

Finally, it has often been argued that perception of self-motion is influenced by the retinal locus of stimulation. Brandt, Dichgans, and Koenig (1973; Dichgans & Brandt, 1978) proposed the *peripheral dominance hypothesis* that peripheral vision is specialized for the perception of self-motion, whereas central vision is specialized for the perception of object motion. However, there is little influence of the retinal eccentricity of the flow pattern on heading thresholds, the only consistent effect being a small improvement when the focus of expansion is at the fovea (Crowell & Banks, 1993; Warren & Kurtz, 1992). In an ideal observer analysis, Crowell and Banks (1994) concluded that human efficiency in extracting information from the flow pattern is comparable across retinal eccentricity (about 10%) but slightly better for lamellar than radial flow everywhere except the fovea. The foveal advantage appears to be due to lower velocity thresholds near the fovea. There is thus no retinal specialization for radial flow patterns: performance depends on the information in the flow pattern, not on the retinal region of stimulation.

In summary, the evidence indicates that the effective information for translational heading is the global radial structure of the velocity field, independent of environmental structure, observer speed, and retinal locus.

2. Curved Paths

Judgments of *circular heading,* one's future course on a circular path, are also quite accurate: thresholds are generally around 1.5° with a probe at a distance of 10 eyeheights (16 m) ahead (Warren et al., 1989, 1991). As with translational heading, the global structure of the velocity field seems to provide the effective information, for performance improves slightly with $\sqrt{N}$ dots ($r = .89$), remains accurate with two-frame dot lifetimes, and is unaffected by speed noise. However, constant errors increase on sharp curves (radius < 50 eyeheights) and at low speeds, and depend on environmental structure; these effects have not been explained satisfactorily but could be due to a small display screen eliminating salient regions of the flow pattern.

One means of recovering path curvature is to integrate over successive translational headings. In this case, accuracy should increase with that of perceived translation, which improves with observer speed (Rieger & Lawton, 1985). In contrast, Turano and Wang (1993) found that the threshold of curvature at which circular paths could be discriminated from linear paths was constant over speed, and remarkably, corresponded to a path radius of 1.5 miles (2,500 m). This suggests that the visual system is detecting path curvature directly from the curvature of the flow pattern rather than deriving it from perceived translation (Lee & Lishman, 1977). For travel on a circular path parallel to the ground plane, the curvature of the flow pattern maps one-to-one to the curvature of the observer's path (Warren et al., 1991). However, Kim and Turvey (1993, personal communication) demonstrated that heading on hyperbolic paths is also judged accurately, when the radius of the osculating circle[8] is changing. It is thus possible that the change in instantaneous path curvature can also be perceived.

In the special case of following a roadway with visible edge lines, Land and Lee (1994) observed that drivers fixate the point on the inside of the curve that is tangent to the line of sight. The angle between the tangent point and the car's axis is related to the curvature of the road and could be used to regulate the steering wheel angle. This behavior also has the effect of eliminating eye rotations, so the retinal flow pattern specifies the curved path (Figure 7) without requiring a decomposition.

3. Translation and Rotation

The issue that has generated the most interest is how the visual system determines heading when the observer is simultaneously translating and rotating ($T + R$), and recent data allow us to narrow the class of relevant models. The earliest studies of simulated observer rotation found poor results (Regan & Beverley, 1982; Rieger and Toet, 1985), casting doubt on the idea that this can be achieved on the basis of optical information alone. However, these experiments either presented a frontal plane, which as we shall see is a degenerate case, or presented arbitrary rotations that did not correspond to pursuit tracking of a point in the scene, including rotation about the line of sight. The current paradigm compares a "moving eye condition," which presents a standard radial flow display (T) but adds a moving fixation point to induce a pursuit eye movement (R), and a "simulated condition," which simulates the retinal flow produced by $T + R$ with a stationary fixation point, so no eye movement actually occurs. This puts optic flow information in conflict with oculomotor information such that relying on the latter would yield chance performance. Warren and Hannon (1988, 1990) found heading thresholds around 1.5° in both conditions—indeed, in the simulated condition it feels as if one's eye is actually moving. This demonstrates that the flow field alone can be sufficient for the decomposition; the issue is the conditions under which this is so.

a. Depth Variation

A repeated finding is that depth variation in the scene is necessary for an accurate visual decomposition, such as a ground plane receding in depth,

---

[8] A circle tangent to the curve, which has the same curvature at the tangent point.

two frontal planes separated in depth, or a discontinuous 3-D cloud of dots (Cutting et al., 1992; Perrone & Stone, 1991; Regan & Beverley, 1982; Rieger & Toet, 1985; Royden et al., 1994; Warren & Hannon, 1988, 1990). In contrast, a single frontal plane yields chance performance in the simulated condition: it generates a radial flow pattern centered at the fixation point, which looks as though one is heading toward the fixation point (Figure 9). In the moving eye condition, on the other hand, performance with a frontal plane is quite accurate. These results provide compelling evidence for motion parallax as the basis for a visual decomposition, although they also suggest that oculomotor information may be used to disambiguate the flow field.

b. Dot Density

As the number of dots is reduced, performance declines but thresholds remain better than 2° with as few as 12 dots 3°–4° apart (Warren & Hannon, 1990) or with half planes of dots that are 6° apart (Perrone & Stone, 1991). Although Rieger and Lawton's (1985) local differential motion algorithm predicts a similar decline with neighborhood size, it cannot account for this level of accuracy over large visual angles, whereas models that are based on generalized parallax can (Heeger & Jepson, 1992; Lappe & Rauschecker,

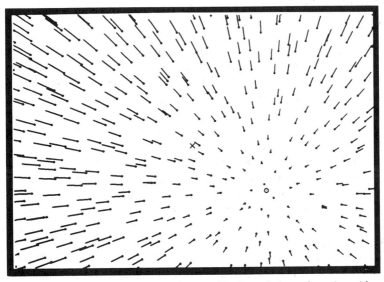

FIGURE 9   Retinal flow field generated by combined translation and rotation with respect to a frontal plane. Observer is translating toward the X while simultaneously rotating because of pursuit fixation of the O on the surface. Note that the radial flow pattern is centered on the fixation point, not the heading point.

1993; Perrone & Stone, 1994). Cutting et al. (1992) argued that the pattern of errors supports their particular version of differential motion parallax, but they did not compare their results against other models that make similar predictions.

c. Noise

When noise is added in the form of dots with uncorrelated motions, performance in the simulated condition remains accurate (thresholds better than 2°) for a ground surface with up to 33% noise dots but deteriorates rapidly for a cloud with as little as 10% noise (van den Berg, 1992). The decomposition is thus highly robust for a ground surface, but the cloud's vulnerability could be seen as consistent with noise–intolerant models. In the moving eye condition, performance was unaffected by noise, consistent with an oculomotor contribution. Van den Berg interpreted his results as support for a rotation subtraction theory, in which distant points specified by the horizon are used to determine the rotational component. Alternatively, good performance with the ground plane could be due to a simple horizon cue: relative motion between the fixation point and the horizon defines a line that intersects the horizon at the heading point. Van den Berg ruled out this strategy by varying the heading point along this line (i.e., the observer was heading into the ground plane) so that the cue was ambiguous and still obtained comparable robustness.

d. Rotation Rate

The preceding experiments supporting a visual decomposition used rates of eye rotation below 2°/s, a consequence of using fixation points on the ground surface. However, when Royden et al. (1992, 1994) manipulated rotation rate about a vertical axis, they reported increasing heading errors at ≥2.5°/s in the simulated condition. In contrast, performance in the moving eye condition was accurate up to 5°/s, indicating an extraretinal contribution. Banks, Ehrlich, Backus, and Crowell (1994) combined different proportions of simulated and actual eye rotation on individual trials and found that perceived heading was completely determined by the oculomotor information. These authors concluded that optical information may be sufficient for the decomposition at low rotation rates, when the gain of the efferent signal is low, but that oculomotor information is required under most conditions.

However, this conclusion is hotly contested. First, van den Berg (1993) objected that arbitrary rotation about a vertical axis failed to simulate pursuit tracking of a point in the ground plane, and he produced data showing accurate performance up to 5°/s. Royden et al. (1994) countered that the improvement was due to the horizon cue and showed that when the cue was eliminated, performance dropped. Second, template models that are based on gaze stabilization assumptions reproduce such errors in the case of rotation about a vertical axis (Lappe & Rauschecker, 1994; Perrone & Stone, 1994). Third, as Royden herself (1994) points out, the element trajectories in her displays of simulated rotation about a vertical axis were indistinguishable from those for movement on a circular path—indeed, observers saw themselves traveling on a circular path. Although the displays may theoretically contain sufficient information, they appear to be functionally ambiguous for human observers, possibly because the visual system has developed competing mechanisms to detect curved paths.

I am persuaded that oculomotor information plays a disambiguating role, but I doubt that Royden et al.'s (1992, 1994) displays are representative of most natural viewing conditions. Such conditions typically include pursuit tracking of surfaces in the scene rather than rotation about a vertical axis, a large field of view, complex structure with textured surfaces and dynamic occlusion, and extended viewing time, all of which could affect performance. Further experiments are needed to determine the influence of these variables. My expectation is that as the visual information is enriched, it will come to dominate the oculomotor information at higher rotation rates.

e. Depth Information

Recent experiments have shown that static information for depth order in the scene can facilitate the decomposition in the simulated condition. Van den Berg and Brenner (1994) reported that static stereo information for depth improved the noise tolerance of a random-dot cloud to the level of a ground plane; the plane was unaffected, presumably because it already contained depth information. Vishton, Nijhawan, and Cutting (1994) showed that performance with a 3-D cloud of squares was accurate when their relative size was consistent with their depth order but at chance when it was inconsistent. This provides intriguing evidence that the visual system can use relative depth information in the decomposition. Although this is consistent with the rotation subtraction theory, depth information could also help determine the translational component directly by resolving variation in the flow field that is due to depth (Equation 11).

4. Moving Objects

Most heading models assume that the environment is rigid, yet people also navigate successfully in the presence of moving objects, as when walking down a crowded street or driving on a busy freeway. Several strategies for dealing with independently moving objects are possible in principle: (1) The simplest approach would be to pool over all motion vectors, but this would yield systematic heading errors. (2) Moving objects could first be segmented on the basis of local information, such as relative motion or dynamic occlusion, and removed from the heading estimation (Adiv, 1985). (3) Observer motion could first be estimated globally and moving objects segmented by removing discrepant regions (Thompson, Lechleider, & Stuch, 1993). (4) Heading and segmentation could be performed simultaneously, on the basis of relative motion (Hildreth, 1992). Using displays of a square object moving in depth in front of a planar background, Warren and Saunders (in press) found that perceived heading was systematically biased in the direction of object motion, but only when the object covered the focus of expansion. Surprisingly, this indicates that the visual system does not segment moving objects before determining heading, consistent with spatial pooling by center-weighted expansion units. This may actually prove to be an adaptive solution for navigating with respect to obstacles on the path ahead: as one approaches a moving object, it increasingly dominates perceived heading. This raises the possibility that heading is more appropriately defined in the frame of reference of other objects rather than the frame of reference of the stationary surround.

5. Neural Mechanisms for Heading

Evidence of neural pathways selective for expansion and rotation was initially provided by Regan and Beverley (1978, 1979b, 1985), who showed, for example, that adaptation to an expanding–contracting rectangle reduced sensitivity to a similar expansion but not to a side-to-side oscillation. Subsequent work in the cat identified units that are sensitive to local expansion (Regan & Cynader, 1979) and found that velocity-sensitive cells in the lateral suprasylvian area tend to be centrifugally oriented, such that their preferred directions radiate from the area centralis (Rauschecker, Grunau, & Poulin, 1987). This could reflect an adaptation to predominant radial flow patterns. Frost and his colleagues have identified separate pathways in the pigeon that appear to be specialized for the detection of self-motion and object motion (Frost, 1985; Frost et al., 1990). In primates, there are a number of motion areas that could support the perception of self-motion (Maunsell & Newsome, 1987). Recent interest has focused on a major motion pathway running from motion sensors in V1, to velocity units in MT selective for both the direction and speed of motion, to large-field units in MST sensitive to patterns of motion (Maunsell & van Essen, 1983a; Ungerleider & Desimone, 1986).

In a provocative study of the dorsal portion MSTd, Saito et al. (1986) reported units selective for expansion–contraction, clockwise–counterclockwise rotation, and translation. This fueled speculation that MSTd cells could serve to decompose the flow pattern into elementary components of div, curl, def, and translation, as suggested by Koenderink and van Doorn (1978). However, when Orban et al. (1992) presented expansion-selective cells with a pure expansion pattern and a spiral pattern that contained an equivalent component of expansion, the level of response dropped for the spiral, indicating that the cell did not extract the expansion. Duffy and Wurtz (1991a, 1991b) found that 63% of MSTd cells actually responded to two or three components presented separately. Graziano, Andersen, and Snowden (1994) subsequently tested simultaneous combinations of expansion and rotation that formed spiral patterns and found a continuum of cells selective for different combinations. Spiral flow is similar to the family of flow patterns produced by surfaces slanted in depth (see Figure 6). The evidence has led these researchers to conclude that MSTd cells do not decompose the optic flow into basic components but rather act as templates for higher order flow patterns.

Further, cells in MSTd have properties that appear suited to the detection of self-motion, including (1) large receptive fields from 20° to 100° in diameter; (2) stronger responses to larger stimuli, indicative of spatial summation; (3) insensitivity to dot density, at least down to 25 dots; (4) dependence on vector direction; but (5) insensitivity to variation in vector speed; (6) a broad overall speed tuning; and (7) an inability to distinguish local object motion from global field motion, even with clear boundary information (R. A. Andersen, 1994; Duffy & Wurtz, 1991a; Orban, Lagae, Raiguel, Xiao, & Maes, in press; Tanaka, Fukada, & Saito, 1989; Tanaka & Saito, 1989). Properties 3–7 directly parallel the results for the perception of translational heading described above, consistent with the notion that the visual system detects the global radial pattern of vector directions, pooling over local vectors and moving objects.

On the other hand, there are objections to the notion that expansion units detect translational heading. First, they exhibit position invariance, responding to an expansion pattern wherever it appears within the receptive field. However, that level of this response does reveal a broad position tuning, such that expansion units could provide a coarse distributed coding of the position of the focus of expansion (Duffy & Wurtz, 1993; Graziano et al., 1994; Orban et al., in press). Second, there is apparently no regular retinotopic tiling of receptive fields, most of which include the fovea. However, there is a distribution of receptive field centers out to eccentricities of 40°–50° (Saito et al., 1986; Tanaka & Saito, 1989).

Finally, there is evidence that cells in other parts of MST are active during pursuit eye movements (Komatsu & Wurtz, 1988, 1989; Newsome, Wurtz, & Komatsu, 1988). It is not clear whether this activity is related to the production of eye movements or a corollary discharge, and it is not known whether it affects the response of properties of MST cells to optic flow. In addition, Roy and Wurtz (1990; Roy, Komatsu, & Wurtz, 1992) found MSTd neurons that are sensitive to binocular disparity, although it is not known whether these cells also respond to optic flow. In sum, although there is no direct evidence that MST participates in the detection of self-motion, and there is disagreement about its possible role in detecting object motion (Graziano et al., 1994; Orban et al., in press), the similarities with the types of units needed for self-motion are striking.

6. Implications for Heading Models

The preceding evidence rules out several classes of computational models as plausible accounts of biological vision. Contrary to the human data, discrete models are highly noise-sensitive, differential and dynamical models require dense continuous fields, and none of them require variation in depth. On the other hand, there is perceptual evidence consistent with generalized motion parallax, rotation subtraction, and template models, and the physiological evidence is most consistent with some form of template model that detects classes of compound flow patterns. As diagrammed in Figure 10, the data suggest that the visual system simultaneously extracts flow information for $\hat{T}$, flow information for $\mathbf{R}$, oculomotor information for $\mathbf{R}$, and depth information, which interact to determine heading. It thus appears that several different types of information are sufficient to determine heading, but none of them are necessary, a situation characteristic of other perceptual phenomena. A robust system will take advantage of such redundancy in the available information, so it can function adaptively under varying conditions. This raises the possibility that no single model is correct, but that each captures an aspect of a more complex perceptual system.

Let me offer a modest proposal that attempts to reconcile these observations in a sketch of a template model (see Figure 11). Following Perrone and Stone (1994), assume MST-like units constitute templates for flow patterns produced by various combinations of $\mathbf{T}$ and $\mathbf{R}$, with a separate 2-D heading map $(\hat{T}_x, \hat{T}_y)$ for each rate and axis of rotation $(R, \hat{R})$. For example, an $R = 0$

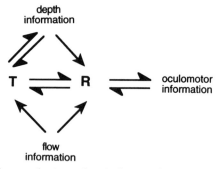

FIGURE 10   Likely contributions of optic flow, oculomotor, and depth information to determining observer translation **T** and rotation **R** on the basis of the current evidence.

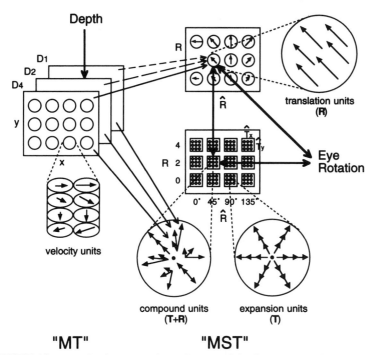

"MT"   **"MST"**

FIGURE 11   Sketch of a proposed template model for decomposing observer translation and rotation. MST-like (medial superior temporal area) units selective for a family of flow patterns are arrayed in a set of ($\hat{T}_x$, $\hat{T}_y$) heading maps, one for each rotation rate (R) and axis ($\hat{R}$). Independent estimates of eye rotation from translational flow and oculomotor information facilitate the corresponding map. Independent depth information contributes via disparity-sensitive MT-like (medial temporal area) velocity units.

map contains expansion units forming a distributed coding of translational heading in retinal coordinates, and the ($R = 2$, $\hat{R} = 45°$) map contains units selective for observer translation plus rotation at 2°/s about a diagonal axis. Other maps are posited for circular paths of different curvature with a ground plane (not shown). Because flow patterns that are due to pursuit fixation are centered on the fovea, so are the receptive fields of these templates, and thus heading relative to the fixation point is specified by the type of pattern, not its retinal position. Given that the translational component is determined by generalized motion parallax, a particular unit must respond to different depth structures. Hence, at each retinal location, a template would receive input from several MT-like units having preferred velocities that correspond to motion in different depth planes ($D = 1, 2, 4, 8 \ldots$). A single MST-like unit is thus sensitive to a family of flow patterns produced by a particular **T** + **R** combination for a variety of depth structures—

including spiral flow patterns generated by planes slanted in depth. Estimates of $\hat{T}$ and $\mathbf{R}$ from optic flow are represented by a peak in the activity distributed over the array of templates.

An independent estimate of $\mathbf{R}$ is provided by other MST units selective for large-field translational motion (Perrone, 1992). Rather than performing explicit subtraction, these units simply facilitate a particular heading map (say, the $R = 2$, $\hat{R} = 45°$ map). Oculomotor information for $\mathbf{R}$ similarly facilitates a specific heading map, and the visual estimate of $\mathbf{R}$ reciprocally influences the perceived eye rotation. Static information for relative depth contributes to both $\mathbf{R}$ and $\hat{T}$ via MT cells tuned to disparity (Maunsell & van Essen, 1983b) or other relative depth information. It contributes to the estimate of $\mathbf{R}$ through connections to MST translation units that are more strongly weighted for more distant depth planes. It contributes to the estimate of $\hat{T}$ through connections to a given MST template in which particular vectors are weighted for particular depth planes. Reciprocally, depth information could feed back via downward projections from the most active MST template to MT units tuned to the corresponding depth plane. Several estimates of $\hat{T}$ and $\mathbf{R}$ thus interact, driving the system to a solution (a peak of activity in a particular heading map) on the basis of whatever information is available.

This scheme is consistent with the current perceptual and physiological evidence and could account for some puzzling aspects of the data. First, when the optic flow is sufficient, it will dominate, but when it is degraded or ambiguous, oculomotor information will dominate. For example, translation plus rotation about a vertical axis at 4°/s will yield competing activity in both the ($R = 4$, $\hat{R} = 0$) heading map and a similar circular heading map; oculomotor information resolves the ambiguity by facilitating one map or the other. Second, depth variation is necessary to activate the appropriate template. With a frontal plane, radial flow from the fixation point will activate competing templates for expansion at the fovea in all heading maps; oculomotor information again resolves the ambiguity by facilitating the map for the appropriate rotation. This would account for the mixed conditions of Banks et al. (1994) in a similar manner. Third, static depth information will improve performance when it is available. Of course, this architecture is highly speculative, and there are equally plausible alternatives. This matter is not yet resolved and remains an active area of research.

B. Perception of Time-to-Contact

There are two lines of evidence that time-to-contact can be perceived: one from perceptual judgments, and the other from the timing of natural behavior. The underlying issue is whether time-to-contact is perceived on the basis of the tau variable or determined from separate estimates of distance and velocity ($T_c = D/V$).

1. Perceptual Judgments

In a paradigm introduced by Schiff and Detweiler (1979), observers view a display of an approaching object that disappears some time before contact and push a button at the judged moment of contact. The consistent result is that judged time-to-contact underestimates actual time-to-contact (measured from the time of disappearance), with a slope of 0.6 to 0.7 out to at least 10 s (Cavallo & Laurent, 1988; McLeod & Ross, 1983; Schiff & Oldak, 1990). This is the case whether the object approaches the observer or vice versa, whether the object is presented in isolation or on a ground surface that provides eyeheight-scaled distance and velocity information, and whether objects have a familiar size. In a different paradigm (Todd, 1981), observers viewed displays of two expanding contours of varying size with no distance or velocity information, and judged which object would arrive first. Seventy-five percent correct difference thresholds were just 40 ms, revealing highly accurate perception of the difference in time-to-contact, specified by $\Delta\tau$. These results clearly indicate that optical expansion patterns alone are sufficient for perception of time-to-contact, consistent with the use of local tau, although they do not rule out a D/V strategy when other information is available. A recent challenge to the autonomy of tau is presented by the finding that relative size can reverse the perceived relative time-to-contact of two approaching objects, presumably because the smaller object appears farther away and is thus seen as arriving later, even though $\Delta\tau$ specifies it will arrive first (DeLucia, 1991; DeLucia & Warren, 1994).

In a direct test of global tau, Kaiser and Mowafy (1993) simulated self-motion through a cloud of dots and had observers push a button when they would pass a colored target dot, which had an off-axis trajectory and disappeared off the screen 1–3 s before contact. Judged time-to-contact underestimated actual time-to-contact only slightly, with a mean slope of 0.84. Global tau is clearly the most relevant time-to-contact variable for guiding locomotion, and these results indicate that it can be used quite accurately.

2. Timing of Action

The observed underestimation in perceptual tasks may not reflect the on-line perception of time-to-contact but could be due to a mental extrapolation paradigm in which observers must imagine the object's behavior for many seconds after the end of the display. In the control of natural behavior, time-to-contact information is continuously available and is used to regulate or initiate an action at a particular margin value (Lee & Young, 1985; Sidaway, McNitt-Gray, & Davis, 1989). For example, leg extension in ski jumping is initiated 194 ms before the lip of the jump, with a standard deviation of only 10 ms (Lee, Lishman, & Thomson, 1982), indicating that perception of time-to-contact is remarkably precise. However, such observational studies do not dissociate tau from other possible strategies. More persuasive are studies of time-to-contact under acceleration (Lee & Reddish, 1981; Lee, Young, Reddish, Lough, & Clayton, 1983), which violate the constant velocity assumption and dissociate several competing strategies. For example, the diving gannet starts folding its wings at a constant tau value of 820 ms before entering the water, rather than at a constant value of actual time-to-contact (taking acceleration into account), a constant height, or a constant velocity. However, this still does not demonstrate that tau is the effective information, for the result is consistent with any instantaneous time-to-contact strategy that assumes a constant velocity.

In a clever manipulation, Savelsbergh, Whiting, and Bootsma (1991) had subjects catch a deflating ball, thereby dissociating optical expansion from D/V information. With monocular viewing, the timing of the grasp shifted later in time by 22 ms, but by only 5 ms with binocular viewing. This demonstrates the effectiveness of optical expansion but also suggests a role for disparity in determining ball size, distance, or time-to-contact, as proposed by Regan and Beverley (1979a). For off-axis approaches, Tresilian (1994) showed that the timing of a manual interception task is more accurate than can be explained by the local tau approximation and depends on visual or proprioceptive information about the angle between the object and the interception point. Thus, perception of off-axis time-to-contact appears to be based on higher order relations such as Equation 5. It is interesting to note that, in an extrapolation task when the interception point is unavailable, there is significantly less underestimation with an off-axis approach than with a direct approach (Schiff & Oldak, 1990), consistent with the local tau approximation that overestimates time-to-contact. It is important to note that actual catching does not appear to be based on a discrete prediction of the time and place of the ball's arrival, as required in an extrapolation task. Rather, hand position is continuously regulated by ongoing information about the current lateral position and time-to-contact of the ball (Peper, Bootsma, Mestre, & Bakker, 1994). Such task-specific control relations are also likely in the guidance of locomotion.

3. Neural Mechanisms for Time-to-Contact

There is some evidence for neural mechanisms that detect looming and time-to-contact. As noted above, there is considerable evidence for expansion-selective units in cat and primate visual cortex. Recordings in the cat have also identified cells sensitive to motion in depth along specific axes (Cynader & Regan, 1978). Recently, Wang and Frost (1992) reported large-field cells in the nucleus rotundus of the pigeon that respond not simply to expansion but to particular values of time-to-contact, over variation in object size and approach speed. The cells were tightly tuned to local expansion specifying a directly approaching object but did not respond to whole-field expansion specifying self-motion and decreased markedly with off-axis approaches as small as 5°. This strongly suggests a mechanism for detecting local tau, reflecting the direct approach constraint.

In summary, the evidence indicates that observers can judge time-to-contact from optical expansion patterns alone with reasonable accuracy, without spatial information about distance, velocity, or size. Although this does not provide conclusive evidence for use of the tau variable, it appears likely that observers rely on global tau during self-motion and local tau for direct approaches. More complex variables are required to account for off-axis interception, such as catching.

C. Vection

Vection is the subjective sensation of self-motion in a stationary observer. A classic example is the *train illusion,* in which an observer seated in a stationary train feels like he or she is moving when a train on the adjacent track pulls out (Helmholtz, 1867/1925, p. 266). The earliest discussion of the phenomenon was by Mach (1875), who also performed the first laboratory experiments using a rotating drum. Two classes of self-motion are usually distinguished: (1) *circular vection* (CV) typically refers to yaw about a vertical axis, as induced in the rotating drum, but *roll vection* can also be induced by a pattern rotating about the line of sight, and *pitch vection* by tipping the surround fore and aft about a lateral axis; (2) *linear vection* (LV), including translation along the anterior–posterior (AP), vertical, or lateral axis, induced by a translating pattern such as an endless belt or moving room. The experienced self-motion is in a direction opposite to the direction of stimulation. Most research has used vection as a means of assessing visual-vestibular-efferent interactions (see Berthoz & Droulez, 1982; Dichgans & Brandt, 1978, for reviews). After recapitulating some basic characteristics, I focus on the effective visual information for vection.

1. Characteristics of Vection

a. Time Course

The mean latency from the onset of stimulation to the start of vection is about 1–2 s for LV (Berthoz et al., 1975) and 2–3 s for CV (Brandt et al., 1973), although there are large individual differences (1–10 s). Latency is independent of the velocity and onset characteristics of the display, that is, whether onset is a step function or a gradual acceleration (over the range of 1° to 15°/s^2). Complete vection, in which the scene appears stationary and all motion is attributed to the observer, does not occur until 8–12 s after onset. This long time delay casts doubt on the functional significance of the sensation of self-motion in the control of behavior. However, the latency is decreased by simultaneous vestibular stimulation, a point not lost on the designers of flight simulators and theme park rides with moving or vibrating seats. Latency is reduced by an impulse acceleration in the corresponding direction (Brandt, Dichgans, & Buchele, 1974), whereas acceleration in the opposite direction can eliminate vection (Young, Dichgans, Murphy, & Brandt, 1973). This suggests that qualitative vestibular information may act to gate visual information, with little subsequent influence (Berthoz et al., 1975; Lishman & Lee, 1973).

b. Velocity

Magnitude estimates of the velocity of self-motion are linear and equal to that of the display up to a saturation speed, at which point they level off. The saturation velocity is about 120°/s for CV (Brandt et al., 1973) and 1 m/s for LV (with a display 0.5 m from the eye; Berthoz et al., 1975). For roll and tilt vection, the saturation velocity is only 10°/s, and there is a curious discrepancy between the sensation of continuous self-motion and a sensation of body tilt that stops at 10°–15° (Held, Dichgans, & Bauer, 1975); this is probably due to conflicting visual information about motion and somatosensory or vestibular information about orientation.

Interestingly, whereas the speed of CV does not depend on the spatial frequency of the stimulus pattern (Dichgans & Brandt, 1978), the speed of LV increases additively with both spatial frequency ("edge rate") and velocity ("flow rate"; Denton, 1980; Larish & Flach, 1990); the same is true for postural sway induced by LV (Lestienne et al., 1977). This may be explained by the fact that flow rate uniquely specifies the observer's rotation speed independent of distance, but it only specifies translation speed if distance is known (T/D); similarly, edge rate only specifies speed if texture size is known. During translation, the visual system apparently relies on both, whereas during rotation, it does not rely on edge rate. However, the speed of CV increases with distance despite constant flow and edge rates (Dichgans & Brandt, 1978), suggesting that perceived distance can influence perceived rotation speed.

c. Frequency and Phase Response

With sinusoidal stimulation, LV is induced only at low temporal frequencies, with a cutoff in the gain of continuous magnitude estimates at around 0.5 Hz (Berthoz et al., 1979; Berthoz et al., 1975). Similarly, the phase of the response drops from near 0° at 0.01 Hz to around 180° at 0.5 Hz. This can be expressed as a linear low-pass system with a time constant of about 1 s (Berthoz & Droulez, 1982). These results are nearly identical to those for visually induced sway (Berthoz et al., 1979), consistent with the idea that self-motion is specified by optical frequencies or accelerations correlated with the dynamics of normal postural sway.

2. Visual Information for Self-Motion

Given an optic flow pattern, what information distinguishes self-motion from object motion? Several hypotheses have been proposed, including a global versus local transformation, stimulation in peripheral versus central vision, and motion of the background versus the foreground.

a. Area of Stimulation

Gibson (1950, 1954, 1968) pointed out that observer movement produces a global transformation of the optic array, whereas object motion tends to produce a local transformation in a bounded region of the array. Exceptions include self-motion in a vehicle and motion of large objects that fill the visual field. While there is evidence that larger areas of stimulation induce more compelling vection, higher velocity CV, and greater postural sway (Brandt et al., 1973; Held et al., 1975; Lestienne et al., 1977), small regions <15° in diameter can also be effective (Andersen & Braunstein, 1985; Howard & Heckmann, 1989). The original train illusion, in which motion is seen through a window, provides such a counterexample. This indicates that the area of stimulation by itself cannot be the full story.

b. Retinal Locus of Stimulation

The peripheral dominance hypothesis states that the peripheral retina dominates vection and spatial orientation, whereas central vision dominates the perception of object motion (Brandt et al., 1973; Dichgans & Brandt, 1978). This derives from similar considerations as the first hypothesis: Because self-motion tends to produce a global transformation, it is more likely than object motion to yield optic flow in the visual periphery, and thus the peripheral retina could have become specialized for detecting self-motion. It could also account for the area effect because larger displays are more likely to encroach on the periphery.

Brandt et al. (1973) reported that a 30° display presented 45°–75° in the periphery was sufficient to evoke CV with an intensity and speed close to full-field stimulation, whereas a central 30° display had no effect at all. Similar results were found for roll vection (Held et al., 1975) and linear vection along the AP axis (Berthoz et al., 1975) and the vertical axis (Johansson, 1977). It quickly came to be accepted that the retinal periphery dominated the perception of self-motion. However, subsequent results call this into question. Andersen and Braunstein (1985) reported LV with central stimulation as small as 7.5°, and, in a direct replication of Brandt et al. (1973), Post (1988) found no effect of the eccentricity of a 30° display on the intensity or velocity of CV. This suggests that the overall pattern of stimulation, not simply the retinal locus of motion, must be considered.

c. Depth Order

Object motion and self-motion generally occur within a stationary environmental frame of reference. Gibson (1968) noted that a moving object occludes and disoccludes more distant background surfaces, whereas self-motion yields motion perspective of the background itself. In principle, the order of surfaces in depth may be given by dynamic occlusion, stereopsis, or static information. There is consistent evidence that both vection and postural adjustments are determined by motion of surfaces perceived to be in the background, rather than the foreground.

Brandt, Wist, and Dichgans (1975) first demonstrated that the latency and velocity of CV were unaffected when a stationary pattern was presented in front of the moving pattern but were greatly reduced when it was presented in the background, where the depth difference was induced by disparity via the Pulfrich effect. Subsequently, Ohmi, Howard, and Landolt (1987) monocularly presented a stationary and a moving pattern that would spontaneously reverse in depth. CV was completely determined by the pattern that was seen in the background. In a critical experiment, Howard and Heckmann (1989) compared area of stimulation, retinal region, and foreground–background by using a 54° × 44° central display that could be perceived as in front of or behind a peripheral display, as specified by disparity. Again, the direction of CV was determined by the background pattern, and there was no difference between central and peripheral displays when they were equated for area. They concluded that vection is primarily controlled by two factors that trade off: area of stimulation and motion of the perceived background surface. Telford, Spratley, and Frost (1992) found the same effect when depth order was specified by dynamic occlusion, and comparable results were reported for both LV and postural sway by Delorme and Martin (1986).

In summary, it now appears that the effective information for vection is background motion or a large area of stimulation, but not peripheral stimulation. Previous evidence for peripheral dominance can be explained by these two factors, for most of the earlier studies either did not equate retinal area or presented central stimulation in the foreground (see Howard & Heckmann, 1989). The theory also accounts for the original train illusion, in which vection is induced by background motion viewed centrally through a window.

IV. VISUAL CONTROL OF SELF-MOTION

Visual control of posture and locomotion involves the use of optical information to modulate stance and gait to adapt to environmental conditions. An account of visual control thus requires understanding both the dimensions of variation of an action and the information by which they are regulated. The standard view has been that various sources of information are used to construct a general-purpose 3-D representation of the scene, on the basis of which path planning is performed and effector commands computed. Alternatively, special-purpose control relations could use task-specific information to regulate action parameters directly, without an intervening model or plan (Warren, 1988). Gibson (1958) originally proposed such "formulae for the visual control of locomotion" that described the information for going forward, steering, and so on. The present section is an elaboration of this approach, including control relations for locomotor tasks such as (1) balance, (2) stepping, (3) steering, including goal seeking and obstacle avoidance, (4) braking, and (5) pursuit and avoidance of moving objects.

A. Affordances and Laws of Control

Particular environmental conditions offer or afford a variety of actions for a given animal, which Gibson (1979) called the *affordances* of the environment. Affordances are simply material properties of environmental surfaces and objects considered functionally, in relation to properties of the animal's action system. For example, a horizontal, rigid surface affords walking; whereas a nonrigid surface affords crawling (Gibson, Riccio, Schmuckler, & Stoffregen, 1987), a stairway affords climbing for individuals with particular leg lengths (Warren, 1984) and an opening affords passage for individuals of a certain body size (Warren & Whang, 1987). The traversibility of the terrain is determined by characteristics such as the size of obstacles relative to leg length (Pufall & Dunbar, 1992), grade relative to limb structure (Kinsella-Shaw, Shaw, & Turvey, 1992), slipperiness relative to foot friction, and compliance relative to leg stiffness (McMahon & Greene, 1978). It has been argued that affordances are perceived on the basis of body-scaled or *action-scaled information* that specifies environmental properties as ratios of the observer's action system (Lee, 1980; Mark & Vogele, 1988; Warren, 1984). For example, the focus of expansion during walking is necessarily at eye level, and thus the frontal dimensions of objects are given in body-scaled units of eye height, specifying whether they should be stepped over, jumped over, or detoured around. It has been shown that altering eye level correspondingly alters both perceived size and perceived affordances (Mark, 1987; Stoper, 1990; Warren & Whang, 1987).

Affordances set the boundary conditions on possible actions. Realizing a particular affordance—stepping over or steering around an obstacle—requires further perceptual guidance. Following Gibson (1958), I have proposed that each such action mode is governed by corresponding *laws of control*, task-specific relationships between optical information and the free parameters of action (Warren, 1988). One would expect to find a set of such control laws for each of the locomotor tasks mentioned above, resulting in gait and postural adjustments that are *functionally specific* to the current state of affairs (Reed, 1988). Specifically, we would expect (1) selective responses to the relevant flow components, (2) directionally specific adjustments, (3) differential adjustments to different classes of flow patterns (e.g., translation vs. rotation), and (4) adaptation to rearrangement of the relation between stimulation and effectors, preserving the functional specificity of adjustments.

B. Visual Control of Standing Posture

The basic requirement of upright stance is to keep the center of gravity (cg) within the static base of support provided by the feet, via synergetic activity at the ankle, knee, and hip (Nashner & McCollum, 1985; Yang, Winter, & Wells, 1990a). Although this is often referred to as *static balance,* the cg actually moves continually within the base of support, providing information about the region of stability under different conditions of terrain and load (Riccio, 1993). The standard model treats stance as an inverted pendulum, with a time constant that is the inverse of the natural frequency of the upright pendulum, which is maintained in an unstable equilibrium by sensory feedback (e.g., McCollum & Leen, 1989; Nashner, 1972). However, it is possible that the postural control system plays a more active role, with its own intrinsic dynamics (Collins & DeLuca, 1993; Dijkstra, Schoner, & Gielen, 1994; Schoner, 1991).

1. Visual Information for Postural Control

The basic theory of visual postural control proposes that AP sway is driven by minimizing the radial expansion and contraction (or "retinal slip") of a frontal surface, thereby anchoring the head to the visual surround with some phase delay (Lee & Lishman, 1975; Paulus, Straube, Krafczyk, & Brandt, 1989; Schoner, 1991). An advantage of such a system is that sway amplitude is appropriately scaled independent of distance, as long as expansion is above the detection threshold. However, this is only the case when looking approximately in the direction of self-motion; for other samples of the flow field (e.g., AP sway parallel to a saggital surface), distance information would be required to scale body sway to the flow rate. Warren, Kay, and Yilmaz (in press) proposed that motion parallax could be used to regulate posture without distance information: translation of the eye produces relative motion between elements at different depths, and minimizing this parallax would compensate for the translation, independent of distance. However, 3-D structure is required, and degenerate cases such as planar environments would yield systematic biases. Thus, expansion and parallax together typically contain sufficient information to control posture, regardless of the sample of the flow field.

2. Experimental Evidence

The role of vision was first demonstrated by the finding that spontaneous sway increases in both the AP and lateral directions when the eyes are closed (Edwards, 1946; Sheldon, 1963; Travis, 1945; Wapner & Witkin, 1950), more so when somatosensory information about the support surface is altered by standing on foam pads or a tilting platform (Berthoz et al., 1979; Hlavacka & Saling, 1986; Lee & Lishman, 1975; Woollacott, Shumway-Cook, & Nashner, 1986). Lee introduced the "swinging room" paradigm, in which the walls and ceiling move above a stationary floor, as a means of placing visual information in conflict with somatosensory and vestibular information and found a visual influence on posture in both infants and adults (Lee & Aronson, 1974; Lee & Lishman, 1975). Although infants often stumble or fall in the swinging room (Bertenthal & Bai, 1989; Butterworth & Hicks, 1977; Stoffregen, Schmuckler, & Gibson, 1987), adult responses on a rigid surface appear to saturate at about 1°–1.5° of ankle rotation, corresponding to a 3–4 cm displacement of the eye. Despite these demonstrations, the functional specificity of postural control has yet to be investigated in detail. For example, the swinging room presents a flow pattern corresponding to translation of the head rather than pitch about the ankles, but we cannot tell from existing measures whether differential responses occur.

a. Frequency and Phase Response

When the eyes are closed, spontaneous postural sway increases at frequencies below 0.5 Hz; similarly, sway is elicited by an oscillating visual scene below 0.5 Hz (Dichgans & Brandt, 1978; Lestienne et al., 1977; Soechting & Berthoz, 1979; van Asten, Gielen, & van der Gon, 1988a, 1988b). The phase of sway with respect to the driver increases from near 0° at 0.1 Hz to almost 135° at 0.5 Hz, with an overall time delay of about 800 ms. Similar results are obtained with both translating (AP) and rotating (roll) displays. Van Asten et al. (1988a) concluded that this behavior is best characterized by a linear, second-order, low-pass system that is driven by optical motion.

b. Effective Information

Although it is possible that posture is regulated by static position or orientation cues, evidence indicates that sway is evoked by optical motion per se (van Asten et al., 1988a, 1988b; Young, 1988). Further, under stroboscopic illumination, postural control deteriorates steadily from 16- to 4-Hz stimulation as continuous motion is eliminated (Amblard, Cremieux, Marchand,

& Carblanc, 1985; Paulus, Straube, & Brandt, 1984). To determine whether posture is selectively driven by the flow components div, curl, and def, van Asten et al. (1988b) simulated AP motion with variously textured surfaces. There were no effects of display type, except for a reduced response with an expanding bull's-eye pattern, in contrast to an checkered bull's-eye pattern. Although this suggests that the combination of div and def is more effective than div alone, the results are inconclusive.

A repeated finding is that the amplitude of spontaneous sway increases with the distance to a frontal surface (Edwards, 1946; Lee & Lishman, 1975; Paulus et al., 1984). This can be explained by assuming that the visual system (1) minimizes expansion and (2) has a motion detection threshold (Paulus et al., 1989). For a given amplitude of sway, optical velocity (e.g., expansion) is inversely proportional to surface distance; thus, at greater distances, a larger sway will occur before the threshold is reached. Oscillating the surface brings the expansion rate above the threshold, and in this case the amplitude of sway remains constant over distance, whether or not stereo information is available (Dijkstra, Gielen, & Melis, 1992; Dijkstra et al., 1994). However, the correlation between driver and sway decreases with distance, suggesting that postural control is not a passive linear system driven by sensory feedback but may be actively generating oscillations in an effort to match the driver.

c. Directional Specificity

Given that heading can be judged with an accuracy of 1°, one might expect to find directional specificity in postural sway, but this has not been tested directly. Most studies have presented optic flow only along the AP axis, which does induce sway that is correlated in the AP direction and uncorrelated in the lateral direction (Delorme, Frigon, & Lagace, 1989; van Asten et al., 1988a). The few studies that have presented both AP and lateral stimulation have reported similar sway amplitudes or correlations in each direction (Andersen & Dyre, 1989; Stoffregen, 1985, 1986), suggesting that sway responses are isotropic.

d. Adaptation to Rearrangement

Because the head can rotate, there is no fixed relation between the sample of the flow field and the position of the effectors; thus, we would expect adaptive control relations between the flow pattern and effector forces. Stoffregen (1985, 1986) tested observers in a swinging room that was moving along the AP axis. When they looked straight ahead, the flow pattern was radial, and when they turned their heads 90° to look at the side wall, the flow pattern was lamellar, yet both classes of flow yielded the same amplitude of AP sway. This is consistent with adaptation to rearrangement. On the other hand, Gielen and van Asten (1990) reported that the direction of sway varies with the direction of gaze, when observers looked diagonally at a display of a hallway oscillating along the AP axis. This may be explained as a response to the parallax between the hallway motion and the fixation marker on the screen (Warren et al., in press).

e. Retinal Region of Stimulation

Opinion has turned against the peripheral dominance hypothesis for postural control as well as vection (Dichgans & Brandt, 1978). It has convincingly been shown that postural sway can be elicited by radial, rotary, or lamellar flow in central vision, and by lamellar flow in the periphery, when equated for visual angle and produced by motion of a background surface (Andersen & Dyre, 1989; de Graaf, van Asten, & Gielen, 1990; Delorme & Martin, 1986; Paulus et al., 1984; Stoffregen, 1985, 1986; van Asten et al., 1988b). Questions remain about whether radial flow in the periphery is effective in inducing postural sway (Stoffregen, 1985), although it is adequate to specify heading (Crowell & Banks, 1993) and time-to-contact (Stoffregen & Riccio, 1990).

C. Visual Control of Locomotion

There is comparatively little research on the visual control of walking and running, largely owing to the technical problem of manipulating large-field optic flow for a moving observer. I briefly describe the few known results and point out problems awaiting investigation.

1. Visual Information during Locomotion

In walking and running, postural control is nested within locomotor control, and the optical transformations become quite complex. The flow pattern includes a constant velocity component that is due to forward progression, a component that is due to eye rotation, sinusoidal components that are due to the stride cycle (which correlate with stride frequency, Cappozzo, 1981, and leg length, Stappers, 1992), and other oscillatory and discrete components that are due to postural sway and perturbations. The visuomotor control system is presumably able to respond to these components selectively to regulate posture and locomotion independently. For example, Cutting et al. (1992) showed that stride-related sinusoidal components do not interfere with perceptual judgments of heading, and Warren et al. (in press) showed that an oscillatory component specifying a postural disturbance modulates sway in a comparable manner with or without a constant component that is due to forward progression. Currently there is no formal analysis of the decomposition of these components.

2. Postural Control during Walking

The biomechanics of postural control during walking, in contrast to stance, require maintaining a dynamic equilibrium in which the base of support is continually changing and the cg is seldom directly above it (Winter, 1987; Yang, Winter, & Wells, 1990b). Thus, postural control must be integrated with stepping, including adjustments of foot placement (Townsend, 1985), and is likely to be phase dependent on the step cycle (Belanger & Patla, 1987; Forssberg, 1979).

a. Frequency and Phase Response

The frequency response of postural sway during walking with an oscillating display has a cutoff around 1 Hz, with a resonance peak at the stride cycle frequency of 0.8 Hz (Kay & Warren, 1995). This wider frequency range could be due to differences in the dynamics of walking and stance and hence in the somatosensory information available. The phase of postural sway with respect to the display also increases as a function of frequency.

b. Functional Specificity

A preliminary study performed in 1983 by Lee, Young, Anderson, Warren, and McCrindle (described in Young, 1988) tested postural responses during running by mounting a tilting room above a treadmill, which did not have a flow component for forward progression. They observed directional body sway in response to a 3° roll of the visual surround about the ankles, but pitching the room fore or aft always evoked backward sway and a shortened flight time, suggesting a nonspecific response to increase stability. More recent experiments have used a "moving hallway" with subjects walking on a stationary floor, which adds a forward progression component. Sudden AP motion of the visual surround induced staggering or falling in children, demonstrating a reliance on visual information for postural control (Schmuckler & Gibson, 1989; Stoffregen et al., 1987). With constant AP motion of the hallway (0.6 m/s), adults reduced their speed when hall motion was opposite the direction of walking, but they made no systematic adjustments when hall motion was in the same direction as walking (Konczak, 1994). Analogous results were reported by using an apparatus that projected moving spots of light on a stationary floor (Ferrandez & Pailhous, 1986; Fluckiger, 1986).

   Functional specificity has been examined in my laboratory by presenting large-screen computer displays of a scene oscillating in different directions to observers walking on a treadmill and recording sway kinematics. The direction and amplitude of compensatory sway depend on the 3-D structure of the scene, consistent with reliance on both optical expansion and parallax (Warren et al., in press). With a frontal plane and a 3-D cloud of elements, sway is directionally specific and isotropic, having equal amplitudes in all directions, but when walking down a hallway, sway is flattened into the lateral plane and is greater in the lateral direction because of the absence of parallax specifying AP motion. There is also evidence of adaptation to rearrangement, for when the treadmill is turned 90° with respect to the hallway, postural adjustments remain directionally specific. Further, walkers respond differentially to displays specifying lateral translation and roll with, respectively, a weaving gait or lateral tilt (Warren et al., 1995). In summary, translational sway appears to be controlled by both optical expansion and motion parallax, yielding functionally specific responses in most 3-D environments but predictable biases with some planar scenes. This suggests that postural control is based on optic flow per se rather than a 3-D representation of the scene.

3. Stepping

To walk or run in rough terrain, foot placement must be controlled in three dimensions to land on clear footholds while maintaining balance, with the appropriate step length, step width, height, and slope and the appropriate swing height to clear obstacles (see Raibert, 1986, for a convergent analysis from robotics). Further, ground reaction force at push-off and landing must be adjusted for the friction and compliance of the surface to avoid slipping, reduce impact shocks, and minimize energy expenditure. Warren, Young, and Lee (1986) examined the control of step length in treadmill running and found that the main control parameter was the vertical impulse applied during push-off $(I = Ft)$, resulting in a longer flight time and thus a larger step (see also Lee et al., 1982). They proposed that vertical impulse could be regulated visually by the time-to-contact with the upcoming foothold, which corresponds to the desired step time and is specified by global tau. However, in studies of overground running, Patla, Robinson, Samways, and Armstrong (1989) and Warren and Yaffe (1989) reported an additional, smaller contribution of AP impulse, which alters forward velocity and is thus comparatively inefficient. This suggests that a global impulse parameter may be modulated by global tau to regulate step length.

Patla and his colleagues have systematically examined the dimensions of variation in walking and identified control strategies for step length and width, stepping over obstacles, and landing on surfaces with varying height, compliance, and friction (see Patla, 1991a, for an overview). In general, these involve modulations of the ipsilateral leg (the swing leg that lands on the target) and the contralateral leg (the stance leg during the adjustments) that occur within one step cycle after a target is cued. For example, stepping over an obstacle involves an increase in vertical impulse in the contralateral leg to raise the body's center of mass and an increase in flexion of the ipsilateral leg at the hip, knee, and ankle so that the toe clears the obstacle (Patla, 1991b). The recruitment of leg muscles depends on the height of the obstacle and proceeds in a proximal to distal order.

These strategies are not simply amplitude-scaled versions of the basic gait pattern but involve different patterns of muscle activity. Determining how such variation can arise from parameter changes in a basic gait is the challenge for the motor side of the problem. On the perceptual side, research is needed to determine the information governing these gait adjustments.

4. Steering

The path of locomotion must be regulated to steer toward goals, pass through openings, and avoid obstacles. Patla (1991b) demonstrated that changing direction during walking involves a large increase in lateral impulse during push-off with the contralateral leg, an increase in torsional impulse about the vertical axis to rotate the body, and abduction of the ipsilateral leg during swing. In contrast to other gait adjustments, subjects require two steps from the cue to overcome inertia and rotate the body, and they prefer to turn in a direction opposite the contralateral foot to minimize impulse and maintain balance. The effective information that regulates this pattern has not been determined empirically.

Although it is possible that steering is based on a full 3-D representation of the environment, in principle one could steer simply on the basis of information about current heading, time-to-contact, and the boundaries of objects. As Gibson (1958) originally proposed, steering toward a goal involves keeping the focus of expansion within the textured contour that corresponds to the goal object, whereas obstacle avoidance requires keeping the focus outside of such contours. The edges of objects and apertures (including their sign) must be distinguished, presumably on the basis of dynamic occlusion, disparity, and so on. Finally, the timing of such avoidance actions could be regulated by tau so that they are initiated sufficiently far in advance to achieve the inertial changes. In an existence proof that such a strategy would work, Duchon and Warren (1994) implemented a simple control law in a real-time mobile robot. Even without an edge-extraction algorithm, the robot successfully steered through a cluttered room by avoiding the region with the shortest time-to-contact, turning through an angle inversely proportional to its distance from the focus of expansion.

Conventionally, it is believed that the visual system requires a series of coordinate transformations to convert the location of an obstacle from retinal to head-centered, body-centered, and finally effector coordinates. This requires accurate kinesthetic information about the relative position and motion of each segment, and error is propagated down the kinematic chain. It is important to note that this problem can be avoided for visual control because the current heading and object edges are both given in the same coordinate frame (e.g., retinal coordinates), and their relationship is intrinsically defined. To steer through a door, for example, the visual angle between the focus of expansion and the doorway directly gives the required change in the direction of horizontal impulse.

5. Braking

Braking to stop in front of an object involves visually regulating one's deceleration, which can be mapped directly into the required effector force ($F = ma$). One possibility is that a constant deceleration is computed from 3-D variables such as object distance (Z), observer velocity (V), or object diameter ($2R$), for example,

$$d = \frac{V^2}{2Z}, \qquad d = \frac{V^2 \tan \theta}{2R}, \tag{14}$$

where θ is the visual angle subtended by the object (Yilmaz & Warren, in press). Alternatively, Lee (1976) showed that braking could be controlled by using the temporal derivative of tau, which provides information about the adequacy of one's current level of deceleration: $\dot{\tau} < -0.5$ specifies that current deceleration is too low and, if maintained, would result in a crash; $\dot{\tau} > -0.5$ specifies that current deceleration is too high and would result in stopping short of the object; and $\dot{\tau} = -0.5$ specifies a constant deceleration that will yield a stop right at the object. Lee suggested that observers could hold $\dot{\tau}$ constant at a safe margin value near -0.5 or use the margin value to determine the required change in deceleration.

Evidence that the $\dot{\tau}$ margin value is perceptually salient was provided by Kim, Turvey, and Carello (1993), who presented displays of a surface approaching at different constant $\dot{\tau}$ values and had observers judge whether the collision would be "hard" or "soft." The critical value was $\dot{\tau} = -0.5$, indicating that observers reliably distinguish "crash" states from "safe" states (but see Kaiser & Phatak, 1993, for a dissenting view). Observational studies of hummingbirds entering a feeding tube (Lee, Reddish, & Rand, 1991), pigeons landing (Lee, Davies, Green, & van der Weel, 1993), and humans running toward a wall (Wann, Edgar, & Blair, 1993) suggest that such approaches are governed by a constant $\dot{\tau}$ but they do not dissociate it from other variables such as distance and velocity.

Yilmaz and Warren (in press) performed a direct test by using closed-loop displays of approach to a road sign in which deceleration was controlled by a spring-loaded mouse brake; a checkerboard ground surface provided static information for distance, velocity, and size. Observers did not hold $\dot{\tau}$ constant during the approach but tended to oscillate about a mean value of -0.51 with successive brake adjustments. The direction and magnitude of brake adjustment depended on the current value of $\dot{\tau}$ and was precisely predicted by the difference between the current $\dot{\tau}$ and a margin value of -0.52. Moreover, the presence or absence of the ground surface had no effect on these values. Thus, observers apparently used $\dot{\tau}$ to determine both the direction and magnitude of change in deceleration, whether or not 3-D information was available. Whether this finding will generalize to other braking tasks remains to be determined.

6. Pursuit and Avoidance of Moving Objects

Locomotion must be controlled not only with respect to the stationary environment but also with respect to other moving objects. In situations such as driving on a crowded highway, it may be adaptive to ignore the background and simply navigate with respect to the moving ensemble. At least three cases should be considered: (1) pursuing or intercepting a moving object, (2) following a moving object at a constant distance, and (3) avoiding or escaping a pursuer. The best studied case is interception, exemplified by the "outfielder problem" of catching a fly ball (Babler & Dannemiller, 1993; Bootsma & Peper, 1992; Michaels & Oudejans, 1992; Peper et al., 1994; Saxberg, 1987a, 1987b; Todd, 1981), but the other cases have received little study (Schiff, 1965).

In principle, control laws for steering and braking could apply to both moving and stationary objects since they regulate the relative motion between observer and object. During pursuit (Gibson, 1958), the optical expansion of the target specifies one is gaining on it, a constant visual angle specifies following at a constant distance, optical contraction specifies that one is losing ground, and deceleration could be controlled by using the $\dot{\tau}$ of the target. However, Probst, Krafczyk, Brandt, and Wist (1984) found that the time required to detect target expansion is elevated three-fold when it is embedded in a radial flow field. It thus remains to be determined whether these control relations would be effective when both the observer and the target are moving.

V. NEW DIRECTIONS

In this chapter, I have attempted to present a coherent picture of how optic flow is used to perceive self-motion and to control posture and locomotion. Let me conclude with a personal list of some new directions and challenges.

1. Perception and Action

Whereas advances have been made in formal analysis and perceptual tests of optical information, the study of how such information is actually used to regulate action is just beginning. Research on natural behavior such as reaching, catching, and locomotion is critical, for it often reveals task-specific solutions that are not evident in general analyses. Observational studies have provided landmark demonstrations of the tight coupling between perception and action but seldom allow us to tease apart competing informational variables and possible control relations. Experimental studies that manipulate the available information and control for alternative strategies are essential but difficult with real-world tasks. The emergence of new technology, including real-time computer graphics, on-line motion analysis, and virtual reality may help make such studies possible.

2. Neural Mechanisms for Detecting Information

The convergence of work on optic flow and visual physiology suggests the beginnings of an Gibsonian account of the neural support for the detection of information. Gibson is often portrayed as antagonistic to the problem of mechanism, but his 1966 book actually focused on this issue and developed the metaphor of a neural system that is "tuned" to higher order patterns of stimulation, actively explores or "hunts" for such information, and detects or "resonates" to it. Since his speculations, we have learned much about principles of neural organization and neural networks that is congenial to this view. The problem of optic flow offers an opportunity for contact between the functional and implementation levels of description by developing an account of neural mechanisms as systems for detecting higher order information.

3. Autonomous Agents and Animate Vision

The notion of task-specific perception and control is having a significant impact in computer vision and robotics. The long-standing AI model of intelligence as symbol manipulation, with chess playing as its apotheosis, is being challenged by a view of intelligence as adaptive behavior by an *autonomous agent* (Beer, 1990; Maes, 1990). Rather than constructing a full, general-purpose representation of the 3-D scene (Marr, 1982), the goal of vision is extracting special-purpose information for the task at hand, as emphasized by recent work on *animate vision* (Aloimonos, 1993; Bajcsy, 1988; Ballard, 1991). Rather than using such a central model to plan any desired action (the model-based approach), adaptive behavior is thought to emerge from the dynamic interaction between a nonrepresentational agent situated in a specific environment (the behavior-based approach) (Brooks, 1991a, 1991b). I view these developments as a—usually unacknowledged—vindication of the ecological approach to perception and action. Interaction between these rapidly developing fields would be fruitful, for common problems such as steering and navigation are being approached in a sympathetic manner (Aloimonos, Rivlin, & Huang, 1993; Raviv & Herman, 1993).

4. Information and Dynamics

An ultimate goal is the integration of an information-based account of perception with a dynamical account of action in a unified theory of adaptive behavior. A theory of action that is based on recent insights from nonlinear dynamics attempts to account for organized behavior in terms of emergent patterns in a complex system, in which the neural components serve as a substrate for self-organization rather than the source of order (Kugler & Turvey, 1987; Schoner & Kelso, 1988). To integrate this view with perception, the challenge is to understand the role played by information both in the pattern formation process and in modulating an organized system to yield adaptive behavior (e.g., Goldfield, Kay, & Warren, 1993; Saltzman & Munhall, 1992). Such a view has recently been applied to the origin of gait patterns and gait transitions (Collins & Stewart, 1993; Diedrich & Warren, 1995; Schoner, Jiang, & Kelso, 1990; Taga, Yamaguchi, & Shimizu, 1991) and can be extended to the dynamics of the visuomotor coupling (Dijkstra, 1994; Kay & Warren, 1995; Schoner, 1991, 1994).

References

Adiv, G. (1985). Determining three-dimensional motion and structure from optical flow generated by several moving objects. *IEEE Pattern Analysis and Machine Intelligence, 7*, 384–401.

Allman, J., Miezin, F., & McGuinness, E. (1985). Direction- and velocity-specific responses from beyond the classical receptive field in the middle temporal visual area (MT). *Perception, 14*, 105–126.

Allum, J. H. J., & Pfaltz, C. R. (1985). Visual and vestibular contributions to pitch sway stabilization in the ankle muscles of normals and patients with bilateral vestibular deficits. *Experimental Brain Research, 58*, 82–94.

Aloimonos, Y. (1993). *Active perception.* Hillsdale, NJ: Erlbaum.

Aloimonos, Y., Rivlin, E., & Huang, L. (1993). Designing visual systems: Purposive navigation. In Y. Aloimonos (Eds.), *Active perception* (pp. 47–102). Hillsdale, NJ: Erlbaum.

Amblard, B., Cremieux, J., Marchand, A. R., & Carblanc, A. (1985). Lateral orientation and stabilization of human stance: Static versus dynamic visual cues. *Experimental Brain Research, 61*, 21–37.

Andersen, G. J., & Braunstein, M. L. (1985). Induced self-motion in central vision. *Journal of Experimental Psychology: Human Perception and Performance, 11*, 122–132.

Andersen, G. J., & Dyre, B. P. (1989). Spatial orientation from optic flow in the central visual field. *Perception & Psychophysiology, 45*, 453–458.

Andersen, R. A. (1994, July) Paper presented at the *Workshop on Systems-Level Models of Visual Behavior,* Telluride, CO.

Babler, T. G., & Dannemiller, J. L. (1993). Role of image acceleration in judging landing location of free-falling projectiles. *Journal of Experimental Psychology: Human Perception and Performance, 19*, 15–31.

Bajcsy, R. (1988). Active perception. *Proceedings of the IEEE 76, 8*, 966–1005.

Ballard, D. (1991). Animate vision. *Artificial Intelligence, 48*, 57–86.

Ballard, D. H., & Kimball, O. A. (1983). Rigid body motion from depth and optical flow. *Computer Vision Graphics Image Processing, 22*, 95–115.

Banks, M. S., Ehrlich, S. M., Backus, B. T., & Crowell, J. A. (1994). Heading judgments with mixtures of real and simulated rotations. *Investigative Ophthalmology and Visual Science, 35,* 2000.

Beer, R. D. (1990). *Intelligence as adaptive behavior.* San Diego, CA: Academic Press.

Belanger, M., & Patla, A. E. (1987). Phase-dependent compensatory responses to perturbation applied during walking in humans. *Journal of Motor Behavior, 19,* 434–453.

Bertenthal, B. I., & Bai, D. L. (1989). Infants' sensitivity to optical flow for controlling posture. *Developmental Psychology, 25,* 936–945.

Berthoz, A., & Droulez, J. (1982). Linear self motion perception. In A. H. Wertheim, W. A. Wagenaar, & H. W. Leibowitz (Eds.), *Tutorials on motion perception* (pp. 157–199). New York: Plenum.

Berthoz, A., Lacour, M., Soechting, J. F., & Vidal, P. P. (1979). The role of vision in the control of posture during linear motion. *Progress in Brain Research, 50,* 197–209.

Berthoz, A., Pavard, B., & Young, L. R. (1975). Perception of linear horizontal self-motion induced by peripheral vision (linear vection). *Experimental Brain Research, 23,* 471–489.

Bingham, G. P. (1993). Optic flow from eye movement with head immobilized: "Ocular occlusion" beyond the nose. *Vision Research, 33,* 777–790.

Bootsma, R. J., & Oudejans, R. (1993). Visual information about time-to-collision between two objects. *Journal of Experimental Psychology: Human Perception and Performance, 19,* 1041–1052.

Bootsma, R. J., & Peper, C. E. (1992). Predictive visual information sources for the regulation of catching and hitting. In D. Elliott & L. Proteau (Eds.), *Vision and motor control* (pp. 285–314). Amsterdam: North-Holland.

Brandt, T., Dichgans, J., & Buchele, W. (1974). Motion habituation: Inverted self-motion perception and optokinetic after-nystagmus. *Experimental Brain Research, 21,* 337–352.

Brandt, T., Dichgans, J., & Koenig, E. (1973). Differential effects of central versus peripheral vision on egocentric and exocentric motion perception. *Experimental Brain Research, 16,* 476–491.

Brandt, T., Wist, E. R., & Dichgans, J. (1975). Foreground and background in dynamic spatial orientation. *Perception & Psychophysics, 17,* 497–503.

Brooks, R. A. (1991a). *Intelligence without reason* (AI Memo No. 1293). Cambridge, MA: MIT Artificial Intelligence Lab.

Brooks, R. A. (1991b). Intelligence without representation. *Artificial Intelligence, 47,* 139–160.

Bruss, A. R., & Horn, B. K. P. (1983). Passive navigation. *Computer Vision, Graphics, and Image Processing, 21,* 3–20.

Butterworth, G., & Hicks, L. (1977). Visual proprioception and postural stability in infancy. A developmental study. *Perception, 6,* 255–262.

Cappozzo, A. (1981). Analysis of the linear displacements of the head and trunk during walking at different speeds. *Journal of Biomechanics, 14,* 411–425.

Cavallo, V., & Laurent, M. (1988). Visual information and skill level in time-to-collision estimation. *Perception, 17,* 623–632.

Clark, F. J., & Horch, K. W. (1986). Kinesthesia. In K. R. Boff, L. Kaufman, & J. P. Thomas (Eds.), *Handbook of perception and human performance* (pp. 1–13 to 13–62). New York: Wiley.

Collins, J. J., & DeLuca, C. J. (1993). Open-loop and closed-loop control of posture: A random-walk analysis of center-of-pressure trajectories. *Experimental Brain Research, 95,* 308–318.

Collins, J. J., & Stewart, I. (1993). Hexapodal gaits and coupled nonlinear oscillator models. *Biological Cybernetics, 68,* 287–298.

Crowell, J. A., & Banks, M. S. (1993). Perceiving heading with different retinal regions and types of optic flow. *Perception & Psychophysics, 53,* 325–337.

Crowell, J. A., & Banks, M. S. (1994). *Ideal observer for heading judgments.* Unpublished manuscript.

Crowell, J. A., Royden, C. S., Banks, M. S., Swenson, K. H., & Sekuler, A. B. (1990). Optic flow and heading judgments. *Investigative Ophthalmology and Visual Science Supplement, 31,* 522.

Cutting, J. E. (1986). *Perception with an eye to motion.* Cambridge, MA: MIT Press.

Cutting, J. E., Springer, K., Braren, P. A., & Johnson, S. H. (1992). Wayfinding on foot from information in retinal, not optical, flow. *Journal of Experimental Psychology: General, 121,* 41–72.

Cynader, M., & Regan, D. (1978). Neurones in cat parastriate cortex sensitive to the direction of motion in three-dimensional space. *Journal of Physiology, 274,* 549–569.

de Graaf, J. B., van Asten, W. N. J. C., & Gielen, C. C. A. M. (1990). *The effect of central and peripheral vision on postural balance of a human viewing a rotating scene.* Unpublished manuscript, Catholic University of Nijmegen, the Netherlands.

Delorme, A., Frigon, J.-Y., & Lagace, C. (1989). Infants' reactions to visual movement of the environment. *Perception, 18,* 667–673.

Delorme, A., & Martin, C. (1986). Roles of retinal periphery and depth periphery in linear vection and visual control of standing in humans. *Canadian Journal of Psychology, 40,* 176–187.

DeLucia, P. R. (1991). Pictorial and motion-based information for depth perception. *Journal of Experimental Psychology: Human Perception and Performance, 17,* 738–748.

DeLucia, P. R., & Warren, R. (1994). Pictorial and motion-based depth information during active control of self-motion: Size-arrival effects on collision avoidance. *Journal of Experimental Psychology: Human Perception and Performance, 20,* 783–798.

Denton, G. G. (1980). The influence of visual pattern on perceived speed. *Perception, 9,* 393–402.

Dichgans, J., & Brandt, T. (1978). Visual–vestibular interaction: Effects on self-motion perception and postural control. In H. Leibowitz & H.-L. Teuber (Eds.), *Handbook of sensory physiology* (pp. 755–804). New York: Springer-Verlag.

Diedrich, F. J., & Warren, W. H. (1995). Why change gaits? Dynamics of the walk-run transition. *Journal of Experimental Psychology: Human Perception and Performance, 21,* 183–202.

Diener, H. C., Dichgans, J., Bruzek, W., & Selinka, H. (1982). Stabilization of human posture during induced oscillations of the body. *Experimental Brain Research, 45,* 126–132.

Diener, H. C., Dichgans, J., Guschlbauer, B., & Mau, H. (1984). The significance of proprioception on postural stabilization as assessed by ischemia. *Brain Research, 296,* 103–109.

Dijkstra, T. M. H. (1994). *Visual control of posture and visual perception of shape.* Doctoral dissertation, Catholic University of Nijmegen, the Netherlands.

Dijkstra, T. M. H., Gielen, C. C. A. M., & Melis, B. J. M. (1992). Postural responses to stationary and moving scenes as a function of distance to the scene. *Human Movement Science, 11,* 195–203.

Dijkstra, T. M. H., Schoner, G., & Gielen, C. C. A. M. (1994). Temporal stability of the action–perception cycle for postural control in a moving visual environment. *Experimental Brain Research, 97,* 477–486.

Dodge, R. (1923). Thresholds of rotation. *Journal of Experimental Psychology, 6,* 107–137.

Droulez, J., & Cornilleau-Pérès, V. (1990). Visual perception of surface curvature: The spin variation and its physiological implications. *Biological Cybernetics, 62,* 211–224.

Duchon, A., & Warren, W. H. (1994). Robot navigation from a Gibsonian viewpoint. *Proceedings of the IEEE Conference on Systems, Machines, and Cybernetics* (2272–2277). Piscataway, NJ: IEEE.

Duffy, C. J., & Wurtz, R. H. (1991a). Sensitivity of MST neurons to optic flow stimuli: I. A continuum of response selectivity to large-field stimuli. *Journal of Neurophysiology, 65,* 1329–1345.

Duffy, C. J., & Wurtz, R. H. (1991b). Sensitivity of MST neurons to optic flow stimuli: II. Mechanisms of response selectivity revealed by small-field stimuli. *Journal of Neurophysiology, 65,* 1346–1359.

Duffy, C. J., & Wurtz, R. H. (1993, November). *MSTd neuronal responses to the center-of-motion in optic flow fields.* Paper presented at the 23rd annual meeting of the Society for Neuroscience (531.9), Washington, DC.

Dyre, B. P., & Andersen, G. J. (in press). Perception of heading: Effect of conflicting velocity magnitude and trajectory information. *Journal of Experimental Psychology: Human Perception and Performance.*

Edwards, A. S. (1946). Body sway and vision. *Journal of Experimental Psychology, 36,* 526–535.

Eskinazi, S. (1962). *Principles of fluid mechanics.* Boston, MA: Allyn & Bacon.

Ferrandez, A. M., & Pailhous, J. (1986, September). *What happens when the head and the legs do not walk at the same velocity?* Paper presented at the annual meeting of the European Brain and Behavior Society, Marseille, France.

Fluckiger, M. (1986). Walking in a moving optical texture. *Perception, 15,* A30.

Forssberg, H. (1979). Stumbling corrective reaction: A phase-dependent compensatory reaction during locomotion. *Journal of Neurophysiology, 42,* 936–953.

Frost, B., & Nakayama, K. (1983). Single visual neurons code opposing motion independent of direction. *Science, 220,* 744–745.

Frost, B. J. (1985). Neural mechanisms for detecting object motion and figure-ground boundaries contrasted with self-motion detecting system. In D. Ingle, M. Jeannerod, & D. Lee (Eds.), *Brain mechanisms and spatial vision.* Dordrecht, the Netherlands: Martinus Nijhoff.

Frost, B. J., Wylie, D. R., & Wang, Y. (1990). The processing of object and self-motion in the tectofugal and accessory optic pathways of birds. *Vision Research, 30,* 1677–1688.

Gibson, E. J., Riccio, G., Schmuckler, M. A., & Stoffregen, T. A. (1987). Detecting the traversability of surfaces by crawling and walking infants. *Journal of Experimental Psychology: Human Perception and Performance, 13,* 533–544.

Gibson, J. J. (1947). *Motion picture testing and research* (AAF Aviation Psychology Research Report No. 7). Washington, DC: U. S. Government Printing Office.

Gibson, J. J. (1950). *Perception of the visual world.* Boston: Houghton Mifflin.

Gibson, J. J. (1954). The visual perception of objective motion and subjective movement. *Psychological Review, 61,* 304–314.

Gibson, J. J. (1958). Visually controlled locomotion and visual orientation in animals. *British Journal of Psychology, 49,* 182–194.

Gibson, J. J. (1966). *The senses considered as perceptual systems.* Boston, MA: Houghton Mifflin.

Gibson, J. J. (1968). What gives rise to the perception of motion? *Psychological Review, 75,* 335–346.

Gibson, J. J. (1979). *The ecological approach to visual perception.* Boston: Houghton Mifflin.

Gibson, J. J., Olum, P., & Rosenblatt, F. (1955). Parallax and perspective during aircraft landings. *American Journal of Psychology, 68,* 372–385.

Gielen, C. C. A. M., & van Asten, W. N. J. C. (1990). Postural responses to simulated moving environments are not invariant for the direction of gaze. *Experimental Brain Research, 79,* 167–174.

Goldfield, E. C., Kay, B. A., & Warren, W. H. (1993). Infant bouncing: The assembly and tuning of action system. *Child Development, 64,* 1128–1142.

Graziano, M. S. A., Andersen, R. A., & Snowden, R. J. (1994). Tuning of MST neurons to spiral motions. *Journal of Neuroscience, 14,* 54–67.

Grossman, G. E., & Leigh, R. J. (1990). Instability of gaze during locomotion in patients with deficient vestibular function. *Annals of Neurology, 27,* 528–532.

Hansen, R. M. (1979). Spatial localization during pursuit eye movements. *Vision Research, 19,* 1213–1221.

Hatsopoulos, N. G., & Warren, W. H. (1991). Visual navigation with a neural network. *Neural Networks, 4,* 303–317.

Heeger, D. J., & Jepson, A. (1990). Visual perception of three-dimensional motion. *Neural Computation, 2,* 129–137.

Heeger, D. J., & Jepson, A. D. (1992). Subspace methods for recovering rigid motion I: Algorithm and implementation. *International Journal of Computer Vision, 7,* 95–117.

Held, R., Dichgans, J., & Bauer, J. (1975). Characteristics of moving visual scenes influencing spatial orientation. *Vision Research, 15,* 357–365.

Helmholtz, H. von (1925). *Handbook on physiological optics* (3rd ed., J. P. C. Southall, Trans.). New York: Dover. (Original work published in 1867)

Hildreth, E. (1992). Recovering heading for visually-guided navigation. *Vision Research, 32,* 1177–1192.

Hildreth, E. C., & Koch, C. (1987). The analysis of visual motion: From computational theory to meuronal mechanisms. *Annual Review of Neuroscience, 10,* 477–533.

Hlavacka, F., & Saling, M. (1986). Compensation effect of visual biofeedback in upright posture control. *Activitas Nervosa Superior (Praha), 28,* 191–196.

Holst, E. von (1954). Relations between the central nervous system and the peripheral organs. *Animal Behavior, 2,* 89–94.

Horn, B. K. P., & Weldon, E. J. (1988). Direct methods for recovering motion. *International Journal of Computer Vision, 2,* 51–76.

Howard, I. P. (1986a). The vestibular system. In K. R. Boff, L. Kaufman, & J. P. Thomas (Eds.), *Handbook of perception and human performance* (pp. 11-1 to 11-30). New York: Wiley.

Howard, I. P. (1986b). The perception of posture, self-motion, and the visual vertical. In K. R. Boff, L. Kaufman, & J. P. Thomas (Eds.), *Handbook of perception and human performance* (pp. 18-1 to 18-62). New York: Wiley.

Howard, I. P., & Heckmann, T. (1989). Circular vection as a function of the relative sizes, distances, and positions of two competing visual displays. *Perception, 18,* 657–665.

Jain, R. (1982). An approach for the direct computation of the focus of expansion. *Pattern Recognition and Image Processing,* 262–268.

Jepson, A. D., & Heeger, D. J. (1992). *Linear subspace methods for recovering translational direction.* MA: Cambridge University Press.

Johansson, G. (1977). Studies on visual perception of locomotion. *Perception, 6,* 365–376.

Johnston, I. R., White, G. R., & Cumming, R. W. (1973). The role of optical expansion patterns in locomotor control. *American Journal of Psychology, 86,* 311–324.

Junger, W., & Dahmen, H. J. (1991). Response to self-motion in waterstriders: Visual discrimination between rotation and translation. *Journal of Comparative Physiology A, 169,* 641–646.

Kaiser, M. K., & Mowafy, L. (1993). Optical specification of time-to-passage: Observers' sensitivity to global tau. *Journal of Experimental Psychology: Human Perception and Performance, 19,* 1028–1040.

Kaiser, M. K., & Phatak, A. V. (1993). Things that go bump in the light: On the optical specification of contact severity. *Journal of Experimental Psychology: Human Perception and Performance, 19,* 194–202.

Kay, B. A., & Warren, W. H. (1995). *Dynamics of the visual-motor coupling during postural control in walking.* Manuscript to be submitted for publication.

Kim, N. -G., Turvey, M. T., & Carello, C. (1993). Optical information about the severity of upcoming contacts. *Journal of Experimental Psychology: Human Perception and Performance, 19,* 179–193.

Kinsella-Shaw, J. M., Shaw, B., & Turvey, M. T. (1992). Perceiving "walk-on-able" slopes. *Ecological Psychology, 4*, 223–239.

Koenderink, J. J. (1986). Optic flow. *Vision Research, 26*, 161–180.

Koenderink, J. J., & van Doorn, A. J. (1975). Invariant properties of the motion parallax field due to the movement of rigid bodies relative to an observer. *Optica Acta, 22*, 737–791.

Koenderink, J. J., & van Doorn, A. J. (1976). Local structure of movement parallax of the plane. *Journal of the Optical Society of America, 66*, 717–723.

Koenderink, J. J., & van Doorn, A. J. (1978). How an ambulant observer can construct a model of the environment from the geometrical structure of the visual inflow. In G. Hauske & E. Butenandt (Eds.), *Kybernetik 1978* (pp. 224–247). Munich: Oldenburg.

Koenderink, J. J., & van Doorn, A. J. (1981). Exterospecific component of the motion parallax field. *Journal of the Optical Society of America, 71*, 953–957.

Koenderink, J. J., & van Doorn, A. J. (1987). Facts on optic flow. *Biological Cybernetics, 56*, 247–254.

Koenderink, J. J., & van Doorn, A. J. (1992). Second-order optic flow. *Journal of the Optical Society of America A, 9*, 530–538.

Komatsu, H., & Wurtz, R. H. (1988). Relation of cortical areas MT and MST to pursuit eye movements. I. Location and visual properties of neurons. *Journal of Neurophysiology, 60*, 580–603.

Komatsu, H., & Wurtz, R. H. (1989). Modulation of pursuit eye movements by stimulation of cortical areas MT and MST. *Journal of Neurophysiology, 62*, 31–47.

Konczak, J. (1994). Effects of optic flow on the kinematics of human gait: A comparison of young and older adults. *Journal of Motor Behavior, 26*, 225–236.

Kugler, P. N., & Turvey, M. T. (1987). *Information, natural law, and the self-assembly of rhythmic movement.* Hillsdale, NJ: Erlbaum.

Land, M. F., & Lee, D. N. (1994). Where we look when we steer. *Nature, 369*, 742–744.

Lappe, M., & Rauschecker, J. P. (1993). A neural network for the processing of optic flow from ego-motion in man and higher mammals. *Neural Computation, 5*, 374–391.

Lappe, M., & Rauschecker, J. P. (1994). On heading detection from optic flow. *Nature, 369*, 712–713.

Larish, J. F., & Flach, J. M. (1990). Sources of optical information useful for perception of speed of rectilinear self-motion. *Journal of Experimental Psychology: Human Perception and Performance, 16*, 295–302.

Lawton, D. T. (1983). Processing translational motion sequences. *Computer Vision, Graphics, and Image Processing, 22*, 116–144.

Lee, D. N. (1974). Visual information during locomotion. In R. B. MacLeod & H. Pick (Eds.), *Perception: essays in honor of J. J. Gibson* (pp. 250–267). Ithaca, NY: Cornell University Press.

Lee, D. N. (1976). A theory of visual control of braking based on information about time-to-collision. *Perception, 5*, 437–459.

Lee, D. N. (1980). Visuo-motor coordination in space-time. In G. E. Stelmach & J. Requin (Eds.), *Tutorials in motor behavior* (pp. 281–295). Amsterdam: North-Holland.

Lee, D. N., & Aronson, E. (1974). Visual proprioceptive control of standing in human infants. *Perception & Psychophysics, 15*, 529–532.

Lee, D. N., Davies, M. N. O., Green, P. R., & van der Weel, F. R. (1993). Visual control of velocity of approach by pigeons when landing. *Journal of Experimental Biology, 180*, 85–104.

Lee, D. N., & Lishman, J. R. (1975). Visual proprioceptive control of stance. *Journal of Human Movement Studies, 1*, 87–95.

Lee, D. N., & Lishman, J. R. (1977). Visual control of locomotion. *Scandinavian Journal of Psychology, 18*, 224–230.

Lee, D. N., Lishman, J. R., & Thomson, J. A. (1982). Regulation of gait in long jumping. *Journal of Experimental Psychology: Human Perception and Performance, 8*, 448–459.

Lee, D. N., & Reddish, P. E. (1981). Plummeting gannets: A paradigm of ecological optics. *Nature, 293,* 293–294.

Lee, D. N., Reddish, P. E., & Rand, D. T. (1991). Aerial docking by hummingbirds. *Naturwissenschaften, 78,* 526–527.

Lee, D. N., & Young, D. S. (1985). Visual timing of interceptive action. In D. Ingle, M. Jeannerod, & D. N. Lee (Eds.), *Brain mechanisms and spatial vision* (pp. 1–30). Dordrecht, the Netherlands: Martinus Nijhoff.

Lee, D. N., Young, D. S., Reddish, P. E., Lough, S., & Clayton, T. M. H. (1983). Visual timing in hitting an accelerating ball. *Quarterly Journal of Experimental Psychology, 35A,* 333–346.

Lestienne, F., Soechting, J., & Berthoz, A. (1977). Postural readjustments induced by linear motion of visual scenes. *Experimental Brain Research, 28,* 363–384.

Lishman, J. R., & Lee, D. N. (1973). The autonomy of visual kinesthesis. *Perception, 2,* 287–294.

Llewellyn, K. R. (1971). Visual guidance of locomotion. *Journal of Experimental Psychology, 91,* 224–230.

Longuet-Higgins, H. C. (1981). A computer algorithm for reconstructing a scene from two projections. *Nature, 293,* 133–135.

Longuet-Higgins, H. C. (1984). The visual ambiguity of a moving plane. *Proceedings of the Royal Society of London, B, 223,* 165–175.

Longuet-Higgins, H. C., & Prazdny, K. (1980). The interpretation of a moving retinal image. *Proceedings of the Royal Society of London, B, 208,* 385–397.

Mach, E. (1875). *Grundlinien der Lehre von den Bewegungsempfindungen* Leipzig: Engelmann.

Mack, A., & Herman, E. (1978). Loss of position constancy during pursuit eye movements. *Vision Research, 18,* 55–62.

Maes, P. (Ed.). (1990). *Designing autonomous agents.* Cambridge, MA: MIT Press.

Mark, L. S. (1987). Eyeheight-scaled information about affordances: A study of sitting and stair climbing. *Journal of Experimental Psychology: Human Perception and Performance, 13,* 360–370.

Mark, L. S., & Vogele, D. (1988). A biodynamic basis for perceiving action categories: A study of sitting and stair climbing. *Journal of Motor Behavior, 19,* 367–384.

Marr, D. (1982). *Vision.* San Francisco: Freeman.

Matin, L. (1982). Visual localization and eye movements. In W. A. Wagenaar, A. H. Wertheim, & H. W. Leibowitz (Eds.), *Tutorials on motion perception* (pp. 101–156). New York: Plenum.

Maunsell, J. H. R., & Newsome, W. T. (1987). Visual processing in monkey extrastriate cortex. *Annual Review of Neuroscience, 10,* 363–401.

Maunsell, J. H. R., & van Essen, D. C. (1983a). The connections of the middle temporal area (MT) and their relationship to cortical hierarchy in the macaque monkey. *Journal of Neuroscience, 3,* 2563–2568.

Maunsell, J. H. R., & van Essen, D. C. (1983b). Functional properties of neurons in middle temporal visual area of the Macaque monkey: II. Binocular interactions and sensitivity to binocular disparity. *Journal of Neurophysiology, 49,* 1148–1167.

Maybank, S. J. (1986). Algorithm for analyzing optical flow based on the least-squares method. *Image and Vision Computing, 4,* 38–42.

McCollum, G., & Leen, T. K. (1989). Form and exploration of mechanical stability limits in erect stance. *Journal of Motor Behavior, 21,* 225–244.

McLeod, R. W., & Ross, H. E. (1983). Optic-flow and cognitive factors in time-to-collision estimates. *Perception, 12,* 417–423.

McMahon, T. A., & Greene, P. R. (1978). Fast running tracks. *Scientific American, 239*(6), 148–163.

Melville-Jones, G., & Young, L. R. (1978). Subjective detection of vertical acceleration: A velocity-dependent response. *Acta Otolaryngologica, 85,* 45–53.

Michaels, C. F., & Oudejans, R. D. (1992). The optics and actions of catching fly balls: Zeroing out optical acceleration. *Ecological Psychology, 4,* 199–222.

Mitiche, A. (1984). Computation of optical flow and rigid motion. In *IEEE Workshop on Computer Vision: Representation and Control.* New York: IEEE Computer Society Press.

Nagel, H. (1981). On the derivation of 3D rigid point configurations from image sequences. In *IEEE Conference on Pattern Recognition and Image Processing* (pp. 103–108). New York: IEEE Computer Society Press.

Nakayama, K., & Loomis, J. M. (1974). Optical velocity patterns, velocity sensitive neurons, and space perception: A hypothesis. *Perception, 3,* 63–80.

Nashner, L. M. (1972). Vestibular postural control model. *Kybernetik, 10,* 106–110.

Nashner, L. M., Black, F. O., & Wall, C. (1982). Adaptation to altered support and visual conditions during stance: Patients with vestibular deficits. *Journal of Neuroscience, 2,* 536–544.

Nashner, L. M., & McCollum, G. (1985). The organization of human postural movements: A formal basis and experimental synthesis. *Behavioral Brain Science, 8,* 135–172.

Negahdaripour, S., & Horn, B. K. P. (1989). A direct method for locating the focus of expansion. *Computer Vision, Graphics, and Image Processing, 46,* 303–326.

Nelson, R. C., & Aloimonos, J. (1988). Finding motion parameters from spherical flow fields (or the advantages of having eyes in the back of your head). *Biological Cybernetics, 58,* 261–273.

Newsome, W. T., Wurtz, R. H., & Komatsu, H. (1988). Relation of cortical areas MT and MST to pursuit eye movements: II. Differentiation of retinal from extraretinal inputs. *Journal of Neurophysiology, 60,* 604–620.

Ohmi, M., Howard, I. P., & Landolt, J. P. (1987). Circular vection as a function of foreground–background relationships. *Perception, 16,* 17–22.

Oman, C. M. (1982). A heuristic mathematical model for the dynamics of sensory conflict and motion sickness. *Acta Otolaryngologica, 44* (Suppl. 392), 1–44.

Orban, G. A., Lagae, L., Raiguel, S., Xiao, D., & Maes, H. (in press). The speed tuning of middle superior temporal (MST) cell responses to optic flow components. *Vision Research.*

Orban, G. A., Lagae, L., Verri, A., Raiguel, S., Xiao, D., Maes, H., & Torre, V. (1992). First-order analysis of optical flow in monkey brain. *Proceedings of the National Academy of Sciences, USA, 89,* 2595–2599.

Patla, A. (1991b). Visual control of locomotion: Strategies for changing direction and for going over obstacles. *Journal of Experimental Psychology: Human Perception and Performance, 17,* 603–634.

Patla, A. E. (1991a). Visual control of human locomotion. In A. E. Patla (Ed.), *Adaptability of human gait: Implications for the control of locomotion* (pp. 55–97). Amsterdam: North-Holland.

Patla, A., Robinson, C., Samways, M., & Armstrong, C. J. (1989). Visual control of step length during overground locomotion: Task-specific modulation of the locomotor synergy. *Journal of Experimental Psychology: Human Perception and Performance, 15,* 603–617.

Paulus, W. M., Straube, A., & Brandt, T. (1984). Visual stabilzation of posture: Physiological stimulus characteristics and clinical aspects. *Brain, 107,* 1143–1163.

Paulus, W., Straube, A., Krafczyk, S., & Brandt, T. (1989). Differential effects of retinal target displacement, changing size and changing disparity in the control of anterior/posterior and lateral body sway. *Experimental Brain Research, 78,* 243–252.

Peper, L., Bootsma, R. J., Mestre, D. R., & Bakker, F. C. (1994). Catching balls: How to get the hand to the right place at the right time. *Journal of Experimental Psychology: Human Perception and Performance, 20,* 591–612.

Perrone, J. A. (1992). Model for the computation of self-motion in biological systems. *Journal of the Optical Society of America A, 9,* 177–194.

Perrone, J. A., & Stone, L. S. (1991). The perception of egomotion: Global versus local mechanisms. *Investigative Ophthalmology and Visual Science, 32,* 957.

Perrone, J. A., & Stone, L. S. (1994). A model of self-motion estimation within primate extrastriate visual cortex. *Vision Research, 34,* 2917–2938.

Poggio, T., Verri, A., & Torre, V. (1991). *Green theorems and qualitative properties of the optical flow* (AI Memo No. 1289). Cambridge, MA: MIT Artificial Intelligence Lab.

Post, R. B. (1988). Circular vection is independent of stimulus eccentricity. *Perception, 17,* 737–744.

Prazdny, K. (1980). Egomotion and relative depth map from optical flow. *Biological Cybernetics, 36,* 87–102.

Prazdny, K. (1981). Determining the instantaneous direction of motion from optical flow generated by a curvilinearly moving observer. *Computer Vision Graphics Image Processing, 17,* 238–258.

Prazdny, K. (1983). On the information in optical flows. *Computer Vision, Graphics, and Image Processing, 22,* 239–259.

Probst, T., Krafczyk, S., Brandt, T., & Wist, E. R. (1984). Interaction between perceived self-motion and object-motion impairs vehicle guidance. *Science, 225,* 536–538.

Pufall, P. B., & Dunbar, C. (1992). Perceiving whether or not the world affords stepping onto and over: A developmental study. *Ecological Psychology, 4,* 17–38.

Raibert, M. H. (1986). *Legged robots that balance.* Cambridge: MIT Press.

Rauschecker, J. P., Grunau, M. W. von, & Poulin, C. (1987). Centrifugal organization of direction preferences in the cat's lateral suprasylvian visual cortex and its relation to flow field processing. *Journal of Neuroscience, 7,* 943–958.

Raviv, D., & Herman, M. (1993). Visual servoing from 2-D image cues. In Y. Aloimonos (Ed.), *Active perception* (pp. 191–226). Hillsdale, NJ: Erlbaum.

Reed, E. S. (1988). Applying the theory of action systems to the study of motor skills. In O. G. Meijer & K. Roth (Eds.), *Complex movement behavior: The motor-action controversy* (pp. 45–86). Amsterdam: North-Holland.

Regan, D. (1986). Visual processing of four kinds of relative motion. *Vision Research, 26,* 127–145.

Regan, D., & Beverley, K. I. (1978). Looming detectors in the human visual pathway. *Vision Research, 18,* 415–421.

Regan, D., & Beverley, K. I. (1979a). Binocular and monocular stimuli for motion in depth: Changing-disparity and changing-size feed that same motion-in-depth stage. *Vision Research, 19,* 1331–1342.

Regan, D., & Beverley, K. I. (1979b). Visually guided locomotion: Psychophysical evidence for a neural mechanism sensitive to flow patterns. *Science, 205,* 311–313.

Regan, D., & Beverley, K. I. (1982). How do we avoid confounding the direction we are looking and the direction we are moving? *Science, 215,* 194–196.

Regan, D., & Beverley, K. I. (1985). Visual responses to vorticity and the neural analysis of optic flow. *Journal of the Optical Society of America A, 2,* 280–283.

Regan, D., & Cynader, M. (1979). Neurons in area 18 of cat visual cortex selectively sensitive to changing size: Nonlinear interactions between responses to two edges. *Vision Research, 19,* 699–711.

Riccio, G. E. (1993). Information in movement variablity about the qualitative dynamics of posture and orientation. In K. M. Newell & D. M. Corcos (Eds.), *Variability and motor control* (pp. 317–357). Champaign, IL: Human Kinetics.

Rieger, J. H. (1983). Information in optical flows induced by curved paths of observation. *Journal of the Optical Society of America, 73,* 339–344.

Rieger, J. H., & Lawton, D. T. (1985). Processing differential image motion. *Journal of the Optical Society of America, A, 2,* 354–360.

Rieger, J. H., & Toet, L. (1985). Human visual navigation in the presence of 3D rotations. *Biological Cybernetics, 52,* 377–381.

Roach, J. W., & Aggarwal, J. K. (1980). Determining the movement of objects from a sequence of images. *IEEE Pattern Analysis and Machine Intelligence, 2,* 554–562.

Roy, J. P., Komatsu, H., & Wurtz, R. H. (1992). Disparity sensitivity of neurons in monkey extrastriate area MST. *Journal of Neuroscience, 12,* 2478–2492.

Roy, J. P., & Wurtz, R. H. (1990). The role of disparity-sensitive cortical neurons in signaling the direction of self-motion. *Nature, 348,* 160–162.

Royden, C. S. (1994). Analysis of misperceived observer motion during simulated eye rotations. *Vision Research, 34,* 3215–3222.

Royden, C. S., Banks, M. S., & Crowell, J. A. (1992). The perception of heading during eye movements. *Nature, 360,* 583–585.

Royden, C. S., Crowell, J. A., & Banks, M. S. (1994). Estimating heading during eye movements. *Vision Research, 34,* 3197–3214.

Saito, H., Yukie, M., Tanaka, K., Hikosaka, K., Fukada, Y., & Iwai, E. (1986). Integration of direction signals of image motion in the superior temporal sulcus of the Macaque monkey. *Journal of Neuroscience, 6,* 145–157.

Saltzman, E. L., & Munhall, K. G. (1992). Skill acquisition and development: The roles of state-, parameter-, and graph-dynamics. *Journal of Motor Behavior, 24,* 49–57.

Savelsbergh, G. J. P., Whiting, H. T. A., & Bootsma, R. J. (1991). Grasping tau. *Journal of Experimental Psychology: Human Perception and Performance, 17,* 315–322.

Saxberg, B. V. H. (1987a). Projected free fall trajectories: I. Theory and simulation. *Biological Cybernetics, 56,* 159–175.

Saxberg, B. V. H. (1987b). Projected free fall trajectories: II. Human experiments. *Biological Cybernetics, 56,* 177–184.

Schiff, W. (1965). Perception of impending collision: A study of visually directed avoidant behavior. *Psychological Monographs, 79* (Whole No. 604).

Schiff, W., & Detwiler, M. L. (1979). Information used in judging impending collision. *Perception, 8,* 647–658.

Schiff, W., & Oldak, R. (1990). Accuracy of judging time-to-arrival: Effects of modality, trajectory, and gender. *Journal of Experimental Psychology: Human Perception and Performance, 16,* 303–316.

Schmuckler, M. A., & Gibson, E. J. (1989). The effect of imposed optical flow on guided locomotion in young walkers. *British Journal of Developmental Psychology, 7,* 193–206.

Schoner, G. (1991). Dynamic theory of action-perception patterns: The "moving room" paradigm. *Biological Cybernetics, 64,* 455–462.

Schoner, G. (1994). Dynamic theory of action-perception patterns: The time-before-contact paradigm. *Human Movement Science, 13,* 415–439.

Schoner, G., Jiang, W. Y., & Kelso, J. A. S. (1990). A synergetic theory of quadrupedal gaits and gait transitions. *Journal of Theoretical Biology, 142,* 359–391.

Schoner, G., & Kelso, J. A. S. (1988). Dynamic pattern generation in behavioral and neural systems. *Science, 239,* 1513–1520.

Shaw, R. E., Turvey, M. T., & Mace, W. M. (1981). Ecological psychology: The consequence of a commitment to realism. In W. Weimer & D. Palermo (Eds.), *Cognition and the symbolic processes: II* (pp. 159–226). Hillsdale, NJ: Erlbaum.

Sheldon, J. H. (1963). The effects of age on the control of sway. *Gerontologia Clinica, 5,* 129–138.

Sherrick, C. E., & Cholewiak, R. W. (1986). Cutaneous sensitivity. In K. R. Boff, L. Kaufman, & J. P. Thomas (Eds.), *Handbook of Perception and Human Performance* (pp. 12–1 to 12–58). New York: Wiley.

Sidaway, B., McNitt-Gray, J., & Davis, G. (1989). Visual timing of muscle preactivation in preparation for landing. *Ecological Psychology, 1,* 253–264.

Simpson, J. I., Graf, W., & Leonard, C. (1981). The coordinate system of visual climbing fibers to the flocculus. In A. F. Fuchs & W. Becker (Eds.), *Progress in Oculomotor Research* (pp. 475–484). Amsterdam: Elsevier.

Soechting, J. F., & Berthoz, A. (1979). Dynamic role of vision in the control of posture in man. *Experimental Brain Research, 36,* 551–561.

Stappers, P. J. (1992). *Scaling the visual consequences of active head movements.* Doctoral dissertation, Technical University of Delft, the Netherlands.

Stoffregen, T. A. (1985). Flow structure versus retinal location in the optical control of stance. *Journal of Experimental Psychology: Human Perception and Performance, 11,* 554–565.

Stoffregen, T. A. (1986). The role of optical velocity in the control of stance. *Perception & Psychophysics, 39,* 355–360.

Stoffregen, T. A., & Riccio, G. E. (1988). An ecological theory of oreientation and the vestibular system. *Psychological Review, 95,* 3–14.

Stoffregen, T. A., & Riccio, G. E. (1990). Responses to optical looming in the retinal center and periphery. *Ecological Psychology, 2,* 251–274.

Stoffregen, T. A., & Riccio, G. E. (1991). An ecological critique of the sensory conflict theory of motion sickness. *Ecological Psychology, 3,* 159–194.

Stoffregen, T. A., Schmuckler, M. A., & Gibson, E. J. (1987). Use of central and peripheral optical flow in stance and locomotion in young walkers. *Perception, 16,* 113–119.

Stoper, A. E. (1990, November). Pitched environments and apparent height. *Paper presented at the 31st annual meeting of the Psychonomic Society,* New Orleans, LA.

Subbarao, M., & Waxman, A. M. (1986). Closed form solutions to image flow equations for planar surfaces in motion. *Computer Vision, Graphics, and Image Processing, 36,* 208–228.

Taga, G., Yamaguchi, Y., & Shimizu, H. (1991). Self-organized control of bipedal locomotion by neural oscillators in unpredictable environment. *Biological Cybernetics, 65,* 147–159.

Talbot, R. E., & Brookhart, J. M. (1980). A predictive model of the visual contribution to canine postural control. *American Journal of Physiology, 239,* R80–R92.

Tanaka, K., Fukada, Y., & Saito, H. (1989). Underlying mechanisms of the response specificity of expansion/contraction and rotation cells in the dorsal part of the medial superior temporal area of the Macaque monkey. *Journal of Neurophysiology, 62,* 642–656.

Tanaka, K., & Saito, H. (1989). Analysis of motion of the visual field by direction, expansion/contraction, and rotation cells clustered in the dorsal part of the medial superior temporal area of the Macaque monkey. *Journal of Neurophysiology, 62,* 626–641.

Telford, L., Howard, I. P., & Ohmi, M. (1992). Multisensory contributions to judgments of heading. *Investigative Ophthalmology and Visual Science, 33,* 959.

Telford, L., Spratley, J., & Frost, B. J. (1992). Linear vection in the central visual field facilitated by kinetic depth cues. *Perception, 21,* 337–349.

Thompson, W. B., Lechleider, P., & Stuch, E. R. (1993). Detecting moving objects using the rigidity constraint. *IEEE Transactions on Pattern Analysis and Machine Intelligence, 15,* 162–165.

Todd, J. T. (1981). Visual information about moving objects. *Journal of Experimental Psychology: Human Perception and Performance, 7,* 795–810.

Todd, J. T., Tittle, J. S., & Norman, J. F. (in press). Distortions of 3-dimensional space in the perceptual analysis of motion and stereo. *Perception.*

Townsend, M. A. (1985). Bipedal gait stabilzation via foot placement. *Journal of Biomechanics, 18,* 21–38.

Travis, R. C. (1945). An experimental analysis of dynamic and static equilibrium. *Journal of Experimental Psychology, 35,* 216–234.

Tresilian, J. R. (1990). Perceptual information for the timing of interceptive action. *Perception, 19,* 223–239.

Tresilian, J. R. (1991). Empirical and theoretical issues in the perception of time to contact. *Journal of Experimental Psychology: Human Perception and Performance, 17,* 865–876.

Tresilian, J. R. (1994). Approximate information sources and perceptual variables in interceptive timing. *Journal of Experimental Psychology: Human Perception and Performance, 20,* 154–173.

Tsai, R. Y., & Huang, T. S. (1981). Estimating three-dimensional motion parameters of a rigid planar patch. *IEEE Transactions on Acoustics, Speech and Signal Processng, ASSP-29,* 1147–1152.

Tsai, R. Y., & Huang, T. S. (1982). Estimating three-dimensional motion parameters of a rigid planar patch: II. Singular value decomposition. *IEEE Transactions on Acoustics, Speech, and Signal Processing, ASSP-30,* 525–534.

Tsai, R. Y., & Huang, T. S. (1984a). Estimating three-dimensional motion parameters of a rigid planar patch: III. Finite point correspondences and the three-view problem. *IEEE Transactions on Acoustics, Speech, and Signal Processing, ASSP-32,* 213–220.

Tsai, R. Y., & Huang, T. S. (1984b). Uniqueness and estimation of three-dimensional motion parameters of rigid objects with curved surfaces. *IEEE Transactions on Pattern Analysis of Machine Intelligence, PAMI-6,* 13–27.

Turano, K. T., & Wang, X. (1994). Visual discrimination between a curved and straight path of self motion: Effects of forward speed. *Vision Research, 34,* 107–114.

Ungerleider, L., & Desimone, R. (1986). Cortical connections of area MT in the Macaque. *Journal of Comparative Neurology, 248,* 190–222.

van Asten, W. N. J. C., Gielen, C. C. A. M., & van der Gon, J. J. D. (1988a). Postural adjustments induced by simulated motion of differently structured environments. *Experimental Brain Research, 73,* 371–383.

van Asten, W. N. J. C., Gielen, C. C. A. M., & van der Gon, J. J. D. (1988b). Postural movements induced by rotation of visual scenes. *Journal of the Optical Society of America, A, 5,* 1781–1789.

van den Berg, A. V. (1992). Robustness of perception of heading from optic flow. *Vision Research, 32,* 1285–1296.

van den Berg, A. V. (1993). The perception of heading. *Nature, 365,* 497–498.

van den Berg, A. V., & Brenner, E. (1994). Why two eyes are better than one for judgments of heading. *Nature, 371,* 700–702.

Verri, A., Girosi, F., & Torre, V. (1989). Mathematical properties of the two-dimensional motion field: From singular point to motion parameters. *Journal of the Optical Society of America, A, 6,* 698–712.

Verri, A., & Poggio, T. (1987). Against quantitative optical flow. In *First International Conference on Computer Vision* (pp. 171–180). Piscataway, NJ: IEEE.

Vishton, P. M., Nijhawan, R., & Cutting, J. E. (1994). Moving observers utilize static depth cues in determining their direction of motion. *Investigative Ophthalmology and Visual Science, 35,* 2000.

Wang, Y., & Frost, B. J. (1992). Time to collision is signaled by neurons in the nucleus rotundus of pigeons. *Nature, 356,* 236–238.

Wann, J. P., Edgar, P., & Blair, D. (1993). Time-to-contact judgment in the locomotion of adults and preschool children. *Journal of Experimental Psychology: Human Perception and Performance, 19,* 1053–1065.

Wapner, S., & Witkin, H. A. (1950). The role of visual factors in the maintenance of body balance. *American Journal of Physiology, 63,* 385–408.

Warren, R. (1976). The perception of egomotion. *Journal of Experimental Psychology: Human Perception and Performance*, 448–456.

Warren, W. H. (1984). Perceiving affordances: Visual guidance of stair climbing. *Journal of Experimental Psychology: Human Perception and Performance*, 10, 683–703.

Warren, W. H. (1988). Action modes and laws of control for the visual guidance of action. In O. Meijer & K. Roth (Eds.), *Movement behavior: The motor-action controversy* (339–379). Amsterdam: North-Holland.

Warren, W. H., & Blackwell, A. W. (1988). Minimum conditions for perception of translational heading. Unpublished data.

Warren, W. H., Blackwell, A. W., Kurtz, K. J., Hatsopoulos, N. G., & Kalish, M. L. (1991). On the sufficiency of the velocity field for perception of heading. *Biological Cybernetics*, 65, 311–320.

Warren, W. H., Blackwell, A. W., & Morris, M. W. (1989). Age differences in perceiving the direction of self-motion from optical flow. *Journal of Gerontology: Psychological Science*, 44, 147–153.

Warren, W. H., & Hannon, D. J. (1988). Direction of self-motion is perceived from optical flow. *Nature*, 336, 162–163.

Warren, W. H., & Hannon, D. J. (1990). Eye movements and optical flow. *Journal of the Optical Society of America, A*, 7(1), 160–169.

Warren, W. H., Kay, B. A., & Hutchinson, A. S. (1995). Visual control of posture during walking: Differential responses to translation and rotation. Manuscript to be submitted for publication.

Warren, W. H., Kay, B. A., & Yilmaz, E. H. (in press). Visual control of posture during walking: Functional specificity. *Journal of Experimental Psychology: Human Perception and Performance*.

Warren, W. H., & Kurtz, K. J. (1992). The role of central and peripheral vision in perceiving the direction of self-motion. *Perception & Psychophysics*, 51, 443–454.

Warren, W. H., Mestre, D. R., Blackwell, A. W., & Morris, M. W. (1991). Perception of circular heading from optical flow. *Journal of Experimental Psychology: Human Perception and Performance*, 17, 28–43.

Warren, W. H., Morris, M. W., & Kalish, M. (1988). Perception of translational heading from optical flow. *Journal of Experimental Psychology: Human Perception and Performance*, 14(4), 646–660.

Warren, W. H., & Saunders, J. A. (in press). Perception of heading in the presence of moving objects. *Perception*.

Warren, W. H., & Whang, S. (1987). Visual guidance of walking through apertures: Body scaled information for affordances. *Journal of Experimental Psychology: Human Perception and Performance*, 13, 371–383.

Warren, W. H., & Yaffe, D. M. (1989). Dynamics of step length adjustment during running. *Journal of Experimental Psychology: Human Perception and Performance*, 15, 618–623.

Warren, W. H., Young, D. S., & Lee, D. N. (1986). Visual control of step length during running over irregular terrain. *Journal of Experimental Psychology: Human Perception and Performance*, 12, 259–266.

Waxman, A. M., & Ullman, S. (1985). Surface structure and 3D motion from image flow: A kinematic analysis. *International Journal of Robotics Research*, 4, 72–94.

Weng, J., Huang, T. S., & Ahuja, N. (1989). Motion and structure from two perspective views: Algorithms, error analysis, and error estimation. *IEEE Pattern Analysis and Machine Intelligence*, 11, 451–476.

Wertheim, A. H. (1987). Retinal and extraretinal information in movement perception: How to invert the Filehne illusion. *Perception*, 16, 289–294.

Whittaker, E. T. (1944). *A treatise on the analytical dynamics of particles and rigid bodies*. New York: Dover.

Winter, D. A. (1987). Sagittal plane balance and posture in human walking. *IEEE Engineering in Medicine and Biology Magazine*, 8–11.

Woollacott, M. H., Shumway-Cook, A., & Nashner, L. M. (1986). Aging and posture control: Changes in sensory organization and muscle coordination. *International Journal of Aging and Human Development, 23*, 97–114.

Yang, J. F., Winter, D. A., & Wells, R. P. (1990a). Postural dynamics in the standing human. *Biological Cybernetics, 62*, 309–320.

Yang, J. F., Winter, D. A., & Wells, R. P. (1990b). Postural dynamics of walking in humans. *Biological Cybernetics, 62*, 321–330.

Yilmaz, E., & Warren, W. H. (in press). Visual control of braking: A test of the tau-dot hypothesis. *Journal of Experimental Psychology: Human Perception and Performance*.

Yoneda, S., & Tokumasu, K. (1986). Frequency analysis of body sway in the upright posture. *Acta Otolaryngol, 102*, 87–92.

Young, D. S. (1988). Describing the information for action. In O. G. Meijer & K. Roth (Eds.), *Complex movement behavior: The motor-action controversy* (pp. 419–437). Amsterdam: North-Holland.

Young, L. R., Dichgans, J., Murphy, R., & Brandt, T. (1973). Interaction of optokinetic and vestibular stimuli in motion perception. *Acta Otolaryngologica (Stockholm), 76*, 24–31.

CHAPTER 9

Ontogenesis of Space and Motion Perception

Philip J. Kellman

I. INTRODUCTION

Thirty years ago, a discussion of the origins and development of visual space and motion perception would have been an exercise in speculation. At best, such a discussion might have included weak inferences from studies of adult performance, some philosophical conjectures, and some inconclusive reports of tests on visually impaired subjects whose sight had surgically been restored. Perhaps most noteworthy at that time were early reports of possible ways to study perception in early infancy (e.g., Bridger, 1961; Fantz, 1958, 1964; E. J. Gibson & Walk, 1960). The ensuing three decades have delivered on the promise of those early reports to produce a scientific understanding of the origins of perception. Although there is more to be learned, and new kinds of questions have replaced those answered, we can now present a reasonably detailed picture of early perceptual abilities.

In this chapter we examine what has been learned about the development of perception of space and motion. In the first part of the chapter, we address space, and in the second, motion. We also find important connections between the two along the way. There are several tasks not undertaken in this chapter. We review little data about developmental neuroanatomy or neurophysiology and consider only selectively the large body of research

Perception of Space and Motion

characterizing sensory discrimination abilities of the infant's visual system. We include findings in which the relation between sensory capacities and perceptual function is fairly clear. This strategy derives only from considerations of space and direct utility. For more comprehensive reviews of basic visual sensitivities, the reader is referred to Banks and Salapatek (1983) or Banks and Dannemiller (1987).

We also confine our attention to *visual* perception of space and motion. Vision is primary in guiding our movements and spatially oriented activity; it provides the most detailed information about objects, spatial layout, and events. Vision has also been a primary focus of research on the development of space and motion perception. Important aspects of spatial and kinematic perception involving auditory space perception, vestibular influences, and intermodal perception are beyond our scope in this chapter.

II. SPACE: THE FIRST FRONTIER

Space is the first frontier in human perceptual and cognitive development. It is the stage on which all objects reside and in which all events unfold. To understand early spatial perception abilities is to understand many of the limits on what else can be perceived, what parts of the world can be comprehended, and what can be learned.

The study of the origins of spatial perception also occupies a central place in perceptual theory. The nature of mature perception may be revealed by understanding what competencies are part of humans' innate endowment and what and how others arise. A classical and persistent view holds that space is a construction from more primitive elements, achieved by experience (Berkeley, 1709/1910; Harris, 1983; Helmholtz, 1867/1925; Piaget, 1954). Originally, this view was advanced on logical grounds (Berkeley, 1709/1910): Vision was held to be inherently ambiguous because of the loss of information in projecting a three-dimensional (3-D)-world onto a two-dimensional (2-D) retina. Assuming this ambiguity, visual perception of the outside world can only be achieved by combining visual sensations with extra-visual information. On most accounts this combination occurred through extensive learning (Berkeley, 1709/1910; Helmholtz, 1867/1925; Piaget, 1954; for a recent revival of this type of account, see Nakayama & Shimojo, 1992). An alternative, ecological view places spatial perception in an evolutionary context: Perceptual systems evolved to deliver useful information about the physical world (Gibson, 1966; Johansson, 1970). Underlying this proposal is a revised analysis of the information available to vision. Kinematic and stereoscopic information can remove many of the ambiguities inherent in the interpretation of single, static, 2-D images. Thus, the logical arguments regarding early visual competence may be dismissed; moreover, the existence of visually guided, spatially oriented behavior in newborns of some other species (E. J. Gibson & Walk, 1960; Hess, 1956) provides at least an existence proof for the possibility of unlearned perceptual mechanisms. None of these considerations settle the issues of perception's origins in human beings, however. In the absence of prevailing logical arguments, these issues must be settled by empirical study. Although investigators have tried to settle them indirectly by making inferences from adult abilities (Gottschaldt, 1926; Senden, 1960; Wallach, 1985), real progress on these issues awaited the development of techniques, over the past few decades, for studying human infants.

A. The Task of Early Space Perception

Before examining specific spatial abilities, it is useful to place them in a functional context. For animate organisms, the functions of space and motion perception are obvious. They guide locomoting through the environment, avoiding hazards, reproducing, acquiring nutrition, and so on. A striking fact for understanding early perceptual ability in *homo sapiens* is that human infants do virtually none of these things. On average, a human infant does not crawl until 6–7 months, does not walk until about 1 year, and does not even reach effectively until 4–5 months. On attaining these milestones, the infant still remains relatively incompetent in finding its own nutrition or escaping danger. Yet by 1 year, the infant's perceptual abilities are adultlike in many, perhaps most, respects, and from the earliest months, infants are engaged in earnest attention to spatial and kinematic features of their environments.

It has been argued (Kellman, 1993; Mandler, 1988) that the function of perception early in life is to underwrite cognitive development. Despite the lack of motor skill, the infant is actively engaged in learning about the physical and social worlds. The perceptual skills available in this period dictate the pace and content of that learning.

The study of the constraints spatial perception places on early learning about the physical and social environments is not far advanced. The foundation of such an analysis must be a clear characterization of early space perception abilities: What spatial properties are perceivable, how, and how well? These questions are our focus.

Besides facilitating early learning, another task of early spatial perception might be learning new perceptual skills. These might be of at least two varieties. One is the more precise extraction and differentiation of information resulting from experience (E. J. Gibson, 1969). The other is that certain detectable stimulus variables might come to specify spatial properties of the environment due to learning. This latter idea has a long history of fervent advocates, although there is little evidence for it in early development. One possible explanation is that the idea is misconceived (Gibson &

Gibson, 1955), but other explanations are possible. Some evidence in adult perception is consistent with the idea that new depth cues can be learned by correlation with old ones (Wallach & O'Leary, 1982). Our profile of early spatial abilities helps make clear which sources of spatial information usable by adults might be products of learning, and those that almost certainly are not.

Sources of information about depth and distance are remarkably numerous. For convenience, we organize them into classes based on similarities in their physical foundations and somewhat by the mechanisms by which they are processed. The four classes are motion-carried information, stereoscopic information, oculomotor information, and pictorial information. This organization differs slightly from some other groupings (e.g., Yonas & Owsley, 1987).

B. Motion-Carried Information about Space

Motion-carried information is arguably the most important source of spatial information for adults, given its precision and informativeness for spatial layout, guidance of locomotion, and skilled action. Motion-carried information is also noteworthy in being unambiguous under very reasonable constraints (e.g., Lee, 1974). For example, the depth ordering of viewed objects given by motion perspective when an observer moves her head back and forth is unequivocal, assuming only that the objects do not move contingent on the observer's movement. Infants do not self-locomote until the second half of their first year, so one might conjecture that motion-carried information would not have developmental priority. The ecological validity of motion information, however, might suggest the opposite. Early learning about the environment might be best served by reliance on only the most accurate sources of information, even if this means that some perceptual situations will be indeterminate (Kellman, 1993).

Spatial information carried by motion is multifaceted. Diverse sources of information reveal diverse aspects of the environment. We consider four: (1) *Optical expansion–contraction* can indicate relative motion between a target and the observer. (2) *Motion parallax or motion perspective* can indicate relative and possibly absolute distance from the observer under some conditions. (3) *Accretion–deletion of texture* can indicate depth ordering of surfaces. (4) The continuously changing optical projection of an object, given by object or observer motion, carries information about its 3-D form, allowing perception of *structure-from-motion* (SFM).

1. Kinematic Information for Approach

The optical projection of an approaching object expands symmetrically as the object comes closer to colliding with the observer. The *time-to-contact* of an object is derivable from the projected boundary's retinal eccentricity and its time derivative (Lee, 1974), and there is some evidence that this information indicates time to contact in adult perception (Lee, Lishman, Roly, & Thomson, 1982). Studies with other species indicate that optical expansion patterns elicit unlearned defensive responses (Schiff, 1965). Early studies of human infants 1–2 months old suggested that optical expansion triggers head retraction, raising of the arms, and blinking (Ball & Tronick, 1971; Bower, Broughton, & Moore, 1970). Later work questioned the interpretation of head and arm movements (Yonas et al., 1977). Infants may move their heads because they track visually the top contour of the pattern, and their relatively undifferentiated motor behavior may lead to the arms following along. To test this hypothesis, Yonas et al. presented a display in which only the top contour moved. Such a display does not specify approach of an object. At 1–2 and 3–4 months of age, infants showed as much or more head and arm movements to the single contour movement display as to the expansion display. It appears that tracking behavior may explain much or all of the apparent "defensive" movements by infants.

Paradoxically, however, it appears that both the tracking hypothesis and the original hypothesis are correct. Yonas et al. (1977) also measured eye blinking to their displays. In contrast to the head and arm movement results, infants blinked reliably more to a display specifying approach than to a single contour. Reliable effects of blinking to approach displays, more than to control displays, have been found in several studies with infants from about 1 month on (Yonas, 1981; Yonas & Granrud, 1985; Yonas, Pettersen & Lockman, 1979).

2. Motion Perspective

Motion perspective is the phantom of perceptual development research to date. A number of investigators have suggested that it may be an innate foundation of spatial perception (E. J. Gibson & Walk, 1960; Yonas & Owsley, 1987). However, evidence specifically implicating or testing motion perspective is thin. E. J. Gibson and Walk (1960) noted lateral head movements by the newborns of certain species in the visual cliff situation that probably indicated use of motion perspective. If such behavior characterizes human infants on the visual cliff, it is less pronounced. Also, human infants cannot even be tested in the standard visual cliff situation until they develop locomotor abilities (around 6 months of age).

Hofsten, Kellman, and Putaansuu (1992) recently reported experimental results related to the development of motion perspective. They presented an array of three vertical bars in a horizontal row, perpendicular to the line of sight, to 14-week-old infants. The infant was placed in a chair that moved laterally back and forth, and the middle bar moved a small amount parallel and in tandem with the chair. In Experiment 1, infants habituated to such an array in which the middle rod moved .32°/s in phase with the moving infant chair. Afterward they were tested with two displays. One was spatially similar in that it consisted of three aligned, stationary rods. The other had three stationary rods, but the middle one was displaced backward 15 cm; this gave the moving infant the same optical change patterns as in habituation. Infants generalized habituation more to the spatially different display having the same optical change as in habituation. Experiment 2 showed that the effect disappeared if the contingent motion was reduced to .16°/s. Experiment 3 tested whether infants in Experiment 1 responded simply on the basis of similarity of optical change patterns or if they were sensitive to the contingency between the optical changes and their own movement, as would be predicted if the optical changes were used as motion parallax information. After habituation, infants saw two test displays differing by whether the center, stationary rod was displaced backward from the flanking rods or forward. Both test displays gave the same magnitude of contingent motion, but only one matched the phase relations used in habituation. Results indicated that infants dishabituated to the changed motion contingency.

The results are consistent with the idea that young infants utilize small contingent optical changes as information about object depth. In the experiments, the dishabituation patterns all fit predictions that were based on sameness or difference of depth position as indicated by motion parallax. However, the results do not uniquely imply this interpretation. The dishabituation patterns also correspond to what would be expected if infants registered and responded to particular optical changes and the contingency (including direction) of these optical changes on the observer's movement. In other words, it is not clear whether the optical changes were taken to indicate depth. One suggestion that these contingent optical changes are special in some way is that infants proved sensitive to velocities well below those found in studies of motion thresholds that used noncontingent motion and stationary observers (see section III. B. 2 below). Although this contrast would fit neatly with the idea that small, contingent motions are encoded as depth, not motion, information, further research will be necessary to bear out, or disprove, this conjecture.

3. Accretion and Deletion of Texture

Accretion and deletion of texture is a source of kinematic information for edges and depth discovered in recent times (Gibson, Kaplan, Reynolds, & Wheeler, 1969; Kaplan, 1969). During relative motion of two opaque surfaces at different depths, texture elements on the further surface will become visible (accretion) or hidden (deletion) at the edges of the nearer surface. In random–dot surfaces in which no other information is available, accretion–

deletion of texture effectively specifies edges, form, and depth ordering of surfaces to adult observers (Andersen & Cortese, 1989; Kaplan, 1969; Shipley & Kellman, 1994).

Kaufmann-Hayoz, Kaufmann, and Stucki (1986) studied shape perception from this kind of information. Three-month-olds who habituated to one shape specified by accretion–deletion dishabituated to a different shape, and vice versa. The result suggests that accretion–deletion effectively specified edges and shape at this early age, although no inferences can be made about depth ordering from the data. Granrud et al. (1984) studied perception of depth ordering by using a reaching procedure. Assuming that infants would reach preferentially to the nearer of two surfaces, they presented moving displays of computer-generated random-dot surfaces with vertical accretion–deletion boundaries specifying nearer and farther surfaces. Infants at both 5 and 7 months of age reached about 50% of the time to areas specified as nearer and 35% to areas specified as farther. (The remaining reaches were to edges or to two or more display regions.)

These results suggest that sensitivity to accretion–deletion information arises early. Later, Yonas and his colleagues raised questions about the basis of infants' responding. They pointed out that ordinary accretion–deletion displays might contain two kinds of information. Besides the actual appearance and disappearance of texture elements, there are different relations between moving texture elements and the boundary between two regions. On one side elements remain in a fixed position relative to the boundary; this side is nearer than the other. In the other region, elements move closer to or further from the boundary over time; this surface is further. Tests with adult subjects show that the latter information (termed *boundary flow*) is usable as depth information when no accretion–deletion of elements at the boundary is present (Craton & Yonas, 1990). Craton and Yonas (1988) reported that 5-month-olds responded to boundary flow information when no accretion–deletion was present. Further work may be needed to indicate whether accretion–deletion alone can specify depth order. The data do suggest that at minimum, accretion and deletion enables infant perceivers to locate the boundaries between regions since the boundaries (required to compute boundary flow) were not given in any other way in the Granrud et al. (1984) and Kaufmann-Hayoz et al. (1986) studies.

4. Structure from Motion

A number of studies indicate an early capacity for detection of 3-D structure from motion (Kellman, 1984; Kellman & Short, 1987a; Yonas, Arterberry, & Granrud, 1987; Arterberry & Yonas, 1988). Infants 14–18 weeks old generalize habituation and dishabituate on the basis of sameness or difference in 3-D form, even when the specific information indicating that form changes between habituation and test periods. Such changes are accomplished by using a new axis of rotation (Kellman, 1984; Arterberry & Yonas, 1988) or by testing transfer from kinematically specified to stationary stereoscopically specified form (Yonas et al., 1987). Since the projective geometric information underlying SFM is equivalent whether the object moves or the observer moves, one might predict that infants would be able to perceive 3-D form from either. This prediction has been shown to be correct (Kellman & Short, 1987a). A more detailed discussion of perception of 3-D form from motion-carried information may be found in the chapter by Kellman in *Perceptual and Cognitive Development,* this series.

C. Stereoscopic Information

Perception of depth from stereoscopic disparity is among the most precise forms of depth information available to adults. In combination with some information about the absolute distance of at least one visible point, it also allows perception of precise metric depth intervals between objects (Wallach & Zuckerman, 1963). Several facts point to innate foundations for this form of depth perception, including the existence of cortical cells sensitive to particular disparities at birth or after minimal visual experience in several species (Hubel & Wiesel, 1970; Pettigrew, 1974; Ramachandran, Clarke, & Whitteridge, 1977).

Evidence suggests that perception of depth from disparity arises by maturation in the early months of life. A number of studies have reported disparity sensitivity in some infants as young as 2–3 months, with most infants first showing sensitivity around the 4th month of life. These studies have used preferential looking methods with stationary displays (Atkinson & Braddick, 1981; Held, Birch, & Gwiazda, 1980) or with random-dot kinematograms (Fox, Aslin, Shea, & Dumais, 1980). These methods are based on the hypothesis that detection of depth specified by disparity leads to greater attention than a comparable flat display. Petrig, Julesz, Kropfl, Baumgartner, & Anliker (1981) found a similar onset of sensitivity by using recordings of visual-evoked potentials (VEPs).

Systematic studies of disparity thresholds have been carried out by Held and his colleagues (Held et al., 1980; Birch, Gwiazda & Held, 1982). In longitudinal studies using a visual preference procedure it was assumed that a striped display containing perceptible depth differences would attract more attention than a comparable flat display. The average ages at which reliable preferences appear are 12 weeks for crossed disparities and 17 weeks for uncrossed. A striking feature of the data is that improvement in stereoscopic sensitivity once it appears is rapid. (see Figure 1) In 3–4 weeks, thresholds change from greater than 60 min to less than 1 min of disparity, the latter measured value limited by the apparatus (Held et al., 1980) and comparable to adult sensitivity under some conditions.

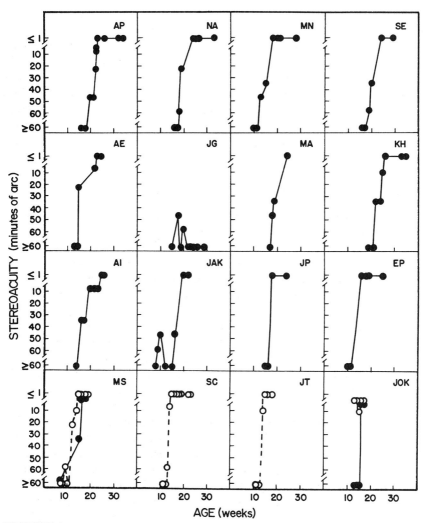

FIGURE 1   Stereoacuity as a function of age. Each data point indicates the smallest disparity for which the infant showed a preference on at least 80% of trials. Filled circles indicate data for uncrossed disparities; open circles indicate data from crossed disparities. From Held, Birch, and Gwiazda (1980); reprinted with permission.

There is some question whether studies of early binocular function indicate use of disparity as depth information or merely sensitivity to disparity. This issue is difficult to resolve with certainty; however, control conditions used in several studies all tend to support the interpretation that preferences for displays containing disparity depend on stereopsis. Held et al. (1980), for example, found that subjects who showed clear preferences for vertical line displays containing horizontal disparity showed no such preferences when the displays were rotated 90° to give 34 min of vertical disparity (a condition that produces rivalry for adults). Fox et al., (1980) reported that infants who preferentially fixated disparities that would have indicated depth to adults did not do so for very large disparities that do not signal depth to adults. In fact, they found a reliable tendency for infants to look away from the latter displays. This result is worrisome in one sense; it suggests that disparities apart from stereopsis might affect infants' fixation. The most straightforward interpretation of the overall pattern of results, however, is that preferential looking found in studies using horizontal disparity depends on stereopsis.

1. Mechanisms Underlying the Onset of Stereopsis

The abrupt onset and rapid rise in stereoscopic acuity seen in longitudinal studies seem consistent with a maturational explanation. Some possibilities include maturation of disparity-sensitive cortical cells, fine tuning of convergence, or changes in visual acuity that might constrain disparity sensitivity. Some evidence suggests that the onset of stereopsis is not dependent on improvements of basic visual acuity (grating acuity). In a longitudinal study measuring both in the same subjects, little or no change in grating acuity is evident during the period in which stereopsis shows its sudden onset (Held, 1993). The same conclusion is supported by Westheimer and McKee (1980). They tested adult stereoacuity under conditions that reduced their acuity and contrast sensitivity to approximately those of a 2-month-old infant. Although these manipulations markedly reduced stereoacuity, they were not adequate to explain the absence of early sensitivity to large disparities. Likewise, development of convergence is an unlikely basis because it would not explain differences in the onset of crossed and uncrossed disparity (Held et al., 1980). In fact, past a certain point, development of precise convergence may await improvements in disparity sensitivity, rather than vice versa (Aslin, 1981; Held et al., 1980). The most likely mechanism for the onset of stereoscopic vision is some maturational change in cortical disparity-sensitive units themselves. Such a dependence of stereoscopic discrimination performance on changes in binocularly sensitive cortical cells has been observed in kittens (Timney, 1981; Pettigrew, 1974). Held (1985, 1988) suggested that cortical changes underly the onset of stereopsis and binocular rivalry; specifically, these changes might reflect development in the segregation of ocular dominance columns in layer four of the visual cortex. In the early months of life, cells in layer four generally receive projections from both eyes. Between birth and 6 months, inputs from the two eyes separate into alternating columns receiving input from the right and left eyes (Hickey & Peduzzi, 1987). Since eye-of-origin information is required for extracting disparity information, this neurological development may be a prerequisite for disparity sensitivity.

D. Oculomotor Information

1. Accommodation

Accommodation is often considered a weak depth cue in adult perception (Hochberg, 1971). There is evidence, however, that it can act as a source of distance information in near space (within 2 m), especially when measured by using an indirect method, for example, via effects on perceived size (Gogel, 1977; Leibowitz, Shiina, & Hennessy, 1972; Wallach & Floor, 1971).

No research has directly addressed accommodation as a source of depth information in human infants. There have been several studies of the development of accommodation, however. An early study (Haynes, White, & Held, 1965) suggested that infants in the first few weeks of life do not adjust accommodation for target distance, maintaining accommodation appropriate for a target at about 19 cm. Accommodative responses improved steadily over the first several months, nearing adultlike responses by 3–4 months. It is probable that the target stimulus used by Haynes et al. was not optimal for testing accommodation, given the visual acuity of the youngest infants (Banks, 1980). Subsequent research indicated that the accommodative responses of 1-month-olds do vary appropriately with target distance, although their accommodative errors are substantially greater than older infants (Banks, 1980; Brookman, 1980; Braddick, Atkinson, French & Howland, 1979; Hainline, Riddell, Grose-Fifer, & Abramov, 1992). The research showing the early presence of accommodative function opens the possibility that accommodation could act as a depth cue from early on. Further research is needed to test this possibility.

2. Convergence

Aslin (1988) discusses some of the reasons that precise assessment of early convergence is difficult. Despite these difficulties, research on the development of vergence has proved to be possible (Aslin, 1977; Slater & Findlay, 1975). Early results indicated that from the first weeks of life, infants make vergence changes appropriate for changes in the distance of viewed targets. Although their convergence is often appropriate for target distance, there is substantial variability across trials and subjects in younger infants. Average accuracy improves steadily through at least 5 months of age. A recent study reported more consistent results (Hainline et al., 1992). Using paraxial photorefraction techniques and targets placed at distances between 25 and 200 cm, they found that most infants even at the youngest age tested (26–45 days) showed appropriate slopes relating convergence to target position. The authors characterized convergence as essentially adultlike, even in the youngest group.

If newborn convergence is reasonably accurate, an important question is what visual information might drive it (Aslin, 1988). What could be the stimulus for eye movements leading to accurate convergence? Given the data on the development of stereopsis, binocular disparity does not seem to be a reasonable candidate before 3–4 months of age. Nor does accommodatively triggered vergence seem plausible since accommodation is much less accurate in the early weeks of life than is convergence. Hainline et al., (1992) suggest two possibilities. First, when targets are sparse or unique, convergence may derive from foveating the target in each eye. Second, correlations in firing of cortical units sensitive to similar retinal positions, but driven by different eyes, could drive convergence. Currently there is little evidence bearing on these hypotheses.

The studies described so far have been concerned with the accuracy of infants' convergence, not with its relevance to depth perception. One study took up the latter issue directly. Hofsten (1977) studied 5-month-olds' reaching behavior under normal viewing and while wearing convergence-altering glasses. He found that reaches were altered appropriately toward positions consistent with convergence information. This result suggests that convergence can provide absolute distance information.

An array of indirect evidence supports the idea that convergence provides distance information much earlier, perhaps from birth. Kellman, Hofsten, Condry, & O'Halloran (1991; Kellman & Hofsten, 1992) studied 8- and 16-week-olds in a situation in which moving observers were tested for motion detection. The visible arrays contained several stationary objects and one moving object that was linked to the observer's moving chair and moved along a path parallel to it. Detection of motion in this situation requires distance information (Gogel, 1982). Infants showed evidence of accurate motion detection when they viewed the displays binocularly, but not monocularly. Although motion detection in the 16-week-old group may have been based on convergence, disparity, or a combination of the two, it is unlikely that disparity is present in many 8-week-olds (Held et al., 1980). The best explanation of 8-week-olds' motion sensitivity in this situation is that it is based on distance information furnished by convergence.

Other results may also plausibly be explained by early availability of distance information from convergence (Granrud, 1987; Slater, Mattock, & Brown, 1990). These studies are discussed in the sections on size and shape constancy.

E. Pictorial Depth Information

A programmatic approach to the development of pictorial depth perception has been carried out by Yonas and his colleagues (see Yonas et al., 1987b, for a review). Many of these studies used reaching as a dependent measure. Paired displays in which pictorial information specified that one object was nearer to the subject than the other were presented to monocular infants.

Preferential reaching to the nearer display was taken to indicate the effectiveness of the pictorial cue.

1. Perspective

A study by Yonas, Cleaves, and Pettersen (1978) used an Ames trapezoidal window (Ames, 1951) to test linear perspective. Five- and 7-month-old infants viewed the trapezoidal window monocularly and binocularly on different trials. Equal reaching to the two sides was observed in the binocular condition, suggesting that binocular information overrode any depth differences signaled by other cues (as would occur for adults in near viewing of such a display). Under monocular viewing, 7-month-olds reached significantly more to the larger side of the window, but 5-month-olds did not. A subsequent study (Oross, Francis, Mauk, & Fox, 1987) provided evidence that infants 7.5 and 9.5 months of age, but not 5.5 months, perceive the illusory oscillation of a rotating Ames window display. These results suggest that perspective signals relative depth to infants by 7 months.

2. Familiar Size

One cue of special importance in evaluating learning effects in space perception is the cue of familiar size. From the geometry of size and distance relations, the combination of a known object size and the projected size can be used to derive the distance from observer to object. Infants' use of familiar size was investigated by Yonas, Pettersen, and Granrud (1982) and Granrud, Haake, and Yonas (1985). As with perspective, 7-month-olds showed evidence of using familiar size, whereas 5-month-olds did not. This is a fascinating outcome because it provides an existence proof for learned information in infant space perception. Perception of distance from familiar size would seem to require accessing memory representations by means of shape and retrieving stored information about object size.

3. Interposition

Granrud and Yonas (1984) studied the effectiveness of interposition information by using displays like those shown in Figure 2. According to this cue, when contours intersect, the one that continues through the intersection is the edge of a surface in front, whereas the contour ending is the edge of a surface going behind the other surface. Thus, in Figure 2a, the left-most part of the display is signaled to be nearer than the middle, which is nearer than the right-most display. In Figure 2b, all contours change direction at the intersections, and no depth order is specified. Finally, Figure 3c provides a control display in which the three panels are separated but have areas identical to those visible in Figure 2a.

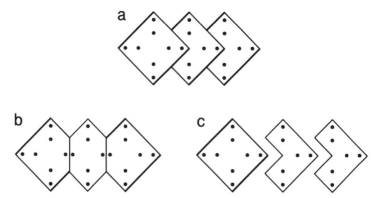

FIGURE 2   Displays used to study depth perception from interposition. (a) Interposition display. (b) Control display, with no interposition information. (c) Control display, with no interposition information and visible areas comparable to (a). Redrawn from Granrud and Yonas (1984).

In their experiments, Granrud and Yonas (1984) tested 5- and 7-month-olds with one eye covered (to remove conflicting binocular information) and all parts of the displays coplanar and equidistant from the subjects. Infants' reaches to different parts of the displays were recorded. In Experiment 1, both 5- and 7-month-olds reached reliably more often to the left-most part of the display in Figure 2a than to the left-most part of the control display in Figure 2b (61% vs. 50% for 7-month-olds and 56% vs. 47% for 5-month-olds). In Experiment 2, the pattern of Figure 2c was used as the control display to ensure that interposition, not relative size of visible areas, produced the patterns of data in Experiment 1. Results indicated that 7-month-olds reached reliably more to the left-most part of the interposition display than to the control display (63% vs. 54%), whereas 5-month-olds showed no reliable difference (56% vs. 54%). Granrud and Yonas interpreted their results as evidence for depth perception from interposition at 7 months but not at 5 months.

4. Shading

In a study by Granrud, Yonas, and Opland (1985), 5- and 7-month-olds were presented with a surface containing a concavity and a convexity. They were also presented, under binocular and monocular viewing, with a photograph depicting a concavity and convexity. Classification of concavity and convexity from shading alone depends on the position of the light source; in some other species as well as in human adults, evidence suggests that illumination from above is assumed in perception of shaded regions (Hershberger, 1970). It was assumed that infants would reach preferentially to an area that appeared nearer than the rest of the surface. Both age groups reached preferentially for the real convexity in both monocular and binocular conditions. Seven-month-olds viewing the photograph reached preferentially for the area specified to be convex by shading information, but only when they viewed the display monocularly. When viewing binocularly, they showed no reaching preference. Five-month-olds showed no reaching preferences to the photographic display under either monocular or binocular viewing. The results suggest that shading alone provides depth information to 7-month-olds but not to 5-month-olds. An elegant feature of this pattern of results is that the perceptual ability under study was inferred from less accurate performance: The older group, but not the younger, appeared to perceive the flat photograph as having depth.

5. Overview of Pictorial Depth

Taken together, the results on a variety of pictorial information sources are remarkably consistent. Sensitivity to all of these sources of information appears to be present by 7 months but not at 5 months of age. The absence of pictorial depth sensitivity in the first half year and the apparent synchrony of the onset of various cues pose an interesting explanatory challenge. The similar timing of initial sensitivity to the various cues has been cited as evidence implicating maturational processes (Yonas & Granrud, 1984). An alternative account that is based on learning might explain the timing of these developments by considering other developmental changes. For example, infants may learn to use these cues after they begin to crawl at around 6 months of age. The importance of locomotion would be consistent with evidence in other species showing connections between self-produced locomotion and sensitivity to visual information about space (Held & Hein, 1963). Analogously, Bertenthal and Campos (1990) provided evidence that crawling experience correlates with human infants' avoidance of the deep side of the visual cliff.

Specific research examining the locomotor hypothesis in relation to pictorial depth cues has been disconfirming, however. Arterberry, Yonas, and Bensen (1989) tested the relation of locomotor experience to sensitivity to linear perspective and texture gradients. Seven-month-olds at different stages of learning to crawl showed no reliable differences in sensitivity. All three groups reached reliably more to an object specified to be closer by perspective or textural information. These findings do not support the hypothesis that crawling experience leads to acquisition of pictorial depth cues.

Other learning accounts for the onset of pictorial depth perception remain possible. For example, infants might learn relationships between static-monocular patterns and depth relations given by motion or stereopsis. One experimental approach that might help to decide the roles of learning and maturation would be training studies, in which a new depth cue correlates with already usable information about depth. Likewise, a longitudinal study that included tests for several different pictorial cues could assess the hypothesis of a single maturational basis by showing how closely in time the various cues really come to operate. Such studies would be complex but useful undertakings.

F. Effects of Distance Perception on Object Perception

Information about distance not only has direct value for perceivers but may also provide information that makes possible constancies in object perception: notably size and shape constancy. In turn, studies of infants' perception of shape and size (and motion, see below) can provide a window into early spatial perception. In this section, we review several findings of this sort, emphasizing the implications for development of space perception. (For a more complete treatment of early object perception abilities, see the chapter by Kellman in *Perceptual and Cognitive Development,* this series.)

1. Size Constancy

Slater, Mattock, and Brown (1990) performed two experiments to assess newborns' size perception abilities. In Experiment 1 they used a visual preference procedure with pairs of objects having identical shapes but differing in distance (23–69 cm) and real size (cubes with 5.1 cm or 10.2 cm sides). In all cases in which retinal size differed, infants showed clear preferences for the object of larger projected size. This finding documented looking preferences for larger projective sizes but did not test size constancy. In the second experiment, Slater et al. used an elegant design to test size constancy apart from the looking preferences found in the first experiment. Subjects were familiarized with either a large cube or a small cube of a constant size over six trials, with distance varying across trials. After familiarization, the large and small cubes were presented successively for two test trials. Distance of the large and small cubes differed so that they had equal projective sizes at the observer's eyes. The cube previously shown during the familiarization period was positioned at a distance that had not been used earlier. Thus, the retinal sizes of both test objects were novel. Specifically, the larger test cube (10.2 cm per side) was positioned 61 cm from the observer, and the smaller cube (5.1 cm per side) was positioned 30.5 cm from the observer.

All of the 12 subjects showed longer test–trial looking to the object whose real size was novel; mean novelty preference was about 84%. A nice feature of the design is that the test configuration in this experiment was presented in the earlier visual preference experiment, at which time it evoked no reliable preference.

These results suggest that size constancy in humans in innate, a conclusion supported by other research (Granrud, 1987; Slater & Morison, 1985). In Granrud's study, rates of habituation were examined to two kinds of sequences of objects in which retinal sizes varied identically. In one sequence, the real object size varied, whereas in the other, it remained invariant. Slower habituation was reported for the former case, suggesting that the changing object size was noticed and sustained subjects' interest.

None of these studies indicate much about the mechanism(s) by which constancy is achieved. Some inferences can be made, however, using a process of elimination. Because objects in the Slater et al. (1990) and Granrud (1987) studies were suspended in midair in front of homogeneous backgrounds, certain relationships of projective size and the area of occluded ground surface (Gibson, 1950) cannot be used as a basis of size perception. These are, therefore, cases in which projective size and viewing distance must combine to determine size accurately. Among possible sources of absolute distance information, relatively few might be available in these displays and usable by newborns. Convergence of the eyes on a viewed target, although estimates of its precision vary somewhat (Aslin, 1977; Hainline et al., 1992; Slater & Findlay, 1975) is the most likely source of information. Accommodative information could in principle be used, but there is no evidence for its use as a depth cue in infancy, and its precision in neonates is poor (Banks, 1980; Hainline et al., 1992). Another possibility is motion parallax. Newborns in the viewing situation used by Slater et al. and Granrud require substantial head support and do not commonly make the self-produced head movements that would be required to generate motion perspective information. Moreover, to maintain subjects' interest, Granrud moved the objects back and forth, a procedure that would at minimum complicate the extraction of distance by optical change contingent on the observer's movement. Thus, convergence is the most likely source of absolute distance information underlying size constancy. The precision of this distance information is not known. However, the data of Slater et al. and Granrud give some indications about precision. On the simple assumptions that projective size is correctly registered and that an object will not be seen as having changed size unless its distance changes discriminably, infants' performance implies that objects are located within an error not exceeding 2.8° of convergence angle in the Slater et al. experiment and about 1.8° in Granrud's experiment. Recent work on infants' convergence indicates that average convergence accuracy in the youngest age group tested (26–45 days) met or exceeded these standards of precision (Hainline et al., 1992).

2. Shape Constancy

In the absence of distance information, recovery of the shape of planar objects slanted in depth (under polar projection) should be impossible. Research with newborns (mean age: 2 days, 8 hr) by Slater and Morison (1985) provides evidence for perception of constant shape despite detectable variations in slant. Earlier work by Caron, Caron, & Carlson (1979) had found such an ability with 12-week-old infants. There is little discussion in these reports of the depth information that supports shape constancy. Because the objects were stationary, motion perspective is a possibility. The requisite head movements would be unlikely in the case of newborns, however, given both their lack of neck strength and the need for head and neck support that would limit movement. A bias for perceiving a symmetric form could explain results for a rectangle at different slants whose projection is trapezoidal. Both the investigations of Caron et al. (1979) and Slater and Morison (1985) found similar effects when the true planar shape was a trapezoid or a rectangle. As in our analysis of the size constancy results, convergence appears to be the likely candidate. It would be useful to test this hypothesis with newborns viewing the displays monocularly or with optically altered convergence.

3. Position Constancy and Motion Perception

Another perceptual outcome that can depend on distance information is perception of objects as remaining stationary (position constancy) or moving during observer motion (Gogel, 1982). Evidence from studies of infants as young as 8 weeks of age suggests that during observer motion, distance information is used to determine which optical displacements indicate real object motion and which are consequences of observer motion (Kellman & Hofsten, 1992; Kellman, Gleitman, & Spelke, 1987). The ability to discriminate moving and stationary objects was eliminated when infants viewed the displays monocularly, suggesting that convergence may also provide the distance information underlying this ability (Kellman & Hofsten, 1992). This topic is explored further in our treatment of motion perception.

G. Summary: Space Perception

Perception of many aspects of the 3-D layout of space, and the use of spatial information to determine other attributes such as object size, shape, and motion, appear to be part of the early competence of human beings. Contact with a 3-D world appears to be present from the beginning, as does some early responsiveness to particular events, such as the approach of an object. What information and processes accomplish this early spatial ability and allow its further development? Motion-carried information about space appears to operate from the beginning of life, although more direct evidence is needed. A variety of spatial abilities requiring some degree of metric information about space, as opposed to merely ordinal depth information, have been unearthed, and binocular convergence is emerging as the likely source of distance information in these cases. The neural bases of stereo-scopic depth perception are innate, but maturation is required to bring this system into operation around 4–5 months of age. Finally, the pictorial cues to depth appear relatively late, sometime in the second half year of life. Whether they depend on maturation, learning, or some combination is unknown.

III. MOTION PERCEPTION

If space is the first frontier, motion is the *raison d'être* of perception. Percep-tual systems exist to guide the motion of organisms, and the properties of objects and environments are important because of the events they make possible. It is therefore no surprise that motion perception is a central topic in perceptual development.

As with space perception, the role of motion perception in infancy is different from its role later in life. Infants' motion perception abilities sub-stantially predate their abilities for skilled action. Responding to threats or foraging for food are possible only in the most limited fashion for the first several months of life. Yet infants are active perceptual explorers of their environment, and they are especially captivated by motion. Why is this the case? A plausible conjecture is that motion is an especially rich source for early learning about the physical and social worlds.

Motion may be special for more than one reason. First, it has a double role, termed by J. Gibson as *dual specification* (Gibson, 1966). Motions of objects and observers are important events to be perceived. At the same time, optical changes given by object or observer motion carry information about unchanging aspects of the environment, such as object form and spatial layout. For early learning, information carried by motion might be primary in specifying both what changes and what persists. A second con-sideration involves the ecological validity of information sources. The lack of knowledge and mobility makes infants less able to correct perceptual errors. Errors could severely distort early physical and social knowledge. On these grounds, it has been argued that information sources that function in early perception should be those with the highest accuracy in specifying properties of the world (Kellman, 1993). Whether or not this functional interpretation is correct, it appears that infants are sensitive to a subset of the information sources usable by adults, and this subset appears to consist of those sources with the highest ecological validity (Kellman, 1993). Much of this early repertoire involves motion-carried information, which, on mathe-matical and ecological grounds, has been argued to be among the least ambiguous information sources in many perceptual domains (Gibson, 1966, 1979; Lee, 1974).

A. Motion and Attention

From the earliest ages, motion attracts attention (Fantz & Nevis, 1967), and infants orient toward moving stimuli by using head and eye movements (Haith, 1983; Kremenitzer, Vaughan, Kurtzberg & Dowling, 1979; White, Castle & Held, 1964). Infants' tendency to fixate and track moving displays has often been exploited in studies of other perceptual abilities (Atkinson, Braddick, & Moar, 1977; Fox et al., 1980; Manny & Klein, 1984; Shimojo, Birch, Gwiazda, & Held, 1984).

The causal direction of the connection between motion and information is not known. Infants might be hard-wired to attend to moving things—a useful adaptation for learning about objects and events. Alternatively, it may be information, not motion, that guides attention. Infants may preferentially attend to events more than static scenes because more or better information about space and objects is available to them from kinematic sources than from static ones.

B. Motion Sensitivity

Motion characteristics can be expressed in terms of time derivatives of spatial position. Tests of motion perception ordinarily involve the first derivative, velocity. Velocity may be subdivided into direction and magnitude (speed), and it is useful to assess visual sensitivity to both of these dimensions. Finally, there are multiple possibilities for the mechanisms that might underly sensitivity to moving stimuli. Research on early motion perception has examined all of these aspects of motion and motion detection.

1. Directional Selectivity

Recent work by Wattam-Bell (1991, 1992) tested the development of directional sensitivity by using behavioral and electrophysiological measures. For direction reversals in oscillating checkerboard patterns, the median ages at which infants first showed detectable visual evoked potentials (VEPs) to stimulus velocities of 5°/s and 20°/sec were 74 and 90 days, respectively. In a later behavioral study, Wattam-Bell (1992) used displays in which a vertical target strip had coherent vertical motion of random dots, against a background consisting of randomly changing dot patterns or opposite direction motion. The target display was always presented simultaneously with an adjacent random or uniformly moving display in a visual preference paradigm. (See Figure 3.) Infants were expected to look longer at the target display if they could detect its motion. The studies used a modified staircase procedure to find the greatest element displacement (d_{max}) in the target display that supported coherent motion detection. Subjects ranged from 8 to 15 weeks of age. Results indicated d_{max} for targets against noise or oppo-

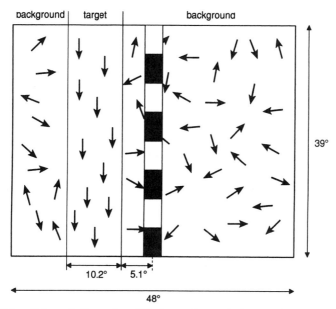

FIGURE 3   Schematic illustration of display used to study directional sensitivity. The two display panels differ by the presence of a vertical strip of coherently moving dots in the center of the left-hand panel. All other motions are random in direction. The center column of rectangles was used to attract infant's attention to the center of the display and disappeared during each trial. From Wattam-Bell (1992); reprinted with permission.

site motion and both increased substantially across the ages tested. For example, at displacement intervals of 20 ms, 8–11-week-olds showed a d_{max} around 0.25°, compared with about 0.65 for 14–15-week-olds and nearly 2° for adults. However, under the smallest d_{max} conditions, even the youngest subjects consistently showed evidence of motion detection.

These results suggest that directional selectivity may be poor, especially in the first 10 weeks of life. Wattam-Bell (1992) suggests that poorer performance of infants during this time may be due to the absence of motion detectors sensitive to larger spatial displacements at relatively short time intervals, that is, detectors sensitive to high velocities. Some support for this conjecture comes from an experiment in which the temporal interval was lengthened: d_{max} increased under these conditions. Evidence about velocity sensitivity is also consistent with this idea.

The weakness of early directional sensitivity has been suggested as a possible explanation of results of studies of perception on the basis of motion-carried information. For example, Slater, Kellman, Spelke, and Johnson (1994; see also Slater et al., 1990) found that newborns differed from 2- to 4-month-olds in their use of common motion as information for the unity of a partly occluded object. They argued that improvements in this ability might depend on maturation of directional selectivity required for accurate registration of the motions of visible parts.

Although directional selectivity may be poor in the early weeks of life, it would be an overstatement to claim it is absent altogether. Whereas the VEP data show no indication of sensitivity before about 10 weeks, the behavioral data indicate earlier ability. The possibility that directional sensitivity is absent at birth also seems paradoxical given that newborns show directionally appropriate responding to moving stimuli, such as saccadic tracking of slowly moving stimuli and optokinetic nystagmus (OKN) responses (Aslin, 1981; Barten, Birns, & Ronch, 1971; Dayton, Jones, Steele, & Rose, 1964). However, it has been argued that these may depend only on subcortical mechanisms (Atkinson & Braddick, 1981).

2. Velocity Sensitivity

Estimates of velocity thresholds in the first half year vary somewhat depending on features of the stimulus used. Volkmann and Dobson (1976) presented a horizontally oscillating checkerboard pattern and a similar but stationary pattern in a preferential looking procedure to 1- to 3-month-olds. The 2- and 3-month-olds clearly preferred the moving display even at 2°/s (the slowest velocity tested); 1-month-olds showed a weak preference. Using rotary motion, Kaufmann, Stucki, and Kaufmann-Hayoz (1985) estimated thresholds, also assessed by a preference procedure, at about 1.4°/s at 1 month and .93°/s at 3 months.

Somewhat higher threshold estimates have come from studies designed to distinguish different mechanisms underlying responses to moving patterns (see below). Using vertical grating stimuli and 75% correct as the threshold criterion, Aslin and Shea (1990) found velocity threshold of about 9°/s at 6 weeks and 4°/s at 12 weeks. Dannemiller and Freedland (1989) estimated threshold at about 5°/s for 16-week-olds and about 2.3°/s for 20-week-olds. However, they found no reliable motion preferences at 8 weeks. Dannemiller and Freedland (1991) studied differential velocity thresholds—the minimum difference in velocity that could evoke a reliable looking preference. They assumed that infants would preferentially fixate the display appearing to move faster. Their subjects reliably distinguished a velocity of 3.3°/s from 2.0°/s but not from 2.5°/s. Although it is difficult to compare stimulus conditions and measurement techniques, these threshold estimates are much higher than velocity thresholds for motion detection in adults; the latter can be as small as 1–2 min of arc/s when stationary reference points are visible (Kaufman, 1974).

Hofsten et al. (1992) suggested that these threshold estimates might understate infant motion detection abilities. As is always true with the visual preference method, a reliable difference in attention requires both that infants can distinguish two displays and that one of the two displays is significantly more interesting or attention holding. It is possible that velocities slower than those at the estimated thresholds are perceptible but not seen as more interesting than stationary patterns.

One reason for suspecting that true thresholds are lower involves motion perspective. Although there is not much direct evidence, there are reasons to suspect that motion perspective provides depth information in infancy (see above). Yet the differential velocity thresholds suggested by Dannemiller and Freedland (1991) would be too large to allow effective use of motion perspective. As Hofsten et al. (1992) calculated, if a child moved her head sideways 4 cm, she or he would be unable to distinguish a target at 69 cm (3.3°/s) from one at 92 cm (2.5°/s).

Using observer-contingent motion and 14-week-old subjects, Hofsten et al. (1992) found sensitivity to a differential velocity of only 0.32°/s, much lower than earlier estimates. Subjects also proved to be sensitive to the contingency of the motion with their own motion. Hofsten et al. suggested two possible reasons for the higher sensitivity they found. First, they used a habituation of looking procedure, which is likely to be a more sensitive method. Second, it is possible that the smaller, observer-contingent motions studied by Hofsten et al. are perceptually processed differently from larger, noncontingent motions. The former motions may be taken to indicate depth positioning of stationary objects, whereas the latter specify object motion.

An interesting application of infants' velocity perception is their anticipatory reaching for moving objects. Research by Hofsten (1980, 1983) indicates that infants reach in a predictive way for objects moving through their field of view. This behavior appears at about the same time (around 4 months of age) as directed reaching for stationary objects (Hofsten, 1980). In these experiments, the moving object was attached to a 74-cm rod that rotated in a horizontal plane around a fixed axis. At its closest point to the infant, the object was 14 cm away. Starting points and velocities were varied, and infants were scored for touching or grasping the object. Careful analysis of the timing and spatial properties of reaches suggested that infants reached with precision of about 0.05 s and with no systematic timing error. Accurate reaching was observed for even the fastest moving objects in the study (60 cm/s); additional observations on several subjects showed accurate reaching for objects moving at 120 cm/s. For various reasons, it is difficult to work back from these remarkable results to specific conclusions about the precision of infant velocity perception. However, the capacity to utilize spatial and motion information in this task appears impressive. Assuming that the development of reaching to stationary objects depends on maturation in the motor system (Field, 1990), the findings also support the idea that accurate 3-D perception precedes skilled motor behavior. Given that predictive reaching and reaching for stationary objects appear at about the same time, it appears that the ability to perceive objects and events with considerable precision must already be in place.

3. Specifying the Effective Stimulus

The study of motion detection abilities is complicated by the fact that a moving stimulus produces multiple changes in a spatial array. Preferential attention to a moving pattern might indicate detection of motion, but there are other possibilities. Positional change of the display or some part of it might be detected. When periodic stimuli are used, such as the checkerboard pattern used by Volkmann and Dobson (1976), the luminance at any point will change periodically. Demonstrated sensitivity might be based on this flicker rather than on motion per se.

Research to distinguish motion (velocity)-sensitive, position-sensitive, and flicker-sensitive mechanisms has been carried out by Aslin and Shea (1990), Freedland and Dannemiller (1987), and Dannemiller and Freedland (1989). Freedland and Dannemiller tested several combinations of temporal frequency and spatial displacement with random black- and white-check patterns. Strength of preference for moving over static displays was not a simple function of velocity. It appears that preference for a moving pattern over a static one is influenced by both spatial displacement and temporal frequency. Their experiments were not designed to distinguish perceived motion from flicker, however. Aslin and Shea (1990) used vertically moving luminance (square wave) gratings to distinguish these possibilities. By varying spatial frequency and velocity, it is possible to separate the effects of flicker and velocity. A response that varied with velocity, for example, might be expected to change if velocity were doubled and spatial frequency halved. Such changes, however, should have no effect on a flicker sensitive mechanism since the temporal frequency remains the same. The results indicated that velocity governed the motion preferences of 6- and 12-week-old infants. The design of their displays allowed Aslin and Shea to rule out some but not all versions of the hypothesis of a position-sensitive mechanism. Dannemiller and Freedland used motion of a single bar flanked by stationary reference bars. Such a display avoids ongoing flicker in any spatial position characteristic of spatially periodic stimuli. Infants' preference patterns were best explained by a velocity-sensitive mechanism. Arguing against a position-sensitive mechanism was the finding that extent of displacement did not predict responses at 16 or 20 weeks of age.

On the whole, these findings are compatible with the hypothesis that infant sensitivity to moving patterns is controlled largely by velocity-sensitive mechanisms.

C. Object and Observer Motion

The primary stimulus for motion is often described as retinal or optical displacement, a change in an object's projected position. Such changes always have two potential causes: object motion or observer motion. The same is true of other stimuli for motion perception such as optical expansion–contraction or convergence changes given with changes in object–observer distance.

These facts have led many theorists to suspect that before extensive learning, object and observer motion should be confused with each other (Helmholtz, 1867, 1925). William James, who conjectured that the world of the newborn is a "blooming, buzzing confusion," had this problem centrally in mind. As neonates, he believed "any relative motion of object and retina both makes the object seem to move, and makes us feel ourselves in motion" (James, 1890, Vol. 2, p. 173). Only through experience can the observer come to infer that particular optical changes indicate motion of an object or of the observer. To describe this account as the prevailing view would be an understatement since until recent years an alternative view had scarcely been articulated. J. J. Gibson (1966, 1979) presented an alternative. He argued that, despite the similarity of a single object's optical change in the two cases, visual information is available to distinguish object and observer motion. The information is relational: When an object moves, its surroundings undergo no optical change. When the observer moves, however, all visible areas undergo optical change. (Any given object's optical change can of course be canceled by appropriate eye or head movements. This subtlety complicates but does not invalidate Gibson's observation of informational differences in object and observer motion.) Given that information exists to distinguish object and observer motion, one might conjecture that visual systems have evolved to be sensitive to these differences.

Until quite recently, there has been little research directly concerned with the origins of human capacities to distinguish object from observer motion. One study was carried out by Kellman et al. (1987). They tested the role of observer-contingent motion in 16-week-olds' perception of partly occluded objects. Earlier work showed that infants of this age perceive a center-occluded object as complete when its visible parts share certain motion relationships (Kellman & Spelke, 1983; Kellman, Spelke, & Short, 1986). In those experiments, stationary observers viewed moving displays. Kellman et al. sought to determine whether the crucial information was provided by perceived motion of objects or merely by certain optical displacements. To contrast these possibilities, they arranged two conditions in which infant observers moved back and forth. In one, subjects viewed a stationary array consisting of a partly occluded rod. In the other, the partly occluded rod was yoked to the infant chair's movement so that it moved back and forth in opposite phase from the subject. (Both the chair and rod rotated rigidly around a fixed point between the infant and the object.)

This arrangement allowed two questions to be asked. First, do infants distinguish cases in which optical displacement arises from object motion from cases in which only the observer moves? Second, if the situations can be distinguished, do they differ in terms of their effect on perceived object unity? The two questions were assessed in different ways. Perceived unity was assessed by habituation and recovery patterns of visual attention. Infants in both groups were habituated to a partly occluded rod, stationary in one case and moving so as to maintain a fixed relationship with the observer (conjoint movement) in the other. After habituation, each subject was tested for looking time to two test displays, whose movement characteristics (stationary or conjoint) matched those of the habituation display. The test displays were an unoccluded complete rod and an unoccluded "broken" display, in which two visible pieces were separated by a gap where the occluder had previously been. If infants perceived the original occluded rod as complete, they were expected to recover attention after habituation to the broken rod but not to the complete rod (Kellman & Spelke, 1983). Perception of motion was assessed by examining overall looking levels during both habituation and test periods. Numerous studies with similar displays had shown that (stationary) infants' looking times to moving displays averaged two to three times longer than to stationary displays. If moving infant observers detected the real object motion during their own movement, they were expected to look longer than moving infants viewing stationary objects, despite the absence of subject-relative change in the conjoint motion condition.

Results suggested that moving infants viewing stationary displays (observer movement condition) did not perceive the displays to be in motion. Their looking times were on the same order as those of stationary infants viewing stationary displays. In contrast, infants in the conjoint movement case appeared to perceive motion: their looking times were two to three times higher than those in the observer motion group. These findings are especially striking in that relative to the subject, there was substantial subject-relative motion in the observer movement condition and none in the conjoint condition. These findings suggest an early capacity of infants to utilize relationships in optical change to perceive the motion and stability of objects during their own motion. In terms of object perception, it is noteworthy that perception of the occluded display as containing a complete object occurred only in the case in which real motion was perceived. (For further discussion see the chapter by Kellman in *Perceptual and Cognitive Development,* this series.)

Subsequent studies tested moving infants' perception of motion and stability more directly (Kellman & Hofsten, 1992; Kellman et al., 1991). The

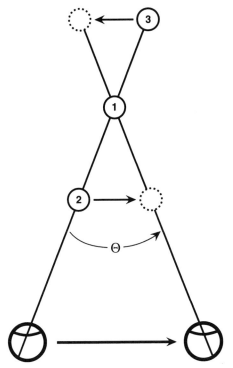

FIGURE 4 Geometry of object and observer motion. When the observer moves (depicted by the moving eye at bottom), a stationary target at (1) undergoes an angular change Θ in visual direction. The same optical change can be given by a nearer object moving in the same direction as the observer (2) or by a more distant object moving in the opposite direction as the observer (3). In this situation, distance information may be required to detect object motion or constant position during the observer's motion.

paradigm used may be understood by reference to Figure 4, which shows some basic geometry of object and observer motion, following the analyses of Gogel (1980, 1982). When the observer moves (depicted as the moving eye in Figure 4), a stationary target at a given distance (1) produces a given optical change (Θ). The same optical change may be produced by a nearer object that moves in the same direction as the observer (2) or a more distant object that moves opposite to the observer (3). When appropriately arranged, detection of whether a viewed target is stationary or moving requires information about the target's distance (Gogel, 1982). In the infant experiments, the observer was laterally moved in a moving infant seat while viewing two or more objects. On any trial, one of the objects moved a short distance along a path parallel to the observer's. The moving object appeared on the left and right side of the display area equally often. Consistent with the geometry of Figure 4, a stationary object was placed on the side opposite to the moving one, at such a distance so as to have the same optical change during the subject's motion. Object size was also adjusted so that the corresponding moving and stationary objects had the same projective size. The subject was thus faced on each trial with objects to the left and right having similar optical projections and displacements. Detecting which was moving and which was stationary required information about target distance. On the basis of other research, it was assumed that infants would preferentially attend to the moving object, if they could distinguish moving from stationary objects under these conditions.

Infants at both 16 and 8 weeks of age showed reliable preferences for the moving object when the object and observer movement were in opposite phase, whereas only 16-week-olds showed the preference when the object and observer moved in the same direction (Kellman et al., 1990; Kellman & Hofsten, 1992). It is not clear why detection of opposite motion was superior for the younger group. Subsequent tests indicated that motion preferences were eliminated under monocular viewing. These results suggest an early capacity for moving observers to perceive the motion and stability of objects. They also implicate binocular information as necessary for this achievement. In particular, the results point to binocular convergence as a source of absolute (egocentric) distance information early in life. Stereoscopic vision is ordinarily present in about half of 16-week-olds and virtually never in 8-week-olds (Held et al., 1980). Also, binocular disparity alone does not specify egocentric distance (Wallach & Zuckerman, 1963). In combination with some source of absolute distance, such as convergence, disparities can specify precise depth intervals (Wallach & Zuckerman, 1963). It is possible that the combination of convergence and disparity allows more precise determination of motion and stability at 16 weeks.

Early detection of motion during observer motion of object and observer motion is fascinating for several reasons. It indicates sophisticated integration of information in infant perception. The character of this integration may also be revealing. The evidence suggests that motion (or stability) perception depends not merely on certain stimulus variables but on perceived distance. The dependence of one perceptual outcome on another is consistent with computational views of perception. Specifically, it suggests multiple levels of representation and computations performed on them (Epstein, 1982; Hochberg, 1974; Marr, 1982).

1. The Bidirectional Geometry of Motion and Distance

The particular computations involving the geometry of motion and distance raise a paradoxical issue. Earlier we described the depth information called motion perspective. Optical changes given by stationary objects to a moving observer provide information about depth and distance. Extracting this information depends on the assumption that objects are stationary. Detecting whether an object is moving or not, when the observer moves, requires the same geometry with different known and unknown quantities. Here, optical changes and distance, given by some other information source, are used to determine whether the object is moving or stationary. The geometry of motion and distance can apparently be used in two ways: to extract distance assuming that the object is stationary or to extract target motion for a given object distance. An important challenge for both infant and adult vision research is to determine the conditions under which this geometry is used to determine motion from distance or distance from motion.

D. Summary: Motion Perception

During the early months of life, infants do not detect motion with the sensitivity matching that of adults. Infants' sensitivity is adequate, however, to detect all but the slowest motions of nearby people and objects, and infant attention is evoked by motion more readily than by any other stimulus dimension. Besides supporting detection of moving targets and their properties, such as direction and velocity, motion processing appears to be disproportionately involved in early perceptual competence. Motion-carried information about objects and space appears to be usable earlier than many other sources of information that operate in adult perception. Even complex interactions between motion and spatial perception, such as combining optical change and distance information to determine object stability or motion during observer motion, are part of the repertoire of infants in the early weeks of life.

IV. CONCLUSION

A. Beyond the Blooming, Buzzing Confusion

Research over the past three decades has radically restructured our ideas about the origins of space and motion perception. An old but durable view that infant development begins with sensory systems providing meaningless, disorganized sensations no longer seems reasonable. Human infants have a smaller perceptual repertoire than do adults, but infants perceive a 3-D spatial environment and events occurring within it. Of course, clear understanding of perception in the newborn is hampered by sensory immaturities and an extremely limited behavioral repertoire. Thus, a general view of the origins of perception must draw on inferences from patterns of behavior in a few observable response systems. Moreover, in many cases the inferences involve data from infants of several weeks or months of age.

The evidence allows us to rule out certain learning hypotheses (such as "touch educates vision" in acquiring 3-D visual perception), but the possibility that there are learning processes we have not imagined is harder to rule out. What is striking about research to date is that no evidence has emerged to support the traditional empiricist view of infants' initial state characterized by William James as a "blooming, buzzing confusion."

Changing the starting point of knowledge has important implications for theories of human cognitive development. Influential accounts of development (e.g., Piaget, 1954; Harris, 1983) and traditional views of perception agree that the infant's first task on the way to achieving knowledge is the interpretation and organization of sensory stimulation. One implication of infant perception research is that evolution may have done much of this work already. There is little evidence for a sensorimotor stage during which the young human being produces perceptions from sensations. Although early perceptual abilities will be refined and supplemented as time goes on, it appears that they are attuned to reality. Thus, the earliest tasks of cognitive development less likely involve constructing reality than learning about it. This changed view of the starting point of development has begun to be reflected in recent accounts of cognitive development (Fodor, 1983; Mandler, 1988; Spelke, Breinlinger, Macomber, & Jacobson, 1992).

B. Perceptual Development and Theories of Perception

Research on the origins of space and motion perception has implications for arguments about the general character of perception (Kellman, 1988). We have mentioned that the constructivist idea of perceptions built from sensations through learning is untenable as an overall picture of early perception. Many findings of early competence, and the importance of motion–carried information, confirm ecological views of perception's origins (E. J. Gibson, 1984; J. J. Gibson, 1966, 1979; Gibson & Gibson, 1955).

Regarding the *process* of perception, the evidence supports a hybrid of claims from inferential and direct theories. Some early abilities to use complex stimulus relationships are consistent with the idea that perception is a direct response of specialized mechanisms to relational variables (E. J. Gibson, 1984; J. J. Gibson, 1979). An example might be the use of accretion–deletion of texture to determine object boundaries and depth order. Yet other early-appearing perceptual abilities suggest less direct processes. The use of distance information in early size, shape, and motion perception, and use of the depth cue of familiar size, implicate processes in which some perceptual outcomes are computed from other perceptual dependent variables or prior representations (Epstein, 1982; Hochberg, 1974; Marr, 1982). A plausible, emerging view is that representations of space, objects, and events are derived from perceptual processes that are computational in character but different from the unconscious inferences that are based on learning described by Helmholtz (1867/1925) in the last century. Instead, perception achieves correspondence with reality because evolved perceptual mechanisms and processes embody constraints about the enduring physical and geometric properties of the world (Shepard, 1984; Johansson, 1970).

C. Kinematic Information and Ecological Foundations

Much of the research on early perception implicates a central role of motion or change information. This is true both attentionally, in that young perceivers attend preferentially to motion, and informationally, in that most or all of the main sources of information carried by motion appear to be useful early in life. The early dependence on kinematic information sources may reflect the more secure ecological foundations of these. Other information sources of high ecological validity, such as stereoscopic depth information, also appear in the first half year. The ambiguities Berkeley (1709/1910) noted in static retinal images involve exactly the information sources that are the last to appear in infants' visual perception. This late onset of perceptual cues involving static spatial relationships applies not only to depth cues but to related perceptual domains, such as object perception (Kellman & Spelke, 1983). Early perception may be "risk averse" in that it depends only on information sources of the highest ecological validity (Kellman, 1993).

D. Interdependence of Space and Motion

We have seen that motion and space are interrelated in early perception, as well as later. Two kinds of interrelations are significant. On one hand, as Gibson (1966, 1979) emphasized, properties of the persisting spatial layout can be given by information carried by motion or change. On the other hand, perception of motion depends in many cases on spatial (distance) information, most centrally in cases of observer motion. Despite the geometric complexity of some of these relationships, or perhaps because of them, there appear to be impressive early capacities to perceive accurately whether objects, the observer, or both are moving through space.

E. Developmental Change

Finally, evidence of early perceptual competence should not obscure the magnitude of developmental change. It is hard to name any perceptual domain in which the precision or speed of infants' information pick-up abilities is comparable to adults. As an example, even the lowest estimates of infant velocity thresholds appear to be an order of magnitude higher than adult velocity thresholds. Moreover, there are whole categories of information in spatial perception, such as pictorial depth information, that are not usable until the second half year of life. Perhaps even more significant are differences that are due to perceptual learning involving the skilled deployment of selective attention (Gibson, 1969). All of these differences imply profound differences in the perceptual worlds of adults and infants. Although some changes with age have been documented, not much is known about the causes of change. Advancing our understanding of mechanisms of perceptual change remains a high priority for future research.

References

Ames, A. (1951). Visual perception and the rotating trapezoidal window. *Psychological Monographs*, Series No. 324.

Andersen, G. J., & Cortese, J. M. (1989). 2-D contour perception resulting from kinetic occlusion. *Perception & Psychophysics, 46*, 49–55.

Arterberry, M. E., & Yonas, A. (1988). Infants' sensitivity to kinetic information for three-dimensional object shape. *Perception & Psychophysics, 44*, 1–6.

Arterberry, M., Yonas, A., & Bensen, A. S. (1989). Self-produced locomotion and the development of responsiveness to linear perspective and texture gradients. *Developmental Psychology, 25*(6), 976–982.

Aslin, R. N. (1977). Development of binocular fixation in human infants. *Journal of Experimental Child Psychology, 23*, 133–150.

Aslin, R. N. (1988). Perceptual development in infancy: The Minnesota symposia on child psychology, Vol. 20. Hillsdale, NJ: Erlbaum.

Aslin, R. N. (1981). Development of smooth pursuit in human infants. In D. F. Fisher, R. A. Monty, & J. W. Senders (Eds.), *Eye movements: Cognition and visual perception* (pp. 31–51). Hillsdale, NJ: Erlbaum.

Aslin, R. N., & Shea, S. L. (1990). Velocity thresholds in human infants: Implications for the perception of motion. *Developmental Psychology, 26*, 589–598.

Atkinson, J., & Braddick, O. (1976). Stereoscopic discrimination in infants. *Perception, 5*, 29–38.

Atkinson, J., & Braddick, O. J. (1981). Development of optokinetic nystagmus in young infants: An indicator of cortical binocularity? In D. F. Fisher, R. A. Monty, & J. W. Senders (Eds.) *Eye movements: Cognition and visual perception.* Hillsdale, NJ: Erlbaum.

Atkinson, J., Braddick, O., & Moar, K. (1977). Contrast sensitivity of the human infant for moving and static patterns. *Vision Research, 17*(9), 1045–1047.

Ball, W., & Tronick, E. (1971). Infant response to impending collision: Optical and real. *Science, 171*, 818–820.

Banks, M. S. (1980). The development of visual accommodation during early infancy. *Child Development, 51*, 646–666.

Banks, M. S., & Dannemiller, J. L. (1987). Infant visual psychophysics. In P. Salapetek & L. B. Cohen (Eds.), *Handbook of infant perception: From sensation to perception* (pp. 115–184). New York: Academic Press.

Banks, M. S., & Salapatek, P. (1983). Infant visual perception. In M. M. Haith & J. Campos (Eds.), *Infancy and biological development* (pp. 435–572). New York: Wiley.

Barten, S., Birns, B., & Ronch, J. (1971). Individual differences in the visual pursuit behavior of neonates. *Child Development, 42*, 313–319.

Berkeley, G. (1910). *Essay toward a new theory of vision.* London: Dutton. (Original work published 1709.)

Bertenthal, B. I., & Campos, J. J. (1990). A systems approach to the organizing effects of self-produced locomot during infancy. In C. Rovee-Collier (Ed.), *Advances in infancy research* (Vol. 6, pp. 1–60), Norwood, NJ: Ablex.

Birch, E. E., Gwiazda, J., & Held, R. (1982). Stereoacuity development for crossed and uncrossed disparities in human infants. *Vision Research, 22,* 507–513.

Bower, T. G. R., Broughton, J., & Moore, M. (1970). Infant responses to approaching objects: An indicator of response to distal variables. *Perception & Psychophysics, 9,* 193–196.

Braddick, O., Atkinson, J., French, J., & Howland, H. C. (1979). A photo refractive study of infant accommodation. *Vision Research, 19,* 1319–1330.

Bridger, W. H. (1961). Sensory habituation and discrimination in the human neonate. *American Journal of Psychiatry, 117,* 991–996.

Brookman, K. E. (1980). Ocular accommodation in human infants. Doctoral dissertation, Indiana University.

Caron, A. J., Caron, R. F., & Carlson, V. R. (1979). Infant perception of the invariant shape of objects varying in slant. *Child Development, 50,* 716–721.

Craton, L., & Yonas, A. (1988). Infants' sensitivity to boundary flow information for depth at an edge. *Child Development, 59,* 1522–1529.

Craton, L., & Yonas, A. (1990). Kinetic occlusion: Further studies of the boundary flow cue. *Perception & Psychophysics, 47,* 169–179.

Dannemiller, J. L., & Freedland, R. L. (1989). The detection of slow stimulus movement in 2- to 5-month-olds. *Journal of Experimental Child Psychology, 47,* 335–337.

Dannemiller, J. L., & Freedland, R. L. (1991). Speed discrimination in 20-week-old infants. *Infant Behavior and Development, 14,* 163–174.

Dayton, G. O., Jones, M. H., Steele, B., & Rose, M. (1964). Developmental study of coordinated eye movements in the human infant: II. An electrooculographic study of the fixation reflex in the newborn. *Archives of Ophthalmology, 71,* 871–875.

Epstein, W. (1982). Percept–percept couplings. *Perception, 11,* 75–83.

Fantz, R. L. (1958). Pattern vision in young infants. *Psychological Record, 8,* 43–47.

Fantz, R. L. (1964). Visual experience in infants: Decreased attention to familiar patterns relative to novel ones. *Science, 146,* 668–670.

Fantz, R. L., & Nevis, S. (1967). Pattern preferences and perceptual–cognitive development in early infancy. *Merrill-Palmer Quarterly, 13,* 77–108.

Field, T. (1990). *Infancy.* Cambridge, MA: Harvard University Press.

Fodor, J. A. (1983). *The modularity of mind: An essay on faculty psychology.* Cambridge, MA: MIT Press.

Fox, R., Aslin, R. N., Shea, S. L., & Dumais, S. T. (1980). Stereopsis in human infants. *Science, 207,* 323–324.

Freedland, R. L., & Dannemiller, J. L. (1987). Detection of stimulus motion in 5-month-old infants. *Journal of Experimental Psychology: Human Perception and Performance, 13,* 566–576.

Gibson, E. J. (1969). *Principles of perceptual learning and development.* New York: Appleton-Century-Crofts.

Gibson, E. J. (1984). Perceptual development from the ecological approach. In M. Lamb, A. Brown, & B. Rogoff (Eds.), *Advances in developmental psychology* (Vol. 3, pp. 243–285). Hillsdale, NJ: Erlbaum.

Gibson, E. J., & Walk, R. D. (1960). The "visual cliff." *Scientific American, 202,* 64–71.

Gibson, J. J. (1950). *The perception of the visual world.* Boston: Houghton Mifflin.

Gibson, J. J. (1966). *The senses considered as perceptual systems.* Boston: Houghton Mifflin.

Gibson, J. J. (1979). *The ecological approach to visual perception.* Boston: Houghton Mifflin.

Gibson, J. J., & Gibson, E. J. (1955). Perceptual learning: Differentiation or enrichment? *Psychological Review, 62,* 32–41.

Gibson, J. J., Kaplan, G. A., Reynolds, H. N., & Wheeler, K. (1969). The change from visible to invisible: A study of optical transitions. *Perception & Psychophysics, 5,* 113–116.

Gogel, W. C. (1977). The metric of visual space. In Epstein, W. (Ed.), *Stability and Constancy in visual perception* (pp. 129–181). New York: Wiley.

Gogel, W. C. (1980). The sensing of retinal motion. *Perception & Psychophysics, 28(2),* 155–163.

Gogel, W. C. (1982). Analysis of the perception of motion concomitant with a lateral motion of the head. *Perception & Psychophysics, 32(3),* 241–250.

Gogel, W. C., & Tietz, J. D. (1974). The effect of perceived distance on perceived movement. *Perception & Psychophysics, 16,* 70–78.

Gottschaldt, K. (1926). Uber den Einfluss der Erfahrung auf die Wahrnehmung von Figuren I. *Psych. Forsch. 8,* 261–317.

Granrud, C. E. (1987). Size constancy in newborn human infants. *Investigative Ophthalmology and Visual Science, 28* (Suppl.), 5.

Granrud, C. E., Haake, R. J., & Yonas, A. (1985). Infants' sensitivity to familiar size: The effect of memory on spatial perception. *Perception & Psychophysics, 37(5),* 459–466.

Granrud, C. E., & Yonas, A. (1984). Infants' perception of pictorially specified interposition. *Journal of Experimental Child Psychology, 37(3),* 500–511.

Granrud, C. E., Yonas, A., & Opland, E. A. (1985). Infants' sensitivity to the depth cue of shading. *Perception & Psychophysics, 37(5),* 415–419.

Granrud, C. E., Yonas, A., Smith, I. M., Arterberry, M. E., Glicksman, M. L., & Sorknes, A. (1984). Infants' sensitivity to accretion and deletion of texture as information for depth at an edge. *Child Development, 55,* 1630–1636.

Hainline, L., Riddell, P., Grose-Fifer, J., & Abramov, I. (1992). Development of accommodation and convergence in infancy. *Behavioral Brain Research, 49,* 33–50.

Haith, M. (1983). Spatially determined visual activity in early infancy. In A. Hein & M. Jeannerod (Eds.), *Spatially oriented behavior.* New York: Springer.

Harris, P. (1983). Infant cognition. In M. M. Haith & J. J. Campos (Eds.), *Cognitive development* (pp. 689–782). New York: Wiley.

Haynes, H., White, B. L., & Held, R. (1965). Visual accommodation in human infants. *Science, 148,* 528–530.

Held, R. (1985). Binocular vision—behavioral and neural development. In J. Mehler & R. Fox (Eds.), *Neonate cognition: Beyond the blooming, buzzing confusion.* Hillsdale, NJ: Erlbaum.

Held, R. (1988). Normal visual development and its deviations. In G. Lennerstrand, G. K. von Noorden and E. C. Campos (Eds.), *Strabismus and ambyopia* (pp. 247–257). NY: Plenum.

Held, R. (1993). What can rates of development tell us about underlying mechanisms? In G. Carl (Ed.), *Visual perception and cognition in infancy. Carnegie Mellon symposia on cognition,* (pp. 75–89). Hillsdale, NJ: Erlbaum.

Held, R., Birch, E. E., & Gwiazda, J. (1980). Stereoacuity in human infants. *Proceedings of the National Academy of Sciences of the USA, 77,* 5572–5574.

Held, R., & Hein, A. (1963). Movement-produced stimulation in the development of visually-guided behavior. *Journal of Comparative and Physiological Psychology, 56,* 872–876.

Helmholtz, H. von. (1925). *Handbook of physiological optics,* Vol. 3. J. P. S. Southall, Ed. and Trans.) New York: Dover. (Original work published 1867).

Hershberger, W. (1970). Attached-shadow orientation perceived as depth by chickens reared in an environment illuminated from below. Journal of Comparative & Physiological Psychology, 73(3), 407–411.

Hess, E. H. (1956). Space perception in the chick. *Scientific American, 195,* 71–80.

Hickey, T., & Peduzzi, J. (1987). Structure and development of the visual system. In P. Salapatek and L. Cohen (Eds.), *Handbook of infant perception,* Vol. I, pp. 1–42. New York: Academic Press.

Hochberg, J. (1971). Perception: Space and movement. In J. W. Kling & L. A. Riggs (Eds.), *Woodworth & Schlosberg's experimental psychology* (pp. 475–550). New York: Holt, Rinehart & Winston.

Hochberg, J. (1974). Higher-order stimuli and inter-response coupling in the perception of the visual world. In R. B. McLeod & H. Pick (Eds.), *Essays in honor of J. J. Gibson,* (pp. 17–39). Ithaca, NY: Cornell University Press.

Hofsten, C. von (1977). Binocular convergence as a determinant of reaching behavior in infancy. *Perception, 6,* 139–144.

Hofsten, C. von (1980). Predictive reaching for moving objects by human infants. *Journal of Experimental Child Psychology, 30(3),* 369–382.

Hofsten, C. von (1983). Catching skills in infancy. *Journal of Experimental Psychology: Human Perception and Performance, 9(1),* 75–85.

Hofsten, C. von, Kellman, P. J., & Putaansuu, J. (1992). Young infants' sensitivity to motion parallax. *Infant Behavior and Development, 15,* 245–264.

Hubel, D. H., & Wiesel, T. N. (1970). Cells sensitive to binocular depth in area 18 of the Macaque monkey striate cortex. *Nature, 225,* 41–42.

James, W. (1890). *The principles of psychology* (Vol. 2). New York: Holt.

Johansson, G. (1970). On theories for visual space perception. *Scandinavian Journal of Psychology, 11,* 67–74.

Kaplan, G. (1969). Kinetic disruption of optical texture: The perception of depth at an edge. *Perception & Psychophysics 6,* 193–198.

Kaufman, L. (1974). *Sight and mind.* New York: Oxford University Press.

Kaufmann, F., Stucki, M., & Kaufmann-Hayoz, R. (1985). Development of infants' sensitivity for slow and rapid motions. *Infant Behavior and Development, 10,* 1–10.

Kaufmann-Hayoz, R., Kaufmann, F., & Stucki, M. (1986). Kinetic contours in infants' visual perception. *Child Development, 57(2),* 292–299.

Kellman, P. J. (1984). Perception of three-dimensional form by human infants. *Perception & Psychophysics, 36(4).*

Kellman, P. J. (1988). Theories of perception and research in perceptual development. In Y. Albert (Ed.), *Perceptual development in infancy. The Minnesota symposia on child psychology, Vol. 20.,* (pp. 267–281). Hillsdale, NJ: Erlbaum.

Kellman, P. J. (1993). Kinematic foundations of perceptual development. In C. Granrud, (Ed.), *Visual perception and cognition in infancy* (pp. 121–193). Hillsdale, NJ: Erlbaum.

Kellman, P. J., Gleitman, H., & Spelke, E. (1987). Object and observer motion in the perception of objects by infants. *Journal of Experimental Psychology: Human Perception and Performance, 13,* 586–593.

Kellman, P. J., & Hofsten, C. von (1992). The world of the moving infant: Perception of objects, motion and space. In C. Rovee-Collier & L. Lipsitt (Eds.), *Advances in infancy research* (pp. 147–184). Norwood, NJ: Ablex.

Kellman, P. J., Hofsten, C. von, Condry, K., & O'Halloran, R. (1991). *Motion and stability in the world of the (moving) infant.* Unpublished manuscript.

Kellman, P. J., Hofsten, C. von, Vandewalle, G., & Condry, K. (1990, April). *Perception of motion and stability during observer motion by pre-stereoscopic infants.* Paper presented at the Seventh International Conference on Infant Studies, Montreal, Quebec, Canada.

Kellman, P. J., & Short, K. R. (1987a). Development of three-dimensional form perception. *Journal of Experimental Psychology: Human Perception and Performance, 13,* 545–557.

Kellman, P. J., & Short, K. R. (1987b, June). *Infant perception of partly occluded objects: The problem of rotation*. Paper presented at the Third International Conference on Event Perception and Action, Uppsala, Sweden.

Kellman, P. J., & Spelke, E. (1983). Perception of partly occluded objects in infancy. *Cognitive Psychology, 15,* 483–524.

Kellman, P. J., Spelke, E., & Short, K. R. (1986). Infant perception of object unity from translatory motion in depth and vertical translation. *Child Development, 57*(1), 72–86.

Kremenitzer, J. P., Vaughan, H. G., Kurtzberg, D., & Dowling, K. (1979). Smooth-pursuit eye movement in the newborn infant. *Child Development, 50*(2), 442–448.

Lee, D. (1974). Visual information during locomotion. In R. B. MacLeod & H. L. Pick (Eds.), *Perception: Essays in honor of J. J. Gibson* (pp. 250–267). Ithaca, NY: Cornell University Press.

Lee, D. N., Lishman, J. R., Roly, & Thomson, J. A. (1982). Regulation of gait in long jumping. *Journal of Experimental Psychology: Human Perception and Performance*.

Leibowitz, H., Shiina, K., & Hennessy, R. T. (1972). Oculomotor adjustments and size constancy. *Perception & Psychophysics, 12,* 497–500.

Mandler, J. (1988). How to build a baby: On the development of an accessible representational system. *Cognitive Development, 3,* 113–136.

Manny, R., & Klein, S. (1984). The development of vernier acuity in infants. *Current Eye Research, 3,* 453–462.

Marr, D. (1982). *Vision*. San Francisco: Freeman.

Nakayama, K., & Shimojo, S. (1992). Experiencing and perceiving visual surfaces. *Science, 257*(5075), 1357–1363.

Oross, S., Francis, E., Mauk, D., & Fox, R. (1987). The Ames window illusion: Perception of illusory motion by human infants. Special Issue: The Ontogenesis of perception. *Journal of Experimental Psychology: Human Perception & Performance, 13*(4), 609–613.

Petrig, B., Julesz, B., Kropfl, W., Baumgartner, G., & Anliker, M. (1981). Development of stereopsis and cortical binocularity in human infants: Electrophysiological evidence. *Science, 213,* 1402–1405.

Pettigrew, J. D. (1974). The effect of visual experience on the development of stimulus specificity by kitten cortical neurones. *Journal of Physiology, 237,* 49–74.

Piaget, J. (1954). *The construction of reality in the child*. New York: Basic Books.

Ramachandran, V. S., Clarke, P. G. H., & Whitteridge, D. (1977). Cells selective to binocular disparity in the cortex of newborn lambs. *Nature, 268,* 333–335.

Schiff, W. (1965). The perception of impending collision: A study of visually directed avoidant behavior. *Psychological Monographs, 79,* Whole No. 604.

Senden, M. von (1960). *Space and sight: The perception of space and shape in the congenitally blind before and after operations* (P. Heath, Trans.). London: Methuen.

Shepard, R. (1984). Ecological constraints on internal representation: Resonant kinematics of perceiving, imaging, thinking, and dreaming. *Psychological Review, 91,* 441–447.

Shimojo, S., Birch, E. E., Gwiazda, J., & Held, R. (1984). Development of verier acuity in infants. *Vision Research, 24*(7), 721–728.

Shipley, T. F., & Kellman, P. J. (1994). Spatiotemporal boundary formation: Boundary, form and motion perception from transformations of surface elements. *Journal of Experimental Psychology: General, 123*(1), 3–20.

Slater, A. M., & Findlay, J. M. (1975). Binocular fixation in the newborn baby. *Journal of Experimental Child Psychology, 20,* 248–273.

Slater, A., Kellman, P. J., Spelke, E., & Johnson, S. (1994). The role of three-dimensional depth cues in infants' perception of partly occluded objects. *Journal of Early Development and Parenting*.

Slater, A., Mattock, A., & Brown, E. (1990). Size constancy at birth: Newborn infants' responses to retinal and real size. *Journal of Experimental Child Psychology, 49*, 314–322.

Slater, A., & Morison, V. (1985). Shape constancy and slant perception and birth. *Perception, 12*, 707–718.

Slater, A., Morison, V., Somers, M., Mattock, A., Brown, E., & Taylor, D. (1990). Newborn and older infants' perception of partly occluded objects. *Infant Behavior and Development, 13*, 33–49.

Spelke, E. S., Breinlinger, K., Macomber, J., & Jacobson, K. (1992). Origins of knowledge. *Psychological Review, 99*(4), 605–632.

Timney, B. (1981). Development of binocular depth perception in kittens. *Investigative Ophthalmology and Visual Science, 21*, 493–496.

Volkmann, F. C., & Dobson, M. V. (1976). Infants responses of ocular fixation to moving visual stimuli. *Journal of Experimental Child Psychology, 22*, 86–89.

Wallach, H. (1985). Learned stimulation in space and motion perception. *American Psychologist, 40*, 399–404.

Wallach, H., & Floor, L. (1971). The use of size matching to demonstrate the effectiveness of accommodation and convergence as cues for distance. *Perception & Psychophysics, 10*, 423–428.

Wallach, H., & O'Leary, A. (1982). Slope of regard as a distance cue. *Perception & Psychophysics, 31*(2), 145–148.

Wallach, H., & Zuckerman, C. (1963). The constancy of stereoscopic depth. *American Journal of Psychology, 76*, 404–412.

Wattam-Bell, J. (1991). Development of motion-specific cortical responses in infancy. *Vision Research, 31*(2), 287–297.

Wattam-Bell, J. (1992). The development of maximum displacement limits for discrimination of motion direction in infancy. *Vision Research, 32*(4), 621–630.

Westheimer, G., & McKee, S. P. (1980). Stereoscopic acuity with defocused and spatially filtered retinal images. *Journal of the Optical Society of America, 70*, 772–778.

White, B., Castle, R., & Held, R. Observations on the development of visually directed reaching. *Child Development, 35*, 349–364.

Yonas, A. (1981). Infants' responses to optical information for collision. In R. N. Aslin, J. R. Alberts, & M. R. Peterson (Eds.), *Development of perception: Psychobiological perspectives: Vol. 2. The visual system* (pp. 313–334). New York: Academic Press.

Yonas, A., Arterberry, M. E., & Granrud, C. E. (1987). Space perception in infancy. In R. Vasta (Ed.), *Annals of child development* (pp. 1–34). Greenwich, CT: JAI Press.

Yonas, A., Bechtold, A. G., Frankel, D., Gordon, F. R., McRoberts, G., Norcia, A., & Sternfels, S. (1977). Development of sensitivity to information for impending collision. *Perception & Psychophysics, 21*, 97–104.

Yonas, A., Cleaves, W., & Pettersen, L. (1978). Development of sensitivity to pictorial depth. *Science, 200*, 77–79.

Yonas, A., & Granrud, C. E. (1984). The development of sensitivity to kinetic, binocular and pictorial depth information in human infants. In D. Ingle, D. Lee, & M. Jeannerod (Eds.), *Brain mechanisms and spatial vision*. Amsterdam: Nijhoff.

Yonas, A., & Granrud, C. E. (1985). Development of visual space perception in young infants. In J. Mehler & R. Fox (Eds.), *Neonate cognition: Beyond the blooming buzzing confusion*. Hillsdale, NJ: Erlbaum.

Yonas, A., Granrud, C. E., & Arterberry, M. E. (1987). Four-month-old infants' sensitivity to binocular and kinetic information for three-dimensional object shape. *Child Development, 58*, 910–917.

Yonas, A., Granrud, C. E., & Pettersen, L. (1982). Infants' sensitivity to relative size information for distance. *Developmental Psychology, 21*(1), 161–167.

Yonas, A., & Owsley, C. (1987). Development of visual space perception. In P. Salapetek & L. B. Cohen (Eds.), *Handbook of visual space perception.* New York: Academic Press.

Yonas, A., Pettersen, L., & Granrud, C. E. (1982). Infants' sensitivity to familiar size as information for distance. *Child Development, 53*(5), 1285–1290.

Yonas, A., Pettersen, L., & Lockman, J. (1979). Young infants' sensitivity to optical information for collision. *Canadian Journal of Psychology, 33,* 268–276.

CHAPTER 10

Auditory Spatial Layout

Frederic L. Wightman
Rick Jenison

I. INTRODUCTION

Everyday sights and sounds are typically described with reference to the environmental object that produced them and not to the physical pattern of stimulation at the sensory receptor. Thus, we say that we see a house rather than an array of points and edges and that we hear a bell rather than a complex of inharmonic partials. This object-oriented view of perception has come to be known as *object perception*. In the case of vision the physical features of environmental objects map directly to patterns of stimulation on the retina. Quite naturally, then, the study of visual object perception concentrates on revealing the details of further processing of the peripheral representation, on such issues as size and shape invariance under various transformations of the retinal image. In contrast, hearing offers no direct peripheral representation of environmental objects. All auditory sensory information is packaged in a pair of acoustical pressure waveforms, one at each ear. While there is obvious structure in these waveforms, that structure (temporal and spectral patterns) bears no simple relationship to the structure of the environmental objects that produced them. The properties of auditory objects and their layout in space must be derived completely from higher level processing of the peripheral input. Thus, many of the issues

Perception of Space and Motion

central to the study of auditory object perception are different from those involved in visual object perception.

The definition of what constitutes an auditory object is an issue of some controversy and considerable importance. Many acoustical waveforms evoke a mental reference to the source of the waveform. These are clearly auditory objects. We hear a church bell, for example, or ice tinkling in a glass. We hear the objects themselves and are generally unaware of the spectral and temporal structure of those waveforms. However, reference to an identifiable physical object may not be a necessary condition for auditory "objectness." As we mention later, waveforms made up of sequences of pure tones can also contain what most would agree are primitive auditory objects, even though no known physical object could have produced the sounds.

That the study of auditory object perception is immature is reflected in the fact that there are few empirical data on the important issues. Thus, while we can be precise here in our descriptions of the physical features of auditory stimuli and somewhat certain about the details of the peripheral encoding of those features, discussion of the higher level processing that subserves auditory object formation and segregation must be speculative. In the context of our discussion of the spatial layout of auditory objects, for example, we can and do review the substantial body of evidence on the factors that determine the apparent spatial positions of single, static sound sources. However, since there are relatively few data on the perception of moving sources and virtually no data on perception of the spatial relations among auditory objects, our treatment of these important issues is limited to an analysis of the potential sources of information and does not attempt to address in detail the questions related to how those sources of information may be utilized.

The chapter begins with a discussion of the peculiarities of acoustical stimuli and how they are received by the human auditory system. A distinction is made, following Gibson (1966), between the ambient sound field and the effective stimulus to differentiate the perceptual distinctions among various simple classes of sound sources (ambient field) from the known perceptual consequences of the linear transformations of the sound wave from source to receiver (effective stimulus). Next we deal briefly with the definition of an auditory object, specifically the question of how the various components of a sound stream become segregated into distinct auditory objects. The remainder of the chapter focuses on issues related to the spatial layout of auditory objects. Stationary objects are considered first. Since much of the material relevant to this subject has recently been reviewed elsewhere (e.g., Middlebrooks & Green, 1991; Wightman & Kistler, 1993), the section concentrates on topics not covered in those previous reports. The sources of information related to the apparent distance of an auditory object is one such topic. The spatial layout of moving auditory objects is discussed next, and in this context we offer a detailed treatment of the acoustics of moving sound sources. A distinction between source movement and observer movement is made to draw attention to the possible role of proprioceptive feedback in the perception of auditory spatial layout. The chapter concludes with a brief treatment of experimental evidence on the importance of input from other senses (vision, primarily) in establishing auditory spatial layout.

II. ACOUSTICAL INFORMATION: THE AMBIENT SOUND FIELD AND THE EFFECTIVE STIMULUS

As we use the term here, *information* is an abstract construct that serves as the bridge between an organism and its environment. It has a structure that is not related to the characteristics of either the transmitting medium or the receptor surface. For example, the "squareness" of a visual object is specified by information (e.g., relationships among visual patterns) that is not defined in terms of the physics of light or the anatomy and physiology of the retina. In the case of auditory objects, the mechanical events that produce them have lawful acoustical consequences in the sound patterns that are represented to the peripheral auditory system. If those patterns map in a one-to-one or many-to-one fashion onto the object properties, then they constitute information that potentially specifies those properties. In principle, then, for any physical property of an environmental object to be recoverable by an organism there must be information available to the perceiver that specifies that property.

The specific property of auditory objects that is of interest here is spatial layout. The information about auditory spatial layout is acoustically conveyed, and thus the stimulus that must be decoded by the perceiver to determine spatial layout is a sound wave. There is information about spatial layout contributed both by the specific type of sound wave that is generated and by the transformations that sound waves undergo in their passage from the source to our ears. This section of the chapter provides an overview of the broad classes of simple sound sources and the characteristics of the waves they produce (the ambient field), and also in this section there is a detailed discussion of the source-to-receiver transformations that convey information about the spatial layout of the sound sources (the effective stimulus).

A. The Ambient Sound Field

Waves in general are important means by which information about a physical event is conveyed to a perceiver. Discussion of wave generation and propagation is beyond the scope of this chapter since both are extraordinarily complex topics, especially in the case of naturally occurring physical events and natural environments. Simplifying assumptions are not only useful but mandatory for our purposes here. In the case of sound-producing events, a convenient assumption is that the sound is produced by a so-called *point* source, or acoustic monopole, and that the propagation equations are linear. Any small object vibrating in a mass of fluid (air) has all the attributes of an acoustic monopole, provided the dimensions of the object are small relative to the sound wavelengths produced and the sound field of interest is several object lengths away. The sound field produced by a monopole is omnidirectional, that is, the same in any direction equidistant from the source.

The sound fields produced by two or more simultaneously active monopoles can be assumed to combine linearly. Thus, an acoustic *dipole,* a very common type of sound source in nature, can be described as the superposition of two spatially separated monopole sources that are 180° out of phase. In contrast with monopole sources, which are omnidirectional, dipole sources have both magnitude and orientation. The structure of the dipole field can best be understood by considering the dipole in terms of its canceling monopoles. The field has an angular dependence with no sound at all produced at 90° to the dipole axis where the sound fields of the constituent monopoles exactly cancel.

The intensity of a sound wave (proportional to pressure squared per unit area) diminishes as the wave travels away from the source. Several factors are responsible for this. One that applies to all sound waves, including those proposed by monopoles and dipoles, is atmospheric absorption. Absorption is the result of nonadiabatic propagation caused by temperature differentials between compressions and rarefactions in the propagating wave and in air depends on temperature, humidity, and wavelength. The attenuation coefficient in air at 20°C with 50% humidity is approximately $1 \times 10^{-10} f^2 / \text{m}$, where f is frequency in Hz. For a monopole source, intensity also decreases with the inverse square of the distance from the source because the total acoustical power is spread out over the surface area of a sphere, the radius of which is the distance from the source. When considering both geometrical spreading and absorption, the intensity (I) of a monopolar source as a function of distance can be written

$$I(r) = \frac{P}{4\pi r^2} e^{-\alpha r},$$

where r is the distance from the sound source, P is the total power produced by the source, and α is the attenuation coefficient. Sometimes the term *attenuation length,* $1/\alpha$, is used to describe the distance over which the intensity decreases to $1/e$. At short distances the decrease in intensity with distance is dominated by spherical spreading, whereas at distances well beyond the attenuation length, absorption is dominant.

The intensity of the sound field produced by a dipole decreases somewhat differently with distance. For a dipole field it is simplest to discuss the decrease in pressure (proportional to the square root of intensity). The equation governing the pressure decrease is complicated, but its essential elements are a magnitude and a direction component. The magnitude part has two terms: one decreasing with the inverse square of distance, and the other linearly. The inverse square dependence dominates the field near the source, and the linear component dominates at large distances.

The characteristics of sound radiation, whether modeled as a monopole or as a dipole, may contribute significant information to aid source identification and to determine spatial layout. As described above, monopoles radiate sound evenly in all directions, but dipoles have a figure–eight directivity pattern. While the compression and rarefaction components cancel in a plane perpendicular to the dipole axis, a pressure gradient does exist in the field near the source that may be useful for tracking a sound source. An example of a dipole source that we are particularly interested in tracking is a flying insect near our ear. There are also more complex sources in nature that can be modeled as the sum of several constituent dipoles.

B. The Effective Stimulus

For our purposes here the effective stimulus is defined in terms of the acoustical pressure waveforms produced by an ambient sound field as they exist just before transduction at the listener's eardrums. For simplicity we assume that the ambient field is produced by one or more acoustical monopoles. The relationship between the ambient field and the effective stimulus is defined by a series of linear transformations of the acoustical waveform that incorporate a number of potential sources of information about the spatial layout of sound sources in the environment. In this section of the chapter we identify the relevant transformations and describe the spatial information that each incorporates. In a later section we examine in detail the evidence on whether the information is perceptually relevant.

The acoustics of the local environment that includes the source and the listener contribute several potentially important sources of information about spatial layout. For example, because of the long wavelengths and slow propagation velocity of sound, the reflections and diffractions of an emitted sound wave off the walls, floor, ceiling, and contents of a typical room enrich the ambient sound field considerably. There is information about the size of the room in the timing of the reflections, information about the wall coverings and contents in the pattern of reverberation, and information about the distance between source and listener in the ratio of direct to reflected sound. If long distances are involved, such as in large rooms or in open spaces, the high-frequency content of the effective stimulus is reduced by atmospheric absorption. There is ample evidence that all of these effects are detectable by a normal-hearing listener.

The listener's shoulders, head, and outer ear structures (especially the pinnae) are significant components of the local acoustical environment and as such contribute additional information relevant to auditory spatial layout. The pattern of reflections and diffractions of an incident sound wave off these structures is heavily dependent on the direction from which the sound arrives, and thus, the information contributed by these effects relates primarily to the direction of auditory objects. The pinnae, in particular, are highly directional, modifying incident sound waves in ways that are specific to each different angle of incidence. As in the case of room effects, there is ample evidence of the detectability of pinna effects.

The fact that we have two ears separated by an acoustically opaque head suggests that information about auditory spatial layout may come from three sources: the effective stimulus at the left ear, the effective stimulus at the right ear, and the difference. These are clearly not independent sources of information. However, there are reasons to believe that all are important. Information from the difference signal, for example, is uniquely independent of the characteristics of the source, and because of the insensitivity of the auditory system to the absolute timing of events, this is the only source of information on the direction-dependent difference in the time-of-arrival of an acoustic waveform. Because of the approximate lateral symmetry of the head, interaural difference information is ambiguous. Interaural time difference, for example, is the same for sources in the front and sources in comparable positions (on the same side of the head, and at the same angles relative to the interaural axis) in the rear. Information from each of the individual ears can potentially resolve these ambiguities.

The information relevant to auditory spatial layout that is contained in the effective stimuli at the two ears can be described as either temporal or spectral patterns. At a formal mathematical level the two descriptions are isomorphic, so one might think the choice is arbitrary. However, when higher level processing of the information is considered, the distinction becomes important because temporal and spectral processing mechanisms in the auditory system are thought to be so different. For this reason, we discuss temporal and spectral separately. Because of the auditory system's relative insensitivity to monaural phase (the phase spectrum of a stimulus at one ear), our discussion of temporal information concentrates on interaural time differences and the temporal patterns of room reflections. Interaural phase, defined as the difference between the phase spectra of the left and right ear stimuli, is relevant only when considering single-frequency components of a stimulus. Our discussion of the spectral information in effective auditory stimuli focuses on the direction-dependent changes in the magnitude components of the complex source-to-eardrum transformation.

III. AUDITORY OBJECTS

It seems obvious that before any discussion of the rules that govern the spatial layout of auditory objects, we should know what an auditory object is. Unfortunately, there is little consensus on what might constitute a satisfactory definition of an auditory object nor on what alternative terms might be better. One alternative that has been proposed is *sound event* (Blauert, 1983), but this term seems to refer more directly to a disturbance of the ambient sound field than to any aspect of the perception of that disturbance. Another alternative is *sound stream* (Bregman, 1990), but this term does not convey the obviously close association between everyday auditory stimuli and the environmental objects that produced them. The term *auditory object* is borrowed from the field of visual perception in which the features of environmental objects map directly to features of the effective stimulus, a pattern of light on the retina. Its use in auditory perception is less satisfying since there is no straightforward mapping of object features to stimulus features. Nevertheless, the fact that auditory percepts in daily life are so naturally and immediately associated with the objects that produced the sounds is undeniable and gives currency, if not clarity, to the term *auditory object*.

The effective stimulus at each ear consists of a one-dimensional acoustical pressure waveform. This waveform contains the superposition of the acoustic outputs from all of the objects in the listener's environment. A complete understanding of what constitutes an auditory object would therefore include specification of the rules, whereby the various components of the single-pressure waveform are segregated into discrete auditory objects. These rules are the object of considerable current interest in the auditory research community (e.g., Bregman, 1990; Handel, 1989), and it is not our purpose to summarize them here. Rather, we focus on the contributions to this segregation process offered by spatial separation. For the purposes of our discussion, it may be helpful to distinguish between two kinds of auditory objects: *concrete* and *abstract*. Concrete auditory objects are formed by sounds emitted by real objects in the environment. Although experimental data are scarce, segregation of concrete objects seems to be primarily determined by spatial and temporal rules. Abstract auditory objects do not often correspond to real environmental objects. They consist typically of more primitive sound elements and are formed by simpler frequency and temporal relations. There has been considerable research on the rules governing the formation of abstract auditory objects (e.g., Bregman, 1990). We concentrate here exclusively on concrete auditory objects.

IV. SPATIAL LAYOUT OF STATIONARY AUDITORY OBJECTS

Much of the experimental literature on auditory spatial layout concerns the accuracy with which the spatial position of a sound-producing object is indicated to a listener, that is, the degree of correspondence between the actual position of the object and its apparent position. It is our view that experiments that focus on accuracy can fail to consider other important features of the auditory percept. For example, consider experiments on monaural listening. The results generally show that the apparent positions of auditory objects are strongly biased toward the interaural axis and the side of the functioning ear. However, those same results are often reported as indicating that monaural localization accuracy is near normal on the side of the functioning ear and progressively poorer off the interaural axis on that side. The emphasis on accuracy obscures the fact that in monaural listening all of the sounds appear to emanate from one place. For reasons such as this, we prefer to ignore the accuracy component of spatial layout altogether, and we discuss only the factors that govern the apparent spatial positions of auditory objects.

The apparent spatial position of an auditory object is defined by its apparent direction and its apparent distance relative to the listener. The potential sources of information for apparent direction and the stimulus features that appear to govern apparent direction have extensively and recently been discussed elsewhere (Middlebrooks & Green, 1991; Wightman & Kistler, 1993). Therefore, the material on apparent direction is only summarized here. Much less attention has been paid to apparent distance, and although data are scarce, they are covered in some detail in this chapter.

A. Acoustical Sources of Information about Static Spatial Layout

The spatial position of each sound-producing object in a listener's environment is specified by several acoustical sources of information that for brevity we call *cues*. Many of the cues are a result of the interactions of the sound waves with the listener's head and pinnae. These interactions are conveniently summarized by a linear transformation, the so-called *head-related transfer function* (HRTF), which represents the changes in the amplitude and phase of the sound wave from the sounding object's position to the listener's eardrum. Mathematically, HRTFs are usually specified in terms of the sound wave's spectrum. Thus, if $X(j\omega)$ is the source spectrum (j is the complex operator and ω is angular frequency) and $Y(jω)$ is the spectrum of the waveform at the eardrum, then the HRTF, $H(jω)$, is given by

$$H(jw) = \frac{Y(jw)}{X(jw)}. \tag{1}$$

More generally, since the HRTF varies with source direction and distance and thus is different at each ear, we must write two equations for $H(jω)$: one for the left ear and one for the right ear. Each depends on source azimuth (θ), elevation (φ), and distance (d) relative to the listener:

$$H_l(\theta, \phi, d, j\omega) = \frac{Y_l(\theta, \phi, d, j\omega)}{X(j\omega)} \tag{2}$$

and

$$H_r(\theta, \phi, d, j\omega) = \frac{Y_r(\theta, \phi, d, j\omega)}{X(j\omega)}. \tag{3}$$

All of the information about sound source position are represented in the pair of HRTFs shown above. These HRTFs vary in complicated ways with changes in source position, so simplifying assumptions must be made to appreciate the essential elements. Two convenient assumptions are that the acoustical space enclosing the source and listener is anechoic and that the listener's head is spherical with pinna–less ears at opposite ends of a diameter of the sphere. The anechoic assumption allows the main effect of distance to be modeled as a simple attenuation of 6 dB for every doubling of distance from the source. The spherical head assumption leads to a greatly simplified account of the effects of diffraction of the sound wave around the head. Figure 1 illustrates the latter point. When ignoring the details for a moment (the spherical model is described in detail in Kuhn, 1977), we see that at each ear variations in source azimuth (or elevation, not shown in the figure) can be expected to produce mainly variations in effective stimulus intensity, a result of the *head shadow* effect when the source is on the opposite side of the head from the ear under consideration. The head shadow effect can be expected to be much larger at high frequencies than at low frequencies. This is because at low frequencies sound wavelengths would be long with respect to the dimensions of the head, and thus the sound waves would travel around the head without attenuation. The covariation of stimulus intensity with azimuth (and elevation) that occurs at each ear individually can be viewed as a potential *monaural cue* to sound source position. Figure 1 also illustrates the potential *binaural cues* to sound source position that are offered by interaural differences (defined by the ratio of the two HRTFs). Note that for all source azimuths other than 0° and 180°, the acoustical path from

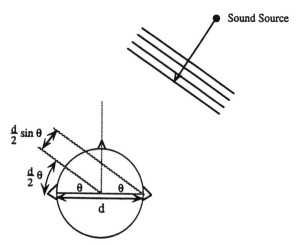

FIGURE 1   Schematic top-down representation of a listener and a sound source. The source is assumed to be sufficiently far from the listener such that the acoustical wavefronts are planar, and the listener is assumed to have a spherical head with ears at opposite ends of a diameter.

source to ear has a different length for the two ears. This path-length difference produces a small difference in the time of arrival of the sound wave at the two ears. The interaural time difference (ITD) varies systematically with source azimuth and is largest for azimuths of $+90°$ and $-90°$. In addition, because of the head shadow effect mentioned earlier, there will be an interaural level difference (ILD) that varies with azimuth in roughly the same way as ITD and is large at high frequencies and small at low frequencies.

The utility of monaural cues is compromised by the fact that some or all features of the sound source waveform must be known for the cue to be unambiguous. In the simple spherical head case described above, while stimulus intensity at a given ear varies systematically with source azimuth, a listener with access only to the effective stimulus at that ear would have no way of knowing whether a weak stimulus was produced by a source on the opposite side of the head or by a weak source. In more general terms, note that (from Equation 3) the effective stimulus at one ear, say the right ear, is defined by the product of the source spectrum and the HRTF:

$$Y_r(\theta,\phi,d,j\omega) = X(j\omega)H_r(\theta,\phi,d,j\omega). \tag{4}$$

Thus, even if a listener had perfect memory for the HRTF at each and every possible source position, a given effective stimulus could unambiguously indicate a specific source position only if the source spectrum were known.

Binaural cues to source position are derived from the ratio of the transduced representations of the two effective stimuli. Thus, the utility of these cues does not require knowledge of the source spectrum since that term appears in both numerator and denominator and hence cancels. Nevertheless, to the extent that the spherical head model is accurate, binaural cues are also ambiguous. Note, as shown in Figure 1, that the difference in acoustical path length from the source to the two ears, which gives rise to the ITD, is the same for sources in front and in the rear. A source at an azimuth of 30°, for example, would produce the same ITD as a source at 150° azimuth. The same could be said for ILDs and for sources at complementary positions above and below the horizontal plane. In fact, the spherical head model predicts conical surfaces projecting outward from the ears along which ITD and ILD are constant and thus along which cues that are based on ITD and ILD would be ambiguous. These are the so-called *cones of confusion*. We should mention here that cone-of-confusion ambiguities could be resolved by head movements, as Wallach (1940) pointed out in his now-classic treatise on the issue. If a listener knew both the direction of movement of the head and the direction of change of the ITD or ILD cue, the direction of the sound source could be derived without ambiguity.

Detailed measurements of human HRTFs (Middlebrooks & Green, 1990; Middlebrooks, Makous, & Green, 1989; Pralong & Carlile, 1994; Shaw, 1974; Wightman & Kistler, 1989a) provide a complete catalog of the potential acoustical cues to apparent sound position and highlight the limitations of the spherical head model. The most prominent features of HRTFs not anticipated by the spherical head model are the directional filtering characteristics of the pinnae and the large listener-to-listener differences in HRTFs. The multiple ridges and cavities of the pinna produce resonant peaks and antiresonant notches in the magnitude response of the HRTF. The frequencies at which these peaks and notches appear are dependent on sound source direction and thus could serve as potential spatial position cues, provided some a priori information about the source was available. Figure 2 shows an example of how the frequency of a given notch in the HRTF changes with sound source elevation. HRTFs from two listeners are shown in this figure to illustrate individual differences. Note that while the general characteristics of the notches are the same from listener to listener, the frequencies at which the notches appear are highly listener dependent.

The spherical head model provides a reasonably accurate prediction of the ITDs derived from actual HRTF measurements. Figure 3 shows ITDs from the horizontal plane HRTFs of a representative listener estimated by Wightman and Kistler (1989a). Also plotted in the figure are the ITDs predicted by

$$\text{ITD} = \frac{d}{2c} (\theta + \sin\theta), \qquad (5)$$

where θ is the azimuth angle as in Figure 1, c is the velocity of the sound wave (cm/s), and d is the interaural distance (cm), chosen for this example to fit the HRTF data shown. While this equation is usually cited as repre-

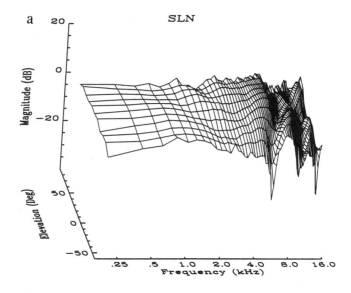

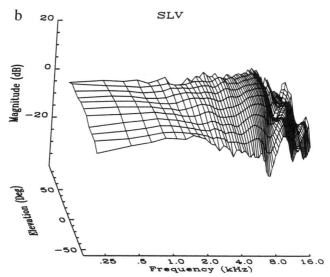

FIGURE 2   Directional transfer functions from two listeners produced by a source at 90° azimuth. Directional transfer functions (DTFs) are head-related transfer functions (HRTFs) divided by the root-mean-square average of the HRTFs from all spatial positions measured. Thus, the DTFs represent the deviation in dB from the average response of the ear. (Adapted with permission from Wightman and Kistler, 1993.)

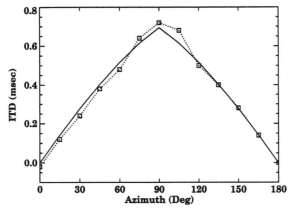

FIGURE 3   Interaural time differences (ITDs), produced by a source at 0° elevation, predicted by the spherical head model (solid line) and measured from a typical listener by using a wideband correlation technique. (Reproduced with permission from Wightman and Kistler, 1993.)

senting the predictions of the spherical head model (e.g., Green, 1976; Woodworth, 1938), it is really just a first-order approximation (Kuhn, 1977). Nevertheless, as Figure 3 shows, it provides an accurate representation of horizontal plane ITDs. Figure 4 (from Wightman & Kistler, 1993) shows a more complete set of ITD data from the same listener. This figure also shows the contours of constant ITD, which for the spherical head model would be circular. Clearly, the spherical head model provides a good first-order approximation to measured ITDs. Just as clearly, ITD is an ambiguous cue to sound source direction since any given ITD signals not one but a whole locus of potential directions.

Interaural level differences derived from HRTF measurements are complicated functions of frequency at each and every source direction, a situation caused at least in part by pinna filtering effects. Figure 5 shows ILD functions derived from a single listener's HRTF measurements at a source elevation of 0 and azimuths of 0° and 90°. Note that even for a source on the median plane (0° azimuth), where ILDs would result only from interaural asymmetries, ILDs are large enough (greater than 0.5 dB, the ILD threshold) to be considered potential sources of information about source position. For a source at 90° ILDs are generally much larger, especially at high frequencies as would be expected because of head shadowing.

The elaborate frequency dependence of ILDs complicates our discussion of them as potential cues to sound source position. We can discuss the interaural level cue either as an *interaural spectral difference,* referring to the entire pattern of ILDs across frequency, or as ILD averaged across one or more frequency bands. Figure 6 illustrates the latter approach. In the upper

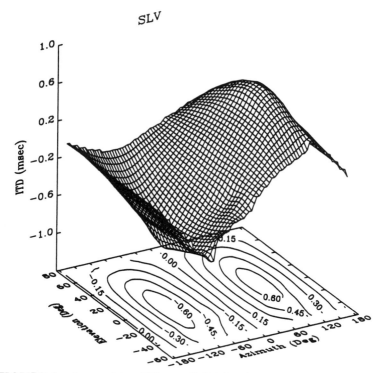

FIGURE 4   Interaural time differences (ITDs) from head-related transfer function (HRTF) measurements from a typical listener plotted as a function of the azimuth and elevation of the sound source. Note the contours of constant ITD below the surface plot. (Adapted with permission from Wightman and Kistler, 1993.)

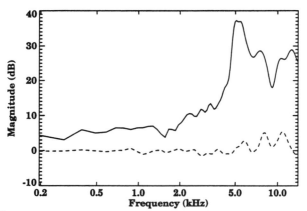

FIGURE 5   Interaural level difference (ILD) as a function of frequency from a typical listener, produced by a source at 0° elevation and 0° azimuth (dashed line) or 90° azimuth (solid line).

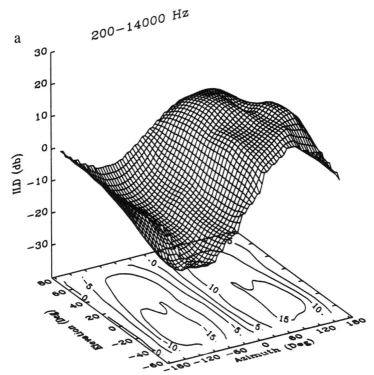

FIGURE 6   Interaural level difference (ILDs) from a typical listener in different frequency regions. Figure 6a shows ILDs across the entire frequency spectrum, and Figures 6b and 6c show ILD in two high-frequency critical bands. (Adapted with permission from Wightman and Kistler, 1993.)

panel we show one extreme, ILD averaged across the entire frequency spectrum. The bottom panels illustrate the other extreme, ILDs in two high-frequency critical bands. Note that the general pattern of ILD as a function of sound source direction is the same regardless of the bandwidth over which ILD is considered or the center frequency of the band. Note also that the general pattern of ILDs is the same as the pattern of ITDs, showing a similar kind of cone-of-confusion ambiguity. Thus, unless a listener could analyze the idiosyncratic details of ILD patterns in narrow bands, ILD information could not be used to disambiguate errors resulting from dependence on ITDs, and vice versa. As mentioned above, information provided by head movements can, in theory, offer such disambiguation.

The acoustical sources of information about the distance of a sound-producing object are not well understood. Nor have they been well documented by systematic measurements. In an anechoic environment, the two most obvious stimulus features that depend on distance are overall level and

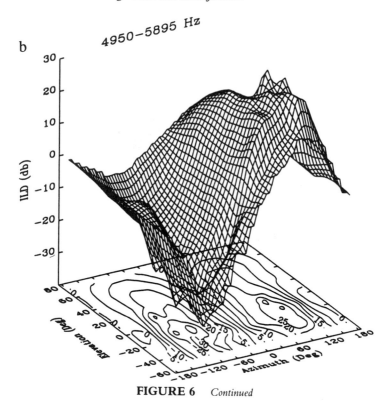

FIGURE 6   *Continued*

spectral content. Overall level decreases by 6 dB for every doubling of the distance between the source and the listener (the inverse square law), and atmospheric absorption gradually attenuates the high-frequency components of a sound as the distance between source and listener is increased (about 2 dB/100 ft at 6 kHz and 4 dB/100 ft at 10 kHz). The utility of both of these monaural cues, of course, depends on knowledge of source characteristics. However, the requirement for a priori knowledge about the source can be eliminated if the perceiver is allowed two or more "looks" at the stimulus from different vantage points. For example, Lambert (1974) pointed out that just two looks at stimulus intensity, as might be obtained if the perceiver's head were rotated, would provide sufficient information for a determination of source distance, without the need for knowledge of source characteristics.

There are two potential binaural distance cues: ITD and ILD; both vary slightly with the distance between source and listener (Coleman, 1963). In the case of ITD, for a source at 90° azimuth, there can be as much as a 150 μs difference in the ITD produced by a near source and a far source. A near source produces a larger ITD than a far source. This change in ITD with

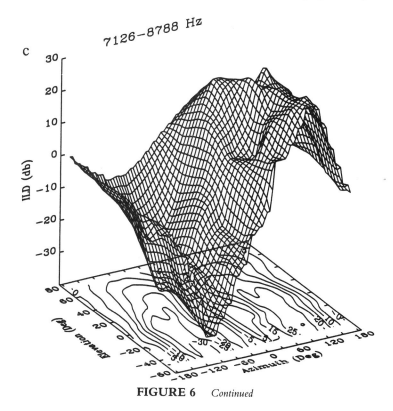

7126–8788 Hz

FIGURE 6 *Continued*

distance occurs because with a source close to the head the extra distance around the head is greater than if the source were far from the head. Distance affects ILDs in a comparable way, although in this case the effect is highly frequency dependent. At low frequencies the distance effect is greatest. For a 300-Hz tone at 90° azimuth, for example, the ILD for a source far from the head (several wavelengths) is about 0.5 dB, but for a source at 44 cm it is over 10 dB. The effects at higher frequencies and at source azimuths off the interaural axis are considerably smaller.

   In a nonanechoic environment, which of course includes nearly all everyday listening situations, there is an additional distance cue provided by the mix of the direct sound wave from source to listener with the reflections of that sound wave off the surfaces of the listening room. When the sound source is close to the head the direct sound dominates since because of the extra distance traveled and absorption at the surfaces, the level of the reflected sound is always lower. However, as the source-to-listener distance increases, the direct sound level decreases, and the ratio of direct to reflected sound level decreases. Given a specific enclosure, then, this ratio is perfectly correlated with source-to-listener distance. Moreover, even though it is a monaural cue, its validity does not depend on a priori knowledge of stimulus characteristics.

B. Acoustical Determinants of Apparent Spatial Position

Our purpose in this section is to review what is currently known about how the acoustical information about the spatial position of stationary sources is actually used. Most of the experiments in this area have considered apparent source direction and apparent distance separately, and for convenience we maintain this separation here. Several comprehensive reviews of this area have appeared recently (Middlebrooks & Green, 1991; Wightman & Kistler, 1993), so the material is only summarized here.

In the vast majority of experiments on the apparent spatial position of stationary auditory objects, only apparent direction (azimuth and elevation) has been considered. Until recently, the dominant theoretical position, epitomized by the duplex theory (Strutt, 1907), was that ITD provided the dominant source of information about apparent direction at low frequencies and that ILD was dominant at high frequencies. The duplex theory derived from the facts that the auditory system was much less sensitive to ITDs at high frequencies than at low frequencies (Joris & Yin, 1992; Yin & Chan, 1988) and from the fact that ILDs are much larger at high frequencies than at low frequencies (see Figure 5). Information provided by pinna filtering was not considered in the duplex theory.

Few empirical data on apparent source direction contradict the duplex theory. However, there are many natural circumstances that reveal the limitations of the theory and that argue for a situation-dependent weighting of the various sources of information about apparent sound direction. Localization of narrowband sounds is one such circumstance. Most narrowband sounds offer conflicting cues to apparent direction, so it is not surprising that they are not often localized accurately. The extreme case of a narrowband sound is sinusoid. Sinusoids offer doubly ambiguous ITD cues. A 1000-Hz sinusoid, for example, could provide a 400-μs ITD leading to the right ear while at the same time indicating a 600-μs ITD leading to the left ear. As Figure 4 shows, each ITD signals a whole range of potential source directions. It should not be surprising that unless a sinusoid has a broadband transient associated with onset or offset, its apparent position is unclear (Hartmann, 1983). Other narrowband sounds are somewhat less ambiguous but still inaccurately localized. The apparent azimuth of a high-frequency noise band is given by ILD, as suggested by the duplex theory (Middlebrooks, 1992). However, the apparent elevation seems to be determined by a learned association between spatial position and the spectral peaks and valleys produced by pinna filtering (Middlebrooks, 1992). The resultant apparent direction is often far removed from the actual source direction and well off the contour of directions indicated by ILD alone. In this case and others (e.g., monaural localization, as described by Butler, Humanski, & Musicant, 1990), the learned association between spatial position and pinna filtering details appears to be a favored source of information about apparent sound direction. In general, the data suggest that in the absence of unambiguous (i.e., wideband) ITD, the information provided by pinna filtering appears to dominate.

If a wideband source contains both low and high frequencies, apparent direction seems to be governed primarily by ITD (Wightman & Kistler, 1992). In the Wightman and Kistler experiments, free-field noise sources were synthesized by using algorithms that were based on listeners' own HRTFs. The *virtual sources* were then presented by means of headphones, affording complete control over the acoustical stimulus. When the ITD information was manipulated to signal one direction and all other cues were left to signal another direction, the listeners' judgments of apparent direction always followed the ITD cue. Thus, even in the presence of opposing ILDs of as much as 20 dB, ITD was dominant. The dominance of ITD occurred for all listeners so long as the stimuli contained energy below about 1500 Hz. When the low frequencies were filtered out, ITD was effectively ignored and judgments of apparent position followed the ILDs and pinna filtering cues.

The importance of the ITD cue is further emphasized by the fact that listeners' make frequent front–back confusions in certain conditions (Oldfield & Parker, 1984a, 1984b; Stevens & Newman, 1936; Wenzel, Arruda, Kistler, & Wightman, 1993; Wightman & Kistler, 1989b). Recall that if apparent direction were governed by ITD, front–back confusions would be expected given the spherical symmetry of the head (Figure 4). While the rate of front–back confusions in everyday life is unknown, with laboratory stimuli and especially virtual source stimuli, front–back confusion rates can be as great as 25% (Oldfield & Parker, 1984a, 1984b; Wightman & Kistler, 1989b). Contours of constant ITD from actual measurements are smooth and regular, as predicted by the symmetry argument, though slightly different for different listeners (Wightman & Kistler, 1993). Contours of constant ILD, on the other hand, are quite irregular and variable from one frequency band to another (Figure 6). We suggest that the fact that listeners make consistent and frequent front–back confusions argues at least indirectly for the dominance of ITD cues and the lesser importance of ILD and pinna filtering cues.

The relative salience of the various acoustical cues to the spatial layout of auditory objects also depends on the "realism" of the cues. In experiments with virtual sources similar to those described above in which ITD was in conflict with other cues (Wightman & Kistler, 1992), we have produced stimuli in which cues in one frequency region conflict with cues in another frequency region. In one condition, for example, the ILD and spectral cues were the same throughout the frequency range (200 Hz–14000 Hz) and signaled, or "pointed to," one of five possible directions on the horizontal plane. The ITD cue in each of four bands (roughly 1.5 octaves wide) pointed to a different direction. Thus, the ITD cue could be said to be "inconsistent" across the frequency range, and the other cues could be said to be "consistent." In other conditions, the ITD cue was consistent and the other cues were inconsistent, and in still other conditions, the frequency range was divided somewhat differently. The results were unambiguous. Listeners' judgments always followed the consistent cue. Even if the ITD cue was inconsistent in a single high-frequency band (above 5 kHz) listeners appeared to ignore ITD and put maximum weight on the ILD and spectral cues that were consistent across the spectrum. Not only does this result suggest that high-frequency ITD cues are encoded as well as low-frequency ITD cues, but it also suggests that cues that are realistic are given greater weight than unrealistic cues. With real sources and real listening environments, it is highly unlikely that either the ITD or the other cues could be inconsistent across the frequency spectrum.

The fidelity of the ITD, ILD, and spectral cues to spatial position is compromised in most natural listening situations by the presence of echoes. These echoes, which to a first approximation are filtered copies of the sound wave, are produced when a sound wave bounces off objects or surfaces in the environment and because of the extra distance they have to travel they reach the listener slightly later than the original or direct sound wave. Typically, the intensities of the echoes are considerably weaker than the intensity of the direct sound, both because of the additional path length and because most objects and surfaces absorb some of the sound energy, particularly at high frequencies. Nevertheless, when the echoes combine with the direct sound, the acoustical cues that signal the spatial position of the sound source are disrupted. With echoes the effective stimulus at each ear consists of the superposition of sounds from a number of different directions. Thus, both the monaural and binaural cues are distorted.

It might be expected that the presence of echoes would seriously impair a listener's ability to determine the spatial layout of sound sources. In fact, in all but the most extreme cases, the echoes are hardly noticed, and localization performance is not impaired (Begault, 1992; Hartmann, 1983). The substantial body of empirical data on this phenomenon can be summarized in the hypothesis that listeners attend only to the first few milliseconds of a stimulus, the time before echoes arrive, to determine the spatial position of a source. The spatial information arriving later, which would be corrupted by echoes, is somehow suppressed. This is the well-known *precedence effect* (Clifton & Freyman, 1989; Wallach, Newman, & Rosenzweig, 1949; Zurek,

1980). Although many of the characteristics of the phenomenon and most of the underlying mechanisms are not well understood, it is clear that the precedence effect is of central importance to the determination of auditory spatial layout in natural listening situations.

Compared with our well-developed understanding of how various sources of acoustical information are combined to determine the apparent direction of auditory objects, relatively little is known about how listeners might form a judgment of apparent distance. Available evidence suggests that perception of auditory distance is not well developed in humans. Apparent distance is typically very different than real distance (e.g., Gardner, 1968; Mershon & King, 1975), and only relative distance can be determined with any accuracy (Cochran, Throop, & Simpson, 1968; Holt & Thurlow, 1969). While there are suggestions in the literature that the distances of familiar sounds are judged more accurately (Coleman, 1962; McGregor, Horn, & Todd, 1985), the classic demonstration by Gardner (1968) shows that in an anechoic room with levels equalized, even the apparent distance of speech is not accurately reported. The most reliable finding seems to be that sounds presented with reverberation are judged to be more distance than the same sounds presented without reverberation (e.g., Mershon & King, 1975).

From several different perspectives inaccuracies in judging the distance of an auditory object are not surprising. First, the primary acoustical correlates of distance, level, and spectrum are unambiguous only if the characteristics of the source are known. Second, in everyday life the absolute distance of an auditory object carries little significance. Direction is clearly much more important, it serves to orient our gaze. Of course, if an auditory object is moving, and especially if that movement is toward the listener, distance carries considerable significance. Experiments on estimation of distance of a moving auditory object typically ask listeners to judge the time at which the object will reach to listener's position, this is called *time-to-contact*. The available data on listeners' judgments of auditory time-to-contact is reviewed in a later section of this chapter.

V. SPATIAL LAYOUT OF DYNAMIC AUDITORY OBJECTS

In everyday life an individual's auditory world is constantly in motion. The orientations of sound-producing objects with respect to a listener's head and ears are ever changing, either because the objects themselves are moving or because the listener's head is moving. In either case, the result is a constantly changing pattern of directional cues at the ears and, if conditions are right, the introduction of additional cues to movement such as the Doppler shift. This section of the chapter describes those additional movement cues in some detail, and we then discuss the available psychophysical data on listeners' processing of dynamic spatial information.

A. Additional Acoustical Information from Moving Sounds

Moving sounds can be described by using the mathematics of kinematics (Jenison & Lufti, 1992). *Kinematics* is the branch of mechanics that describes pure motion that uses the variables of displacement, time, velocity, and acceleration. Doppler shifts, changes in ITD (described earlier) and intensity, can be shown to have dependencies that are based on kinematics. In addition to ITD, Doppler shift, and time-varying intensity, the first differentials of these observed variables may directly be sensed as well. Figure 7 shows the geometry of the sound source moving relative to an observer. φ_t is the angle of the incident wavefront at any time t and is dependent on the distance D_t to a point p on the median plane. θ_0 is the angle at the anticipated closest point of approach (CPA), and β is the angle of the source trajectory relative to the median plane. Angle β is equivalent in magnitude to $\theta_0 + \pi/2$. R_t is the distance from the sound source to the observer.

Movement of either the sound source or the observer changes the relative wavelength of the sound waves. This change is known as the *Doppler shift*. The well-known lawful dependence of the Doppler shift on velocity of the sound source relative to an observer is

$$\omega = \frac{\omega_0}{(1 - M \cos \varphi_t)},$$

where ω_0 is the intrinsic frequency, ω is the shifted frequency, M is the Mach number defined as velocity divided by the speed of sound, and φ_t is the angle of trajectory relative to the observer (see Figure 7). The frequency shift depends only on the velocity component directed toward the observer. This result holds true regardless of the time history of the trajectory. The

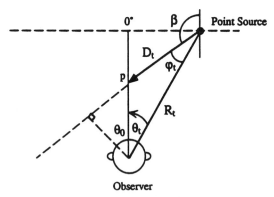

FIGURE 7   Schematic diagram showing angular relations between a listener and a sound source that is moving along a straight path (represented by the arrow).

Doppler-shifted frequency at a given time and position is affected only by the source's velocity and frequency at the instant the wave is generated. Furthermore, the source need not be traveling at a constant velocity or in a straight line for it to apply. When the sound source is far from the observer and approaching (φ_t is small, thus $\cos[\varphi_t]$ is near 1), the angle φ_t changes very little, hence little change in the frequency shift. However, the magnitude of the shift will be at its maximum. Since the sound source is approaching the observer, the shift is toward a higher frequency. As the sound source approaches the observer, φ_t increases rapidly, resulting in a rapid decrease in frequency. As the sound source passes and recedes, there is a corresponding decrease in frequency relative to the intrinsic frequency of the sound source. This of course is the experience we have all had listening to a passing train whistle that decreases in pitch as it passes by and recedes into the distance.

These observed variables, ITD, time-varying intensity, and Doppler, along with their first-order differentials with respect to time, all have characteristic spectrotemporal patterns. Zakarauskas and Cynader (1991) analyzed intensity patterns for actual moving sound sources along various trajectories and derived mathematical expressions for the observed variables that are related to the inverse-square distance relationship. Jenison (1994) extended these analyses to include Doppler and ITD patterns. The simplest trajectory is that of the rectilinear approach with constant velocity as shown in Figure 8. For illustration, the starting point for the moving sound source in these examples is located some distance R_s directly on the median line as shown in the Figure 8.

The characteristic patterns for the three sound source trajectory angles (β) of 90°, 120°, and 150° are shown in Figure 9. For the purpose of this

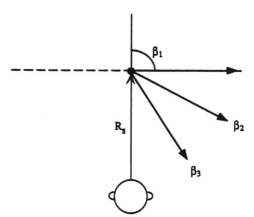

FIGURE 8   Schematic diagram showing three example trajectories for a moving sound source.

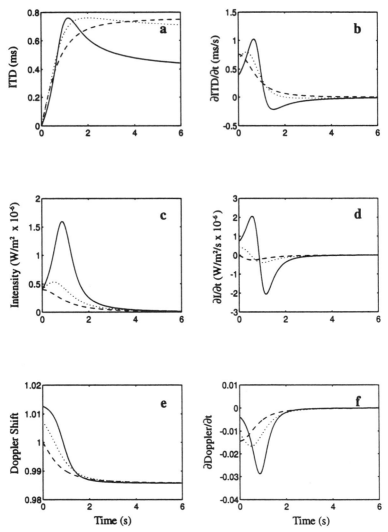

FIGURE 9   Results of kinematic analysis of the interaural time difference (ITD); (a), intensity (b), and Doppler shift (c) cues produced by a moving sound source. The rates of change of those cues are shown in (b), (d), and (f).

example, we have assumed a source of moderate intensity, a velocity of 5 m/s, and a starting distance from the observer of 5 m. Note that all of the ITD functions begin at 0 delay because of the midline starting point. The intensity functions will also start at the same intensity for a given distance from the observer. In the case of the Doppler shift, the shift is toward a higher frequency when the sound is approaching the observer and toward a lower frequency when receding. So for β_1 equal to 90°, the frequency shift will start at unity and decline. For the cases of β_2 and β_3, where the source is initially approaching, passes through a CPA and then recedes, the frequency shift will initially be greater than unity and then decline.

Jenison (1994) has shown that acoustical kinematics sufficiently convey velocity (trajectory and speed) information regarding the moving sound source directly from the observed Doppler shift together with time-varying ITD. Although the theoretical analyses show that sufficient information is available to the observer regarding higher order variables such as the velocity and time-to-contact of the moving sound source, it remains to be known whether the human observer has sufficient sensory mechanisms to detect this information, particularly under conditions of uncertainty.

Most of the empirical research on perception of moving sound sources has focused, either directly or indirectly, on the question of whether dynamic spatial changes are processed with some kind of specialized *movement detectors*. There is considerable neurophysiological evidence that differential information lawfully related to motion is directly detected by the visual system (Maunsell & VanEssen, 1983). Recent evidence suggests that there are also direction-sensitive neurons spatially segregated in auditory cortex (Stumpf, Toronchuk & Cynader, 1992). Other findings suggest that neural processing of auditory motion involves mechanisms distinct from those involved in processing stationary sound location (Spitzer & Semple, 1991, 1993; Stumpf, Toronchuk, & Cynader, 1992). Thus, while converging physiological evidence supports the existence of motion sensitive neurons, the psychophysical evidence for specialized motion detectors is inconclusive. The two lines of research that have addressed this question involve measurements of the *minimum audible movement angle* (MAMA) and measurements of auditory motion aftereffects.

The MAMA experiments are variations of the classical *minimum audible angle* (MAA) experiments conducted with stationary sources. They are both detection or discrimination experiments that measure the threshold for discriminating small changes in spatial parameters. In the case of MAAs, what is measured is the smallest spatial separation of two static sources that can reliably be detected. The MAMA represents the smallest amount of spatial displacement or movement of a single source that can reliably be detected. Although both experiments can inform us about the processing capabilities of the auditory system, it is important to note that since they involve discrimination or detection paradigms, the extent to which the results can be generalized to questions about apparent spatial position may be quite limited. In other words, that listeners can discriminate between two sources at slightly different spatial positions does not necessarily imply that the apparent positions of the sources were different. Similarly, discrimination between a moving source and a static source does not necessarily imply that movement itself was perceived.

While the investigators involved in the MAMA research may quibble over details, most would probably agree that the results do not support the existence of specialized motion detectors in the auditory system. Measured MAMAs, when expressed in terms of the total angle traversed at threshold, are roughly the same as or slightly larger than the MAAs measured with stationary sources, or about 2° (Grantham, 1986; Harris & Sergeant, 1971; Perrott & Musicant, 1977; Perrott & Tucker, 1988). A simple explanation of the basic MAMA results is that the listener takes an acoustic "snapshot" of the position of the source at the beginning and end of its trajectory (Grantham, 1986) and discriminates on the basis of static positional changes. Not all the available data support this view, but the exceptions are relatively minor (Perrott & Marlborough, 1989).

Gibson (1966) took issue with the notion of a series of perceptual snapshots, which requires fusion or composition to account for the perception of a single moving object. By redefining information for motion perception, Gibson eliminated the need for a concept such as fusion. Since motion information is available to the observer, even through discrete looks, the additional step of reconstruction to a continuous event is simply not necessary. To Gibson, the mechanics of the mediating sensory system were not germane to the perception of motion. To have "dynamic event perception," in contrast to the less elegant "motion perception plus inference," it must be shown that even though dynamic properties, such as mass and inertia, are not present in the optic (or acoustic) array, they are specified by the kinematics. That is, the information regarding the physical motion of an object is conveyed through the kinematics, whether discrete or continuous.

Research on motion aftereffects provides indirect evidence on the question of the existence of specialized motion detectors. The idea is that exposure to an adapting stimulus that is moving in one direction fatigues the neural elements that respond to movement in that direction. The aftereffect, a perception of movement in the opposite direction, is presumed to reflect the spontaneous activity of the neural elements sensitive to movement in the opposite direction. Movement aftereffects are common in vision, one variation of which is called the *waterfall illusion* (Sekular & Pantle, 1967).

Grantham (1989, 1992) has reported reliable though weak evidence for motion aftereffects in audition. After prolonged exposure to a free-field adapting stimulus that was moving in the horizontal plane, listeners' judgments of the direction of movement of a subsequently presented probe stimulus were slightly biased in a direction opposite to that of the adapting stimulus. While the effects were disappointingly small, the results were nevertheless suggestive.

Some of the research on perception of moving sound sources has been less concerned with the existence of specialized motion detectors and more broadly focused. For example, several studies have attempted to quantify the relative salience of the various sources of acoustical information that signal source movement. These experiments ask listeners to indicate the time at which a moving source is closest to them (time to interception) or the time at which they would make contact with the source (acoustic tau). In a theoretical study, Shaw, McGowan, and Turvey (1991) analyzed the acoustic intensity field produced by collinear relative movement between a sound source and an observer and showed the acoustic tau to be related to the inverse of the relative change in average intensity. Jenison (1994) extended the analysis to the more general case, including *time-to-interception,* showing that time-averaged intensity and time-varying ITD and their corresponding first-order derivatives are sufficient for conveying both collision and interception information.

Empirical studies of auditory time-to-contact or time-to-interception include research reported by Rosenblum, Carello, and Pastore (1987) in which listeners heard sound sources over headphones. Three stimulus variables were manipulated: interaural time difference, overall level, and Doppler shift. Each was presented both in isolation and in competition so that each indicated a different point of closest approach or interception. The results suggested that while any of the three stimulus parameters could accurately indicate point of closest approach, overall level was the dominant cue. The authors argue that overall level should be dominant since it is the only cue of the three that is, in all environmental circumstances, unequivocal. Todd (1981) investigated how well subjects could discriminate time-to-contact for visual stimuli by simulating two simultaneously approaching objects on a computer display. Subjects were asked to judge which object would arrive first. We have recently launched analogous experiments that examine subjects' ability to discriminate the arrival of two sound sources. Sounds were synthesized according to the simple kinematics of a moving sound composed of three harmonics by using ITD, average intensity, and Doppler shift. A sound arriving to the left of the listener was mixed with a sound arriving differentially in time to the right of the observer. Subjects were asked to choose which sound would arrive sooner. Figure 10 shows preliminary results from 24 subjects. In Todd's experiment, relative time-to-contact was 75% correctly discriminated when the difference in time-to-contact was about 50 ms. In contrast, the relative auditory time-to-contact in our preliminary studies was 75% correctly discriminated when the difference was about 300 ms. Schiff and Oldak (1990) examined observers' accuracy in using visual and acoustical estimates of time-to-arrival from film and sound-recorded approaching vehicles. Their data indicate that sighted subjects were significantly more accurate in estimating time-to-arrival with sight than sound, however, visually impaired subjects performed as well as

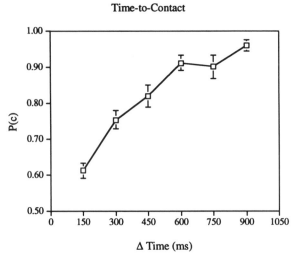

FIGURE 10   Average psychometric function from 24 listeners in the time-to-contact experiment. Percentage correct discriminations between two sounds arriving at different times is plotted as a function of the arrival time difference.

or better than the sighted subjects with only the acoustic channel. Although the evidence is only suggestive at this point, human observers have the capacity to efficiently estimate relative time–to–contact regardless of how the information is conveyed as long as the temporal window for estimation is within several seconds. This restricted window should not be surprising given the pattern of the observables described above. Significant changes in ITD, intensity, and Doppler occur only in a spatial region (hence the temporal region as well) about the CPA. This relationship holds for subtended angle in the visual domain as well.

Head movements provide a somewhat different kind of dynamic auditory stimulus from movement of the sound source. Because head movements typically involve changes only in the direction of the sound source with respect to the head there is very little Doppler shift and very little change in overall level. However, interaural parameters change more rapidly with head movements than with typical source movement. In addition, head movements provide additional information to the perceiver by means of proprioceptive feedback from the neck musculature. Although there has been speculation about the role of head movements for decades, there have been few empirical studies of their role (Pollack & Rose, 1967; Simpson & Stanton, 1973; Thurlow & Runge, 1967). Only recently has empirical research begun to provide firm evidence of the importance of head movements for perception of the spatial layout of auditory objects.

Given a stationary auditory object in the environment there is a change in the angular relation of the object and a listener's head that accompanies normal head movement. This change in relative orientation produces a systematic and predictable change in the pattern of spatial cues (ITD, ILD, and spectral cues) produced by the object at the listener's ears. If these normal changes in the spatial cues are disrupted, the apparent position of the auditory object is often disturbed. Young (1931) reported one of the first demonstrations of this phenomenon. In this experiment, sounds were routed to the ears through rubber tubes attached to fixed ear trumpets. With this arrangement the normal coupling between a listener's head movements and changes in the acoustical stimulus at the ears was eliminated. Listeners reported all sounds as originating behind the head, outside of the listeners' visual fields, regardless of the actual position of the sound source. Similar front–back confusions are reported in the modern studies of virtual sound sources that are synthesized and presented to listeners by means of headphones (Wightman & Kistler, 1989b).

As mentioned above, front–back confusions are not entirely unexpected given the rough spherical symmetry of the head and the salience of ITD cues. The idea that in everyday life a listener's head movements might provide the information needed to avoid them is usually attributed to Wallach (1940). Wallach showed that if a listener could monitor the direction of change in ITD that accompanied a head movement, the front–back ambiguity could be avoided. For example, suppose a sound is presented at an azimuth of 45° and an elevation of 0° (on the horizontal plane, roughly 45° to the right of the median plane). A front–back confusion would be represented by an apparent azimuth report of roughly 135°. If the listener's head moved to the right, the ITD produced by the source initially at 45° would decrease because the angle of the source relative to the head would approach 0°, the point of minimum ITD. However, if the source were actually at 135° azimuth, the ITD would have increased. Thus, the direction of change in ITD unambiguously indicates whether the source was in the front or in the rear.

In spite of the simplicity and face validity of Wallach's (1940) arguments, conclusive evidence that head movements are used to resolve front–back confusions has not appeared. One obvious reason for this is that experiments that control both head movements and the associated auditory stimulus dynamics have been technically too demanding until recently. Advanced technology now allows synthesis of virtual sources in such a way that the effects of head movements can directly be studied. Using magnetic head trackers and real-time convolution devices such as the Convolvotron (Foster, Wenzel, & Taylor, 1991), one can monitor a listener's head position continually during an experiment and adjust the synthesis algorithms dynamically (20–40 times per second) to simulate a stationary source. As the listener's head moves, the device compensates for changes in the relative positions of the stationary virtual source and the head by using different left–right pairs of HRTF-based filters for each updated head position. The movement compensation is smooth and the resultant percept of an external sound source in a stationary position is compellingly realistic (Wenzel, 1992).

We have recently begun some research on the role of head movements that takes advantage of the new technology and attempts to clarify some of the issues raised by the earlier work (Wightman, Kistler, & Andersen, 1994). The essential elements of the paradigm were as described in earlier work (Wightman & Kistler, 1989b). Listeners localized virtual sources (2.5 s wideband noise bursts) in two conditions. In one, the virtual stimuli were presented over headphones with no head tracking, and the listeners were asked not to move their heads during the test. In the other, a magnetic head tracker was used to sense head position, and the virtual synthesis algorithms were modified in real time according to the head tracker's reports. In the second condition, listeners were encouraged to move their heads during stimulus presentation if they felt it would facilitate localization. Apparent position judgments were made verbally after each stimulus presentation. Preliminary results from a single listener are shown in Figure 11. Note that in the head stationary condition this listener made frequent front–back confusions, as evidenced by the off-diagonal responses in the front–back panel. In the head-movement condition, however, the front–back confusions were nearly eliminated. The listeners' gave no indication of other differences between the two conditions, either in their apparent position judgments or in their subjective reports. Thus, in contrast with suggestions in the literature, apparent source distance was the same with and without head movements (cf. Simpson & Stanton, 1973), and the images were equally well externalized in the two conditions (cf. Durlach et al., 1992). We conclude on the basis of these results that the primary role of head movements is resolution of confusions about the spatial layout of auditory objects.

VI. THE ROLE OF AUDITORY–VISUAL INTERACTIONS IN THE SPATIAL LAYOUT OF AUDITORY OBJECTS

The sensory environment of most individuals includes both visual and auditory objects, and in many cases sound-producing objects can be seen as well as heard. Thus, while it is useful and informative to consider audition alone when discussing the spatial layout of auditory objects, it is important to be mindful of the potential role played by vision. Indeed, some auditory–visual interactions are quite powerful and their consequences well documented.

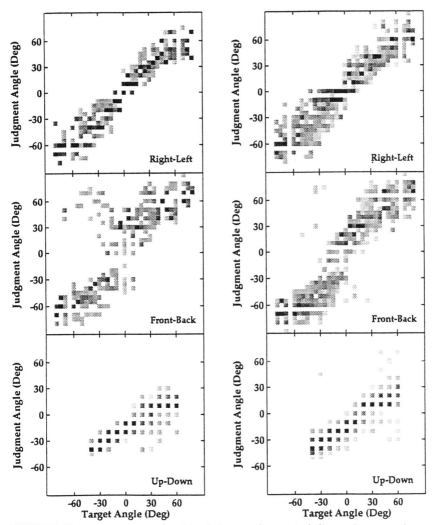

FIGURE 11   Apparent source position judgments from a single listener in an experiment in which the listener heard virtual sources presented over headphones. In one condition (left panels) the listener was required to hold his or her head still, and in the other condition (right panels) the listener was encouraged to move his or her head and the virtual stimuli were modified in real time according to the listener's head position to simulate a stationary external source. Each judgment of apparent azimuth and elevation is represented in three panels that reflect the extent (expressed as an angle from −90° to +90°) to which the judged position is on the right or left (top), in the front or back (middle), and above or below the horizontal plane (bottom). The darkness of each symbol represents the number of judgments that fell in the local area of the symbol.

The so-called *ventriloquism effect* is perhaps the best known of the auditory –visual interactions (e.g., Pick, Warren, & Hay, 1969). The typical manifestation of the effect is a strong biasing of the apparent position of an auditory object in the direction of a simultaneously present visual object. Evidence of the potency of this effect is familiar to anyone who has watched the image of someone speaking at the movies or on television. While the sound of the voice clearly seems to originate at the mouth of the person speaking, the actual source of the sound, a loudspeaker, is usually displaced far to one side. Clearly one's perception of the spatial layout of auditory objects will be heavily influenced by whether or not the source of the sound is visible.

Additional evidence for auditory–visual interactions comes from research on visual facilitation (e.g., Warren, 1970). Visual facilitation refers to the fact that the variance of localization judgments is lower when listeners hear the test stimulus in a lighted room than when they hear it in the dark. The source of sound is invisible in either case, and whether the listener makes the response in the light or the dark is irrelevant to the outcome. It is as if the listener is able to establish a frame of reference within which to place the auditory objects, and the presence of the frame of reference facilitates localization. Some investigators argue that eye movements, even in the absence of visual input, are the basis of the facilitation effect (Jones & Kabanoff, 1975), but the issue is far from being resolved. What is especially interesting about the visual facilitation effect is that it occurs only in adults. Children as old as 12 years do not show the effect (Warren, 1970).

VII. CONCLUSION

The study of auditory object perception in general and the spatial layout of auditory objects in particular is in its infancy. In the case of the spatial layout of single stationary sound sources in anechoic space much is known about the sources of information and how that information is processed. The salience of ITD cues, the importance of monaural spectral cues derived from pinna filtering, the role of head movements, and so forth, have been thoroughly documented in studies of single stationary sources. Relatively few investigators have ventured beyond the relative security of this constraint so that experiments involving nonanechoic listening conditions and moving sources are scarce, and studies of multiple sources are virtually nonexistent. The potential sources of information are reasonably well understood, but how that information might be used in the auditory system is completely unknown.

The state of affairs in hearing contrasts sharply with the relative maturity of the study of visual spatial layout, in which research on such complex topics as optic flow has been in progress for decades. One reason for the slower progress on the hearing side may be that the experiments are technically more demanding. For example, it is easier to present an arbitrary visual pattern to a retina than an arbitrary sound waveform to an eardrum. Technology is changing this situation rapidly, so we can expect significant advances in our understanding of auditory object perception in the near future.

Acknowledgments

The authors are indebted to Doris Kistler and many others in the Hearing Development Research Laboratory for their assistance in preparing this chapter and in conducting the research that led to it. Preparation of the manuscript was supported in part by research grants from the National Institutes of Health (National Institute of Deafness and Other Communicative Disorders), National Aeronautics and Space Administration, and Office of Naval Research.

References

Begault, D. (1992). Perceptual effects of synthetic reverberation on three-dimensional audio systems. *Journal of the Audio Engineering Society, 40*, 895–904.

Bregman, A. (1990). *Auditory scene analysis*. Cambridge, MA: MIT Press.

Butler, R., Humanski, R., & Musicant, A. (1990). Binaural and monaural localization of sound in two-dimensional space. *Perception, 19*, 241–256.

Blauert, J. (1983). *Spatial hearing: The psychophysics of human sound localization*. Cambridge, MA: MIT Press.

Clifton, R., & Freyman, R. (1989). Effect of click rate and delay on breakdown of the precedence effect. *Perception & Psychophysics, 46*, 139–145.

Cochran, P., Throop, J., & Simpson, W. E. (1968). Estimation of distance of a source of sound. *American Journal of Psychology, 81*, 198–207.

Coleman, P. D. (1962). Failure to localize the source distance of an unfamiliar sound. *Journal of the Acoustical Society of America, 34*, 345–346.

Coleman, P. D. (1963). An analysis of cues to auditory depth perception in free space. *Psychological Bulletin, 60*, 302–315.

Durlach, N. I., Rigopulos, A., Pang, X. D., Woods, W. S., Kulkarni, A., Colburn, H. S., & Wenzel, E. M. (1992). On the externalization of auditory images. *Presence, 1*(2), 251–257.

Foster, S. H., Wenzel, E. M., & Taylor, R. M. (1991, October). Real time synthesis of complex acoustic environments. Paper presented at the *IEEE Workshop on Applications of Signal Processing to Audio & Acoustics*, New Paltz, NY.

Gardner, M. B. (1968). Proximity image effect in sound localization. *Journal of the Acoustical Society of America, 43*, 163.

Gibson, J. J. (1966). *The senses considered as perceptual systems*. Boston: Houghton Mifflin.

Grantham, D. W. (1986). Detection and discrimination of simulated motion of auditory targets in the horizontal plane. *Journal of the Acoustical Society of America, 79*, 1939–1949.

Grantham, D. W. (1989). Motion aftereffects with horizontally moving sound sources in the free field. *Perception & Psychophysics, 45*(2), 129–136.

Grantham, D. W. (1992). Adaptation to auditory motion in the horizontal plane: Effect of prior exposure to motion on motion detectability. *Perception & Psychophysics, 52*(2), 144–150.

Green, D. M. (1976). *An introduction to hearing*. New York: Wiley.

Handel, S. (1989). *Listening: An introduction to the perception of auditory events*. Cambridge, MA: MIT Press.

Harris, J. D., & Sergeant, R. L. (1971). Monaural/binaural minimum audible angle for a moving sound source. *Journal of Speech and Hearing Research, 14,* 618–629.

Hartmann, W. M. (1983). Localization of sound in rooms. *Journal of the Acoustical Society of America, 74,* 1380–1391.

Holt, R. E., & Thurlow, W. R. (1969). Subject orientation and judgment of distance of a sound source. *Journal of the Acoustical Society of America, 6*(2), 1584.

Jenison, R. L. (1994). *On acoustic information for auditory motion.* Manuscript submitted for publication.

Jenison, R. L., & Lutfi, R. A. (1992). Kinematic synthesis of auditory motion, *Journal of the Acoustical Society of America, 92,* 2458.

Jones, B., & Kabanoff, B. (1975). Eye movements in auditory space perception. *Perception & Psychophysics, 17,* 241–245.

Joris, P. X., & Yin, T. C. T. (1992). Responses to amplitude-modulated tones in the auditory nerve of the cat. *Journal of the Acoustical Society of America, 91,* 215–232.

Kuhn, G. F. (1977). Model for the interaural time differences in the azimuthal plane. *Journal of the Acoustical Society of America, 62,* 157–167.

Lambert, R. (1974). Dynamic theory of sound-source localization. *Journal of the Acoustical Society of America, 56,* 165–171.

Maunsell, J. H. R., & van Essen, D. C. (1983). Functional properties of neurons in middle temporal visual area (MT) of Macaque monkey: I. Binocular interactions and the sensitivity to binocular disparity. *Journal of Neurophysiology, 49,* 1148–1167.

McGregor, P., Horn, A. G., & Todd, M. A. (1985). Are familiar sounds ranged more accurately? *Perceptual and Motor Skills, 61,* 1082.

Mershon, D. H., & King, L. E. (1975). Intensity and reverberation as factors in the auditory perception of egocentric distance. *Perception & Psychophysics, 18*(6), 409–415.

Middlebrooks, J. C. (1992). Narrow-band sound localization related to external ear acoustics. *Journal of the Acoustical Society of America, 92*(5), 2607–2624.

Middlebrooks, J. C., & Green, D. M. (1990). Directional dependence of interaural envelope delays. *Journal of the Acoustical Society of America, 87*(50), 2149–2162.

Middlebrooks, J. C., & Green, D. M. (1991). Sound localization by human listeners. In M. Rozenzweig and L. Porter (Eds.), *Annual review of psychology* (Vol. 42, pp. 135–159). Palo Alto, CA: Annual Reviews Inc.

Middlebrooks, J. C., Makous, J. C., & Green, D. M. (1989). Directional sensitivity of sound-pressure levels in the human ear canal. *Journal of the Acoustical Society of America, 86*(1), 89–108.

Oldfield, S. R., & Parker, S. P. A. (1984a). Acuity of sound localization: A topography of auditory space: I. Normal hearing conditions. *Perception, 13,* 581–600.

Oldfield, S. R., & Parker, S. P. A. (1984b). Acuity of sound localization: A topography of auditory space: II. Pinna cues absent. *Perception, 13,* 601–617.

Perrott, D. R., & Marlborough, K. (1989). Minimum audible movement angle: Marking the end points of the path traveled by a moving sound source. *Journal of the Acoustical Society of America, 85,* 1773–1775.

Perrott, D. R., & Musicant, A. D. (1977). Minimum auditory movement angle: Binaural localization of moving sound sources. *Journal of the Acoustical Society of America, 62,* 1463–1466.

Perrott, D. R., & Tucker, J. (1988). Minimum audible movement angle as a function of signal frequency and the velocity of the source. *Journal of the Acoustical Society of America, 83,* 1522–1527.

Pick, H. L., Warren, D. H., & Hay, J. C. (1969). Sensory conflict in judgments of spatial direction. *Perception & Psychophysics, 6,* 203–205.

Pollack, I., & Rose, M. (1967). Effects of head movements on the localization of sounds in the equatorial plane. *Perception & Psychophysics, 2,* 591–596.

Pralong, D., & Carlile, S. (1994). Measuring the human head-related transfer functions: A novel method for the construction and calibration of a miniature in-ear recording system. *Journal of the Acoustical Society of America, 95,* 3435–3444.

Rosenblum, L. D., Carello, C., & Pastore, R. E. (1987). Relative effectiveness of three stimulus variables for locating a moving sound source. *Perception, 16,* 175–186.

Schiff, W., & Oldak, R. (1990). Accuracy of judging time to arrival: Effects of modality, trajectory, and gender. *Journal of Experimental Psychology: Human Perception and Performance, 16,* 303–316.

Sekular, R., & Pantle, A. (1967). A model for after-effects of seen movement. *Vision Research, 7,* 427–439.

Shaw, B. K., McGowan, R. S., & Turvey, M. T. (1991). An acoustic variable specifying time-to-contact. *Ecological Psychology, 3,* 253–261.

Shaw, E. A. G. (1974). Transformation of sound pressure level from the free field to the eardrum in the horizontal plane. *Journal of the Acoustical Society of America, 56*(6), 1848–1861.

Simpson, W., & Stanton, L. (1973). Head movement does not facilitate perception of the distance of a source of sound. *American Journal of Psychology, 86,* 151–160.

Spitzer, M. W., & Semple, M. N. (1991). Interaural phase coding in auditory midbrain: Influence of dynamic stimulus features. *Science, 254,* 721–724.

Spitzer, M. W., & Semple, M. N. (1993). Responses of inferior colliculus neurons to time-varying interaural phase disparity: Effects of shifting the locus of virtual motion. *Journal of Neurophysiology, 69,* 1245–1263.

Stevens, S. S., & Newman, E. B. (1936). The localization of actual sources of sound. *American Journal of Psychology, 48,* 297–306.

Strutt, J. W. (1907). On our perception of sound direction. *Philosophical Magazine, 13,* 214–232.

Stumpf, E., Toronchuk, J. M., & Cynader, M. S. (1992). Neurons in cat primary auditory cortex sensitive to correlates of auditory motion in three-dimensional space. *Experimental Brain Research, 88,* 158–168.

Thurlow, W. R., & Runge, P. S. (1967). Effect of induced head movements on localization of direction of sounds. *Journal of the Acoustical Society of America, 42*(2), 480–488.

Todd, J. (1981). Visual information about moving objects. *Journal of Experimental Psychology: Human Perception and Performance, 7,* 795–810.

Wallach, H. (1940). The role of head movements and vestibular and visual cues in sound localization. *Journal of Experimental Psychology, 27*(4), 339–368.

Wallach, H., Newman, E., & Rosenzweig, M. (1949). The precedence effect in sound localization. *The American Journal of Psychology, 62,* 315–336.

Warren, D. H. (1970). Intermodality interactions in spatial localization. In W. Reitman (Ed.), *Cognitive psychology* (pp. 114–133). New York: Academic Press.

Wenzel, E. M. (1992). Localization in virtual acoustic displays. *Presence, 1*(1), 80–107.

Wenzel, E. M., Arruda, M., Kistler, D. J., & Wightman, F. L. (1993). Localization using nonindividualized head-related transfer functions. *Journal of the Acoustical Society of America, 94,* 111–123.

Wightman, F. L., & Kistler, D. J. (1989a). Headphone simulation of free-field listening: I. Stimulus synthesis. *Journal of the Acoustical Society of America, 85,* 858–867.

Wightman, F. L., & Kistler, D. J. (1989b). Headphone simulation of free-field listening. II. Psychophysical validation. *Journal of the Acoustical Society of America, 85,* 868–878.

Wightman, F. L., & Kistler, D. J. (1992). The dominant role of low-frequency interaural time differences in sound localization. *Journal of the Acoustical Society of America, 91*(3), 1648–1661.

Wightman, F. L., & Kistler, D. J. (1993). Sound localization. In R. Fay, A. Popper, & W. Yost (Eds.), *Springer series in auditory research: Human psychophysics* (pp. 155–192). New York: Springer-Verlag.

Wightman, F. L., Kistler, D. J., & Andersen, K. J. (1994). Reassessment of the role of head movements in human sound localization. *Journal of the Acoustical Society of America, 95,* 3003.

Woodworth, R. S. (1938). *Experimental Psychology.* New York: Holt.

Yin, T. C. T., & Chan, J. C. K. (1988). Neural mechanisms underlying interaural time sensitivity to tones and noise. In G. M. Edelman, W. E. Gall, and W. M. Cowan (Eds.), *Auditory function: Neurobiological bases of hearing* (pp. 385–430). New York: Wiley.

Young, P. T. (1931). The role of head movements in auditory localization. *Journal of Experimental Psychology, XIV* (2), 95–124.

Zakarauskas, P., & Cynader, M. S. (1991). Aural intensity for a moving source. *Hearing Research, 52,* 233–244.

Zurek, P. (1980). The precedence effect and its possible role in the avoidance of interaural ambiguities. *Journal of the Acoustical Society of America, 67,* 952–964.

CHAPTER 11

Dynamic Touch

M. T. Turvey
Claudia Carello

I. THE NATURE OF DYNAMIC TOUCH

A kind of touch that is prominent in everyday manipulatory activity involves the hand supporting the manipulated object and in contact with only a part of it. Both statically and in motion, the manipulated object affects the tensile states of the muscles and tendons of the hand and arm and, thereby, the patterning of activity in the ensembles of muscle and tendon receptors. Muscle and tendon deformations (induced by the forces and torques engendered by holding and manipulating) characterize the haptic subsystem of dynamic touch, more so than deformations of the skin and changes in joint angles (Gibson, 1966). Dynamic touching, therefore, is the kind of touching that occurs when a utensil (e.g., a fork), a tool (e.g., a hammer), or any medium-sized object (e.g., a book), is grasped and lifted, turned, carried, and so on. It contrasts with the two haptic subsystems (Gibson, 1966) of cutaneous touch (e.g., an object resting on the skin) and haptic touch (e.g., the hands enveloping an object and sweeping thoroughly and freely over its surfaces). The latter have been the subject of most experimental inquiry (e.g., Katz, 1925/1989; Klatzky, Lederman, & Reed, 1989; Lederman & Klatzky, 1987). With respect to manipulatory activity and locomotion guided by a hand-held implement (e.g., Burton, 1992, 1993), dynamic

Perception of Space and Motion

touch, rather than the cutaneous and haptic versions, plays the most significant role. Dynamic touch is implied whenever an object is grasped and wielded, whenever a solid surface is palpated or vibrated, and whenever a hand-held implement is brought into contact with other objects.

As with any perceptual system, experimental analysis of dynamic touch should address its exteroperceptive, proprioperceptive, and exproprioperceptive capabilities and the exterospecific, propriospecific, and expropriospecific information supporting these capabilities. These terms are mostly familiar. *Exteroperception* refers to the perception of the layout and changes in layout of adjacent material surfaces, that is, the perception of objects and events, respectively. *Proprioperception* refers to the perception of the orientations and movements of the body's segments relative to each other and to the body. The preceding two terms are close to the classical usages popularized by Sherrington (1906). The term *exproprioperception,* in contrast, is nonclassical. It was introduced by Lee (1978) to distinguish the perception of the orientations and movements of body and its segments as units relative to the environment. In significant part, the encouragement for the latter term is the fact that the study of optical information reveals mathematically distinct optical structure governing self- or ego-motion from that governing perception of the body's segments (Gibson, 1979). In the research on dynamic touch to be summarized below, all three perceptual capabilities will come under scrutiny. Their study will be shaped by the expectation that each depends on different forms of mechanical stimulation, more precisely, exterospecific, propriospecific, and expropriospecific information, respectively.

A. A Law-Based, Dynamical Systems Perspective

Wielding an object, probing surfaces with a hand-held implement, and palpating or vibrating a solid medium are kinds of dynamical systems. In a very general and abbreviated form, a dynamical system is represented by

$$\dot{x} = F(\dot{x}, t; c, N), \tag{1}$$

where $\dot{x}$ is a state variable such as displacement, $\dot{x}$ is its rate of change, t is time, c is a parameter such as mass, rotational inertia, coefficient of stiffness, coefficient of friction, and so forth, N is noise, and F is the physics (the relevant laws of motion and change) governing the time evolution of the state. Usually there is more than one state variable, more than one parameter, and more than one source of noise. Whereas the state variables during the "running" of a dynamical system assume different values at different points in time, the parameters are time independent, remaining at one and the same value. The time invariance of parameters confers on them a special quality: They express the specific way in which a system's states are coupled to the forces imposed on it by its surroundings (Rosen, 1988). Parameters give a system its specific identity independent of the multiplicity of changes that might occur in the system's states.

Patently, in wielding, probing, and palpating, the forces (torques and impulses) and the states (motions and deformations) vary with time. Providing an invariant coupling between those time-dependent forces and states, however, are the parameters of wielding, probing, and palpating. A major theory of perception, that advanced by Gibson (1959, 1966, 1979), is founded on the assumption that perception is specific to invariants of transforming energy distributions related lawfully to properties of the environment, the body, and the body–environment juxtaposition. In the case of dynamic touch, the energy distributions (playing out on the tissues of the body) are mechanical, and they undergo transformations in the course of wielding, probing, and palpating. Frequently, the goals of perception by dynamic touch are persistent environmental properties and persistent body–environment relations, such as the length of a held instrument, the size and distance of a probed surface, and the position of the hand relative to the dimensions of a held and manipulated object. On Gibson's view, we may suppose that these persistent environmental properties and body–environment relations are linked to the persistent aspects of the dynamics, those that are time-invariant, in short, the dynamics' parameters.

Accordingly, the strategy for understanding dynamic touch seems to be as follows: (1) define the dynamical system; (2) identify the parameters that couple the (muscular and other) forces impressed on the system to the system's states; (3) determine, for the given property of hand-held object or adjacent surface layout, the parameter or parameters that constrain fully the perception; and (4) provide a reasoned basis for the relation between the pertinent parameter(s) and the perception (Carello, Fitzpatrick, & Turvey, 1992).

B. The Need for Model Systems

The success of the strategy defined by (1)–(4) above depends on the availability of "model experimental systems." Such model systems are, to begin with, carefully contrived simplifications of the complex process of interest. Their second characteristic is that they permit the behavior of specific observables to be studied as a function of one parameter, or relatively few parameters, in a reproducible fashion (Haken, 1988). Any identified model system should allow for the development of new concepts whose dynamics can be checked rigorously through further studies of the model system and its close variants (Haken, 1988). These new concepts can then be applied to the original complex system or process. In the identification of model systems for dynamic touch, an important requirement will be that well-established physical concepts are expressed by the systems and are open to creative exploitation as the systems are subject to investigation. We take considerable care in the next section, therefore, to establish the dynamics of wielding. This formal base provides the rationale for the experimental manipulations and analyses described in the sections that follow.

II. DYNAMICS OF WIELDING

When an object is held firmly in the hand and wielded, the object's motion is most aptly described as a rotation in three space about axes through a fixed point O. Consequently, the dynamics of wielding an object are expressible through Euler's equations of rotational motion. In unexpanded form, these equations are expressed as

$$\frac{d\mathbf{J}}{dt} = \dot{\mathbf{J}} + \omega \times \mathbf{J}, \tag{2}$$

where $d\mathbf{J}/dt$ is the absolute rate of change of the angular momentum vector $\mathbf{J}$ about the spatial axes fixed at O, $\dot{\mathbf{J}}$ is the rate of change of the angular momentum vector about axes that are fixed in the object and rotate with it, ω is the instantaneous angular velocity vector, and $\times$ is the vector or cross product. Given that $d\mathbf{J}/dt = \mathbf{N}$, the torque vector, Equation 2 can be written as

$$\mathbf{N} = \dot{\mathbf{J}} + \omega \times \mathbf{J}. \tag{3}$$

Since $\mathbf{J} = \mathbf{I} \cdot \omega$, where $\mathbf{I}$ is the inertia tensor and $\dot{\omega}$ is the angular acceleration vector, Equation 3 can be expressed more usefully for present purposes as

$$\mathbf{N} = (\mathbf{I} \cdot \dot{\omega}) + \omega \times (\mathbf{I} \cdot \omega), \tag{4}$$

where $\cdot$ is the scalar or dot product. Of all the quantities in Equation 4, only $\mathbf{I}$ is time independent. In the course of wielding, $\mathbf{I}$ is an invariant that couples the time-varying rotational forces $\mathbf{N}$ to the time-varying motions as quantified by ω and $\dot{\omega}$. In perceiving the persistent properties of a hand-held occluded object by dynamic touch—for example, its length, shape, or weight—Equation 4 suggests that such perceiving must be constrained by $\mathbf{I}$.

A. Moment of Inertia and the Inertia Tensor

An object's inertia for turning depends not just on the object's constituent masses but on how far away they are from the axis of rotation. Thus, as an object's masses are distributed further from the axis, the greater becomes its resistance to rotational acceleration about that axis. More specifically, an object's moment of inertia is the sum of all of its masses multiplied by their distances squared from the axis. In the general case, however, an object's rotational inertia cannot be quantified by a single number. In three-space motion about axes through a point O, an object exhibits different resistances to rotational acceleration in different directions and is representable, therefore, only by a quantity consisting of many numbers. This "hypernumber" (Moon & Spencer, 1965, 1986) arises from the fact that (1) the turning force about each axis factors into a force tangent to the rotational motion and a force normal or radial to the rotational motion and (2) that there are inertial forces resisting both. If the component of torque is N_x, then the moment of the inertia force opposing the torque's tangential component is the moment of inertia about the x-axis, and the moment of the inertia force opposing the torque's radial component is the centrifugal moment or product of inertia about an axis perpendicular to the xy plane formed by the given axis x and a coplanar axis y orthogonal to it. It follows that, for any arbitrary coordinate system $Oxyz$, the hypernumber representing the rigid body's resistance to rotational acceleration about O is a tensor consisting of nine numbers: three quantifying the moments of inertia I_{xx}, I_{yy}, I_{zz}, and six quantifying the products of inertia, I_{xy}, I_{xz}, I_{yx}, I_{yz}, I_{zx}, I_{zy} (e.g., Goldstein, 1980; Symon, 1971). This is the inertia tensor **I**, or more appropriately I_{ij}, introduced in Equation 4; it is represented by a 3×3 symmetric matrix with the moments of inertia on the diagonal. Because $I_{ij} = I_{ji}$, the inertia tensor reduces to six independent numbers.

B. Invariants of the Inertia Tensor I_{ij} about O

The components of I_{ij} with respect to any particular origin are obtained by starting with the corresponding components of I_{ij} taken with respect to the object's center of mass and adding to them the product of the object's mass m and the squared distance of its center of mass (CM) to the new origin (assuming the new axes to be parallel to the axes through the object's CM). The equations that use this parallel axis theorem are of the form

$$I_{xx} = m \ (y^2 + z^2) + I_{xx}{}^*,$$
$$I_{xy} = m \ xy + I_{xy}{}^*, \tag{5}$$

where the asterisk signifies moment or product referring to the center of mass as origin (e.g., Goldstein, 1980; Kibble, 1985). In performing the calculation, the axes through the center of masses are so chosen as to be the central symmetry axes of the body about which the products are zero (i.e., $I_{xy} = m \ xy$).

The calculation of I_{ij} is done with respect to a rectangular coordinate system with its origin at O, that is, $Oxyz$. Obviously, there are indefinitely many sets of three perpendicular axes that can be anchored at O. For each choice of $Oxyz$, the components of I_{ij} will differ. It is the case, however, that scalar properties of I_{ij} can be identified that are invariant over the indefinitely many possible variations of $Oxyz$. The most prominent two are the trace (the sum of the three moments of inertia on the diagonal) and the determinant (e.g., Borisenko & Tarapov, 1979). By using the Einstein summation convention (e.g., Boas, 1983), these are given by I_{ii} and $I_{1i}I_{2j}I_{3k}\delta_{ijk}$, respectively, where δ_{ijk} is the Kroenecker delta or unit matrix (e.g., Boas, 1983). Given the arbitrariness of $Oxyz$, it must be expected that coordinate-system independent scalars such as the trace and determinant have meaning for dynamic touch rather than the particular moments and products calculated in any arbitrarily chosen $Oxyz$.

The trace and the determinant are grounded in coordinate-system independent quantities, or invariants, of a more fundamental kind, namely, the eigenvalues of I_{ij}. These scalars are referred to the only nonarbitrary coordinate system at O, that for which the axes are the principal axes or eigenvectors of I_{ij} (e.g., Goldstein, 1980; Kibble, 1985; Symon, 1971). For a second-order symmetric tensor such as I_{ij}, there are three eigenvalues and three orthogonal eigenvectors. In the coordinate system with the eigenvectors as the axes, I_{ij} is in diagonal form with the eigenvalues on the diagonal and all other entries equal to zero (i.e., no products of inertia, for example, Goldstein, 1980; Kibble, 1985; Symon, 1971). The eigenvectors are the principal axes, and the eigenvalues are the principal moments of inertia.

For any object wielded about a fixed point O, the moments and products of inertia can be computed by means of Equation 5. The resultant tensors can then be diagonalized to yield the eigenvalues (e.g., Boas, 1983; Goldstein, 1980; Symon, 1971). The eigenvalues or principal moments of inertia are referred to by I_1, I_2, and I_3 (with 1, 2, 3 standing in correspondence to largest, intermediate, and smallest). Referring back to the tensor invariants, the trace of I_{ij} is equal to the sum of the three eigenvalues, and the determinant of I_{ij} is equal to the product of the three eigenvalues. As intimated above, all of I_{ij}'s invariants are tied to its eigenvalues. For dynamic touch, it can only be the eigenvalues, independent as they are from choice of coordinate system, that matter. The particular moments and products calculated in any arbitrarily chosen $Oxyz$ cannot have any special significance. In more general terms, the preceding is further argument for modeling dynamic touch in respect to its coordinate-independent physical states and not in respect to representations that are coordinate-dependent descriptions (see Hayward, 1992, for a corresponding sentiment). The significance of this argument should become apparent below.

C. A Hypothesis about the Role of the Inertia Eigenvalues, Inertia Eigenvectors, and Inertia Ellipsoid in Dynamic Touch

In respect to the principal axes and principal moments, Equation 4 is expressed in expanded form as

$$I_1\dot{\omega}_1 - \omega_2\omega_3 (I_2 - I_3) = N_1 \qquad (6)$$

together with two similar equations obtained by cyclic permutation of 1, 2, and 3. What Equation 6 highlights is that, for any arbitrary wielding of an object in three space, the time-varying motions and the time-varying torques are coupled through all three eigenvalues and that the resultant deformation of the muscles and tendons is constrained in a time-independent way by all three eigenvalues. The preceding is reinforced by geometric considerations. If all possible axes p are passed through O, and lengths OA, equal in magnitude to $(I_p)^{-1/2}$, laid off on each axis, the locus of the points A is an ellipsoid called the *momental ellipsoid* or *ellipsoid of inertia* of the object at O. The principal axes of the ellipsoid coincide with the principal axes of inertia of the body at O. In short, I_{ij} is characterized uniquely by a quadric surface with semiaxes of lengths $(I_1)^{-1/2}$, $(I_2)^{-1/2}$ and $(I_3)^{-1/2}$ (e.g., Borisenko & Tarapov, 1979; Lovett, 1989). This geometric entity captures the distribution of the mass of an object "in the mean" (Starzhinskii, 1982). It is evident that the ellipsoid provides an invariant geometric rendering of the invariant mechanical parameter I_{ij} of the dynamics defined by Equation 4. Consequently, if perception by dynamic touch is constrained by I_{ij}, then it must be constrained by the inertial ellipsoid. The perception of object orientation, whether the object is an attachment to the body, such as an implement held in the hand, or a body part, such as an arm, should be constrained by the directions of the inertial ellipsoid. Similarly, for an attachment to the body or a body segment itself, the perception of its magnitudes—such as length, width, and weight—should be constrained by the linear dimensions of the inertial ellipsoid.

III. PERCEIVING OBJECT LENGTH

Figure 1a depicts an apparatus for investigating the perception of the length of a wielded rod without the benefit of vision. In a typical experiment, the subject's right arm rests on an arm support such that the elbow is kept in a fixed position and the wielding takes place about the wrist joint. A screen occludes the right upper limb and the grasped object. To the subject's left is a visible board oriented vertically in a plane perpendicular to the subject's sagittal plane. The position of this board is under the subject's control. It can be moved by means of mechanical or electrical controls manipulable by either the left hand or the feet. Typically, the range of the board's movement is from a location aligned with the position of the right wrist to a distance of approximately 2.5 m from the right wrist. On a trial, one end of an object such as a wooden or metal rod is placed into the subject's right hand by the experimenter. The subject's task is to wield the object by motions about the wrist joint and to adjust the report board so that its visible position coin-

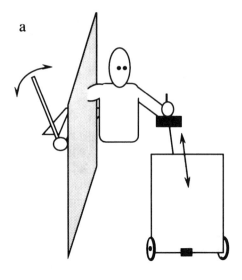

a

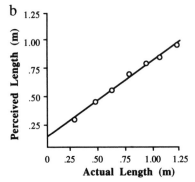

b

FIGURE 1 (a) The subject wields a rod out of view and adjusts the position of a visible surface to coincide with the felt location of the rod tip. (b) Perceived length is a function of actual length. (Adapted from Solomon & Turvey, 1988. Copyright by the American Psychological Association. Adapted with permission.)

cides with the felt distal tip (the end farthest from the hand) of the object, that is, the point reachable with the object.[1] The wielding motions are otherwise unrestricted and the subject can wield the object and manipulate

---

[1] Although some investigations of the haptic touch subsystem have reported that cross-modal matches yield different perceived lengths from ipsemodal matches (e.g., Jastrow, 1886; Kelvin & Mulik, 1958), this is not always the case (Chan, Carello, & Turvey, 1990; Davidon & Mather, (1966). This issue was addressed directly for length perceived by dynamic touch and no difference was found between visual and haptic matches (Carello, Peck, & Fitzpatrick, 1993).

the board for as long as is needed to arrive at a confident judgment. (Usually, wielding the object and positioning the report board occur simultaneously.) No feedback is given about the accuracy of the judgment. Across trials, the lengths of the objects vary, with a unique randomization for each subject. No foreknowledge is provided about the particular lengths and their range, but subjects might be provided (depending on the experiment) with foreknowledge of the common shape of the objects (e.g., by practice with a visible rod).

Figure 1b gives the results from the original experiment (Solomon & Turvey, 1988, Experiment 1) using the preceding method. The rods were aluminum and ranged in length from 0.305 to 1.219 m in increments of 0.152 m. As can be seen from Figure 1b, perceived length was essentially a linear function of actual length. The intercept was approximately zero, and longer lengths tended to be underestimated. Despite having no prior knowledge of the lengths used, and despite the opportunity to place the report board at any distance from 0 to 2.5 m, subjects' responses tracked rod lengths within their actual range.

A. Isolating the Significance of Moment of Inertia

Figure 1b provides evidence of a haptic ability to perceive the extents of nonvisible hand-held objects. Because the haptic perceptual system is affected only by forces, perceived length cannot be based on an object's actual length, which is a geometric quantity (of dimension L) and not a quantity of the required kinetic type (involving the dimension M, that is, mass). The analysis of section II pointed to an object's rotational inertia (of dimensions ML^2) as the invariant kinetic quantity likely to constrain the perception of object properties. Figure 2 shows how the significance of rotational inertia to the perception of length was first demonstrated (Solomon & Turvey, 1988, Experiment 5). There were nine aluminum rods: three of length 0.610 m and mass 0.209 kg, three of length 0.762 m and mass 0.261 kg, and three of length 0.914 m and mass 0.313 kg. To each rod a metal cube of 0.127 kg was attached. Within a triplet of rods of identical magnitudes, the attachment was made at three different locations—one fourth, one half, and three fourths of the rod length from the hand. Manipulating the position of the attached metal cube, therefore, distinguished the rods in a triplet according to rotational inertia about the wrist joint (greatest for the three-fourths attachment and least for the one-fourth attachment) but left them identical in mass and length. Inspection of Figure 2a shows that perceived length is a function of both rod length and the position of the attached metal cube. Figure 2b shows how the one-to-many relation of Figure 2a is rendered one-to-one by expressing perceived length as a function of I_{xx}. In this initial study, I_{xx} was calculated for each rod modeled as a thin cylinder with near-a

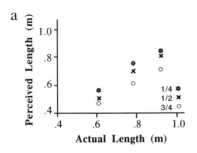

b

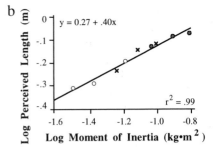

c

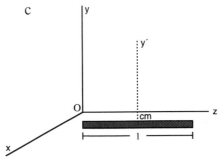

FIGURE 2   (a) For a given rod length, perceived length will vary as a function of the position of an attached mass (Solomon & Turvey, 1988, Experiment 5). (b) This one-to-many relation is rendered one-to-one by expressing perceived length as a function of I_{xx}. (c) With the axis of rotation a point O in the wrist, the x-axis runs through O horizontally, the y-axis runs vertically, and the z-axis runs longitudinally through the rod. This convention is used throughout. (Adapted from Solomon, Turvey, & Burton, 1989b. Copyright by the American Psychological Association. Adapted with permission.)

zero diameter, rotated about a point O approximate to one end of the rod (representing the rotation point in the wrist). Under the preceding simplification, the two largest moments of inertia of an object with an axis of cylindrical symmetry (I_{xx} and I_{yy} by the convention of Figure 2c) are given by

$$I_{xx} = I_{yy} = (mL^2/12) + ma^2, \qquad (7)$$

where m = mass, L = length, and a = the perpendicular distance from axis of rotation O to the parallel axis through CM. The third and smallest moment of inertia (I_{zz}), that about the axis of cylindrical symmetry, is taken to be zero by the simplifying assumption of negligible diameter.

The results summarized in Figure 2 are in agreement with the moment of inertia hypothesis and are counter to the hypothesis that object mass determines object length perception. These two hypotheses can be further contrasted through the simple manipulation of moving O relative to a rod's longitudinal axis; that is, by grasping the to-be-wielded rod at different points along its length. This manipulation results in different magnitudes of I_{xx} as is evident from Equation 7. Given that a is the perpendicular distance from O to the parallel axis through CM, variations in a produce variations in I_{xx} for a rod of fixed magnitudes. By Equation 7, I_{xx} is greatest when O corresponds to points at the ends of the rod and is least when O is at the middle, that is, at CM. If perceived length is tied to I_{xx}, then it should decrease systematically and symmetrically as the position along a rod's length at which it is grasped and wielded approaches the CM, even though rod length and rod mass are constant. Several experiments have tested and confirmed the preceding predictions (Solomon & Turvey, 1988, Experiments 7 and 8; Solomon, Turvey, & Burton, 1989a). In these experiments, because the subject is grasping at intermediate positions and not just the extremes, he or she must often make a judgment in the apparatus of Figure 1a about where the tip of the rod could reach if it were grasped at its most proximal end. Performing this task calls for an implicit translation of the point of origin for the length measure. A grasp at $\frac{3}{4} L$ would leave only one fourth of the grasped rod in front of the hand. In contrast, with the grasp at $\frac{1}{4} L$, three fourths of the rod length would be forward of the hand. By Equation 7, I_{xx} for these two hand positions is the same and greater than that of $\frac{1}{2} L$. If subjects can execute the length measure, and if perceived length were governed by the values given by Equation 7 over variations in a, then perception should depend nonlinearly on hand position with a minimum at $\frac{1}{2} L$. Figure 3 shows the nonlinear effect of hand position on perceived length observed by Solomon et al. (1989a). As expected, however, the perceived lengths of Figure 3 are linearly dependent on I_{xx} when expressed in double logarithmic coordinates.

The results given in Figures 2 and 3 are not sufficient to establish the moment of inertia hypothesis. There are other quantities in the dynamics of wielding that are closely connected with an object's resistance to rotational acceleration. Notable among them are torque N_i, as is evident from Equations 4 and 6, kinetic energy, and work. In the act of wielding, N_i is time varying. It is a transformation in contrast to I_{ij} which is an invariant. Perhaps subjects base their judgments of a persistent object property such as length on the maximal value or time average of N_i (or of kinetic energy or of work) over a bout of wielding rather than on the invariant rotational inertia. Experiments that counter this interpretation involve direct manipulations of the wielding dynamics. For example, the motions of a wielded rod about the wrist joint can be constrained to a repetitive, nearly planar motion of fixed amplitude and frequency. The combination of keeping the amplitude constant (by imposing physical limits on the displacements of the rod in the plane perpendicular to the ground) and varying the frequency of

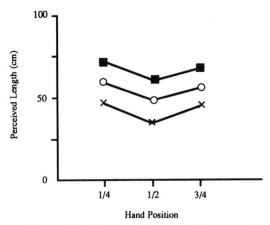

FIGURE 3   A rod grasped in the middle has a smaller I_{xx}—and is perceived to be shorter—than a rod grasped one fourth from either end. The curve parameter is rod length. (Adapted from Solomon et al., 1989a.)

wielding (by means of a metronome) across trials was found to have no effect on perceived length, despite the systematic variations in kinetic energy, mean work, and mean N_i (Solomon & Turvey, 1988, Experiment 4). In this latter experiment, the tangential acceleration of the rod's CM would be given by $a\,\dot{\omega}$, where ω is the metronomically determined angular velocity. Consequently, variations in ω would have been accompanied by variations in $a\,\dot{\omega}$ and, perforce, variations in N_i, given its proportional dependence on tangential acceleration (e.g., den Hartog, 1948).

Another way to manipulate N_i is through the planes of wielding. In a strictly vertical plane, gravity aids and opposes the motion in different phases; in a strictly horizontal plane, gravity's contribution is uniform throughout the motion. The difference in the contribution of gravity means a difference, on the average, in the torques needed to produce the controlled rotational motion. Experiments on wielding in vertical and horizontal planes have found no effect of the plane of motion on perceived length (Solomon et al., 1989a).

Related to the issue of an independence of perceived length from N_i is its independence from the muscular synergies producing the three-space motions of the held object. A particularly simple demonstration of this independence is an experiment in which wielding a rod in a horizontal plane parallel to the ground is achieved either with the palm facing downward, an overhand grasp, or with the palm facing upward, an underhand grasp. Wielding with the overhand grasp involves the flexor and extensor carpi radialis; wielding with the underhand grasp involves the flexor and extensor ulnaris muscle group. Compared with the more common experimental situation described above, in which a rod is wielded in a vertical plane perpendicular to the ground plane, the preceding styles of wielding constitute 90° counterclockwise and clockwise rotations of the forearm. The three wielding orientations not only engage different muscle groups but different torsional states within the forearm musculature. The experimental outcome is that perceived length is constant over these variations in muscle synergies and torsional magnitudes (Solomon et al., 1989a). This conclusion will be underscored in section IV.

B. The One-Third Scaling

In the experiments summarized in III.A, the dependency of perceived length on moment of inertia can be expressed through a power function that is approximately of the form $\alpha I_{xx}^{1/3}$. The significance of a one-third scaling is that for rods of uniform density, perceived length will be a linear function of actual length and will closely match actual length depending on the value of α. This conclusion follows from simple dimensional considerations. Because of the cylindrical symmetry of rods, volume can be expressed as the product of length and cross-sectional area. Area is proportional to the square of the rod's diameter, thus Volume $\propto$ Length $\times$ (Diameter)^2. It follows, therefore, that for a solid cylinder of uniform density, Mass $\propto$ Volume, meaning that Mass $\propto$ Length $\times$ (Diameter)^2. If the diameter of a set of objects conforming to cylindrical symmetry were either constant or negligible, then object mass would increase in direct proportion to object length. Consequently, $I_{xx} \propto$ (Length)^3 given that $I_{xx} \propto$ Mass $\times$ (Length)^2 and Mass $\propto$ Length. Hence, if perceived length conforms to $\alpha I_{xx}^{1/3}$, then it will increase as a positive linear function of actual length.[2]

The above has relevance to the obvious question of whether subjects in the experiments summarized in III.A were perceiving length, as argued, or moment of inertia. A moment of inertia sensation has been reported by Kreifeldt and Chuang (1979), and evidence for an ability to distinguish among objects in terms of rotational inertia has been reported by Knowles and Sheridan (1966).[3] Informally, within the task and apparatus depicted in Figure 1a, subjects report that they feel the tip of the wielded rod and that they attempt to position the report board at a point in alignment with the

[2] Although the power functions from experiments on perceiving length by dynamic touch are reasonably similar in exponents, they differ most notably in their respective constant coefficients. For a discussion of the origins of such differences see Borg and Marks (1983) and Rule (1993).

[3] These investigators required subjects to distinguish among unseen shafts that differed according to the moment of inertia of an affixed metal cylinder. The distinctions were to be made by twisting the shaft by means of a knob. Discussions of the results were restricted to inertia, but rotational inertia was the relevant independent manipulation.

felt tip. That is, they do not seem to be judging an object's resistance to rotational acceleration but its length. In this important respect, the one-third exponent commonly seen is precisely what would be expected if rod length were the object of perception.

C. Manipulating the Inertia Tensor

If wielded objects are perfectly cylindrical and of negligible width, then (1) Equation 7 applies, and (2) $I_{zz} = 0$. To move experimentally beyond the moment of inertia hypothesis as expressed by Equation 7 and toward the inertia tensor hypothesis as based in Equations 4 and 6, cylindrical symmetry needs to be broken and all of an object's linear dimensions need to be relevant to the calculations of rotational inertia. The conceptual move allied to the preceding experimental move necessitates an appreciation of the issue of selecting a coordinate system $Oxyz$. As spelled out in Section II.B., any number of arbitrary coordinate systems can be defined at O. In the initial work on perception by wielding, the significance of this arbitrariness was not fully understood. It was assumed that the subsystem of dynamic touch had to extract from the pattern of moments—defined within a coordinate system—the invariant form consisting of eigenvectors and eigenvalues; that is, dynamic touch had to effect a "functional diagonalization" of I_{ij} (Solomon & Turvey, 1988; Solomon et al., 1989b; Turvey, Solomon, & Burton, 1989). The present understanding, however, is that because the diagonalized tensor is the only nonarbitrary form, the coordinate system defined by the eigenvectors—the symmetry axes of the object about O—is the coordinate system of dynamic touch. That is, in perceiving by wielding, the relevant coordinate system for dynamic touch is always defined locally and uniquely by the symmetry of the mass distribution of the hand-held object about the point of rotation.

Equation 6 suggests that, in the general case, all three eigenvalues constrain perception of length. Irregular objects with nonzero magnitudes of all three eigenvalues, I_1, I_2, I_3, are easily constructed. Figure 4 depicts several that have been used in experiments on perception of extent. Although more complicated than simple solid cylinders, the lengths of the longitudinal dimensions of rods with attached branches are perceived reliably (Pagano & Turvey, 1993). For these objects, despite their departures from perfect cylindrical symmetry, I_1 and I_2 (the intermediate eigenvalue) remain highly correlated. Multiple regression in double logarithmic coordinates reveals that the actual stem length is predictable from a product of I_1 and I_3 (the smallest eigenvalue), with I_1 raised to the 0.39 power and I_3 raised to the -0.04 power, with both exponents highly significant. The outcome of the same regression with perceived stem length as the dependent quantity yielded a similar product of $I_1^{0.42} I_3^{-0.01}$, but with only I_1 significant

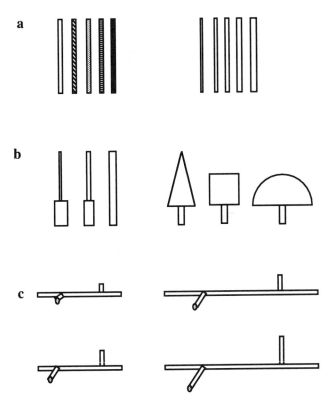

FIGURE 4   A variety of objects with nonzero magnitudes of all three eigenvalues, I_1, I_2, I_3. (a) Different material compositions and different diameters. (b) Inhomogeneous materials and shapes. (c) Irregular objects with branches at right angles to each other and the stem; the proportion of branch length to stem length can vary.

(Pagano & Turvey, 1993). That the major and minor eigenvalues might both affect length perception, but in opposite ways, was demonstrated unequivocally by Fitzpatrick, Carello, and Turvey (1994) by using several kinds of objects, namely, solid cylinders that varied in radius, objects that were hybrids of cylinders of different materials and dimensions, and objects that conformed to basic geometrical solids (see Figure 4). For many of these objects, cylindrical symmetry was again broken with I_1 and I_2 different in magnitude but still highly correlated. Figure 5 shows, for the experiments of Fitzpatrick et al. (1994), the dependency of perceived length on the derived power function in I_1 and I_3. Whereas perceived length increased with I_1, it decreased with I_3.

A reasonable conjecture is that the most general function governing the perception of the lengths of objects by wielding is expressible as the ordered

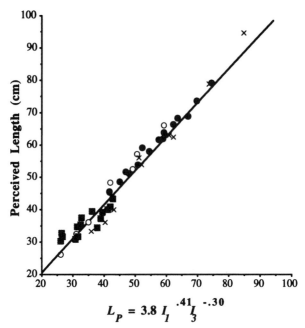

$$L_p = 3.8 \, I_1^{.41} \, I_3^{-.30}$$

FIGURE 5   Perceived length is predictable from a power function in I_1 (positive exponent) and I_3 (negative exponent). Symbols represent different experiments with different objects. (Adapted from Fitzpatrick et al., 1994.)

pairs ($[I_1, I_2, I_3], L_p$), where $[I_1, I_2, I_3]$ refers to a scalar given by the eigenvalues in combination, and L_p is perceived length. The preceding conjecture represents, however, an incomplete account of extent perception by dynamic touch. The mapping of an object's spatial dimensions to I_{ij} is noninvertible. Whereas a particular I_{ij} is defined uniquely by the mass distribution of a given object, the reverse is not true: Any given I_{ij} would describe indefinitely many objects with very different mass distributions. From a mathematical-physical perspective, the mapping from I_{ij} to specific spatial dimensions is not possible without additional restrictions; despite this, L_p was unambiguous in the experiments reviewed in the present section. Traditional approaches to perception would assume that the uniqueness of the mapping from I_{ij} to L_p reflects assumptions embodied in the perceptual apparatus. In visual perception research, for example, computations of motion from structure are said to be constrained by an assumption that the world is rigid (e.g., Marr, 1982; Ullman, 1979). A thoroughgoing ecological approach to perception, however, prohibits the arbitrary ascription of internal constraints and preestablished assumptions about the world (e.g., Turvey & Carello, 1981; Turvey, Shaw, Reed, & Mace, 1981). Within this approach, the specificity of perception to properties of I_{ij} must be understood through general principles.

IV. THE INERTIA TENSOR FIELD AND THE CHALLENGE OF PERCEIVING A CONSTANT OBJECT EXTENT OVER FREE MOVEMENTS OF A MULTISEGMENTED LIMB

The research discussed in section III was in respect to conditions of wielding in which the three-space rotations occurred about a point in the wrist with the other joints of the upper arm fixed. In part, the restriction was imposed to facilitate calculating I_{ij} and measuring the subject's perception of the distance reachable with the tip of the hand-held object. Everyday interactions with objects, however, rarely place such restrictions on the movements of the upper limbs. Many common tasks involve free wielding of hand-held objects, with all joints contributing—singly or in combination at any particular point in time—to an object's motions in three-space as the goals of a given task are achieved.

Producing three-space motion of a hand-held object about different points of origin (wrist, elbow, shoulder, hip, and ankle) would seem to pose a difficulty for the understanding established in Section III that perceived extent is a (single-valued) function of rotational inertia. Grasp a stick firmly at one end and wield it with the eyes closed, first, with motions of the hand about the wrist, second, with motions of the forearm about the elbow while prohibiting motions of the hand about the wrist, and third, with motions of the whole arm about the shoulder while prohibiting separate motions about either the elbow or the wrist. The impression is that the length of the stick seems to be the same in each case. On the understanding that perceived extent relates to the object's rotational inertia, this apparent constancy is puzzling. To reiterate, the resistance of an object to rotational acceleration is expressed as the mass of the object multiplied by the distance squared of the object (i.e., its CM) from the point about which it is rotated. As the distance from the rotation point increases, the object's resistance to a change in its rotational velocity increases as the square of the distance. Thus, a hand-held stick's rotational inertia is considerably greater for wielding about the elbow than about the wrist and considerably greater, in turn, for wielding about the shoulder than about the elbow. Accordingly, at first blush, one might expect perceived extent to differ across the three conditions of wielding rather than remain constant.

Related considerations, having to do with the performatory aspects of the limbs, compound the puzzle. When swung and waved, the human arm behaves as a kinematic chain, with the torques and motions associated with any one cylindrical-like segment affecting the torques and motions associated with the others in both pronounced and subtle ways (Bernstein, 1967; Schneider, Zernicke, Schmidt, & Hart, 1989). Skilled actions involving movements of the whole arm often require a richly variable dynamic of the kind made possible (actively and passively) by the arm's articulated cylinders and an ability to register continuously the spatial magnitudes of a hand-held object to constrain the patterning, timing, and magnitude of the arm's muscular forces. Lawn tennis, table tennis, badminton, hockey, baseball, and cricket come immediately to mind as examples of such activities within the realm of sport. Because of the very obvious role of vision in the control and coordination of these acts, the role of dynamic touch is likely to go unnoticed. Without dynamic touch, however, the scaling of muscular forces to the hand-held object's dimensions could not achieve the fluency and autonomy required by these skilled behaviors (Cooke, Brown, Forget, & Lamarre, 1985; Forget & Lamare, 1987). It would seem, however, that the preceding performatory and perceptual requirements are at odds with each other: In that dynamic touch is, by definition, tied to dynamics, requiring a highly variable movement dynamics would seem to contravene the requirement that the perceptual subsystem of dynamic touch yield constant spatial perceptions.

The resolution of the difficulties raised in the preceding paragraphs is to be found in the notions of a time-dependent inertia tensor, which possesses a time-independent aspect. When wielding occurs only about the wrist, the point of rotation for I_{ij} can be taken to be in the wrist ($I_{ij \text{ wrist}}$). However, when wielding freely about the wrist, elbow, and shoulder, each of the three joints can be taken as the point of reference for a different rendering of I_{ij}, namely, $I_{ij \text{ wrist}}$, $I_{ij \text{ elbow}}$, and $I_{ij \text{ shoulder}}$, respectively, as shown in Figure 6. Given that I_{ij} can be defined at each "point" in the space of points constituted by the body's joints, it is importantly the case that the body, in the act of wielding an object, comprises an I_{ij} field. This I_{ij} field must be time dependent. Because of movement about the wrist, the distance of the object from O_{elbow} and, therefore, the mass distribution of the object about O_{elbow} will change from instant to instant, meaning that $I_{ij \text{ elbow}}$ will vary as a function of time. Similarly, because of movement about the wrist and the elbow, the distance of the object from O_{shoulder} and, therefore, the mass distribution of the object about O_{shoulder} will change from instant to instant, meaning that $I_{ij \text{ shoulder}}$ will vary as a function of time. In contrast, $I_{ij \text{ wrist}}$ does not vary as a function of time because the distance of a firmly grasped object from O_{wrist} and, therefore, the mass distribution of the object about O_{wrist} does not change. Thus, while it is the case that the I_{ij} field must necessarily be time varying, there is an aspect of the field that is invariant with respect to time. By the hypothesis of Gibson identified in section I, one might expect that perceived object magnitude will vary as a function of $I_{ij \text{ wrist}}$ in free wielding, as well as in restricted wielding about O_{wrist}, O_{elbow}, and O_{shoulder},

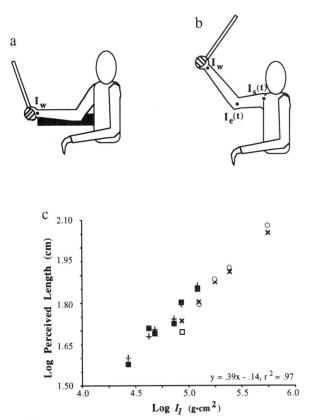

FIGURE 6 (a) When wielding occurs only about the wrist, the point of rotation can be taken to be in the wrist. (b) When wielding freely about the wrist, elbow, and shoulder, each of the three joints can be taken as the point of reference for a different rendering of I_{ij}. (c) Whether rotation is free or restricted to the wrist, perceived length is a function of I_1 defined at the wrist. Symbols represent different conditions in different experiments. (Adapted from Pagano et al., 1993.)

because in all cases $I_{ij \text{ wrist}}$ quantifies an invariant of the changing flux of mechanical energy available to the haptic perceptual system. This prediction has been confirmed by using the method and apparatus depicted in Figure 1a. As shown in Figure 6, perceived length (for solid cylindrical objects with or without attached metal disks) was found to be a (single-valued) function of the largest eigenvalue of $I_{ij \text{ wrist}}$ for wielding about the wrist, elbow, and shoulder singly and for wielding about all three joints simultaneously (Pagano, Fitzpatrick, & Turvey, 1993).

Returning to the apparently competing performatory and measurement demands on an upper limb during actions involving a hand-held implement, haptic perception of the spatial properties of the implement would be a problem of great complexity if it were based on the time-dependent torques and motions necessary to the fluency and success of the act. The complexity would be compounded if the time-varying I_{ij} of the limb had to be factored into the computations. The research of Pagano et al. (1993) suggests that the haptic subsystem of dynamic touch circumvents the implied computational complexity by capitalizing on that aspect ($I_{ij \text{ wrist}}$) of the time-varying play of mechanical forces on the body's tissues that does not change and that connects physically with the spatial features of the object.

V. PERCEIVING SHAPE

Many manipulatory activities involving tools and instruments seem to depend on the manipulated object's shape. The notion of "shape" refers to the property of a surface or object that depends on neither orientation nor position in space and that is indifferent to uniform scalings. Mathematically speaking, shape is a geometrical structure that is invariant, respectively, over isometries and homotheties (Koenderink, 1990). With respect to the definition of visible shape, Koenderink advocates measures grounded in the principal surface curvatures. For any point on a surface, the principal curvatures are the absolute maximum and the absolute minimum attained by the normal curvature. In a similar vein, Burton, Turvey, and Solomon (1990) suggested that the definition of tangible shape—tangible, that is, in the manner of dynamic touch—must be grounded in the principal moments (eigenvalues) of I_{ij}. Specifically, they advocated the ratio of the major and minor eigenvalues, which are the absolute maximum and absolute minimum moments of inertia, respectively, attainable about the given point of rotation. The ratio I_1 / I_3 (or $I_{\max} / I_{\min}$) would be independent of coordinate system and largely unaffected by scale.

In their Experiment 1, Burton et al. (1990) had blindfolded subjects wield freely (rotational motion about all three joints of the arm) an object in the right hand and an object in the left hand. The objects were five geometric solids (hemisphere, cylinder, parallelepiped, cone, and pyramid) of nearly identical weight (as depicted in Figure 4). The objects were wielded by means of handles of a fixed size attached to the base of each object. The subjects' task was to report same or different. A significant difference was found between the mean number of hits (*same* objects judged as same) of 10.44 (out of a maximum of 20) and the mean number of false alarms (*different* objects judged as same) of 4.55 (also out of a maximum of 20). The results suggested that although solid objects of different shapes were distinguishable, shapes nonetheless were often judged to be different even when they were the same. In a second experiment a procedure was used in which subjects attempted to judge which of three occluded objects was different (e.g., two hemispheres and one cone) with no foreknowledge of either the

FIGURE 7   The subject wields an object of a particular shape out of view and chooses a match from among visible objects. (Adapted from Burton, Turvey, & Solomon, 1990.)

kind or number of shapes in the experimental set. The objects were wielded one at a time, with the subjects free to repeat wieldings as often as needed to reach a decision. Results revealed that the identification of which of the three objects was different exceeded chance (a mean of 13.7 out of 20 vs. a chance expectation of 6.7) and that identification was more accurate in some combinations than others.

In the third and fourth experiments of the series, subjects identified the particular object being wielded. Burton et al. (1990) had subjects select, from among the set of five geometric solids visible to them, that object corresponding in shape to the wielded object (which differed from the visible candidates in size). On a trial, a subject grasped with the right hand the given object's handle and wielded it freely; the left hand could be used to point to the likely shape (see Figure 7) or the shape was simply named. There were three major observations. First, subjects were able to perform this task at a level significantly exceeding chance (approximately one third vs. one fifth). Second, performance was the same for the geometric objects at three different sizes (approximately 520, 760, and 1,020 g). Third, the confusions to which subjects were most liable were predicted strongly by the proximity of the I_1/I_3 ratio of one object to that of another (i.e., cones and pyramids, and cubes and short cylinders). The upshot is that there seems to be a crude ability to distinguish among object shapes by wielding, but a great deal more research would be needed to determine whether shape as commonly defined for visual perception is the property perceived by dynamic touch.

VI. PERCEIVING LENGTH UNDER CONDITIONS OF MINIMAL WIELDING

Although the focus of the experiments summarized in the preceding sections has been the properties perceptible by wielding, it is nonetheless the case that haptic exteroperception accompanies the mere holding of an otherwise unsupported object. That is, we seem to be able to feel the dimensions of a hand-held object even when our explorations of its dynamics are purposely limited. Typical examples are one's implicit awareness of the dimensions of a half-filled coffee cup held steadily above a desk during an intense conversation with the arm bent and the elbow resting on the desk's surface or of the book resting on the palm of the hand during the careful reading of a particularly difficult paragraph.

The investigation of the capabilities of dynamic touch with minimal movement was begun by Hoisington (1920). He had subjects raise and lower a horizontally aligned rod grasped at one end through a few centimeters' distance while maintaining the alignment and then raising and lowering a second rod in the same fashion and judging its length as smaller or larger than the first rod. His subjects successfully discriminated rod lengths. Burton and Turvey (1990) replicated Hoisington's observations by using the experimental procedure depicted in Figure 1a (without the wielding). Their experiments involved even less movement on the part of the subject than Hoisington's experiments had; whereas Hoisington's subjects lifted the rods vertically from a support preliminary to making a judgment, Burton and Turvey's subjects had the rods placed directly into the hand that was already in the posture at which the perceptual judgments were to be made.[4] Rods of 45, 61, 76, 91, 107, and 122 cm were perceived by Burton and Turvey's subjects to be 41, 58, 77, 91, 109, and 111 cm.

What forces are involved in balancing a rod horizontally and perceiving its length under these conditions of minimal wielding? A rod can be balanced horizontally through vertical forces by a single support at its CM. Otherwise, to balance a rod horizontally through vertical forces, two points of support are minimally required. If both supports are to one side of CM, then one support must supply a vertically upward reactive force, the other a vertically downward reactive force. Hoisington (1920) hypothesized that haptic perception of rod length under the conditions of his experiments was

---

[4] Hoisington (1920) performed one experiment (Experiment A–X in his series notation) that involved observers merely holding rods without lifting them from a lower position. The outcome was the same as in his lifting experiments, but the implications were not discussed.

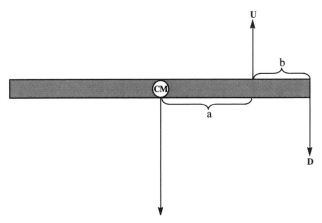

FIGURE 8   The vertical forces needed to balance a rod horizontally with two points of support. The upward force (U) is at a distance a from the center of mass (CM); the downward force D is at a distance b from U. (Adapted from Carello et al., 1992.)

understandable through a force gradient given by the ratio of downward-to-upward forces impressed upon the hand during the holding of a rod. In his length-discrimination task, with a rod grasped at its end, a downward force (D) was provided at the heel of the hand and felt as an upward "kick," and an upward force (U) was provided at the middle phalanges of the index finger and felt as a downward "pressure."

An important prediction of this D to U force gradient, as Hoisington (1920) realized, was that for a given rod, the perception of its length should decline with increased separation of pressure and kick. Consider Figure 8, which depicts D (felt as kick) and U (felt as pressure) together with the downward pull of gravity through CM. To achieve a horizontal alignment of the rod, a balance must be established among these forces (F) and the moments of these forces or torques; $N =$ (force) $\times$ (moment arm), where the moment arm is the length of the perpendicular dropped from the center of moment (the point or axis about which the rotation would take place if it could) to the line of force. Consequently, balancing a rod horizontally requires satisfaction of the following conditions: ΣF(vertical) $= 0$, ΣF(horizontal) $= 0$, and $\Sigma N = 0$. For the present case, there are no forces or components of forces in the horizontal direction; all forces are in the vertical direction. Summing the forces yields

$$U - D - Mg = 0. \tag{8}$$

Let the Ns be calculated about the point of application of U, the center of moment. Then,

$$Db - Mga = 0, \tag{9}$$

where M is the rod mass, g is the constant acceleration due to gravity, and a and b are the distances of Mg and D, respectively, from U. Substituting and rearranging yield

$$D/Mg = a/b, \tag{10}$$

$$U/Mg = (a + b)/b, \tag{11}$$

and

$$D/U = a/(a + b). \tag{12}$$

According to Equation 12, D/U (or kick/pressure) is greater the smaller the value of b or, equivalently, the smaller the distance separating D (or kick) and U (or pressure). Hence, Hoisington's (1920) prediction: For any given rod, the greater the separation of kick and pressure, the shorter will be its perceived length. This prediction of Hoisington's was tested experimentally by Carello, Fitzpatrick, Domaniewicz, Chan, and Turvey (1992) together with a conjecture by Hoisington that the gradient between kick and pressure could be registered satisfactorily by any parts of the body. In more general terms, this conjecture of Hoisington's reads: If the pattern of forces impressed upon the body is what matters, rather than the anatomy by means of which those forces are felt, then variations in the anatomical localizations of the same force pattern should yield length perceptions of the same magnitude. Carello et al. (1992) confirmed the conjecture of anatomical independence and the gradient hypothesis through an examination of the conditions depicted in Figure 9. For a fixed distance between D and U (see Figure 8), perceived length was the same regardless of points of contact (D at the base of one hand and U at the forefinger, or D at the base of one hand and U at the forefinger of the other hand, or D at the base of one hand and U at the knee); for increasing distances between D (at the base of one hand) and U (at the forefinger of the other hand), perceived length was found to decrease systematically.

Hoisington's (1920) D/U gradient hypothesis is not of a kind with the inertia tensor hypothesis developed and confirmed in preceding sections. Its focus is on the forces at play in preserving a fixed-rod orientation rather than a parameter of the dynamics that couples the forces to the object's motion (see section I.A). Whether a force gradient is actually needed can be checked by reducing the number of anatomical contact points from two to one. Figure 10 shows how this was done by Carello et al. (1992). In respect to preserving static equilibrium, Equations 10 and 11 express the balance of the rod in terms of one contact point and gravitational torque, N_g. In the conditions of Figure 10, Carello et al. found rods of 76, 91, 107, and 122 cm to be perceived as 75, 96, 109, and 123 cm in length with no difference between the one-point and two-point contact conditions. Given the inap-

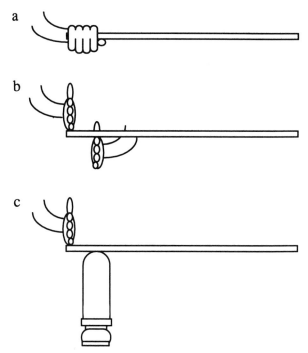

FIGURE 9   The same distance h (see Figure 8) can be achieved (a) across the palm of a single hand, (b) from the bottom edge of one hand to the top edge of the other hand, or (c) from the bottom edge of one hand to the top of the knee.

plicability of Hoisington's force gradient to one contact point, the candidate mechanical quantities become N_g, moment of inertia, and static moment. The static moment is the first moment of the mass distribution given by the integral of the products of the point masses and their respective position vectors and usually calculated as the product of the object mass M and the length of the perpendicular from the object's CM to its center of moment (the point or axis about which the rotation would take place if the rod were set in motion).

In evaluating the contributions of the first moment and second moment of the mass distribution (moment of inertia), Burton and Turvey (1990) used rods of three different lengths with (1) two masses attached, one mass at a distance one eighth of the rod length from one end and one mass of the same magnitude at the same distance from the other end; (2) one mass of the same magnitude as those in (1) attached at a distance of one eighth of the rod length from an end; and (3) no masses attached. When grasped at their midpoints, the static moments of these rods would be greater for the single attached mass rather than the double attached mass (and, thereby, statically

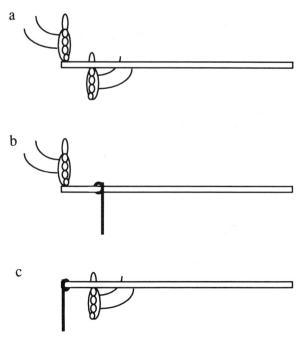

FIGURE 10   (a) Two points of anatomical contact in which the right hand provides downward force (D), and the left hand provides upward force (U) (See Figure 8). (b) One point of anatomical contact provides D, and an environmental support provides U. (c) One point of anatomical contact provides U, and an environmental support provides D.

balanced) conditions, whereas the reverse would be true for the moments of inertia. Experiments contrasting holding the rods steady and horizontal to the ground plane versus wielding them freely about an axis in the wrist produced two different dependencies of perceived length on number of attached masses. When held steady, perceived length was essentially the same for one and two attached masses; in contrast, when wielded, perception was greater when two masses were attached rather than one. The pattern of results points to a difference between the mechanical quantities of relevance to minimal and free rod wielding. The particular form of the pattern and close examination of the partial F values in the multiple regression of perceived length on both first and second moments suggests, however, that it is not a clear-cut distinction. The moment of inertia is implicated in both wielding conditions, although its contribution in the minimal situation (holding steady) is markedly reduced. It appears that the first moment is a contributor to the perception of length without movement, perhaps the major contributor, but its contribution can be compromised by that of the second moment.

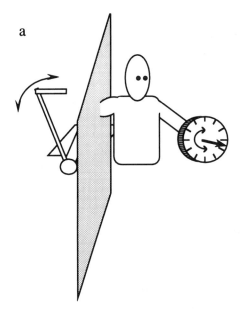

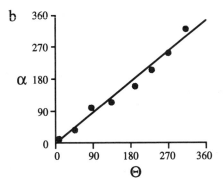

FIGURE 11 (a) The subject wields an L-shaped rod out of view and adjusts the position of a visible marker to point in the felt direction of the branch. (b) Perceived orientation, quantified by the circular statistic α is a function of actual orientation θ, both measured in degrees. (Adapted from Turvey et al., 1992. Copyright by the American Psychological Association. Adapted with permission.)

To evaluate the contrasting contributions of the first moment and N_g, Carello et al. (1992) decorrelated these quantities by manipulating the perpendicular to the line of force, $a \cos \theta$, where a is the length of the line joining the center of moment to the CM (see Figure 8), and θ is the inclination to the ground plane. They reasoned that for rods of three different lengths held steadily at $\theta = 0°$, $45°$, and $90°$, θ should prove nonsignificant if perceived length was constrained solely by the first moment and significant if perceived length was constrained, in contrast, by N_g. Although multiple regression revealed that the static moment accounted for considerably more of the variance in perceived length, the effect of θ was, nonetheless, highly significant. Evidence for N_g challenges the guiding assumption that perception by dynamic touch is constrained by the invariant of the holding dynamic, namely, the static moment. In response, Carello et al. (1991) raised the issue of whether θ's significance might have arisen from its contribution to muscle torsion rather than N_g. As of now there are no experiments that could adjudicate on this issue, and the basis of length perception under conditions of minimal wielding remains unclear.

VII. PERCEIVING HAND–OBJECT AND OBJECT–HAND RELATIONS

When an object is grasped and wielded, two kinds of directional perceptions are of significance: How the object or its segments are directed relative to the hand, and how the hand is positioned relative to the object (e.g., where along its length is the object grasped?). As the preceding section has underscored, the contribution of the haptic perceptual system to the control of manipulatory activity involving tools and implements occurs primarily through the subsystem of dynamic touch and functions, presumably, in the tuning (see Greene, 1972; Turvey, 1977) of the coordinative structures or muscular synergies involved in the activity. This tuning is not only in respect to the constant spatial dimensions of a hand-held object but also in respect to the constant hand-to-object and object-to-hand spatial relations during wielding. In short, the tuning is based on both exterospecific information and expropriospecific information.

As identified in sections II to V, the eigenvalues of I_{ij} constrain the exteroperceptive abilities of human dynamic touch. The main goal of section VII is to show that the eigenvectors of I_{ij} constrain dynamic touch's exproprioperceptive abilities. To reiterate, the eigenvectors or principal directions refer to those axes about which the off-diagonal terms, or products of inertia, are zero. They are the symmetry axes of the object about its rotation point O.

A. Dependence of Orientation Perception on Products of Inertia, Object Size, and Style of Wielding

The first experiments directed at the issue of perceiving the orientation of an object relative to the hand used L-shaped objects and the report apparatus depicted in Figure 11a (Turvey, Burton, Pagano, Solomon, & Runeson,

1992). The central principal axes of such an object are orthogonal Cartesian axes passing through its CM about which the products of inertia (and, thereby, the dynamical reactions) are zero. If an L-shaped rod is grasped at one end and wielded by motions about the wrist, then, by definition, the axes of rotation will not be the central principal axes, products of inertia will exist, and dynamical reactive forces will be present throughout the wielding. Now it is important to note that for a fixed system of coordinates with origin at the wrist, the products and moments of inertia will vary with how the rod is placed in the hand. Let the longer piece of the L-shaped rod be called the *stem,* let the shorter piece be called the *branch,* and let the stem be the piece that is held. Then it is clear that the rod can be placed in the hand such that, if the longitudinal axis of the stem parallel to the body's sagittal plane is the x-axis, then the branch can be oriented in the yz plane at any angle between $0°$ and $360°$. For each orientation of the rod—meaning the angle made by the branch in the yz plane—there will be a different alignment of the rod's mass in the wrist-based coordinate system.

Table 1 presents the orientation dependent I_{ij}s for an L-shaped wooden rod, composed from a stem of 35 cm and 28 g and a branch of 9 cm and 7.2 g, held firmly in the hand at eight different orientations corresponding to $0°$, $45°$, $90°$, $135°$, $180°$, $225°$, $270°$, and $315°$. The angles are the orientations of the branch of the L-shaped rod in the coordinate system defined through a fixed point in the wrist (see Figure 2c). The tensors are calculated for a system of rectangular coordinates with origin at a point in the wrist. (The x- and z-axes are parallel to the ground plane and the y-axis is parallel to the gravitational plumb line.) Inspection of Table 1 reveals how the components of I_{ij} are defined uniquely for a given angle of orientation and how they change with angle.

In the initial experiment (Turvey et al., 1992, Experiment 1), eight set-

TABLE 1   Inertia Tensors of L-Shaped Rods in a Variety of Orientations[a]

Θ (in degrees)	Tensor components (g·cm²)					
	I_{xx}	I_{yy}	I_{zz}	I_{xy}	I_{xz}	I_{yz}
0	22524	20562	1967	0	0	−4970
45	22545	20586	2098	−104	706	−5239
90	22814	20719	2416	−224	999	−5970
135	23211	20640	2734	−213	706	−6701
180	23421	20562	2865	0	0	−6970
225	23211	20640	2734	213	−706	−6701
270	22814	20719	2416	224	−999	−5970
315	22545	20586	2098	104	−706	−5239

[a] Adapted from Turvey, Burton, Pagano, Solomon, and Runeson (1992). Copyright by the American Psychological Association. Adapted with permission.

tings of the L-shaped rod were used, ranging from 0° to 360° in 45° steps, with the branch pointing straight upward for a setting of 0°. Subjects were not informed that the number of possible positions of the L-shaped object was limited in this way. The object could be wielded in any way preferred as long as the wrist stayed at the designated place on the arm of the chair and the stem stayed in the same place in the hand (see Figure 11a). There was no time limit within a trial for shaking the L-shaped object. Each person reported his or her judgment of the branch's orientation by turning the circular dial mounted on the visible report board until the arrow on the dial corresponded with the perception of the orientation of the occluded L-shaped object. Given that a subject estimated a given orientation on four separate trials during the course of the experiment, circular statistics[5] were used to calculate the mean perceived angle for each orientation. As can be seen from Figure 11b, perceived orientation quantified by the circular statistic α matched actual orientation. The check by a multiple regression of the dependence of perceived orientation on the elements of I_{ij} (see Table 1) revealed that although moments and products of inertia both contributed to perceived orientation, the examination of the partial Fs suggested that the contribution of the products was greater.

An important aspect of circular statistics is the provision of several useful measures in respect to the perception of orientation by dynamic touch. As remarked, the circular statistic providing the dependent measure in Figure 11b is α, the measure of the resultant angle of the judgments (see footnote 5). In addition to α, there is r, which measures the coherency of the various judgments and h, the homing coefficient, which measures how closely the perceived orientations "homed in" on the actual target orientation. The h is like the r coefficient, except that it takes into account whether the judgments were accurate. Thus, if most subjects judged the rod set at 45° as 180°, they might have a high r but a low h. Because dynamic touch is essentially exploratory, with the relevant invariant quantities revealed over actively induced variations in the forces and motions, h might depend on the kinds of explorations permitted in the task depicted in Figure 11a. Turvey et al. (1992, Experiment 2) found that h was greater when subjects were permit-

---

[5] An arithmetic mean is not generally suitable for judgments of angle because of the periodic nature of a circle. For example, for an L-shaped object at 315°, a judgment of 15° and a judgment of 255° are both within 60° and should be considered equally accurate. However, the arithmetic average of these two judgments would be 135°, which differs from the setting by 120°. Trigonometric functions are suitably circular, but they cycle twice in a circle, and thus, there would not be a unique value for every point on the circle. The preceding difficulties are overcome by circular statistics (Batschelet, 1965, 1978). The main component of this method is finding an average judgment by taking the sine and cosine of each judgment, summing these judgments over repetitions, and transforming this sine and cosine combination back into the angle they pertain to. This method yields the resultant of the vectors described by each of the component angles (see Turvey et al., 1993, for examples of the method).

ted to wield freely than when they were restricted to motions in either the vertical or horizontal planes. All three wielding conditions, however, produced reliable discriminations of the orientations of the L-shaped object.

If there is truly a capability to perceive the orientation of an object in the hand, then it should be the case that orientation perception is size independent: Objects of different sizes but at the same orientation should be perceived at the same orientation. At the same time, however, it might be expected that the accuracy of perception will depend on size. Larger versions of the same object will be characterized by larger moments and products of inertia. Consequently, the asymmetry of the second moments of the mass distribution relative to the hand should be more easily detectable for larger L-shaped objects. In terms of circular statistics, α should be affected by object orientation but not by object size, and h should be affected by object size and not by object orientation. These predictions were confirmed in an experiment (Turvey et al. 1992, Experiment 3) in which three L-shaped rods were used distinguished by the size of the branch—6.0, 11.5, and 16.25 cm.

B. Support for the Eigenvector Hypothesis Comes from Experiments That Break the Covariation between Space Axes and Symmetry Axes

Although the experiments using L-shaped objects provide general support for the I_{ij} hypothesis, they are not able to confirm the specific hypothesis that the perceptual ability to perceive orientation is tied to the eigenvectors. For L-shaped objects, there is a confounding of an object's spatial orientation (expressed as vectors in the space axes O_{xyz}) and its eigenvectors (the symmetry axes of the second moment of the mass distribution). To evaluate the eigenvectors hypothesis, objects different from L-shaped objects must be used, specifically, objects for which the covariation between spatial orientations and eigenvectors is broken.

In two experiments reported by Pagano and Turvey (1992), the wielded object consisted of a stem with two branches forming a V perpendicular to the stem. Two coordinate systems can be identified for this object. One coordinate system provides a reference frame for the spatial orientation of the branches relative to the stem and is depicted in Figure 12a. This reference frame consists of angles within the plane of the branches about axes coincident with the central axes of the stem. The second coordinate system (anchored at the object's point of rotation in the wrist) provides a reference frame for calculating I_{ij} and, in turn, the eigenvectors of the object and is depicted in Figure 12b. Each eigenvector is defined by three xyz coordinates of these axes. By differentially weighting the branches, it is possible to construct V objects such that, when the objects are oriented similarly within

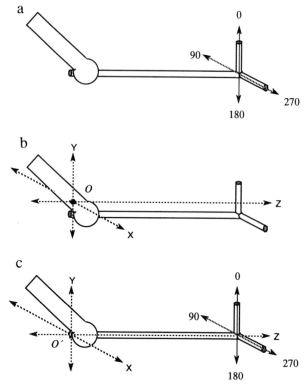

FIGURE 12 (a) The subject holds the stem of a rod that ends with two branches forming a V perpendicular to the stem. A coordinate system provides a reference frame for the spatial orientation of the branches relative to the stem. (b) A second coordinate system (anchored at the object's point of rotation O in the wrist) provides a reference frame for calculating I_{ij} and, in turn, the eigenvectors of the object. (c) The orientation of the eigenvector pointing in the z direction of the spatial axes; the eigenvector e_3, about a point O′ at the end of the stem. (Adapted from Pagano & Turvey, 1992.)

the former reference frame, their eigenvectors are oriented differently within the latter reference frame. If perception of object orientation through dynamic touch is dependent only on the actual geometric orientation of the object, differentially weighted objects should be perceived to be at the same orientation within the spatial reference frame. If, however, the perception of object orientation is tied to the object's eigenvectors, differently weighted objects with coincident orientations within the spatial reference frame will be perceived to be at different orientations within that reference frame.

In one experiment, the more clockwise of the two branches of a V object was weighted in one third of the trials, the more counterclockwise branch was weighted in one third of the trials, and neither branch was weighted in one third of the trials. Subjects were asked to perceive the orientation of both branches by using a variant of the report procedure shown in Figure 11A. Two rotatable pointers rather than one allowed them to report the orientation of the V. The predicted outcome was as follows: If perceived orientation is specific to the inertial eigenvectors, then perceived orientations should be drawn away from the branch's spatial orientation to the orientation of the object's rotational-inertia symmetry axes. That is, in the conditions in which the more clockwise branch is weighted, perceived orientations of the V should be more clockwise, and in the conditions in which the more counterclockwise branch is weighted, perceived orientations of the V should be more counterclockwise. These expectations can be expressed most straightforwardly through the orientation of the eigenvector e_3 pointing in the z direction of the spatial axes about a point O' at the end of the object opposite from that of the V (see Figure 12c). By the transformation law of tensors (e.g., Borisenko & Tarapov, 1979), I_{ij} calculated at O in Figure 12b can be transformed into I_{ij} at O' in Figure 12c. Table 2 shows the orientations of the spatial bisector and the z eigenvector or e_3 for the three different V objects of the experiment, and Figure 13 shows the fit of perceived orientation to the spatial orientation of the object (Figure 13a) and to e_3 (Figure 13b).

In a second experiment, Pagano and Turvey (1992) had subjects perceive the orientation of the weighted branch only. As in the first experiment, it was expected that subjects' perceptions of orientation would be drawn away from the weighted branch's spatial orientation and to the orientation of e_3 about O'. Specifically, under conditions in which the unweighted branch was 90° clockwise with respect to the weighted branch, perceived orientation of the weighted branch should be more clockwise. Likewise, under conditions in which the unweighted branch was 90° counterclockwise with respect to the weighted branch, the perceived orientation of the weighted branch should be more counterclockwise. Whereas the eigenvectors hypothesis predicts that perceived orientation should be drawn in the direction of the weighted branch for the conditions of the first experiment, it predicts that it should be drawn in the direction of the unweighted branch for the conditions of the second experiment. Though different, both predictions followed from the understanding that perceived orientation is a function of I_{ij}'s eigenvectors rather than the actual spatial orientation of either branch. The confirmatory results of Pagano and Turvey's second experiment are shown in Figure 14.

C. Perceiving Where an Object Is Grasped

As implied in the introduction to the present section, exproprioception by dynamic touch involves both object-to-hand relations and hand-to-object

TABLE 2   Spatial Orientation of the Bisector and e_3 (in Degrees) about O as a Function of the Actual Orientation (in Degrees) of the Two Branches in Each Condition of Figure 13

Actual orientation		Bisector	e_3
Branch 1	Branch 2	orientation	orientation
0	90	45	43.9
90	180	135	133.9
180	270	225	223.9
270	360	315	313.9
0	90	45	25.5
90	180	135	115.5
180	270	225	205.5
270	360	315	295.5
0	90	45	62.8
90	180	135	152.8
180	270	225	242.8
270	360	315	332.8

relations. The latter are the focus of the present subsection. Consider Figure 15, when a homogeneous cylindrical object is grasped at different positions along its length (i.e., different y-coordinates of CM), the corresponding I_{ij} varies with both rod size and hand position. With respect to the grasped homogeneous solid cylinders depicted in Figure 15a, the components of I_{ij} are identical with the exception of the sign of I_{yz} for hand positions of 0.25 and 0.75 of rod length; for the hand at 0.5, I_{xx} and I_{yy} are smaller and I_{yz} equals zero. Analysis shows that I_{yy} and I_{yz} predict the rotation point, with I_{yz} the more important of the two implying that I_{yz} should be the major constraint on perceiving where an object is grasped. Pagano, Kinsella-Shaw, Cassidy, and Turvey (1994) found that, when subjects grasped and wielded homogeneous cylinders, perceived hand position matched actual hand position. To provide a strong test of the hypothesis that perceived grasp is tied

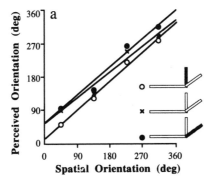

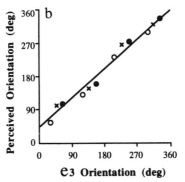

FIGURE 13   (a) The fit of perceived orientation to the spatial orientation of objects is biased toward the weighted branch of the V. (b) Perceived orientation is a function of e_3. (Adapted from Pagano & Turvey, 1992.)

to I_{ij}, particularly to its off-diagonal terms, inhomogeneous objects were used that broke the symmetries responsible for the relations identified above between grasp position and I_{ij}. The moments and products of inertia of uniformly cylindrical objects were changed by appending weights to such objects at locations either above or below the hand (see Figure 15b). Perceived hand position was expected to depend systematically on I_{ij}, in particular on I_{yz}, but not on actual hand position. If perceived hand position depends primarily on I_{yz}, then the simple regression of perceived hand position on I_{yz} should have an intercept of 0.5. that is, if one's perceived grasp relative to the object's mass distribution is constrained by I_{yz}, then the greater the deviation of I_{yz} from zero, the more deviant should perceived hand position be from the object's midpoint, regardless of actual hand

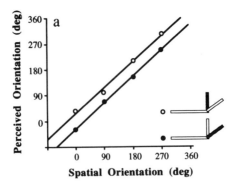

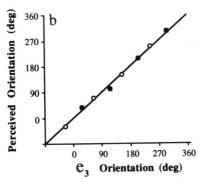

FIGURE 14   (a) Perceived orientation of the weighted branch is biased toward the un-weighted branch. (b) Perceived orientation is a function of e_3. (Adapted from Pagano & Turvey, 1992.)

position. Further, the direction of the deviation, greater than or less than the midpoint, should depend on the sign of I_{yz}. Pagano et al. confirmed these expectations as shown in Figure 15c and the more basic understanding that these perceptions were constrained by the eigenvectors, as shown in Figure 15d. For the objects held in the manner of Figure 15a, the eigenvectors or principal axes about O differ from $Oxyz$ by a rotation in the yz plane. One eigenvector, therefore, is coincident with the x-axis, and the location of the remaining two eigenvectors is quantified by a rotation about the x-axis. This rotation of the eigenvectors would be downward for homogeneous rods held below the midpoint (CM above the hand), upward for those held above the midpoint (CM below the hand), and zero (i.e., coincident with the z-axis of $Oxyz$) for those held at the midpoint. The latter feature means that for an eigenvector rotation of 0°, perceived hand position should equal 0.5. The degree to which the principal axes were rotated predicted perceived hand position as Figure 15d reveals.

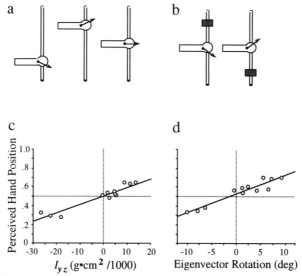

FIGURE 15   (a) The rotation of the eigenvector e_3 of a homogeneous solid cylinder depends on where it is grasped. (b) For rods grasped in the middle, the rotation of e_3 of a solid cylinder with an attached mass depends on how far the mass is from the grasp and whether the mass is above or below the hand. (c) The more the value of I_{yz} departs from zero, the more perceived grasp departs from 0.5. (d) Perceived grasp is a function of the direction of e_3 in O_{xyz}. (Adapted from Pagano et al., 1994. Copyright by the American Psychological Association. Adapted with permission.)

VIII. DYNAMIC TOUCH AND THE "MUSCULAR SENSE"

The next two sets of empirical findings to be summarized (in sections IX and X) address ancient issues in experimental psychology, namely, perception of the body (with the related notion of a body image) and perception of weight (with the associated phenomenon of the size–weight illusion). As will become apparent, the findings suggest that both issues are linked to I_{ij}. Because both issues traditionally have been related to the "muscular sense," it is valuable at this juncture to bring into focus the classical conception of this "sense" and its alignment with the ideas about dynamic touch developed thus far in this chapter.

Although recognition of a muscle sense can be traced to scholars in the sixteenth century, the first major discussion of its nature was by Charles Bell in 1826 (Boring, 1942). Bell suggested that muscular tissue may contain receptors capable of signaling how a muscle activated by the central nervous system is actually behaving (proprioception) and of distinguishing the effects of external loads from those of central neural innervation (exteroception). He advanced two hypotheses. First, that muscle contains sensory and motor fibers and, second, that these muscular sensory fibers are the basis for experiencing the orientations of limbs and limb segments and the properties of surfaces and objects with which the body is in contact. Confirmation of the first hypothesis was in place in the nineteenth century (see Boring, 1942; Granit, 1955). In contrast, confirmation of the second hypothesis was achieved late in the present century, and then primarily in respect to the positions and movements of body segments (e.g., Burgess, Wei, Clark, & Simon, 1982; Goodwin, McCloskey, & Matthews, 1972). In both the last and present century, the exteroceptive aspect of Bell's second hypothesis has largely been ignored.

The anatomy and physiology of the receptive organs in the muscle are currently well-known (for an overview, see Shepherd, 1988). The fibers making up the bulk of the muscle and responsible for displacing limb segments are the extrafusal fibers. In parallel with them are modified muscle fibers, termed *intrafusal,* enveloped by receptive structures known as *muscle spindles.* A muscle spindle is a transducer sensitive to muscle length that transmits signals centrally over two afferent routes: the spindle primary, or group Ia afferents, and the spindle secondary, or group II, afferents. The sensitivity of these afferents to muscle length and its changes can be centrally modulated by static and dynamic γ motoneurons that induce contractions in the small intrafusal fibers present within the capsule of a spindle. Static γ motoneurons bias the Ia and II afferents primarily to muscle length; dynamic γ motoneurons affect only the Ia afferents, biasing them to changes in muscle length (Evarts, Bizzi, Burke, DeLong, & Thach, 1971). In addition to the muscle spindles are Golgi tendon organs embedded in the tendon at the end of a muscle and, therefore, in series with the extrafusal muscle fibers. Golgi tendon organs act as sensitive tension receptors, responding to muscle tensions of 0.1 g and smaller (Binder, Kroin, Moore, & Stuart, 1977).

Acceptance of Bell's first hypothesis was accompanied by rejection of his second hypothesis. The rejection was empirical, anatomical, and logical. Experiments had failed to find evidence of a perception of limb position when joint receptors were temporarily disabled and muscle receptors were fully functioning (e.g., Goldscheider, 1898; Provins, 1958) and of a perception of muscle lengthening when tendons were pulled (Gelfan & Carter, 1967). Anatomical studies had failed to find evidence for muscle afferent pathways to the cortex suggesting that the muscular sense organs were "private measuring instruments" (Granit, 1955) limited to servicing spinal reflexes (e.g., Rose & Mountcastle, 1959). Logical considerations ruled out a proprioceptive role for muscle receptors given that neither spindles nor tendon receptors could register muscle length per se, and it seemed apparent that absolute muscle length had to be registered if limb position and movement were to be perceived (Merton, 1964; Rose & Mountcastle, 1959). The outcome of these criticisms was a rejection of muscle sense and a promotion of "joint sense." In direct favor of joint sense was evidence that joint receptors were tuned to respond over narrow angles within the range of joint movement (Skoglund, 1956) and that pathways from the joint receptors to the cortex could be identified (Rose & Mountcastle, 1959).

The possibility that Bell's second hypothesis had been rejected on false grounds became apparent when Goodwin et al. (1972) and Matthews and Simmons (1974) found positive evidence for a proprioceptive role of muscle receptors in experimental settings analogous to those that had previously provided negative evidence. It now seems as if previous research had examined displacements that were too small and too slow and had focused subject's attention on inappropriate aspects of the experimental task. Of particular importance was the finding that stimulation of the spindles through vibrations applied to the biceps led subjects to experience the arm as more extended (the intrafusals as more elongated) than was actually the case (Goodwin et al., 1972). With the discovery of muscle afferent pathways to the somatosensory and motor cortex (Shepherd, 1988), and the accumulation of results indicating that joint receptors are activated only at extreme positions (e.g., Clark & Burgess, 1975), Bell's muscle sense was reestablished and its hypothesized proprioceptive role confirmed.

One might argue that both achievements were reinforced by Burgess et al.'s (1982) suggestion of how to address the logical counterpoint that muscle receptors cannot specify degree of flexion or extension because they do not signal absolute length: The pattern of spindle activity defined over the antagonistic musculature at a joint is unique to joint angle. The implication is that perceiving the orientations of limbs and limb segments is not based in a measure suited to trigonometric calculations of joint angles such as length but rather is based in large scale deformation quantities that are specific to those dispositions. The receptive machinery embedded in the muscles and tendons associated with a limb segment provides quantification of strain differences (extrafusal vs. intrafusal) in different directions, rates of change of strain differences in different directions, stress differences in different directions, and (potentially) rates of change of stress differences in different directions. Collectively, the spindles and Golgi organs respond to the deformation of muscle, that is, its change of shape or nonrigid motion, and to the changes in deformation over time. That they can provide a field[6]

---

[6] What is a field? The field notion was referred to in section IV and will appear again in section IX. This seems a good place to provide an intuitive sketch of its meaning. A useful answer to the preceding question can be extracted from a fluid in motion (Krieger, 1992), for example, the flow of water constituting a simple stream in a meadow. To every point in space occupied by the water, a velocity vector can be assigned; at a larger scale, these local vectors link up into flow lines. Of importance, the field values (the velocity vectors) at nearby points cannot be arbitrarily different from each other, that is, they cannot be independent of each other. If they were, then there would be discontinuity and no flow. A field tends to be reasonably smooth.

description of muscle deformation is suggested by a detailed consideration of a given muscle (Matthews, 1964). The soleus muscle of the cat is made up of about 25,000 extrafusal and 300 intrafusal muscle fibers supplied by about 150 α and 100 γ motoneurons, respectively. Its sensory innervation is provided by about 50 spindles with 50 primary afferents and 50 to 70 secondary afferents and about 45 tendon organs with roughly the same number of tendon afferents. Evidently, muscle constitutes a richly variable receptive structure that can be potentially informative about a wide variety of properties. It was Ruffini's guess (1897) that the sensory organs of the muscle may closely match those of the eye and ear in sophistication of function. The growing evidence for the spatial abilities of dynamic touch confirm that, at the very least, there are important parallels.

IX. PERCEIVING LIMB POSITION BY DYNAMIC TOUCH

Consideration now turns to research directed at the possibility that the understanding of dynamic touch summarized in sections II–VII may apply not only to how one perceives "attachments to the skin," such as tools and instruments and the hand's relation to them, but also to the very traditional concern of how one perceives the body itself. Preliminary to a discussion of the experiments, and following Pagano and Turvey (in press), an argument is provided that the body, its limbs, and its limb segments are describable through I_{ij}s defined about the respective rotation points in the joints. This argument leads to the hypothesis that a person's knowledge about the dimensions and directions of his or her body and its appendages is given continuously by the eigenvalues and eigenvectors of the respective tensors.

The existence of an internally stored "model of oneself" or body "schema" (Head, 1920) on the basis of some combination of past and current sensory information (Parsons, 1990) is typically regarded as necessary for proprioceptive abilities. As originally defined by Head and Holmes, it was a "combined standard, against which all subsequent change in posture is measured (1911–1912, p. 187)." More recently, it has been defined as an

---

Furthermore, it is evidently the case that the water in a stream is connected to sources, springs, and mountains. Turning to bulk muscle as a (sensory) field, the sources are the spindles and Golgi tendon organs. The field in muscle is the signaling properties of these receptors, their "leakage" so to speak. Although it has a very large number of degrees of freedom—the signals produced by each receptor under stress—a muscle field like a fluid flow limits the point-to-point arbitrariness of its sources and, therefore, its degrees of freedom, by overarching constraints such as continuity. In contrast to the customary strategy of taking the properties of the individual receptors as the right degrees of freedom, the experimental results and arguments presented here imply that the right degrees of freedom for the muscular sense must be attributed to the field. As Weinberg (1983, p. 16) admonishes, "You may use any degrees of freedom you like to describe a physical system, but if you use the wrong ones, you'll be sorry."

abstract internal representation of the body's spatial and mechanical properties "containing the internal model of the body and including the set of basic
motor mechanisms and of algorithms for their coordination" (Gurfinkel &
Levik, 1991, p. 152; see also Parsons, 1990). A common assumption is that
the coordinates of a distal extremity can only be obtained from stored
knowledge of limb lengths taken in conjunction with joint angles (Craske,
Kenny, & Keith, 1984; Gurfinkel & Levik, 1979, 1991). Studies involving
muscle–tendon vibration seem, however, to be at odds with this assumption. Craske (1977) induced errors in perceived limb position by vibrating
the tendons of the limb in question. Of importance, the perceived limb
positions were often impossible; when either the biceps or triceps tendons
were vibrated, the forearm was often perceived to be at an angle of extension beyond that which is anatomically achievable. In a similar experiment
by Lackner and Taublieb (1984), subjects perceived the location of the right
hand to be dissociated from the forearm when the right biceps brachii was
vibrated. Although the vibration caused the perceived location of both the
hand and forearm to become displaced relative to their actual locations, the
displacement of the forearm was perceived to be much grater than the
displacement of the hand so that the hand seemed to be left behind and no
longer spatially contiguous with the forearm. Anatomy precludes previous
experience with such limb configurations. These results—demonstrating
that the range of perceived joint angles is not limited to the actual range of
joint angles (Craske, 1977) and the perceived locations of limb segments are
not limited to those that are anatomically possible (Lackner & Taublieb,
1984)—suggest that perception of limb position occurs contrary to, or simply in the absence of, a stored body scheme. The perceived dispositions of
the limbs at a given point in time appear to be a function of stimulation
occurring at that moment.

A simple extension of the I_{ij} field introduced in section IV leads to a
conception of the body scheme that is flexible and "on-line", namely, the
body scheme is the disposition of each limb and limb segment perceived
according to the instantaneous states of the I_{ij} field during self-induced
movements (Pagano & Turvey, in press). An I_{ij} field for the body arises
from the fact that the dispositions of the limb distal to each joint O can
be represented geometrically by the magnitudes and directions of the ellipsoid of inertia at each O (see Figure 16). As discussed in section II.C, the
ellipsoid of inertia is potentially definitive of object structure for dynamic
touch (Pagano & Turvey, 1993). The "body scheme," more precisely referred to as the perceptual consequences of the I_{ij} field, may be represented
geometrically by ellipsoids of inertia, one at each O. The importance of the
ellipsoid of inertia lies in the fact that it is a geometric representation of the
way in which forces act on an object or limb. It is a rendering of the way in
which I_{ij} quantifies the geometric nature of an object's mass distribution. In

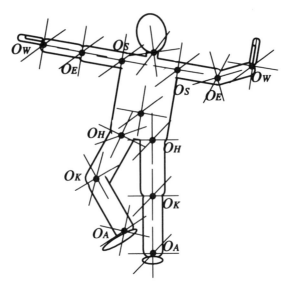

FIGURE 16   An I_{ij} field for the body defined at centers of rotation O_i for each of the primary body segments.

consequence, it may provide an alternative to models of proprioception that propose separation representations for kinematic and dynamic (force) parameters, with coordinate transformations required to reconcile differences between the two (see Flanders, Helms Tillery, & Soechting, 1992). In principle, the I_{ij} field is sufficiently structured to be informative not only about postures but also about transformations of postures. Like the contrast between the optic array (at a fixed point of observation) and the transforming optic array (at a changing point of observation, see Gibson, 1966, 1979, 1986), the specifying ability of the I_{ij} field should be enhanced by transformations over time.

Relevant to the implementation of experiments directed at this I_{ij}-field hypothesis is the fact that the universal biological shape of limbs is cylindrical. Bodies of animals are composed of cylindrical parts, approximately round or elliptical in cross-section with a readily identifiable longitudinal axis (Wainwright, 1988). The spatial orientation of a cylindrical object can be defined by the orientation of the longitudinal axis. For example, the geometric orientation of a limb segment can be determined from the angle created in spatial coordinates by the longitudinal axis, such a method being analogous to specifying the orientation of limb through joint angles. An alternative, and specifically dynamic, definition of a cylindrical object's orientation assumes it to be in motion about an endpoint corresponding to a relevant joint. The spatial orientation of one of the object's eigenvectors about that point will be coincident with the geometric orientation of the longitudinal axis. This is because the point of rotation for a limb segment, located at a joint, is typically on the longitudinal axis of that segment. It is the case, however, that the haptic system is stimulated by mechanical quantities and not by purely geometric properties such as an object's longitudinal dimension. The inertial eigenvectors are mechanical parameters and thus may quantify properties of tissue deformation patterns. They are the directions of the maximal resistance, the minimal resistance, and an intermediate resistance to rotational acceleration. The coincidence of the longitudinal axis orientation and the orientation of an eigenvector allows one to know about the former by means of the latter through dynamic touch (e.g., motions of the limbs). That is, generalizing from what has been shown to be the case with hand-held objects, the specific hypothesis is that one can know about the spatial orientation of a limb by detecting its eigenvectors. By breaking the coincidence between the eigenvectors and the longitudinal axis of the arm one can ask, therefore, whether the perception of limb orientation is a function of a limb's eigenvectors or of its geometric orientation.

A. Pointing to a Visual Target with the Arm Is Pointing with Its Eigenvectors

In a series of experiments, the eigenvectors of the arm were manipulated by asking subjects to hold an object with small appended weights (Pagano & Turvey, in press). The object was cross-shaped, consisting of two wood dowels—a stem and a branch—attached perpendicularly at their midpoints. When held in the manner shown in Figure 17a, the stem of the object points in the same direction as the arm. That is, the longitudinal axis of the cylindrical stem is parallel to the longitudinal axes of the forearm. Thus, the tasks "point the arm in a particular direction" and "point the stem in a particular direction" are one and the same. Masses were added to the cross-piece to alter the eigenvectors of the arm-rod system. Figure 17b depicts three examples of the mass conditions of the hand-held object (e.g., 100 g at 16 cm on each side of the stem or 200 g at 16 cm on the left branch or 200 g at 16 cm on the right branch) and the relation of the object to the segments of the upper arm. The particular asymmetric mass conditions identified rotated the z eigenvector of the arm 2.1° to the right or to the left of the eigenvector's direction (coincident with the arm's longitudinal axis) in the symmetric mass condition.[7] In all three conditions the geometric orientation of

---

[7] The orientation of the z eigenvector, or e_3, was computed for each arm-plus-object combination by using regression equations and procedures provided by Reynolds (1978; see also Chandler, Clauser, McContville, Reynolds, & Young, 1975; Clauser, McContville, & Young, 1969) applied to the body dimensions of one representative subject. From these regression equations the mass, distance of segment CMs from the point of rotation in the shoulder, and

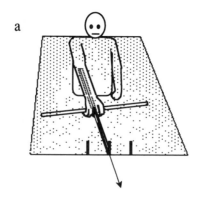

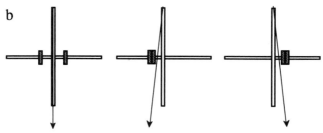

FIGURE 17   (a) The subject wields a cross under an occluding screen and points at a designated visible target. Here, the eigenvector in the z direction of the arm plus cross is coincident with the eigenvector of the arm. (b) Depending on how masses are attached to the cross, the eigenvector can point in the same direction as the arm or be deflected to the right or left. (Adapted from Pagano & Turvey, in press.)

the arm (as specified by shoulder joint angles) is identical and by manipulating the eigenvectors in a horizontal plane, N_g remains invariant over each of the three mass conditions.[8]

principal moments of inertia for the limb segments were computed. The parallel axis theorem was then used to transform the principal moments of inertia for each segment about its respective CM to moments and products of inertia about the shoulder, and these quantities were combined with those for the weighted object to get the moments and products of I_{ij} about O for the limb-plus-object combination of each mass condition.

[8] It has been hypothesized that detection of gravitational torque N_g acting at each joint may account for the perception of limb orientation (Worringham & Stelmach, 1985; Worringham et al., 1987). The torque produced at a joint because of gravity is proportional to the limb's angle relative to the gravitational vertical. N_g is minimal when the limb's CM is vertically aligned with respect to the joint and maximal when CM is horizontally aligned. It is possible that individual joint torques and neighboring joint torque patterns can contribute to the limb position sense (Worringham & Stelmach, 1985). That is, proprioception may be a function of an N_g field. There are several reasons, however, to expect that proprioception is a function of I_{ij}

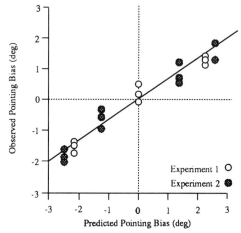

FIGURE 18   Pointing bias is a function of the difference between the direction in spatial coordinates of e_3 and spatial coordinates of the target. (Adapted from Pagano & Turvey, in press.)

A simple task to ask subjects to perform is that of pointing the occluded arm (plus object) to a target, as shown in Figure 17a. One would expect that, relative to the subject's pointing in the symmetrical mass condition, the subject would point farther to the right when the left side was weighted and farther to the left when the right side was weighted. This expectation would follow from the hypothesis that the perceived orientation of the arm depends on the arm's eigenvectors. The actual angular positions of Targets A, B, and C shown in Figure 17a relative to the point of rotation in the shoulder were 20.4°, 8.7°, and −3.8°, respectively, where 0° would be pointing directly forward on a line perpendicular to the plane containing the targets. For each of the three targets (and for the mass conditions of two separate experiments), Figure 18 shows the mean pointing direction as a function of the direction predicted from the target position and e_3. For example, with a 200-g mass placed 16 cm to the left of the hand (rotating

---

rather than N_g. First, changing the load on a limb also changes N_g at every position, thus N_g cannot provide reliable limb position information unless an inference process is used to compare N_g at one angle to N_g of the same limb at some other angle (Worringham & Stelmach, 1985). Second, N_g acts only with respect to the gravitational vertical and fails, therefore, to address one's ability to perceive limb orientations in planes perpendicular to gravity. Even within the vertical plane, N_g is not determinate; a mass oriented 45° above the horizontal, for example, has the same N_g as an equal mass 45° below the horizontal. In contrast, I_{ij} is indifferent to planes of motion. Significantly, I_{ij} is gravity independent. It is the three-space expression of the second moments of an object's mass (kg) distribution about a fixed point, it is not tied to an object's weight (kg ms^{-2}).

e_3 2.1° to the left), subjects should point the arm at 18.3° for Target A, 6.6° for Target B, and −5.9° for Target C. That is, they should point 2.1° to the right of each target. The close fit of the data in Figure 18 to that predicted is marred only by slopes that depart from 1. This deviation is most likely attributable to the inevitable degree of error in calculating a limb's I_{ij} (see footnote 7).

B. In Matching the Postures of the Arms, One Matches Their Eigenvectors

A person's impression of the elbow's position seems to reflect forearm orientation rather than the elbow's joint angle. Soechting (1982) asked subjects to point the right arm at a target and then reproduce with the left arm either the right-elbow joint angle or the orientation of the right forearm in space. The standard deviation of error was significantly greater for matching joint angle than for matching limb orientation. Similar experiments by Worringham, Stelmach, and Martin (1987) also demonstrate that subjects are less accurate at perceiving joint angles than perceiving forearm inclination. Of importance, they found errors in joint angle perception to be biased toward matching forearm inclination. These results can be taken as evidence that perception of a limb's orientation is a function of spatial variables rather than joint angles, where these spatial variables for limb orientation are defined relative to an absolute frame of reference anchored either in the body (e.g., the trunk) or in the environment (e.g., gravitational or spatial vertical and horizontal axes, Soechting, 1982; Soechting & Ross, 1984). Additional experiments have shown that the limb is perceived according to its orientation in space rather than its endpoint's (e.g., finger's) position in space (Helms Tillery, Flanders, & Soechting, 1991; see also Flanders et al., 1992). These experiments suggest that the perception of forearm inclination is tied to a "spatially oriented" variable, a direction that is independent of the joint angles composing that particular inclination and one that can in principle be quantified with reference to the environment in which the limb is embedded. In this regard, the eigenvectors of the forearm are specific to the orientation of the forearm's mass distribution in space, not the particular joint angles that gave rise to that orientation, nor the geometric position of the endpoint in space. Accordingly, the eigenvectors of I_{ij} may account for the spatially oriented nature of proprioception described by Soechting and colleagues (see Flanders et al., 1992, for a review) and may do so without the need to identify any particular coordinate system.

The experimental procedure to test these ideas was that depicted in Figure 19 (Pagano, 1993). It used a matching procedure in which the perceived orientation of an arm is reproduced with the contralateral arm (McCloskey, 1973; Soechting, 1982; Soechting & Ross, 1984; Velay, Roll, & Paillard,

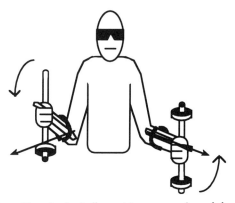

FIGURE 19   The subject rhythmically positions a cross in each hand by rotating at the elbow and tries to match the orientation of the two arms. Instead, the eigenvectors of the arms plus crosses are matched where eigenvector orientation depends on whether masses are attached above, below, or on either side of the arm. (Adapted from Pagano, 1993.)

1989; Worringham et al., 1987). The variation on this basic procedure was to have subjects execute their postural matches in the context of a rhythmic activity, with recordings of limb positions made by a sonic three-space motion recording device. Throughout the experiment, the right arm served as the target arm, and the left arm served as the matching, or pointing, arm. Subjects began half of the trials with the target arm in the up position (roughly 75° with respect to horizontal) and the pointing arm in the down position (roughly −30° with respect to horizontal), and in the remaining trials subjects began with the target arm in the down position and the pointing arm in the up position. The experimenter began each trial by switching on a metronome that repeatedly sounded a triplet of tones, with 2.0 s separating the three tones. This continuous repetitive pattern lasted for the duration of each trial. When the subject was ready, Tone 1 acted as the signal to move the target arm about the elbow to some angle intermediate between the positions of the target arm and the pointing arm. Tone 2 signaled the subjects to move the pointer to an angle such that the pointer was parallel to the target. Tone 3 signaled the subject to return both arms to their starting positions, completing the cycle of three tones with their corresponding movements. This cycle was repeated without interruption for the 30-s duration of the trial, with 2.0-s intervals between each tone and each cycle. The relative angles of those points in a trial at which the subject was matching the two arms were averaged to obtain the mean relative pointing angle.

Masses were attached to a hand-held object such that the inertial eigenvectors of the target arm were rotated upward (200 g attached to the upper branch), downward (200 g attached to the lower branch), or unperturbed (100 g attached to the upper branch and 100 g attached, at the same distance from the stem, to the lower branch, see Figure 19). It was expected that if subjects perceive the orientation of the target arm according to its eigenvectors, the pointing arm would be oriented above, below, or even with the target arm, respectively. As predicted, compared with pointing in the symmetrical mass condition, the trend was for the subjects to orient the pointing arm higher when the upper portion of the target arm was weighted and lower when the lower portion of the target arm was weighted. Thus, the relative pointing directions corresponded to the directions in which the eigenvectors were rotated by the added weight.

X. WEIGHT PERCEPTION AND THE SIZE–WEIGHT ILLUSION

Of the various capabilities of dynamic touch, none have figured so prominently in the historical development of experimental psychology as the perception of an object's weight. In *The Sense of Touch,* Weber (1834/1978) established the conceptual and methodological foundations for psychophysics and an empirical approach to perception on the basis of his documentation of the relation between variations in weight and variations in a person's weight judgments. The law for which he is famous was originally demonstrated with data from experiments in which subjects discriminated among objects in weight by hefting them. Weber proposed that the pressure an object exerted on the skin, and its resistance to the forces acting upon it such as those used in hefting or wielding, were of significance to weight perception. Perceived heaviness, he observed, was related to both object mass and object size. The size–weight illusion reported originally by Charpentier (1891) and Dresslar (1894) confirmed this proposed dependence of weight perception on mass and extent. In modern times, Stevens and Rubin (1970) have provided the most comprehensive demonstration of the size–weight illusion. Figure 20a is representative of their data. As can be seen, whereas perceived heaviness increases with increases in object mass, it decreases with increases in volume. Larger objects of the same mass are perceived as lighter. Although many demonstrations of the illusion involve vision—the subject is allowed to view the wielded objects—experiments have shown that vision is not essential to the effect (Ellis & Lederman, 1993; Masin & Crestoni, 1988; Pick & Pick, 1967). It is perhaps ironic that this phenomenon substantiating Weber's insight on the significance of both mass and extent has proven to be the major obstacle to a theory of weight perception. For many investigators of the phenomenon it has seemed that an account was needed in which independent sensations of mass and extent are combined mentally to transform the sensation of mass into a perception of heaviness (e.g., Anderson, 1972; Gregory, 1974; Sjöberg, 1969). For

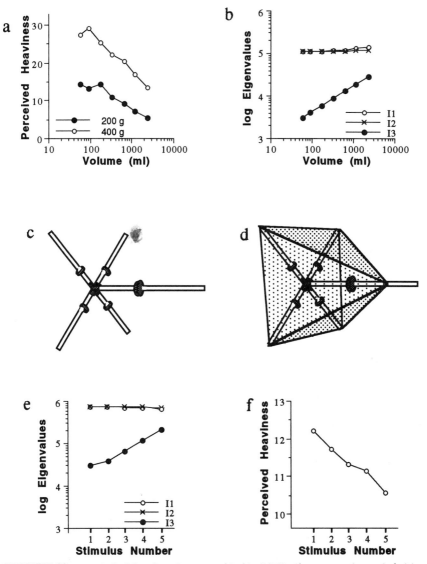

FIGURE 20   Typical of data from Stevens and Rubin (1970), a larger mass (open circles) is perceived as heavier than a smaller mass (filled circles), but for a given mass perceived heaviness decreases with increasing volume. (b) The pattern of eigenvalues for one of those mass conditions. (c) A tensor object was constructed so that attached masses could be moved on the shaft and on the branches of the cross to manipulate independently I_1, I_2, and I_3. (d) Subjects were allowed to see the objects covered with paper. (e) Attached masses can be placed so as to produce a stimulus set with the desired pattern of eigenvalues. (f) Perceived heaviness decreases with an increase in I_3. (Adapted from Amazeen & Turvey, in press.)

many others it has seemed that the illusion implies that the centrally produced force commands (needed to move an object) are mentally registered (for a review, see Jones, 1986) and may be used in a matching procedure that reveals a discrepancy between the forces expected to be appropriate (generated on the basis of perceived object size) and those that are actually needed (e.g., Davis & Brickett, 1977; Woodworth, 1921).

The classical accounts summarized in the preceding paragraph seek to address the overall form of the size–weight illusion, but they do not attempt to address its complexity as expressed by power functions each specific to a particular combination of mass and volume (see Stevens & Rubin, 1970). Further, not all forms of the preceding accounts of the illusion are simultaneously accounts of what might be referred to as normal weight perception (Jones, 1986). Given the major facts about weight perception, Amazeen and Turvey (in press) proposed that both weight perception and the so-called size–weight illusion should be functions of I_{ij}. The major facts are that weight perception is enhanced by wielding and hefting, depends on both the magnitude of mass and its distribution, and varies complexly with variations in the magnitude of mass and its distribution. These facts point to a persistent property quantifying the relation between the distribution and magnitude of an object's mass that is structurally rich and meaningful in the context of the actions revealing weight. Only I_{ij} would seem to satisfy these requirements.

A. Perceived Heaviness Depends on Rotational Inertia

Rods wielded about one end can be of constant mass but of different moments of inertia simply by virtue of the position along the rod of an attached mass. Amazeen and Turvey (in press) used a conventional magnitude estimation procedure of having subjects assign numbers to occluded wielded rods relative to a standard rod with the arbitrary weight of 10. Within an experiment, the standard rod was wielded every sixth trial. With rods of constant mass and fixed length, perceived heaviness increased with increasing distance of the attached mass from the hand-held end of the rod. Rotational inertia was similarly seen to determine perceived heaviness when rods were of constant mass but of different lengths and, therefore, volumes. The independence of these heaviness judgments from N_i was demonstrated in an experiment in which the angular frequency of wielding within a single plane was manipulated systematically by means of a metronome, as in Solomon and Turvey (1988, Experiment 4). The lower the frequency, the smaller the average absolute magnitude of angular acceleration. Thus, by this manipulation, N_i could be varied independently from I_{ij}. The results revealed no contribution of the average angular acceleration and, therefore, of the average N_i, to the weight judgment made during a bout of wielding. Perceived weight was solely a function of I_{ij}.

B. Investigating the Size–Weight Illusion through "Tensor Objects"

Given the evidence that weight perception is tied to I_{ij}, the question can be raised of whether the complex pattern of data found in experiments demonstrating the size–weight illusion is also predictable from I_{ij}. Amazeen and Turvey (in press) computed the tensors for the objects of Stevens and Rubin's (1970) comprehensive study. In that study, filled cylinders grasped in the hand were hefted (rotated) by motions about the elbow. Multiple regression then revealed that 99% of the variance in the weight judgments in Stevens and Rubin's study was accommodated by I_{ij}, with all three eigenvalues being significant. Closer examination of the sets of objects that systematically increased in volume but remained equal in mass, the ones that yield the weight judgments shown in Figure 20a, revealed a particular pattern of change in the relation among the three eigenvalues. Specifically, I_1 and I_2 were approximately identical and unchanging over the stimulus set, but I_3 changed across the stimuli, becoming increasingly similar to I_1 and I_2 as the volume of the wielded cylinders became larger. The pattern is shown in Figure 20b. Amazeen and Turvey (in press) conjectured that if objects of constant mass and volume could be constructed to simulate the pattern of eigenvalues in Figure 20b, then the weight judgments given to these objects should conform to that shown in Figure 20a. A tensor object was created to achieve the desired simulation. It is depicted in Figure 20c. As shown, the tensor object consisted of two rods forming a cross with arms of equal lengths and with a third rod perpendicular to the plane of the cross and affixed to the cross at its center. Algorithms built on the parallel axes theorems for moments and products of inertia, Equation 5, specified where metal disks of certain magnitudes should be placed on the parts of the tensor object so as to produce a particular relation among the three eigenvalues. A number of tensor objects were constructed that conformed, as a set, to the patterning of eigenvalues across experimental stimuli shown in Figure 20b. In one experiment conducted with this set, the individual tensor objects were wielded behind a curtain. In another experiment, the individual tensor objects were wielded in view. The objects in this latter experiment, however, were covered with paper as shown in Figure 20d to occlude the rods and to obscure the differences across the objects in the positions of the metal disks. The paper covering made the sameness of the tensor objects in linear dimensions and volume visually apparent. The results of the two experiments were identical and are shown in Figure 20e: As expected, perceived heaviness for the tensor objects of equal mass and volume decreased with increasing I_3 in the context of constant I_1 and I_2. The complement of the two experiments conducted on tensor objects conforming to the eigenvalue pattern of Figure 20b was an experiment with a set of tensor objects ordered such that all three eigenvalues increased systematically and in parallel. An eigenvalue pattern of the preceding kind characterized the object sets in Stevens and Rubin (1970) that yielded systematic increases in perceived heaviness; they were sets in which the stimuli increased in mass independently of volume. The complementing experiment with tensor objects of fixed mass and volume produced the expected systematic increase in perceived heaviness with increasing I_1, I_2, and I_3. In summary, both weight perception and the so-called size–weight illusion seem to be systematically determined by I_{ij}.

XI. SELECTIVELY PERCEIVING PARTS OF AN OBJECT

Grasp a pencil between thumb and index finger and wiggle it. While wiggling, attend to the portion of the pencil that lies in front of the point of grasp. Now attend to the portion that lies behind the point of grasp. It does seem that distinct impressions of the fore and aft extents can be had with reasonable accuracy. As will become apparent, efforts to understand this ability to perceive segments of a wielded object highlight how analyses that are not based on the full inertia tensor can lead to awkward and false conceptions. It will also become apparent that as the selectivity of dynamic touch is examined further, the need for a physical description beyond that provided by tensors is required.

The first experimental test of spatially selective dynamic touch was provided by Solomon and Turvey (1988, Experiment 9). Across trials, rods of different lengths were grasped at points intermediate between their ends. Subjects attempted to perceive, on the basis of wielding, the effective reaching length of "just that portion of the rod extending beyond the position of the hand grip." Thus, for a rod of 60 cm held at a point three fourths of the rod length measured from the end closest to the subject, the correct response should be 15 cm. Figure 21 presents the mapping between perceived fractional length and actual fractional length found in Experiment 9 of Solomon and Turvey (1988) by using the basic procedure depicted in Figure 1a. In that experiment, subjects wielded rods of 0.61 m, 0.76 m, and 0.91 m at hand positions of one fourth, one half, and the three fourths of the rod length. The data were analyzed in terms of their dependence on I_{xx} of the whole object and I_{xx} of the fraction, assuming the cylindrical objects to be of negligible circumference. The analysis indicated that only the fractional I_{xx} mattered; perception was independent of the total I_{xx}. The latter fact suggested to Solomon and Turvey that subjects separated off the torques

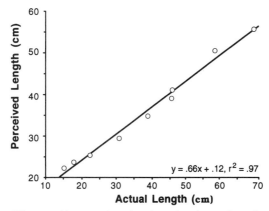

The graph shows: y-axis "Perceived Length (cm)" ranging from 20 to 60; x-axis "Actual Length (cm)" ranging from 10 to 70. Equation on plot: $y = .66x + .12$, $r^2 = .97$

FIGURE 21   When a rod is grasped at a location other than at the end, perceived length of the portion in front of the hand is a function of the actual length of that portion. (Adapted from Solomon & Turvey, 1988. Copyright by the American Psychological Association. Adapted with permission.)

and motions associated with the fraction from those associated with the rod as a whole. The hypothesis thus proposed was that the haptic subsystem of dynamic touch could invert the principle of equipollence (or equivalence of torques): N_x can be decomposed into component torques, and principal moments can be decomposed into component principal moments.

A subsequent study was directed specifically at the dependence on fractional I_{xx} and independence from total I_{xx} as the testable form of the inversion of equipollence hypothesis. Occluded rods were held at one half or three fourths of their lengths. On one third of the trials the rods were free of additional weights (Condition A), on one third of the trials a metal disk was attached at a point below the CM (Condition B), and on the remaining one third of the trials the same metal disk was attached at a point above the CM (Condition C), with both points of attachment noncoincident with the hand position. In Experiment 1, subjects had to perceive the distance reachable with the extent of rod forward of the hand; in Experiment 2, they had to perceive the distance reachable with the whole rod "if it were held at its proximal end." These two experiments of Solomon et al. (1989b) and their results are schematized in Figure 22. For simplicity, only the situations in which the hand is at the midpoint of the rod are depicted. The expectations for the midgrasp were that in the fractional-length experiment the conditions would order as Condition A = Condition B < Condition C, whereas in the whole-length experiment they would order as Condition A < Condition B = Condition C. These patterns conformed to a dependence of perception on fractional I_{xx} in Experiment 1, with fractional I_{xx} measured from the fraction's proximal end (within the grasp), and a dependence of perception on total I_{xx} in Experiment 2, as total I_{xx} would be defined for different

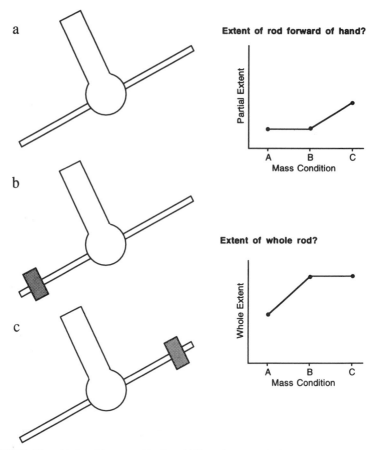

FIGURE 22   (a) A rod is grasped in the middle with no attached masses, (b) a mass behind the hand (c) and a mass in front of the hand. The pattern of perceived extents for these mass conditions depends on whether the task is perceiving partial length or whole length.

Os by the parallel axis theorem. The strong implication of the experiments of Solomon et al. was that subjects could essentially split the mass distribution of a hand-held rod, attending selectively to the designated fraction indifferent to the mass distribution of the remainder. Specifically, Solomon et al. advanced two hypotheses. First, that when the task is to perceive the whole length of the rod, regardless of hand position, the haptic subsystem of dynamic touch behaves like a mechanism that registers the dynamics of the whole hand-held object through the principle of superposition or parallel composition, I_{xx} total $= I_{xx}$ fore $+ I_{xx}$ aft. Second, when the task is to perceive the rod extent forward of the grasp, dynamic touch behaves as another kind of mechanism, one that filters the required fragment of the rod through subtraction, I_{xx} total $- I_{xx}$ aft $= I_{xx}$ fore. The problem with these hypotheses is that inversion of the principle of equivalence of forces is not physically feasible. Given I_{xx} total $= 10$ (for example), an indefinitely large number of paired values would satisfy the decomposition (e.g., 9 and 1 or 3 and 7). Other constraints—external to rigid body mechanics—would have to be brought in to achieve the correct pair of I_{xx} fore and I_{xx} aft.

The selective facility of dynamic touch isolated by Solomon and Turvey (1988) and Solomon et al. (1989b) was extended to the limiting case of holding a rod stationary by Burton and Turvey (1991). Other experiments on the limiting case of dynamic touch—detailing the contribution of the first moment to perceived extent—were summarized in section VI. The experiments of Burton and Turvey paralleled those of Solomon et al. in design but focused on total and fractional first moments. The fit between expectation and outcome was evaluated by the multiple regression of perceived extent against the partial static moment (that of the segment forward of the hand) and the full static moment (that of the entire rod pivoting about its proximal end). Essentially, when subjects were instructed to perceive the fraction, the partial static moment was significant and the full static moment was not; in contrast, when the subjects were instructed to perceive the whole rod, the full static moment was significant and the partial static moment was not. As Burton and Turvey underscore, the multiple regression technique provides a method for determining and quantifying selectivity in dynamic touch. Further, because subjects were denied the opportunity to vary systematically the patterning of torques, motions, and tissue deformations, it is reasonable to suppose that their demonstrated facility to attend to a part or to the entirety of a hand-held object was covert. Similar visual and auditory abilities to attend covertly to one of two spatially or temporally overlapping figures or events are well established but not especially well understood (e.g., Johnston & Dark, 1986).

A. The Ability to "Fractionate" Entails Both Eigenvalues and Eigenvectors

In Section VII.C a feature of dynamic touch was discussed that might seem to depend on the mechanism proposed to address the selective report of a rod fraction. When a cylindrical object is grasped, perceiving the hand position through dynamic touch might require the hypothesized process of decomposing I_{xx} total into I_{xx} fore and I_{xx} aft—hand position would be given by the ratio of the two partial moments. Instead of the preceding decomposition, however, it was shown in section VII.3 that perceiving hand position is based on I_{ij} taken in its entirety. Perceiving where the hand grasps a wielded cylindrical object is a linear function of the angle between the z-unit vector of $Oxyz$ (the spatial coordinate system) and the inertial eigenvector in the yz plane (Pagano et al., 1994). A reasonable assumption, therefore, is that the ability to perceive the length of a rod segment forward of the hand entails specification of the hand relative to the rod and, as such, implicates I_{ij}'s eigenvectors. This raises the question, therefore, of whether the perception of the magnitude of a rod segment might be a function of a quantity composed of a magnitude (e.g., the major eigenvalue) and a direction (its corresponding eigenvector) defining, thereby, the fractionation capability as one of perceiving a magnitude in a particular direction relative to the hand. Referring to Figure 22, if there is a particular combination of eigenvalues and eigenvectors governing the selective perception of a rod fraction, then it will have to be of the same magnitude for the different mass distributions depicted by Conditions A and B. The strong motivation for the decomposition hypothesis is the experimental observation that the perceived length of the attended segment is unaffected by the physical dimensions of the unattended segment.[9] At all events, dispensing with the idea that I_{ij} is uniquely decomposable suggests the following general hypothesis about perceiving the extent of a segment of a hand-held object: The eigenvalues of I_{ij} support the magnitude aspect ("extent"), and the eigenvectors of I_{ij} support the directional aspect ("forward of the hand"), with the eigenvalues and eigenvectors forming a single quantity constraining perception.

B. Perceiving One of Two Things in the Hand May Involve Spinors

Hold two objects in one hand. For example, grasp a metal dining fork between the thumb and index finger at the same time that a short pencil is held between the base of thumb and index finger and against the palm. Now wield them while maintaining a firm grip on both. One seems to have nonvisual impressions of the different magnitudes of the two objects. The

---

[9] Chan (1994) has reported a failure to replicate this basic pattern of results. Two peculiarities of his method and one limited analysis may be responsible, however (Burton, Santana, & Carello, 1995). First, although his subjects also adjusted a marker to coincide with the felt position of the rod tip, they could read the values on the tape measure from which the experimenter recorded their length reports. Second, the length and moment of inertia of the rod portion in front of the hand did not vary in two of his experiments. Given that the task was to perceive different lengths, demand characteristics may have led subjects to order the rods according to some other property that did vary, such as the inertia of the back portion. Finally, in the third experiment, in which moment of inertia in front of the hand varied (although length did not), two out of three numbers in each of two critical comparisons did not differ. These equalities, which would be expected from the decomposition hypothesis, were not revealed in the analysis, however, because Chan averaged over the two sets of comparisons. Granted that one number in each set differed, his results are, at best, equivocal. Coupled with the fact that perceived lengths in all three experiments grossly under-estimated actual partial lengths, these data are an unreliable basis for challenging previous results (Burton et al., 1995).

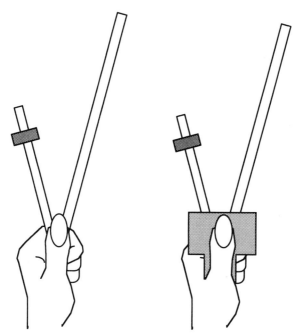

FIGURE 23 (a) Rods of different lengths, with or without attached masses, are held firmly at an orientation 15° to either side of the thumb. (b) Those same rods inserted into a wooden handle (again 15° to either side of the thumb) cannot independently move and constitute a single object. (Adapted from Turvey et al., 1995a.)

same seems to be the case for held, branched objects, such as a carpenter's L square grasped at the vertex. In short, the ability to perceive selectively the lengths of things in particular directions is general, and as argued in the preceding section, may be an ability that is based in both the eigenvalues and eigenvectors of I_{ij}. This hypothesis was tested in experiments in which subjects wielded two rods grasped unimanually, as depicted in Figure 23a, and in experiments in which subjects wielded a single object with two distinct branches, as depicted in Figure 23b. Appropriate variations in I_{ij} were brought about by varying rod lengths and attaching metal disks to the rods. For both situations in Figure 23, perceived length of the attended rod (1) varied systematically with actual length, (2) was close in value to the actual length, and (3) was influenced by the magnitude of the unattended rod. Further, perceived length of the attended rod was found to be a function of I_1 (of the two-rods system, Figure 23a, or the two-rods-and-handle system, Figure 23b) and the rotation of the eigenvectors about the y-axis of the $Oxyz$ coordinate system as long as the sense of the rotation, clockwise or anticlockwise, was made dependent on the direction of the attended rod

(Turvey, Carello, Fitzpatrick, Pagano, & Kadar, 1995a,b). The data, there-fore, were consistent with the expected ability and the hypothesis about its basis in both the eigenvalues and eigenvectors of I_{ij}. At the same time, the data raise new and complex issues about the physical descriptions under-lying the capabilities of dynamic touch.

To present the results most revealingly, let A designate the attended rod, let L and R designate the left and right rod, respectively, and let the sub-scripts m and n index rod identity. The two major observations can then be summarized as follows: (1) $A(L_m) = A(R_m)$ (i.e., the perceptual conse-quences of attending to a given rod in a particular pair of rods is the same whether the rod is to the left or to the right of the thumb), and (2) $A(L_m) \neq A(R_n)$ and $A(R_m) \neq A(L_n)$ when $L \neq R$ (i.e., the perceptual consequence of attending to one rod in a given asymmetric configuration of a rod pair is different from that of attending to the other rod in the same asymmetric configuration). The angle Θ of the eigenvectors' rotation about the y-axis of $Oxyz$ measured anticlockwise from the x-axis (perpendicular to the longi-tudinal axis of the thumb) is calculable from the coordinates of the eigenvec-tors in $Oxyz$. What Figure 24 highlights is the anomalous nature of selective perception by dynamic touch. Observation 1 indicates that the same I_1 in conjunction with two different eigenvector orientations in $Oxyz$ ($\Theta = 90°$ $+ \Gamma°$ and $\Theta = 90° - \Gamma°$) composed one and the same single quantity to produce one and the same perceptual effect. Observation 2 indicates that the same I_1 in conjunction with a single Θ composed two quantities to produce two different perceptual effects. If Θ were truly single valued, then Obser-vation 1 would have to read $A(Lm) \neq A(R_m)$, and Observation 2 would have to read $A(L_m) = A(R_n)$ and $A(R_m) = A(L_n)$. It seems, therefore, that the situation of wielding a given object configuration is double valued—for the given object configuration in connection with the hand that wields it, the given rotation about y of the eigenvectors within $Oxyz$ can be $\Theta = 90°$ $+ \Gamma°$ and $\Theta = 90° - \Gamma°$. Wielding a given object configuration to attend to L and then wielding to attend to R is tantamount to a (physically impermiss-ible) sign change in the x-coordinate of the eigenvector in the xz plane as depicted in Figure 24c.

If one orientation of a rigid body is transformed into another, as in Figure 24a, then the new configuration would be given by the three coordinates of a select point (e.g., the object's CM) and a rotation. The former would be an element in the set of all triplets of real numbers $\mathbf{R}^3$ and the latter would be an element in the group of rotations in 3-dimensional space, that is, the (special orthogonal [SO][10]) rotation group SO(3). The "configuration space" for objects such as those depicted in Figure 23 is usually taken to be $\mathbf{R}^3 \times$ SO(3). Now given that the physical state of an object in the hand, as

---

[10] An orthogonal matrix is one for which the inverse equals the transpose.

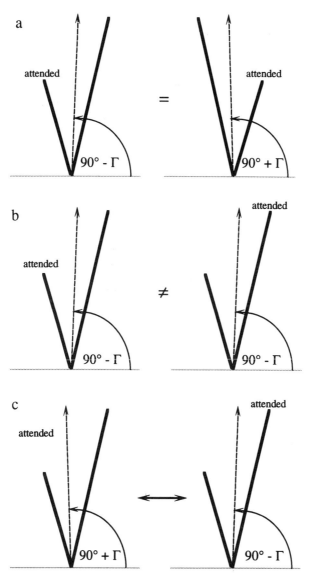

FIGURE 24 (a) For attended rods of the same length but with a change in sign on the eigenvector orientation, perceived length is the same. (b) For attended rods of different values of length but with the same eigenvector, perceived length is different. (c) Wielding a given object configuration to attend to L (left rod) and then wielding to attend to R (right rod) is equivalent to a sign change in the x-coordinate of the eigenvector in the xz plane.

expressed by I_{ij}, is entirely dependent on its configuration in three space, then $\mathbf{R}^3 \times SO(3)$ would also seem to be the object's "state space." The main lesson from Figure 24, however, is that the state of a wielded object is not identical with its configuration, that is, with I_{ij}. The statement that "state differs from configuration" is, in a possibly revealing sense, just another way of expressing the psychological phenomenon of attention. From a strictly physical perspective, however, the implication of the inequality is that explaining the observations depicted in Figure 24 may require a mathematical object or quantity different in its geometry from I_{ij} and from tensors and vectors (first-order tensors) in general. There are two important hints as to its nature. One hint is the apparent two valuedness of a given physical configuration in the experiments (the $\pm$ x-coordinate of the eigenvector in Figure 24c). The other hint is provided by realizing that no rotation—the so-called identity transformation that leaves a physical configuration exactly as it was—is the same as rotation by 2π. A good guess, therefore, is that we are looking for a mathematical object that changes sign under a 2π rotation, meaning that for any given configuration it is two valued.

To any rotation is associated a quantity R known as a *rotation operator* or *spinor transformation* (or *quaternion,* in Hamilton's [1853] formulation, Misner, Thorne, & Wheeler, 1973):

$$R = \cos (\theta/2) - i \sin (\theta/2)(\sigma_x \cos \alpha + \sigma_y \cos \beta + \sigma_z \cos \gamma). \quad (13)$$

In Equation 13, Θ is the angle of rotation, α, β, and γ are the angles between the axis of rotation and the coordinate axes, and the σ_i are the spin matrices:

$$\sigma_x = \begin{vmatrix} 0 & 1 \\ 1 & 0 \end{vmatrix}, \quad \sigma_y = \begin{vmatrix} 0 & -i \\ i & 0 \end{vmatrix}, \quad \sigma_z = \begin{vmatrix} 1 & 0 \\ 0 & -1 \end{vmatrix}. \quad (14)$$

R reverses sign on a rotation through an odd multiple of 2π, but this reversal never shows up in the transformation laws of tensors. For example, the transformation law for a vector $\mathbf{X}$ is

$$\mathbf{X} \to \mathbf{X}' = R\mathbf{X}R\dagger, \quad (15)$$

where $R\dagger$ is the conjugate transpose obtained by taking the conjugate complex of every element in the matrix and then interchanging rows and columns. Given the two factors, R and a sign change in each, rotation by 2π leaves the sense of the vector (together with its magnitude and direction) unchanged. The change of sign does show up when a particular two-component quantity is considered that transforms according to the law

$$S \to S' = RS. \quad (16)$$

S is a spinor object which like the spinor transformation R reverses sign every 2π rotation (e.g., Altman, 1986; Goldstein, 1980; Naber, 1992; Misner et al., 1972).

If spinors are significant to understanding dynamic touch, then the rotation group SO(3) cannot be appropriate for modeling the state space of wielded objects. However, because SO(3) models three-dimensional space, the relevant group must necessarily be a group that maps onto SO(3). That is, for every one of the transformations in the relevant group there must be a corresponding transformation of SO(3), that is, a real orthogonal transformation in ordinary three-dimensional space. The relevant group has been suggested in Equations 13 and 14. Homomorphic[11] with SO(3) is SU(2), the group of 2 × 2 complex unitary unimodular matrices[12]—any relation among the matrices of SO(3) is satisfied also by the matrices of SU(2) (e.g., Altman, 1986; Goldstein, 1980; Naber, 1992).

Recall that the inertia ellipsoid is a geometric representation of I_{ij} through its eigenvectors and its eigenvalues. The inertia ellipsoids of the objects depicted in Figure 23 are tilted relative to the hand, as indexed by the rotation of the eigenvector in Figure 24. This tilt or rotation can be expressed through an *attitude spinor* (Hestenes, 1994a, 1994b). That is, the tilt of the ellipsoid can be conceived of as a rotation A and expressed, therefore, through Equation 13. Because there will be two complementary versions of A for a given physical configuration and, therefore, a given inertia ellipsoid, the physical descriptions of the objects depicted in Figure 23 will be double valued. In consequence, a spinor hypothesis of selective dynamic touch can be advanced: Perceiving the right rod of a two-rod configuration involves one version of the attitude spinor, say A, and perceiving the left rod involves the other version, −A. Using the preceding convention, regression analyses conducted on the data of the experiments schematized in Figure 24 found that I_1 and the components of ±A corresponding to degree of rotation and the direction of the rotation axis accounted for approximately 90% or more of the variance in perceived length (Turvey et al., 1995b). Inspection of the calculated attitude spinors revealed a physical basis for perceiving different left and right rods as different, and for perceiving the same rod in a given two-rod object as the same whether it was on the left or the right.

A further examination of the spinor hypothesis was conducted through the selective perception of a part of a single rod that is grasped at a point intermediate between its ends, similar to what had been the case in the original experiments on selective dynamic touch. Given a rod held initially with its longitudinal axis perpendicular to the ground, perception can be directed at the segment above the hand or at the segment below the hand.

---

[11] A mapping from one group to another that preserves the algebraic operations is referred to as a *homomorphism*.

[12] A unitary matrix satisfies the equation $\mathbf{A}\,\mathbf{A}^\dagger = 1$ or $\mathbf{A}^\dagger = \mathbf{A}^{-1}$, where the transpose conjugate designated by the dagger is obtained from A by taking the complex conjugate of each element; thus, the equation says that the inverse equals the transpose conjugate. A unimodular matrix has a determinant of +1.

By positioning the grasp at the rod's midpoint, the simple addition of a metal disk to the rod above or below the hand can be used to manipulate the attitude of the rod's ellipsoid of inertia relative to the hand. An attachment above will tilt or rotate the ellipsoid downward, and an attachment below will tilt or rotate the ellipsoid upward, in a vertical plane perpendicular to the ground plane. In this case, the meaning of a spinor's double-valuedness is plainly on display. A spinor represents an oriented rotation, with two such orientations for any given rotation (Hestenes, 1986). The two orientations for any given upward or downward rotation in the experimental situation just described are distinguished only by the rotation angle (θ versus $2\pi - \theta$) and the sense of the rotation axis (positive for all θ rotations and negative for all $2\pi - \theta$ rotations). The experiment confirmed the hypothesis that attending to the segment above the hand and attending to the segment below the hand corresponded to the two oriented rotations represented by A and $-A$, respectively: Perceived partial length above was a function of I_1 and θ and perceived partial length below was a function of I_1 and $2\pi - \theta$ (Turvey et al., 1995a). Apparently, perceiving a magnitude in a particular direction involves I_{ij} characterizing the hand-held object's physical configuration and $\pm A$ characterizing the object's connection to the body. In the experiments just described, $\pm A$ relates a frame rigidly attached to the wrist (a "wrist frame") to the frame of eigenvectors of the wielded object. It seems, therefore, that the most general account of the (nonvisual) spatial-perception abilities expressed in the wielding of objects will involve both inertia tensors and attitude spinors.

XII. PERCEIVING SURFACE LAYOUT AND HAND-HELD PROBES BY PROBING

As noted above, the centrality of dynamic touch to everyday activity is obscured by the fact that it is usually part of a coordinated effort among perceptual systems. It is hard to appreciate the contribution of dynamic touch to manipulating a pencil or calipers or a baseball bat that are also being guided visually. The capabilities of dynamic touch seem most intuitively obvious, perhaps, in the use of a cane by a blind person to explore paths and doorways or to find obstacles and brinks. A haptic implement is used explicitly by the individual to perceive an object or arrangement of surfaces at some remove from that person's body. In that use, the long cane is not substantively different from the use of vibrissae, beaks, claws, horns, and so on by animals so equipped (Burton, 1993; Gibson, 1966). Each of these attachments to the skin is a medium that allows the tissues of the body to be deformed by properties of the things that the medium strikes or scrapes. The deformations engendered by contact between implement and surface are likely to be affected not only by the implement, as in the foregoing discussions, but by the nature of the contact as well.

Pursuit of an understanding of perceiving object properties by wielding has used a strategy that serves equally well to develop an understanding of perceiving surface properties by means of hand-held probes. To reiterate, define the system, identify the parameters that couple the muscular (and other) forces impressed upon the system to the system's states, determine for a given property the parameters that fully constrain the system, and provide a reasoned basis for the relation between the pertinent parameters and the perception (see section I). In the case of probing—that is, when contact between an implement and the surface occurs—the forces include not only muscular forces but contact forces (shocks and impulses) as well. The parameters are the constants of the probe (such as I_{ij}), of the surface (e.g., elasticity), and of the configuration of rod and surface at contact (e.g., angle). When a rod is used to strike a surface, short-duration deformations of the body's tissues produced by contact are superimposed on the relatively long-duration deformations brought about by wielding. The results reviewed in section III indicate that the latter deformations are patterned by I_{ij}. The short-duration deformations are likely to depend on the conditions of contact. Several examples illustrate the successes and the remaining challenges of this approach.

A. Perceiving a Probe versus Perceiving by Means of a Probe

Consider the case of perceiving the distance of a horizontal surface located somewhere below the hand that is exploring it with a stick. The distance will determine whether that surface is one that requires a step up, a step down, or is a brink or obstacle that must be negotiated around. When the surface is tapped with the stick, the reaction to the impulse forces at the pivot point in the wrist is scaled to the distance of the pivot point from the center of percussion[13] of the probe. The center of percussion P is obtained by dividing the moment of inertia by the static moment (den Hartog, 1948). Additionally, for a given probe, the angle of inclination, ϕ, of the probe at contact will vary. A role for ϕ may arise from the shearing strain on the forearm that is fixed by the surface location (Chan & Turvey, 1991). Shearing strain is proportional to the ratio of the angle through which the tissue is twisted (approximately $90° - \phi$) and the length of the tissue. The torsion for a given surface location is constant because the surface restrains the degree of rotation. We should reasonably expect perception of the distance of a surface below the hand to be a function not only of I_{ij} but of P and ϕ as well.

---

[13] The center of percussion is defined as that point in a rotating rigid body that can be struck without causing an acceleration at O. It is the "sweet spot" in a hitting implement such as a baseball bat or a tennis racket. The location of the center of percussion is not fixed but depends on the location of O.

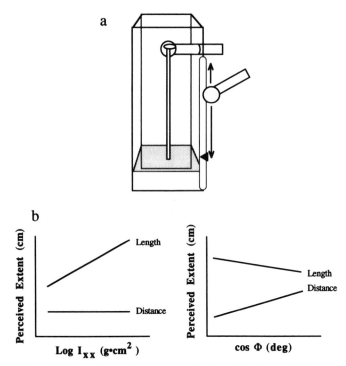

FIGURE 25   (a) The subject probes an unseen horizontal surface and indicates its distance or the probe length with a report apparatus visible outside of the occluding box. Only the marker for surface distance is shown. (Adapted from Chan & Turvey, 1991.) (b) Perceived length and perceived distance are different functions of I_{xx} and cos φ. (Copyright © 1991 by the American Psychological Association. Adapted with permission.)

Experiments that led to this hypothesis by Chan and Turvey (1991) took the following form, depicted in Figure 25a. The surface to be probed was the inside floor of a large box; the box had a "false bottom" that could be set at a variety of heights. The subject's hand was inserted through a hole in the side of the box and probes were supplied by the experimenter from the opposite, open side of the box. The probed surface, the hand, and the probe were all occluded from the subject's view. An adjustable marker attached to pulleys on the outside of the box was used by the subject to indicate the location of the horizontal surface. In some experiments, subjects were also asked to indicate on a separate apparatus the length of the probe (with the order of distance and length reports counterbalanced over trials and the markers reset after each report). When the surface distance is coincident with the length of the probe (i.e., angle is not a factor), perceived distance can essentially be considered equivalent to perceived length with contact. Under those circumstances, by using the same up and down movement to strike the surface or swing the rod in the absence of a surface (i.e., perceived length without contact), perceived surface distance was a function of log I_{xx} (no other components of I_{ij} were tested) and P ($r^2 = .995$), whereas perceived probe length was a function of log I_{xx} alone ($r^2 = .986$). Chan and Turvey's final experiment disentangled probe length from surface distance and found perceived distance to be a function of ϕ as well, $D_p = 1.6 \cos \phi^{.95} I_{xx}^{.25} P^{.18}$ ($ps < .001$ in a multiple regression, $r^2 = .96$). The roles of I_{xx}, P, and ϕ were again distinct (Figure 25b) for perceived length, $L_p = 4.3 I_{xx}^{.21} P^{.06}$ (only log I_{xx} and P were significant in a multiple regression, $r^2 = .90$).

These distinct roles for ϕ, I_{xx}, and P in perceiving the length of a probe and the distance of a probed surface provided the focus for a series of experiments in which the surface was a vertical wall in front of the subject (Carello et al., 1992). The distance of a vertical surface is relevant to steering and decelerating during forward locomotion. Note that in comparison to the experiments of Chan and Turvey (1991) the conditions of a different surface orientation entail a different orientation with respect to gravity, different muscle synergies, and different torques. In replication of the basic finding when surface distance and probe length were coincident, this time with the movement of the probe from side to side, perceived length with contact was a function of log I_{xx} and P ($r^2 = .997$), whereas perceived length without contact was a function of log I_{xx} alone ($r^2 = .995$). Decoupling surface distance from probe length allowed another style of exploration, a hammering motion in the saggital plane and the introduction of angle as a variable (Figure 26). A series of experiments carefully disentangled angle, I_{xx}, and P from probe length and surface distance (e.g., so that both near and far surfaces could be associated with steep or shallow angles, small or large values of I_{xx} or P, etc.). The experiments verified people's ability to attend selectively to length or distance (perceived distances ranged from 20 to 45 cm for actual surface distances of 18 to 48 cm, and perceived lengths ranged from 60 to 100 cm for actual rod lengths of 61 to 91 cm). Analyses showed that the selective perception of length was not dependent on the perception of distance nor was the selective perception of distance dependent on the perception of length. Rather, perception of those properties was dependent on different complexes of parameters, even though the exploratory movements were putatively identical. Those complexes comprised measurable mechanical parameters associated with wielding and striking with an implement (Figure 26b). In a departure from Chan and Turvey's last experiment, however, these experiments found no reliable role for P in perceiving surface distance. Tellingly, perhaps, the status of P as a dynamical parameter is less clear and less secure than that of I_{xx}. As already noted, I_{ij} couples a system (object with fixed rotation point) and its environment (forces) unequivocally. Ascribing such a role to P (viz., coupling states of the axis to impulsive forces of contact) is equivocal. It is, to be sure, an

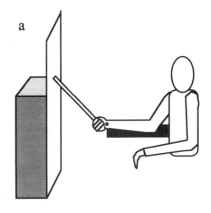

a

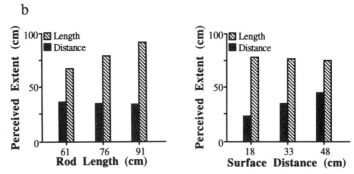

b

FIGURE 26   (a) The subject probes an unseen vertical surface (for simplicity, the occlusion screen is not shown) and indicates its distance or the probe's length with a report apparatus of the kind shown in Figure 1a. (b) Perceived rod lengths and perceived surface distances are in the appropriate ranges and are not confused with one another. (Adapted from Carello et al., 1992.)

indicator of the relevance of contact parameters, but beyond its appearance in power laws generated from data, its place in a parameter complex derived from first principles remains elusive.

B. Size Perception by Dynamic Touch

A greater degree of clarity has been obtained from the effort to understand the perception of size by striking (Barac-Cikoja & Turvey, 1991, 1993, 1995). The size to be perceived was that of a gap between two vertical surfaces (Hanley & Goff, 1974). Nonvisual size perception of this sort is relevant to whether an aperture is large enough to permit passage of the body or a body segment. The inner edges of the gap were struck by a probe somewhere along its length by use of repetitive horizontal movements about a rotation point O in the wrist. O was positioned on the bisector of the angle α defined by the hand-and-probe's excursion between the walls of the gap. Aperture size was indicated by the adjustment of the visible distance between two comparable surfaces (Figure 27a). All things being equal, the larger the gap, the greater the angular excursion. However, all things are not equal—the distance of the gap affects angular excursion; the strike point along the probe and the probe characteristics affect the reactive forces.

In the experimental situation, the "law of size constancy" is identical in form to that in vision. Actual gap size is equal to the product of $\tan \alpha$ and the distance from O to the gap. In the experiments of Barac-Cikoja and Turvey (1991), the variables manipulated were aperture size α, distance b of the point of contact along the probe with the gap measured from O, mass m of the probe plus hand, location of the center of mass a of the probe plus hand, and moment of inertia I_{yy} of the probe plus hand about O. (Thinking of a rod parallel to the ground, as in Figure 2c, the z-axis is its longitudinal axis, the y-axis is vertical and perpendicular to z, the x-axis is horizontal and perpendicular to z.)

The major results were (1) perception of a given size decreases with b, (2) for the same α, different sizes are perceived as different, (3) perception of a given size decreases with increasing I_{yy}, (4) discrimination among a given set of sizes decreases at a specific rate as b increases, and (5) all of the preceding hold regardless of whether the subject knows the distances of the apertures and whether the subject has foreknowledge of the different rotational inertias of the rods (Figure 27b). In summary, haptically perceived size did not abide by the law of size constancy. Rather, the forces felt at O are scaled to the muscular forces applied at the system's CM to arrest its movement (Barac-Cikoja & Turvey, 1991). What follows shows how that scaling is possible.

Mechanical analysis of the torques, impulse forces, and motions of striking between spatially separate surfaces reveals a collective dimensionless quantity λ that, for a given rod, aperture, and distance, is invariant over muscular forces, resultant impulsive torques, and motions (see Barac-Cikoja & Turvey, 1991, 1993):

$$\lambda = \sin(\alpha/2) \times [1 - (2a/b) + (ma^2/I_{yy})] = \sin(\alpha/2) \times \delta. \qquad (17)$$

It is a scalar quantity, or zero-order tensor, that connects the muscular forces imposed upon the probe to the reactive forces impressed upon the tissues of the body. Haptic perception of aperture size was found to be a single-valued function of λ (Figure 27c). In each of the seven experiments conducted by Barac-Cikoja and Turvey (1991), this collective parameter predicted successfully the interdependent effects of angular displacement, distance of surfaces, and the mechanical properties of the implement. It also predicted

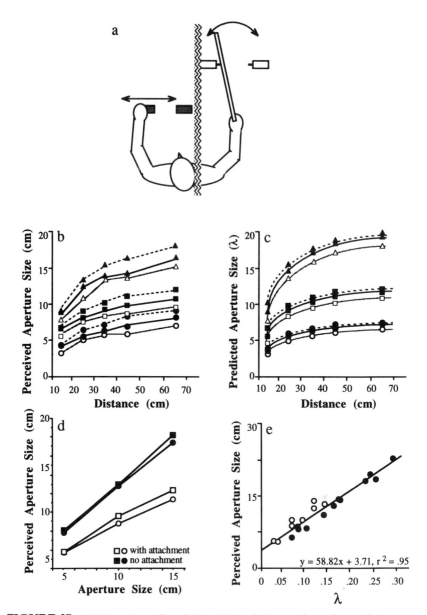

FIGURE 27 (a) Top view of a subject striking the inner edges of a gap between two wooden blocks while adjusting the visible gap between two report blocks. (b) Each set of three lines represents a different angular excursion; within a set, the curves represent a different I_{yy} for the same angle. (c) The predictive power of λ is seen in the separation of the three sets of lines, the relative ordering within a set, and the decreasing slope with distance. (Figures 27a, 27b, and 27c adapted from Barac-Cikoja & Turvey, 1991.) (d) Perceived aperture size as a function of actual aperture size depends on whether rotation is about the wrist (circles) or elbow (squares) and, especially, whether the contact is with the finger or an attachment. (e) With the preceding conditions, perceived size is a single-valued function of λ. (Adapted from Barac-Cikoja & Turvey, 1993. Copyright by the American Psychological Association. Adapted with permission.)

the rate at which the resolution of size by dynamic touch declined with b. The upshot is the λ hypothesis of size perception by haptic probing:

$$\text{perceived size} \propto \lambda$$

or

$$\text{Perceived size} \propto \sin(\alpha/2) \times \delta. \tag{18}$$

Inspection of Equation 18 suggests close similarity in structure to the law of size (S) constancy developed for vision

$$S = \tan \Theta \times D, \tag{19}$$

where Θ is the angle subtended by the object and D is its distance. Insofar as the sine and tangent functions are, for small angles, closely similar, the difference in trigonometric functions between Equations 18 and 19 may not be very significant in quantitative terms. Qualitatively, however, their origins in their respective equations are significantly different: The sine function of Equation 18 arises from a consideration of the components of the reactive force generated at contact (see Barac-Cikoja & Turvey, 1991, 1993). This aspect aside, it is important to compare the δ of Equation 18 with the D of Equation 19. Because $I_{yy} = mK_y^2$, where K_y is the radius of gyration,[14] δ can be rewritten as

$$\delta = 1 - (2a/b) + (a^2/K_y^2). \tag{20}$$

Further, because k_y^2/a is the distance p of the center of percussion from O, the expression for δ can be written even more simply as

$$\delta = 1 - (2a/b) + (a/p). \tag{21}$$

What Equation 21 brings out is the fact that δ is a configuration of different kinds of distances from O, namely, to center of mass (a), to point-of-contact (b), and to center of percussion (p). Intuitively, these points define the constant geometric structure of the probing. During rotational probings about a fixed point O, these distances remain invariant. Collectively, as the single quantity δ, they scale the angle through which the probe moves (more precisely, the component of the contact force associated with a given angular displacement). It can be seen from Equations 21 and 18 that if p equals $b/2$, then perceived size would completely be determined by $\sin(\alpha/2)$. This would be analogous to the "law of retinal size," meaning a complete absence of size constancy under the perceptual conditions of dynamic touch.

---

[14] The radius of gyration of a rigid body is the distance from O to a point at which a concentrated particle of mass equal to that of the body would have the same moment of inertia as the body.

Two important predictions follow from the identity of $\sin(\alpha/2)$ with $S/2b$ (where S is gap size). First, λ will approximate S as $2b/\delta$ approximates 1 (when the dimensionless δ is multiplied by whatever the unit quantity needed to bring it into the same scale as b). More specifically, perceived size should equal S if $2b/\delta = 1$, underestimate S if $2b/\delta < 1$, and overestimate S if $2b/\delta > 1$. The second prediction is closely related to the first, having to do with the discriminative capacity of dynamic touch in perceiving size by striking. As summarized above, Barac-Cikoja and Turvey (1991) observed that the rate at which perceived size changes with S declined systematically with b, the distance to the point of contact. That is, the range of perceived sizes for a given range of actual Ss shrunk with distance, suggesting a systematic reduction in haptic size discrimination. Of importance, this decline in resolving power is paralleled by λ, which likewise shrinks in its range, as a function of b, for a given range of actual sizes. Inspection of Equations 17 and 21 suggests, however, that size discrimination must be tied to more than b. Equation 22 presents the partial derivative of λ with respect to S:

$$\frac{\partial \lambda}{\partial S} = \frac{1}{2b} - \frac{a}{b^2} + \frac{a}{2bp}. \tag{22}$$

Given Equation 18, it follows from Equation 22 that only when $\partial\lambda/\partial S = 1$ (given λ multiplied by whatever the unit quantity needed to bring it into the same scale as S) will perceived size change at the same rate as S. For $\partial\lambda/\partial S > 1$, perceived size will change faster than S; for $\partial\lambda/\partial S < 1$, perceived size will change slower than S. In summary, the rate of change of perceived size with respect to S should be determined by the right-hand side of Equation 22; that is, by a particular configuration of the invariant mechanically significant distances comprising probing about O, namely, a, b, and p. The discriminative capacity of dynamic touch is predictable, in principle, from the dynamics. The predictions that were based on $2b/\delta$ and $\partial\lambda/\partial S$ were confirmed in the experiments of Barac-Cikoja and Turvey (1993).

The latter experiments also extended the scope of the λ hypothesis by evaluating it under conditions of probing involving different limb segments. Use of the hand versus use of the forearm versus use of the whole arm means (1) different muscular synergies and different sites of tissue deformation and (2) different distances from the axes about which the rotational probing motions occur and different angular excursions of the rod for the same point of contact along the rod and for the same aperture size. Methods for calculating λ for any body segment-cutaneous appendage combination were developed. Probing by motions about different joints, with hand-held rods that differed in rotational inertia, yielded perceptions of aperture size that varied in direct proportion of λ. An additional comparison was made between probing with and without an attachment to the skin. Figures 27c and 27d show that probing gaps with a hand-held rod and probing gaps with the bare index finger, both conducted through rotations about the y-axis in the wrist, are similar when expressed in relation to λ. When probing the environment with appendages, perception by dynamic touch seems to obey the same principles whether contact is made with a receptor-rich biological probe (a finger) or with a "neurally inert" stick (Burton, 1993).

Equation 19 is derived from a Euclidean geometric analysis of size at a distance and involves no dynamics. The psychological version replaces S by perceived size and D by perceived distance. It is commonly referred to as the *size–distance invariance hypothesis* (Kilpatrick & Ittelson, 1953). In contrast to the psychological version of Equation 19, Equation 18 is derived from an analysis of the dynamics rather than the Euclidean geometry of probing distal surfaces and can, in principle, accommodate the facts of size perception strictly through observables (i.e., measurable quantities). A direct comparison of the λ hypothesis and the size–distance invariance hypothesis was conducted by Barac-Cikoja and Turvey (1995). Subjects were required to perceive both gap size and gap distance. As in section XII.A, no causal connection was found between the two perceptions—all of the variance in perceived size was found to be accountable for by mechanical parameters, in this case λ. It was concluded that evoking perceptual entities in explanations of size perception is required only when the stimulus analysis is incomplete.

C. Perceiving Behavioral Possibilities by Probing

Thus far, we have considered probing for which the subject's response is magnitude production, providing a visual match for the perceived property. However, of course, perceivers are not in the business of matching sizes and distances but perceiving whether those sizes and distances permit certain activities: stepping up or down, walking between, and so on. Indeed, we took care to note the behavioral relevance of each of the studied properties. This concern respects Gibson's assertion that organisms perceive *affordances*, the behavioral possibilities of an environment layout. Whereas the preceding experiments could each be said to tap a property of behavioral relevance, none was assessed directly. An affordance response was the basis of Burton's (1992) investigation of haptically perceiving gaps in the substrate. In particular, he examined whether a person could determine by probing whether a gap in the surface of support could be stepped over without requiring a gait adjustment. Subjects stood on a walkway fashioned from

FIGURE 28   Subjects either walk along a series of platforms or stand at the front edge of a gap and explore it with an aluminum rod. They judge whether the gap could be stepped over without breaking stride, would require some adjustment of an ordinary walking gait, or could not be crossed. (Adapted from Burton, 1992.)

several movable platform segments. A gap between segments could be introduced anywhere along the walkway (Figure 28). Gap size was manipulated and explored, first, with a single probe by blindfolded subjects, who were selected to be of extreme heights. This last manipulation is characteristic of affordance experiments because it leads to differences in the action system—in this case, leg length—that should lead to different perceptions by the two groups (e.g., Carello, Grosofsky, Reichel, Solomon, & Turvey, 1989; Mark, 1987; Warren, 1984).

As expected, the taller subjects designated larger gaps as crossable than did the shorter subjects. When gap size was scaled by leg length, the difference between the two groups of subjects was eliminated. This is a standard affordance finding, albeit the first in the realm of dynamic touch. In subsequent experiments, probe properties were manipulated. In contrast to the preceding probing experiments, however, probe variables had little influence on perceived crossability. Rod length, not inertia, contributed significantly to the regression. The importance of rod length was through its contribution to the amount that a subject would have to lean to reach the far side of the gap with the probe. Because leaning changes the posture used during locomotion, differences are not unexpected. However, this is the first dynamic touch task in which the mass distribution of the probe was inconsequential. The affordance response is the obvious difference from the host of magnitude production and magnitude estimation tasks used previously. Why this should matter is still a matter of speculation. However, we might imagine a parallel with vision: Judgments of absolute sizes and distances may differ if done monocularly or binocularly, whereas the guidance of locomotion is unaffected. Information about affordances is not dependent on the vagaries of the energy medium.

This last point gets a potentially important interpretation in a comparison of dynamic touch with vision in the perception of the affordance of a slanted surface for supporting upright stance (Fitzpatrick, Carello, Schmidt,

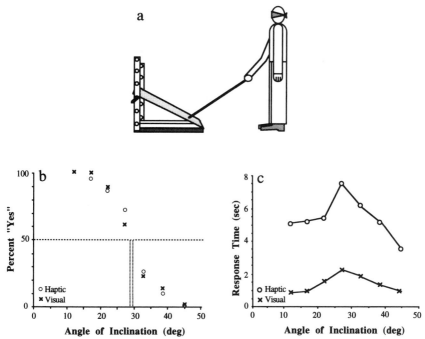

FIGURE 29   (a) A blindfolded subject explores a surface (whose slant can be adjusted) with a wooden probe. Without the blindfold, the subject simply looks at the surface. In each case, the task is to determine whether a given slant would support stable upright posture. (b) The transition between slants that would support stance and slants that would not does not differ for the two perceptual systems. (c) Exploration time increases around that transition point for both perceptual systems. (Adapted from Fitzpatrick et al., 1994, with kind permission from Elsevier Science Ltd., The Boulevard, Langford Lane, Kidlington OX5 1GB, UK.)

& Corey, 1994). A 1-m^2 platform 1 m in front of an observer was slanted up from the floor 0° to 45° (in 5° or 1.7° increments in two experiments). In blocked trials, participants either looked at the slanted surface or, blindfolded, probed it with a 120-cm stick and reported whether a given slope could be stood on stably without requiring bending at the hip (Figure 29a). The perceived transition between supporting stance and not supporting stance did not differ for the two perceptual systems (Figure 29b). Moreover, for both perceptual systems, the exploration time required to reach that determination peaked at the transition and dropped dramatically before and after (Figure 29c).

These results suggest that both the haptic and visual perceptual systems are suited to detecting action-based properties necessary for the coordination and control of action. Also, they provide support for Gibson's assertion that information is free of the peculiarities of sensory system; it is, rather, higher order relations manifest in a number of structured energy distributions (Fitzpatrick et al., 1994; Gibson, 1966).

> The equivalence of different stimuli for perception and behavior has long been a puzzle, but it ceases to be puzzling if we suppose that it results from equivalent stimulus information being carried by different forms of stimulus energy. . . . It is not surprising that patterns in the flux of sound, touch, and light from the environment may be equivalent to one another by invariant laws of nature" (Gibson, 1966, p. 55).

D. Taking Stock

One additional puzzle remains unresolved in the research on probing. The experiments on perceiving a gap size—which provide the best illustration of the sort of strategy that we are championing—are the only ones that require inclusion of the limb segment in the calculation of inertia. If λ is calculated on the basis of the rod inertia alone, it loses its predictive power. However, inclusion of the limb segment in the calculation of inertia does not improve the account of data in perceiving length by contact, perceiving distance of either a vertical or horizontal surface, or perceiving length without contact. The conditions that demand inclusion of the limb are not as yet clear.

XIII. DISTANCE PERCEPTION BY VIBRATIONS OF SOLID MEDIA

Dynamic touch has many variations. Registration of patterns of mechanical vibration of the surfaces on which organisms stand and move is often the basis for the perception of distal objects and events. Prey burrowing at a distance of 50 cm are detected by the desert scorpion (*Paruroctonus mesaensis*) on the basis of the temporal structure and amplitude difference in compressional (horizontal) and Rayleigh (retrograde elliptical) wave fronts transmitted in the sand (Brownell, 1984). Spiders locate prey in the web on the basis of the vibrations produced by the prey's impact with the web and its subsequent attempts at escape (Barrows, 1915; Burgess & Witt, 1976). The capability of registering mechanical waves propagated in sand or fibrous matter involves bodily contact with the medium and sensory mechanisms—such as the slit sensilla of scorpions and the lyriform organs of spiders—responsive to the deformation in the body's tissues produced by the waves. Kinsella-Shaw and Turvey (1992) conjectured that human limbs in contact with a solid medium should, by virtue of their mechanoreceptors, be capable of functioning like the limbs of scorpions and spiders. That is, distal objects should be perceptible by humans on the basis of mechanical waves in a solid medium (see Katz, 1925/1989).

A model system for investigating this possibility consists of perceiving the distance of an object on a single taut strand vibrated manually. The dynamics are given by the one-dimensional wave equation:

$$\partial^2 u / \partial x^2 = (1/v^2)(\partial^2 u / \partial t^2), \tag{23}$$

where $u = u (x, t)$, a function locating each point x on the string at every instant of time t, and v equals $(T/\mu)^{1/2}$, with T the tension (horizontal component of force on the strand) and μ the linear density. The apparatus shown in Figure 30a is so designed as to guarantee the application of the preceding equation, it is referred to as *a minimal haptic web* (Kinsella–Shaw & Turvey, 1992). In the basic experiment, a metal disk of approximately 1 kg was affixed to the taut strand at different distances from the position of the subject's right hand grasping the strand. The disk and taut strand were occluded. Visible to the subject, and manipulable by the left hand, was a report apparatus that allowed the subject to position a marker at the felt distance of the metal disk (see Figure 30b). The subject was required to set the strand into motion by tugging and pushing at the point of grasp. Typically, subjects used an impulse strategy meaning that they would give the strand a sharp single shake, wait awhile, and then repeat the action. There was no limit on the number or frequency of such impulse perturbations. For actual distances of 30.5, 61, 91, 122, and 152 cm, the mean perceived distances were 48.3, 66, 83.4, 101.6, and 141.6 cm in one experiment and 33.7, 58.4, 89.4, 105.4, and 136.2 cm in a second experiment in which subjects received practice in the task before the experiment proper (Kinsella–Shaw & Turvey, 1992).

Given that people can perceive distances of things in the minimal haptic web, there must be a mechanical quantity that constrains this ability in the manner of I_{ij} and λ in the research described above. In Equation 23, the elastic force $\partial^2 u / \partial x^2$ is coupled to the strand's motions $\partial^2 u / \partial t^2$ by the constant μ/T. According to the strategy identified in Section I.A, the requisite quantity must entail μ/T in some form. For a taut strand of a given material, μ is fixed. In contrast, T can be varied by varying the weight of the attached metal disk and the position of the hand relative to the two stanchions to which the strand is attached (see Figure 30). T is least at the center of the strand and greatest at points close to the attachments. These "middle" and "end" hand positions were used in an experiment in which the metal disk was positioned at four different distances from the hand, with the same four distances for both hand positions. Calculations revealed that T increased with distance when the hand was at the middle and decreased with distance when the hand was at the end. When subjects made judgments about the distance of the attached metal disk, the rate at which perceived distance changed with actual distance was approximately 0.9 for the hand in the middle and 0.2 for the hand at the end. That is, there was a marked interaction between hand position and the distance of the attached object,

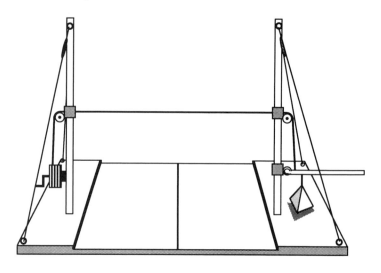

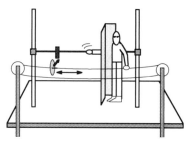

FIGURE 30   (a) The minimal haptic web instantiates the one-dimensional wave equation. (b) A subject moves the strand on which an occluded mass is attached and indicates with a visible marker the felt location of that attached mass. (Adapted from Kinsella-Shaw & Turvey, 1992.)

suggesting an influence of T on spatial perception within the minimal haptic web.

In addressing the preceding data, Kinsella–Shaw and Turvey (1992) suggested that an important quantity is τ, the time it takes a transient wave to travel between two points on a segment of the strand under a given tension. τ is computed as the distance between the points divided by the appropriate v (see Equation 23). Thus, as T increases, v increases with a consequent decrease in the τ between any two points on the segment. τ is the time scale of the deviation from, and return to, the equilibrium state of the strand. This time scale is informative about the distance of the object from the hand. Given two distance d_1 and d_2 of the same object and two tensions T_1

and T_2 corresponding to the two object-strand configurations, the wave return times over the distances d_1 and d_2 will be d_1/v_1 and d_2/v_2, respectively. In that v is proportional to T, specifically, to $(T)^{1/2}$, τ is directly related to d and inversely related to T. It was hypothesized, therefore, that perceived distance of an object from the hand was based on the wave travel time τ. By this hypothesis, perceived distance must vary with d raised to a positive power and with T raised to a negative power. Consistent with the hypothesis, multiple regression in logarithmic coordinates of the data from the experiment examining middle and end positions of the hand revealed exponents of 0.55 and -0.13 for d and T, respectively.

A very different hypothesis follows from an interpretation of the ability to "echolocate," which has features in common with the spatial ability exhibited in the minimal haptic web. In echolocating, use may be made of the time differential between when the probe sound was emitted and when the reflected sound returned. With respect to dynamic touch and vibrating solid media, the question can be raised of whether subjects use the time differential, Δt, between when the hand initiated the perturbation, t_1, and when the reflected wave returned to the hand, t_2. Subjects could base an estimate of object distance from the hand on the relative differences in Δt across the various distances of the attached metal disk: larger values of Δt would mean larger distances. Kinsella-Shaw and Turvey (1992) conducted experiments in which the subject grasped the strand but did not actively perturb it. The perturbation was introduced by the experimenter at the location of the metal disk. The experimenter perturbed the strand by raising it to a set altitude, releasing it abruptly, and then arresting its motion immediately on return to the initial position. The judgments under these passive conditions (in which the subject received only three discrete incident waves) were less accurate than in the active case (described above) in which the subject perturbed the strand freely. Despite the lowered accuracy, judgments of distance were systematically dependent on actual distance, in contradiction of the Δt hypothesis.

XIV. IMPLICATIONS OF RESEARCH ON DYNAMIC TOUCH FOR PERCEPTION IN GENERAL

Theories of perception have been dominated by the study of vision and, to a lesser extent, by the study of audition. Whereas the study of touch contributed significantly to the early understanding of sensory receptors (Boring, 1942, 1950; Granit, 1955), original formulations of concepts such as *local sign* (Lotze, 1856/1885), as well as the first round of analyses of psychophysical functions (Weber, 1834, 1978), it has contributed minimally to the specifics of perceptual theory. As Neisser (1976) has suggested, the limited role of touch in theory building has been due largely to (1) no isolable organ corresponding to the eye-retina system and the ear-cochlear system and (2) no available means to control the relevant stimuli, especially in the general case of active touch. With respect to Point 2, the advantage of studying dynamic touch over the other subsystems of touch (see section I) is that it does permit control of the relevant stimuli. The research summarized in this chapter represents a significant advance in the understanding of touch precisely because dynamic touch permits full exploitation of rotational and contact dynamics, branches of physical analyses that have been developed rigorously over the past three centuries. The information detected by dynamic touch is contained in structured distributions of mechanical energy and these are addressable experimentally. Consequently, given the extensive body of research now available on touch in its dynamic form, the traditional neglect of touch phenomena in the development of perceptual theory can be redressed. In the following, some general theoretical conclusions from the experiments reviewed in this chapter are enumerated.

A. Extraction of Physical Invariants

Perhaps the most important conclusion is that a perceptual system extracts physical invariants from the changing flux of stimulation. This conclusion comports with central themes of Gibson (1959, 1966, 1979). Ambient patterned energy distributions are hypothesized by Gibson to contain structure specific to their sources in the environment. In developing the implications of the specificity of structured energy arrays to their causes, Gibson (1966) speculated that "if the invariants of this structure can be registered by a perceptual system, the constants of neural input will correspond to the constants of stimulus energy, although the one will not copy the other" (p. 267). Research on dynamic touch suggests that the latter speculation of Gibson's might be developed along tensorial lines (Fitzpatrick et al., 1994; Pagano et al., 1993).

I_{ij} of an object about a given point O is a physical invariant, that is, a quantity independent of the coordinate systems at O (e.g., rectangular, curvilinear, and those of both kinds produced through arbitrary rotations) by which it might be expressed. Wielding an object about O defined, for example, at the wrist, incurs a time-dependent tissue deformation pattern that is (1) constrained by the rigid arm-plus-rod dynamics and (2) expressed in the intrinsic coordinate system defined by the muscles and tendons of the forearm (see Pellionisz & Llinás, 1985). At any given point in time, an array of numbers can be assigned to the states of the forearm's tissues. These numbers, referring as they do to the particular strain states, would be very different from the numbers by which the rigid body dynamics are described. Moreover, there would be more of them given that the number of independent dimensions—muscles and tensors—to which quantities can be assigned exceeds the number of dimensions needed to formulate motions and torques in three space.[15] Nonetheless, a reasonable hypothesis is that a linkage must exist between the deformable body dynamics and the rigid body dynamics (Solomon, 1988; Solomon & Turvey, 1988; Solomon et al., 1989b). The tensile states of muscles and tendons produce torques and motions of hand and object, these in turn affect the tensile states of muscles and tendons. The two kinds of dynamics are circularly causal and coimplicative. Within this circular causality, an invariant deformation pattern D_{kl} (considered as a tensor of rank two for simplicity) can be assumed to exist in correspondence with I_{ij}. Put simply, D_{kl} is I_{ij} in deformation quantities (for the strategies used to define such quantities, see Fung, 1993). The defining property of a tensor is the transformation law that identifies the way the tensor's component quantities in one coordinate system are related to its component quantities in another coordinate system. The transformation of the p components of a tensor guarantees that the new components q determine the same tensor. The precise form of this transformation law depends on the physical or geometric meaning of the tensor (e.g., Borisenko & Tarapov, 1979). In summary, D_{kl} is related to I_{ij} by a transformation law.

On similar grounds it can be hypothesized that the invariant I_{ij} about O is also rendered as A_{mn} (similarly considered as a tensor of rank two for simplicity), the tensorial quantification of the invariant pattern of afferentation induced by D_{kl} and expressed in the intrinsic coordinate system defined by the neural activity in the muscular and tendon afferents. There is, therefore, a rendering of I_{ij} in at least three natural coordinate systems. These renderings, by definition, are not expressed identically and must differ in their details. However, because they are all renderings of the same physical fact, the same invariant, they must be identical at the tensorial level of description. A tensor is a quantity that possesses a specified system of components in every coordinate system and that changes under a transformation of coordinates. Thus, I_{ij}, D_{kl}, and A_{mn} are renderings of the same fact in different coordinate systems. Given the preceding arguments, a neural formulation of the sensitivity of dynamic touch to physical invariants poses the question of "how are neuronal networks organized such that they can embody and functionally support the necessary geometrical transformations?" (Pellionisz & Llinás, 1985, p. 251)

From the broader perspective of perceptual theory, a general theory of the extracting of invariants would replace theories of "constancy" in perception (Gibson, 1979). Classically, these latter theories have been devised

---

[15] Special issues are raised when the transformation is between coordinate systems that are dimensionally unequal, but suggestions for their resolution are to be found in the literature (e.g., Pellionisz, 1986; Pellionisz & Llinás, 1985).

(primarily in respect to vision) to explain how a perceiver can have impressions of unchanging shape, size, orientation, and so on in the face of changing sensory input. The form taken by these theories has often assumed an internal calculation involving mental representations of one or more physical quantities, as noted in the next subsection.

B. Percept–Percept Coupling

The focus of the experiments summarized in the present chapter has been lawful regularities underlying perceptual capabilities. They are of significance, additionally, to interpretations of perception as a computational or reasoning-like process. Characteristic of ratiomorphic interpretations is the problem of how to formalize the mechanism by which nominally distinct stimulus attributes become linked in perception. Such accounts would consider, for example, the perception of object extent (section III) as conditioned on the *perceptions* of diameter, composition, mass, and shape and the perception of aperture size (section XII) as conditioned on the *perceptions* of angle, distance, mass, and rotational inertia. As examples of these accounts, percept–percept coupling (e.g., Epstein, 1982), and perceptual integration (e.g., Ashby & Townsend, 1986; Klatzky et al., 1989; Reed, Lederman, & Klatzky, 1990) are founded on the assumption that the processing of one property is contingent on variations in the perception of another property, one that often seems to be irrelevant (such as object size when wielding to perceive object weight, see section X; or surface distance when probing to perceive rod length, see section XII).

In contrast to the notion of mental quantities that must be combined algorithmically, the experiments on dynamic touch reveal perception to be a function (in its standard sense of a single-valued mapping) of physical quantities such as I_{ij} and λ that gather together, in a lawfully prescribed manner, the potentially separate dimensions of length, diameter, composition, mass, and shape (in the case of I_{ij}) and angle of contact, distance of contact, probe mass, and probe rotational inertia (in the case of λ). Where research on dynamic touch has explicitly pitted physical quantities of the preceding kind against formulations involving "percepts" (the perceived values of component dimensions), the finding has been that the appropriate physical quantities make the inclusion of perceived quantities superfluous (e.g., section XII).

C. Coordinate Systems

Questions of what constitutes the proper coordinate system for a particular perceptual achievement often arise. With respect to the perceptual control of upper-limb movements, for example, a shoulder-centered rectangular coordinate system has been advanced by some investigators (e.g., Flanders et al., 1992; Soechting, Helms Tillery, & Flanders, 1990), whereas others have proposed coordinate systems anchored elsewhere, both within and outside the body (e.g., Alexander, 1992; Blouin, Teasdale, & Fleury, 1992). The results from investigations of dynamic touch (section IX) suggest that the major issue is not the particular coordinate system in which parameters for the perceptual control of the limbs are rendered but rather the nature of the parameters themselves—for example, I_{ij} rather than geometric orientation or joint angles. As the potentially relevant quantity for the nonvisual perception of limb orientation, I_{ij} is coordinate-system independent. For each choice of coordinate system O_{xyx}, the components of I_{ij} will differ, but the nature in which the tensor specifies material properties does not change. Different translations of O result in different tensorial components (i.e., the independent elements in the matrix change), but the manner in which the tensor transforms is such that it continues to be specific to the object or limb property it quantifies. A reasonable conjecture from the results on dynamic touch is that perceptual systems are tied to physical invariants and not to any preferred coordinate system.

D. Smart Perceptual Systems

The findings on dynamic touch have encouraged an interpretation of perceptual systems as *smart, determinate, soft,* and *scaled* (Carello et al., 1991; Solomon, 1988; Solomon & Turvey, 1988). The qualifier smart is in reference to the exploitation of special aspects of the situation in adapting to the complexities of a perceptual task (Bingham, 1988; Runeson, 1977). The reviewed results suggest that perceptual systems capitalize routinely on physical invariants. The qualifier determinate is in reference to the frequently observed functions by which perceptions map uniquely to physical quantities (see, for example, Figures 2, 5, 13, 14, 15, 27).

The qualifier soft is in reference to the observations that dynamic touch in the wielding and probing modes can act as different kinds of measuring instruments. Reinforcing the qualifier soft are those observations that suggest that any given meter can be assembled over different anatomical structures and that different meters can be assembled over the same anatomical structure (sections VI and XII). The broad theoretical importance of the designation soft is the implication that the functioning of a perceptual system is specific to general dynamical principles rather than to particular anatomical components.

The qualifier scaled is in reference to the finding that perception of a dimension (e.g., length) closely approximates its actual magnitude (see Figures 1, 2, 21, 26). This is so, even though the quantity of which the perception is a function (such as I_{ij}) is in units of a different kind. Arriving at an understanding of scaling may demand an operator characterization of perceptual systems. The following operators have been enumerated in respect to dynamic touch and extent perception: a differential operator that describes the motion of the wielded object, an integral operator that yields I_{ij}, an orthogonal operator that diagonalizes I_{ij}, and an operator that renders the eigenvalues as an extent. Collectively, the preceding composition of operators has been referred to as the *haptic operator* (Solomon, 1988; Solomon & Turvey, 1988; Solomon et al., 1989a, 1989b). In physical theory, the major operators are mathematical shorthand for laws. Thus, the primary motivation for an operator formulation would be to establish a framework in which a perceptual system's "smart" abilities can be characterized in lawful terms.

E. Specificity to Information

It is usually agreed that the different classes of perceptual experience are specific to something. Extensions of the nineteenth century doctrine of specific nerve energies have tended to identify the "something" with anatomy. For example, exteroperception is specific to exteroceptors—the organs of vision and audition—and proprioperception is specific to proprioceptors—the receptive mechanisms of skin, joints, muscles, and tendons. Gibson (1966) rejected anatomical specificity, and the reviewed research on dynamic touch reinforces his reasons for doing so. The three major information kinds, identified in section I, are exterospecific, propriospecific, and exypropriospecific. According to Gibson (1966, 1979), all three information kinds are available (in greater or lesser degree) to each perceptual system and are detectable by each perceptual system. By Gibson's hypothesis, the specificity of perception is not to anatomy but to information. In the research reviewed in this chapter, dynamic touch was shown to be exteroceptive, proprioceptive, and exproprioceptive, consonant with the understanding that these three kinds of perception do not depend on specialized receptors. The individual mechanoreceptors imbedded in muscle and tendon respond to the local mechanical perturbations arising from local tissue distortion. However, when they are incorporated into an "organ of sensitivity" (Gibson, 1966), and behave collectively, they can respond in distinct ways to the transformations and invariants of patterns of mechanical energy engendered by the environment, the body, and environment–body relations.

F. Limits of Specificity

Two major experimental goals within Gibson's (1959, 1966, 1979) program are to discover specificity (1) between properties of structured energy distributions and properties of the environment, body, and environment–body relations and (2) between perception and properties of structured energy distributions. Of importance, there is no requirement in Gibson's perspective that a structured array be fully specific to its source: Structured arrays can only be as specific to their sources as the laws of physics allow (Gibson, 1960). For a wielded object, the structured array of different resistances to rotational acceleration in different directions, I_{ij}, is informative about its linear dimensions, but it is not perfectly so. Stated more directly, the eigenvalues of I_{ij} cannot predict the length of an object with probability one (as determined, for example, by a multiple regression). The results summarized in section III suggest that I_{ij} can constrain perceived length within the "ballpark" of actual length, but this need not be the case for all objects. It depends on how they are constructed.

Another closely related limitation on specificity can be conveyed by the experiments on probing reviewed in section XII. In those experiments, the energy distribution was mechanical, the nominal environmental property was gap size, and the nominal perception was of gap size. The demonstrated specificity of perceived size to λ meant the nonspecificity of perceived size to actual size. Specificity of Type (2) above was demonstrated but not specificity of Type (1), at least not when the environmental property was defined strictly as the size of a gap in meters. The property λ of the mechanical energy distribution is not specific to aperture size but to the configuration of the fixed spatial and kinetic properties defining a given situation of probing a separation between surfaces. With respect to vision, Koffka (1935; see also Gibson, 1950) spoke of size-at-a-distance to underscore that size per se was not perceivable in separation from distance. It may be the case that for dynamic touch and aperture perception by probing, the perceptible property is not size per se but size-at-a-distance-contacted-with-a-particular-implement. For probing about a fixed point O, there is no discernible property in the mechanical forces and motions that relates invariantly to aperture size.

XV. CONCLUDING REMARKS

Perceiving what is in the hand and perceiving by means of what is in the hand are logically continuous. This continuity encompasses perceiving by keratinous appendages such as vibrissae and claws as well (see Burton, 1993, for a review). Gibson (1966) argued that extended perception—where the obtaining of information is at some remove from the body and its receptors—highlights the irrelevance of sensations for perception. Whether an object or surface is touched with the skin, a claw or nail, or a tool, it is the object or surface that is felt, not the impressions on the skin. It is also felt at the end of the appendage, not where the mechanoreceptive neurons are. Moreover, the variety of appendages that can be drafted for perception illustrates that the critical requirement is informational—susceptible to physical influence—not anatomical. As summarized in the preceding section, the implications of research on dynamic touch for perception in general are far reaching and include consideration of fundamental observables (including a principled characterization of properties that should not be perceivable), the nature of measurement, and a treatment of process that respects comparable issues in physical theory. In short, the study of dynamic touch has given rise to a programmatic strategy for addressing perception.

Acknowledgment

Preparation of this manuscript was supported by National Science Foundation Grants SBR 94-10982 and SBR 94-22650. The research reported here was conducted under National Science Foundation Grants BNS 87-20144, BNS 90-11013, and SBR 94-10982.

References

Alexander, G. E. (1992). For effective sensoriomotor processing must there be explicit representations and reconcilitation of differing frames of reference? *Behavioral and Brain Sciences, 15*, 321–322.

Altman, S. L. (1986). *Rotations, quarternions, and double groups.* London: Oxford University Press.

Amazeen, E., & Turvey, M. T. (in press). Weight perception and the haptic "size–weight illusion" are functions of the inertia tensor. *Journal of Experimental Psychology: Human Perception and Performance.*

Anderson, N. H. (1972). Cross-task validation of functional measurement. *Perception & Psychophysics, 12*, 389–395.

Ashby, F. G., & Townshend, J. T. (1986). Varieties of perceptual independence. *Psychological Review, 93*, 154–179.

Barac-Cikoja, D., & Turvey, M. T. (1991). Perceiving aperture size by striking. *Journal of Experimental Psychology: Human Perception and Performance, 17*, 330–346.

Barac-Cikoja, D., & Turvey, M. T. (1993). Perceiving size at a distance. *Journal of Experimental Psychology: General, 122*, 347–370.

Barac-Cikoja, D., & Turvey, M. T. (1995). Does perceived size depend on perceived distance? An argument from extended haptic perception. *Perception & Psychophysics, 57*, 216–224.

Barrows, W. M. (1915). The reactions of an orb-weaving spider, *Epiera sclopetaria* Cl, to rhythmic vibrations of its web. *Biological Bulletin, 29*, 316–332.

Batschelet, E. (1965). *Statistical methods for the analysis of problems in animal orientation and certain biological rhythms.* Washington, DC: American Institute of Biological Sciences.

Batschelet, E. (1978). Second order statistical evaluation of directions. In K. Schmidt-Koenig & W. T. Keeton (Eds.), *Animal migration and homing* (pp. 1–24). Berlin: Springer-Verlag.

Bernstein, N. (1967). *The coordination and regulation of movement.* New York: Pergamon.

Binder, M. D., Kroin, J. S., Moore, G. P., & Stuart, D. G. (1977). The response of Golgi tendon organs to single motor unit contractions. *Journal of Physiology, 271*, 337–349.

Bingham, G. P. (1988). Task-specific dynamics and the perceptual bottleneck. *Human Movement Science, 7*, 225–264.

Blouin, J., Teasdale, N., Bard, C., & Flaury, M. (1992). The mapping of visual space is a function of the structure of the visual field. *Behavioral and Brain Sciences, 15,* 326–327.

Boas, M. L. (1983). *Mathematical methods in the physical sciences.* New York: Wiley.

Borg, G. A. V., & Marks, L. E. (1983). Twelve meanings of the measure constant in psychophysical power functions. *Bulletin of the Psychonomic Society, 21,* 73–75.

Boring, E. G. (1942). *Sensation and perception in the history of experimental psychology.* New York: Appleton-Century-Crafts.

Boring, E. G. (1950). *A history of experimental psychology* (2nd ed.). New York: Appleton-Century-Crofts.

Borisenko, A. I., & Tarapov, I. E. (1979). *Vector and tensor analysis with applications.* New York: Dover.

Brownell, P. H. (1984). Prey detection by the sand scorpion. *Scientific American, 251,* 86–97.

Burgess, P. R., Wei, J. Y., Clark, F. J., & Simon, J. (1982). Signalling of kinesthetic information by peripheral sensory receptors. *Annual Review of Neuroscience, 5,* 171–187.

Burgess, P. R., & Witt, P. N. (1976). Spider webs: Design and engineering. *Interdisciplinary Science Reviews, 1,* 322–335.

Burton, G. (1992). Nonvisual judgment of the crossability of path gaps. *Journal of Experimental Psychology: Human Perception and Performance, 18,* 698–713.

Burton, G. (1993). Non-neural extensions of haptic sensitivity. *Ecological Psychology, 5,* 105–124.

Burton, G., Santana, M.-V., & Carello, C. (1995). Haptic decomposition is anchored in the inertia tensor. In R. J. Bootsma & Y. Guiard (Eds.). *Studies in perception and action, III.* Hillsdale, N.J.: Erlbaum.

Burton, G., & Turvey, M. T. (1990). Perceiving the lengths of rods that are held but not wielded. *Ecological Psychology, 2,* 294–324.

Burton, G., & Turvey, M. T. (1991). Attentionally splitting the mass distribution of a hand-held rod. *Perception & Psychophysics, 50,* 129–140.

Burton, G., Turvey, M. T., & Solomon, H. Y. (1990). Can shape be perceived by dynamic touch? *Perception & Psychophysics, 5,* 477–487.

Carello, C., Fitzpatrick, P., Domaniewicz, I., Chan, T.-C., & Turvey, M. T. (1992). Effortful touch with minimal movement. *Journal of Experimental Psychology: Human Perception and Performance, 18,* 290–302.

Carello, C., Fitzpatrick, P., & Turvey, M. T. (1992). Haptic probing: Perceiving the length of a probe and the distance of a surface probed. *Perception & Psychophysics, 51,* 580–598.

Carello, C., Grosofsky, A., Reichel, F., Solomon, H. Y., & Turvey, M. T. (1989). Perceiving what is reachable. *Ecological Psychology, 1,* 27–54.

Carello, C., Peck, A., & Fitzpatrick, P. (1993). Haptic and visual matches for haptically perceived extent are equivalent. *Bulletin of the Psychonomic Society, 31,* 13–15.

Chan, T.-C. (1994). Haptic perception of partial-rod lengths with the rod held stationary or wielded. *Perception & Psychophysics, 55,* 551–561.

Chan, T.-C., Carello, C., & Turvey, M. T. (1990). Perceiving object width by grasping. *Ecological Psychology, 2,* 1–35.

Chan, T.-C., & Turvey, M. T. (1991). Perceiving the vertical distances of surfaces by means of a hand-held probe. *Journal of Experimental Psychology: Human Perception and Performance, 17,* 347–358.

Chandler, R. F., Clauser, C. E., McContville, J. P., Reynolds, H. M., & Young, J. W. (1975). *Investigation of inertial properties of the human body: Final report, Apr. 1, 1972–Dec. 1974* (AMRL-TR-74-137). Dayton, OH: Aerospace Medical Research Laboratories, Wright-Patterson Air Force Base.

Charpentier, A. (1891). Analyse experimentale de quelques elements de la sensation de poids [Experimental study of some aspects of weight perception]. *Archives de Physiologie Normales et Pathologiques, 3,* 122–135.

Clark, F. J., & Burgess, P. R. (1975). Slowly adapting receptors in the cat knee joint: Can they signal joint angle? *Journal of Neurophysiology, 38,* 1448–1463.

Clauser, C. E., McContville, J. P., & Young, J. W. (1969). *Weight, volume and center of mass of segments of the human body* (AMRL-TR-69-70; NASA CR-11262). Dayton, OH: Aerospace Medical Research Laboratories, Wright-Patterson Air Force Base.

Cooke, J. D., Brown, S., Forget, R., & Lamarre, Y. (1985). Initial agonist burst duration changes with movement amplitude in a deafferented patient. *Experimental Brain Research, 60,* 184–187.

Craske, B. (1977). Perception of impossible limb positions induced by tendon vibration. *Science, 196,* 71–73.

Craske, B., Kenny, F. T., & Keith, D. (1984). Modifying an underlying component of perceived arm length: Adaption of tactile location induced by spatial discordance. *Journal of Experimental Psychology: Human Perception and Performance, 10,* 307–317.

Davidon, R. S., & Mather, J. H. (1966). Cross-modal judgments of length. *American Journal of Psychology, 79,* 409–418.

Davis, C. M., & Brickett, P. (1977). The role of preparatory muscle tension in the size-weight illusion. *Perception & Psychophysics, 22,* 262–264.

den Hartog, J. P. (1948). *Mechanics.* New York: Dover.

Dresslar, F. B. (1894). Studies in the psychology of touch. *American Journal of Psychology, 6,* 313–368.

Ellis, R. R., & Lederman, S. J. (1993). The role of haptic vs. visual volume cues in the size-weight illusion. *Perception & Psychophysics, 53,* 315–324.

Epstein, W. (1982). Percept–percept coupling. *Perception, 11,* 75–83.

Evarts, E. V., Bizzi, E., Burke, R. E., DeLong, M., & Thach, W. T. (1971). Central control of movement. *Neuroscience Research Progress Bulletin, 9,* No. 3.

Fitzpatrick, P., Carello, C., & Turvey, M. T. (1994). Eigenvalues of the inertia tensor and exteroception by the "muscular sense." *Neuroscience, 60,* 551–568.

Fitzpatrick, P., Carello, C., Schmidt, R. C., & Corey, D. (1994). Haptic and visual perception of an affordance for upright posture. *Ecological Psychology, 6,* 265–287.

Flanders, M., Helms Tillery, S., & Soechting, J. F. (1992). Early stages in a sensorimotor transformation. *Behavioral and Brain Sciences, 15,* 309–362.

Forget, R., & Lamarre, Y. (1987). Rapid elbow flexion in the absence of proprioceptive and cutaneous feedback. *Human Neurobiology, 6,* 27–37.

Fung, Y. C. (1993). *Biomechanics: Mechanical properties of living tissue* (2nd ed.). New York: Springer-Verlag.

Gelfan S., & Carter, S. (1967). Muscle sense in man. *Experimental Neurology, 18,* 469–473.

Gibson, J. J. (1950). *Perception of the visual world.* Boston: Houghton Mifflin.

Gibson, J. J. (1959). Perception as a function of stimulation. In S. Koch (Ed.), *Psychology: A study of science* (Vol. 1 pp. 456–501). New York: McGraw-Hill.

Gibson, J. J. (1960). The concept of the stimulus in psychology. *American Psychologist, 15,* 694–703.

Gibson, J. J. (1966). *The senses considered as perceptual systems.* Boston: Houghton Mifflin.

Gibson, J. J. (1979). *The ecological approach to visual perception.* Boston: Houghton Mifflin.

Gibson, (1986). *The ecological approach to visual perception* (2nd ed.), Hillsdale, NJ: Erlbaum.

Goldscheider, A. (1898). *Gessammelte Abhandlungen, Vol. 2, Physiologie des Muskelsinnes* [Collected works, Vol. 2, Physiology of kinesthesis]. Leipzig: Barth.

Goldstein, H. (1980). *Classical mechanics.* Reading, MA: Addison-Wesley.

Goodwin, G. M., McCloskey, D. I., & Matthews, P. B. C. (1972). The contribution of muscle afferents to kinesthesia shown by vibration induced illusions of movement and by the effects of paralysing joint afferents. *Brain, 95,* 705–748.

Granit. R. (1955). *Receptors and sensory perception.* New Haven, CT: Yale University Press.

Greene, P. H. (1972). Problems of organization of motor systems. In R. Rosen & F. Snell (Eds.), *Progress in theoretical biology* (Vol. 2, pp. 303–338). New York: Academic Press.

Gregory, R. L. (1974). *Concepts and mechanisms of perception.* New York: Scribner.

Gurfinkel, V. S., & Levick, Y. S. (1979). Sensory complexes and sensorimotor integration. *Human Physiology, 5,* 269–281.

Gurfinkel, V. S., & Levick, Y. S. (1991). Perceptual and automatic aspects of the postural body scheme. In J. Paillard (Ed.), *Brain and space.* (pp. 147–162). New York: Oxford University Press.

Haken, H. (1988). *Information and self-organization.* Berlin: Springer-Verlag.

Hamilton, W. R. (1853). *Lectures on quarternians.* Dublin: Hodges & Smith.

Hanley, C., & Goff, D. P. (1974). Size constancy in extended haptic space. *Perception & Psychophysics, 15,* 97–100.

Hayward, V. (1992). Physical modeling applies to physiology, too. *Behavioral and Brain Sciences, 15,* 342–343.

Head, H. (1920). *Studies in neurology: Vol. 2.* London: Oxford University Press.

Head, H., & Holmes, G. (1911–1912). Sensory disturbances from cerebral lesions. *Brain, 34,* 102–254.

Helms Tillery, S. I., Flanders, M., Soechting, J. F. (1991). A coordinate system for the synthesis of visual and kinesthetic information. *Journal of Neuroscience, 11,* 770–778.

Hestenes, D. (1986). *New foundations for classical mechanics.* Norwell, MA: Kluwer Academic.

Hestenes, D. (1994a). Invariant body kinematics: I. Saccadic and compensatory eye movements. *Neural Networks, 7,* 65–77.

Hestenes, D. (1994b). Invariant body kinematics: II. Reaching and neurogeometry. *Neural Networks, 7,* 79–88.

Hoisington, L. B. (1920). On the non-visual perception of the length of lifted rods. *American Journal of Psychology, 31,* 114–146.

Jastrow, J. (1886). Perception of space by disparate senses. *Mind, 11,* 539–554.

Johnston, W. A., & Dark, V. J. (1986). Selective attention. *Annual Review of Psychology, 37,* 43–76.

Jones, L. A. (1986). Perception of force and weight: Theory and research. *Psychological Bulletin, 100,* 29–42.

Katz, D. (1989). *The world of touch* (L. Krueger, trans.). Hillsdale, NJ: Erlbaum. (Original work published 1925)

Kelvin, R. P., & Mulik, A. (1958). Discrimination of size by sight and touch. *Quarterly Journal of Experimental Psychology, 10,* 187–192.

Kibble, T. W. B. (1985). *Classical mechanics.* London: Longman.

Kilpatrick, P., & Ittelson, W. H. (1953). The size-distance invariance hypothesis. *Psychological Review, 60,* 223–231.

Kinsella-Shaw, J., & Turvey, M. T. (1992). Haptic perception of object distance on a single-strand vibratory web. *Perception & Psychophysics, 52,* 625–638.

Klatzky, R. L., Lederman, S., & Reed, C. (1989). Haptic integration of object properties: Texture, hardness, and planar contour. *Journal of Experimental Psychology: Human Perception and Performance, 15,* 45–57.

Knowles, W. B., & Sheridan, T. B. (1966). The "feel" of rotary controls: Friction and inertia. *Human Factors, 8,* 209–215.

Koenderink, J. J. (1990). *Solid shape.* Cambridge, MA: MIT Press.

Koffka, K. (1935). *Principles of Gestalt psychology.* New York: Harcourt, Brace.

Kreifeldt, J. G., & Chuang, M.-C. (1979). Moment of inertia: Psychophysical study of an overlooked sensation. *Science, 206,* 588–590.

Krieger, M. H. (1992). *Doing physics.* Bloomington: Indiana University Press.

Lackner, J. R., & Taublieb, A. B. (1984). Influence of vision on vibration-induced illusions of limb movement. *Experimental Neurology, 85,* 97–106.

Lederman, S., & Klatzky, R. L. (1987). Hand movements: A window into haptic object recognition. *Cognitive Psychology, 19,* 342–368.

Lee, D. N. (1978). The functions of vision. In H. L. Pick, Jr. & E. Saltzman (Eds.), *Modes of perceiving and processing information.* (pp. 159–170). Hillsdale, NJ: Erlbaum.

Lotze, R. H. (1885). *Mikrokosmus* (Vol. 1, 4th ed., E. Hamilton & E. E. C. Jones, Trans.). Edinburgh: Clark (Original work published 1856).

Lovett, D. R. (1989). *Tensor properties of crystals.* Philadelphia: Adam Hilger.

Mark, L. S. (1987). Eyeheight-scaled information about affordances: A study of siting and stairclimbing. *Journal of Experimental Psychology. Human Perception and Performance, 13,* 361–370.

Marr, D. (1982). *Vision.* San Francisco: Freeman.

Masin, S. C., & Crestoni, L. (1988). Experimental demonstration of the sensory basis of the size–weight illusion. *Perception & Psychophysics, 44,* 309–312.

Matthews, P. B. C. (1964). Muscle spindles and their motor control. *Physiology Review, 44,* 219–288.

Matthews, P. B. C., & Simmons, A. (1974). Sensations of finger movement elicited by pulling upon flexor tendons in man. *Journal of Physiology, 239,* 27–28.

McCloskey, D. I. (1973). Differences between the senses of movement and position shown by the effects of loading and vibration of muscles in man. *Brain Research, 61,* 119–131.

Merton, P. A. (1964). Human position sense and sense of effort. *Symposia of the Society for Experimental Biology, 18,* 387–400.

Misner, C. W., Thorne, K. S., & Wheeler, J. A. (1973). *Gravitation.* San Francisco: Freeman.

Moon, P., & Spencer, D. E. (1965). *Vectors.* Princeton, NJ: Van Norstrand.

Moon, P., & Spencer, D. E. (1986). *Theory of holors.* Cambridge, England: Cambridge University Press.

Naber, G. L. (1992). *The geometry of Minkowski space-time.* New York: Springer Verlag.

Neisser, U. (1976). *Cognition and reality.* San Francisco: Freeman.

Pagano, C. C. (1993). *Inertial eigenvectors as the basis for the perception of limb direction.* Unpublished doctoral dissertation, University of Connecticut, Storrs.

Pagano, C. C., Fitzpatrick, P., & Turvey, M. T. (1993). Tensorial basis to the constancy of perceived extent over variations of dynamic touch. *Perception & Psychophysics, 54,* 43–54.

Pagano, C. C., Kinsella-Shaw, J., Cassidy, P., & Turvey, M. T. (1994). Role of the inertia tensor in haptically perceiving where an object is grasped. *Journal of Experimental Psychology: Human Perception and Performance, 20,* 276–284.

Pagano, C. C., & Turvey, M. T. (1992). Eigenvectors of the inertia tensor and perceiving the orientation of a hand-held object by dynamic touch. *Perception & Psychophysics, 52,* 617–624.

Pagano, C., & Turvey, M. T. (1993). Perceiving by dynamic touch the extents of irregular objects. *Ecolotical Psychology, 5,* 125–151.

Pagano, C. C., & Turvey, M. T. (in press). The inertia tensor as a basis for the perception of limb orientation. *Journal of Experimental Psychology: Human Perception and Performance.*

Parsons, L. M. (1990). Body image. In M. W. Eysenck (Ed.), *The Blackwell dictionary of cognitive psychology.* (pp. 46–47). England: Oxford, Basil Blackwell.

Pellionisz, A. (1986). Tensor network theory of the central nervous system and sensorimotor modeling. In G. Palm & A. Aertsen (Eds.), *Brain theory* (pp. 121–146). Berlin: Springer-Verlag.

Pellionisz, A., & Llinás, R. (1985). Tensor network theory of the metaorganization of functional geometries in the central nervous system. *Neuroscience, 16,* 245–273.

Pick, H. L., & Pick, A. D. (1967). A developmental and analytic study of the size-weight illusion. *Journal of Experimental Child Psychology, 5,* 362–371.

Provins, K. A. (1958). The effect of peripheral nerve block on the appreciation and execution of finger movements. *Journal of Physiology, 143,* 55–67.

Reed, C., Lederman, S., & Klatzky, R. L. (1990). Haptic integration of planar size with hardness, texture, and planar contour. *Canadian Journal of Psychology, 44*, 522–545.

Reynolds, H. M. (1978). The inertial properties of the body and its segments. In E. Churchill, J. T. Laubach, J. T. McConville, & I. Tebbetts (Eds.), *Anthropometric source book: Volume I. Anthropometry for designers.* (chap. IV). NASA Reference Publication 1024, Scientific and Technical Information Office.

Rose, J. E., & Mountcastle, V. B. (1959). Touch and kinesthesis. In J. Field, H. W. Magoun, & V. E. Hall (Eds.), *Handbook of physiology* (Vol. 1, pp. 387–429). Washington, DC: American Physiological Society.

Rosen, R. (1988). Similarity and dissimilarity: A partial overview. *Human Movement Science, 7*, 131–153.

Ruffini, A. (1897). Observations on sensory nerve-endings in voluntary muscles. *Brain, 20*, 368–374.

Rule, J. (1993). Analyzing coefficients of psychophysical power functions. *Perception & Psychophysics, 54*, 439–445.

Runeson, S. (1977). On the possibility of "smart" perceptual mechanisms. *Scandinavian Journal of Psychology, 18*, 172–179.

Schneider, K., Zernicke, R. F., Schmidt, R. A., & Hart, T. J. (1989). changes in limb dynamics during practice of rapid movements. *Journal of Biomechanics, 22*, 805–817.

Shepherd, G. M. (1988). *Neurobiology* (2nd ed.). New York: Oxford University Press.

Sherrington, C. (1906). *The integrative action of the nervous system.* New Haven, CT: Yale University Press.

Sjöberg, L. (1969). Sensation scales in the size-weight illusion. *Scandinavian Journal of Psychology, 10*, 109–112.

Skoglund, S. (1956). Anatomical and physiological studies of knee joint innervation in the cat. *Acta Physiologica Scandinavia, 36*, (Suppl. 124), 1–101.

Soechting, J. F. (1982). Does position sense at the elbow reflect a sense of elbow joint angle or one of limb orientation? *Brain Research, 248*, 392–395.

Soechting, J. F., Helms Tillery, S. I., & Flanders, M. (1990). Transformation from head-to-shoulder-centered representation of target direction in arm movements. *Journal of Cognitive Neuroscience, 2*, 32–43.

Soechting, J. F., & Ross, B. (1984). Psychophysical determination of coordinate representation of human arm orientation. *Neuroscience, 13*, 595–604.

Solomon, H. Y. (1988). Movement-produced invariants in haptic explorations: An example of self-organizing, information-driven, intentional system. *Human Movement Science, 7*, 201-223.

Solomon, H. Y., & Turvey, M. T. (1988). Haptically perceiving the distance reachable with hand-held objects. *Journal of Experimental Psychology: Human Perception and Performance, 14*, 404–427.

Solomon, H. Y., Turvey, M. T., & Burton, G. (1989a). Gravitational and muscular influences in perceiving length by wielding. *Ecological Psychology, 1*, 265–300.

Solomon, H. Y., Turvey, M. T., & Burton, G. (1989b). Perceiving extents of rods by wielding: Haptic diagonalization and decomposition of the inertia tensor. *Journal of Experimental Psychology: Human Perception and Performance, 15*, 58–68.

Starzhinskii, V. M. (1982). *An advanced course of theoretical mechanics.* Moscow: MIR Publishers.

Stevens, J. C., & Rubin, L. L. (1970). Psychophysical scales of apparent heaviness and the size–weight illusion. *Perception & Psychophysics, 8*, 225–230.

Symon, K. (1971). *Mechanics.* Reading, MA: Addison-Wesley.

Turvey, M. T. (1977). Preliminaries to a theory of action with reference to vision. In R. E. Shaw & J. Bransford (Eds.), *Perceiving, acting, and knowing.* (pp. 211–266). Hillsale, NJ: Erlbaum.

Turvey, M. T., Burton, G., Pagano, C. C., Solomon, H. Y., & Runeson, S. (1992). Role of the inertia tensor in perceiving object orientation by dynamic touch. *Journal of Experimental Psychology: Human Perception and Performance, 3,* 714–727.

Turvey, M. T., & Carello, C. (1981). Cognition: The view from ecological realism. *Cognition, 10,* 313–321.

Turvey, M. T., Carello, C., Fitzpatrick, P., Pagano, C. C., & Kadar, E. E. (1995a). Spinors and selective dynamic touch. Manuscript submitted for publication.

Turvey, M. T., Carello, C., Fitzpatrick, P., Pagano, C. C., & Kadar, E. E. (1995b). Two-valuedness of spinors and selective dynamic touch. In R. J. Bootsma & Y. Guiard (Eds.), *Studies in perception and action, III.* Hillsdale, NJ: Erlbaum.

Turvey, M. T., Shaw, R. E., Reed, E. S., & Mace, W. M. (1981). Ecological laws of perceiving and acting: In reply to Fodor and Pylyshyn (1981). *Cognition, 9,* 237–304.

Turvey, M. T., Solomon, H. Y., & Burton, G. (1989). An ecological analysis of knowing by wielding. *Journal of the Experimental Analysis of Behavior, 52,* 387–407.

Ullman, S. (1979). Against direct perception. *Behavioral and Brain Sciences, 3,* 373–415.

Velay, J. L., Roll, R., & Paillard, J. (1989). Elbow position sense in man: Contrasting results in matching and pointing. *Human Movement Science, 8,* 177–193.

Wainwright, S. A. (1988). *Axis and circumference: The cylindrical shape of plants and animals.* Cambridge, MA: Harvard University Press.

Warren, W. H. (1984). Perceiving affordances: Visual guidance in stair climbing. *Journal of Experimental Psychology: Human Perception and Performance, 10,* 683–703.

Weber, E. H. (1978). *The sense of touch* (H. E. Ross, Ed. and Trans.). London: Academic Press. (Original work published 1834)

Weinberg, S. (1983). Why the renormalization group is a good thing. In A. Guth, K. Huang, & R. Jaffe (Eds.), *Aymptotic realms of physics* (pp. 1–19). Cambridge, MA: MIT Press.

Woodworth, R. S. (1921). *Psychology: A study of mental life.* New York: Holt.

Worringham, C. J., & Stelmach, G. E. (1985). The contribution of gravitational torques to limb position sense. *Experimental Brain Research, 61,* 38–42.

Worringham, C. J., Stelmach, G. E., & Martin, Z. E. (1987). Limb segment inclination sense in proprioception. *Experimental Brain Research, 66,* 653–658.

Index